101 727 870 9

THE  CHILD

THE BATTERED CHILD

FIFTH EDITION

Revised and Expanded

EDITED BY

Mary Edna Helfer, R.N., M.Ed., Ruth S. Kempe, M.D.,
and Richard D. Krugman, M.D.

THE UNIVERSITY OF CHICAGO PRESS

Chicago and London

MARY EDNA HELFER, R.N., M.ED., is senior instructor in the Department of
Preventive Medicine, University of Colorado School of Medicine, and director of Continuing
Medical Education Outreach at the University of Colorado Health Sciences Center and
the Colorado Area Health Education Program.

RUTH S. KEMPE, M.D., is associate professor emerita of pediatrics and
psychiatry at the University of Colorado School of Medicine.

RICHARD D. KRUGMAN, M.D., is dean of the School of Medicine and professor
in the Department of Pediatrics at the University of Colorado.

The University of Chicago Press, Chicago 60637
The University of Chicago Press, Ltd., London
© 1968, 1974, 1980, 1987, 1997 by The University of Chicago
All rights reserved. Published 1997
Printed in the United States of America

06 05 04 03 02 01 00 99 98 97   1 2 3 4 5
ISBN: 0-226-32627-6 (cloth)

Library of Congress Cataloging-in-Publication Data

The battered child / edited by Mary Edna Helfer, Ruth S. Kempe,
Richard D. Krugman. —5th ed. rev. and expanded.
        p.   cm.
    Includes bibliographical references and index.
    ISBN 0-226-32627-6 (alk. paper)
    1. Child abuse—United States.   2. Child abuse—United States—
Prevention.   3. Abused children—United States.   I. Helfer, Mary
Edna.   II. Kempe, Ruth S.   III. Krugman, Richard D., 1942–   .
HV6626.52.B375   1997
362.76'0973—dc21
                                                    97-7789
                                                      CIP

⊗ The paper used in this publication meets the
minimum requirements of the American National Standard
for Information Sciences—Permanence of Paper for
Printed Library Materials, ANSI Z39.48-1984.

This fifth edition

is dedicated to Ray E. Helfer

Contents

PART 3 INTERVENTION AND TREATMENT

PART 4 PREVENTION

Foreword to the Fifth Edition

RICHARD D. KRUGMAN AND RUTH S. KEMPE

With very few exceptions, if one wishes to
prevent something bad from happening, the development
of something good must come first.
RAY E. HELFER, "An Overview of Prevention"

Ray Helfer, until his untimely death in 1992, was a leader in the effort to understand and eliminate the maltreatment of children. The epigraph above symbolizes his crisp, clear approach to prevention. Few have had the comprehensive grasp of the field, the trenchant perception of its entirety, that he did, and fewer still have written as eloquently about the problem and its potential solutions. Ray could dream about the future in the most creative terms,[1] but he never failed to mold those dreams into creative plans—for example, the Children's Trust Funds, which he designed to provide funds for the prevention of child abuse and neglect and which he modeled after the Highway Trust Funds that build the interstate highway system in the United States. Ray had the remarkable ability to look at the world and its problems from a variety of perspectives. He showed all of us how to see life through the eyes of a five-year-old by shooting pictures from three feet off the floor so we could see things as a young child does.

While prevention was his passion, child neglect was his demon. He decried the neglect of neglect, writing often about the devastating toll the neglect of children takes on their physical and emotional well-being. He advocated for effective treatment for abused children and their families and pushed for well-coordinated, effective community programs to serve these families. No government—national, state, or local—ever met his challenge.

For all of us, in different but constant ways, Ray was a beloved friend, colleague, teacher, mentor—and, to Mary Edna and their children, husband and father. His early departure has left a significant void—but one that will surely be filled over time by the thousands of professionals in every field who were inspired both by his enthusiasm and by his optimism that together we would be able to eliminate child abuse and neglect as we have other public health problems of children.

This edition is dedicated to his memory and his work.

1. Helfer, R. E., "Child Abuse and Neglect: Assessment, Treatment, and Prevention—October 21, 2007," *Child Abuse and Neglect: The International Journal* 15, suppl. 1 (1991): 5–15.

Preface to the Fifth Edition

A decade has passed since the last edition of *The Battered Child* was published. The field has continued to expand significantly but, as the preface to the fourth edition of the volume stated, not every area has progressed as rapidly as some. The atmosphere then was felt to be one of "gains and losses." Little has changed in this regard. In fact, a decade later, we find ourselves as professionals advanced by a great deal of new knowledge about all forms of abuse and neglect of children but falling further behind in applying what we know to improving services for children.

The preface to each previous edition of this book has reported substantial progress in gathering knowledge and exploring new methods of intervention. The preface to the fourth edition also reflected some concern about our ability as a society to translate the information explosion into effective programs for change. Clearly, one reason for this gap is the large number of children and families to be served; another is the difficulty in maintaining quality and flexibility within an institutional social agency response.

We have lost Ray Helfer since the fourth edition appeared. Just as Ruth Kempe took Henry's position as co-editor of the fourth edition, Mary Edna Helfer has taken Ray's place in this edition. Richard Krugman, who had the singular opportunity of having both Henry and Ray as mentors, has joined the latest "Helfer and Kempe" editors.

The format of the book remains the same as it was for the preceding editions, although 90% of the content is new. The first part provides an overview and general background of the components of the ecology of child abuse and neglect. Part 2 focuses on assessment of the various forms of abuse and neglect, while the Part 3, longer than that in any previous edition, covers intervention and treatment. Part 4, on prevention and policy, expands on some of the previous editions but, as has been noted by the volume's various editors for the last thirty years, is still too short.

Over the last decade, thousands of professionals and volunteers have worked diligently to try to assist the millions of children and families affected by child abuse and neglect. These dedicated men and women have had too few resources and too little organized information on which to base their practice over this period of time. Consequently, it is to them that this work is directed—we hope it will be useful in their worthy efforts.

We wish to thank all the contributors to this volume. Some have participated in the earlier editions; many more are new to this one, the fifth edition of *The Battered Child*. All have provided us with their time and perspective. Without them, this edition would not be possible. We also wish to thank Mary Roth and the staff at the C. Henry Kempe National Center for the Prevention and Treatment of Child Abuse and Neglect, and John Tryneski and Mary Caraway of the University of Chicago Press for their editing skill and support.

M.E.H., R.S.K., AND R.D.K.

Preface to the Fourth Edition

The seven years that have lapsed since the publication of the third edition of *The Battered Child* have seen some significant progress in several, but not all, areas within this complex field. On the positive side, considerable experience has been gained in understanding family assessment, treatment, and the physical and developmental effects of abuse and neglect. A literal explosion of information and interest has occurred in the area of sexual abuse. These gains are depicted in this edition. On the negative side, there have been considerable setbacks in the national commitment to the problems faced by these children and their families. This has resulted in the domino effect of less research, fewer protective service workers, retreat into the isolation of the past by many departments of social services, fewer cases substantiated after a report has been received, and an overall decrease in available services for those caught up in the cycle. Were these adversities not sufficient, we lost a friend and advocate when Henry Kempe died early in 1984. I have appreciated the continued support, encouragement, and help from Ruth Kempe as we have worked together on this edition.

In this atmosphere of gains and losses, the fourth edition presents some new and exciting approaches, information, ideas, and suggestions.

The editors have kept the standard format which has stood the test of time. Part I, Context, establishes the foundations upon which these abnormal rearing practices are laid by presenting the historical, cultural, epidemiological, developmental, and psychological bases for child abuse, neglect, and sexual exploitation. Each of these five chapters are revised or rewritten, except Dr. Steele's classic monograph on the psychodynamic factors. This has not been changed, a tribute to the insight of this remarkable man.

Part II, Assessment, has been expanded significantly. Six of the eleven chapters are new, four have undergone major revision, and two remain unchanged. Every component of the multidisciplinary team assesssment is covered in depth. This section provides all disciplines with detailed discussions of their roles in carrying out comprehensive assessments of the members of the family.

Part III, Intervention and Treatment, has been broadened by the addition of three new chapters on treatment, a new chapter on the role of law enforcement, and a greatly expanded discussion of the law and laywers.

The least amount of progress has occurred in the area of prevention. This is discussed in Part IV in an overview, a revision of the parent-infant relationship chapter, and a new look at our national priorities. Prevention approaches are difficult to undertake until our skills, knowledge, national commitment, and public readiness are in the right combination, as yet not realized on a large scale. The potential is still great.

This edition ends with some final thoughts and eight recommendations for future directions.

The editors are encouraged by the enormous grass roots concern that has emerged during the past seven years. These special people will make a difference.

R.E.H.

Preface to the Third Edition

Nineteen eighty marks the twentieth year since the phrase "the battered child" was coined in the attempt to bring to the attention of the country and the world the plight of abused and neglected children. This goal has clearly been achieved. Programs have been developed, laws passed, insight gained, and yet the problem persists. One and one-half percent of the children in the United States are reported annually to protective service units as victims of suspected abuse and neglect. The important word in the previous sentence is *annually*. Every year another one and one-half percent is added to the toll.

Twelve years have passed since the publication of the first edition of *The Battered Child*. Finding sufficient material to fill that edition was difficult. The opposite is true for the third edition: we found it difficult to limit the contributions.

Considerable discussion was held over the question of the title. Is it appropriate to preserve the title *The Battered Child* when the field has expanded far beyond the severely physically battered child? This book seems to be well entrenched as a primary source of current knowledge on the subject. Rather than change the title and start anew, the editors and publisher decided to maintain the title and expand the concept to include the vast array of manifestations of abuse and neglect of children. The material covered in this third edition is not, therefore, limited to physical abuse.

Part I reviews the background material, an understanding of which is necessary to put the problem of abuse and neglect into perspective. This section has been completely rewritten, and new authors have been added. Basic concepts are discussed, the historical and cross-cultural aspects reviewed, the way stress and crises (including parental alcohol and heroin addiction) affect and influence parent-child interactions is analyzed, and the devastating influences abuse has on the child's development are summarized. Dr. Steele has completely rewritten and updated his chapter on psychodynamics, a piece of work that truly is another classic.

In Part II the issues of assessment are discussed, both for the child and the family. This section contains many practical suggestions for all professionals confronted with the awesome obligation of evaluating a suspected case of child abuse. In addition to discussions of radiological assessment and pathology, six new contributions review interviewing techniques, physical findings, failure to thrive, child neglect, sexual abuse, and abuse by burning.

Part III includes seven chapters, all of which deal with current methods of intervention and treatment, both short- and long-term. Protective services, child therapy, law enforcement, and foster placement—all these difficult subjects are reviewed. Discussions of the community consortium, the roles of the lawyer, and the consequences of abuse round out this section on intervention.

Part IV is included with great hope and expectation—at last, a section on prevention. This has been a long time coming, too long indeed. Preventive programs are beginning to yield results. The future looks bright. Some states are implementing these preventive concepts as part of the routine services to new parents and their babies. We await the long overdue involvement of the school system in this endeavor. Its contribution could be most significant.

In the mid-1970s Vice-President Mondale pioneered federal legislation for the benefit of children. The results have been gratifying. How desperately do our children need a political advocate in the 1980s.

The editors are committed to improving the plight of every abused and neglected child. Our society cannot afford to do anything less. We are indebted to the contributors for their work. Together we are turning the corner and moving toward prevention.

R.E.H.   C.H.K.

Preface to the Second Edition

There are fifteen women in a house of correction just outside one of our larger cities. All of them are there for the same reason: they have been convicted of crimes against children—cruelty or manslaughter. Geraldine is one of these women. Still young, she was reared in a traumatic, motherless atmosphere, ran away from home as a teenager, became pregnant, married an emotionally ill college graduate, and began to have more children after placing her first child up for adoption. Her second child died in its first year of life from the effects of severe physical abuse. The third was born in prison.

The "justice" achieved by the criminal court after sentencing her to from two to four years in prison is exemplified by the sentencing judge's response to a request for early parole. No one knew who killed the baby—the mother, the father, or both—but a confession had been obtained from the mother, so she was tried and convicted; the father, remaining at home and now on welfare, cares for the prison-born child. An attempt was made to have Geraldine released so that a program of social and psychiatric treatment could be initiated. The judge, emotional and removed from the reality of the situation, chided proponents of the therapeutic program and suggested that he would approve early parole only if the mother submitted to sterilization.

Geraldine is still in prison, but in another year she will be freed and reunited with her emotionally disturbed husband and her new baby, with (no doubt) more babies to come; the process of criminal rehabilitation has again been flouted. And in the same institution there are fourteen other women convicted of similar offenses.

In spite of the Geraldines, there is evidence of slow but definite progress. Since *The Battered Child* was published in 1968, understanding has deepened, many more people have become involved, some courts have improved, treatment programs are being developed all over the country, and abuse and neglect are generally recognized at a much earlier point in the child's life. For example, in 1972 almost ten thousand cases of suspected abuse and neglect were reported in New York City alone. This fact is encouraging to many, since the feeling is that the lid is now off and solutions must and will be found.

A second book, *Helping the Battered Child and His Family* (Lippincott, 1972), has been published; the mass media have shown increasing interest and willingness to be helpful; and a few foundations have expressed interest in funding service and research projects. The biggest lack remains the apathy of federal agencies in the field of child welfare. Time is even changing this.

In the second edition of *The Battered Child*, the editors have deleted material no longer applicable, updated other contributions, and added more recent information. A chapter on the New York experience has been added. The section on the reporting laws, pathology, and X-ray has been extensively revised. Certain discussions, covered in greater detail in

Helping the Battered Child and His Family, have been removed and duplication avoided. The classic chapters by Steele and Pollock and by Davoren, however, have been left untouched.

Adequate demographic data which provide up-to-date evidence of the true incidence of significant child abuse in the United States are not available. Comparing current reporting of child abuse under state laws, we find that many communities are running a rate of 375 reports of suspected abuse per million population per year. No one has tried to compare the reported rate of suspected child abuse to the actual incidence—only a house-to-house, block-to-block intensive study can give us this information. Even so, such a ratio would only be valid in the community studied, because the number of reports compared to the true incidence depends on many variables, including physicians' interest and education, community attitudes, receptivity of the public agencies—especially the child-protective services—and, of course, the police and the juvenile courts.

In the absence of detailed information on incidence, it is still possible to assess the experience of a large metropolitan area such as New York City through the report of the Select Committee on Child Abuse authorized by the New York State Assembly. It provides information which can be used quite readily by other metropolitan areas and is a valuable contribution to the study of a difficult problem in a major center.[1]

The editors are convinced that recognition and treatment of battered children will accelerate during the seventies. The involvement and interest of both professionals and lay workers are encouraging. Geraldine, her husband, and her family see it differently, however. They will continue to withdraw, and their children will run the risk of repeated injury, until many more devoted and informed individuals proliferate into every nook and cranny of our service agencies, police, hospitals, courts, schools, and, above all, our communities.

R.E.H.   C.H.K

---

1. The New York City data are confusing in that the state requires the reporting of both abuse and neglect. There is no specific way of separating the New York City report into these two categories of the abnormal rearing problem. In 1972, therefore, the New York City rate for *both* entities was 1,200 per million population.

Preface to the First Edition

Tens of thousands of children were severely battered or killed in the United States in 1967. This book is written about and for these children. Who are they, where do they come from, why were they beaten, and—most important—what can we do to prevent it?

Presented herein is a multidisciplinary approach to the problem. There is both agreement and controversy among the contributors, but each has one goal in mind—to provide the reader with all of the available information which can hopefully be utilized to change the fate of these children and their parents.

We would like to express our sincere appreciation to all of the contributors and their staffs for sharing with us their experiences and research in the field of child abuse. We are also greatly indebted to Miss Katherine Oettinger and Dr. Arthur Lesser and their staff at the Children's Bureau for their continued help and support. Miss Jean Rubin, a former member of the Children's Bureau, was most helpful during a critical period in our study.

Each of our patients has provided us with a unique learning experience. We would like to express our appreciation not only to these children but also to their parents, who for the most part have been cooperative and helpful in making this work possible.

R.E.H.   C.H.K

Context

Part 1: Editors' Comments

More and more we have recognized the complexity of the context—cultural, social, and individual—in which child maltreatment occurs. The field of child abuse and neglect has grown dramatically over the past thirty years. Originally thought to be a problem that affected less than a thousand children a year in the United States, child abuse, we now realize, has occurred throughout history and in many different cultures. The context in which abuse is currently understood is quite a bit more advanced than it was a few decades ago.

The character that child abuse issues take on in each country also reflects the context in which the abuse occurs. For less developed countries, the issues of children's survival—related to poor nutrition and inadequate health care—overshadow questions about whether children are maltreated. In many countries, the prevalence of child labor—with its concomitant loss of developmental and educational opportunity—reflects an older social structure similar to that seen in Europe and the United States a century ago and described here in chapter 1. Child labor, child prostitution, and street children are pressing problems for many developing countries at the end of this century simply because they affect so many children; dealing with physical and emotional abuse are, in this context, less of a societal priority.

Part 1 gives new meaning to the adage "Where you stand depends on where you sit." The cross-cultural, economic, sociological, ecological, legal, and psychiatric perspectives outlined here will provide the reader with a useful background in which to consider the volume's sections on assessment, invention and treatment, and prevention ahead. The wise student of this subject will immediately recognize that looking at the problem from only one of these perspectives will hamper a true understanding of how we might address all the individual, family, and societal effects of child maltreatment.

1

Children in a World of Violence: The Roots of Child Maltreatment

ROBERT W. TEN BENSEL, MARGUERITE M. RHEINBERGER, AND SAMUEL X. RADBILL

> Moral ideas do not necessarily unfold with the
> flow of time. They have a tendency to cling to what is old
> and thereby hallowed.
>
> OWSEI TEMKIN, *Respect for Life*

Violence against children has been manifested in every conceivable manner: physically, emotionally, through neglect, by sexual exploitation, and by child labor. In 1895, the Society for the Prevention of Cruelty to Children summarized many of the ways London children were battered: by boots, crockery, pans, shovels, straps, ropes, thongs, pokers, fire, and boiling water. It described neglected children who were miserable, vermin-infested, filthy, shivering, ragged, nigh naked, pale, puny, limp, feeble, faint, dizzy, famished, and dying. Children were put out to beggary by those responsible for their pallor, emaciation, and cough; children were held in the clutches of idle drunkards and vagrants; little girls were victims of sexual abuse. Children were slaves of injurious employment in circuses, were displayed as monstrosities in traveling shows, and were exploited in diverse other modes (1, p. 875).

Child maltreatment is not a new phenomenon. It has existed since the beginning of recorded history. "Child abuse thrives in the shadows of privacy and secrecy. It lives by inattention" (2). Our current concept of what constitutes child maltreatment is a result of redefining and relabeling. It stems from a change in our consciousness and from an awareness of previously accepted child-rearing practices that are now considered unacceptable by the majority of society and are often illegal (2–4).

ROBERT W. TEN BENSEL, M.D., M.P.H., is a professor in the Department of Pediatrics and in the School of Public Health, University of Minnesota.

MARGUERITE M. RHEINBERGER, J.D., M.P.H., works for the Allina Foundation, Allina Healthsystem. She is currently completing a graduate degree in mass communication at the University of Minnesota.

SAMUEL X. RADBILL, M.D., now deceased, was with the Graduate School of Medicine, University of Pennsylvania.

The Right to Live

In ancient times, when might was right, the infant had no rights until the right to live was ritually bestowed. Until then, the infant was a nonentity and could be disposed of with little compunction. The newborn had to be acknowledged by the father; what the father produced was his to do with as he wished. Proclaiming the child as his own not only assured life and welfare but also inheritance rights (5). Children's rights were also a prerogative of parenthood. As the head of the family, the father had the ultimate authority; even the mother was subordinate.

With some, the child was not really of this world until he or she had partaken of some earthly nourishment. A drop of milk or honey or even water could ensure life to the newborn. An eighth-century story tells of a grandmother who, outraged by her daughter-in-law's numerous brood of daughters, ordered the next-born daughter to be slain. Her servants kidnapped the baby—another girl—as soon as she was born, before she could be put to the mother's breast, and tried to drown her in a bucket of water. A merciful neighbor, however, rescued the infant and put a little honey in her mouth, which she promptly swallowed. The child was thus protected and her right to live assured. In British New Guinea, traditionally an infant was taken to the banks of a stream and the infant's lips moistened with water. The baby that did not accept the water was thrown away.

To determine fitness to live, the Germans would plunge the newborn into an icy river. This was done not only to toughen the child but to test its hardiness. Some North American Indians threw the newborn into a pool of water and saved it only if it rose to the surface and cried. Elsewhere there were other ordeals for survival.

In the Society Islands, a parent could not kill with impunity a child who had survived for a day; in some places, the child was safe even after a half-hour of survival.

The child was a nonperson in some societies until it received a name, which identified it as an individual. The Christian child was not granted full heavenly recognition until it was christened, at which time a "Christian" name was bestowed. The soul of a child that died before baptism was believed not to go to heaven but to be condemned to everlasting limbo. The body of such a child could not be buried in hallowed ground but instead was disposed of elsewhere (6).

Illegitimate children have long been outlawed and especially liable to abuse. "Born in sin," they were without benefit of clergy or inheritance. Illegitimate children were unwelcome, ostracized, and often abandoned or killed by their despondent mothers. If the babies survived, they were subject to degradation and maltreatment. The church offered protective institutions that hid the mothers' identity, hoping to encourage compromised mothers to spare their infants. A study in 1917 indicated that of the four to five thousand illegitimate children born in Chicago every year, one thousand disappeared completely. In 1915, Norway adopted a law that conferred rights upon such children—including the right to a father's name, to parental support, and to inheritance equal with that of siblings born in wedlock (7). Only within recent years has some alleviation from the stigma of illegitimacy been granted in the United States.

Infanticide, Exposure, and Abandonment

In every ancient society of which records exist, infanticide was practiced. Legally, infanticide has been defined as the willful and intentional killing of a child, as condoned by the parents or by society. In antiquity, infant indicated a human being from birth to seven years of age, whereas the twentieth-century definition of infant is a human being from birth to one year of age.

Langer (8), in his article "Infanticide: A Historical Survey" writes, "Infanticide has, from time immemorial, been the accepted procedure for disposing not only of the sickly infants, but of all such newborns who might strain the resources of the individual family or larger community." The earliest evidence consists of the remains of infants interred in building walls at the city of Jericho in 7000 B.C.. Diodorus Siculus, Greek historian during the late first century B.C., reported that the Ceylonese put to death weak or infirm children and discarded those that had no courage or could not endure hardship. The Greeks did not want any cripples to grow up, believing their defects would pass to their offspring; consequently, they allowed only healthy newborns to be kept alive. Plato accepted this practice (9), and Aristotle recommended a law prohibiting crippled children from being reared. Even Soranus, a second-century Greek physician, instructed midwives to examine each child at birth and to get rid of any not fit to be raised. The Roman Law of Twelve Tables also forbade the raising of defective children. Exposure of children to the elements was practiced widely, and the Roman law gave the father power to control the life and death of his children. The concept that children were property further justified infanticide. Aristotle said, "The justice of a master or a father is a different thing from that of a citizen, for a son or a slave is property, and there can be no injustice to one's own property." (10) Egyptians, on the other hand, sentenced parents who killed their child to hug the corpse for seventy-two hours, thinking that it was not fit for those who gave life to the child to die but that they should be punished in a way which would arouse repentance and deter them from further life-taking attempts (11, pp. 40, 83).

With the onset of Christianity, Greek and Roman ideas about human life began to change. The law or public opinion began discouraging infanticide: in A.D. 374, Roman law deemed infant killing to be murder. The fourth-century A.D. is a significant time in history because Constantine the Great (the first Christian emperor) decreed in 315 and in 322 that the state should provide maintenance and education for poor children and should prevent the exposure, sale, and murder of infants. Thus, the state's responsibility for the welfare of children (*parens patriae*) was officially established (12).

During the Middle Ages (from A.D. 476 to 1453), infanticide was considered to be a "crime against nature" and was punished with extreme harshness. Society was exceptionally harsh with women who killed their children. Eventually, infanticide became a "privileged crime" and was punished less severely than before. In today's society, women frequently are given less severe or alternative sentences when they are found guilty of infanticide, whereas men are frequently sentenced to prison for killing their children (13).

As late as 1843, infanticide was practiced in Germany, where the first-born sons of certain noble families were interred in the walls of buildings to ward off evil spirits. Various cultures have practiced infanticide since that time, either sporadically or fairly regularly. For instance, India found it necessary to pass the Infanticidal Act in 1875 to prohibit Hindu women from throwing their female infants into the Ganges River. In China today, limiting women to only one child has lead to the current practice of killing female infants in preference of having a male child. The result is a lower ratio of adult females in the population.

Currently, at the end of the twentieth century, a major dilemma is the question of abortion, whether it represents a form of infanticide as the killing of an individual or a justifiable moral and medical practice as guaranteeing women's freedom of self-determination.

Child-Rearing Modes

Lloyd de Mause writes of the Western world, "The history of childhood is a nightmare from which we have only recently begun to awaken" (13). He outlines the major modes of parent-child relationships as they progressed from the beginning of recorded history to the present and defines these modes and the centuries during which various child-rearing patterns predominated. Modes changed gradually and, as de Mause notes, progressed at different rates for different family lines, classes, and geographic areas. De Mause also notes that in the countries he studied only the most advanced areas made steady progress in providing humane care to their infants and children.

The general child-rearing modes as described by de Mause are the *infanticide mode,* from antiquity through the fourth century A.D.; the *abandonment mode,* from the fifth century through the thirteenth; the *ambivalent mode,* from the fourteenth century through the seventeenth (a period marked by the "discovery of the child"); the *intrusive mode,* in the eighteenth century (physical discipline peaked during this time); and the *socializing mode,* from the nineteenth century to the present (these time periods indicate only generally when these child-rearing practices predominated).

The oldest and most extreme form of abandonment was the outright selling of children by their parents into slavery. This was legal in societies such as those of Babylon and Greece. The Early Christian church attempted to control abandonment. In the seventh century, Theodore, the archbishop of Canterbury, ruled that a man could not sell his son into slavery until after the boy was seven years old. Selling children into slavery also occurred in Russia and in the Americas up to the mid-nineteenth century. Children were also used as political hostages and as security for debts.

Child-Rearing Practices

From the Dark Ages and the Middle Ages (the fifth through the thirteenth centuries), little information about children survives in writing and in art, a comparative lack of interest that seems to be reflected in the way children were cared for. Indeed, a few pictures depict them more as potential souls to swell the population of heaven than as earthly bodies that might thrive and bring joy on earth. It is important to remember that, despite almost continuous childbearing, families might end up with only a few surviving children due to the very high mortality rates from miscarriages, accidents, and disease.

Until recent times, any child-rearing practices in common use in a given period were considered totally appropriate. Today some of these practices would be considered, at best, neglectful of the needs of normal childhood or even abusive, especially when carried to extremes.

From ancient times through the eighteenth century, there was no safe mode of artificial feeding, so children of the affluent (and most children from other families who could afford it) were fed by a wet nurse for the first two or three years of life. Wet nurses were often carelessly chosen, and the foster care they provided was often fraught with danger. The risks to children included being starved, overlaid (suffocated), neglected, or physically abused (14). Some of the wet nurses were known as "angel makers"; they not only allowed or helped their charges to die but sometimes even collected multiple insurance claims on each death. Illegitimate children were particularly at risk when placed in foster care, per-haps because there was little supervision.

Infants were commonly swaddled, often placed on a board and always tightly wrapped, to restrict movement for at least the first few months of life, a practice not conducive to health or robust development. Late physical development was probably related to swad-dling, but we possess no information about what effect such confinement and enforced passivity had on emotional development. Infants do sleep a great deal, and caring for them was no doubt much more "convenient" when the child could be carried and set down much like a parcel.

To soothe a fretting infant or young child, nurses or parents often resorted to genital manipulation. Playing with a child sexually was not unusual then and was sometimes con-sidered an amusement for both.

Once a child's swaddling was discontinued, the delayed control of toileting was ac-complished by the use of purges, suppositories, and enemas. In the eighteenth century, total control of toilet function by those means was replaced to some extent by the potty chair and toilet training. Training was begun at a very early age and performed in the punitive mode of the times, the contest of wills considered an important issue in winning over the child to parental discipline.

It was during the eighteenth century that the concept of neglect was introduced in England, largely as a side effect of the Gin Epidemic of 1720–1751. The availability of cheap gin helped to encourage alcoholism, which affected many parents and nurses as well as others in England (and elsewhere in Europe, where alcohol in many forms has been no less a problem). The College of Physicians identified fetal alcohol syndrome in infants of alcoholic mothers. Hogarth's classic illustration *Gin Lane* (fig. 1.1) shows how destructive gin was to all except the gin shop owner and the pawnbroker. Henry Fielding, a magistrate and the author of the novel *Tom Jones,* wrote of the effects of alcohol and helped to en-courage better government control of liquor, and the child neglect and abuse it often trig-gered (15).

When a child reached the age of seven years, infancy was over but so was childhood,

1.1 William Hogarth (1697–1764), *Gin Lane.*

for children were then expected to learn the tasks of adulthood. The young son in a noble family was apprenticed to the household of a knight or lord, to learn the art of warfare and the customs of the privileged. How much book learning he also acquired varied, for services of a clerk were cheap and, as a result, the boy might himself never need to know how to write or read. The boy of a humbler station was apprenticed to a master to learn a trade or profession or to serve as a farm laborer. He might learn weaving, clerking, or stonecraft, and he would be dependent on his master for everything. Daughters might be kept at home or also sent into servitude as a lady-in-waiting or as a housemaid. Sometimes girls were taught to read and write at those monasteries or church schools that taught boys. Most often, though, they were taught only household skills.

The church encouraged education not only for the benefit of monasteries and convents, which needed competent monks and nuns, but also to develop competence in those who would be of importance to the parish. For children of peasants and the poor, however, opportunities seldom came for education or advancement, and they had little choice but to join their parents in hard labor.

Thus, most children, regardless of social class, may have spent only a very small part of their childhoods with their parents. Presumably they were loved, but conditions of life were hard, and the lonely fate of children was taken for granted.

There is more evidence that as the social fabric of Europe became more stable in the sixteenth and seventeenth centuries, children were noticed and valued—but in an ambivalent way. Much of their value seemed to be related to exploitation, especially of their work potential, by parents and others. Children were worked, overworked, mutilated so they could beg more effectively, sold by parents into indenture (an equivalent of slavery), and encouraged to prostitute themselves. By the time of the Industrial Revolution in the eighteenth century, indenture and apprenticing were common practices (see the following section, on child labor).

During this period, more emphasis was placed on education and schools. Parents had begun to be more aware of their children's potential capabilities but also had begun to have very high expectations of their ability to work and help care for their parents' needs. The tendency to apply severe moralistic standards to children's behavior was combined at that time with the higher expectations for good conduct and the firm belief in physical punishment. If a child was not respectful, tractable, and totally obedient, severe physical punishment by parents, teachers, and overseers alike was considered morally right (this is the intrusive mode described by de Mause). Since the belief of the times was that parents owned their children, parents accordingly had the authority to decide by their own set of rules what was best for the child. Beatings were considered effective moral training, applied to future kings and peasants alike. Sanction for physical punishment had many sources; one law from the Middle Ages states, "If one beats a child until it bleeds, then it will remember—but if one beats it to death, the law applies."

By the nineteenth century, the family was better established as a stable unit of society, and children were included as integral and working members of that unit. Social observers became more concerned with the effect that the behavior of adults had on children—particularly, the lack of recognition of the frequent sufferings that children underwent. The writings of Charles Dickens, Victor Hugo, and Leo Tolstoy dramatized the plight of children and generated much popular sympathy for their travails.

Such sympathy was expressed most often through the work of private charities in each community, as well as in the development of institutions such as orphanages. These institutions were founded with wise intentions, but their success was often undermined by several factors: lack of medical knowledge of infectious diseases, poor sanitation, and an absence of good public health practices (which made any public institution dangerous for one's health then). Venality, greed, and callousness by caretakers often meant the children were still malnourished and maltreated. Mortality rates remained high. Nonetheless, society as a whole was becoming more aware of children and their needs, and more ready to take advantage of the new opportunities for change.

Many of the changes that have come about in the twentieth century in the way we take care of children reflect advances in medical knowledge, which have led to better health and drastically reduced the child mortality rates. Other changes reflect social advances that have improved living conditions, education and work opportunities for everyone, and public awareness of social issues and political action. Still other changes reflect the greatly increased knowledge we have gained through psychology and the other social sciences about children, their physical and psychological development, and finally about their emotional needs.

As we can count more reliably on the survival of our children, and as we recognize more clearly their place in our future, we see an increasing social and political investment in ensuring their well-being. We also see new recognition of the importance of every phase of a child's development, including infancy, to his or her future.

Child Labor

Child labor, under the apprenticeship system, in workhouses, in orphanages, as well as in industry, also brutalized children, leading to sporadic outbursts of anguish (4). When the English evangelist George Whitefield established the Bethesda Orphan House in Georgia in 1738, he preached: "Lord, do Thou teach and excite them to labor." However, the cruel punishment inflicted on the children there raised such an outcry on the part of the community that such strict discipline had to be ameliorated (16). Johann Peter Frank (1745–1821), the German physician who founded the science of public health, was shocked by the agrarian child labor used in continental viticulture, which resulted in youngsters becoming deformed and misshapen. He advocated laws in the eighteenth century to provide age limits for specific kinds of work and to prohibit forcing weak children to do the heavy work of artisans and making half-grown boys to do the labor of men. However, another century passed before such laws were enacted.

The guilds of the Middle Ages regulated the work of children, not out of compassion but to prevent competitive cheap labor. The statute of artificers in 1562 gave the government regulatory control over apprentices, binding children to their master by indenture for seven years, a system of enslavement that endured until 1815. In the seventeenth century, six-year-old children toiled in the clothing industries, and the great demand for children in the factories after the Industrial Revolution burst forth, early in the eighteenth century, led to further excruciating exploitation. "Pity those little creatures," Josiah Quincy wrote in 1801, when child labor was viewed as beneficial not only to society but to the child as well. He found children from four to ten years old employed in cotton mills "with a dull dejection" in their countenances. They were battered both physically and psychologically (4). A ghastly machine, jocularly called "Sherrington's Daughter," was used to punish "idle" children. It bent their heads down between their knees so that blood flowed from their nose and ears.

There was no protection for children employed in the mills, where they were mercilessly beaten and overworked, until the child labor laws initiated reforms during the nineteenth century. Children were transported to the American colonies in droves to be apprenticed until they reached the age of twenty-four. Pauper children in almshouses that ostensibly sheltered them were sold into apprenticeship and treated atrociously. Colonial newspapers constantly advertised for runaway children. As late as 1866, a Massachusetts legislative report hailed child labor as a boon to society. Writing on child labor laws in 1891, Abraham Jacobi, the father of American pediatrics, cried out against the employment of "mere babies" in the mines and as chimney sweeps. He deplored inexpensive child labor supplied to greedy industry by the poorhouses. The working child was even more abused in rural areas (17).

Chimney sweeps were a particularly sad lot. William Blake called them England's disgrace, "little black things among the snow crying 'weep!' 'weep!' in notes of woe." These waifs were purposefully kept small and thin so that they could more easily clamber up narrow, clogged flues. Auenbrugger, famous in medical history for his book on thoracic percussion, wrote a libretto in 1781 for the *Chimney Sweep Opera* in Vienna and three years later was ennobled for his humanitarian work on behalf of the poor (18).

Sexual Abuse

Historically, sexual offenses against children were common and child sexual exploitation has been present from the earliest recorded writings. More than most aspects of human behavior, sexuality has been the focus of great variations in attitudes, both public and private. The widespread prevalence of sexual abuse throughout history contrasts markedly with the ostensible abhorrence of such practices by society. In antiquity, the first mention of the duty of the adult male to respect his position of power by not engaging in illicit sexual activities appears in the Hippocratic Oath (circa 460–377 B.C.): "Whenever I go into a house, I will go to help the sick and never with the intention of doing harm or injury. I will not abuse my position [of authority] to indulge in sexual contacts with the bodies of women or men, whether they be freemen or slaves." Children should have been added to this list, but at the time children were considered to have the status of "slaves." Sexual abuse of children in antiquity was not addressed very openly, since taking liberties with a child was often considered merely casual use of an unimportant object rather than a threat to the more important sexual institution of marriage.

Another widely prevalent sexual attitude was the view that a woman or child was the property of a man and therefore to be used as he saw fit. Thus, marriages were contracted for very young children, solely for the political, commercial, or property value of such unions. The same applied to marriages for women that were used to form alliances in this way, without regard for the women's wishes. In some cultures, daughters, as well as wives, were loaned to guests as an act of hospitality. We find this in Irish heroic tales, in French medieval literature, and among the Eskimos and Native American tribes of North America. Neither was it always a disgrace to hire out girls for sexual use; the child was a marketable commodity. Daughters and sons were sometimes sent out into the streets as prostitutes; the money they earned was used to supply or augment the family income.

A variety of defloration rites at puberty or in preparation for marriage could be painfully abusive, yet these rites were not just indulged but often enforced publicly (19, p. 347). Some Hindus considered it disgraceful for a girl to remain unmarried after the onset of menstruation; as a result, premenstrual copulation was extensively practiced under cover of marriage. About 20% of these marriages involved girls of twelve or thirteen. The deaths of these children during their first sexual act were not rare, but they were usually concealed (20).

Incest

Laws, codes, and regulations represent society's consensus of its values and ethics. Out of everyday life comes the insight that certain boundaries to human behavior must be established because of the harm that would otherwise be caused. As a result, certain behaviors must be strictly interdicted and controlled. Rituals and taboos (prohibitions) regarding control over sexuality exist in all cultures. Religious laws also control sexuality, and most criminal laws have their basis in religious laws. The word *incest* means "unchaste and low; acting like an animal." Incest is a nearly universal taboo that has been present since antiquity. Incest applies universally to adults or adolescent males who are involved sexually with children in the nuclear family. Most writers say that the incest taboo marks the beginning of human advancement toward civilization.

The Code of Hammurabi (circa 2150 B.C.) states in law number 154, "If a man be known to his daughter, they shall expel that man from the city" (21), "To know" has been translated as "to conceive a child." The Code of Hammurabi was written in stone and placed in the center of the city of Babylon so all would know the law. The laws of Moses (circa 1300 B.C.) contain God's incest prohibition, "None of you shall approach to any that is near the kin to him to uncover their nakedness" (Lev. 18:6). In early Judeo religion, incest was a sin; in secular society, it was a crime. The major societal punishment was banishment. The Hebrew Bible states that offenders "shall be cut off from among their people" (Lev. 18:29).

Incest was especially devastating to the child because of the taboo. The taboo often extended to adoption, fosterage, milk-brotherhood (that is, those who were nursed by the same woman), and other intimate relationships similar to blood kinship. When it extended to housemates in general, children were prudishly separated at home and in schools. Some primitive tribal peoples terminated association of boys between five and ten years of age with their mothers and sisters. Even where sexual freedom among children of the same household existed, illicit marriage was strictly forbidden. Father-son incest was doubly taboo.

Many arguments have been propounded by anthropologists as to why incest was taboo; some authors argue the growing impact of civil values and religion. While the taboo was primarily ethical and religious, exogamy tended to preserve family unity and to maintain better intrafamily and community relationships. The Catholic Church limited marriage to the fourth degree of kinship in the first and second centuries and expanded that limitation to the seventh degree in the tenth century. This prohibition was intended to force individuals to marry outside their own villages: "The only way to prevent so many closed societies, hostile toward one another, was to multiply the relationships of kinship existing between villages, and with this end in view, to encourage exogamous marriages. The greatest theologians, Saint Augustine and Saint Thomas Aquinas, seem to have understood this was the reason for the prohibition of incest" (22). A moral code imposed psychological restraint and seemed to produce certain genetic advantages in line with the general belief that family inbreeding intensified hereditary traits.

Today most states in this country define *family* as the extended family, including adoptive families and stepfamilies, not just blood relatives. Accordingly, the concept of incest has been broadened to "intrafamilial sexual abuse."

Incest, pedophilia, and other sexual acts were classified in Dante's *Inferno* (early fourteenth century) as violent acts against "God, nature, and art." Laws were meant to control "crimes against nature" and "unnatural acts." Punishment was for the perpetrator to be constantly bombarded by "flakes of fire." Hell, fire, and brimstone have for centuries been associated with sexual crimes.

Sexual deviation was considered an unnatural act, and people believed that nature would punish the perpetrator with disease or neurosis. Freud reflected, "The law only forbids men to do what their instincts incline them to do; what nature itself prohibits and punishes, it would be superfluous for the law to prohibit and punish" (23). A major issue is, How does society control individuals who can't restrain their sexual impulses or individuals in whom personal guilt or other mechanisms are not present to control their sexual arousal toward children?

Susan Brownmiller reasons, "The unholy silence that shrouds the intrafamilial sexual abuse of children and prevents a realistic appraisal of its true incidence and meaning is rooted in the same patriarchal philosophy of sexual private property that shaped and determined historic male attitudes toward rape . . . for if woman was man's original corporal property, then children were, and are, a wholly owned subsidiary" (24).

There are complex reasons for the incest taboo. Whatever the reasons, it still remains that incest, the universal crime, violates a taboo that is as forceful among primitive peoples as among sophisticated moderns. It is behavior that disrupts or destroys the social intimacy and sexual distance upon which family unity depends.

However much incest has been considered a taboo, it is well to remember that of the 345,000 children reported as sexually abused in 1994, a substantial proportion were indeed sexually abused by people from their own family (25).

Dr. Stanley Hirsch, a former director of the National Institutes of Health states, "Our culture's collusion to avoid the most basic issues, death and sexuality, is amazing, yet understandable in the context of our striving for control and our fear of noncontrol. Death and sexuality imply both mysteries of life and the loss of control over life" (26).

Pedophilia

The history of pedophilia (sexual love of children) is largely hidden and repressed. It has not been written about or prohibited by law to any great extent. In "On Love and Friendship," Aristotle wrote that one should never confuse love with sexual passion. Furthermore, according to Richard Taylor, "Few ancients thought of it [sexual activity] as having any essential connection with love and friendship" (27).

Pedophilia has existed since ancient Greek times. Greek society tolerated men who were boy lovers, or "pederasts," as long as their relationships did not disturb the basic family. Thus, a double standard existed: sexual relationships with boys were tolerated outside the family but not among family members. "Plutarch said the reason why freeborn men and boys wore a gold ball around their necks when they were young was so that men could tell which boys it was all right to abuse [sexually] when they found a group in the nude" (28).

Sexual abuse of children by nonfamily members has occurred from the past to the present with few if any societal sanctions. During the Renaissance, Italian aristocrats often asked for sexual favors from young boys. Prostitution involving children was considered almost universal.

In 1898, Richard von Krafft-Ebing coined the term *pedophilia erotica* as "a morbid disposition, a psychosexual perversion, in which a sexually needy person is drawn to children." Thus, it has only been within the last one hundred years that we have begun to acknowledge that there are adults, usually males, who are sexually drawn (but not exclusively) to young boys. Girls have also been victims of pedophiles. The pedophile in Victorian England was often associated with child prostitution, which was considered "the vilest feature of the whole Victorian scene" (29).

During the later nineteenth century, Kingdon elaborated on a fascination with young girls that presented in a more subtle form: "This was the cult of the love of little girls. It originated at Oxford where professors entertained young girls at tea parties. Among its literary voices were W. E. Henley, Francis Thompson, Robert Louis Stevenson, and Algernon Swinburne" (30).

We are only now realizing the depth and pervasiveness of the problem of pedophilia. It is as if we have denied children who are abused outside the family the equal protection of the law. As adults, we have largely been ignorant of the hazards that the world presents to children, especially those children who, for various reasons, are vulnerable to the sexual advances of skilled pedophiles.

Pornography

Throughout history, we can find records of the existence of child pornography. Pornography involving children existed among the highest levels of society; Montaigne (31) commented that such obscene literature found a ready market in his time.

With the introduction of photography in 1839, pornographers lost no time in taking pictures of children in seductive poses. Prior to that time, drawings had been widely available, primarily among the aristocracy of society. One of the most influential writers of children's books in the nineteenth century was Lewis Carroll, whose real name was the Reverend Charles Dodgson; as a photographer, he had a fascination with girls. He openly admitted, "I am fond of all children, except boys" (32). Naked children also intrigued him. In a letter to a friend he wrote, "I wished I dared dispense with all costume. Naked children are so perfectly pure and lovely . . . " (32). He even made reference to nude photography of children in his diary entry of 21 May 1867. On that day he recorded that "Mrs. Latham brought Beatrice, and I took a photograph of the two, and several of Beatrice alone sans habiliment [without clothes] (33, 34). Carroll's book *Alice in Wonderland* was actually a result of his fascination with Alice Liddell, one of his favorite photographic subjects (fig. 1.2). Lewis Carroll was persuaded by his friends to stop photographing nude children, but he then proceeded to paint nude children, which required even longer periods of sitting with his young models (35).

The advancement in technology has increased the easy dissemination of pornographic materials through computers. Such material, providing a much wider range of information and explicit sexual activities depicted, is now accessible by a vast audience (see chapter 19).

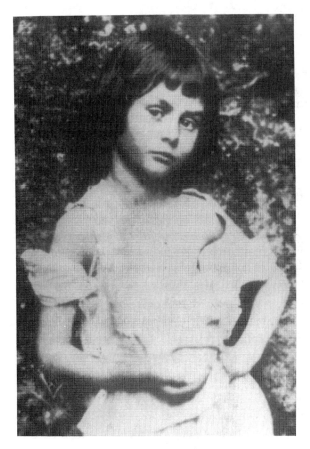

1.2 Alice Liddell (the Alice of *Alice in Wonderland*), photographed as a child by Charles Dodgson (Lewis Carroll).

Prostitution

Age-of-consent laws were enacted to protect children from sexual abuse. Beginning in England with King Edward I, during the thirteenth century, it has been illegal for an adult to have intercourse with a girl under age twelve. In 1576, the age of consent was lowered to ten; then raised to thirteen in 1875 and to age sixteen in 1885. The law then was used to prosecute adults who were taking advantage of, or promoting, child prostitution. Most child prostitutes lived with their families and "brought home as large a share of their earnings as their elders could make them" (29). Prostitution was largely a form of child labor for boys or girls or a last resort for young women. Brothels staffed by children aged fourteen and under were a standard feature of the London underworld. Virgins were at a "premium" (36).

The commissioners of public charities and correction of New York City in 1869 stated that there were thirty thousand children in the city streets, their main occupation being beggary and pilferage; the girls were prostitutes by the age of fifteen, and the brevity of their lives, shortened by syphilitic disease, the only check upon the increase of their numbers. To break up this career, the commissioners advocated that children in the streets be arrested and sent to the Juvenile Retreat on Randall's Island: the Children's Aid Society would then secure reputable homes for them (37).

Sexual Violence and Rape

Rape was common in the unbridled days of the past, especially during wartime. It is depicted in the Bible as well as in Greek and Roman history, and it played a prominent part in the drama of historic violence. Hercules violated the fifty daughters of Thestius, and Helen of Troy was deflowered by Theseus at the age of seven, according to one story, and according to another at the age of twelve.

Flagellation was a common form of sexual abuse. One sadistic little girl of six abused a boy of seven, who bore his martyrdom with dull resentment but liked his beatings because the pain gave him a thrill of bitter delight (38). Voluptuous sensation could lead seductive youngsters to instigate beatings purposely. Nineteenth-century newspapers frequently featured lurid accounts of children battered in devious ways for the satisfaction of the sexual lust of sadists. These sex torturers placed ads in the papers to obtain children, using code words which were understood by the initiates. German law finally put a stop to advertisements for immoral purposes.

Advancement of Children's Rights

Esteem for the child was slow to appear. Until the Middle Ages, childhood was over almost as soon as the child was weaned. Among the Israelites, weaning took place at the age of three; then the little boy could enter the house of God along with the men; at thirteen, the age of puberty, he was counted as one of the men. Medieval children were sent away from home by the age of seven for upbringing; this custom eventuated in the apprentice system. The Italians thought this custom showed a particularly English lack of affection toward children (39). In the thirteenth century, children began to appear in art, portrayed with various childhood attractions. By the sixteenth century, the moral philosophy of men like Erasmus, himself a wronged illegitimate orphan, and Montaigne, raised by an indulgent father, stirred the hearts of many to adopt nonviolent methods of rearing children and wakened compassionate solicitude for the oppressed and the handicapped child. Their ethics carried over to the seventeenth century and later, influencing men like Rousseau, a libertine who had fathered at least six illegitimate children, all of whom vanished before he turned humanitarian and wrote, "Speak less of the duties of children and more of their rights" (40).

In the seventeenth century, there was a shift from communal living arrangements to family groups, and society was thrilling more deeply to the charms of children. The child gradually achieved a place of honor in the family, and the family attained an independent status (6). Step by step, the child was increasingly idolized. In the eighteenth century, Samuel Richardson's novel *Pamela* spoke out against child abuse, as did Sir Walter Scott's book

The Heart of Midlothian in the nineteenth century. Victor Hugo's Cosette, the foster child who was abused as a household drudge in *Les Misérables,* and the many young characters in nearly all of Dickens's sentimental Victorian novels, stirred up growing popular ferment for humane treatment of children.

By 1871, the New York State Medical Society could rightly say, in a resolution supporting foundling asylums, that humanity recognized the right of every newborn to be protected and supported.

The potential for child abuse in an adult's manner of punishing children was recognized, and brought to light by the famous Mary Ellen case of 1874. This landmark case also focused attention on the novel issue of allowing the state to intervene to protect the rights of children (41, 42). The historical accounts of the Mary Ellen case vary in some degree, but the basic facts are consistent. Mary Ellen was a child who was severely abused by her stepmother (fig. 1.3). Her constant screams were overheard by a dying woman in an adjoining room. The woman invoked the help of a Methodist missionary, Mrs. Wheeler, who visited her. Mrs. Wheeler searched endlessly for some person or some organization who could provide assistance to Mary Ellen. She was refused help on the bases that she had no actual proof these beatings had occurred and that she did not have a right to protect Mary Ellen because Mary Ellen was not her legal ward. In a last desperate attempt, Mrs. Wheeler turned to Henry Bergh, founder and president of the New York Society for the Prevention to Cruelty to Animals (NYSPCA). Bergh did not let her down. He argued, "The child is an animal. If there is no justice for it as a human being, it shall at least have the rights of the stray cur in the street. It shall not be abused" (41). Jacob Riis, a police reporter, wrote about the case in his coverage of the trial: "I saw a child brought in, carried in a horse blanket, at the sight of which men wept aloud, and I heard the story of Mary Ellen told again, that stirred the soul of a city and roused the conscience of a world that had forgotten; and, as I looked, I knew I was where the first chapter of the children's rights was being written" (41). This was a prophetic statement; after the Mary Ellen case, society intervened to protect other abused children. Custodial rights to Mary Ellen were terminated, and Mrs. Wheeler's family adopted her (fig. 1.4). Within a year, Bergh formed the New York Society for the Prevention of Cruelty to Children (NYSPCC) which was formally incorporated in 1875 (fig. 1.5). In 1876, The NYSPCA and NYSPCC merged in the American Humane Association, its mission being to rescue both animals and children from inhumane treatment.

By the beginning of the nineteenth century, the public conscience had been aroused on behalf of the oppressed, the neglected, and the handicapped. Schools sprang up for the blind, the deaf, and the mentally retarded, so that exceptional children were no longer jettisoned.

By the end of the century, Abraham Jacobi exclaimed that the greatest improvement in public morals consisted in acknowledgment that the right to protection is among the inalienable rights of all beings, especially the feeble. Pointing at the large numbers of abandoned children devoid of the care and protection of the family circle, whose parents were in hospitals, in prisons, or dead, he declared these all had a claim to the aid of the community (43).

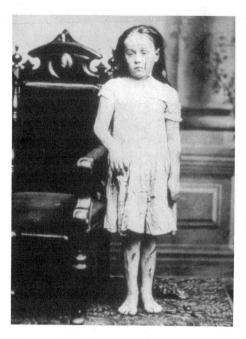

1.3 Mary Ellen, abused as a child by her step-mother, 1874.

1.4 Mary Ellen, rescued from abuse and adopted by Mrs. Wheeler, circa 1875.

1.5 Intervention by the New York Society for the Prevention of Cruelty to Children, circa 1875.

Protective Services for Children

Child welfare began in Mesopotamia six thousand years ago, when orphans had a patron goddess to look after them (44). The Rig-Veda also mentions another deity among the ancient Hindus who rescued the exposed child and endowed him with legal rights (45). The gods reflected a mirror image of mankind, affording a picture of what went on among the people.

The Bible commands, "Do not sin against the child" (Gen. 42:22). The laws of Solon, in 600 B.C., required the commander of an army to protect and raise, at government expense, children of citizens killed in battle; the wives of Roman emperors extended child welfare. Then there was jolly old St. Nicholas Thaumaturgos during the third century, who was the patron saint of children and protector of the feebleminded.

In the main, protective services have always consisted of placing children in institutions or under foster care. Despite good intentions, children have suffered physical and psychological damage under this system. However, without such intervention, they were even more apt to be maimed and killed.

Institutional Care

At a very early period, Athens and Rome had orphan homes; *brephotrophia* were mentioned in 529 in the laws of Justinian. With the rise of Christianity, the church provided for foundlings: every village had a *xenodochium,* a hospice for pilgrims and the poor, which embraced children (46). By the sixth century, the *brephotrophia* at Trier included a marble receptacle in which a child could be safely deposited secretly. Similar institutions throughout France in the seventh century were the antecedents of the welfare systems of the nineteenth century.

The first foundling hospital was established by Datheus, the archpriest of Milan, in 787. This was followed by the Hospital of the Holy Spirit, started by Pope Innocent III in 1066. The next major foundling hospital was established in Florence in 1444 and was known as the Hospital of the Innocents. It was started by the Guild of Silkworkers and was supported by the Medici's power and authority. This is where "pediatrics" began. One of the Andrea Della Robbia bas-relief medallions of a swaddled infant from the facade of the Hospital of the Innocents was chosen as the logo of the American Academy of Pediatrics in 1930.

The next major foundling hospital was started in Paris by the priest Vincent de Paul. In 1650, he became extremely concerned about the number of children being abandoned on the steps of the cathedral of Notre Dame. Records of the day indicate that there were up to a hundred thousand children abandoned each year in France. He turned to the women of the church and to the community for help in establishing the Paris foundling hospital. Because of his efforts on behalf of foundlings, he was eventually declared the patron saint of charitable organizations (47).

The foundling hospital in London was established "for the maintenance of education of exposed and deserted young children" by Sir Thomas Coram (48). This foundling hospital attracted the attention of the British painter and engraver William Hogarth, who designed the hospital's coat of arms as part of the invitation to the performance of Handel's *Messiah*. The royalties from the *Messiah* were donated to the foundling hospital (49).

In Naples, with a population of about four hundred thousand and a birthrate of fifteen thousand births a year in the nineteenth century, there were over two thousand foundlings in the asylum. The foundling hospital of St. Petersburg was the most magnificent in Europe. The Russians were very proud of it and endowed it munificently. Upward of twenty-five thousand children were enrolled regularly in its books. About one in four died; in addition, the foundling hospitals did not prevent exposure or infanticide (50).

British law, which also applied to the American colonies, initiated early involvement of government in public welfare. The main reliance was on almshouses, where, to offset expense and save the young from the sin of idleness, children were forced to work even as young as at age five or six years.

Children fared badly under the dismal routine of institutions. They suffered from deprivation and starvation, and little consideration was given to their recreational needs. A visitor to a foundling asylum was dejected by the sight of children sitting all day long bound to potty chairs (51). Few survived. Those who did were starved, overworked, cuffed, degraded, despised, and unpitied. In Paris, a street beggar could buy an infant at the Hôtel Dieu for twenty sous and then maim it so that it would attract pity and more liberal alms, or a wet nurse could buy a replacement for an infant entrusted to her care who had died (51).

Foundling homes, orphanages, and almshouses offered little surcease from death. Protestant countries were convinced that such charities encouraged immorality; in addition, they objected to the cost and believed foster care was cheaper. To avoid the failings of institutional life, children were farmed out to foster care as soon as possible.

In the United States, the first foundling home was the New York Foundling Asylum, built on Randall's Island in New York in 1869. In 1873, over 1,300 infants were found abandoned and over 122 infants were found dead in the streets and alleys of New York City. Abandoned babies were also taken to almshouses. Times of wars and social upheaval saw an increased use of foundling hospitals and orphanages. An extremely high death rate for abandoned infants was noted, with as many as 90% of them dying from malnutrition. The Nursery and Children's Hospital in New York City was established in 1854 to provide care for the children of mothers who couldn't nurture their own children.

Foster Care

Foster care was also mentioned in antiquity. Removal to private homes often subjected children to maltreatment and neglect, but it did give them a sporting chance of survival. Even so, 80% of illegitimate children put out to nurse in London during the nineteenth century perished.

A German report of 1881 stated that 31% of illegitimate children died under foster care, allegedly from natural causes but actually from freezing, starvation, or deliberate destruction. Seldom were foster parents called to account. In spite of such gross irregularities, foundlings made out better under foster care than they did in foundling institutions.

The Pennsylvania Society to Protect Children from Cruelty estimated in 1882 that about seven hundred infants perished annually in Philadelphia from abuse and neglect. The society urged the establishment of special children's asylums combined with a system for placement in foster homes based upon those current in Europe (52).

When children spent their entire childhoods in a succession of foster homes, the lack of security of a permanent home life marred their emotional development and sowed seeds of unhappy consequences in later life. Tansillo's poem *La Balia* ("the nurse") decried the eighteenth-century fashion of surrogate care under some wretch of vulgar birth and frail conduct, just out of jail, or of some strumpet. In England, Jonas Hanway (1712–1786) reported that only one out of seventy children entrusted to parish care grew up, only to be crippled and sent out into the streets to beg, steal, or fall into prostitution; Hanway brought about parliamentary reform that required all young foster children to be registered. The *British Medical Journal* in 1903 chided the system of "baby farming" and urged the licensing of foster parents and inspectors to see that children were properly cared for (53).

The pros and cons of institutional care versus foster care have long been debated. Advanced in favor of the latter were less cost and the blessings of family life, while supporters of institutions argued the cost would be insignificant with proper economy and that surrogate parents gave little service for the pittance they received but from which they still expected to profit.

Hundreds of thousands of children and their families have been helped by the wise use of foster care. Contact with the child by one or both parents, when possible, not only aids the child's mental development but also boosts the morale of the foster parents and their respect for the child. Despite studies done by the Child Welfare League in 1965, and the study conducted by the Columbia School of Social Work, there is still an uneasy feeling that the thousands of children adrift in the foster care system need to be rescued (54).

Child Protection Laws

Traditionally, the father's authority, like the royal prerogative, could be asserted without question, but through the years this absolute authority has been increasingly limited by statutes and the changing climate of public opinion. The father's authority was modified in Rome in 450 B.C. and again in A.D. 4. The Christian church fathers in the fourth century, in line with the Judaic injunction "Thou shalt not kill," equated infanticide with murder. This was a landmark in the history of children's rights. A succession of imperial edicts after that guaranteed the child's right to life.

In medieval times, the church governed birth, marriage, and death, establishing the rules for law and medicine. A penance was set for overlaying (lying upon) a child. In the twelfth century, a penance was also incurred by caregivers when infants in their charge died of scalding. Refusal to nurse an infant and the death of a child by the mother's hand likewise brought church censure. The bishop of Bamberg in the twelfth century forbade the killing of girl babies because it was then such a widespread practice in his domain, but a thirteenth-century German law permitted a man distressed by poverty to exterminate or sell his children, provided he did not sell them to pagans or, in the case of girls, into prostitution.

The secular courts steadily increased their jurisdiction over infanticide. In 1224, overlaying was so prevalent that the statutes of Winchester penalized women just for keeping infants in bed with them. Church admonitions were repeated so often, many people's eyes must have been shut to reality. The royal court of Henry I assumed authority when a child was killed by anyone other than the parent. When Henry VIII broke off from the Church of Rome, secular authorities took complete jurisdiction. The laws became more stringent, although many modifications were made through the years. Rapid urbanization made concealment more difficult, and society began to reevaluate the worth of the child (55).

In spite of shocking evidence to the contrary, numerous inquests of battered children returned a verdict of natural death. In his inimitable fashion, Charles Dickens, in *Oliver Twist* (1839), describes the ordinary inquest:

> Occasionally, when there was some more than usually interesting inquest upon a parish child who had been overlooked in turning up a bedstead, or inadvertently scalded to death when there happened to be a washing . . . the jury would take it into their heads to ask troublesome questions, or the parishioners would rebelliously affix their signatures to a remonstrance. But, the impertinencies were speedily checked by the evidence of the surgeon, and the testimony of the beadle; the former of whom had always opened the body and found nothing inside (which was very probable indeed), and the latter of whom invariably swore whatever the Parish wanted. (56)

Oscar Wilde, in a letter to the *Daily Chronicle,* 27 May 1897, from personal experience in the Reading jail, wrote an impassioned plea for prison reform, especially regarding children incarcerated even before adjudication. "The cruelty that is practiced by day and by night on children in English prisons," he said, "is incredible . . . Every child is confined to its cell for 23 hours out of 24 . . . If an individual, parent or guardian, did this to a child he would be severely punished. The Society for the Prevention of Cruelty to Children would take the matter up at once . . . But our society does worse . . . Inhuman treatment of a child is always inhuman by whomsoever it is inflicted." Tiny children were fed revolting food, which he described in detail. They were terrorized by the prison system. "No child under fourteen years of age should be sent to prison at all," he declared (57).

When young children were imported for sexual misuse, the Society for the Prevention of Cruelty to Children became involved with the white slave question and was instrumental in passing protective laws against this kind of child abuse. The Mann Act also particularly protect girls. The Lindbergh Law against kidnapping was another step in the progress of child protective laws.

A significant step was separation of minors from adult criminals and the institution of juvenile courts. A juvenile court was established in Chicago at the turn of this century, and in 1907 the Los Angeles Police Department began to specialize in juvenile affairs, creating in 1910 a separate juvenile bureau. This police department in 1970 set up a desk for abused children and in 1974 established the first battered child police unit to handle physical and sexual abuse of children.

Prior to 1964, there were no effectual child abuse reporting laws. In 1961, during the American Academy of Pediatrics' conference on child abuse, chaired by Dr. C. Henry Kempe, the first model child abuse law was drafted. Experience and increased insight into the psychodynamics of the abusive parent led to revisions. First the law was aimed at case finding and deterrent punishment, but soon it was apparent that the entire family was often involved in the "battered child syndrome."

The Child Abuse Prevention and Treatment Act (Public Law 93-247) was passed on 31 January 1974; its passage established a National Center on Child Abuse and Neglect (NCCAN). The definition of child abuse used in the Child Abuse Prevention and Treatment Act is essentially unchanged, "Child abuse and neglect means the physical or mental injury, sexual abuse, negligent treatment, or maltreatment of a child under the age of 18 by a person who is responsible for the child's welfare under circumstances which indicate the child's health or welfare is harmed or threatened thereby."

In 1978, child sexual abuse was incorporated into the federal Child Abuse Prevention and Treatment Act. The definition of sexual abuse included rape, molestation, and child pornography. With these new definitions of child sexual abuse came expanded mandatory reporting requirements which were tied to federal funding of state programs. The federal government also began at that time to increase funding for studies and dissemination of information (58).

Dr. Vincent de Francis, director of the Children's Division of the American Humane Association, argued a less popular view of the importance of child neglect: "We are concerned about the abused child, but the children are abused in many ways, not purely the battered child, we have children who are sexually abused, we have children who are neglected in a host of ways. If we are going to address ourselves to the problems of children who need help, we must address ourselves to the entire problem" (59). The book *Making an Issue of Child Abuse: Political Agenda Setting for Social Problems* (59) provides a contemporary historical view of how child abuse became a major issue in the United States and was placed on the nation's political agenda.

Child Abuse as a Pediatric Problem

Except for medical care of the injured child, the problems of the battered child in the past ordinarily were not the concern of physicians. Their mission was to heal the sick, not to deal with social problems. The cross the child had to bear was the responsibility of society. The physicians were implicated not in the course of practice but, rather, in company with other compassionate citizens charged with a moral obligation to protect children. They did not handle social, psychological, cultural, religious, or economic afflictions, shunned politics, left morals to the theologians, and scrupulously avoided any controversial police activity that might conflict with the sacred Hippocratic principle of confidentiality. They divulged privileged communications only when the public health required it, as during the plague. Child abuse, child labor, juvenile delinquency, and similar social questions historically were ethical and moral problems, not strictly medical ones.

Nevertheless, the medical profession was not unmindful. Abraham Jacobi, when he was president of the New York State Medical Society in 1882, formed a committee to cooperate with the Society for the Prevention of Cruelty to Children in formulating legislation to improve child labor laws.

In 1946, John Caffey, a pediatrician and a radiologist, described six infants with subdural hematomas and long bone fractures in the absence of any history of trauma. Caffey noted that fractures of the cranium are not infrequently associated with infantile subdural hematomas. He also noted that in none of these cases was there a history of injury toward the child to which the injuries could be reasonably attributed. In no case was there clinical evidence of generalized or localized skeletal diseases which predisposed to pathological fractures. Caffey described the differential diagnosis of cortical thickening of bones in the absence of disease. In one of the cases, the infant was "clearly unwanted by both parents and this raised the question of intentional maltreatment of the infant." He finally surmised that the fractures of the long bones were caused by the same traumatic forces which were presumably responsible for the subdural hematomas (60).

In 1974, Caffey made another major contribution when he published his article "The Whiplash Shaken Infant Syndrome." He presented evidence which indicated that many so-called battered babies are really shaken babies. He advocated a "nationwide educational campaign against the shaking, slapping, jerking, and jolting of infants' heads."

Dr. Fredrick Silverman reinforced the findings of striking roentgenologic manifestations of unrecognized trauma. Again, the history from the caretaker was important in disclosing no history of trauma. The unsuspected finding of fractures on routine X rays prior to surgery was noted. Silverman also documented the evolution of healing lesions over time (61).

Finally, when Wooley and Evans (62) blasted the medical profession in 1955 for its reluctance to concede that the multiple injuries to children were committed willfully, the profession began to pay attention.

Dr. C. Henry Kempe and his colleagues in Denver studied all the different features of child abuse from 1956 to 1961. In 1961, Dr. Kempe was chairman of the program committee for the American Academy of Pediatrics and organized a multidisciplinary conference with the emotive title of "The Battered Child Syndrome." This conference, and its provocative title, triggered an impassioned outburst on behalf of abused children. A bandwagon effect was generated. The Children's Bureau provided generous grants for study of the subject, and the American Humane Society carried out surveys, issued pertinent publications, and convened national symposia considering many different angles. Centers were set up to look into the basic causes of abnormal child-rearing processes that increase child abuse and to initiate new methods of dealing with them.

Dr. Kempe created one of the first child protection teams in the nation at the Colorado General Hospital in Denver in 1958. The other two were started by Helen Boardman and by Elizabeth Elmer who were social workers based respectively at Children's Hospital of Los Angeles and Children's Hospital of Pittsburgh. Both clearly recognized the role of parents as abusers and initiated programs for the families. The landmark article "The Battered Child Syndrome" (63), was published in 1962 in the *Journal of the American Medical Association*. It contained the results of a survey of district attorneys who had reported that a large number of children were being severely beaten. Because of the multidisciplinary nature of the problem, several colleagues were co-authors of the paper including Dr. Fred Silverman, a pediatric radiologist; Dr. Brandt Steele, a psychiatrist; Dr. William Droege-

1.6 Ray E. Helfer, M.D.   1.7 C. Henry Kempe, M.D.

mueller, then a recent graduate of the University of Colorado School of Medicine; and Dr. Henry Silver, a pediatrician.

This article and the attendant publicity alerted medical professionals to the problem of child abuse for the first time on a national level. The initial response of society and the government was to pass laws requiring physicians and other health professionals to report "suspected" cases of abuse and neglect. Between 1963 and 1968, all fifty states enacted mandatory reporting laws. These were the most rapidly adopted pieces of legislation in the history of the United States. Laws dealing with child abuse are very controversial, with discussions continuing as to which has the greater priority, the children's right to protection or the family's right to raise their children in the way they see fit (see chapter 4). A "child abuse" heading first appeared in the *Quarterly Cumulative Index Medicus* in 1965, under which about forty articles were listed.

Kempe, Steele, and their colleagues were instrumental in stimulating the development of individual therapy programs for abusive and neglectful parents. In 1967, a lay therapist program using nonprofessionals to support and befriend abusive and neglectful parents was established. In the following year, 1968, the first edition of *The Battered Child* edited by Ray E. Helfer (fig. 1.6) and C. Henry Kempe (fig. 1.7) was published (64). Research was begun on the role of the "health visitor" in the prevention of early childhood injuries using verified cases.

Since that time, professionals have become aware of the complexity of the roots of child abuse and neglect and are realizing that it is necessary to take a multidisciplinary approach to understand, treat, and work toward prevention of the problem. Social work, legal, health, psychology, education, and law enforcement professionals must work together to bring about effective intervention and prevention.

The field has continued to gain momentum, both at the national and international level. The First International Congress on Child Abuse and Neglect was held in Geneva, Switzerland, in 1976 and has been held every other year since that time. The Tenth International Conference was held in Kuala Lumper, Malaysia, in 1994, the eleventh in Dublin, Ireland, in 1996. In 1977, the International Society for the Prevention of Child Abuse and Neglect was established, and the first issue of the *Child Abuse and Neglect: The International Journal* was published with C. Henry Kempe as editor.

Summary

Fortunately, child maltreatment has been recognized over the last three decades as an issue of genuine concern for societies throughout the world. Despite the continued reluctance of many people to acknowledge that child abuse and neglect do exist, progress has been made in identifying and better understanding the problem and its roots.

The primary approach to treatment has shifted from the punitive to the therapeutic. Child protection laws are now oriented toward nonpunitive protection of children, helping families in crisis, preserving good standards of parental behavior, and providing basic services for optimum care of children in a family relationship. "To cure is the voice of the past, to prevent the divine whisper of today" (53).

Broad issues such as cultural diversity are reflected in the Indian Child Welfare Act of 1978 and the Permanency Planning Act of 1980, which seek to protect cultural heritage while responding to the needs of children whose families can no longer take care of them. In addition to the work of the various professionals, more awareness has developed among the general public of the need for better care for children. This has led to more community involvement and the mobilization of volunteers and resources in an attempt to develop positive interventions and prevention programs.

No single person, discipline, or institution can solve the problem of child maltreatment. History has shown, however, that society has begun to revise its valuation of children—no longer counted as chattel, they are recognized as important contributors to the future.

References

1. Burdett, H. C. 1895. *Burdett's Hospital and Charities Annual.* New York: Scribner.
2. Bakan, D. 1971. *The Slaughter of the Innocents.* Boston: Beacon Press.
3. de Mause, L. 1974. The Evolution of Childhood. In *The History of Childhood,* ed. L. de Mause, 1–73. New York: Psychohistory Press.
4. Bremner, R. H. 1974. *Children and Youth in America: A Documentary History.* Vol. 2, *1866–1932.* Cambridge, Mass.: Harvard University Press.
5. Harper, R. F. 1904. *The Code of Hammurabi, King of Babylon about 2000 B.C.* 2d ed. Chicago: University of Chicago Press.

6. Aries, P. 1962. *Centuries of Childhood: A Social History of Family Life,* trans. R. Baldick. New York: Knopf.

7. Slinger, W. H. 1919. *Child Placing in Families.* New York: Russell Sage.

8. Langer, L. 1973–74. Infanticide: A Historical Survey. *History of Childhood Q.* 1:353–62.

9. Plato. 1898. *The Dialogues of Plato,* trans. B. Jowett. New York: Random House.

10. Aristotle, qtd. in Jones, J. W. 1956. *The Law and Legal Theory of the Greeks: An Introduction.* Oxford: Clarendon Press.

11. Booth, G. 1721. *Historical Library of Diodorus the Sicilian.* London: n.p.

12. Jones, T. 1978. *In the Twilight of Antiquity.* Minneapolis: University of Minnesota Press.

13. de Mause, L. 1980. Our Forbearers Made Childhood a Nightmare. In *Traumatic Abuse and Neglect of Children at Home,* ed. G. J. Williams and J. Money, 14–20. Baltimore: Johns Hopkins University Press.

14. Ashby, H. T. 1922. *Infant Mortality.* 2d ed. Cambridge: Cambridge University Press.

15. Rogers, P. 1979. *Henry Fielding: A Biography.* New York: Scribner's.

16. Radbill, S. X. 1976. Reared in Adversity: Institutional Care of Children in the Eighteenth Century. *Am. J. Diseases of Children* 130:751–56.

17. Tillman, E. B. 1958. Rights of Childhood. Ph.D. diss., University of Wisconsin.

18. Willius, F. A. 1950. Historical Comments. In *Diagnosis and Treatment of Cardiovascular Disease,* 4th ed., vol. 1, ed. W. D. Stroud. Philadelphia: F. A. Davis.

19. Crawley, E. 1902. *The Mystic Rose: A Study of Primitive Marriage.* New York: Macmillan.

20. *Indian Medical Gazette.* 1890. Editorial. Sept.

21. Handcock, P., ed. 1932. *The Code of Hammurabi.* New York: Macmillan.

22. Flandrin, J. 1976. *Families in Former Times: Kinship, Household, and Sexuality in Early Modern France.* New York: Cambridge University Press.

23. Freud, S. [1913] 1950. *Totem and Taboo.* New York: W. W. Norton.

24. Brownmiller, S. 1975. *Against Our Will: Men, Women, and Rape.* New York: Simon and Schuster.

25. Daro, D., and Wiese, D. 1995. NCPCA Annual Fifty State Survey. Chicago: National Committee for the Prevention of Child Abuse and Neglect.

26. Hirsch, S. 1980. Speech delivered in Washington, D.C. National Institutes of Health.

27. Taylor, R. 1981. *Good and Evil: A New Direction.* New York: Macmillan.

28. Keill, N. 1971. *Varieties of Sexual Experience.* New York: International University Press.

29. Chesney, K. 1970. *The Anti-Society: An Account of the Victorian Underworld.* Boston: Gambit.

30. Kingdon, F. 1961. Literature and Sex: Sex and Today's Society. In *Encyclopedia of Sexual Behavior,* vol. 2, ed. A. Ellis and A. Abarbanel, 631–40. New York: Hawthorn Books.

31. Montaigne, M. de. 1991. *The Essays of Michel de Montaigne,* trans. and ed. M. A. Screech. New York: Penguin Books.

32. Charles Dodgson, qtd. in Macdonald, G. 1979. *Camera Victorian Eyewitness: A History of Photography, 1826–1913.* New York: Viking.

33. Charles Dodgson, qtd. in Cohen, M. N. 1978. *Lewis Carroll's Photographs of Nude Children.* Philadelphia: Phillip H. and A. S. W. Rosenbach Foundation.

34. Cohen, M. N. 1978. Lewis Carroll, Photographer of Children: Four Nude Studies. New York: Clarkson, Potter, Inc.

35. Gernsheim, H. 1969. *The History of Photography from the Camera Obscura to the Beginning of the Modern Era.* London: Thames and Hudson.

36. Evans, H. 1979. *Harlots, Whores, and Hookers: A History of Prostitution.* New York: Taplinger.

37. *Harper's Weekly.* 1869. 13:91.

38. Moll, A. 1913. *Sexual Life of the Child,* trans. Eden Paul. New York: Macmillan.

39. Tuchman, B. W. 1978. *A Distant Mirror: The Calamitous Fourteenth Century.* New York: Knopf.

40. Rousseau, J.-J. 1933. *Emile.* New York: Dutton.

41. Riis, J. 1894. *Children of the Poor.* New York: Putnam.
42. Lazoritz, S. 1990. Whatever Happened to Mary Ellen? *Child Abuse and Neglect: International J.* 14:143–49.
43. Robinson, W. J. 1909. *Collectanea Jacobi,* vol. 6. New York: Critic and Guide.
44. Radbill, S. X. 1973. Mesopotamian Pediatrics. *Episteme* 7:283.
45. Pinkham, M. W. 1941. *Woman in the Sacred Scriptures of Hinduism.* New York: Columbia University Press.
46. Radbill, S. X. 1955. History of Children's Hospitals. *Am. J. Diseases of Children* 90:411–16.
47. Doherty, W. J. 1978. *Saint Vincent de Paul and His World,* rev. ed. [originally written by Monseignor Jean Calbert; updated, revised, adapted, and modernized]. Vatican City: Palazzo San Callisto in Trastevere.
48. Nichols, R. H., and Wray, F. A. 1935. *The History of the Foundling Hospital.* London: Oxford University Press.
49. Paulson, R. 1974. *Hogarth: His Life, Art, and Times.* New Haven, Conn.: Yale University Press.
50. Sanger, W. W. 1898. *History of Prostitution.* New York: Medical Publishing Co.
51. Peiper, A. 1965. *Chronik der Kinderheilkunde,* 4th ed. Leipzig.
52. Crew, J. J. 1882. *Care of Deserted Infants.* Philadelphia: Pennsylvania Society to Protect Children from Cruelty.
53. *British Med. J.* 1903. 17:154-55.
54. *Philadelphia Inquirer.* 1979. Editorial. 16 Apr.
55. Damme, C. 1978. The Worth of an Infant under Law. *Med. History* 22:1–24.
56. Dickens, Charles. 1839. *Oliver Twist.* Harmondsworth: Penguin.
57. Wilde, O. 1931. The Case of Warder Martin. In *The Writings of Oscar Wilde,* vol. 4. New York: Wise and Co.
58. U.S. Department of Health, Education, and Welfare. 1978. *Child Sexual Abuse: Incest, Assault, and Sexual Exploration.* Washington, DC: U.S. Government Printing Office.
59. de Francis, Vincent. Qtd. in Nelson, B. J. 1984. *Making an Issue of Child Abuse: Political Agenda Setting for Social Problems.* Chicago: University of Chicago Press.
60. Caffey, J. 1946. Multiple Fractures in the Long Bones of Infants Suffering from Chronic Subdural Hematoma. Am. J. Roentgenology 56:163–73.
61. Silverman, F. N. 1953. The Roentgen Manifestations of Unrecognized Skeletal Trauma in Infants. *Am. J. Roentgenology* 69:413–27.
62. Wooley, P. V., and Evans, W. A. 1955. Significance of Skeletal Lesions in Infants Resembling Those of Traumatic Origin. *JAMA* 158(7):539–43.
63. Kempe, C. H.; Silverman, F. N.; Steele, B. F.; Droegemueller, W.; and Silver, H. K. 1962. The Battered Child Syndrome. *JAMA* 181(1):17–24.
64. Helfer, R. E., and Kempe, C. H. 1968. *The Battered Child.* Chicago: University of Chicago Press.

2

Culture and Child Maltreatment

JILL E. KORBIN

The relationship between culture and child maltreatment is complex, politically charged, and fraught with unresolved issues. The challenge in understanding child maltreatment from the vantage point of different cultures is to encompass cultural diversity and to ensure equitable standards of care and protection for all children. In this chapter, I will consider culture and child maltreatment in four areas: definitions, incidence and prevalence, etiology, and practice.

Culture and the Definition of Child Maltreatment

Definitional problems have hampered progress in understanding the relationship between culture and child maltreatment. Imprecision and the lack of operational criteria in the definition of child maltreatment have received considerable attention in the literature (1). These definitional problems are exacerbated in cross-cultural and multiethnic comparisons.

Examples of practices that would be differentially defined as abusive or neglectful by different cultural groups are abundant in the cross-cultural record. Cross-cultural research has not yielded a universally ideal parenting strategy. Rather, child rearing must be viewed within the social and historical context in which it is embedded (2–6). While anthropology has characteristically emphasized that all cultural practices are relative, numerous anthropologists have increasingly directed attention to cultural practices that even when understood in context are detrimental and harmful to individuals (7, 8).

Descriptions of cultural practices are written in what is termed the *ethnographic present*, that is, the specific period in time which an individual anthropologist studied such practices and presented them in the literature. Use of the ethnographic present does not necessarily imply that such cultural practices still occur. Terms of cultural or ethnic groups that I use in this chapter are those employed by the authors of the studies I cite.

Documenting cultural practices that appear abusive from the standpoint of one group but not another only moves the child maltreatment field so far. Establishing a universally accepted definition of child maltreatment, however, has been fraught with difficulties. A cataloguing of the painful and difficult experiences that children may undergo around the

JILL E. KORBIN, Ph.D., is professor of anthropology at Case Western Reserve University.

world would be extensive. It is equally instructive to consider Euro-American child care practices through the eyes of other cultures.

As but one example, western pediatricians advise that it is developmentally important for infants and young children to sleep independently, in their own beds and rooms (9). Rural Hawai'ian-American-Polynesian women with whom I worked in the 1970s, in contrast, asked me to verify that white parents actually isolated infants and young children in separate beds, and worse, in separate rooms, alone for the entire night. While this may seem like a benign example in that no physical injuries are inflicted on the children, many cultures believe that isolating children for the night is not only detrimental to social development but also potentially dangerous. These women responded to my explanations about the dangers of overlaying with incredulity; they contended that it would be impossible to sleep through the struggles of a suffocating infant or toddler. From an evolutionary and cross-cultural perspective, McKenna and colleagues (10) have suggested that there are advantages to co-sleeping, including the hypothesis that parents and children coordinate breathing and sleep cycles, thus preventing Sudden Infant Death Syndrome (SIDS) related to apnea.

The literature on culturally informed definitions of child maltreatment has followed three basic strategies. First, theoretical constructions have been formulated based on ethnographic descriptions of child-rearing practices, as well as deviation from those practices, and on international accounts of child maltreatment (4, 5, 11–13). Second, studies with specific cultural and/or ethnic groups have sought to identify the diversity of conceptions of child abuse and outline the parameters for cultural misunderstanding of culturally appropriate practices (14). And, third, studies employing vignettes have sought to systematically study cultural and professional definitions and perceptions of the seriousness of hypothetical incidents of child abuse and neglect (15–17).

All three strategies have strengths and weaknesses. In the first two, definitions are often anecdotal or based on small and nonrepresentative samples. Theoretical models for definitions have been suggested in these works, but these models have not been subjected to empirical verification. These works, however, have usefully underlined the importance of considering cultural meanings and definitions in addressing child maltreatment. In the third strategy, we find that although vignette studies are methodologically rigorous, they do not necessarily reflect behavior (11). Nonetheless, vignette studies have indicated cultural differences in child-rearing beliefs and values that may exert a strong influence on definitions of child maltreatment (15, 16).

Cultural Conflict in Defining Child Maltreatment

Cultural conflict in defining child maltreatment generally arises as a result of disagreement concerning cultural differences in child care. In reality, it is the dominant culture in any society that sets the prevailing child-rearing standards, just as it sets the standards for other behaviors. As indicated in figure 2.1, the greater the divergence in child care practices and beliefs, the greater the potential for cultural conflict in definitions of maltreatment (18). At the level of cultural differences, definitions of child maltreatment have a substantial com-

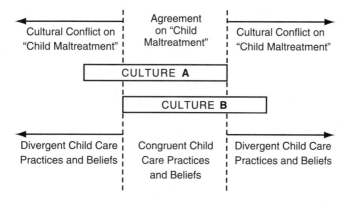

2.1 Cultural conflict in defining child maltreatment.

ponent of relativity. Cultural practices must be understood within their context. Explanation and understanding, however, do not preclude trying to assure equitable standards of child protection. The majority of attention in the literature has been directed to documenting legitimate cultural practices that are defined as abuse by one group but not by another. This documentation is critical if we are to avoid misidentifying culture as abuse or abuse as culture (19).

Nevertheless it is important for us to recognize that cultural practices are not necessarily benign simply because they are cultural. First, cultural practices must be viewed in the context of ongoing change in each society. What is well suited to one situation may not be suited at all to another. Laotian and Cambodian refugees in the United States, for example, bring with them child care patterns that enlist sibling caretaking and community responsibility for child supervision. Some of these refugees express surprise that the dominant culture in the United States, as reflected through schools and child protection agencies, looks askance at sibling caretaking by children as young as eight—something that is unremarkable in Laos and Cambodia (20) and, indeed, in much of the world.

Second, some cultural practices may cause injury or be harmful to children. Child care behaviors that are entirely normative may in fact reduce the well-being of children in general or categories of children in particular (21). However, culturally sanctioned normative behaviors are usually not inflicted with malintent, regardless of harm that may ensue, and are not, strictly speaking, defined as child maltreatment. This does not mean, however, that intervention is impossible. In an area of the Southwest, lead poisoning in young Hispanic children was linked to indigenous medications used to cure *empacho,* a bolus of the stomach that must be purged (22, 23). Educational and community awareness efforts were successful in diminishing the harmful form of these substances, and thus the incidence of lead poisoning, while not minimizing the cultural importance or necessity of treating *empacho.*

Idiosyncratic Violation of Cultural Norms Intracultural diversity, or idiosyncratic departure from cultural standards, is a critical domain for culturally informed definitions of child maltreatment. All cultures contain individuals who deviate from cultural standards and norms (24, 25), including those concerning parenting and child care (4). The continuum of acceptable to unacceptable behavior within any culture must be clearly understood: this is the level at which we can best differentiate cultural practices from maltreatment.

Differentiating cultural differences from child maltreatment has been hampered in current child protection work largely because child protection workers are usually restricted in their community contacts to problematic individuals and families rather than being educated about the range of culturally acceptable and unacceptable behaviors. For example, children left alone and unsupervised frequently prompt child maltreatment reports among the Navajo (26). Parents who are reported for these behaviors may justify their behavior as traditional Navajo child-rearing patterns of sibling caretaking and responsibility training. However, in Hauswald's interviews with thirty Navajo mothers, none thought that young children should be left alone for extended periods with siblings of less than thirteen years of age. These mothers disapproved of leaving children alone overnight without adult supervision. Still, neglect cases in the community involved children as young as five years of age being left for long periods to baby-sit even younger siblings (26). This, then, is not a cultural pattern but, rather, a departure from cultural norms and values, exacerbated by problems of poverty, unemployment, and alcoholism.

Finkelhor and Korbin (12) have suggested that culturally informed definitions of child maltreatment must include any related behavior that is proscribed, preventable, and proximate. Starr (27) similarly includes the cultural and societal standards within which an act is judged. Thus, cultural practices are not, strictly speaking, abuse since they are not proscribed—at least not by the group in question. We can, accordingly, consider the relative harm and benefit of diverse cultural practices (7) without necessarily assigning the label of child abuse to an entire cultural group. Idiosyncratic departure, however, is proscribed, even within the culture in which it occurs.

Finally, it is important to consider more precisely what designates membership in a culture. Cultures and ethnic groups have too often been regarded as homogeneous. Broad classifications of African American, Asian American, Native American, or European American do not necessarily or invariably correspond to the reality of every member's day-to-day life. Each of these broad categories contains multiple and distinctive cultures, as well as intracultural diversity along the lines of generation, acculturation, education, income, gender, age, and past experience. Further, individuals evince great diversity in the degree to which they participate in identifying with their culture's values and practices (28, 29).

Culture and the Incidence and Prevalence of Child Maltreatment

When international efforts to address child maltreatment were being initiated, C. Henry Kempe (30) suggested that child abuse was present in all societies and that preventing it was a matter of arousing public and professional willingness to recognize the problem. In most Western societies, once child abuse is officially recognized, prevalence data are reasonably similar (31–33). International efforts to call attention to the problem have seen an increase in the awareness of multiple forms of child maltreatment around the world. Publications in *Child Abuse and Neglect: The International Journal* represent a wide array of regions and nations.[1] Emphases, not unexpectedly, have varied. Some societies have elected to address problems of child labor or child prostitution, while others have explored intra-familial child maltreatment. This growing international literature on child maltreatment makes it abundantly clear that child abuse and neglect is not restricted to Western societies.

Despite increasing awareness of the issue around the world, child abuse and neglect are often difficult to recognize in small populations, especially when national-level data is not available. Because child maltreatment is a low base rate behavior, it may occur very infrequently in a small population during a single year of anthropological fieldwork. Among the Inuit, for example, anthropologist Graburn observed a few cases of what could be described as the classic battered child. These cases were rare, but their very existence, however minimal, contradicted past literature on Inuit peoples and Graburn's own overall impression of nurturant, indulgent, and nonpunitive Inuit parenting. A description of these cases was not published for many years after Graburn's fieldwork (34), thereby leaving intact a literature that would lead one to believe that child abuse was virtually nonexistent among Inuit peoples living in traditional circumstances (34, 35). Similarly, in my own fieldwork among rural Hawai'ian-Polynesian-Americans, child maltreatment seemed so aberrant from the larger pattern of loving and attentive care to children that the few cases that came to my attention also did not find their way into the literature for many years (36).

Additionally, it is often difficult to determine the incidence or prevalence of child mal-treatment in societies with high rates of child mortality (especially high mortality rates among infants and children under five years of age). Neglect as a component in differential child survival may be difficult to distinguish from disease or malnutrition in individual cases even though demographic analyses have yielded categories of children at risk (37). Some children may fail to receive the level of care required to ensure their survival, but the cause of death may be attributed to factors beyond parental control. While her analysis has generated controversy (38), Scheper-Hughes (39) has described a pattern of classification of child illness in a Brazilian favela which tolerates parental withdrawal of care from chil-dren who are thought to be unlikely to thrive.

In the United States, the literature is contradictory, but speculation persists about dif-ferential rates of child maltreatment among cultural or ethnic populations. Reporting bias and the confounding of social class and ethnicity are equally, if not more, compelling ex-planations for these differential rates than those that rely on differences in cultural values or child-rearing practices.

Neither of the two national incidence studies (40, 41)—the results of which were pub-lished in 1981 and 1988, respectively—found a significant relationship between race, cul-ture, or ethnicity, and the incidence, type, or severity of child maltreatment. Both studies classified children as "black," "white," or "other." As I explained in my discussion above, these broad classifications have limited usefulness in helping us to understand cultural dif-ferences more accurately.

1. The number of manuscripts from diverse nations that have been published is extensive, and listing them all is beyond the space limitations of the present chapter. I recommend the reader consult *Child Abuse and Ne-glect: The International Journal.*

Jason and colleagues (42), using data from the state of Georgia's Department of Protective Services, found that African Americans were disproportionately reported for child abuse, unrelated to reporting bias. Horowitz and Wolock (43) found that while African Americans were overrepresented in abuse and neglect reports, their distribution was equal to their representation in the federal Aid to Families with Dependent Children program.

Lauderdale and colleagues' research in Texas (44) also found an overrepresentation for African Americans. In a within-group analysis, European Americans had the highest rate of physical abuse relative to other types of maltreatment, and African Americans and Mexican Americans had higher proportions of neglect. Lauderdale et al. speculated about the cultural reasons for these differences, basing their inquiry on the literature on socialization and personality patterns.

Additionally, these researchers found a significant rural-urban difference within ethnic groups. African Americans living in rural areas showed the lowest rates of abuse, even though African Americans demonstrated the highest rates of abuse of all ethnic groups when area of residence (either urban or rural) was not included in the analysis. Rates for Mexican Americans also were lower than European American rates when residence area was included in the analysis. We can, of course, construct many possible interpretations of these findings and envision multiple implications. The most obvious is to study the workings of rural African American communities, the strengths of which may be weakened with increasing urbanization. We cannot, however, dismiss the possibility of bias in the reports.

Light's (45) reanalysis of Gil's (46) data compared incidence rates of child abuse for African Americans and European Americans in four northern and four southern states. In the northern states, European Americans accounted for 27.3% of child abuse and neglect cases, while in the southern states, European Americans accounted for 72.9% of the cases. This discrepancy was not attributable to the proportions of African Americans and European Americans in the population. Rather, at the time the data were gathered, in 1967, social welfare services and facilities for African American children in the South were extremely scarce. Child abuse and neglect in the African American population tended to be handled informally, within kin and community networks, and without recourse to public agencies. In the North, however, most case reports involved exactly those poor, ethnically diverse families who utilized public welfare services. What at first examination might well have appeared to be a difference tied solely to residence could also be related to the relative availability of social services.

Numerous researchers have in fact identified reporting bias by race and social class in the literature on child maltreatment (e.g. 47). Hampton and Newberger's reanalysis (48) of the 1981 National Incidence Study (40) found that class and race were the best predictors of whether an incident of child maltreatment was reported by hospitals. Impoverished African American families were more likely to be reported than affluent European American families, even if the severity of the abusive incident was comparable. O'Toole et al. (17) found that vignettes were more likely to be identified as abuse if a lower-class caretaker was involved. A recent study found that drownings were more likely to be reported to child protective services (CPS) if, among other variables, the family was nonwhite and poor (49).

Reporting bias is evident not only in the United States. A government report in New

Zealand in the early 1970s (50) found that Polynesian (primarily Maori) children were overrepresented in child abuse and neglect reports. Twenty years later, Kotch et al. (51) found that Polynesian (particularly Maori and Samoan) children are still more likely to have injuries and fatalities attributed to maltreatment than are white children.

Not only are child abuse and neglect cases influenced by reporting bias based on the ethnicity of the alleged perpetrator or the identity of the reporter (52), but they are also influenced by neighborhood and community socioeconomic factors and the severity of an agency's caseload. Child protection workers' judgments about the seriousness of abuse and neglect vignettes were influenced by the overall severity of cases coming in to their agencies. Child protection workers in socioeconomically disadvantaged areas with more severe abuse and neglect caseloads had a higher threshold in judging the severity of abuse vignettes, while those in socioeconomically advantaged areas had a comparably lower threshold (53).

The argument about ethnic differences in rates of child abuse and neglect cannot, however, be wholly dismissed on the basis of detection and reporting errors and bias. Self-reports on the Conflict Tactics Scales (CTS) indicate that lower socioeconomic status is a risk factor for violent behaviors toward children (54, 55). Although violence toward children occurs in all social strata, such violence—particularly, severe violence—is more likely to take place in poor families. Gelles (56) further focused the analysis to indicate that one subset of the poor—particularly, young mothers with young children living below the poverty line—is at the greatest risk of violent behavior toward children.

Despite these findings on socioeconomic status, self-report data on the CTS in the first National Family Violence Study did not find a significant difference between African Americans and European Americans in reported violent acts toward children (54). In the 1975–1985 National Family Violence Restudy, however, the rates of severe violence toward African American children increased, as did the ratio of African Americans to European Americans for severe violence toward children. That African American children did not experience the nearly 50% reduction in severe violence found for the population as a whole (57) was explained by self-reports on the CTS that African Americans were more likely to use an object when hitting a child (58).

The data available, then, leave many issues unresolved. Both official reporting data and self-report data indicate that impoverished families show higher rates of reported child maltreatment (59, 54). Garbarino and Ebata (11) argue that it is under conditions of socioeconomic deprivation and stress that cultural differences manifest themselves most clearly. Giovannoni and Billingsley (60) found that it is the poorest of the poor, across ethnic groups, who neglect children. Ethnic groups at greatest risk of poverty, then, appear to demonstrate increased incidence and prevalence of child maltreatment. There is no convincing evidence that allows us to separate the effects of socioeconomic status from the effects of cultural or ethnic identity on rates of reported child abuse and neglect. A critical problem is that the search has nevertheless ensued for cultural factors that are related to maltreatment. This search has been largely speculative and has generated much debate on both the risk factors and the protective factors afforded by diverse cultures.

Population-based survey research on the prevalence of child sexual abuse has not supported the existence of ethnic differences in rates of child sexual abuse. Priest's survey of students attending historically African American colleges (61) indicated rates similar to those found in other surveys. Finkelhor's Boston study (62) did not find an association between ethnicity and child sexual abuse. Russell's prevalence study in San Francisco (63) included four ethnic groups (Latina, Asian, African American, and European American) and found no significant ethnic differences in intrafamilial abuse. Wyatt (64) specifically sampled for equal representation of African Americans and European Americans and found no significant ethnic differences in the prevalence of child sexual abuse. The two national incidence studies also did not find a relationship between race and sexual abuse.

Culture and the Etiology of Child Maltreatment

Considering the problems of definitional ambiguity and inadequate estimates of incidence and prevalence, as discussed above, it is potentially more productive to examine the ways that cultural factors promote or impede child maltreatment. The various pathways, common and divergent, that may lead to child maltreatment in different cultural groups are poorly understood.

We must determine a definitional starting point for exploring the etiology of maltreatment. Among Koreans in the United States studied by Ahn and Gilbert (65), a grandfather touching the genitals of his preschool grandson was understood as an expression of pride in the young child who would carry on the family line. As such, it was regarded not as abusive but as customary—that is, as within normative standards of behavior. Their Korean respondents recognized, nevertheless, that such behavior was regarded differently in this country. In contrast, African Americans and European Americans in this study regarded the touching of children's genitals as unacceptable, noting that there was no reason for it. However, kissing between parents in front of children, regarded benignly by European Americans and African Americans, was regarded as sexually inappropriate by Korean Americans (65). All three groups, then, considered some behaviors unacceptable, even if these behaviors differed from one group to another. Why do some individuals violate the rules of behavior in each group, whatever those rules may be? And how are those behaviors related to child maltreatment?

We need to achieve a better understanding of what is considered sexually charged or dangerous to children in diverse societies. Parental bathing or co-sleeping with children in societies in which these behaviors are not part of the cultural repertoire would be an indication for risk of maladaptive parenting styles or sexual abuse. In Japan, however, where such behaviors occur outside the usual context of sexuality, their existence would not necessarily indicate an increased risk for sexual maltreatment. But since we know that child sexual abuse does occur in Japan (66)—as well in the United States (62, 63) despite differing child care patterns—we are prompted to ask, What are the convergent or divergent pathways leading to sexual misuse?

In addition to our need for definitional clarity, we need reliable and valid estimates of incidence and prevalence to make progress in understanding culture's contribution to child maltreatment. In the previous section, I discussed the overrepresentation of poor and ethnic populations in child abuse and neglect reports. Such differences in reporting have led some researchers to search for cultural practices that would presumably cause these differential rates. With rare exception, studies do not link the cultural practice that is thought to lead to higher incidence or prevalence of child maltreatment with these rates in a systematic way. This has led, in turn, to speculation, in the absence of empirical justification, about what cultures are more or less prone to abusive and neglectful behaviors toward children. Better research is badly needed on the relationship between child-rearing beliefs and practices and abusive behavior. In exploring the relationship between culture/ethnicity and child maltreatment, the cultural variable must be "unpacked" (67–69). In other words, because culture is not monolithic, it should not be viewed as being uniformly distributed or having a uniform impact on all its members.

A few exceptional studies, however, do consider the relationship between cultural practices and child maltreatment report rates (70–72). For instance, Samoan Americans are overrepresented and Japanese Americans underrepresented for abuse in Hawai'i, a difference Dubanoski and Snyder (71) attribute to Samoan values concerning physical punishment and increased aggressiveness. This kind of work takes an important step in trying to elucidate the differences between cultural groups that may increase the risk of child abuse. However, intracultural variability must also be considered. Because Dubanoski and Snyder do not measure actual physical punishment within each population, they assume that the value placed on physical discipline is causally linked to actual physical discipline. In fact, though, we do not have data on the distribution of the value accorded to physical punishment within the Samoan and Japanese populations studied or on whether or not such values predict which Samoans or Japanese will abuse (or be reported for abuse). Moreover, Samoan child protective service providers consider physical discipline one of the areas that is likely to be misunderstood by non-Samoans (14). Further, other factors, such as socioeconomic status or the disruption and change involved in the migration of Samoans, could also have explanatory value.

Addressing the issue of both intercultural variability and intracultural variability, Dubanoski (70) also compared Hawai'ian American and European American child maltreatment reports. Hawai'ian Americans were overrepresented, while European Americans were underrepresented in the state of Hawaii's child abuse reports. Looking within the Hawai'ian American population, Dubanoski suggests that child-abusing Hawai'ian American families were low on 'ohana (extended family) involvement.

Culture and Child Maltreatment: Risk Factors and Protective Factors

Culture provides the context for the complex interaction of risk factors and protective factors that respectively contribute to or prevent the occurrence of child maltreatment. Since regularities in the antecedents and consequences of child-rearing practices have been identified cross-culturally (73–75), regularities in the antecedents and consequences of child abuse and neglect should be similarly amenable to cross-cultural research (5, 76).

In searching for the contribution of culture to the etiology of child maltreatment, we must note that intracultural variability can equal or exceed intercultural variability. For example, peer aggression is more likely to be negatively sanctioned in extended than in nuclear households, regardless of the culture in which the family resides (73). In extended families, fighting between children potentially draws more adults into the fray and discord than in nuclear households, in which only the parents (or perhaps only the primary care-taker) need negotiate the aggression. Etiological variables therefore must be demonstrated to have explanatory power both within and between cultures (5).

While current knowledge leads to the conclusion that child abuse occurs in all cultures, we also have reason to believe that there is a differential distribution cross-culturally based on the balance of risk factors and protective factors (4, 5). The most suggestive cross-cultural evidence to date is based on the balance between the embeddedness of child rearing in a larger sociocultural context and the various categories of children at risk for maltreatment. Unfortunately, there is at this point a paucity of cross-cultural research on the contribution of the psychological characteristics or pathology of caregivers.

Embeddedness of Child Rearing in the Larger Sociocultural Context   The presence of social networks and social supports to children and families, as well as a positive balance between supports and strains, has been posited to be important to child well-being and the prevention of child maltreatment (77–79). The cross-cultural literature supports the hypothesis that social networks and the embeddedness of child rearing in a larger social context are crucially significant protections against child maltreatment (4, 5).

The cross-cultural record suggests that children with diminished social networks are vulnerable to maltreatment (80). For example, children from intertribal marriages among the Samia of East Africa were at increased risk of neglect. If the children were not well cared for, neither the mother's kin nor the father's necessarily felt that the children fell under their jurisdiction (81).

Social networks have the potential to serve multiple protective functions for children (82, 5). First, networks provide the personnel for assistance with child care tasks and responsibilities. Second, networks provide options for the temporary and/or permanent redistribution of children. And, third, networks provide the context for collective standards and, therefore, for the scrutiny and enforcement of such standards.

In the United States, the acceptance of physical discipline has been linked to child maltreatment (46, 83). While physical discipline may be accepted by a community, the presence of protective networks may counterbalance this potential risk factor by providing safeguards against excess. If child care tasks and children are shared, rather than considered the property of one or two biological parents, a situation is more likely to develop in which "no one needs an invitation to intervene in the case of an overly severe spanking" (84). Among rural Hawai'ian-Polynesian-Americans, relatives do not hesitate to yell from one house to the next that a spanking has gone on long enough or is too severe a response to the child's misbehavior. Children told me that they often screamed or cried more quickly and loudly than a spanking warranted as an effective strategy to summon help and disarm an angry parent (5, 36).

Cross-culturally, parents are more likely to display warmth rather than rejection toward their children if other adults are available to assist with child care tasks (73, 76). However, it must be cautioned that not all network involvement is positive (85). Not all networks are good networks. Just because abundant kin are in proximity does not necessarily mean that those individuals will be helpful or supportive. Further, if individuals in a child's network are themselves abusive or neglectful, they may reinforce maltreating behaviors. Potentially abusive or neglectful parents may take solace or comfort in the idea that they are not "bad" parents but simply behaving like everyone else around them (86, 87).

Values Placed on Children and Categories of Vulnerable Children   The cross-cultural literature suggests that child maltreatment is less likely in cultures in which children are highly valued for their economic utility, for perpetuating family lines and the cultural heritage, or as sources of emotional pleasure and satisfaction. Nevertheless, generalized cultural values placed on children are not sufficient, in and of themselves, to prevent child maltreatment.

The cross-cultural record suggests categories of children who are at greater risk of maltreatment. Their disvalue or undervalue may be expressed in a range of behaviors. Such children may be subjected to deliberate infanticide, physical abuse and neglect, sexual misuse, psychological maltreatment, or economic exploitation. Some categories of children at increased risk can be identified through demographic analyses of differential mortality patterns, while other categories can be identified only with a thorough understanding of the cultural context (21, 37). All such categories, however, may be exacerbated or mitigated by the particular cultural context in which they occur.

Health and nutrition status. While the direction of cause and effect is difficult to determine, children whose health or nutritional status is compromised may be at increased risk of maltreatment. The apathetic, anorexic, and unresponsive behaviors of malnourished children may fail to elicit the parental solicitousness that would improve their health status and thereby their behavior (88). Cultural beliefs may further compromise an already malnourished child (89, 90). In areas of Mexico and Central America, a child displaying behaviors indicative of malnourishment may instead be perceived as *chipil,* or angry at the mother during weaning and envious of the new sibling. The child is punished or ignored for perceived bad behavior instead of being fed to ameliorate the underlying cause.

Gender. Cultural beliefs about proper care of sons versus daughters can compromise certain children's health and survival (21, 91). Cultural context determines the impact of gender on child maltreatment. The economic status of women and their utility in agricultural work accounts for differences in the male/female ratio—thought to result from female infanticide and selective neglect in childhood—in different parts of India (92). A marked cultural preference for sons, however, does not mean that parents actively dislike or seek to compromise the well-being of their existing daughters (91, 93). In the community in India studied by Poffenberger (93), sons were regarded as delicate flowers while daughters were thought to be much hardier, like stones, able to withstand more hardship than their brothers. The distribution of community resources, such as medical care, reflected these beliefs. In a twenty-year perspective on an Indian community, Minturn (94) found that greater accessibility and lower health care costs of a local clinic greatly improved the likelihood of sur-

2.2 Split pants for Chinese toddlers diminish the potential for parent-child conflict concerning toilet training. (Photograph courtesy of M. Korbin.)

vival for girls. Although in recent years more attention has been directed toward bias against females, the cultural context may also act to the detriment of males. In Greece, for example, higher cultural expectations of sons translates into harsher punishments for boys, which has the potential for spilling over into abuse (95). And in Jamaica, male children are at greater risk of maltreatment because of the matrifocal structure of families (96).

Developmental stage. Children may be more vulnerable to maltreatment at different developmental stages. In the United States, toddlers and adolescents, both of whom display oppositional behaviors, may be at greater risk for abuse (54). Toddlers who do not meet parental standards in the course of toilet training are at increased risk of abuse, including burns inflicted by being dunked in scalding hot water (97). Risks associated with developmental stage, however, must be viewed within the specific cultural context. Among some Native American groups, toilet training became harsher with the adoption of wooden floors that were harder to clean than the previous dirt floors (98). In China, young children who have not yet mastered control of elimination are dressed in pants slit open (see figure 2.2). Elimination can thus be accomplished with minimal mess, diminishing the potential for a battle of wills between parent and child.

Behavioral and personality characteristics. Categories of undervalued children cannot necessarily be identified by evident characteristics but vary with the values a culture confers on personality and physical attributes. A characteristic valued in one society may be disvalued in others. For example, among the Yanomamo of Venezuela, aggressiveness is highly valued in young male children who are encouraged to be "fierce," even to the extent of hitting their fathers (99). In contrast, among the Machiguenga of the Peruvian Amazon, aggressiveness and anger are so highly disvalued that toddlers who have frequent tantrums are subjected to scalding baths (100).

Cultural Competence in Child Maltreatment Work

While an exhaustive discussion of cultural competence is beyond the scope of this chapter, the importance of acquiring cultural competence in child abuse prevention and intervention cannot be minimized (101). Cultural sensitivity and cultural awareness, although prerequisites to competence, are not sufficient. Most individuals, particularly those engaged in human services, regard sensitivity as a marker of a good and decent person. Cultural competence, however, requires us to gain additional knowledge and skills that we can apply strategically in dealing with diverse populations. The People of Color Leadership Institute (102) has identified a continuum of cultural competence; its endpoint goal—the attainment of "advanced cultural competence"—calls on us to advocate for cultural competence not only in the child protection system but throughout society as a whole (103).

The professional literatures in international health and medical anthropology (104–7) have demonstrated repeatedly that program acceptance and efficacy depend not simply on resolving issues of access and availability but just as much on achieving congruence with the needs and cultural beliefs of the target community.

Several writers have suggested cultural values can impede use of child protection agencies, such as familialism (a strong emphasis on and loyalty to the family group rather than a focus on individual members), among the Chinese (16) or African American concerns about "not putting your business into the street," particularly with outsiders (108). In Long's example of sexual abuse in a Native American community (109), relatives recognized the perpetrating uncle's behavior as wrong, and regarded the child as victimized, but opposed the mother's reporting of the abuse to a European American agency. As a result, the mother pursued protection of her child along more culturally congruent lines. Working with a therapist, she developed contingency arrangements, such as leaving her daughter with other relatives when the uncle was present. By maintaining integration in the clan network, the mother selected the most effective protection strategy for her child. Reintegration of the abused child into a network of known individuals who opposed the perpetrator's behavior—even though they were unwilling to extrude him from the group—and who would help to protect the child in the future was a better bet than trying to pursue a prosecution that would have excluded the mother and the child themselves from this support network.

Just because some cultural groups oppose the involvement of child protection agencies in their lives, however, does not mean that they spurn any wider network or helping services for assistance with family problems and issues, including those related to child maltreatment. For example, in many African American communities, the church is an important vehicle for help with family matters, one that has gone largely unrecognized and underutilized by official social service agencies (110).

Treatment Modalities and Strategies

The concept of cultural competence suggests that treatment will be most effective when it is compatible and congruent with the client's cultural values, beliefs, and behaviors (111). Obviously, this is not a simple or monolithic matter. Tharp's review of the literature on the treatment of culturally diverse children (67) suggests that there are three models of cultural compatibility.

The first model proposes cultural specificity, with distinct modalities of treatment for different cultures. One variant of this culturally specific model is to utilize indigenous treatments and healers. For example, *ho'o'ponopono* is a traditional form of family discussion and conflict resolution among Hawai'ians (112) that has been utilized in child abuse intervention. Another variant is to design treatment modalities for specific cultures. Tharp points out that even though the issue of cultural compatibility in treatment is not a new debate, very few culture-specific treatment modalities have been developed. An example is *cuento* therapy, developed for Puerto Rican children, which adapts the traditional use of folktales in child socialization to foster discussion of current difficulties (113).

The second model involves "two-type" treatment approaches that view the majority culture on one side and all children of color on the other. In this view, problems such as poverty and racism are viewed as the underlying causes of difficulties among children of color. This approach holds that strategies to resolve or address these root problems will be sufficient. The diversity within and among different cultures becomes unimportant in the context of broader social issues.

And, third, there are universalistic strategies which assume that the same treatment and intervention will work, with perhaps slight variation, for all groups. Tharp suggests that because universalistic strategies start with the individual, rather than the wider social network, therapists may encounter substantial barriers to the success of intervention with children from cultures in which families and social networks are primarily important. He suggests that treatment strategies start with the larger network of individuals involved with a child. Above all, treatment interventions must be contextualized (67).

No set of generalizations about any cultural or ethnic population will be sufficient to deal with all cases of child maltreatment among culturally diverse populations. The importance of intracultural variability, and the need to specify what is significant about the cultural context (to "unpack" the cultural variable), precludes the development of a library-like card catalog of strategies for working with specific cultural groups. While acquiring knowledge of general cultural patterns provides an important starting point, we must assess each individual, family, and neighborhood on their own merits.

Conclusions and Future Directions

What, then, do we know about the relationship between culture and child maltreatment, and what do we need to know? First, we must take as a given that cultures vary in their definitions of optimal, deficient, and even adequate parenting and that these concepts powerfully influence definitions of child abuse and neglect. We must also be aware that all cultural practices are not necessarily good for the individuals who experience them (7). The child protection field must more carefully evaluate what a specific cultural practice entails, how it fits with the cultural context, what its distribution is within the population, and what impact it has on members of the culture.

Less attention has been paid in the literature to intracultural variability, or the continuum of behaviors that are accepted within any cultural group. Child abuse or neglect is generally not "cultural," in the sense of a whole group acting to the explicit detriment of its children. Instead, maltreatment generally involves individuals acting outside of their culturally accepted continuum of behaviors and practices. Coming to a fuller understanding of intracultural variability and the ways in which individuals negotiate their culture's definitions of rule breaking or deviant behavior is a critical direction for us to take.

Second, the evidence is somewhat contradictory concerning the impact of culture on the incidence and prevalence of child maltreatment. The importance of culture is difficult to determine due to imprecise definitions of both culture and maltreatment, due to possible bias in reporting, and due to the confounding of social class and culture. Current estimates of differences among cultures in rates of child abuse and neglect are equally likely to reflect these problems than true differences in incidence and prevalence. The field would greatly benefit from improved epidemiological data that address these deficits.

Third, culture is likely to be important in the etiology of child maltreatment in providing the context for identifying factors that are risk-enhancing or risk-reducing. The interrelationships of such variables both across and within cultures are poorly understood, however. Culture is not causal in and of itself but functions in the constellations of risk factors and protective factors that different cultures afford. In particular, those of us in the field must work toward improving our understanding of intracultural variability.

And, finally, cultural competence is critical in addressing and resolving family troubles and bolstering family strengths. Prevention and intervention strategies must consider client variables and perspectives, including cultural affiliation. This is not a simple matter: it demands a long-term commitment to developing our knowledge and skills for working across and within the diverse populations that constitute modern society.

References

1. National Research Council, Panel on Research on Child Abuse and Neglect. 1993. *Understanding Child Abuse and Neglect.* Washington, D.C.: National Academy Press.
2. Eisenberg, L. 1981. Cross-Cultural and Historic Perspectives on Child Abuse and Neglect. *Child Abuse and Neglect: International J.* 5(3):299–308.
3. Gelles, R. J. 1987. What to Learn from Cross-Cultural and Historical Research on Child Abuse and Neglect: An Overview. In *Child Abuse and Neglect: Biosocial Dimensions,* ed. R. Gelles and J. Lancaster, 15–30. New York: Aldine de Gruyter.
4. Korbin, J. E., ed. 1981. *Child Abuse and Neglect: Cross-Cultural Perspectives.* Berkeley and Los Angeles: University of California Press.
5. Korbin, J. 1987. Child Maltreatment in Cross-Cultural Perspective: Vulnerable Children and Circumstances. In *Child Abuse and Neglect: Biosocial Dimensions,* ed. R. Gelles and J. Lancaster, 31–55. New York: Aldine de Gruyter.

6. Sternberg, K., and Lamb, M. 1991. Can We Ignore Context in the Definition of Child Maltreatment? *Development and Psychopathology* 3(1):87–92.

7. Edgerton, R. B. 1992. *Sick Societies: Challenging the Myth of Primitive Harmony.* New York: Free Press.

8. Keesing, R. 1982. Introduction to *Rituals of Manhood: Male Initiation in Papua New Guinea,* ed. G. Herdt, 1–43. Berkeley and Los Angeles: University of California Press.

9. Lozoff, B., and Zuckerman, B. 1988. Sleep Problems in Children. *Pediatrics in Review* 10(1): 17–24.

10. McKenna, J.; Mosko, S.; Dungy, C.; and McAninch, J. 1990. Sleep and Arousal Patterns of Co-Sleeping Human Mother/Infant Pairs. *Am. J. Physical Anthropology* 83:331–47.

11. Garbarino, J., and Ebata, A. 1983. The Significance of Cultural and Ethnic Factors in Child Maltreatment. *J. Marriage and the Family* 45(4):773–83.

12. Finkelhor, D., and Korbin, J. 1988. Child Abuse as an International Issue. *Child Abuse and Neglect: International J.* 11(3):397–407.

13. Korbin, J. 1987. Child Abuse and Neglect: The Cultural Context. In *The Battered Child,* 4th ed. rev., ed. R. E. Helfer and R. S. Kempe, 23–41. Chicago: University of Chicago Press.

14. Gray, E., and Cosgrove, J. 1985. Ethnocentric Perception of Childrearing Practices in Protective Services. *Child Abuse and Neglect: International J.* 9(3):389–96.

15. Giovannoni, J., and Becerra, R. 1979. *Defining Child Abuse.* New York: Free Press.

16. Hong, G., and Hong, L. 1991. Comparative Perspectives on Child Abuse and Neglect: Chinese versus Hispanics and Whites. *Child Welfare* 70(4):463–75.

17. O'Toole, R.; Turbett, P.; and Nalepka, C. 1983. Theories, Professional Knowledge, and Diagnosis of Child Abuse. In *The Dark Side of Families: Current Family Violence Research,* ed. D. Finkelhor, R. Gelles, G. Hotaling, and M. Straus. Beverly Hills, Calif: Sage.

18. Korbin, J. 1994. Sociocultural Factors in Child Maltreatment: A Neighborhood Approach. In *Safe Neighborhoods: Foundations for a New National Strategy for Child Protection,* ed. G. Melton and F. Barry. New York: Guilford.

19. Abney, V., and Gunn, K. 1993. Culture: A Rationale for Cultural Competency. *APSAC Advisor* 6(3):19–22.

20. Ima, K., and Hohm, C. 1991. Child Maltreatment among Asian and Pacific Islander Refugees and Immigrants: The San Diego Case. *J. Interpersonal Violence* 6(3):267–85.

21. McKee, L. 1984. Sex Differentials in Survivorship and Customary Treatment of Infants and Children. *Medical Anthropology* 8(2):91–108.

22. Baer, R., and Ackerman, A. 1988. Toxic Mexican Folk Remedies for the Treatment of Empacho: The Case of Azarcon, Greta, and Albayalde. *J. Ethnopharmacology* 24:31–39.

23. Trotter, R.; Ackerman, A.; Rodman, D.; Martinez, A.; and Sorvillo, F. 1983. Azarcon and Greta: Ethnomedical Solution to Epidemiological Mystery. *Medical Anthropology Q.* 14(3): 3, 18.

24. Edgerton, R. B. 1976. *Deviance: A Cross-Cultural Perspective.* Menlo Park, Calif.: Cummings.

25. Edgerton, R. B. 1985. *Rules, Exceptions, and Social Order.* Berkeley and Los Angeles: University of California Press.

26. Hauswald, L. 1987. External Pressure/Internal Change: Child Neglect on the Navajo Reservation. In *Child Survival: Anthropological Perspectives on the Treatment and Maltreatment of Children,* ed. N. Scheper-Hughes, 145–64. Dordrecht, Holland: D. Reidel.

27. Starr, R. H., ed. 1988. *Child Abuse Prediction: Policy Implications.* Cambridge, Mass.: Ballinger.

28. Harwood, A., ed. 1981. *Ethnicity and Medical Care.* Cambridge, Mass.: Harvard University Press.

29. Sue, S. 1988. Psychotherapeutic Services for Ethnic Minorities. Two Decades of Research Findings. *Am. Psychologist* 43(4):301–8.

30. Kempe, C. H. 1978. Recent Developments in the Field of Child Abuse. *Child Abuse and Neglect: International J.* 2(4):261–67.

31. Badgley, R. 1984. *Sexual Offenses against Children.* Ottawa: Canadian Government Printing Center.

32. Mrazek, P.; Lynch, M.; and Bentovim, A. 1981. Recognition of Child Sexual Abuse in the United Kingdom. In *Sexually Abused Children and Their Families,* ed. P. Mrazek and C. H. Kempe, 35–50. New York: Pergamon Press.

33. Oates, R. K., ed. 1990. *Understanding and Managing Child Sexual Abuse.* Sydney: Harcourt Brace Jovanovich.

34. Graburn, N. 1987. Severe Child Abuse among the Canadian Inuit. In *Child Survival: Anthropological Perspectives on the Treatment and Maltreatment of Children,* ed. N. Scheper-Hughes, 211–26. Dordrecht, Holland: D. Reidel.

35. Briggs, J. 1975. The Origins of Non-Violence: Aggression in Two Canadian Eskimo Communities. *Psychoanalytic Study of Society* 6:134–203.

36. Korbin, J. 1990. Hana'ino: Child Maltreatment in a Hawai'ian-American Community. *Pacific Studies* 13(3):6–22.

37. Scrimshaw, S. 1978. Infant Mortality and Behavior in the Regulation of Family Size. *Population Development Rev.* 4:383–403.

38. Nations, M., and Rebhun, L. 1988. Angels with Wet Wings Won't Fly: Maternal Sentiment in Brazil and the Image of Neglect. *Culture, Medicine, and Psychiatry* 12:141–200.

39. Scheper-Hughes, N. 1992. *Death without Weeping: The Violence of Everyday Life in Brazil.* Berkeley and Los Angeles: University of California Press.

40. National Center on Child Abuse and Neglect. 1981. *Study Findings: National Study of the Incidence and Severity of Child Abuse and Neglect.* Washington, D.C.: Department of Health, Education, and Welfare.

41. National Center on Child Abuse and Neglect. 1988. *Study Findings: Study of National Incidence and Prevalence of Child Abuse and Neglect, 1988.* Washington, D.C.: Department of Health, Education, and Welfare.

42. Jason, J.; Amereuh, N.; Marks, J.; and Tyler, C. 1982. Child Abuse in Georgia: A Method to Evaluate Risk Factors and Reporting Bias. *Am. J. Public Health* 72(12):1353–58.

43. Horowitz, B., and Wolock, I. 1981. Material Deprivation, Child Maltreatment, and Agency Interventions among Poor Families. In *The Social Context of Child Abuse and Neglect,* ed. L. Pelton. New York: Human Sciences Press.

44. Lauderdale, M.; Valiunas, A.; and Anderson, R. 1980. Race, Ethnicity, and Child Maltreatment: An Empirical Analysis. *Child Abuse and Neglect: International J.* 4(3):163–69.

45. Light, R. 1973. Abused and Neglected Children in America: A Study of Alternative Policies. *Harvard Educational Rev.* 43:556–98.

46. Gil, D. 1970. *Violence against Children: Physical Child Abuse in the United States.* Cambridge, Mass.: Harvard University Press.

47. Newberger, E.; Reed, R.; Daniel, J.; Hyde, J.; and Kotelchuck, M. 1977. Pediatric Social Illness: Towards an Etiologic Classification. *Pediatrics* 60:178–85.

48. Hampton, R., and Newberger, W. 1985. Child Abuse Incidence and Reporting by Hospitals: Significance of Severity, Class, and Race. *Am. J. Public Health* 75(1)45–58.

49. Feldman, K. W.; Monastersky, C.; and Feldman, G. K. 1993. When Is Childhood Drowning Neglect? *Child Abuse and Neglect: International J.* 17(3):329–36.

50. Fergusson, D.; Flemming, J.; and O'Neill, D. 1972. *Child Abuse in New Zealand.* Wellington: Government Press.

51. Kotch, J. B.; Chalmers, D. J.; Fanslow, J. L.; Marshall, S.; and Langley, J. D. 1993. Morbidity and Death Due to Child Abuse in New Zealand. *Child Abuse and Neglect: International J.* 17(2):233–47.

52. Carr, A., and Gelles, R. J. 1978. Reporting Child Maltreatment in Florida: The Operation of Public Child Protective Service Systems. Report to the National Center on Child Abuse and Neglect.

53. Wolock, I. 1982. Community Characteristics and Staff Judgements in Child Abuse and Neglect Cases. *Social Work Research and Abstracts* 18:9–15.

54. Straus, M.; Gelles, R.; and Steinmetz, S. 1980. *Behind Closed Doors: Violence in the American Family.* New York: Anchor.

55. Gelles, R. J., and Straus, M. A. 1988. *Intimate Violence.* New York: Simon and Schuster.

56. Gelles, R. 1992. Poverty and Violence towards Children. *Am. Behavioral Scientist* 35(3): 258–74.

57. Straus, M., and Gelles, R. 1986. Societal Change and Change in Family Violence from 1975 to 1985 as Revealed by Two National Surveys. *J. Marriage and the Family* 48:465–79.

58. Hampton, R.; Gelles, R.; and Harrop, J. 1989. Is Violence in Black Families Increasing? A Comparison of 1975 and 1985 National Survey Rates. *J. Marriage and the Family* 51:969–80.

59. Pelton, L., ed. 1981. *The Social Context of Child Abuse and Neglect.* New York: Human Sciences Press.

60. Giovannoni, J., and Billingsley, A. 1970. Child Neglect among the Poor: A Study of Parental Adequacy in Families of Three Ethnic Groups. *Child Welfare* 49(4):196–204.

61. Priest, R. 1992. Child Sexual Abuse Histories among African-American College Students: A Preliminary Study. *Am. J. Orthopsychiatry* 62(3):475–76.

62. Finkelhor, D. 1984. *Child Sexual Abuse. New Theory and Research.* New York: Free Press.

63. Russell, D. 1986. *The Secret Trauma: Incest in the Lives of Girls and Women.* New York: Basic Books.

64. Wyatt, G. E. 1985. The Sexual Abuse of Afro-American and White American Women in Childhood. *Child Abuse and Neglect: International J.* 9:507–19.

65. Ahn, H. N., and Gilbert, N. 1992. Cultural Diversity and Sexual Abuse Prevention. *Social Service Rev.* (Sept.): 410–427.

66. Ikeda, Y. 1982. A Short Introduction to Child Abuse in Japan. *Child Abuse and Neglect: International J.* 6 (4):487–90.

67. Tharp, R. G. 1991. Cultural Diversity and the Treatment of Children. *J. Consulting and Clinical Psychology* 59(6):799–812.

68. Whiting, B. B. 1976. The Problem of the Packaged Variable. In *Historical and Cultural Issues.* Vol. 1 of *The Developing Individual in a Changing World,* ed. K. Riegel and J. Meacham. Chicago: Aldine.

69. Weisner, T.; Gallimore, S.; and Jordan, C. 1988. Unpackaging Cultural Effects on Classroom Learning: Native Hawaiian Peer Assistance and Child-Generated Activity. *Anthropology and Education Q.* 19:327–53.

70. Dubanoski, R. 1981. Child Maltreatment in European- and Hawaiian-Americans. *Child Abuse and Neglect: International J.* 5(4):457–66.

71. Dubanoski, R., and Snyder, K. 1980. Patterns of Child Abuse and Neglect in Japanese- and Samoan-Americans. *Child Abuse and Neglect: International J.* 4(4):217–25.

72. Ritchie, J., and Ritchie, J. 1981. Child Rearing and Child Abuse: The Polynesian Context. In *Child Abuse and Neglect: Cross-Cultural Perspectives,* ed. J. Korbin, 186–294. Berkeley and Los Angeles: University of California Press.

73. Minturn, L., and Lambert, W. 1964. *Mothers of Six Cultures. Antecedents of Child Rearing.* New York: Wiley.

74. Whiting, B. B., and Whiting, J. W. M. 1975. *Children of Six Cultures: A Psycho-Cultural Analysis.* Cambridge, Mass.: Harvard University Press.

75. Whiting, B. B., and Edwards, C. 1988. *Children of Different Worlds: The Formation of Social Behavior.* Cambridge, Mass.: Harvard University Press.

76. Rohner, R. 1986. *The Warmth Dimension: Foundations of Parental Acceptance-Rejection Theory.* Beverly Hills, Calif.: Sage.

77. Garbarino, J., and Crouter, A. 1978. Defining the Community Context for Parent-Child Relations: The Correlates of Child Maltreatment. *Child Development* 49:604–16.

78. Garbarino, J., & Sherman, D. 1980. High Risk Neighborhoods and High Risk Families: The Human Ecology of Child Maltreatment. *Child Development* 51:188–98.

79. Garbarino, J., and Kostelny, K. 1992. Child Maltreatment as Community Problem. *Child Abuse and Neglect: International J.* 16:455–64.

80. LeVine, S., and LeVine, R. 1981. Child Abuse and Neglect in SubSaharan Africa. In *Child Abuse and Neglect: Cross-Cultural Perspectives,* ed. J. Korbin, 35–55. Berkeley and Los Angeles: University of California Press.

81. Fraser, G., and Kilbride, P. 1980. Child Abuse and Neglect—Rare, but Perhaps Increasing, Phenomenon among the Samia of Kenya. *Child Abuse and Neglect: International J.* 4(4): 227–32.

82. Garbarino, J. 1977. The Human Ecology of Child Maltreatment. *J. Marriage and the Family* 39(4):721–35.

83. Straus, M. 1991. Discipline and Deviance: Physical Punishment of Children and Violence and Other Crime in Adulthood. *Social Problems* 38(2):133–54.

84. Olson, E. 1981. Socioeconomic and Psychocultural Contexts of Child Abuse and Neglect in Turkey. In *Child Abuse and Neglect: Cross-Cultural Perspectives,* ed. J. Korbin, 96–119. Berkeley and Los Angeles: University of California Press.

85. Thompson, R. 1994. Social Support and the Prevention of Child Maltreatment. In *Protecting Children from Abuse and Neglect,* ed. G. Melton and F. Barry, 40–130. New York: Guilford.

86. Korbin, J. 1989. Fatal Maltreatment by Mothers: A Proposed Framework. *Child Abuse and Neglect: International J.* 13:481–89.

87. Korbin, J. 1997. "Good Mothers," "Baby Killers," and Fatal Child Maltreatment. In *Small Wars: The Cultural Politics of Childhood,* ed. N. Scheper-Hughes and C. Sargent. Berkeley and Los Angeles: University of California Press. In press.

88. Chavez, A.; Martinez, C.; and Yaschine, T. 1975. Nutrition, Behavior Development, and Mother-Child Interaction in Young Rural Children. *Federation Proceedings* 34(7):1574–82.

89. Foster, G., and Anderson, B. 1978. *Medical Anthropology.* New York: Wiley.

90. Werner, E. 1979. *Cross-Cultural Child Development: A View from Planet Earth.* Monterey, Calif.: Wadsworth.

91. Lane, S., and Meleis, A. 1991. Roles, Work, Health Perceptions, and Health Resources of Women: A Study in an Egyptian Hamlet. *Social Science and Med.* 33(10):1197–208.

92. Miller, B. 1981. *The Endangered Sex: Neglect of Female Children in Rural North India.* Ithaca, N.Y.: Cornell University Press.

93. Poffenberger, T. 1981. Child Rearing and Social Structure in Rural India: Toward a Cross-Cultural Definition of Child Abuse and Neglect. In *Child Abuse and Neglect: Cross-Cultural Perspectives,* ed. J. Korbin, 71–95. Berkeley and Los Angeles: University of California Press.

94. Minturn, L. 1984. Changes in Differential Treatment of Rajput Girls in Khalapur: 1955–1975. *Medical Anthropology* 8(2):127–32.

95. Agathonos, H.; Stathacoupoulou, N.; Adam, H.; and Nakou, S. 1982. Child Abuse and Neglect in Greece: Sociomedical Aspects. *Child Abuse and Neglect: International J.* 6(2):141–45.

96. Sargent, C., and Harris, M. 1992. Gender Ideology, Childrearing, and Child Health in Jamaica. *Am. Ethnologist* 19(3):523–37.

97. Feldman, K. 1987. Child Abuse by Burning. In *The Battered Child,* 4th ed. rev., ed. R. E. Helfer and R. S. Kempe, 197–213. Chicago: University of Chicago Press.

98. Honigman, J. 1967. *Personality in Culture.* New York: Harper and Row.

99. Chagnon, N. 1968. *Yanomamo: The Fierce People.* New York: Rinehart and Winston.

100. Johnson, O. 1981. The Socioeconomic Context of Child Abuse and Neglect in Native South America. In *Child Abuse and Neglect: Cross-Cultural Perspectives,* ed. J. Korbin; 56–70. Berkeley and Los Angeles: University of California Press.

101. Green, J. W. 1982. *Cultural Awareness in the Human Services.* Englewood Cliffs, N.J.: Prentice-Hall.

102. National Resource Center on Child Sexual Abuse. 1993. Cultural Competence Continuum. *NRCCSA News* 1(5):3.

103. Abney, V. D., and Gunn, K. 1993. Culture: A Rationale for Cultural Competency. *APSAC Advisor* 6(3):19–22.

104. Coriel, J., and Mill, J. 1990. *Anthropology and Primary Health Care.* Boulder, Colo.: Westview Press.

105. Lozoff, B.; Kamath, K.; and Feldman, R. 1975. Infection and Disease in South Indian Families: Beliefs about Childhood Diarrhea. *Human Organization* 34(4):353–57.

106. Nichter, M. 1989. *Anthropology and International Health: South Asian Case Studies.* Boston: Kluwer.

107. UNICEF. 1990. *The State of the World's Children, 1990.* New York: Oxford University Press.

108. Lieber, L., and Baker, J. 1976. Parents Anonymous—Self-Help Treatment for Child-Abusing parents: A Review and an Evaluation. Paper presented at the First International Congress on Child Abuse and Neglect, Geneva, Switzerland.

109. Long, K. 1986. Cultural Considerations in the Assessment and Treatment of Intrafamilial Abuse. *Am. J. Orthopsychiatry* 56(1):31–136.

110. Pinderhughes, E. 1982. Afro-American Families and the Victim System. In *Ethnicity and Family Therapy,* ed. M. McGoldrick, J. Pearce, and J. Giordano. New York: Guilford.

111. McGoldrick, M.; Pearce, J.; and Giordano, J., eds. 1982. *Ethnicity and Family Therapy.* New York: Guilford.

112. Shook, E. V. 1989. *Ho'o'ponopono: Contemporary Uses of a Hawaiian Problem-Solving Process.* Honolulu: East-West Center.

113. Constantion, G.; Malgady, R.; and Rogler, L. 1986. Cuento Therapy: A Culturally Sensitive Modality for Puerto Rican Children. *J. Consulting and Clinical Psychology* 54:639–45.

3

The Role of Economic Deprivation in the Social Context of Child Maltreatment

James Garbarino

In the last two decades, public awareness of child maltreatment as a major social issue has increased dramatically—from an estimated 10% of the adult population defining it as a major problem in the mid-1970s to a documented 90% doing so by the 1980s (1). Creating this public awareness, creating a professional infrastructure of protective services, and initiating intensive efforts aimed at prevention have been major accomplishments, but now the hardest work begins.

This hardest work involves systematic efforts to incorporate our understanding of the social context of child maltreatment into our efforts to develop effective strategies for prevention and treatment among the populations at highest risk. Focusing on social context will inevitably take us to the issue of economic deprivation and poverty, and to what Wilson (2) calls the "underclass," where poverty and violence are pervasive and conventional human service models are often inappropriate and ineffective (3). In this chapter, I will examine some of the special issues confronting efforts to understand and deal with the role of economic deprivation in the social context of child maltreatment.

Background and Overview

To speak of social context is to invoke an ecological perspective, a perspective that directs our attention simultaneously to two kinds of interaction. The first is the interaction of the child as a biological organism with the immediate social environment as a set of processes, events, and relationships. The second is the interplay of social systems in the child's social environment. This dual mandate—to look both *inward* to the day-to-day exchanges that form a child's life in his or her family and *outward* to the large forces that shape social contexts—is both the beauty and the challenge of human ecology.

Ecology is the study of relationships between and among organisms and environments. Ecologists explore and document how an individual and its surroundings mutually shape each others' development. Like the biologist who learns about an animal by studying its habitat, sources of food, predators, and collective behavior, the student of human development must address how people live and grow in their environment—which is largely a social one. And, while all students of animal ecology must accommodate their theories to

James Garbarino, Ph.D., is director of the Family Life Development Center and professor in the Department of Human Development and Family Studies, College of Human Ecology, Cornell University.

the purposeful actions of the organism, the human ecologist must go further and seek to incorporate into any speculative framework the cognitive complexity of the organism-environment interaction—the social and psychological maps that define human meaning.

The most important characteristic of this ecological perspective when we ask questions and want explanations about individual behavior and development is that it reinforces our inclination to look inside the individual *and* simultaneously encourages us to look beyond the individual to the environment. It emphasizes development in context.

An ecological perspective constantly reminds us that child development results from the interplay of biology *and* society, from the characteristics children bring with them into the world and the way the world treats them, from nature *and* from nurture. In this, it reflects what Pasamanick (4) calls "social biology." In contrast to sociobiology, which emphasizes a genetic origin for social behavior (5), social biology concentrates on the social origins of biological phenomena (for example, the impact of poverty on infant morbidity). Nevertheless, the two perspectives are not mutually exclusive. Indeed, sociobiologists see the *historical* (that is, evolutionary) origins of biological phenomena (namely, gene pool characteristics) in social phenomena (in other words, the differential life success of individuals) because of the *social* implications of the *genetically based* behavior of individuals (5). These scientists seek to explain how the social impact of biologically rooted traits affects the survival of organisms and thus the likelihood that those particular genetic patterns will be passed along to surviving offspring.

Children face different opportunities and risks for development because of their mental and physical makeup *and* because of the social environment they inhabit—and, in addition, because of the way each affects the other (6). Social environment affects the very physical makeup of the child; genetic factors affect social relations.

My goal here is to make use of a systems approach to clarify the complexity we face in attempting to understand the interplay of biological, psychological, social, and cultural forces in child maltreatment. A systems approach can help us discover the connections among what might at first seem to be unrelated events. It also can help us see that what often seems like an obvious solution may actually only make the problem worse. Forrester (7) concludes that because systems are linked, and therefore influence each other (via "feedback"), many of the most effective solutions to social problems are not readily apparent and may even be "counterintuitive." According to Hardin (8), the first law of ecology is, "You can never do just one thing." Intersystem feedback ensures that any single action may produce and exacerbate unintended consequences. This will become apparent as we proceed.

When we ask the question, "Does X cause Y?" the answer is always, "It depends." We cannot reliably predict the future of one system without knowing something about the other systems with which it is linked. And even then prediction may be very difficult. We see this when we ask, "Does neglect harm development?" We answer, "It depends on the child's age, the quality of the parent-child attachment, and what happens to remediate the immediate consequences of neglect. In short, it depends."

There is considerable debate about the exact processes that translate economic deprivation into developmental risk for children, but there is consensus that economic deprivation does represent a challenge to the coping resources of individuals, families, and communities (9). For example, the connection between unemployment and developmental crisis is mainly indirect, but it is real nonetheless. Unemployment tends to diminish resources and precipitate problems in mental health and welfare. Male identity and parental status have traditionally been tied to occupational position. Unemployment diminishes that identity and gives rise to ambiguity or even outright conflict in the family. Further, in families where unemployment exists, family members spend more time together, and thus more opportunity for abuse arises.

This emotional threat is compounded by the very practical fact that employment is the principal source of basic health and welfare services. Unemployment thus precipitates crises in both the psychic and the fiscal economy of the family. Both increase the likelihood of risky conditions for children and decrease the likelihood that such risky conditions will be observed and attended to effectively.

This is particularly significant for workers in financially marginal employment, where reserves are minimal or nonexistent—"one paycheck away from disaster," as they are often described. Such financial vulnerability heightens the importance of access to social resources. One source of concern is the growing recognition that the politically tolerable level of "normal" unemployment has been steadily increasing—from 4% in 1950 to 7% by 1986. The mid-1990s have seen a reversal of this trend overall; however, some minority groups continue to show high levels of unemployment.

But even the meaning of these data is changing, since public accounting methods no longer include those people too discouraged to seek work or others who are employed only part-time. The impact of employment per se on family economics has itself changed. During the 1960s, for example, earning a minimum wage produced sufficient income to lift a family of three above the poverty line. Until 1996, that same minimum-wage job left a family 25% below the poverty line (and recent increases in the minimum wage have not eliminated this problem).

These changes parallel inadequacies in the standards for assessing the poverty level, standards that exclude many families who lack adequate resources to meet basic needs such as health care. As "recessions" occur, they produce double-digit levels of unemployment, with localized "hot spots" in excess of 20% (a condition that exists chronically among some minority groups in the United States, for whom "the Great Depression" is not a historical memory but, rather, an ongoing reality). Deteriorating economic conditions, characterized by increases in the number of people falling below the poverty level, are a major force driving the human ecology of risk in early childhood (10).

In addition to the well-established connection between poverty and infant mortality, researchers have identified a link between economic deprivation and physical abuse and neglect of children, certainly the bottom line when it comes to indicators of child welfare and family functioning (11–14). Their studies report a correlation between low income and the risk for child maltreatment on both the individual and community level. The rate of child maltreatment (all forms of child abuse and neglect combined) computed as part of the three federally financed national incidence studies (in 1981 and 1988 and 1996) increased by a factor of ten when we compared families with income in the affluent range to families living in poverty (15). Studies of maltreatment rates at the community level tell the same story (16, 17).

Economic crisis can generate an epidemic of threats to the functions of child welfare because it exacerbates the problem of "social toxicity" (6, 18). This happened during the 1980s in unemployment "hot spots" around the country as child maltreatment rates followed climbing unemployment rates. In Oregon, for example, where a depressed lumber industry prompted double-digit unemployment rates, officials reported a 46% increase in child maltreatment for 1981 (19). An upsurge in the need for child welfare services and other human services typically coincides with a diminished capacity of established institutional services to respond to the multiplying caseload during troubled economic times. As an economic crisis unfolds, it simultaneously increases demand for state-supported services across the spectrum, from health care to food stamps, and typically decreases the tax revenues available to finance such services. A further disturbing trend is the finding that "economic recovery"—such as occurred in the mid-1980s (with unemployment dipping below 7% in 1987)—did not, and increasingly does not, reach the growing underclass, where unemployment, poverty, and demographic adversity are becoming ever more entrenched and chronic (2).

While most industrialized societies entitle all families to maternal and infant health care and basic child support subsidies (see chapter 23), ours does not (20–22). This gap is part of the social context of child maltreatment in the United States. Although the federal budget includes a substantial commitment to "entitlement" programs, five-sixths of the allocated funds goes to programs that disproportionately assist affluent adults, while relatively little goes to families which need the services of child welfare agencies (23). As Bronfenbrenner (24) noted, this may explain why correlations between measures of income or socioeconomic status and basic child negative outcomes are often higher in the United States than in other "modern" societies. Low income is a better predictor of child development deficits in the United States than in other countries because our social policies tend to exaggerate rather than minimize the impact of family income on access to child maltreatment preventive and rehabilitative services.

Many Americans have become accustomed to an affluent material standard of living that probably cannot be sustained in the future for large numbers of people much of the time (25). Data from the economic depression of the 1930s, when expectations were considerably lower, predict a pattern of increasing frustration, anger, depression, and hostility under such straitened personal and financial circumstances. Such negativity increased developmental risk for children, with child maltreatment manifesting as the outcome of greatest concern. Accordingly, it is those sorts of responses to economic deprivation that most concern us here.

Add to this the geographic concentration of economically marginal families, as communities become more homogeneous (for instance, through clustered public housing). In Cleveland, for example, the proportion of poor families living in neighborhoods where the majority of families are poor grew from 23% in 1960 to 69% in 1990 (26). These trends hold true in most American cities.

The developmental effects on children caught in these situations are profoundly disturbing. Children become the incidental and deliberate targets of concentrated and often unmitigated rage and despair, in the form of neglect and abuse. Children "cost too much" when their caregivers cannot generate enough income to meet popular expectations, which they themselves share, for participating in the monetarized economy of day-to-day modern life.

We should note that the magnitude of these correlations between poverty and child maltreatment may reflect an effect of a social policy. It seems reasonable to assume that in a society in which low income is *not* correlated with minimal access to basic human services (for example, in societies providing universal availability of maternal-infant health care), these correlations between poverty and child maltreatment would be smaller; in a society totally devoid of policies to ameliorate the impact of family-level differences in social class, on the other hand, the correlations might be even larger. The key is discerning how social class (a "status" variable) is translated into the experiences of children and parents (the "process" variables). More and more, the focus of such efforts is economic inequality (rather than simple income levels). Eron and his colleagues (27) have concluded that violence and aggression are correlated to income disparities. The Luxembourg income study (28) reveals that among modern, industrialized societies the United States has the biggest gap between rich and poor. Whereas the wealthiest 10% makes six times as much as the poorest 10% in the United States, the comparable figure for Canada is four times (and for Sweden, two times). All of this points to the psychological and cultural translation of income into the immediate social environment of children.

Tulkin's (29) classic analysis of the concept of cultural deprivation made this clear. On the one hand, it is not the culture of those living in poverty in some general sense that matters most. Rather, what really matters are those aspects of that culture which translate into an inability to meet the basic developmental needs of children (for instance, whether or not caregivers "accept" infant attachment, whether or not they "give up" too quickly on sick children, and whether or not it is normative to reject children with disabilities [30]).

It is easy to attribute blame for being poor, generally incorrectly, to the beliefs and values of the poor, but it is much harder to recognize that in fact these beliefs bear no one-to-one correspondence with socioeconomic outcomes. There are multiple ways to escape poverty. Having said that, we can go still further to note that there are multiple possible consequences of being poor.

The community plays a vital role in "deciding" this issue. By establishing a strong and attentive system of prenatal and maternal child health care, and by making such care easy to gain access to and difficult to avoid it, a community can do much to dissociate poverty and infant mortality (22). By adopting a passive stance and allowing the "free market" to rule, a community can strengthen the links between poverty and early child death (18).

This hypothesis merits additional empirical exploration, but it is consistent with the observation that socioeconomic status is a more potent predictor of child development outcomes in the United States than in some European societies. Furthermore, a replication of the study that I directed in Omaha (16, 11), which was conducted in Montreal by Bouchard, revealed a weaker association of socioeconomic status and child maltreatment rates, presumably because of that city's welfare politics, which diminish the link between household income and the availability of basic services (31). The direct correlative links between social class and social pathology constitute the first meaning of high risk—such as the finding that poverty is a risk factor because it is associated with higher rates of infant mortality, child abuse, and similar maladies.

Child Maltreatment in Social Context

Child maltreatment takes place in a social as well as a psychological and cultural context. Prevention, treatment, and research should incorporate this contextual orientation (32). For many purposes, this means identifying and examining high-risk neighborhoods as well as high-risk families as the likely settings for outbreaks of child maltreatment (17).

The role of social support systems in enhancing family functioning is to link social nurturance and social control (6). Such support systems "provide individuals with opportunities for feedback about themselves and for validations for their expectations about others, which may offset deficiencies in these communications within the larger community context" (33, p. 12).

A study by Freudenburg and Jones (34) of twenty-three communities experiencing rapid population growth found that all but two of these communities also experienced a disproportionate increase in crime; this suggested that changes in a community's social structure which accompany rapid growth result in a breakdown of social control. As the "density of acquaintanceship" (that is, the proportion of a community's residents who know one another) decreases, criminal activity increases. These findings may constitute important elements in expanding our understanding of some child maltreatment cases.

Another issue concerns the negative effects of "out migration" from neighborhoods that are beginning to decline and "turn bad." Out migration may have debilitating effects on local social networks (35) and create still more confounding effects as a result of people's choosing to live somewhere on the basis of perceived similarities to the residents or avoiding neighborhoods based upon their bad reputation.

Beyond these obvious "selection factors," neighborhoods differ on the basis of ethos. Some areas are more vital and coherent, even among middle-class families (36), and they share common problems. However, many areas evince a weak ethos. A survey in South Carolina (37) revealed that on a scale of 1 to 7—with 7 indicating high involvement—the average score for neighborhood residents was 2+ in response to the question, "How involved are you in other people's children?" The same survey revealed that most people could not name one agency that had been particularly helpful on behalf of children.

Previous research has sought to explore and validate the concept of social impoverishment, both as a characteristic of high-risk family environments and as a factor in evaluating prevention and recovery programs aimed at child maltreatment. The starting point was identifying the environmental correlates of child maltreatment (38, 16). This provided an empirical basis for "screening" neighborhoods to determine high- and low-risk areas. The foundation for this approach is the well-documented link between low income and child maltreatment noted earlier.

Two Meanings of "High Risk"

My colleague and I used the statistical technique of multiple regression analysis to illuminate two meanings of "high risk" (16). The first meaning refers to areas with a high absolute rate of child maltreatment (based on cases per unit of population). In this sense, concentrations of socioeconomically distressed families are most likely to be at high risk for child maltreatment. In the first city we studied (Omaha, Nebraska), socioeconomic status accounted for about 40% of the variation across neighborhoods in reported rates of child maltreatment.

However, it is the second meaning of "high risk" that is of greatest relevance here. "High risk" can also be taken to mean that an area has a higher rate of child maltreatment *than would be predicted solely on the basis of its socioeconomic character.* Thus, two areas with similar socioeconomic profiles may have very different rates of child maltreatment. In this sense, one area is "high risk" while the other is "low risk," although both may have higher rates of child maltreatment than other, more affluent areas. Much of the variation among community rates of child maltreatment is therefore linked, as we discovered, to *variations* in socioeconomic and demographic characteristics.

The View from the Trenches

To put some meat on the bones of our statistical analysis, we conducted a small set of interviews to illuminate the important but elusive variable of "community climate." To shed some light on this factor, we interviewed community leaders in "North," a community with a "higher than predicted" rate of child abuse, and "West," a community with a "lower than predicted" child abuse rate. We used a sixteen-item questionnaire based upon prior research (11).

Our hypothesis, what we expected to find, was that in the high-abuse community social service agencies would mirror the high social deterioration characteristic of the families and the community in general, while, conversely, in the low-abuse community a strong, informal support network among the social service agencies would manifest. The results of the small number of interviews supported this hypothesis.

The interviews with civic professionals complement our statistical analyses and provide further indication of the serious difficulties facing the North community as a social system. The extremity of the negative features of the environment—poverty, violence, poor housing—seems to be matched by a negative community climate—a lack of community identity and a fragmented support systems network (17).

The final piece of evidence available to us in our analysis concerns child deaths resulting from maltreatment. Such child deaths are a particularly telling indicator of the bottom line in a community. There were nineteen child maltreatment deaths reported for the four community areas we studied during the period 1984–1987. Eight of these deaths occurred in North, a rate of 1 death for each 2,541 children. For West, the rate was 1 death for each 5,571 children. The fact that deaths caused by child maltreatment were twice as likely in North seems consistent with the overall findings of our statistical analyses and interviews. This is an environment which is truly a conspiracy of ecological events against children.

Community Violence and Domestic Violence

Our studies highlight both the general impact of poverty on the conditions of life for children and the specific existence of community climate variables at work which are not wholly dependent on low income. The existence of these forces is a fact of life for everyone involved in promoting child abuse prevention and delivering child protective services. While the role of poverty is often considered in protective service decision making and child abuse treatment program design, and while community unrest and social deterioration are often noted as relevant social problems, rarely are these factors considered in relation to the stresses they place on those individuals providing human services, especially in the context of pervasive violence.

Human service workers increasingly find themselves serving children and families who live in community environments that are chronically violent. These include some large public housing developments and socially deteriorated, low-income neighborhoods in cities across the nation (39–41).

Children living in these areas are not only more frequently exposed to crime, they are also more likely to be victims of child abuse and neglect. We have found that for census tracts having high crime rates, child maltreatment rates were up to four times higher than the citywide average. These incidents of domestic violence interact dynamically with the incidents of public violence: some of the disorderly incidents outside a family's own home are in fact related to someone else's domestic conflicts, so children and parents are exposed to violence in other families indirectly, as part of their life experience as neighbors and friends. Furthermore, international research (42) demonstrates that children exposed to domestic violence are much more vulnerable to the negative effects of violence in the larger community.

Implications for Delivering Social Services to High-Risk Families

In considering the social policy issues that emerge when we deal with child maltreatment where it happens most frequently, we must be concerned not only with the fact that high-risk families live in high-risk neighborhoods. We must also confront the fact that the people who provide services to families in high-risk communities are also at risk for crime victimization in the course of their day-to-day work.

For example, one of the regional directors of the Department of Children and Family Services reported that at any given time at least two of his forty caseworkers were unable to work because of injuries sustained while going to and coming from the homes of the families they served. Many more service workers have experienced significant trauma and live constantly with fear when asked to investigate cases in the urban "war zone" (39). Our research on the level of violence and trauma in the life of Head Start staff members serving high-risk neighborhoods reveals the same phenomenon—60% of the staff had experienced traumatic violence (43).

Successful child abuse prevention and child protective services must address the issues of powerlessness, traumatization, and immobilizing fear that impede effective family life and social development for a significant and growing proportion of children in urban areas with large underclass populations. Part and parcel of this is understanding the needs of professionals who work in these environments.

These professionals themselves often feel powerless, traumatized, and afraid. How do they make sense of prevention and protection missions in neighborhoods so violent they fear for their own personal safety? How are they to bring persuasive messages of family safety? Should everyone concerned simply accept lower standards for child protection in such environments? Should they fall silent, and concentrate on protecting themselves, when confronted with harsh, even violent, child rearing?

Halpern (44) has identified such "domains of silence" as a critical impediment to the delivery of effective family services, most especially among paraprofessionals recruited from high-risk populations. The significance and seriousness of this impediment will become clearer as we examine the social policy considerations that arise from understanding the impact on children of living in dangerous environments and utilizing this understanding as a context for addressing child maltreatment. To accomplish this, we must start with a commitment to incorporate human ecology perspective into all our efforts to prevent— and, when necessary, intervene in—child maltreatment.

Conclusion

The U.S. Advisory Committee on Child Abuse and Neglect has concluded that our nation faces a child maltreatment "emergency." Rates of child maltreatment continue to increase in many areas, and public agencies are pushed beyond their capacity to respond (45). The link between poverty and child maltreatment continues to be a powerful feature of the problem (15). In the current socioeconomic climate, poverty for families has been increasing and, in urban areas, becoming ever more geographically concentrated in segregated neighborhoods (46). That being the case, it is little wonder that the problem of child maltreatment is worsening in these urban areas of concentrated poverty (45).

We must, accordingly, call attention to an important reality about neighborhood life: social momentum is a powerful force. When things are going badly, the tendency is for all the social systems to be pulled down together. It takes extraordinary energy and effort to resist such negative social momentum—say, a political leader of special talent, commitment, and resources; or a powerfully effective social program that creates its own positive momentum in the neighborhood.

Child maltreatment is a symptom not just of individual or family trouble but of neighborhood and community trouble as well. Indeed, it may well combine with those negative community forces to jeopardize still further the development of children. We know that many children can absorb and overcome an experience involving one or two risk factors. When the risk factors add up, however, they may precipitate developmental crisis and impairment (47). This, we believe, is the situation faced by abused and neglected children living in the urban war zone.

The central challenge is to deal with the aggregation of negative social indicators. Fortunately, as social indicators, they can be responsive to social change, which we can concertedly hope to mobilize and shape for the better. As we plan and implement child abuse prevention initiatives, we must at the same time recognize that the task of keeping the wider social context in view is not easy.

Indeed, if we hope to have a significant effect when working in neighborhoods of concentrated poverty and social disorganization, we must introduce powerful efforts to reverse negative social momentum. And we must do so with an appreciation for the compounding of social problems that community violence engenders in the lives of victimized children.

This is the difficult course we must follow. Translating this broad conclusion into specific policy and programming is a formidable endeavor. One appealing approach is to identify "prevention zones," which could then become the targets for comprehensive, sustained intervention by a wide range of public and private agencies. Only through implementing such programs, it would seem, can we hope to reverse the destructive pressure of negative social momentum observed in some poor neighborhoods and replace it with the positive momentum observed in others.

Leadership here means an inspired willingness to go beyond cosmetic public relations and invest major resources to make a better community for children. We have reason to hope that fewer children would suffer maltreatment as a result.

References

1. National Committee for Prevention of Child Abuse. 1988. Public Attitudes and Actions Regarding Child Abuse and Its Prevention: The Results of a Louis Harris Public Opinion Poll. Chicago: NCPCA.
2. Wilson, W. J. 1987. *The Truly Disadvantaged: The Inner City, the Underclass, and Public Policy.* Chicago: University of Chicago Press.
3. Schorr, L. 1988. *Within Our Reach: Breaking the Cycle of Disadvantage.* New York: Anchor.
4. Pasamanick, B. 1987. Social Biology and AIDS. *Am. Psychological Assoc. Division Thirty-seven Newsletter* (winter): 1ff.
5. Wilson, E. 1978. *On Human Nature.* Cambridge, Mass.: Harvard University Press.
6. Garbarino, J., and Associates. 1992. *Children and Families in the Social Environment,* 2d ed. New York: Aldine de Gruyter.
7. Forrester, J. 1969. *Urban Dynamics.* Cambridge, Mass.: Harvard University Press.
8. Hardin, G. 1966. *Biology: Its Principles and Implications.* San Francisco: W. H. Freeman.
9. Fisher, K., and Cunningham, S. 1983. The Dilemma: Problem Grows, Support Shrinks. *APA Monitor* 14(2): 1ff.
10. Moen, P.; Kain, E.; and Elder, G. 1981. Economic Conditions and Family Life: Contemporary and Historical Perspectives. Paper presented at the National Academy of Sciences, Assembly of Behavioral and Social Sciences, Committee on Child Development Research and Public Policy, New York.
11. Garbarino, J., and Sherman, D. 1980. High Risk Neighborhoods and High Risk Families: The Human Ecology of Child Maltreatment. *Child Development* 51: 188–89.
12. National Center on Child Abuse and Neglect. 1981. *Study Findings: National Study of the Incidence and Severity of Child Abuse and Neglect.* Washington, D.C.: U.S. Department of Health and Human Services.
13. Pelton, L. 1978. Child Abuse and Neglect: The Myth of Classlessness. *Am. J. Orthopsychiatry* 48: 608–17.

14. Steinberg, L.; Catalano, R.; and Dooley, D. 1981. Economic Antecedents of Child Abuse and Neglect. *Child Development* 52:975–85.

15. Pelton, L. 1994. The Role of Material Factors in Child Abuse and Neglect. In *Protecting Children from Abuse and Neglect: Foundations for a New National Strategy,* ed. G. Melton and F. Barry. New York: Guilford.

16. Garbarino, J., and Crouter, A. 1978. Defining the Community Context of Parent-Child Relations. *Child Development* 49:604–16.

17. Garbarino, J., and Kostelny, K. 1992. Child Maltreatment as a Community Problem. *Child Abuse and Neglect: International J.* 16:454–55.

18. Garbarino, J. 1995. Raising Children in a Socially Toxic Environment. San Francisco: Jossey-Bass.

19. Birch, T. 1982. *Child Abuse and Unemployment.* Chicago: National Committee for Prevention of Child Abuse.

20. Kahn, A., and Kammerman, S. 1975. *Not for the Poor Alone: European Social Services.* Philadelphia: Temple University Press.

21. Kammerman, S., and Kahn, A. 1976. *Social Services in the United States: Policies and Programs.* Philadelphia: Temple University Press.

22. Miller, A. 1987. *Maternal Health and Infant Survival.* Washington, D.C.: National Center for Clinical Infant Programs.

23. Fallows, J. 1982. Entitlements. *Atlantic Monthly* 250(1):5ff.

24. Bronfenbrenner, U. 1986. Ecology of the Family as a Context for Human Development. *Developmental Psychology* 22:723–42.

25. Giarini, O. 1980. *Dialogue on the Wealth of Nations.* New York: Pergamon.

26. Korbin, J., and Coulton, C. 1994. *Neighborhood Impact on Child Abuse and Neglect: Final Project Report to the National Center on Child Abuse and Neglect.* Washington, D.C.: U.S. Department of Health and Human Services.

27. Eron, L. D.; Guerra, N.; and Huesman, L. R. 1996. In *Aggression: Biological, Developmental, and Social Perspectives,* ed. F. Feshbach and J. Zagordska. New York: Plenum.

28. Rainwater, L., and Smeeding, T. 1995. U.S. Doing Poorly—Compared to Others. *News and Issues* [New York: National Center for Children in Poverty] (fall/winter):4–5.

29. Tulkin, S. 1972. An Analysis of the Concept of Cultural Deprivation. *Developmental Psychology* 6:326–39.

30. Scheper-Hughes, N. 1987. Culture, Society, and Maternal Thinking: Mother Love and Child Death in Northeast Brazil. In *Child Survival: Anthropological Perspectives on the Treatment and Maltreatment of Children,* ed. N. Scheper-Hughes, 187–210. Boston: D. Reidel.

31. Chamberland, C.; Bouchard, C.; and Beaudry, J. 1986. Abusive and Negligent Behavior toward Children: Canadian and American Realities. *Canadian J. Behavioural Science* 18(4):391–412.

32. Garbarino, J.; Stocking, S.; and Associates. 1980. *Protecting Children from Abuse and Neglect: Developing and Maintaining Effective Support Systems for Families.* San Francisco: Jossey-Bass.

33. Caplan, G., and Killilea, M., eds. 1976. *Support Systems and Mutual Help.* New York: Grune and Stratton.

34. Freudenberg, W. R., and Jones, T. R. 1991. Attitudes and Stress in the Presence of Technological Risk: A Test of the Supreme Court Hypothesis. *Social Forces* 69(4):1143–68.

35. Fitchen, J. 1981. *Poverty in Rural America: A Case Study.* Boulder, Colo.: Westview Press.

36. Warren, R. 1978. *The Community in America.* Boston: Houghton Mifflin.

37. Melton, G. 1992. It's Time for Neighborhood Research and Action. *Child Abuse and Neglect: International J.* 16(4):909–13.

38. Garbarino, J. 1976. A Preliminary Study of Some Ecological Correlates of Child Abuse: The Impact of Socioeconomic Stress on Mothers. *Child Development* 47:178–85.

39. Dubrow, N., and Garbarino, J. 1989. Living in the War Zone: Mothers and Young Children in a Public Housing Development. *Child Welfare* 67(1).

40. Marciniak, E. 1986. *Reclaiming the Inner City: Chicago's Near North Revitalization Confronts Cabrini-Green.* Washington, D.C.: National Center for the Urban Public Affairs.
41. Merry, S. 1981. *Urban Danger: Life in a Neighborhood of Strangers.* Philadelphia: Temple University Press.
42. Kostelny, K. 1993. The Psychological and Behavioral Effects of Political Violence on Palestinian Children Living in the Occupied West Bank. Ph.D. diss., Erikson Institute/Loyola University, Chicago.
43. Garbarino, J.; Dubrow, N.; Kostelny, K.; and Pardo, C. 1992. *Children in Danger: Coping with the Consequences of Community Violence.* San Francisco: Jossey-Bass.
44. Halpern, R. 1990. Community-Based Early Intervention. In *Handbook of Early Childhood Intervention,* ed. S. J. Meisels and J. P. Shonkoff. Cambridge: Cambridge University Press.
45. Melton, G., and Barry, F., eds. 1994. *Protecting Children from Abuse and Neglect: Foundations for a New National Strategy.* New York: Guilford.
46. Garbarino, J. 1990. The Human Ecology of Early Risk. In *Handbook of Early Childhood Intervention,* ed. S. J. Meisels and J. P. Shonkoff. Cambridge: Cambridge University Press.
47. Sameroff, A., and Fiese, B. 1990. Transactional Regulation and Early Intervention. In *Handbook of Early Childhood Intervention,* ed. S. J. Meisels and J. P. Shonkoff. Cambridge: Cambridge University Press.

The Legal Context of Child Abuse and Neglect:
Balancing the Rights of Children
and Parents in a Democratic Society

Donald C. Bross

Few can be induced to labor exclusively for posterity;
and none will do it enthusiastically. Posterity has done
nothing for us; and theorize on it as we may, practically we
shall do very little for it, unless we are made to think, we
are, at the same time, doing something for ourselves.

ABRAHAM LINCOLN, speech given 22 February 1842, Springfield, Illinois

Certain enduring subjects continue to make the protection of children difficult from a legal perspective. These subjects are pertinent to all of the legal developments concerned with child protection. Although some of these issues (child witness law and practice, for example) are being thoroughly analyzed (1), others remain to be fully elaborated and refined. I will focus on two such issues in this chapter: the nature of the legal relationship between children and parents, and the degree of access to information about any particular child that a democratic society requires to assure all children at least minimally adequate care. By choosing these topics of core importance, topics which need to be thoroughly addressed and developed, I intend to illustrate both the progress achieved and the work remaining to be done in establishing legal protections for children. If we do not consider these topics adequately, the legal foundation for child protection becomes more difficult to secure.

Until we attain widespread consensus and clarity about the legal meaning of the child-parent relationship, the interpretation of child protection laws remains unpredictable, a continuing source of uncertainty for parents, policy makers, lawyers, judges, and society in general. Many assumptions are made about the nature of the legal ties binding child and parent, and these assumptions are not always shared, especially not in multiethnic, multireligious, and multicultural nations such as our own. Nonetheless, common to all these assumptions are implications about the nature and extent of parental authority. It is crucially

DONALD C. BROSS, PH.D., J. D., is professor in the Department of Pediatrics at the University of Colorado School of Medicine and director of education and legal counsel at the C. Henry Kempe National Center for the Prevention and Treatment of Child Abuse and Neglect.

important that we reach a common understanding of parental authority, particularly as it relates to questions of confidentiality and accountability.

Assuming we all agree that in our democratic society every child has a right to receive at least minimally adequate care, we must have legal means of ascertaining the level of each child's safety. Knowledge of children's safety depends on obtaining information about their current health, development, and supervision. The degree to which providing this information about the child's safety is a matter of the parents' free choice depends on how the nature of the legal relationship between child and parent is defined. I contend that our power to govern children in democracies (to nurture, train, and educate them—in other words, to "raise" them) is strongly dependent on parents' power to exercise responsible oversight (in effect, "use it or lose it"—use responsible parental authority or lose control of our children). Accordingly, I argue that parents' right to privacy should be yielded only to the degree that particular information is needed to establish that each child is safe and receiving minimally adequate care.

The Parent-Child Legal Relationship

The social and legal covenant which ties the generations together cannot be taken for granted. It is not clear what compels parents to care for children. In fact, some parents do not care for their children at all, some love their children very much but not at all well, and others do well enough that their children grow up to join in the work of the world. Some children even grow up to extraordinary virtuosity, occasionally partially crediting their parents. Parents have great power over our lives when we are young: power to do us great good and great harm. What inducements exist to assure adequate parenting, and how does the law maximize these inducements without curtailing individual liberties or attempting what only parents can provide?[1]

Given that so many children are well-enough raised by their parents, and that the law is a notoriously inefficient means for the resolution of problems,[2] one option is to keep law completely out of child care efforts and hope for the best. Some indeed agree that government should keep completely out of the lives of families. But given estimates that over one thousand children are murdered annually by caregivers in the United States alone (3), we must consider this option unacceptable. Simply deciding that some social and legal response is necessary to protect children, however, is far from knowing what should be done and comprehending the details of what is appropriate. The reality is that parents and children enjoy the benefits of family best when they are left alone together—yet parents and children can injure each other. Parents and children need each other—but how

---

1. The inducements arguably are minimal. This is true in part because of the ultimate difficulty of knowing what is best for a given child and, therefore, the uncertainty of knowing how to design inducements for parenting that will always be appropriate. For an example of the indeterminacy of knowing what was best for one child, see Morris's "The Best Interests of the Child" (2).

2. Compared to combat and other forms of violence, of course, the inefficiencies and injustices of law seem more acceptable. Neither is this intended to imply that improvements cannot or should not be made in the law.

much should children suffer from their parents' mistakes? How can the rights of parents and children be balanced?

Accountability in free enterprise and in democratic systems is normally assured by those most affected by wrongful private or public actions. Children prosper or suffer at the hands of others, and yet children cannot be relied upon to enforce "good enough" caregiving by parents. Human children are not born free of dependency on others, cannot care for their caregivers in the beginning, and do not hold the power of full citizenship to seek enforcement of their interests. The full benefits of law, including the power to make enforceable agreements, are enjoyed completely only with full citizenship, that is, when sufficient maturity is achieved. However, even though freedoms are legally granted as a function of chronological maturity, at least some legal *protections* for all members of a democracy begin early in life. These rights of protection are in effect before children are in a position to require or assure that their rights will be supported, but there is a point in each citizen's life when, regardless of age, he or she first begins to enjoy some of the benefits of law provided by society. In democratic countries, what rights for children will be permitted to accrue and when this accruement will occur for each new person fall under a special domain—an imperfect one—of the common law.

The implicit task of child rearing in a democracy is to raise children with sufficient care that they survive physically, mentally, and socially to take care of themselves as adults, to become essentially self-governing. Self-governance means that a person is not greatly troubling to others, especially not to the extent that any external, formal, institutional means of social control must be brought to bear.

The implicit task of children is "simply" growing up as best their circumstances permit. If possible, children should grow up to contribute to the general good, including being able to care for others. When we care well enough for children, what we are doing for ourselves in the long run is assuring the future.

On the one hand, however, the immediate demands of child care are so pressing that these philosophical and legal perspectives seem remote and unreal aspects of daily family life. Any parent at any time may instead decide to ask, "What has my child done for me lately?" Society must, consequently, provide great leeway to parents to encourage their active involvement in child rearing, in recognition of the fact that the state cannot be a parent, even a poor one, and in recognition of the fact that no one can know what is "best" for children in many situations. This inducement—that parents will be free and left alone to raise their children according to their own image of the "good"—is perhaps the most significant inducement to be a parent offered by democracies.

On the other hand, there is continuing concern that the care provided by parents and the institutions of society is inadequate, that it fails to equip our young to maintain and improve modern political and economic life, and that it thus, in effect, jeopardizes the future. When parents demand that their children meet parental needs irrespective of, or even in violation of, the children's needs, the future is robbed by abusive and neglectful care*takers* (since in this instance parents cannot rightfully be called care*givers*). Such conflicts between different views and interests often must be worked out within the law. Many considerations enter into establishing a legal context for settling disputes about child care. I propose that meeting the standard of reasonably adequate care of their children, ceteris paribus, is a fair price to ask parents to pay for the great power they wield over their children in a democracy. I further propose that parents' rights to privacy and children's rights to accountability must be balanced in such a way as to enable democratic societies to assure reasonably adequate care for all children.

Individual Rights in the Common-Law Democracies

Common-law democracies place enormous emphasis on the individual, to the point that individualism can be criticized as detrimental, even destructive, to the interests of the greater community. Nevertheless, the emphasis on the individual's rights is one of the main characteristics setting common-law countries apart from others.

Autonomy is cherished in democracy. Individual choice and responsibility are presumed, and there must be a clear justification to suspend that presumption. This is true, first of all, with respect to interference by the government in the affairs of a private individual. Our basic assumption is that governmental intervention in private conduct is harmful per se and, therefore, the government must show clear justification for the harm it thus causes. In the second place, autonomy is also considered a significant value with respect to interference of one private citizen in the interests or rights of another. Any significant harm caused requires substantial justification; otherwise, a number of legal remedies may be available to the injured person.

Given these values, when one child is treated worse than another child, what is the justification? When a child enjoys no autonomy, what is the justification? When a person fails to act beneficially toward a child over whom he or she holds control, perhaps harming the child by repudiating or subordinating the child's rights, what is the justification? Some might say that families are so private that they are beyond the reach of law. Others concede that families are inherently private but at the same time consider family life an inherently social process and thus subject, at least in some ways, to the concerns of society (4).

For a child, no less than for an adult, an analysis of individual interests should include an examination of the principles of beneficence and autonomy. Autonomy means allowing individuals to make their own choices unless those choices unreasonably infringe on the interests of others. Autonomy also assumes reasonable competence, that is, competence of a level which permits independent functioning. Practicing beneficence means avoiding harm to others. These ideas constitute the major focus of ethical debates and are hence appropriate as well to the analysis of parental and child interests and rights.

Possible justifications for loss of autonomy include:

- that autonomy is not possible due to incompetency stemming from mental illness, retardation, coma, or some other disability;
- that autonomy has been forfeited by the commission of culpable acts;
- that autonomy has not yet been achieved because competency has not yet been attained.

All of these can apply to a particular child, and the third applies to all young children.

Possible justifications for doing harm which might be acceptable are:

- that longer-term and more important interests of the person injured are thereby served;
- that the harm is *de minimis,* meaning, not important;
- that the harm cannot be avoided and that the harm was fairly distributed among individuals;
- that the interests of the common good are so overwhelming in a given instance that a particular degree of individual harm is rationalized.

These principles apply in general, whether to the power of the parent over a child or to the power that might be brought to bear by a state agency over a parent. However, parental discretion is given greater legal leeway in virtually every instance than is the exercise of state power. States cannot act with damaging effect in an arbitrary or capricious manner without facing the prospect of legal redress for damages caused. Parents can and do act arbitrarily and capriciously to the detriment of children without risking the possibility of legal censure—not, at any rate, until their action or its result is excessive. We can find many historical and contemporary examples of statutes and judicial decisions that presume not only against state interference with parents but in favor of the idea that deliberate harm to a child is acceptable so long as it is a parent who does the harm. Legitimizing parents' infliction of physical harm on children in the name of discipline, but not permitting state action against parents without compelling justification, is one example the law affords of the great scope of parental discretion (5, 6).

Statutes and case law decisions are, however, gradually moving away from presuming that harm to a child must in all likelihood have been for the good to requiring that any significant harm caused to a child, even by a parent, must be demonstrably justifiable or else the use of authority by the caregiver can be called into question. Moving away from the presumption that harm caused to a child by a parent is justifiable does not mean that the presumption of parental authority is discarded. What it does mean is that a balancing test is brought into the case and applied, a balancing in which the harms of state interference and the harms of state noninterference in a particular family situation will be more evenly weighed.

The duties of noninterference are evident throughout the common law, as we have seen. In the common-law countries, duties of noninterference historically and to this day are imposed first of all on the government. Governmental duties of support are primarily duties of protection, limiting governmental interference in the lives of citizens and limiting the interference of citizens with each other. There are few "fundamental" governmental duties of economic or social support in common-law countries; this is in contrast to political systems ranging from the totalitarian, which claim "ownership" or "dominion" over citizens, to the paternalistic, which mandate an enormous array of services that are not easily refused. In many democratic countries, however, what seems to be changing is that recognition and acceptance of the principle that parents owe a variety of "fundamental" duties to their children is growing. Parental duties of care, support, and "noninterference" with the child's development—which complement the sweeping powers, including the power of "interference" in their children's lives for good or ill, that parents have assumed heretofore—are being clarified to a greater degree than in the past. Defining these terms practically is a difficult task, but one that is taking place daily nevertheless in ordinary and emergency judicial proceedings.

Deciding on a Basis for Parental Rights and Responsibilities

Parental Duties as Assumed Responsibilities

One factor traditionally considered in the enforcement of duties is the extent to which a duty has been assumed by an individual. By accepting and taking on a duty, an individual may waive at least some rights to object to interference if he or she performs that duty to the detriment of the person whom the individual had volunteered to assist. This concept is found in tort law where a person who attempts to rescue another person to whom he or she originally owed nothing may find him- or herself held accountable for breach of the duty assumed if the rescue is done badly.

Parental duties normally are *assumed* by individual, deliberate action. This "volunteering" for parenthood is an important basis for the statutorily and judicially imposed contingent duties which follow the birth of a child. These imposed duties reflect the special nature of childhood. In effect, the assumption of the special *powers* reserved to parents when they care for children brings with it the assumption of concomitant *duties* which society considers part of the "package." William Blackstone, the renowned English legal scholar, stated the common law this way:

> The duty of parents to provide for the *maintenance* of their children, is a principle of natural law: an obligation . . . laid on them by their own proper act, in bringing them into the world: for they would be in the highest manner injurious to their issue, if they only gave their children life, that they might afterwards see them perish. By begetting them, therefore, they have entered into a voluntary obligation, to endeavor, as far as in them lies, that the life which they have bestowed shall be supported and preserved. (7, p. 178; emphasis in original)

The "glue" that binds the generations together under this approach is one of "waiver," in the sense that whether or not parents intended to be reasonably responsible, in becoming parents, they have waived their right to object to their duty to posterity.

The Principle of "Exchange" in Defining Children's and Parents' Rights

Another way to examine the process through which parental power is accorded great deference and yet freighted with responsibility is by looking at the trade-off of authority and responsibility. In the words of the nineteenth-century American jurist James Kent, "The rights of parents result from their duties" (8, lect. 29, p. 225). The association between the beginning of enforceable rights for each individual and the child-parent relationship hinges on the obvious dependency of children on adults, and to the necessity for someone competent to exercise sufficient authority to meet those dependency needs. The historical and reasonable preference has been that such authority should be exercised by the child's parents. There is also implicit or explicit acknowledgment that parents must be given extensive authority not only to meet the child's developmental needs but also to enable them to contend with the demands of parenting (9, pp. 105–7; 10, pp. 24–25). Thus power is assumed by and conceded to parents because it is good for both parent and child.

Needs and benefits from the child-parent relationship which must be considered, from the parent's perspective, to encourage child rearing include:

- relatively exclusive authority, including independence from arbitrary or capricious governmental interference, in making child-rearing decisions;[3] and
- relatively satisfying child-parent relationships.[4]

Needs and benefits from the child-parent relationship which must be considered as crucial from the child's perspective include:

- protection from danger, including the elements and severely adverse human contact; and
- opportunities for development, which requires appropriate kinds of nutrition, attachment, stimulation, separation, and exploratory activities, none of which can be obtained adequately by a child without a human parent.

Any true "balancing test" of parent and child relationships, however, is evolutionary thinking, from the historical perspective:

> The doctrine of parental absolutism that evolved during the Babylonian, Hebrew, Greek, and finally the Roman societies died a natural death. In its place, the concept of presumptive parental rights has arisen. Today, the parent-child relationship is characterized as a presumptive parental right: American society presumes that a child's parent(s) wants to act in the child's best interests. These presumptions are only overcome when the facts in a particular case dramatically indicate otherwise. The presumption of right rests with the parent. (11, p. 325)

The modern notion of balancing assumes that children can have interests separate from parents and from the family and that these interests and rights should not only be weighed but even weighed equally—balanced, in fact—against the interests and rights of others. The current implication that children have *independent* interests, not to mention rights, cannot be taken for granted either culturally or legally.

Many changes have occurred since the Roman law that gave fathers control of the lives and estates of their offspring until their own death. This law was based on the principle that what a person had begun could, as a matter of entitlement, be ended by the same individual (7, p. 181). In contrast, to argue today that parents are given powers over children—who

---

3. One way for society to further this interest would be to give parents the right to vote in elections as proxies for each individual child. One implication of this relatively exclusive authority is the right of parents to sacrifice some interests of a child for the benefit of other children or the "family."

4. Attachment to the child as a love object and experience of emotional gratification from child care are intrinsic to ideal parenting situations. However, use of a child to satisfy a parent's needs for sex or violent discharge of anger is considered by almost everyone to justify societal intervention on behalf of the child. In other words, some of the parent's needs can, and often will, be met from child care, while other needs must be met in other ways. In extreme situations—for instance, when a parent is willing to sacrifice essential interests of the child for the sake of religious observance—"martyring" the child is prohibited (*Prince v. Massachusetts,* 321 U.S. 158 [1944]).

are to be free and independent eventually—only in exchange for duties or responsibilities to be fulfilled on behalf of those same children is "natural" within the common-law framework. Common-law cultures are marked by the great extent to which principles of contract have become dominant in politics and culture as well as in law.

Child-Parent Relationships as a Factor in Defining Powers and Duties

Although modern society can impose an "exchange" principle on child-parent relationships, just as the Roman law imposed a "what has been started can be ended" principle on them, both the "waiver" and "contractual" approaches have a coldness to them. Real families are composed of flesh and blood, emotions, and personal—not merely abstract and philosophical—relationships. The importance of human intimacy is reflected in many preferences in legal decisions and statutes for the "blood tie" between parent and child. While there are many good reasons that biological parents tend to take on the primary opportunity for nurturing their children, biological definitions of the child-parent relationship are not adequate for many purposes, nor are they entirely adequate for legal analysis. For example, the biological or genetic relationship between emancipated child and parent remains constant, but the law generally enforces no parental power over the older, emancipated child.

A more functionally based definition of the child-parent legal relationship would reflect growing popular recognition of the importance of continuing interactions between a given child and parent. The first set of interactions between them are indeed biological, as the father and mother join to conceive and the mother then provides essential conditions for life during pregnancy. Once a child is born, however, the process of childhood visibly combines nature with nurture.

Infants have more than just clear "preferences" for certain people, as adults have hierarchies of preference—they have basic needs for special relationships. While some people might deny the importance of infant attachments, the general view of child development specialists is that infants' primary relationships are so important to their development that they cannot thrive without them (9, 10). Yet an infant's psychological relationship with an adult to whom it isn't related biologically, no matter how strong the attachment, has not necessarily overridden legal support for the biological parent-child relationship. While the presumption for biological parents remains potent, and often determinative,[5] court decisions increasingly are recognizing that the quality of the ongoing parent-child relationship is often the best means for determining the "best interests" of the child. One set of cases in which the U.S. Supreme Court has given great weight to active and continuing parent-child relationships concerns stepparent adoptions.

> When an unwed father demonstrates a full commitment to the responsibilities of parenthood by "com(ing) forward to participate in the rearing of his child," his interest in personal contact with his child acquires substantial protection under the Due Process Clause. At that point it may be said that he "act(s) as a father towards his children." *But the mere existence of the biological link does not merit equivalent constitutional protection.* The actions of judges neither create nor

5. See, for example, *In re. J.C.,* 608 A.2d 1312 (N.J. 1992), and *In re K.L.F.,* 608 A.2d 1327 (N.J. 1992), in which psychological bonds between children and foster parents were not sufficient cause to terminate the biological parent-child legal relationship.

sever genetic bonds. "[T]he importance of the familial relationship, to the individuals involved and to the society, stems from the emotional attachments that derive from the intimacy of daily associations, and from the role it plays in 'promot[ing] a way of life' through the instruction of children as well as from the fact of blood relationship." (12; emphasis added)[6]

The result of such decisions is to clarify that biological parents who are uninvolved in caring for a child can waive their legally enforceable power over that particular child. Parental authority is thus a "biology plus" proposition. Another way to interpret such developments is that the courts are beginning to pay better attention to the significance of parental love and caring from the perspective of children.

To discuss the role of a parent only in terms of power and duties, moreover, is to risk missing an important distinction between power, authority, and good parenting. Children need a parent who is authorita*tive*, but this does not imply that a parent must be authoritar*ian* (13). Indeed, the authoritarian parent—the parent who relentlessly demands submission to his or her authority for its own sake—may well do the same harm to children that authoritarian and totalitarian governments everywhere have been known to cause the people they control. Democratic societies depend on citizens who know the difference between "authoritative" and "authoritarian" and who mostly opt for the former.

The Essential Importance of Children's Access to Society

As long as we concede that one basis for civilization is accountability for any completely unacceptable actions that private individuals take against each other, such as unjustified child endangerment or recklessly inflicted injury, we must acknowledge that we need relevant information to permit us to determine whether or not individual citizens have been or are being victimized. The discovery of a murder victim's body abrogates many aspects of the decedent's privacy if they might be pertinent to a criminal inquiry. Analogously, people able and willing to ask for help consciously waive some of their rights of privacy by the very act of seeking assistance. Such situations clarify that privacy and confidentiality are not monolithic and absolute; individuals may cede some privacy rights without relinquishing all rights to privacy. It is also true, of course, that some disclosure of normally private information about a person may be justified by circumstances, without all private information about that person becoming available automatically to everybody without restriction (14).

For cultural, legal,[7] and developmental (10) reasons, at least some parts of family life are considered a private matter. The right of family privacy, however, is not absolute: it is a right exercised by *individuals,* and the use of "family" in a "corporate" sense, as if it

6. See also *Michael H. v. Gerald D.,* 491 U.S. 110 (1989).

7. See, for example, *Roe v. Wade,* 410 U.S. 113, 152 (1973), finding a protected area of privacy for abortion decision; *Griswold v. Connecticut,* 381 U.S. 479, 484–85 (1965), concluding that use of contraception is a private concern; *Loving v. Virginia,* 388 U.S. 1, 12 (1967), holding that marriage is a private decision; and *Prince v. Massachusetts,* 321 U.S. 158, 166 (1944), stating that family relationships are protected from governmental interference.

were inevitably a uniform identity completely subsuming its members, can be dangerously misleading. Husbands and wives can and do waive confidentiality about private matters in some divorce custody disputes, and one or the other may have to refer to the courts to decide whether or not a child's confidentiality is to be maintained about a certain matter (1, 1:52–55). Many cases illustrate that adults are quite capable of stating that they are acting in a child's interests by either trying to obtain the release of confidential information or trying to prevent it when, in fact, they are acting in actual or potential conflict with the child's interests.

The issues of confidentiality and accountability are not limited to family and juvenile law. As with other potential conflicts between confidentiality and accountability, the decision on who is to have access to information about a child's well-being can determine a child's health, life, or death. For example, efforts to control sexually transmitted diseases and mental health commitment proceedings raise conflicts between the privacy of emancipated minors and protection of the public.

Mechanisms to Assure the Access of Children to Society

Home visitation—the child checked at home by a public health worker—is very common in western Europe, where it is considered a normal routine by parents and children (15). Universal home visitation has been proposed for the United States (16). In this country, mandatory child abuse and neglect reporting laws are currently one important means of assuring that children's well-being can be verified when suspicious circumstances arise. Such laws can be viewed as guaranteeing children's right of access to society. Mandatory school attendance for children over the age of five is yet another policy which legally guarantees that children will be visible to their larger society.

Developing a "Need to Know" Basis for Access to Information about a Child's Status

Other circumstances can arise on an ad hoc basis that involve issues of confidentiality about a child's health or well-being. Potential conflicts exist between parents' desire to know that their offspring is using drugs or alcohol, seeking treatment for mental illness, seeking contraceptives, or seeking an abortion and the minor's desire for confidentiality. For many years statutes have been enacted to limit the sharing of such information with parents on the assumption that parental notification in these cases would deter some minors from seeking needed care.

In divorce custody disputes, one parent may wish information about a therapist's sessions with a child to be heard in court, while another parent may oppose such admissions. In child abuse and neglect hearings, many statutes have abrogated the physician-patient testimonial privilege in order to permit statements about a child's medical condition to be heard notwithstanding parental objections (14, pp. 162–63). This breach of confidentiality is necessary to determine whether or not a child's condition provides evidence of abuse or neglect.

One way to analyze the decisions being made both in legislatures and in courtrooms is to determine to what extent a "need to know" principle has evolved. Judges generally are unwilling to make decisions involving the life of a child unless they have the evidence necessary to make a reasonable judgment. Legislatures have been unwilling to make confidentiality so absolute a privilege that society's need to know that children are receiving reasonably adequate care cannot be met. The better legal scholars argue that those who are in a position to make decisions for the child must be able to receive any information they need about a child's situation, whatever their legitimate role on behalf of the child, whether the caretaker is a parent, relative, care-giving professional, or member of society at large. Conversely, those who are not responsible for advising the parent, judge, or other legitimate decision-maker should not be made privy under law to the child's personal circumstances.[8]

The concept that "need to know" should determine access to information about a child is somewhat of an oversimplification, but it is intended to empower those who must act on behalf of a child. It is consistent with developments, at least in the United States, which require that medical professionals and others disclose information to patients or clients necessary to permit true informed consent. it is a standard rigorous enough to guide the control of military secrets in this country and in other common-law countries. Only by establishing clear laws and guidelines for enabling access to information about children by parents and by other individuals (in law enforcement agencies, public health and medical settings, and schools) charged with children's well-being can minimally adequate care for children be assured. Laws specifying and clarifying the conditions warranting access to information guard against the overreaching of any individual or agency charged with providing adequate care for a child.

As data systems improve, a more complete picture of a child's life, including records of the child's health care, can begin to include information about all who have had access to the information. Audit trails will increase the probability of detecting and sanctioning the improper release of data.

Summary

The importance of healthy child-parent relationships in resolving some of our most pressing social concerns will direct general attention increasingly to issues of family law. Situations arise frequently in which the character of individual child-parent legal relationships must be considered outside the confines of private family life—situations such as divorce custody disputes and reports of possible child maltreatment. Although the presumption of parental authority retains primacy, legal thinking is shifting from abstract principles of dominion and equity to the practical issues of psychological and emotional attachment, that is, of determining who has been most important in caring for an individual child. Legal decisions increasingly are focusing on the adequacy of actual care afforded a given child when disputes about the child's care arise: if parents do not actively and adequately care for their children, then the presumption of their parental authority is deemed to be no longer enforceable.

Only by assuring some access to society for all children can adequate care for children

8. This is essentially the thesis of Weisberg and Wald with respect to *civil,* but not criminal, proceedings for child protection (14, pp. 143–212).

be assured by a democratic society. A framework for balancing parents' rights of privacy and children's rights to accountability continues to develop. Mandatory child maltreatment reporting laws, health visitation programs, and public education help assure children's access to general societal networks outside the home. When accountability for a child's care must be balanced against the parents' desire for privacy, any information necessary to determine if a child is physically and mentally safe must be made available.

References

1. Myers, J. E. B. 1992. *Evidence in Child Abuse and Neglect Cases.* 2d ed. vols. New York: Wiley.
2. Morris, N. 1984. The Best Interests of the Child. *Univ. Chicago Law Rev.* 51:447–516.
3. McClain, P. W.; Sacks, J. J.; Froehlke, R. G.; and Ewigman, B. G. 1993. Estimates of Fatal Child Abuse and Neglect, United States, 1979 through 1988. *Pediatrics* 91:338–43.
4. Garbarino, J. 1988. *The Future As If It Really Mattered.* Longmont, Colo.: Bookmakers Guild.
5. Hiner, N. R. 1979. Children's Rights, Corporal Punishment, and Child Abuse. *Bull. Menninger Clinic* 43:233–48.
6. Herman, N. R. 1985. A Statutory Proposal to Prohibit the Infliction of Violence upon Children. *Family Law Q.* 19:1–52.
7. Blackstone, W. 1765. *Commentaries on the Laws of England,* 1:446–54. Quoted in *Child, Family, and State: Problems and Materials on Children and the Law,* 2d ed., by R. H. Mnookin and D. K. Weisberg, 178. (Boston: Little, Brown, 1989).
8. Kent, J. [1826–30] 1873. *Commentaries on American Law.* 12th ed. Edited by O. W. Holmes. Boston: Little, Brown.
9. Goldstein, J.; Freud, A.; and Solnit, A. J. 1973. *Beyond the Best Interests of the Child.* New York: Free Press.
10. Goldstein, J.; Freud, A.; and Solnit, A. J. 1979. *Before the Best Interests of the Child.* New York: Free Press.
11. Fraser, B. F. 1976. The Child and His Parents: A Delicate Balance of Rights. In *Child Abuse and Neglect: The Family and the Community,* ed. R. E. Helfer and C. H. Kempe. Cambridge, Mass.: Ballinger.
12. *Lehr v. Robertson,* 463 U.S. 248, 261 (1983).
13. Kempe, R. S. 1993. Personal communication.
14. Weisberg, R., and Wald, M. 1984. Confidentiality Laws and State Efforts to Protect Abused or Neglected Children: The Need for Statutory Reform. *Family Law Q.* 18:143–212.
15. Kempe, C. H. 1976. Approaches to Preventing Child Abuse: The Health Visitors Concept. *Am. J. Diseases of Children* 130:941–47.
16. U.S. Advisory Board on Child Abuse and Neglect. 1991. *Creating Caring Communities: Blueprint for an Effective Federal Policy on Child Abuse and Neglect.* Washington, D.C.: U.S. Department of Health and Human Services; Administration for Children, Youth, and Families.

5

Psychodynamic and Biological Factors in Child Maltreatment

Brandt F. Steele

The term *child maltreatment* covers a large, complex group of human behaviors characterized by traumatic interactions between parents or other caretakers and the infants and children of all ages under their care, as well as between strangers and children during casual contact. It includes many varieties of physical, emotional, and sexual abuse and various forms of neglect, all of which can occur alone or in combination. Such maltreatment is biologically maladaptive insofar as, to a greater or lesser extent, it damages immature members of our species in ways that interfere with their optimal physical, emotional, cognitive, and social development and their adaptive survival abilities. What is thus distorted is nothing less than the basic task of life—that, after ensuring our own survival, we take part in producing the next generation in the best condition possible, to ensure the survival of our species. The roster of child maltreatment perpetrators is lengthy, including biological parents, stepparents, siblings, other relatives, adoptive parents, foster parents, and parental paramours, as well as baby-sitters, day-care workers, teachers, scoutmasters, family friends, doctors, ministers, and strangers.

Maltreatment is an extremely complex problem, its ramifications extending into the fields of medicine, sociology, law, psychology, child development, religion, psychiatry, biology, and anthropology. All these disciplines have something significant to contribute to the elucidation and comprehension of maltreatment phenomena. Child maltreatment is not a psychiatric illness in the ordinary sense of that phrase, but it can best be understood in dynamic psychological terms. My own approach is to examine the problem within a bio-psycho-social framework, with some emphasis on psychoanalytic concepts of human development and mental functioning (1).

The most fundamental biological element in human maturation and development is the phenomenon of neoteny: the human infant has a longer period of immaturity and dependency between birth and adult status than has any other mammal. Thus, far fewer patterns of behavior are genetically determined, and much more time is required early in the life cycle for learning the intricacies of interactions and the meanings of experiences that guide later behavior. The challenges and strains endemic to this period of prolonged dependency

Brandt F. Steele, M.D., is professor emeritus of psychiatry at the University of Colorado School of Medicine and serves on the staff of the C. Henry Kempe National Center for the Prevention and Treatment of Child Abuse and Neglect.

give rise to the phenomena of child maltreatment. Although the basic behaviors and mental patterns of abusers have not changed appreciably in the past forty years, ongoing research has furthered our comprehension of these abusive behaviors and mind-sets.

Generational Repetition of Maltreatment

Since the early study of "battered children" in the 1960s (2), it has been clear that parents and other caregivers tend to treat children under their care in much the same fashion as they themselves were raised (3–6). A simple example:

> Two boys, two-and-a-half and four years old, respectively, were in the hospital with severe burns of the palms of their hands and told us how their father had burned them for playing with matches after being told not to. Their father readily admitted doing it and said it was the best method of dealing with such misbehavior. When asked how he knew it was the best, he said, "When I was their age and played with matches, mother burned my hands. As a matter of fact, the Zippo lighter I used on the kids is the same one mother used on me."

Typically, the repetition is more subtle and somewhat varied, although often accompanied by the same sense of justification and righteousness. This father was not amoral; like all of us, he learned right and wrong from his parents. He happened to have identified with a hand-burning mother. Criticism has often been directed against the validity of retrospective histories as data to support theories of the generational transmission of child maltreatment. Ideally, scientific validation would require prospective studies from infancy to adulthood, although a researcher's continued involvement with a family would introduce other distorting influences. In the case cited above, the internal consistency of the data is very compelling and reveals a foreshortened life history in the current interaction between parent and child.

Probably only about one-fourth of all people abused as children grow up to be diagnosed as abusers (although abused children do tend to develop many other kinds of relationship problems and personality disorders). On the other hand, it is rare for a child care professional to see anyone who has maltreated children who does not give a personal history of significant neglect, with or without accompanying abuse, in his or her own childhood.

To understand the origin and transmission of maltreatment patterns across generations, it is necessary to explore and assess the interactions between infants and their caregivers in the earliest months of life. In 1938, Benedek (7) described how infants adapt to the realities of their environment and internalize the behavior of caregivers. Later, in 1959, Benedek went on to explicate how deeply imbedded memories, conscious and unconscious, of what it was like to be a child and to be cared for in certain ways become the template guiding an individual's patterns of parenting as they are evoked by the birth of offspring (8). Recent decades have seen a growing interest in attachment theory and its particular relevance to the dynamics of maltreatment.

Attachment

Infants' problems with maternal deprivation had been studied by John Bowlby in the early 1950s (9). Later, out of his concern over the severe reactions of infants separated from their mothers, he wrote about the close tie existing between them (10). Using his own observations, along with ideas from the ethologist Lorenz's work on imprinting (11) and data from Harlow's research on monkeys (12), Bowlby developed a theory of the psychological attachment of human infants to their mothers.

Basically, the theory describes how baby mammals seek and move to their mother for nourishment and protection and how they automatically return to her if separated, especially in case of perceived danger. In nonhuman primates, the infant-mother dyad is mutually cooperative—the newborn infant clinging to mother's fur, and mother actively retrieving and holding her infant—after a few weeks, the baby can run to her. In humans, the helpless infant can only signal distress, while the mother must instigate all feeding, holding, and protection after sensitively recognizing the baby's state and needs. It takes many months for a human baby to develop the active motor skills required to maintain the proximity that is seen in nonhuman primates and other mammals shortly after birth.

There is a very significant difference between an infant's attachment to its mother and the mother's bonding to her baby. Newborn human infants, if not seriously premature or congenitally defective, will, like all primates and mammals, begin to attach to whomever fate has provided as a primary caregiver. This is an automatic, genetically programmed process, necessary for survival: the baby adapts to whoever supplies basic needs for nourishment, protection, stimulation, and company. This is a gamble, as there is no guarantee the supplier will be a healthy, empathic caregiver. At first, the attachment is essentially to the maternal function itself, and can exist with any person who performs that function. Only around the beginning of the fourth month of life does the infant develop the ability to recognize the specific individual to whom he or she is attached.

The mother's response to her newborn, however, is not a biologically obligatory, automatic process necessary to her survival. Her bonding will be immediately influenced by her health during pregnancy, the relative ease or pathologic difficulty of delivery (13), and the acceptability to her of the baby's sex. The long-lasting residues of her total life experience also determine the character of her bonding, beginning with her attachment to and identification with her own mother and extending to her relationships with all other significant persons in her formative years. Crucial to this process are the feelings she has about the baby's father, her own self-image, whether the baby was planned or wanted, her socioeconomic status, whether she is isolated or has support of family or others, plus whatever fantasies she has both of what she wants or expects from a baby and of what it means to be a mother. The baby is at the mercy of whatever fate has provided, and his (or her) future depends on what kind of past history his caregiver can draw from to guide parenting behavior.

The material and human environment in which the baby lives and to which he must adapt is his total world, the only world he knows, and to him it is normal. In this world, he will learn verbal language, the mother tongue, that will last for the rest of his life. In similar fashion, he will learn an equally potent language of interpersonal relationships that will guide his self-concepts and his interactions with others in the future. The first others will be the people in whatever family structure makes up his home—father, siblings, relatives, servants, and so on—to whom he will attach in varying degrees. In order to understand his development and later life, we must explore the quality and content of these first attachment experiences.

Bowlby (14) used his psychoanalytic framework to describe how the infant internalizes the experiences with his attachment figures to create an "internal working model" that becomes the guide for his subsequent interpersonal relationships. This model, composed of knowledge of the environment integrated with his own abilities, also determines the character of his later adult bonding and parenting behavior and, hence, is similar to Benedek's (8) concept that the parent's memories of being cared for as a child provide the template for parenting. In addition, the internalized model also holds much of the material that will appear later in the adult individual's transferences to other adults.

Following Bowlby's lead, Mary Ainsworth (15) developed the technique of "strange situation"; she evaluated the quality of one-year-old infants' attachment to their mothers by observing the infants' responses to their mothers' idiosyncratic behaviors. Based on the assumption that the quality of the baby's attachment will be demonstrated by the baby's behavior under the stress of separation and reunion with the mother, or of being alone with a stranger, her technique identified three distinct types of attachment: secure, avoidant, and ambivalent. Her work opened a new field for exploring and understanding mother-infant interactions and child development, thereby stimulating an enormous amount of research and generating an abundant literature. Among the many who have corroborated and extended Ainsworth's pioneer work are Main and Solomon (16), who added a fourth category of attachment (disorganized/disoriented); Main (17); Sroufe, Egeland, and Kreutzer (18); and Egeland (19)—all of whom have demonstrated how the individual's early attachment style persists for many years and continues to influence personal relationships and interactions during later life.

The infant's development involves continuing interaction between his maturing biological structures and functions and his surrounding environment, particularly whatever material is available for him to perceive and integrate. From birth on, he is dependent upon the idiosyncratic input of his particular caregivers. A valuable perspective on this process has been noted by Sander (20–23) in his studies of the development of the infant's self-regulating ability. He describes how the infant works on a contingency basis, giving signals and getting responses ("If I do *a,* then *b* happens"). In an ideal mother-infant relationship, the interaction proceeds harmoniously: The baby's physiologic metabolic state is registered in the brain as "hunger-discomfort" and, in turn, stimulates neuronal impulses to motor areas that instigate crying and random muscular activity. The empathic mother recognizes the baby's crying and motor activity as a sign of hunger, offers her breast, and coos and talks to her baby, holding him close, while he sucks until satisfied. He relaxes, his physiological equilibrium is restored, and he is psychologically comforted. The mother is also pleased by seeing her baby's positive response to her ministrations.

For the infant, the cycle of discomfort, signaling, feeding, tension relief, and pleasurable satisfaction is repeated many times, and the neural circuits and psychic states become "validated" by the mother's adequately reliable response. He, at the same time, becomes entrained and adapted to his mother's own basic rhythms and feeding manners, which she, in turn, has adjusted to her baby's individual temperament and needs. Similar cycles of infant signal and caregiver response occur in all other aspects of providing for the basic needs of the infant—nourishment, protection, stimulation, and human company. It is in this repetitive, mutually rewarding system, described by Benedek (7) as "symbiotic," that the lasting unconscious memories of being parented begin to be encoded, along with the early primitive origins of a sense of self and of basic trust and confidence that the world can be good to one. The infant thrives in a milieu of empathic care supplied by a good attachment object.

Neglect, Abuse, and Lack of Empathy

All forms of maltreatment can be conceptualized as neglect insofar as the full welfare of the child has not been adequately recognized and provided for by the caregiver. Although all physical abuse and some sexual abuse can be seen as behaviors that do actual physical and emotional harm, they inevitably involve the disregard or neglect of beneficial response to the child's age-appropriate needs and protection. Such neglect seems to be the outward expression for the caregiver's lack of empathy. Empathy is biphasic: first, the caregiver sensitively perceives and integrates the child's cues, to attain accurate understanding of the child's state and needs of the moment; second, the caregiver actually provides an appropriate response to the perceived need. Empathy is a learned talent, acquired through being empathically cared for in early life. This early origin of empathy has been recognized since the work of Olden (24, 25) and Josselyn (26) in the 1950s, and is clearly described by Anna Freud:

> Due to their inability to care for themselves, infants and children have to put up with whatever care is given them. Where child management is not extremely sensitive, this causes a number of disturbances, the earliest of which are usually centered around sleep, feeding, elimination, and the wish for company. . . . Inconsiderate handling of the infant's early needs has some further repercussions for pathological development. In his growth toward independence and self-reliance, the child accepts the mother's initial gratifying or frustrating attitude as a model which he imitates and recreates in his own ego. Where she understands, respects, and satisfies his wishes as far as possible, there are good chances his ego will show equal tolerance. Where she unnecessarily delays, denies, and disregards wish fulfillment, his ego is likely to develop more of the so-called "hostility toward the id," a readiness for internal conflict, which is one of the prerequisites of neurotic development. (27, pp. 155–57)

Gray and colleagues (28, 29) observed mothers in the delivery room when they first greeted their newborns in extro-uterine life and again in their interactions with their infants during the first feedings. At this time, the mother's bonding potential and empathic ability can easily be correlated with her total life experience, from early attachment to current perinatal events. A fairly accurate prediction can be made of the mother's prospects either for good parenting or for child neglect and abuse. The presence of empathy is an integral part of the generational transmission of good parenting, and its lack is crucial in the transmission of maltreatment. Careful evaluation of the mother-infant interaction provides essential information about the status and quality of the infant's attachment and the mother's bonding, what problems may exist, and what needs to be treated. Such data also point the way to how interventions early on can prevent neglect and abuse later. A technique of thorough evaluation of parent-child interactions has been developed and described by Haynes-Semen and Hart (30).

The clinical picture of these concepts can be very subtle or, as in the following vignette, deceptively simple:

> Cheri, an attractive, intelligent, verbal young woman was referred for evaluation of child abuse. When asked what had been happening, she answered, in a subdued voice and mildly depressed mood, with carefully chosen words, "I never felt really loved or cared about by anybody all my life. When my baby was born, I thought he would love me. When he cried so much, it meant he didn't love me, so I hit him." Kenny, eighteen days old, was in the hospital with a fractured skull. Later, Cheri added details: although she had rarely been physically punished as a child, she had been exposed to a good deal of violence between other family members.

In this brief vignette, it is easy to see how the experiences of deprivation and exposure to aggression in Cheri's early childhood became embedded in her memories and how her "internal working model" has resurfaced to guide her parenting behavior. Her lifelong feeling of emptiness and yearning for love has led her to turn to her baby to supply the love she felt she could never get from the adult world. She cannot empathically understand Kenny's crying as the only technique he has of expressing the discomfort of hunger and his need for help. Instead, she misinterprets his crying as criticism and rejection of her as unlovable, attacking her already fragile narcissism and low self-esteem. In identification with her own unempathic aggressive parents, she lashes out and hits him. She lives out what she learned was "normal" in the only world she knew.

As a result, Kenny's rudimentary contingency system is shattered; his signal for help produced a hit on the head instead of a nourishing breast. There is no motherly validation of his neuro-psychic functions; his own state and effort are irrelevant. If such disregard of his signals were repeated, even if he were not again hit, Kenny would soon not respond to his own internal discomfort but wait helplessly until Cheri felt it convenient to do something. He would be at great risk of failing to thrive. This pattern of disregard and nonvalidation of an infant's signal spreads into all other aspects of caregiver-infant interactions. Lacking a consistent reliable system to which he can adapt, the child sustains distorted cognitive, emotional, and social development. The blockage of the infant's self-regulatory functions becomes the base of what psychologists have traditionally called a lack of internal locus of control and a consequent submission to external loci of control, a symptom commonly seen in children and adults who have been maltreated.

The deficits in self-esteem, sense of identity, security, and interpersonal relationships can all be understood as the consequence of inadequately empathic care during early development. Emotional neglect and abuse are almost inseparable, as both cause damage to the sense of self and identity and interfere with the normal process of separation and individuation.

Deficits in empathy can be greatly improved in both adults and children through the learning experience of being cared for by an adequately empathic therapist, who, in a way, functions as a new and different attachment object. What results is concomitant improvement in self-esteem, sense of identity, security, and interpersonal relationships. New parents are often open to such interventions. The pioneering work of the psychoanalyst Heinz Kohut (31), in recent years in his promulgation of "self psychology," has provided a framework for understanding and treating the psychopathological residues of the deprivation of empathic care in early life.

Trauma: Neglect and Abuse

The deleterious effects of child maltreatment can be generically described as the consequences of trauma. The concept of trauma is borrowed from medicine, where it defines bodily damage such as fractures, lacerations, and burns caused by the impact of some object or substance. In maltreatment, the term has been broadened to include damage to the child's psychological, cognitive, emotional, and social functions caused by the behaviors of caregivers and others.

Psychological trauma occurs when there is an imbalance—when a stronger, noxious stimulus overwhelms a weaker coping ability of the child. Consequently, the child's psychic functions are disturbed and disabled.

Even neonates possess an innate mechanism for coping to some degree with excessive stimuli; this mechanism is described as a "stimulus barrier" or "stimulus screen," and it can lead to a shutdown of perception or withdrawal (32). An example is the prolonged, quiet non-REM sleep observed in neonates after they have been circumcised without anesthesia (33). Gradually, during the daily experience of empathic care, infants acquire more sophisticated and effective coping strategies and defenses. Until then, the developing infant must depend on his caregiver to prevent trauma, a situation clearly described by Anna Freud:

> Even if the neonate is considered protected against excessive stimulation by a high threshold of excitation, the older infant may be thought of as potentially traumatized all the time since his rudimentary ego has no ability to cope with over-stimulation from either external or internal sources. What comes to his rescue normally are the ministrations of his mother who, by providing care, protection, and comfort, assumes the role of a protective shield, holds off external excitations, and alleviates internal stimuli. It is only in the second year of life that this function of the protective shield (auxiliary ego) gradually passes over from the mother to the child himself and is taken over by his own ego. (34, p. 37)

In maltreatment, this process is highly distorted. For example, in the case of Cheri (described in the preceding section), her unempathic behavior fails to assuage her infant son Kenny's internal discomfort, adds another external source of pain, does not validate his neuro-psychic pattern of discomfort-comfort cycles, and fails to provide an empathic model to integrate into his own psyche.

The medical profession's early approach to the problem of child maltreatment primarily addressed physical abuse and inevitably focused on the overt injury as the cause of trauma, according less attention to the comparatively subtle emotional repercussions. Physical abuse is easily recognized and documented by x rays, photos, descriptions, and measurements. However, fractures, bruises, burns, and lacerations, do not, per se, lead to the long-lasting emotional, cognitive, and social problems that trouble a physically abused child. Many, if not most, children have been injured by falling off a bicycle or out of an apple tree, burned by accidentally touching a hot object, bruised during games or by shutting a car door too quickly, or cut in unfortunate encounters with sharp edges. With ordinary sympathy and care, there are no lasting effects, maybe even something to brag about. It is the psychologically shattering effect of the injury being inflicted by the very persons to whom the child looks for safety and care that is traumatic. There is no place to go for comfort: the source of help has become a source of attack; the normal coping mechanism is absent. Ordinarily, a child accidentally bruised or burned, even fractured, can go to mother, who will pick up, hold, and comfort him and kiss the hurt spot to "make it all better"—and who will get medical care if needed. If, however, mother is the one who has hit her child or pushed her child's hand against a hot stove for disobediently touching something, the child has no recourse except to suffer and wait for the environment to improve. Even in serious accidental injuries that result in hospitalization, much of the child's enduring psychic damage is due to the separation from his parents and the loss of their normal supportive care.

Much of the psychiatric and psychological literature on the concepts of trauma and "post-traumatic stress disorder" has tended to exaggerate the etiological role of stimulus strength while disregarding the importance of coping ability. *DSM-III* lists as its first criterion for post-traumatic stress, "Existence of a recognizable stressor that would evoke significant symptoms of distress in almost everyone" (35, p. 238). This assessment is far from true. War experience, from which much of our knowledge of post traumatic stress disorder has been gained, indicates that combat infantrymen can become symptomatic before actually meeting the enemy, on the first day of combat, or not until after over 120 days of frontline combat, or at any time in between. The stressors have been relatively uniform; it is the variable inadequacy of coping ability that determines when breakdown will occur, but this is not mentioned in *DSM-III*. *DSM-IV* (36) does not include the "almost everyone" phrase, but it still fails to refer to the lack of coping ability. Even with natural disasters such as flood and hurricanes, the traumatic impact of stress is much diminished by the helpful response of neighbors, the Red Cross, and others who enhance individual coping ability, just as mother used to assuage the hurts. Vaillant described the process succinctly: "[I]t is not stress that kills us. It is effective adaptation to stress that permits us to live" (37, p. 374).

Physical Abuse

Maltreatment in the form of physical abuse, epitomized as "the battered child syndrome" (2), has remained the most obvious and easily recognized sign of impaired caregiver-child interactions. As we have seen, fractures, bruises, burns, lacerations, human bites, and damage to internal organs can readily be documented by hospital records of overt symptoms, x rays, photographs, measurements, and verbal descriptions. Such data help challenge the variable, inconsistent, illogical explanations of children's injuries given by caregivers and provide the legal basis for protective intervention by various agencies.

Ordinary medical care can usually correct the children's physical trauma, but it does not address the long-term psychic damage. It is well-established now that parents and other caregivers who physically abuse their charges almost always give histories of having been physically abused themselves; they have identified with their abusers and with the idea that punishment is a proper and necessary means of discipline, often supported by religious belief and cultural "norms" (for example, Spare the Rod and Spoil the Child). As a rule, abusive parents do not intend to really damage the child but believe that punishment will make the child shape up and do better.

Identification with the aggressor is a defense mechanism, one frequently used in the attempt to cope with physical abuse, as I noted above, in the case of the hand-burning father. Such identification is at the same time identification with the parent authority and hence becomes part of the child's superego, contributing eventually to the sense of rightness adult abusers have about their punitive behavior. For example, Sam G., a husky Army drill sergeant, had severely beaten his toddler son "for disobedience and lack of respect" when the boy kept making noise after being told to stop. This man told how his own father had beaten him many times for not being respectful and obedient, and he was now inculcating these virtues of respect and obedience to authority in new Army recruits. He believed it was necessary and appropriate to punish his son for the boy's own good. Sam had identified with his own abusive father-aggressor and made his father's ideals part of his internal working model. He also carries the memory of being a bad, disobedient boy and sees in his son a reincarnation of his own bad self and, therefore, someone deserving of punishment. Despite the fact that Sam is a six-foot-two-inch tall, two-hundred-pound powerful adult, his self-esteem is fragile. The boy's disobedience is felt as a threat or attack on Sam's own self-image or narcissism, triggering an aggressive response in self-defense. In addition to his predisposition to be aggressive, Sam displays a corresponding lack of empathic understanding of his child. It would seem unlikely that Sam would unleash such severe aggression if he could experience adequate empathy.

Dorothy, a young woman who had scalded her two-year-old baby for a toilet-training error and was responding well to therapy, came to my office one day after seeing her baby's pediatrician. She had asked him what to do about the baby's beginning at times to bite her. He had told her, "When he bites you, bite him back; that will teach him to stop." Dorothy said, "I thought about it and decided not to follow that advice. If I bite him back, that teaches him biting is the right thing to do, doesn't it?" A wise young mother had learned how to be empathic.

Emotional Abuse and Neglect

In contrast to the relative ease and certainty of describing physical abuse and neglect, the concepts of emotional abuse and neglect are more subtle and elusive, harder to describe and define. It is hard to put into meaningful terms the lack of caring and empathy, how much love was not there, the lack of interaction and stimulation; it is like trying to describe the contents of a vacuum. Equally difficult is trying to communicate the sense of emptiness and hurt created by verbal abuse and denigration. Common expressions are like those of Cheri: "I never felt loved or cared for." "No one ever listened to me." "I could never please mother; she always found fault in what I tried to do." "Dad called me stupid." "I could never get a real response from mother; she might just as well have been stuffed." "Father was a giant self-centered tyrant. You had to be careful what you said or asked him or he'd explode." "Everything was my fault." Children do not really know how to think of themselves except by the way they are verbally described and treated by caregivers, especially by their primary attachment figures.

Neglect and Lack of Empathy

Empathy is a learned talent, acquired through being empathically cared for in early life. Just like verbal language, it is developed through imitation and internalization of caregiver behaviors and is a basic element of the internal working model's effect on the intergenerational transmission of either good or inadequate parenting patterns.

All forms of maltreatment can be conceptualized as neglect insofar as the total welfare of the child has not been fully recognized and provided for by the caregivers. Neglect appears in many forms, well described by Polansky and colleagues (38). It is easily seen in failure to provide adequate nutrition, clothing, cleanliness, vaccinations, safety, and protection when such failure is not due solely to poverty or other deficits and events beyond the caregiver's control but is the result of the caregiver's lack of empathy and true devotion.

All of the above forms of neglect can contribute to the development of what is called "nonorganic failure to thrive." Too often this syndrome is attributed to the simple factor of inadequate caloric intake, while its contributing elements receive less attention. Caregivers whose deficit of empathy does not let them really "hear" the infant's hunger cries or "see" the lack of weight gain are also likely to not pick up, hold, and carry around the baby very much, to instead leave him alone in the crib a great deal, and to not talk or play much with the infant. Lack of such sensory stimulation and human interaction can lead to the deficit in motor skills and delays in language development that are often seen in maltreated infants (39).

Babies seem to have an innate urge to vocalize and communicate. The caregiver, by talking with the baby, aids and fine-tunes the process by approving and guiding the baby's sounds into recognizable words. This forms the basis of the mind's symbolic functions, upon which all later cognitive learning depends. Lack of caregiver interactions in the verbal field constitutes a serious type of neglect.

Part of the primary caregiver's function is to interpret reality for the infant. By providing her baby with materials to touch and taste and move and by guiding his earliest exploratory activity, a mother teaches him what is safe to do or not to do and, through her own actions, presents a model for imitation. Later, the caregiver provides cognitive verbal explanations and admonitions about how people function. For example, such information about sexuality is crucially important for the child's later ability to manage innate sexual drives appropriately.

In addition to neglecting the child's basic needs—for survival and growth—the mother or other caregivers may fail to meet the child's psychic needs for stimulating education and human company, as well as failing to model the behaviors for mutually beneficial interpersonal relationships. Sometimes when a baby is just learning how to make the transition from being spoon-fed to finger food and spoon use, he will try to put some food into the caregiver's mouth, imitating what was done to him. Such food is not likely to be what the caregiver would most prefer, but if it is rejected or the baby's hand is slapped, his chance to identify with the empathic caregiver is distorted and his own empathy and grasp of the golden rule will be impaired.

Sexual Abuse

Although sexual abuse of children has been known throughout history, it has been more acknowledged, more reported, and more studied this past quarter century than ever before. Currently, the heightened interest of society in general and of the feminist movement in particular has made the sexual abuse of children a prime concern (40–44). Sexual abuse is more complex in its origin, expression, and impact than other forms of child maltreatment. The term *sexual abuse* essentially covers any kind of activity of a sexual nature with a child that is beyond the child's age-appropriate abilities and understanding. It includes touching and fondling of genital areas and breasts, sensuous stroking of skin areas, kissing, and progressing on to penile or digital penetration of the vagina, mouth, or anus. It may involve, in more extreme cases, bruising, lacerations, or burning of genitals or, in the worst cases, kidnapping, torture, and death.

This wide variety of sexually oriented behaviors is uniquely human. From a biological standpoint, humans differ from all other animals in that their sexual interactions and copulation are relatively undetermined by reproductive physiology. Although the instinctive sexual drive is strong in both males and females, it is not closely correlated with estrus, ovulation, or annual environmental or hormonal cycles. In the human female, there is significant time difference between estrus and ovulation, and her arousal and receptivity are random. The human male is not dependent on olfactory perception of female estrus to initiate sexual arousal but can become aroused spontaneously or by many other outside stimuli. The lack of specific biologically determined patterns of sexual arousal—plus a highly elaborated, complex sense of pleasure—permits humans, beginning in early life, to develop an enormous variety of sensual experiences that eventually lead to sexual activity. It may well be that, as Freud (45) said, "Anatomy is destiny," but how anatomy is *used* is learned, not innate, and human ingenuity can produce abundant variations that are far afield from simple copulation for reproduction. What people consider appropriate or inappropriate is based on cultural ideas that range from extremely permissive attitudes toward both adults and children to extremely punitive restrictions and prohibitions that almost deny the real existence of sexuality. In addition, culturally based reluctance to publicly talk about sexuality is widespread. The incest taboo has been more effective in preventing discussion of incest than in preventing incest itself, and until very recently victims have seriously hesitated ever to disclose their suffering lest they be shamed or blamed.

Sexual abuse of children of all ages in the family is not an isolated phenomenon occurring in an otherwise healthy life situation. It is the obvious, overt, symptomatic expression of seriously disturbed family relationships and is always preceded by more or less emotional neglect or mistreatment. Parents or other caretakers involved in sexual abuse are, in most ways, quite similar to those who are simply physically abusive and neglectful and, as noted above, may at different times express any of these destructive behaviors. Sexual abusers suffer from the same severe lack of self-esteem, have a poorly integrated sense of identity, tend to be somewhat socially isolated, and have a history of emotional deprivation, perhaps of physical abuse, and often of very chaotic family life in their early years. As with physical abusers, sexual abusers often present with a history of generational repetition of abuse, especially incest in various forms. Raybin (46) reported homosexual incest involving three generations, and Raphling, Carpenter, and Davis (47, p. 54) described multiple incestuous relationships existing in a family for over three generations. Gebhard and colleagues (48) noted that men imprisoned for sexually molesting children had often been the victims of sexual molestation themselves as children. Dysfunctional families can provide the child with aberrant role models and variant acts that become part of the child's pattern of sexual expression. Some sexual abusers describe extremely chaotic living conditions during their childhood, with multiple changes of caregiving figures and exposure to extremely atypical, flamboyant sexual activities. For instance, one man said, "My father was a drunk and my mother was a whore. There were always other men and women coming into the house, and very free sexual activity of all kinds, heterosexual and homosexual." In addition to the obvious impressions made by role models in such family groups, abusers also acquire a deeper and compelling identification with the sexually abusive adults known in early childhood. This often gives incest a sort of moral approval in the subculture of some families, as is clearly evident when fathers say with some degree of righteous indignation, "My father had sex with all my sisters, so why shouldn't I sleep with my daughters?" Mothers also, in identification with their own mothers, seem unable to protect daughters from sexual abuse and, in many instances, condone or actually promote the incestuous relationship between husband and daughter. Both fathers and mothers may righteously justify their incestuous activities by the rationalization that it is best for the child to learn about sex from a loving family member than from "no-good" peers.

Different studies of various populations have reported that anywhere from 5% to 80% of sexual abusers have been sexually abused themselves; probably 40% to 50% is average (49, 50). Sometimes the abuse is a literal repetition, as when a man seduces his nephew at the same age at which he himself was seduced by his uncle.

Women are infrequently as sexually abusive to children as are men; however, those women who are abusive do much the same things. They are most likely to become sexually stimulating to infants and very young children during the ordinary tasks of bathing, dressing, and diaper changing, a process known as "sexualized attention" (51). Men likewise can be sexually stimulating during play. It is not clear how often nowadays caregivers stimulate the genitals of fussy babies to comfort and quiet them, although it was said to be a common practice in the past.

What is considered acceptable and what is deemed abusive differs markedly across cultures. In Turkey, for instance, it has been thought appropriate to verbally admire and kiss a baby's genitals during diaper changing (52). Recently, a professional woman of Turkish ancestry told me her mother and grandmother had considered this to be normal behavior in their childhoods.

The various kinds of sexual abuse occur in different settings and are committed by different kinds of people. Within the family setting, sexual abuse is called incest; outside the family, pedophilia. The most common type of incest is fathers or stepfathers with daughters and stepdaughters, followed by fathers and stepfathers with sons and stepsons. Incest between both biological siblings and step-siblings is probably just as common, especially in the less serious form of early exploratory activity that does not persist (53). Although they do not have the biological relationship of traditional family settings, temporary or long-term paramours can initiate sexual relationships with their partner's children just as stepfathers do, but without the legal cover of marriage. Compared to men, the incidence of incest by women is extremely low. Accurate statistics are not available, but maternal incest with sons and stepsons does occur more often than is recognized. It is reported in Japan (54), where excessive closeness between mother and sons persists beyond infancy and she "teaches them to masturbate, helps them to ejaculate, and tells them how frequently they may do so." This can later progress to consummated incest but does not cause as much dismay as it would in Western culture. Reports of molestation of girls by women, in contrast, are still very infrequent.

Psychoanalytic theory, erroneously, I believe, tended to relate incest to the living out of the child's own oedipal fantasies. It seems highly unlikely, however, that a father could not resist even strong seductive behavior of a daughter if he cared to. Clinically, it is evident that the sexually abusive father intends to satisfy his own sexual desires while unempathically ignoring his daughter's age-appropriate needs and neglecting his duty of protector. The daughter has been taught to be obedient, has often been groomed through previous sexualized attention, and may love her father and wish to please him. In addition, both father and daughter often share a feeling that the wife-mother has to a significant degree been unavailable and uncaring or rejecting. Both incest partners are trying via sexuality to assuage their feelings of loneliness and emptiness that originated in early life deprivation which persisted and interfered with normal progression through what Mahler, Pine, and Bergman (55) described as the separation-individuation phase of development (56). As Furman (57) puts it, "Mother has to be there to be left." In some cases, though, the incestuous father has almost the opposite problem: he experienced such a satisfying, overly close dependency on his mother that she did not allow him to psychologically grow or individuate; consequently, he tries to recreate such helpless dependency in later adult relationships. An incestuous father may also use sex to establish a sense of control and self-worth, as well as to repair an already fragile narcissism and a distorted patriarchal sense of parental rights.

It is sad but sometimes true that mothers contribute, either knowingly or unconsciously, to the incest of their daughters. Possibly 40% to 50% of mothers of incest victims have been incest victims themselves and have experienced other forms of neglect and abuse. It is not entirely clear why some mothers insist, despite obvious behavioral changes in their husbands and daughters, they did not know incest was going on. Most likely, a previous lack of closeness, empathy, and trust hampered communication between family members, added to a self-protective defense mechanism of denial by the mother and the inability of the daughter to trust her mother enough to ask for help. The mother, too, out of past deprivations and disregard, with low self-esteem, can feel no confidence that her own needs and feelings will be listened to and may well fear that if she reports the incest, her husband will be sent to jail and the finances and reputation of the whole family will be destroyed. Such fears are justified in view of the fact that society has treated incest as a crime that must be punished. The mother may also feel much guilt and wonder what is wrong with her that led her to choose and marry a man who would do such things. Sometimes the incest is unconsciously instigated by mother, as in the following case:

> During a lecture to women members of Society's League Against Molesters (SLAM), I mentioned that both fathers and daughters involved in incest needed and deserved treatment. One woman stood up and very loudly berated me for even suggesting a perpetrator be treated; they should be locked up, jailed, and the key thrown away. She told how at age fourteen she had been sexually abused by her father, but nothing was done about her report. She added that what made it even worse was that her father has sexually abused her own fourteen-year-old daughter when she sent her up to spend the summer with him on his ranch.

Pedophilia is the term usually used to describe sexual abuse of children by someone outside the family. The perpetrators are essentially similar to incest perpetrators as far as general history and dynamics are concerned. They differ from incest perpetrators, however, in their persistent focusing on children as a primary, even exclusive, object choice for sexual satisfaction. They also tend to believe more in the idea that sex is the proper and best way to express love between adult and child. In its extreme form, this accounts for the Rene Guyon Society, whose motto is "Sex before eight or else it's too late," and NAMBLA, the North American Man-Boy Love Association (58). Women are rarely pedophilic; it is almost exclusively a male behavior. Most pedophilic men have not been discovered until well into adult life; they may continue into their seventies, gradually becoming less active. Some have victimized hundreds of children. Although not recognized until later, most begin their victimizing when they are in puberty and adolescence. Since the early 1980s, increasing awareness and special attention has been focused on juvenile sex offenders (59), some of whom begin as early as four years of age. There are many theories of the etiology of sexual aberrations (60, 61); the most compelling theory is that such aberrations develop in a dysfunctional family, just as do other forms of maltreatment. In the personal history of pedophilics, there is an extremely high (estimated as high as 95%) incidence of having been sexually abused in childhood.

Some pedophilic perpetrators have specific preferences or targets, such as four-year-old blonde girls or latency-aged boys, while others molest either girls or boys of any age. Girls are molested more often than boys. Many men, out of their own experience of being abused, are perceptive—not to say empathic—observers of children and are expert at picking up vulnerable victims. For instance, they look for children wandering alone around a housing project who appear lonely, dejected, and at loose ends and then offer them conversation and interest, as well as candy or money. Such men can be clever actors, or con men, very adept at grooming their victims (62).

Sequelae of Sexual Abuse

In addition to the many sequelae characteristic of all other forms of abuse and neglect—poor sense of identity, low self-esteem, deficient empathy, lack of trust, generational repetition, poor interpersonal relationships, loneliness, emptiness, impaired attachment style, depression, and personality disorders—sex abuse victims have residues specifically related to sexual molestation. Included are complete suppression of all sexual interest and avoidance of all sexual activity, lack of pleasure during sexual activity, change from heterosexual to homosexual choice in both men and women, pedophilia, sadomasochistic behaviors, psychosomatic disorders, poor anger control, prostitution (both male and female), submission to further abuse and rape, or a decision never to have children. Many variations on these themes are described by Goodwin (63), Steele (64), Kramer (65–67), Russell (68), and Ryan (69). Unwanted vaginal penetration has a particularly devastating effect in some cases, seeming to attack the very core of existence. One victim said, "I always thought I could grow up and get away from all the beatings and criticism and be free to live. But when my father put his penis in my vagina it was the end. All hope was lost. My spirit had been killed. And mother did not care. That's when I cut my wrists." Shengold (70) has aptly described the psychic damage as "soul murder."

When girls report incest to their mothers or other attachment figures and are told that they have caused the abuse, or that they have fantasized it and are lying, or that it really couldn't have happened because father would never have done such a thing, they are devastated, feel abandoned, begin to doubt their own perceptions, and develop an uncertain ability to test reality and know what is real. In other cases, the overstimulation of the incest experience can overwhelm the ego in vulnerable children and lead to dissociation. In the 1980s, one manifestation of dissociation, "multiple personality disorder," was reported in rapidly increasing numbers as a sequela of sexual abuse, especially incest, that had taken place during the victims' earlier years. The almost fadlike quality of interest in and diagnoses of multiple personality disorder led to the publication of two books on sexual abuse sequelae (71, 72). The validity of the multiple personality diagnosis continues to be controversial: many allege that the memories of sexual abuse are actually induced by therapists, and the claims of some patients having dozens, even more than a hundred, distinct separate personalities seem to be, shall we say, overenthusiastic. Such extreme statements can lead to doubt about other, more reasonable descriptions of this disorder as a sequela of sexual abuse.

Suggestions have been tendered that the consequences of sexual maltreatment should be conceptualized and treated as post-traumatic stress disorder. This approach could be technically correct, but it is misleading. The psychic meanings and coping mechanisms activated by sexual trauma are unique and extremely different from those following the trauma of battle, natural disasters, auto accidents, and other forms of child maltreatment; they require a specific understanding and response.

Inappropriate and unwanted sexual invasions are felt as attacks on the most intimate, private sense of self, and this outrage is compounded by loss of control over one's own body. Boys are more likely to feel uncertainty about, or to undergo a change of, gender identity, while girls tend to feel a more pervasive damage and degradation of their femininity and a devaluation of what they could offer in life through their love.

Sense of Self and Identity

The lack of validating responses to an infant's attempts to communicate his needs leads him to disregard his internal perceptions as irrelevant, to feel that his primitive sense of self has no practical value, is ineffectual and, therefore, worthless. No coherent positive sense of self can then develop. If, at the same time, the child is verbally criticized and denigrated, or physically punished, the result is a mutually reinforcing combination of lack of approval and active disapproval, leading to a fragile, unintegrated identity. When such insecure individuals become mothers themselves, their poor identity and low self-esteem can profoundly disturb their process of bonding to their own infants and indicate high risk for future problems. For example:

> Linda, nineteen, was having her first baby. She told how she had been abandoned by her mother at six months and been bounced around among various relatives for many years of foster care. Linda's husband had abandoned his two previous wives after the birth of their first babies. He reluctantly spent a few minutes with her in the labor room and, when she cried out with a labor pain, told her that he and his mother suffered more pain from hemorrhoids than she was having. The day after birth, while holding her new daughter, amid other signs of poor bonding, Linda said, "I think she looks like my husband, but he says she looks like me. Looks like me, poor kid." And she repeated, "Looks like me, poor kid."

Linda demonstrates the lasting residual effects of lack of empathic care in early years and insecure attachment, in addition to a tragically low self-esteem and the sense of worthlessness that interferes with her finding someone who could really care about her. And she quickly endows her new daughter with her own poor identity and worthless self-image. Within a few weeks, the baby was seen in the emergency room with mild bruising. Soon afterward, the parents told the visiting nurse they could not stand the baby's crying and asked the nurse to take custody and remove the baby before the father harmed it seriously.

A most explicit description of problems of identity and self-image and their origin and expression was given by Bertie O.

> "I look in a mirror and hardly know it's me. Sometimes I'm like my mother, sometimes like my grandmother. Sometimes I'm like my husband Jack's mother. Sometimes I'm like his grandmother. Jack wants me to be first like one and then the other. Everybody wants me to be somebody else."

At another time she said, "When I'm alone, I'm more like my grandmother than anyone else in the world; I'm quieter, more calm, peaceful, and more loving. I can be like her, the way I want to be, but when someone comes in and says, 'Why don't you do this way or that way' or criticizes me, I'm all lost and confused. I try to become like everything they say. I hardly know who I am. I'm still so scared of mother that I get anxious if she has been angry at me. I'll pull the shades down and lock the door and keep the chain on. If she got mad enough and thought I said anything against her, she'd come out and beat me within an inch of my life."

The highlights of Bertie's history will help us to understand her statements. She was a firstborn child. Bertie's mother frequently berated her because the pregnancy had ruined her mother's figure, damaged her pelvic organs, and disrupted her marriage because Bertie's father began then to be unfaithful. From infancy into early childhood, the mother repeatedly attacked Bertie with her fists, razor strops, or wire coat hangers—and occasionally slapped her even in adult life. Her mother and father engaged in many battles; once, in her early teens, Bertie witnessed her mother shooting at one of the father's paramours, the bullet going through the woman's housecoat, missing her body. Another time, Bertie's father had used his service revolver to shoot the TV set because he didn't like the program.

With her strict, pseudomoralistic policeman father, Bertie had a rather warm relationship, which the mother constantly tried to disrupt by telling each how bad the other was. Bertie was her grandmother's favorite, and she returned the love without hesitation. "She was the only woman I've never been afraid of," Bertie said. Bertie's mother tried unsuccessfully to break this attachment, too, by criticizing the grandmother and often preventing their getting together.

Just before marriage, Bertie asked her gynecologist for a contraceptive diaphragm, but she was refused one because she was still a virgin. She got pregnant on the honeymoon and was dismayed and angry. She did not want the baby and had recurrent dreams of a difficult delivery producing a girl who both looked like her own baby photos and would ruin her youth, deny her freedom and happiness, and shatter her chances for a good marriage. Although Bertie never told the dreams to anybody, she frequently talked to Jack, her husband, about her fear that he would spoil the baby and her concern about how soon she could start disciplining it.

When her baby, Cindy, was a month old, she was found to have a broken leg from "getting her leg caught between the slots of her crib and turning over." At three months of age, Cindy was brought to the hospital with a fractured skull and bilateral subdural hematomas, "cause unknown." Two weeks later, Bertie was brought to the hospital in a hysterical, semidissociative, confused state, cowering and saying over and over, "Please don't let them beat me. Make them stop fighting. Take the guns away." She had attempted suicide by taking a lot of pills, none of which were dangerous. That morning, she had been presented with irrefutable evidence that she had been stealing money and items of apparel from friends when on social visits—something that had been previously suspected but which she had denied. (In the past, Bertie's mother had been picked up twice for shoplifting, but the charges were dropped.) After the accusation, Bertie had gone to the bathroom, looked in the mirror, and thought, "This is all true, even if I didn't know it. My husband will hate me and leave me. I'm as bad as my mother. I don't remember it, but I must have hurt my baby, too. I deserve to die." She took the pills and collapsed. The almost psychotic, regressive state she fell into cleared in a few days, as she continued to talk about memories of past events and emotions.

Bertie had identified not only with her mother's aggression and stealing, and with her belief that a baby will damage a mother's physical and marital well-being, but also with both her father's and mother's strict disciplinary attitudes; the bit of empathy she learned from her grandmother was utterly overwhelmed. At the same time, Bertie had a persistent feeling of being a trapped, naughty, frightened, helpless child who has to try to please everybody. Truly, she knows not who she is.

Fantasies about the unborn baby are essentially universal, largely determined by the mother's life history and her own self-perception. It is normal to identify with one's parents and also to see one's self in one's children. Parents often say, "He's as bad as I was when I was a kid" or "She's just as feisty as I was; it must be a family trait." Some abusers describe a feeling of "I have hit myself" and crying after punishing their baby. Thus, we find in operation a kind of three-generational identity: "I am my parent, myself, and my child." The defense mechanism of identification with the aggressive parents sets the pattern of abuse, and since such identification with parents becomes part of the superego, it accounts for the sense of righteousness often expressed by abusers. In contrast to the usual concept of identification as "I am like him," the identification with the child is "He is like me"— Fenichel describes this as "reverse identification" (73, p. 40). It is not a projection—"It is not me; it is him"—because it doesn't involve denial.

The rather fluid tripartite identification plays an integral part in the single abusive act, as the caregiver repeats the action of the caregiver who had earlier abused him and at the same time sees his own child as the reincarnation of himself as a "bad kid." This process is also present in the way caregivers view a child in general, even the way a mother views her unborn child during pregnancy. Penny had responded well to therapy and was treating her two-year-old son rather well when she decided to have another baby. She soon was pregnant and feeling pleased until she first felt the baby moving, around the beginning of the second trimester; she then became severely emotionally upset, "Last night I suddenly realized that all along I've thought the baby was another boy and I would know how to take good care of him. Then I thought, 'What if it's a girl? I'm likely to treat it like mother treated me, and she'll be as angry at me as I am at mother. It will be a mess.'" This instigated intense therapeutic work on Penny's past; she attached and did well with her second baby, which was, indeed, a girl. If this conflict had remained unconscious, the baby girl would have been at high risk for abuse.

Low self-esteem and poor identity are common in abusers of all kinds and account for their inability to cope well with inevitable life stresses and their vulnerability to any behavior or event that is perceived as an attack on their fragile narcissism. Thus, something as "normal" as a car battery going dead or a refrigerator or washing machine breaking down can create a sense of helplessness and can disrupt all daily routines. If it is a child's behavior that is perceived as a failure to respect or satisfy the caregiver's needs of the moment, it can be the crisis that precipitates physical abuse. The child is seen as the reincarnation of the caregiver's bad self, for which he was punished when he was a child, prompting the caregiver to shift his identification to his own punitive caregivers and to punish the child with a sense of full justification.

Insofar as low self-esteem is the sequela to being unempathically cared for in early years, the child becomes distrustful of the adults closest to him. This lack of trust can be unconsciously transferred to other adults in later life and can seriously interfere with any or all interpersonal relationships. It thereby becomes difficult to develop closeness or even to feel safe enough to ask for help or support, which in turn further magnifies helplessness, negative self-image, and expectations of rejection.

Caregiver Perceptions of the Child

Holly, a young mother, came for evaluation of abuse, bringing her twenty-two-month-old Sammy with her. During the interview, she would alternately tell him, "Stop doing that. Come here!" and "Stop bothering me. Go away," whacking him on the buttocks each time. In the midst of this, he emptied an ash tray, wiped it with Kleenex, and replaced it on the desk. When I noted this rather precocious behavior, Holly expressed pleasure and pride in his accomplishments and told how he helped her a great deal with household tasks. However, she had not allowed him any real freedom or pleasure during this visit, and she said, "My mother says Sammy ought to have his butt blistered every time he turns around."

Holly's five-and-a-half-month-old boy was in the hospital with fractures of the skull and pelvis, and she acknowledged having beaten him. She said he had been a good baby at birth but had gradually become very unsatisfactory; he was "stubborn and lazy and would do nothing for himself," would get sick deliberately to frustrate her, and would look at her with great anger in his eyes. His present punishment had occurred when she was under more than average stress from marital conflict and was feeling very alone and uncared for and, therefore, especially needy of compliant, helpful behavior from her two boys. Understanding of her behavior could be gained from her statement that "My mother never cared about me, never listened to me or what I wanted. I was never anything but a servant in her house." Her inadequate empathy was evidenced on another occasion when she described how important it was to not spoil children by picking them up when they cried. Then she added, "But I know children need to be loved, too, so I've made it a practice to pick my little babies up and hold them for ten minutes twice a day." At other times, she alluded to severe physical punishment she had received in childhood.

It is obvious that Holly is seriously deficient in empathy for her two sons, has unrealistically high expectations for their behavior, and believes in the value of punishment. Her parenting behavior has been profoundly influenced by her early life experience with her mother.

Possibly most incidents of infant abuse are inflicted by mothers, since they are usually the primary caregivers and spend most time with their babies. But when circumstances cause fathers to take over the caregiving tasks, they too can be just as abusive, or even more abusive.

Henry J. had passed his examinations and was unemployed while awaiting appointment to the police force. His wife was working to support them, so he took care of their three boys. He was soon beyond his abilities and became angry that the boys did not appreciate how hard he was trying. John, age sixteen months, had not been minding orders. Henry said, "He's old enough to know what I mean when I say 'Come here,' and when he doesn't mind me, I give him a gentle tug on the ear." John was in the hospital with deep lacerations behind both ears and multiple bruises and abrasions over his body. Donny, age three and a half months, was hospitalized with fractures of the left clavicle and left femur, a subdural hematoma, as well as malnutrition. Henry said Donny refused to eat the potatoes he had fried for him. "He'd hold them in his mouth for hours, and I'd have to hit him to make him swallow them." About Robert, age five, Henry said, "He is perfect, maybe too perfect, but he hardly ever has to be disciplined any more." Henry thought Robert caused Donny's injuries.

Henry described his own father as having been very strict and as having used his hands, boards, and straps to punish Henry and his brother. "Dad said he was teaching us how to behave and not get into trouble or be delinquent." Henry's brother had since been charged with child abuse in another state. Henry had little empathy for his sons and no knowledge of good child care; he was stressed by his unemployment and his wife's absence. He saw his boys as disobedient, frustrating tormentors and acted out his identification with an abusive father.

In addition to attributing to the child the image of his own bad childhood self, the caregiver often labors under a prevalent misperception that a child should behave in ways far beyond his age-appropriate abilities. This is evident in the caregiver's almost unconscious desire and demand that the child provide the love and care needed to make up for deficits in the caregiver's early life, as we saw earlier in the case of Cheri. As subtle variation of this theme is seen in the case of adoptive parents who need a child to make up for their own infertility and to enhance their self-esteem. Some data indicate that abuse and neglect occur more often in adoptive situations than in nonadoptive ones; this may possibly be related to the similar circumstances of parents deciding to have a child to save a fragile marriage. Babies cannot repair marital or parental problems—they complicate life while making it joyful. Foster parents, despite good intentions, can be overwhelmed and end up punishing or returning children whose behavior has become highly disturbed and unmanageable because of previous abuse:

> A very religious young couple found they were infertile and decided to adopt two Hispanic infants who had been abused and put up for adoption. The couple was planning to do missionary work with Hispanic and Indian families in the southwest to teach good child care and thought that because they were Anglos, they would be more accepted if they had two Hispanic babies themselves. However, they found the babies were difficult, quite uncooperative, and disobedient, and in response they soon resorted to severe physical abuse. The mother told her minister she was concerned about how hard she was hitting the children, and he told her to interpose something impersonal between herself and the children. She then used boards, a belt, and a hairbrush with a sense of righteousness.

Cultural factors can profoundly affect caregiver attitudes toward children. The Christian doctrine of original sin has justified the punishment of children to "drive the devil out of them." So do Old Testament admonitions: "Do not withhold discipline from a child; if you beat him, he will not die" (Prov. 23:13 Revised Standard Version). "If you beat him with the rod, you will save his life from Sheol" (Prov. 23:14 RSV). "He who spares the rod hates his son, but he who loves him is diligent to discipline him" (Prov. 13:24 RSV).

Punishment does work in stopping disapproved behavior, but only temporarily. The same misbehavior is later resumed, or other misbehaviors appear instead, often in more severe forms. Punishment per se does not create good behavior. Desirable behavior (or, at least, what is considered to be desirable behavior) is developed not through punishment but through approval, by approving of the child when he exhibits good behavior—which, after all, he can learn only from the good role models provided him. Punishment leads to fear, distrust, and insecure attachments; approval leads to cooperation and security.

Historically, our culture, especially the legal system, has considered parental rights to raise children as parents see fit to be primary and to override any rights of their offspring. In ancient Roman law, many principles of which we still follow, the *patria potestas* gave the *paterfamilias* absolute authority over his children. By law, the father could, if he wanted, expose his children, sell them, or kill them, and all property they acquired remained under his control. Less drastic forms of the concept of children as property persist to this day. Children are expected, in many forms of maltreatment, to disregard their own feelings and needs and adapt to excessive, distorted parental desires and demands. In custody cases, the child's welfare is often lost sight of during the contention for parental rights of access and the mutual accusations of wrongdoings of adversarial parents.

The combination of increased general knowledge of child development and of the average age at which children reach certain abilities, plus the general competitiveness of our society, plus the parental need for children to do well to enhance parental self-esteem can lead parents to unwarranted perceptions of a child as somehow defective and below par: "Johnny isn't getting as many A's in school as Willy next door." "Mary isn't walking and talking as soon as Betty did." "When I was Joe's age, I was winning tennis games; he's just lazy." In such situations, children's normal individual differences and temperaments are disregarded, and unempathic parents can respond with verbal criticism, denigration, and punishment, conveniently disregarding their own role in creating the alleged problems.

Aggression, Violence, Delinquency, and Crime

Despite the current almost frantic concern about aggression in our own society and around the world, a historical perspective reveals that there is nothing really new about the subject except that recent technology and weaponry have escalated the lethality of aggression in all levels from the interpersonal to the international. Aggression has always been part of the human condition. Throughout history, the desires for power, position, prestige, and possessions, as well as the drives of envy and jealousy, have led to wars of conquest, revolutions, assassinations, riots, ordinary murder, and individual punishments. Humans share with our animal relatives the biological ability to unleash aggression, an instinct of self-preservation and self-enhancement. Nor should we discount the pattern of aggressive reaction to perceived danger that Cannon (74) described as part of the "fight or flight" response, characteristic of all members of the animal kingdom. Humans, with our much greater brain capacity, however, are less thoroughly programmed and possess extensive means of modifying our aggressive potential by either restraining it or justifying its release.

For example, baboon tribes of the same subspecies will severely attack others from a group that looks and smells different and crosses a territorial boundary. Humans, too, use the perception of difference as reason or excuse for verbal disapproval or physical attack, but we use a much greater list of differences. Our word "barbarian" comes from the ancient Greeks who denigrated as stupid, uncivilized aliens those people who did not speak Greek and whose vocalization sounded like "bar bar bar." There is a pervasive tendency in humans to interpret the perception of differences as possibly or probably dangerous and as warranting an aggressive response. Ethnic differences lead to wars to establish national territories. Religious differences lead to wars and persecution or burning of heretics. Skin color differences lead to many kinds of intolerance, discrimination, and violence. The common denominator, in a way, is the human tendency to believe "I'm right," "he's wrong," and "I need to protect myself and my integrity." We go to war if our national security is threatened.

Aggression and empathy are incompatible; it would seem unlikely that a person could release aggression if he or she had empathy for the victim. Maltreatment in early childhood leads to lack of empathy, as well as low self-esteem, vulnerability, and a tendency to perceive the outer world as untrustworthy and dangerous. We are surrounded by many traditions and cultural customs and moral rules about behavior and what is right and wrong. But much of these basics are acquired by the child through the idiosyncratic admonitions and behavior of his primary caregivers, long before he has contact with the outside world (75, 76). Often, as maltreated children begin to interact with people outside the family in neighborhood and school, early signs of delinquency become apparent in the form of poor interpersonal social behavior, aggression, and learning difficulties (77). Having been neglected in various ways, maltreated, children feel empty and continue to seek a sense of being accepted; they easily join with anyone who sees the world as they do and selfishly exploit others without regard for them.

Such behavior often coincides with the normal pattern in adolescence to individuate and separate from parents and identify with peers. For maltreated children, these peers are often gang members who feel as they do and provide a mutually accepting and supportive new family. The diagnostic criteria for what is variously called "antisocial personality," "conduct disorder," or, in legal terms, "delinquency," include various combinations of behaviors—lying, stealing, fighting, academic difficulties, truancy, vandalism, resistance to authority, poor interpersonal relationships, sexual promiscuity, running away from home, cruelty to animals, and abuse of other children. Such children and adolescents exhibit low self-esteem, fragile identity, dysphoria, distrust and suspicion of adults, and serious deficits in empathy, all of which can be correlated with maltreatment in their dysfunctional families of origin (78) and understood as one kind of sequela to maltreatment. Although there is some tendency for delinquent behavior to decline significantly or disappear during the third decade of life, it is typically the matrix out of which the persistent antisocial trend develops into adult criminal "careers." It is well known that the great majority of criminals in our prisons have histories of significant maltreatment in early childhood and records of previous delinquency.

Some children subtly identify with criminal parents, while other children are overtly encouraged by parental approval for delinquent acts. For example, a six-year-old girl who was emotionally neglected, and whose brother had been physically abused, brought her mother a woman's gold wristwatch which she had slyly picked up from her teacher's desk at the end of school. Her mother thanked her and said, "That shows you love me, doesn't it," and did nothing about the theft despite her daughter's open confession.

Similarly, children who have been exposed to domestic violence, either as victim or as observer, tend to identify with the aggressors, or with aggression itself as a normal component of interpersonal relationships, and have quite an idiosyncratic view of violence:

> R.A., age thirty-three, an aggressive, violent criminal who had been delinquent since the age ten or twelve and had spent eleven years off and on in prison, wrote, "Violence is in a way like bad language—something that a person like me has been brought up with. Something I got used to very early on as part of the daily scene of childhood, you might say. I don't at all recoil from the idea. I don't have a sort of inborn dislike of the thing like you do. As long as I can remember, I have seen violence in use all around me—my mother hitting the children; my brothers and sisters all whacking one another, or other children; the man downstairs whacking his wife, etc. You get used to it. It doesn't mean anything in these circumstances." (79, 93).

Despite R.A.'s disclaimer, his remarks demonstrate that his nonchalant acceptance and use of violence are part of his internal working model, learned from experience in early life. Most abusive caregivers are not nearly as imbued with aggression as a normal way of life as R.A. was. Their release of aggressive attack against a child is reactive to specific events that they see as disobedience or deliberate disappointment of their needs and expectations. The child's "bad behavior" is somehow interpreted as an attack on the caregiver's already fragile self-image, the child considered as bad as the caregiver himself was as a child and consequently deserving of the same punishment or rejection that was meted out to him when he was young. We have seen several variations on this theme in the other cases discussed above.

The Clinical Picture

The following condensed case history presents with unusual clarity many of the commonly seen elements of physical and sexual abuse.

> Laura G. was an attractive young woman, age twenty-six, poised, friendly, and verbal. She was the wife of a noncommissioned career officer in the armed forces. Her reasons for coming to us were anxiety over marital problems, depression, and worry over her physical and emotional abuse of her elder son.
>
> Laura herself was the elder of two children of parents who lived in very marginal economic circumstances on the outskirts of a small, rural town. Her father was mildly alcoholic; her mother more severely so. Her parents frequently argued and occasionally fought rather violently.

Laura had felt her mother was never interested in her and had seemed far away and inattentive when Laura tried to talk to her. Laura recalled that even as a little child she worked very hard to do things to please her mother but never seemed able to do so and was often the subject of mild criticism. She felt deprived, rejected, and hopeless. Her younger brother, Joe, was her mother's favorite, the one to whom her mother gave all her love. Laura's relationship to Joe was always ambivalent—some love and companionship mixed with envy and hatred.

Laura had been deeply attached to her father from her earliest years. She felt very close to him and believed he returned her warmth, cared for her, and listened to her. Her father, however, was not always kind. He often beat her with his hands or belt until she was black and blue, and his favorite saying was, "I'll knock you through the wall." Sometimes he made her hold two bare electric wires in her hands while he turned on a current to shock her (he was an electrician by trade). He explained to her that he gave her the shocks to remind her that he was the boss and that she must obey him. Despite such abuse, she felt close to him and liked to be around him and do things which pleased him. He would often praise her and give her credit for things she did well when she tried to help him. She spent much more time with him than she did with her mother, and when Laura was about four years old, her father had begun to extend his affectionate cuddling into some degree of genital fondling. She remembers him asking, "You want me to make it feel good down there?" and her answering, "Yes." By the time Laura was seven, her father was having regular sex play with her; this soon progressed to intercourse, which took place frequently for the next several years. Laura enjoyed the closeness and pleasure of the sexual activity, but also felt it was somehow wrong, because her father admonished her not to tell other people. She was puzzled about just what was "wrong," as her father seemed to gain pleasure from the activity, had asked her to do it, and had always taught her to obey him. In addition, her mother did not seem to disapprove, even though she was aware of what was happening between Laura and her husband.

The mother and father were rarely affectionate with each other and were often in open conflict. The mother rejected the father sexually and often told him to leave her alone. They usually slept in different rooms. There was no doubt that Laura's mother was aware of the incest, because sometimes after she had had an argument with her husband, she would encourage Laura to go and sleep with him. Sometimes the mother would ask Laura to get money from the father after Laura slept with him and bring it back to her so that she could buy a bottle of liquor.

When Laura was thirteen, her father became depressed, as far as she knew because of his endless difficulties in trying to make a living. He committed suicide in the bedroom of their home, using a shotgun to blow off part of his face and the top of his head, while Laura was helping her mother cook dinner. Laura was utterly devastated as well as shocked. Three days later, after the funeral, on a cold, gray, rainy day, Laura and her mother came back home and went into the bedroom. It smelled bad, and Laura opened the shutters and the windows to let in light and air. She recalls, "I looked around the room, and there I saw bits of flesh and hair on the wall and on the ceiling, all that was left of my father. He was the only one I ever loved, and the only person who ever loved me."

The next year, when she was fourteen, Laura acquired a steady boyfriend. He was friendly and affectionate to her and spoke in a way when they were alone that made her feel very beautiful and fine. She began having intercourse with him frequently and enjoyed it. In public, however, he fought with her and treated her as "something to wipe his feet on." She could not stand the mistreatment and broke up with him. Years later, she still dreamed about him and fantasized about him, even though she realized life with him would not have been good.

At fifteen, she began dating cadets at an air force base. She loved being treated "like a lady" by these somewhat older young men. Frequently, the relationships became sexual affairs, but they did not seem meaningful to her and did not last very long. She became more promiscuous, and she described having had affairs with thirty-two different men when she was between the ages of eighteen and twenty-one and, at times, "carrying on" with as many as three men in one day. At twenty-two, she met and married a man who was very kind, patient, and considerate of her. He listened to her and tried to do things to please her and to make her happy. In spite of what seemed to her an ideal marriage, she continued periodically to have affairs and, at times, found her husband physically repulsive. By the time we knew her, she felt that, by her behavior, she had "ruined" him and changed him from a kindly person to an angry, punitive one. She avoided sex with him and was often very critical of him, despite all his efforts. Although it was not really necessary, Laura often worked part-time in order to "get money to help the family finances," thus reducing the financial burden on her husband, and also to get away from the house. At these jobs she often met the men with whom she would become involved.

Toward Jimmy, the older of her two sons, Laura had been extremely ambivalent. At times she had felt love for him and, in general, had taken good physical care of him. Yet, she was more likely to be filled with feelings of disgust and hatred, and had often wished that she could get rid of him or that he would die. She expected him to be quite capable and obedient; accordingly, to punish him for various misbehaviors, she would beat him with her fists or whip him with a belt or board. She seemed to be aware that fundamentally Jimmy was a rather normal little boy, but she said, "He has all my faults, and I have tried to beat all his phobias and other problems out of him. I know it's not sensible, but I can't control myself. I think he must be me, and I'm a combination of my mother and my father. My mother would never pay any attention to me, and my father would beat me. I say to Jimmy, 'I'll knock you through the wall,' just like daddy used to say to me."

Laura had a curious mixture of feeling guilty over her mistreatment of the boy and yet, at the same time, feeling justified in her anger with him because of his ostensible deficits and failures. She also believed that she had brainwashed her husband into following her pattern of screaming and yelling at this boy, to whom he had previously been very good. Laura felt she had ruined both her husband and her elder son, but her guilty responsibility could not eliminate her anger. She would say, "I want to get rid of them both. I want them both to die. But I've thought of suicide myself, because I've been ruining them." Although Laura did not drink regularly or excessively, she was more likely after a social evening with a few drinks to get into quarrels with her husband and to have more trouble with Jimmy, with the likelihood of abuse.

With her younger son, Benny, Laura had a completely different relationship. She loved him dearly and held for him a warmth and affection she had not previously known she was capable of feeling. She surmised that he was like her younger brother, Joe, to whom her mother had given all her love and affection, and that she was imitating her own mother in this favoritism. Laura was bewildered by these very intense and yet discrepant feelings. She was quite puzzled about her own identity, which she expressed at various times in such thoughts as, "I think Jimmy must be me, and I'm a combination of my mother and my father." "When I would talk to my mother, she would be far away and not answer. I do the same thing with Jimmy. It was father who used to beat me; now it seems Jimmy is me, and I'm beating him the way father beat me. Little Benny is my brother, Joe. Mother gave all her love and protection to Joe, and I am very kind and loving to him." Another time she said, "I don't know yet who I really am. I am beginning to think I am somebody and I know a little bit about who I am, but I'm having trouble becoming it and being something. I don't know whether I am my mother or my father or my brother, or a combination of all of them, or whether I am my children."

After her marriage, Laura periodically made an attempt to establish some sort of friendly relationship with her mother, and there were occasional visits. But they never did reach any true emotional rapport, not could they discuss the events of Laura's early life. With her brother, Joe, she had a distant, hostile relationship. While there was no evidence of overt incestuous activity between Joe and his mother, she seemed to have exploitatively tried to keep him close to her and had hampered his separation and individuation. He eventually became seriously disturbed, and once, when he threatened to kill his mother, Laura offered her sanctuary and protection. At that time there was some feeling of closeness, but it was soon ruptured by her mother's inconsiderate disregard of Laura's feelings and criticisms of her behavior.

Superficially, Laura appeared to be a popular, attractive, young married woman with two children, similar to many other young wives who lived around a military base with husbands whose career was in the armed services. Yet she was seriously troubled, behaviorally and psychologically, both in her marriage and in her child-rearing functions. In this tragic history we see the themes of economic difficulty, alcoholism, social isolation, parental conflict, maternal deprivation, sibling rivalry, physical abuse, incest, untimely death of a parent, and suicide.

As an adult, Laura shows many of the characteristics commonly met with in a parent who maltreats people. She suffers from a mild chronic depression, very low self-esteem, inability to experience pleasure or find satisfaction for her lasting emptiness and need for love and attention, lack of a coherent and consistent sense of identity, and misperceptions of her children. The striking split between good and bad objects, the uncoordinated ego functions, and the unintegrated components of identity are similar to those described as characteristic of "borderline states." These psychological difficulties seem to be clearly related to the experiences Laura had with her caretakers in her early life and the necessity for her to adapt to them somehow. She has identified with several parts of the inconsistent caretaking behaviors of both her mother and her father, and she also maintains a self-concept closely related to the self-concept she had as a child. She transfers and attributes to adults in her present environment and to her own children as well the attitudes and feelings she directed toward the important figures of her early life.

Her sexual behavior seems to be a frantic, desperate, compulsive search for a man to love and be loved by and at least partly stems from her unresolved grief over the death of her father by suicide. She overidealized her father, clinging especially to the loving side of her ambivalence toward him, has never fully relinquished her attachment to him, and has been unable to find an adequate replacement for the warm closeness she had with him, including the incest. Her promiscuity is undoubtedly related to the sexualization of this early love relationship with her father. Yet, the desperateness of her search also suggests it has deep roots in an effort to find a substitute for the lack of basic, empathic love from her mother in her early life. Her inability to gain full satisfaction or pleasure from sexual activity stems partly from the fact that, in itself, sexual activity cannot replace the lack of a deep, early sense of being empathetically loved and cared for. It also partly originates from her residual guilt about her relationship to her father, which is not so much a feeling of having done something wrong sexually with him but, rather, one of not having been able, even in her most warm and loving sexual surrender to him, to make him happy enough to prevent his suicide.

Laura was aware that her sexual behavior was not really acceptable in society. Yet, again, this was not totally a feeling of guilt over sexuality but more a sense that she was ineffectual and never good enough for other people. It was not a strong, inner sense of having done something wrong for which she deserved punishment, nor did she give any evidence of feeling guilt about sexual behavior that had displaced her mother in her father's affections. In fact, her earliest powerful superego identifications are with the mother who encouraged the sexual relationship with the father, and with the father who instigated and appreciated the sexual relationship. Because Laura is still unconsciously fixated to the loving, sexual father of her childhood who was also abusive, she has had the recurrent tendency to attach herself to men who not only love her but who are also cruel to her, fight with her, or attack her physically. By criticizing and frustrating her husband who was originally quite affectionate and considerate to her, she managed to change him into a person who is mean to her and maltreats her child, thus recreating the father of her childhood.

Laura relives another part of the childhood drama in her ambivalent behavior toward her older son, Jimmy, whom she misperceives as almost a reincarnation of her own childhood self. In identification with her father, she loves Jimmy at times but also abuses him, hitting him, using a belt on him, and repeating to him the same words her father used— "I'll knock you through the wall." At other times, she repeats the behavior of her mother toward herself and is unresponsive, inattentive, and unempathic toward Jimmy. With her younger son, Benny, she repeats the kind, preferential care which her mother gave to Laura's younger brother, Joe, and she also lavishes on Benny the love she wishes she had had as a little girl, gaining some vicarious pleasure from this.

In view of Laura's disturbing experiences in early life and her multiple, inconsistent identifications with her parents, it is not surprising that she is significantly hampered in her child caring activities and has become what we call an abusive parent. Her tendency to repeat the past and get herself involved in unhappy experiences is an example of moral masochism in the sense described by Berliner (80) as "self-defeating or destructive behavior" issuing from attachment to a sadistic love object. Difficulties in experiencing pleasures or enjoying life generally, as well as constantly recurring patterns of getting into difficulty, are characteristic of most of the maltreating caretakers I have known. This masochistic tendency makes such persons increasingly vulnerable and unable to cope with the troublesome crises and difficulties that inevitably occur in all people's lives, especially in the care of children.

The process of responding to the parents of one's earliest years, the identification with them, and the persistence of these identifications into adult life is not in any way abnormal. It is, in fact, an entirely normal part of the psychic development of all children. As I noted before, the problem lies in the kind of parent available for the identification process. Laura identified with both the punitive and loving aspects of her father and with the aloof, rejecting, uncaring aspects of her mother, as well as with her mother's loving care of a younger son. In her social interactions, Laura maintained superficially close sexualized relationships with men and more distant, often antagonistic, relations with women. In therapy, she established positive relationships with three successive male therapists whom she felt "understood" her. She had managed to get sexually involved with one of them. She remained suspicious and cool toward female personnel in the clinic.

Summary

Human beings are born as helpless babies who for a long time are dependent for care and for protection on whatever caregivers fate has provided for them. In this setting, through attachments to and interactions with his caregivers, an infant learns what the external world is like, who he himself is, and what to do and not do in order to survive. By the end of the first year, he has learned some basic concepts of the only world he knows, as well as how to understand and behave in it; this internal working model will unconsciously guide much of his future relationships and behavior. What he has learned depends upon the "curriculum" presented by his specific caregiver-teacher; it can be either good and useful or distorted and destined for trouble. The origins both of good child care and of child maltreatment lie in these early relationships. Our goal of preventing maltreatment can be realized if we use this knowledge to create interventions that help parents develop good caregiving patterns in pre-, peri-, and postnatal periods.

References

1. Steele, B. F. 1994. Psychoanalysis and the Maltreatment of Children, *J. Am. Psychoanalytic Assn.* 42:1001–25.
2. Kempe, C. H.; Silverman, F. N.; Steele, B. F.; Droegemueller, W.; and Silver, H. K. 1962. The Battered Child Syndrome. *JAMA* 181:17–24.
3. Steele, B. F., and Pollack, C. 1968. A Psychiatric Study of Parents Who Abuse Infants and Small Children. In *The Battered Child*, ed. R. E. Helfer and C. H. Kempe. Chicago: University of Chicago Press.
4. Steele, B. F. 1970. Parental Abuse of Infants and Small Children. In *Parenthood: Its Psychology and Psychopathology*, ed. E. J. Anthony and T. Benedek. Boston: Little, Brown.
5. Steele, B. F. 1980. Psychodynamic Factors in Child Abuse. In *The Battered Child*, 3d ed. rev., ed. C. H. Kempe and R. E. Helfer. Chicago: University of Chicago Press.
6. Steele, B. F. 1985. Generational Repetition of the Maltreatment of Children. In *Parental Influences in Health and Disease*, ed. E. J. Anthony and G. H. Pollack. Boston: Little, Brown.
7. Benedek, T. 1938. Adaptation to Reality in Early Infancy. *Psychoanalytic Q.* 7:200–215.
8. Benedek, T. 1959. Parenthood as a Developmental Phase: A Contribution to the Libido Theory. *J. Am. Psychoanalytic Assn.* 7:389–417.

9. Bowlby, J. 1953. Some Pathological Processes Set in Train by Early Mother-Child Separation. *J. Mental Sciences* 99:265–72.

10. Bowlby, J. 1958. The Nature of the Child's Tie to His Mother. *International J. Psychoanalysis* 39:350–73.

11. Lorenz, K. 1952. *King Solomon's Ring.* New York: Thomas Y. Crowell Co.

12. Harlow, H. 1958. The Nature of Love. *Am. Psychologist* 3:673–85.

13. Lynch, M., and Roberts, J. 1977. Predicting Child Abuse: Signs of Bonding Failure in the Maternity Hospital. *British Med. J.* 1:624–26.

14. Bowlby, J. 1969. *Attachment.* New York: Basic Books.

15. Ainsworth, M. 1969. Object Relations, Dependency, and Attachment: A Theoretical Review of the Infant-Mother Relationship. *Child Development* 40:969–1025.

16. Main, M., and Solomon, J. 1990. Procedures for Identifying Infants as Disorganized/Disoriented during the Ainsworth Strange Situation. In *Attachment in the Preschool Years: Theory, Research, and Intervention,* ed. M. Greenberg, D. Cicchetti, and E. Commings. Chicago: University of Chicago Press.

17. Main, M. 1993. Discourse, Prediction, and Recent Studies in Attachment: Implications for Psychoanalysis. *J. Am. Psychoanalytic Assn.* 41 (supp.): 204–44.

18. Sroufe, L.; Egeland, B.; and Kreutzer, T. 1990. The Fate of Early Experience Following Developmental Change: Longitudinal Approaches to Individual Adaptation in Childhood. *Child Development* 61:1363–73.

19. Egeland, B. 1991. Mediators of the Effects of Child Maltreatment on Developmental Adaptations in Adolescence. In *The Effects of Trauma on the Developmental Process,* ed. D. Cicchetti and S. Toth. Vol. 8, Rochester Symposium on Developmental Psychopathology. Rochester, N.Y.: Rochester University Press.

20. Sander, L. W. 1962. Issues in Early Mother-Child Interaction. *J. Amer. Acad. Child Psychiatry* 1:141–66.

21. Sander, L. W. 1975. Infant and Caretaking Environment: Investigation and Conceptualization of Adaptive Behavior in a System of Increasing Complexity. In *Explorations in Child Psychiatry,* ed. E. J. Anthony. New York: Plenum.

22. Sander, L. W. 1980. Panel: New Knowledge about the Infant from Current Research: Implications for Psychoanalysis. *J. Am. Psychoanalytic Assn.* 28:181–98.

23. Sander, L. W. 1987. Awareness of Inner Experience: A Systems Perspective on Self-Regulatory Process in Early Development. *Child Abuse and Neglect: International J.* 11:339–46.

24. Olden, C. 1953. On Adults' Empathy with Children. *Psychoanalytic Study of the Child* 8:111–26.

25. Olden, C. 1958. Notes on the Development of Empathy. *Psychoanalytic Study of the Child* 13:505–18.

26. Josselyn, I. 1956. Cultural Forces, Motherlessness, and Fatherlessness. *Am. J. Orthopsychiatry* 26:264–71.

27. Freud, A. 1965. *Normality and Pathology in Childhood.* Vol. 6, *The Writings of Anna Freud.* New York: International University Press.

28. Gray, J.; Cutler, C.; Dean, J.; and Kempe, C. H. 1976. Perinatal Assessment of Mother-Baby Interaction. In *Child Abuse and Neglect: The Family and the Community,* ed. R. E. Helfer and C. H. Kempe. Cambridge, Mass.: Ballinger.

29. Gray, J.; Cutler, C.; Dean, J.; and Kempe, C. H. 1977. Prediction and Prevention of Child Abuse and Neglect. *Child Abuse and Neglect: International J.* 1:45–53.

30. Haynes-Seman, C., and Hart, J. 1988. Interactional Assessment: Evaluation of Parent-Child Relationships in Abuse and Neglect. In *The New Child Protection Team Handbook,* ed. D. Bross, R. D. Krugman, M. R. Lenherr, D. A. Rosenberg, and B. D. Schmitt. New York: Garland.

31. Kohut, H. 1977. *Restoration of the Self.* New York: International University Press.

32. Esman, A. H. 1983. The "Stimulus Barrier": A Review and Reconsideration. *Psychoanalytic Study of the Child* 38:193–207.

33. Emde, R. N.; Harmon, R. J.; Metcalf, D.; Koenig, K.; and Wagenfeld, S. 1971. Stress and Neonatal Sleep. *Psychosomatic Med.* 33:491–97.

34. Freud, A. 1970. A Discussion with Rene Spitz. Vol. 7, *The Writings of Anna Freud.* New York: International University Press.

35. American Psychiatric Association. 1980. *Diagnostic and Statistical Manual of Mental Disorders,* 3d ed. Washington, D.C.: APA.

36. American Psychiatric Association. 1994. Diagnostic and Statistical Manual of Mental Disorders, 4th ed. Washington, D.C.: APA.

37. Vaillant, G. E. 1977. *Adaptation to Life.* Boston: Little, Brown.

38. Polansky, N.; Chalmers, M.; Buttonweiser, E.; and Williams, D. 1981. *Damaged Parents: An Anatomy of Child Neglect.* Chicago: University of Chicago Press.

39. Martin, H. P. 1980. The Consequences of Being Abused and Neglected: How the Child Fares. In *The Battered Child,* 3d ed. rev., ed. C. H. Kempe and R. E. Helfer. Chicago: University of Chicago Press.

40. Herman, J. L. 1981. *Father-Daughter Incest.* Cambridge: Harvard University Press.

41. Meiselman, K. C. 1978. *Incest: A Psychological Study of Causes and Effects with Treatment Recommendations.* San Francisco: Jossey-Bass.

42. Mrazek, P. B., and Kempe, C. H., eds. 1981. *Sexually Abused Children and Their Families.* Oxford: Pergamon Press.

43. Schechter, M., and Roeberg, L. 1987. Sexual Exploitation. In *Child Abuse and Neglect: The Family and the Community,* ed. R. E. Helfer and C. H. Kempe. Cambridge, Mass.: Ballinger.

44. Sgroi, S. 1975. Sexual Molestation of Children: The Last Frontier in Child Abuse. *Children Today* 4:18–21, 44.

45. Freud, S. [1924] 1976. The Dissolution of the Oedipus Complex. In vol. 19, *Standard Edition of the Complete Psychological Works of Sigmund Freud,* ed. and trans. James Strachey, 173–79. New York: W. W. Norton.

46. Raybin, J. B. 1969. Homosexual Incest. *J. Nervous and Mental Disorders* 148:105–10.

47. Raphling, D. L.; Carpenter, B. L.; and Davis, A. 1967. Incest: A Genealogical Survey. *Archives Gen. Psychiatry* 16:505–11.

48. Gebhard, P. H.; Gaynes, G. H.; Pomeroy, W. B.; and Christenson, C. R. 1965. *Sex Offenders: An Analysis of Types.* New York: Harper and Row.

49. Finkelhor, D. 1987. Child Sexual Abuse: Two Models. *J. Interpersonal Violence* 2:348–66.

50. Doll, L. S.; Joy, D.; Bartholow, B. N.; Harrison, J. S.; Bolan, G.; Douglas, J.; Saltzman, L.; Moss, P.; and Delgado, W. 1992. Self-Reported Childhood and Adolescent Sexual Abuse among Adult Homosexual and Bisexual Men. *Child Abuse and Neglect: International J.* 16:855–64.

51. Haynes-Seman, C., and Krugman, R. 1989. Sexualized Attention: Normal Interaction or Precursor to Sexual Abuse. *Am. J. Orthopsychiatry* 59:238–45.

52. Olson, E. A. 1981. Socioeconomic and Psychocultural Contexts of Child Abuse and Neglect in Turkey. In *Child Abuse and Neglect: Cross-Cultural Perspectives,* ed. J. E. Korbin. Berkeley and Los Angeles: University of California Press.

53. Laviola, M. 1992. Effects of Older Brother–Younger Sister Incest: A Study of the Dynamics of Seventeen Cases. *Child Abuse and Neglect: International J.* 16:404–21.

54. Kitihara, M. 1989. Incest—Japanese Style. *J. Psychohistory* 17:446–50.

55. Mahler, M.; Pine, F.; and Bergman, A. 1975. *The Psychological Birth of the Human Infant.* New York: Basic Books.

56. Steele, B. F. 1991. The Psychopathology of Incest Participants. In *The Trauma of Transgression: Psychotherapy of Incest Victims,* ed. S. Kramer and S. Akhtar. Northwale, N.J.: Jason Aronson.

57. Furman, E. 1982. Mothers Have to Be There to Be Left. *Psychoanalytic Study of the Child* 37:15–28.

58. DeYoung, M. 1988. The Indignant Page: Techniques of Neutralization in the Publications of Pedophilic Organizations. *Child Abuse and Neglect: International J.* 12:583–91.

59. Ryan, G., and Lane, S., eds. 1991. *Juvenile Sexual Offending.* Lexington, Mass.: D. C. Heath.

60. Ryan, G. 1991. Theories of Etiology. In *Juvenile Sexual Offending,* ed. G. Ryan and S. Lane. Lexington, Mass.: D. C. Heath.

61. Steele, B. F., and Ryan, G. 1991. Deviancy: Development Gone Wrong. In *Juvenile Sexual Offending,* ed. G. Ryan and S. Lane. Lexington, Mass.: D. C. Heath.

62. Singer, M.; Hassey, D.; and Strom, K. 1992. Grooming the Victim: An Analysis of a Perpetrator's Seduction Letter. *Child Abuse and Neglect: International J.* 16:877–86.

63. Goodwin, J., ed. 1989. *Sexual Abuse: Incest Victims and Their Families.* Chicago: Year Book Publishers.

64. Steele, B. F. 1990. Some Sequelae of the Sexual Maltreatment of Children. In *Adult Analysis and Childhood Sexual Abuse,* ed. H. B. Levine. Hillsdale, N.J.: Analytic Press.

65. Kramer, S. 1983. Object-Coercive Doubting: A Pathological Defensive Response to Maternal Incest. *J. Am. Psychoanalytic Assn.* 31 (supp.): 325–51.

66. Kramer, S. 1990. Residues of Incest. In *Adult Analysis and Childhood Sexual Abuse,* ed. H. Levin. Hillsdale, N.J.: Analytic Press.

67. Kramer, S. 1991. Psychopathological Effects of Incest. In *The Trauma of Transgression: Psychotherapy of Incest Victims,* ed. S. Kramer and S. Akhtar. Northvale, N.J.: Jason Aronson.

68. Russell, D. 1989. *Sexual Exploitation: Rape, Child Sexual Abuse, and Workplace Harassment.* Beverly Hills: Sage.

69. Ryan, G.; Lane, S.; Davis, J.; and Isaac, C. 1987. Juvenile Sexual Offenders: Development and Correction. *Child Abuse and Neglect: International J.* 11:385–89.

70. Shengold, L. 1989. *Soul Murder: The Effects of Childhood Abuse and Deprivation.* New Haven, Conn.: Yale University Press.

71. Kluft, R. P., 1985. *Childhood Antecedents of Multiple Personality.* Washington, D.C.: American Psychiatric Press.

72. Kluft, R. P., ed. 1990. *Incest Related Syndromes of Adult Psychopathology.* Washington, D.C.: American Psychiatric Press.

73. Fenichel, O. 1945. *The Psychoanalytic Theory of the Neuroses.* New York: W. W. Norton.

74. Cannon, W. B. 1932. *The Wisdom of the Body.* New York: W. W. Norton.

75. Parens, H. 1987. Cruelty Begins at Home. *Child Abuse and Neglect: International J.* 11:331–38.

76. Silver, L. B.; Dublin, C.; and Laurie, R. 1969. Does Violence Breed Violence? Contributions from a Study of the Child Abuse Syndrome. *Am. J. Psychiatry* 126:404–7.

77. Steele, B. F. 1982. Discovery of Children at Risk for Juvenile Delinquency. In *Early Childhood Intervention and Juvenile Delinquency,* ed. F. N. Dutile, C. H. Foust, and D. R. Webster. Lexington, Mass.: D. C. Heath.

78. Steele, B. F. 1982. Effects of Abuse and Neglect on Psychological Development. In *Frontiers of Infant Psychiatry,* ed. J. Call, E. Galenson, and R. Tyson. New York: Basic Books.

79. Parker, T., and Allerton, R. 1962. *The Courage of His Convictions.* New York: W. W. Norton.

80. Berliner, B. 1958. The Role of Object Relations in Moral Masochism. *Psychoanalytic Q.* 27:38–56.

Assessment

Part 2: Editors' Comments

Part 2 is the largest section of this book, reflecting both the expansion of clinical knowledge and the expenditure of professional effort over the years in trying to better diagnose all forms of child abuse and neglect. While relatively few research dollars have flowed into this area, we nonetheless have managed to develop a fairly well-accepted empirical approach to recognizing abused children. Assessment is best accomplished as a multidisciplinary approach, bringing together the perspectives and methods of social work, medicine, law enforcement, and mental health professionals. Each chapter in part 2 offers important new information on the assessment skills needed by our profession. It is only when all the relevant, and invariably interconnected, facts are brought together in what are called "staffings," "case conferences," or "team meetings" that accurate assessment of the child's and family's situation can occur.

New to this edition are chapters on psychological maltreatment (chapter 17), Munchausen syndrome by proxy (chapter 18), and unusual forms of maltreatment (chapter 19). These forms of child abuse and neglect further expand the concept of "the battered child" from its original formulation and give all students and practitioners of assessment more to learn and deal with every year.

Communication in the Therapeutic Relationship: Concepts, Strategies, and Skills

MARY EDNA HELFER

Since the health provider/patient relationship is a transaction between human beings, the success of that transaction depends almost entirely on how well they understand each other, i.e., how well they communicate.

MICHELE TOLELA, "Communication" (1)

ommunication is our most important medium for social contact and personal develop-ment. It is also our most prolific behavior; most of our daily activities involve com-munication. The average American spends about 70% of his or her active hours communi-cating—listening, speaking, reading, and writing (2, p. 1). Communicating with others is so central to our existence that even in our attempts not to communicate, we still "say" something. Interacting with others is as vital to our survival in the social environment as the exchange of oxygen and carbon dioxide is to our survival in the physical environment.

Consider how helpless we become when unable to communicate. Even newborns are required to communicate from the very moment of birth to maintain their existence. Our self-identity, in part, is an outcome of our communication efforts (3), and our behavior is adopted and adapted in response to the communication we receive and the messages we transmit to others. Communication is the means we utilize to interact with and alter our environment. An individual's livelihood depends on the ability to influence the actions of others through communication. The satisfaction of our basic needs and, ultimately, the survival of our species are dependent upon mastery of an intricate set of communication rules and behaviors.

Although all persons communicate, the ability to do so skillfully and with purpose rarely occurs as a natural gift. Knowledge, practice, and experience are required to develop precise, predictable, effective, and satisfying techniques of interaction.

MARY EDNA HELFER, R.N., M.Ed., is senior instructor in the Department of Preventive Medicine, University of Colorado School of Medicine, and director of Continuing Medical Education Outreach at the University of Colorado Health Sciences Center and the Colorado Area Health Education Program.

Communication in the Therapeutic Relationship

In the clinical setting, the interview is the most important tool available to physicians and other health care providers. As Dr. Mack Lipkin stated:

> The interview is the major medium of care. It determines the problems to be addressed and helped. It forms the physician (provider), patient (client) relationship so central to the satisfaction of both practitioner and patient (client). It determines one's knowledge of the life context of the illness (or problem) which may hold the secrets of etiology and healing. It is the medium of patient (client) education about the illness (or problem), the diagnostic process, and the therapy. (4, p. vii)

A formal language system enables us to express very complex or abstract ideas to another person. Speech is the verbal medium used by the patient to inform the health provider of symptoms and concerns, and it is used, in turn, by the provider to respond to the patient's needs (5). The manner in which the content of speech is expressed, moreover, provides information which is as important as the words themselves. The volume, rate, pitch, inflection, intensity, and continuity all convey cues to the emotional state of the patient and are sometimes referred to as *paralanguage* (6). Paralanguage may communicate a message which could cause the interviewer to question how literally he or she should accept the overt message transmitted by the spoken word alone. Active listening is required if the interviewer wants to hear both components of speech. A good practitioner must, of necessity, be a good communicator. During the interview with the patient/client, the skilled provider must accomplish several differing objectives. The three central functions of the medical interview, which were first described by Bird and Cohen-Cole (7) and modified by Lazare (8) and Lazare and colleagues (9), are:

1. gathering data to understand the patients' problems;
2. developing rapport and responding to the patients' emotions;
3. educating the patients about their illness and motivating them to adhere to treatment plans.

The unspoken dialogue—that is, the pattern of nonverbal communication—is equally important (10). It is the medium most frequently used to communicate emotion and subtleties of meaning which could not be conveyed if we were restricted to a single mode of communication. The nonverbal behavior of the patient/client is an indicator of his or her emotional state. Patients/clients express their emotional state through facial expression, body posture, movement, tone of voice, inflection, and physical manifestations of the autonomic nervous system response (flushed face, breathing patterns, tearing, sweaty palms, and so on). The interviewer who is interested in understanding his or her patient's/client's emotional state must look for these cues and recognize their importance in the communication process.

The nonverbal behaviors of the practitioner may be the most critical component of the emotional interaction with patients or clients. Appropriate body posture, body movements, facial expression, tone of voice and rate of speech, touch, and the space between the interviewer and the patient/client convey an attitude of concern and warmth far beyond any words that may be uttered (11). Nonverbal behaviors have the capacity of combining, resulting in an astonishing number and variety of cues. These combinations may be thought of as a "vocabulary" of the unspoken dialogue.

The verbal and nonverbal combine to yield a constellation of cues with specific meanings. Sadness, for example, is mirrored in the face of a depressed patient, who may also exhibit a downturned mouth; a low, slow, monotonous voice; downcast eyes; slumped shoulders; sighing respiratory movements; and a general decrease in body movement. An angry patient may present clenched teeth and fixed jaw, increased rate and volume of speech, increased muscle tension, flushed face, and increased perspiration to the observer.

The interviewer must avoid making judgments based on isolated signals from any given system. Communication may be very clear when all systems agree. As interviewers, however, we usually must learn to listen actively and observe the entire range of communication behaviors to determine the degree of congruence between them—and, when we notice discrepancies, we always must help the patient clarify the true meaning of his or her communication.

Special Considerations Relating to Child Abuse

Communicating with abusive or neglectful parents presents some very special problems and requires very special skills. This is probably one of the most difficult, if not the most difficult, kind of therapeutic interpersonal relationship to establish. There are very few clinical situations which generate such strong feelings of anger, hostility, and frustration in health care providers as dealing with parents who have abused their children. It may be very difficult for the emergency room nurses, physicians, and social workers to feel any empathy for the parents after caring for the maltreated child. Few of us were trained to communicate extensively with someone whom we dislike or whose behavior upsets us. We struggle, often very clumsily, using interactional techniques that do not help us achieve our goals of building rapport and gathering data.

Two key factors involved in learning to overcome this problem are: first, to understand these people in as much depth as possible—to put the effort into getting to know them, the childhood they came from, and how they arrived where they are; and, second, to work hard to distinguish between their feelings and their actions. You do not like what they are doing, or have done, to their child, but you can—in fact, you must—accept how they are feeling and develop a communication system with them as people. This will not be an easy task, but when the shell is broken through, the provider finds real, feeling people in desperate need of help who are rarely able or willing to ask for it.

Nonverbal behaviors can sometimes communicate empathy more effectively than verbal statements. A sympathetic look, eye contact, attentive listening, and/or attentive silence can accomplish a great deal toward letting the parents know you are in tune with their distress as well as very concerned about their child. Focusing on how the parents feel at the present time, faced with the consequences of their actions, is helpful. Again, we need not condone or accept the parents' behavior but, rather, should try to understand their feelings (these complexities are discussed more fully in other chapters in this book; see especially chapters 5, 8, 16, 23, 26, and 28).

There are five basic skills that can be developed and used to facilitate the provider's empathic response to parents' emotional distress (12).

Reflection. Reflection is the most direct response skill. Emanating from Rogerian psychology (13), reflection is the provider's statement of an observed emotion exhibited by the parent—for example, "I can see you seem very sad (or anxious) right now." This response demonstrates to the parent that the interviewer is concerned about him or her as a person in addition to being concerned about the child who has been maltreated. If the parent does not acknowledge the emotion reflected by the provider, denies it, or refuses to discuss personal emotions (or, in the case of some abusive parents who were themselves abused as children, cannot discuss feelings), the provider should respect this reaction. On the other hand, if the provider does not acknowledge the emotions expressed by the parent, the parent may feel less understood and undermine the potential for building rapport. It is a cardinal rule of interviewing to respond to patients'/parents' feelings when they appear. Lack of any acknowledgment may be interpreted by the parent as lack of interest.

Legitimation. Legitimation is very similar to reflection but, in addition, specifically communicates acceptance and validation of the emotions expressed by the parent—for example, the interviewer may tell an angry parent, "I can understand your anger under the circumstances; anyone would be angry under those circumstances." In the case of anger, health care providers do not have to agree with the parents' reason for feeling angry, but we should try to understand the parents' anger from their viewpoint.

Personal support. The provider should make an effort to convey to the parents that he or she is personally available to help them if they are receptive to any help.

Partnership. Parents may be more receptive to treatment plans and/or placement decisions for the child if they are included and feel a sense of participation in the discussion and decision process. Increasing the abusive parents' participation in the planning for a treatment program may enhance their self-esteem and increase their coping skills.

Respect. Respect for the parents, or for whatever progress they make, is frequently best conveyed by nonverbal behaviors; however, explicit comments can enhance rapport with an abusive parent—for instance, "You're doing a good job dealing with this very difficult situation, despite the uncertainty involved."

Utilizing these five skills may enhance the potential for compromise and negotiation when it is time to develop a long-term treatment program.

Providers also experience feelings about abusive parents that must be internally acknowledged. Personal awareness and acceptance of the feelings triggered by the parent increase the providers' coping skills and ability to provide care to the child and his or her parent. Therapists may elect to discuss their personal reaction with the parent as part of a long-term therapeutic relationship.

The "Patient"

In dealing with child maltreatment, the professional care provider must first identify who the patient is. Some professionals may feel it is the child, others the mother or father, or possibly the siblings and grandparents. Approaching an interview with a predetermined notion that any one of these individuals is the *only* true patient will be most confusing to an inexperienced professional. Child abuse or neglect is a symptom indicating that a family's interactional system has broken down. Consequently, the whole family must be perceived as *the patient* and approached and handled accordingly. As Peabody pointed out in a classical article: "One of the essential qualities of the physician is interest in humanity, for the secret of the care of the patient is caring for the patient" (14). As difficult as this complex caring may be for the provider to generate when faced with a case of child maltreatment, as difficult as it may be to care for the entire family and not just side with the maltreated child, it is critical to the success of any intervention or treatment plan.

Unique, often strong, emotional ties bind the various members of a family together. At times, these ties are not easily understood, especially when a wife returns to the husband who beats her or a little girl runs to the father who sexually abuses her. These complex ties must be appreciated and considered when the professional is trying to establish a communication system with this family; using all the skills at his or her disposal, pulling out all the interpersonal and interactional stops, will be necessary.

Any time a parent is being interviewed about a child, a conflict of interest arises that professionals must learn to appreciate. The parent is emotionally very tied to the child and feels responsible for what happens, or has happened, to the child. If the child has pneumonia, for example, and the doctor asks, "Did he take his medicine?" or, even worse, "Did you give him his medicine?" an immediate conflict is provoked with the parent. The doctor comes across as all good, the parent as all bad or, at least, blameworthy. Consider how a parent suspected of child abuse reacts when asked, "Who hurt your child?" or, even worse, "Did *you* hurt your child?"

When a professional knows, with a reasonable degree of certainty, that something of a very negative nature has happened to a child, the rule is, *do not ask* the parent. Stating the problem, as you see it, is always preferable. For example saying, "Your child has been hurt; tell me about it" is much preferable to asking, "Who hurt your child?" or even asking, "How did your child get hurt?" The parent is much less defensive with the former approach, and the conflict of interest, while still present, is less an interference.

Abusive parents have considerable difficulty using nonverbal communication skills. Even the few skills they do have are often misread by inexperienced professionals. Abusive parents often do not look at people eye to eye, they may only rarely cry or show other facial expressions, they may sit slumped in a chair, and they may be very aggressive or very passive. Most of the skills we learn in graduate school or medical school to establish rapport may be of little use as we try desperately to communicate with these sensory-muted parents (see chapter 28). Sometimes an interviewer feels as though he or she is trying to establish rapport with a robot.

Verbal expression may be equally muted. Since young adults who were abused as children are trained not to trust others and trained to believe that all people hurt others, they are likely to be guarded in their interaction and not likely to verbally respond to someone who says, "I'm here to help you," or, "I'm here to ask you a few questions." A much more appropriate opening is the reflection, "You must have had a rough week," or, "You look tired," or, "You're probably really concerned about your child."

Abusive parents are not reared to demonstrate motivation. Why be motivated? Tomorrow is no better than today; today is just as bad as yesterday. Professionals find it very difficult to establish a communication system with someone they view as unmotivated. When parents do not show up, follow directions, call, say thanks, ask questions, smile, and so forth, we are turned off. And yet, there *is* motivation there, shown in a variety of subtle ways. The parents may peek through the window, hoping you will come back; show up late, hoping you will still be there; bring their abused child to school, hoping someone will recognize their cry for help.

The potential for a productive interview will be enhanced if the interview is conducted in a professional and nurturing manner. The interviewer can give the parent or client support and a sense of being understood, as well as providing an opportunity to "tell his story." A nurturing and supportive attitude is critical, for without a sense of being understood, the parent may withhold or distort information that is essential for accurately assessing the child's injuries. Developing appropriate treatment strategies will also be compromised by inaccurate or incomplete data.

Understanding Emotional Responses

In order for an abusive parent to feel understood, the *professional care provider* must identify or acknowledge the emotions the parent brings to the interview. *Empathy* is a term indicating one person's appreciation, understanding, and acceptance of someone else's emotional situation (12, 15). The communication of this understanding is one of the most helpful, meaningful, and comforting interventions an interviewer can accomplish with an abusive parent. A physician/provider can significantly help build rapport and trust by responding to all the parents' emotions with empathy.

Emotional Reactions   One of the emotional reactions abusive parents may exhibit is actually the absence of any observable emotion. The consequences and emotional impact of the abuse may be so great they simply deny it happened. This can make the parent less responsive to treatment programs.

Anger exhibited by patients can also be particularly troublesome. It frequently provokes rejection by members of the care-providing team and sends the patient on a shopping expedition for another doctor, social worker, or emergency room, wasting valuable time and causing duplication of efforts. Anger may be expressed in a readily recognized form of direct confrontation and criticism or in a disguised, indirect form. Bowden and Burstein describe several types of anger which are frequently encountered in dealing with patients (16). Parents may be voicing a legitimate complaint about a given situation; they may be displacing their anger by venting feelings generated at a different time in another context; they may be angry as a result of a process of assimilating the hard truths of their situation within themselves; or they may be characterologically angry.

In dealing with situational anger, we should listen and assess the complaint in an accepting and nonjudgmental manner. Usually the anger is temporary, and if we give it the opportunity to run its course, an improvement in the openness and frankness with which the patient can talk with the physician or other provider may well result.

Displaced anger is carried over from a previous setting or interaction. This may be an unconscious adaptive mechanism which permits the patient to vent feelings of anger while maintaining a positive image with the health professional team members on whom he or she feels most dependent for care of the child. All team members need to recognize and learn to deal with displaced anger, as most of them will have opportunities to be the recipients of such anger. The quality and depth of the parent's feelings should be acknowledged. This may prompt some dissipation of the feeling and shift the focus to the more legitimate source of anger. Displaced anger is basically transitory and, if permitted open expression, may clear the way for improved communication.

Anger as a reaction to an internal process is not a reflection of the current interpersonal transactions but a reflection of the patient's assimilating the knowledge of his or her situation. This type of anger is often seen in people who have suffered an acute reduction in their sense of adequacy and competence, such as patients developing a serious illness or a parent who may feel inadequate based on the abuse or neglect that has taken place.

Dealing with characterologically angry parents is most difficult. Their critical early childhood experiences with help givers—such as physicians, teachers, and parents—have convinced them in many pervasive and preverbal ways that such helpers are more likely to take advantage of them than to do them any actual good. They frequently are very rigid in their beliefs and attitudes, appear hyperalert during the interview, and seem unable to accept emotional support from team members. They rely heavily on projection as an adaptive mechanism. They often give a history of growing up in a hostile, nonnurturing environment, describing their parents as persons who always overpowered or degraded them. Their past experiences have convinced them that helpers are in reality punishers and are potentially dangerous people who cannot be trusted.

When working with individuals whose basic characters are built on anger, the care provider—obviously a help giver him- or herself—must be open and candid while communicating with them. Ambiguity may be viewed as a threat. A consistent, authoritative, and, above all, benign posture may prove beneficial in working with these patients. Their anger is likely to erupt if the provider seems inconsistent or vacillates in making decisions. They despise weakness in themselves and others. Their areas of strength and competence should be maximized during any interactions with them, thereby enhancing their self-esteem and reducing conflict. In extreme cases, these patients may act or appear paranoid or sociopathic and often require psychotherapeutic intervention.

Depression   Bowden and Burstein also describe a variety of depressive states and discuss some of the basic mechanisms underlying various stages of depression (16). It is essential for care providers to educate themselves and develop a thoroughgoing awareness of the several stages of depression that are frequently encountered while interacting with highly stressed patients.

Mourning is viewed by Bowden and Burstein as a healthy, normal reaction to loss; it usually follows a predictable course as the person works through a problem and resolves the stress. The loss may be physical, such as a crippling injury; an emotional loss, such as the separation from an abused or neglected child; or a loss of self-esteem, such as the parent may experience when feeling he or she has failed as a parent. The parents or caretakers of an injured child, for example, may appear very sad, as evinced by their crying, downcast expression, or other nonverbal behavior. They may experience, and demonstrate, decreased interest in their other routine activities and responsibilities. In some cases, denial may be their first psychological response to loss. Very little emotion may be exhibited as a parent tries to block out the reality of his or her situation by saying, "This can't be really happening to me." This stage usually progresses to one of displaced anger—the parent holds someone or something else to be responsible for the problems.

The sense of loss, which will facilitate a parent's moving to the grief stage, should be recognized. Grieving is a vital process if the parent is to move on to reintegration and reinvolvement in trying to cope with their loss or failure. What is actually being grieved over may not be readily apparent to the interviewer, for what is important and internal for one person may have little meaning to another. On occasion, the provider is confronted with an individual who has every apparent reason to go through the grieving process but does not exhibit appropriate verbal or nonverbal behavior. These individuals must undergo additional assessment and possibly psychiatric care.

Secondary or reactive depression is usually exhibited in parents as a sense of worthlessness, guilt, or hopelessness about their situation and environment. Bowden and Burstein describe three causes of secondary depression. A common psychological pattern appears which may be very applicable in understanding the emotional state of many abusive parents. There is a gap between the way these parents want to function, or feel they should function, and the way they are actually able to function. Bowden and Burstein state:

> The childhood experiences of patients with secondary depression predispose them to this reaction pattern in response to stress. Such children were often treated as inadequate and incompetent by their overly critical parents. Memories of statements such as, "You can't do anything right," are common. In addition, as children, these persons harbored much anger toward their parents but felt guilty and afraid of expressing it, and they developed the pattern of turning the anger and self-reproach inward. (16, p. 79)

Anxiety Anxiety is a common and expected reaction for an abusive parent to exhibit; after all, the great majority of parents experience some degree of anxiety—it comes with the territory. Sometimes anxiety, fear, and anger are not distinguishable: anxiety often lends to anger, and many parents may feel a generalized anger, not unlike free-floating anxiety, that cannot be focused on one particular person. Physicians and other providers are frequent targets for this anger. This is unfortunate, since some seemingly angry parents may alienate the very people who can be most helpful to them during their emotional crisis. When providers are aware of these reactions, they can often deal with them better and with fewer maladaptive consequences for the patient (17).

A cardinal rule of good interviewing, as I have stated earlier, is to respond to a patient's feelings as soon as any appear. The physician/provider who avoids acknowledging a parent's feelings may give the parent the message that he or she is afraid of the feeling or, worse, uninterested.

Stress of Illness   Strain and Grossman (17) have described various stresses of illness: several are particularly relevant to interacting with an abusive parent.

One such stress is the threat of separation. The child's injuries, especially when the possibility of hospitalization is involved, can generate in parents an acute fear of separation from someone the parent loves and whom he or she may perceive as necessary for comfort and support.

Another stress of illness suffered by abusive parents is the threat of loss of love. Many parents may feel that their abusive behavior will make them even more unattractive or unlovable to the people around them. Providers must refrain from judgmental comments that would reinforce this belief and focus on the parent as well as the child as a "patient" in need of help.

The parents must, in addition, deal with the normal adaptive tasks of illness, such as maintaining emotional balance, preserving social and/or family relationships, and coping with the current situation. For the abusive parents, coping with the unknown is very difficult. They may have to cope with an enormous uncertainty in predicting the outcome of the child's injuries, whether there may be legal consequences associated with the abuse, whether they can trust those who indicate a desire to "help" them, and what will happen when the child recovers from the injuries.

These parents are also called upon to adapt to a variety of health care providers as well as social services, police, and legal representatives. This broad spectrum of personalities with different interests and approaches can represent a manageable task for some parents and an impossible, overwhelmingly stressful one for others.

Guidelines for Facilitating the Interview

An important component of eliciting history from a parent is for the interviewer to furnish the parent with a cognitive understanding of why some questions are being asked. The importance and potential benefit of understanding the total environment and the family dynamics pertaining to a particular child may not be immediately obvious to the parent. If we do not provide them with a clear explanation of the purpose of the interview, the parents may not in turn provide the information needed to obtain a "comprehensive overview" of the current living situation, family interaction patterns, and any crisis that may have contributed to the parental neglect or abuse. The process of verbalizing their situation may act as a stimulus for parents to participate in thinking about alternative solutions to help resolve the problems that contributed to the abuse.

I would like to propose several specific suggestions of methods to facilitate an interaction, especially one whose purpose is to establish rapport as well as to gather certain factual information. Each of these suggested techniques requires considerable practice to implement. The concepts will not be difficult to grasp; setting them in action will be another matter. Some providers find that the skill of interviewing comes very naturally; others struggle with each new (and old) interaction. Consideration of these guidelines will be helpful in both situations.

The open-ended question. Many use this technique effectively. It can help an interviewer gather the most accurate and unbiased information and determine the ability of the patients to organize their thoughts and tell their own stories. The open-ended question can be used to gain both cognitive and affective information: "Describe the nature of your pain." "Tell me how you felt about your father's death." Interviewers must use this technique skillfully, or the interview may get out of control. If the open-ended question does lead a patient/client only to unproductive rambling, we can move to more specific, direct closed-ended questions (see chapters 8 and 12 about interviewing children).

The closed-ended question. Most providers are skilled in utilizing this form of questioning—so skilled, in fact, that some use nothing but closed-ended questions to gain information. "Do you have a cough?" "When did your father die?" This type of question is usually easy to answer and usually brings forth specific information. When used judiciously, it is most helpful. When used exclusively, however, it can destroy rapport. Questions should proceed from open-ended to closed-ended as the information needed becomes more specific (see chapter 8).

Labeling. This is a useful tool for building a positive relationship with the parent(s). The timely use of labeling or reflection can often break through the most resistant barriers. In order to learn the skill of labeling one must first recognize what should be labeled. Interviewers can hardly say, "That last question must have really upset you," unless they recognized that the person they are interviewing was in fact disturbed by the last question. A more appropriate response is, "It must be difficult for you to talk to me." After a provider has established a therapeutic relationship of trust with a parent, the provider may also label his or her own feelings: "I'm feeling very frustrated; I keep getting mixed messages." "It is easier for me to talk to you when you look at me." "I really had a bad week." *Never* say, "I know how you feel," unless you really have experienced *exactly* the same situation and are willing to talk about it in some detail. A better statement is, "If that had happened to me, I might have felt just as you did." Well-timed and appropriate labels can turn a difficult interview into one that is not only informative but productive for both individuals. Rapport follows. Keep in mind that labels are most effective when they are placed on both the parent's and the interviewer's feelings and reactions. Labeling enhances a positive interaction.

Confrontation. This technique allows the interviewer to confront the parent with any discrepancies between the verbal or logical component of his or her message and the nonverbal or kinesic cues he or she exhibits. Such confrontation is always based on specific observations with no inference made regarding motive. For example, "You say you had a good relationship with your mother, but you always look away from me when you talk about her." "You say things are going well at home, but you look very sad when you talk about Johnny's father." Confrontation may help the patient elaborate on these conflicting cues and help the parent get in touch with his or her feelings. Confrontation is one of the more difficult skills to acquire because it entails "listening on all channels" and is not part of our repertoire of routine social behaviors. Confrontation is risky to the interaction and is best used after some degree of rapport has been built.

Silence. The thought of sitting quietly, waiting for the other person to say something, makes some individuals most uncomfortable. Even a short five-to-ten-second pause may seem endless. This technique often allows both individuals to gather their thoughts and gain the courage to speak them. The use of silence can be self-defeating, however, if tensions rise to such a peak that thoughts and speech vanish. Silence must be used judiciously.

Checking. Checking is the most important information-gathering skill and the least utilized (18). Language has complex meanings that can be easily misinterpreted. An interviewer may have been given inaccurate or misleading information about a parent, or the interviewer's attention may wander when the parent is speaking. It is essential to check with the patient to confirm or discredit the accuracy of the information received. This can be accomplished by the interviewer's providing a brief summary of the information gathered to the parent and checking on the accuracy or interpretation of the data.

The Structure and Setting of the Interview

Careful consideration must be given to the structure and setting of the interview if we want to get the most from any interaction with a parent. Doctors and social workers often pay little attention to these matters and then wonder why an interview went poorly. Comfort and privacy are crucial.

Opening the interview sets the tone for the interactions. Abusive parents need some structure when they are anxious and don't know what will happen. It is important to introduce yourself and explain your role (physician, social worker, or whatever) first. Next, tell the parent what is happening now to deal with the immediate issues related to the child's injuries, and then discuss the long-term plan. The issue of confidentiality (see chapters 8 and 12) must be directly addressed and the parent fully informed as to who will have access to the information gathered during the interview.

During the course of the interview, the interviewer must intersperse some key techniques that help facilitate both rapport building and data gathering. Using the skills described above will aid immensely in accomplishing these two goals. Considerable practice is required to become comfortable with these skills, so the more often the interviewer uses them, the more effective they are likely to be.

Closure to the interview is of major importance. The interviewer must not close abruptly, say thanks, and leave. The parents' final impression and feeling of satisfaction will depend, in large part, on how the final minutes of the interview are handled. If the interview is complete, with no expectations for another meeting, then summary statements and questions are in order: "Let me review what I've heard," or, "Let's summarize a few major issues once again." If another meeting is anticipated, then the agenda and timetable should be set: "When we meet again, we need to talk about . . . ," or, "I want to finish up with . . ." A time and place must be set for the next discussion. In either situation, final or temporary closure, the parent must be given the opportunity to bring up points or issues: "Is there anything else we should discuss before we close?" The parent should always be told with whom the information obtained will be shared and what the next step will be.

Finally, no discussion on the structure and setting of an interview would be complete without mentioning a few additional suggestions to help achieve the goals of rapport building and data gathering.

1. Incorporate the more personal issues within less personal matters. It is quite easy for an interviewer to flow from less personal to personal; for example, in inquiring about the parent's parents, asking questions about how the interaction between parents and children went when the patient was a child is very natural and nonthreatening.

2. Use discretion in taking notes during an interview. Writing constantly is distracting; on the other hand, not writing anything may indicate disinterest: a happy medium is necessary. It is best, however, not to take notes when discussing very personal or sensitive issues. You will remember the main points until the interview time is over and can record them immediately afterward to insure accuracy. The patient may become very conscious of the interview process if the interviewer is absorbed in note taking, and the urgency of the emotional material may consequently be lost.

3. The concept of tracking/nontracking is important to understand, for a care provider can make very good use of this technique during an interview. Some do it automatically, others find it most difficult. Tracking is following through on a patient's/client's statement to obtain more details. For example, if a patient/client says, "My mother and I look a lot alike," your tracking response might be, "In what way?" Nontracking, in contrast, is to come to closure on a given issue by switching to another topic or question. Both tracking and nontracking can facilitate an interview when used skillfully.

4. The interviewer's dress and posture can say a great deal to the patient or client.

5. Opinion and judgmental statements present difficult issues. Giving your opinion during the interview, when expressed with care, can facilitate the discussion. If, however, these opinions are felt to be judgmental, the patient may well clam up, and rapport will be lost at least momentarily.

There are many ways to improve one's interviewing techniques. The most important thing to keep in mind is that interviewing is a skill; and skills can be learned and improved with practice. They must eventually become automatic, much like a driver's reactions when a car hits a piece of ice and skids. This practice is best done under observation, preferably using videotape. This enables an interviewer to obtain immediate and helpful feedback.

Michele Tolela gives an excellent summary of the communication process necessary for delivering services in situations of child abuse and neglect:

> Communication is a complex process—it is not a discrete phenomenon beginning with the first word spoken between two people and ending when the last word has been heard. Communication has a history in the past and pitfalls for the future. We should look at communication as a complex process that has to be learned, that can be learned. (1, p. 92)

References

1. Tolela, M. 1967. Communication: A Three Part Series. *Pennsylvania Med. J.* 70:76–78, 84–85, 91–92.

2. Berlo, D. K. 1960. *The Process of Communication.* New York: Holt, Rinehart, and Winston.
3. Miller, G., and Steinberg, M. 1975. *Between People: A New Analysis of Interpersonal Communication.* Chicago: Science Research Association.
4. Cohen-Cole, S. A. 1991. Foreword to *The Medical Interview.* Mosby Year Book, Inc.
5. Cassell, E. J., and Skopek, L. 1977. Language as a Tool in Medicine: Methodology and Theoretical Framework. *J. Med. Education* 77:197–203.
6. Mehrabian, A., and Ferris, S. R. 1967. Inferences of Attitudes from Nonverbal Communication in Two Channels. *J. Consulting and Clinical Psychology* 31:248–52.
7. Bird, J., and Cohen-Cole, S. A. 1990. The Three Function Model of the Medical Interview: An Educational Device. In *Models of Consultation—Liaison Psychiatry,* ed. M. Hale, 65–88. Basel.
8. Lazare, A. 1989. Three Functions of the Interview. In *Outpatient Psychiatry: Diagnosis and Treatment,* ed. A. Lazare, 153–57. Baltimore: Williams and Wilkins.
9. Lazare, A.; Lipkin, M.; and Putnam, S. M. 1992. The Functions of the Medical Interview. In *The Medical Interview,* ed. M. Lipkin, S. M. Putnam, and A. Lazare. New York: Springer-Verlag.
10. Burgoon, J., and Saine, T. 1978. *The Unspoken Dialogue: An Introduction to Nonverbal Communication.* Boston: Houghton Mifflin.
11. Shea, S. C. 1989. Nonverbal Behavior: The Interview as Mime. In *Psychiatric Interviewing: The Art of Understanding,* ed. S. C. Shea, 135–77. Philadelphia: W. B. Saunders.
12. Cohen-Cole, S. A., and Bird, J. 1985. Interviewing the Cardiac Patient, Pt. 2: A Practical Guide for Helping Patients Cope with Their Emotions. *Quality Life Cardiovascular Care* 2:7–12.
13. Carkuff, R. R. 1969. *Helping the Human Relations.* 2 vols. New York: Holt, Rinehart, and Winston.
14. Peabody, F. W. 1927. The Care of the Patient. *JAMA* 88:877–82.
15. Licthenberg, J.; Bornstein, M.; and Silver, D.; eds. 1985. *Empathy.* Hillsdale, N.J.: Analytic Press.
16. Bowden, C. L., and Burstein, A. G. 1979. *Psychological Basis of Medical Practice: An Introduction to Human Behavior.* 2d ed. Baltimore: Williams and Wilkins.
17. Strain, J. J., and Grossman, S. 1985. Psychological Reactions to Medical Illnesses and Hospitalization. In *Psychological Care of the Medically Ill: A Primer in Liaison Psychiatry,* ed. J. J. Strain and S. Grossman. New York: Appleton.
18. Cox, A.; Hopkinson, K.; and Rutter, M. 1991. Psychiatric Interviewing Techniques, Pt. 2: Naturalistic Study—Eliciting Factual Information. *British J. Psychiatry* 138:283–91.

The Assessment of Child Abuse:
A Primary Function of Child Protective Services

MICHAEL W. WEBER

I n today's child protective services (CPS) agencies, assessing the level of risk to children's safety is the most prominent concern. This prominence is a new phenomenon and high-lights a dilemma within child protective services and within policy debates about how our society protects its children. This chapter will explore the role which social services has historically played within CPS and how this role has changed over the past twenty years. With that end in mind, I will review the role which assessments play in current CPS prac-tice, examine a number of policy and practice issues regarding the roles of social services and assessment within the CPS system, and discuss the current dilemma surrounding assessment.

I. History of Social Services within Child Protective Services

Two major structural shifts have led to the way child protective services operate today. First of all, social work practice has diminished as legal practices and priorities have assumed an increasingly dominant role; second, responsibility for child protection is no longer ex-ercised mainly by the private sector but, rather, by the government.

The period from the mid-1960s to the mid-1980s might be called the years when child protective services flourished. There was a wide public consensus about the role which CPS should play within society, and those who publicly opposed CPS were viewed as uncaring about children. Enough public support existed for CPS that even when federal spending for social services was cut back beginning in 1981, child abuse initiatives were the only child welfare programs which regularly received legislative funding.

During these years of CPS prominence, particularly during the early 1980s, eight in-terrelated trends emerged: these factors shape the child protection practice of today.

1. Lack of Consensus about the Role of CPS

In the early 1980s, parents who had been found by CPS to have abused their children took to the courts for the first time to affirm their innocence. Lawsuits were filed and won by parents who claimed that their rights had been violated and their children had been removed from their home without sufficient cause. After a nationally publicized trial of a large group of families in Scott County, Minnesota, for sexual abuse of their children, the not-guilty

MICHAEL W. WEBER is associate director of the National Committee to Prevent Child Abuse.

verdict (which many CPS and law enforcement professionals consider to be the result of an inadequate prosecution) led to the formation of the Victims Of Child Abuse Legislation (VOCAL) organization. Now a nationwide organization, VOCAL is the preeminent voice of those who consider existing CPS legislation and practice far too intrusive into family life. Persons on this side of the debate about the role of CPS would limit its involvement only to families in which abuse is serious and substantiated by extensive evidence. This emphasis on the level of evidence available heightened efforts within CPS to assure that investigation of reports of child maltreatment included a search for legally admissible evidence and contributed to a reluctance to take any action without a significant amount of such evidence.

On the other side of the debate are advocates for the children who die at the hands of their parents. These advocates decry the lack of protection afforded by relatives, neighbors, churches, schools, and CPS. The most extreme of these advocates go so far as to advocate for CPS removal of children upon the receipt of any abuse report, to assure the protection of the child during the agencies' response to the report.

Both of these incompatible positions regarding the role of CPS are reflected in legislation introduced in a number of states since the mid-1980s. One consistent response of CPS agencies to this new debate about their appropriate role has been to pay more attention to gathering evidence which would justify the actions they take and which would clearly be admissible in court.

2. Court Procedures

The new debate about how intrusive CPS should be often resulted in families contesting the court action brought against them by CPS. The advice that families charged with child abuse had formerly been given—to cooperate fully because court action was in their best interest and because opposition might result in permanent loss of child custody—was no longer so intimidating. The past predilection of judges to listen only to the information presented by CPS staff was changed by the growing participation of private attorneys or public defenders in these hearings, assuring that parental rights were not violated and that action would be taken only on the basis of evidence convincing enough to be legally admissible in a courtroom.

The new phenomenon of contested court actions meant that CPS had to pay far more attention to ensuring that the professional conclusions drawn about child abuse were substantiated by legally admissible evidence. Although a small minority of cases ultimately resulted in court action to remove children from parental custody, the loss of a few court cases prompted CPS staffs to seek significant training by lawyers to assure that the CPS cases proceeding to court would be legally sound. This training and the heightened attention to preparing for potential legal action furthered the emphasis on investigation and the collection of evidence admissible in court.

3. Criminalizing Child Abuse

Growing awareness of parental child abuse intensified public debates about what grounds CPS needed to justify intervening in the privacy of a family home. Of particular relevance to this discussion were the notorious cases of extreme parental abuse, either physical or sexual. The general public was appalled at the extensive nature of the problem and was particularly dissatisfied with the lackluster official response, even when the CPS system had determined that the child abuse had occurred. Ordinarily the sanction against parents was that they would lose custody of their children, but the public was increasingly demanding that abusive parents face prosecution and punishment as well.

In the early 1980s, laws in many states did not permit greater sanctions against abusive parents than their loss of custody of the abused child. Public dissatisfaction with this situation combined with the emerging public awareness of domestic violence. The public recognized that treatment of children or women which would be criminal if perpetrated on strangers was not illegal if it occurred within families. New legislation was passed in most states which made the maltreatment of children not only the basis of child protection action to limit or terminate parental custody but also the basis for criminal prosecution for assault.

While these new laws reflected more appropriately society's rejection of intrafamilial abuse, they also further heightened the emphasis within CPS on legally admissible evidence. Not only was substantial evidence of abuse necessary for CPS to initiate interventional action, but that evidence also had to be legally admissible in criminal trials. After jurisdictions lost a number of criminal prosecution cases in court because CPS staff, in the course of their response to a report of abuse or neglect, had inadvertently contaminated the criminal investigation or the evidence, even greater emphasis was placed on investigative procedures which were compatible with criminal prosecutions.

4. Recognition of Sexual Abuse

The attention which Dr. C. Henry Kempe, in the 1960s, originally drew to child abuse focused on physical abuse. During the 1980s the public recognized the parallel problem that children are also sexually abused by their parents. The earliest examples of such abuse were uncontested cases recognizing that the abuse had taken place. But after it was clear, as in the Scott County cases mentioned above, that litigation could exonerate the accused parent, parents contested findings of sexual abuse with increasing frequency.

Characteristically, sexual abuse is seldom substantiated by concrete evidence. Physical abuse is attested to by bruises and broken bones. Neglect is evinced by patterns of sickness in children, by photographs of filthy houses, by cupboards without food, and by intolerable hygiene of children as observed by persons outside the home. Sexual abuse, on the other hand, almost always occurs in private, so usually no witnesses are available, and seldom does physical evidence remain by the time the abuse is reported. The exception is physical damage caused to children or the presence of sexually transmitted diseases, but often this evidence is conclusive of sexual abuse only for very young children. In addition, even though this evidence convincingly demonstrates that abuse must have occurred, it usually gives little indication of the perpetrator's identity.

Thus, with its increased attention to the problem of child sexual abuse, child protection was confronted with a form of abuse seldom substantiated by traditional types of physical evidence at the same time that the necessity of collecting such evidence was gaining new prominence.

5. Emergence of Child Abuse Teams

During the 1980s, child protection staff recognized that they often needed to consult with medical, legal, school, or mental health staff to understand a family's history and current situation more fully or to provide more appropriate intervention for the child who had allegedly experienced abuse or neglect. However, legislation restricting the use of personal data prevented CPS staff from discussing specific cases with other professionals without first obtaining the permission of the family, even though the consultation was required before the family could be informed that a report of maltreatment had been filed and even though the family was unlikely to grant permission for such consultation.

In response, the legislatures of most states enacted laws authorizing the appointment of multidisciplinary "child abuse teams," to directly bring the specialties of other related professions to assist child protective services efforts. Such teams are appointed by or work with CPS agencies and can include a variety of professionals or other community members with some specific contribution to make to the assessment of the case on hand. Ordinarily such teams include medical, mental health, education, and legal professionals, but they might also include staff of other social service agencies, members of the clergy, law enforcement personnel, or investigators.

Most agencies appoint ongoing teams which meet regularly to consult on cases which are proving particularly difficult for the CPS staff; however, new teams can be convened or new team members can be added for consultation on individual cases. The advantage of an ongoing team is the familiarity the members develop with CPS procedures, the cross-disciplinary respect earned through positive contributions made in the consultations, and the collective specialization gained by intensive review of multiple cases. The privacy of the families is protected, since the laws authorizing the appointment of such teams binds all team members with the data privacy requirements governing the child protection agency. While these teams can be used to consult on cases at any stage in the CPS process, more and more frequently the teams are called in during the CPS agency's initial response to a report of abuse and neglect, both because of the increasing complexity of reported child maltreatment and because of the increasing public attention to the way cases are handled at the time of the initial report.

6. Media Coverage of Child Abuse

In the mid-1980s, parental disputes of child abuse charges and the emergence of severe sexual abuse cases caught the attention of the media.

In some cases, the media reported the ongoing battles of parents against a CPS finding of child maltreatment. The parents were frequently portrayed as victims of an overaggressive CPS staff, which had concluded without significant evidence that the parents had abused their children. Usually it was the parents' story which was publicly portrayed, while the CPS agency insisted that it could not publicly comment about the case or even acknowledge that such a case existed.

During the same period, media coverage of child abuse tragedies tended to follow an increasingly familiar pattern. A child died or was severely abused by his or her parents; the child protection services agency had received a report and had taken no action or insuffi-cient action to protect the child; the media learned of the maltreatment and sought to report what had happened, including whether the CPS agency had acted responsibly; the CPS agency refused to discuss the situation, citing data privacy regulations. The typical media portrayal of CPS was of a government agency with no public accountability which had not done its job of protecting children.

This scenario was usually followed by the creation of a mayor's or governor's task force or blue-ribbon commission. One or more CPS staff members were then found not to have taken every reasonable action to protect the child; a reorganization of the CPS agency was instituted; the task force recommended smaller caseloads, more training, and clearer policies; and elected officials provided the funds for CPS programs which might have been requested and denied earlier.

Because it appeared so prevalently throughout the country, this media pattern became a primary concern of managers of CPS agencies and of the elected official responsible for those agencies. Fear of becoming embroiled in this scenario directed a great deal of CPS attention to gathering all possible information on each individual case. Partially this was to assure that should a child abuse tragedy occur, the CPS agency would be able to document that it had fulfilled its responsibility by conducting a thorough investigation and thus could be absolved of any blame for the tragedy. But, additionally, this attention to investigation stemmed from the growing assumption that with sufficient information, child abuse could be predicted and children protected.

7. The Development of Risk Assessment Tools

The emergence of child abuse investigation as a professional specialty and the intense in-terest in preventing any child abuse tragedy from happening with an agency's purview led to the development and almost universal implementation of formal protocols for assessing the level of risk faced by children who came to the attention of child protective service agencies.

A number of risk assessment protocols have been developed, but reviewing two of the earliest that were formulated will be sufficient for this discussion. The model developed by the state of Illinois emphasized the structured gathering of information about the presence of any factors within a family which research had shown to be highly correlated with abuse of children within a family. This tool was used as the first response to a report of abuse or neglect, and the information could be collected and analyzed quickly. The cumulative in-formation on a number of factors led to a determination of low, medium, or high risk.

A significantly different model, developed by ACTION For Children, was intended to be used periodically during the entire course of a child protection case and to assemble a wider range of information about the family. A major disincentive against using this tool was the extensive amount of time required to complete the risk assessment as well as the extensive training and supervision required to enable the staff to use the tool.

The development of these tools both caused and affected the kind of child protective services practiced during the 1980s. The fear of becoming fodder for a media event heightened the desire of elected officials and administrators for an easy and effective test to ascertain which families should receive CPS intervention in order to arrest any child abuse tragedies in the making. Conversely, the use of a structured risk assessment tool which bore some resemblance to a medical diagnosis led to confidence within CPS that risk could be reliably measured and, accordingly, that abuse could be predicted and prevented. This sense of confidence was in turn reflected by CPS managers, who, at least implicitly, indicated to elected officials that if sufficient funds were granted to CPS agencies to conduct thorough investigations and to perform risk assessments consistently, the potential for severe abuse could be anticipated and tragedies avoided. The media events surrounding tragedies when they did occur were then, in one sense, holding CPS agencies accountable for the promises they made that increased funding would prevent—or at least reduce—child abuse and tragedy.

8. Child Abuse Registers

One final factor emerging in the 1980s which significantly affects today's child protective services practice was the registration of perpetrators of child abuse.

As increased societal attention was focused on child abuse, a number of child abusers responded by developing patterns of evasion. Some abusive parents would move from jurisdiction to jurisdiction; consequently, CPS agencies in the new location would not be aware of past findings of abuse within the family. This would limit the likelihood that any new report of an abusive incident would be recognized and handled as fitting into a wider context of previous abusive behavior. Some parents whose abusive behavior resulted in physical injury to a child would use multiple medical facilities so that the patterns of repeated abuse would not be identified.

In response, some state legislatures created child abuse registers, which list persons officially found to have abused children. Usually such registers include both intrafamilial abuse and third-party abuse, such as that perpetrated by child care staff or school personnel.

While the creation of these registers did give CPS agencies the information needed to identify patterns of abuse, it also intensified the ongoing emphasis on thorough CPS investigation and evidence collection. Because persons whose names appeared on a register of perpetrators could contest their inclusion on such a list via a judicial or quasi-judicial venue, the pressure on CPS agencies increased. The expectation of CPS was not just that those staff identify parents whose behavior had been determined to be abusive and whose actions would thus warrant careful evaluation if subsequent reports were received but also that those staff provide the evidentiary basis to legally justify the inclusion of a parent's or other individual's name on a child abuse register.

II. Current Child Protection Practice: Historical Perspective

Current child protection practice decisively demonstrates the influence of the eight major factors described above, which emerged during the 1980s. These factors inaugurated a shift from the early history of child protection. In those days, child protection practice centered on social workers rescuing children and placing them in better situations; little emphasis was accorded to changing the family, to mastering the investigative process, or to assuring the legal rights of parents.

Between 1974, the time when the federal Child Abuse Prevention and Treatment Act (CAPTA) (Public Law 93-247) precipitated the emergence of child protective services as a specialized field within the governmental sector, and the mid-1980s, CPS was a service still characterized by the traditions of social work. The emphasis was on changes in the client's life, usually the child's. The methods used tended to be urging and exhorting parents either to change or to give up custody of their child voluntarily. Even use of the court was seen as a therapeutic tool to precipitate change in the clients' lives rather than as a forum for settling a legal dispute. The role of the CPS worker involved visiting the family to assess the situation in order to determine the appropriate course of action, but CPS assessments then were not highly structured and did not follow a formal protocol which could be characterized as an investigation.

In the mid-1980s, in contrast, the protection of children became almost exclusively a governmental role. As a result of the eight factors described above, responding to reports of child abuse, specifically by conducting investigations, became the core role of CPS. The new methodologies that were developed focused on working at better means of determining what had actually occurred in the child's life. The skills of professionals from other disciplines who served on the child abuse teams were most commonly used to help determine whether the child had been abused. A primary concern of CPS leadership, both elected and appointive, was on gathering enough information to prevent the occurrence of a child tragedy.

In addition to the eight sociological factors cited above, two additional influences have played a major role in shaping current child protection practice. The first of these additional influences is legislation, particularly the 1980 Foster Care and Adoption Assistance Act (Public Law 96-272). The federal policy for child welfare consisted primarily of this piece of legislation from its passage until the 1993 passage of the Family Preservation and Family Support Act (Public Law 103-66).

The 1980 legislation resulted from the recognition of two systemic facts: (1) that far too many children in foster care could have been kept with their families if the child welfare system had attempted to make changes in the child's home rather than simply removing the child from the home, and (2) that once children entered foster care, they often did not return to their parents' home, even after the threat of abuse no longer existed. To rectify these problems, Public Law 96-272 required that the child welfare agency (ordinarily child protective services) make "reasonable efforts" to keep the child within his or her family home rather than placing the child in foster care and, if the child was removed to foster care, to return the child home as quickly as possible. The law did not define what constituted "reasonable efforts," and the provisions for enforcement focused on documenting that the child protection agency and the court had followed certain stipulated procedures.

In addition, to augment this federal legislation, most states were passing their own legislation (sometimes regulations) to direct the procedures of child protection. Almost invariably, these laws governed the beginning stages of the child protection process—the acceptance of child abuse reports from the public and the investigation of those reports—with no comparable specificity about the services a family should receive from CPS or about how or when a CPS case should be closed.

The second additional major influence shaping CPS practice today has been the programmatic consensus of CPS leadership and frontline staff, particularly as reflected in professional standards of practice. The National Association of Public Child Welfare Administrators (NAPCWA) published in 1988 their *Guidelines for a Model System of Protective Services for Abused and Neglected Children and Their Families* (1). The Child Welfare League of America (CWLA), in 1989, issued a new edition of its *Standards for Service for Abused or Neglected Children and Their Families* (2). And the 1994 edition of *Standards for Agency Management and Service Delivery* (3), issued by the Council on the Accreditation of Services for Families and Children, includes a section entitled "Protective Services for Children." All of these professional standards reflect a number of commonalities about the provision of child protective services:

- CPS is to be a specialized function of the child welfare system and should be a governmental function
- CPS must be part of an array of services which includes prevention and early intervention services, with CPS providing only a crisis intervention role
- The primary goal is to have children remain safely with their parents, with "reasonable efforts" being taken to preserve family integrity and out-of-home placement being a last resort
- Services must be provided by trained professionals, and staff must be culturally competent to meet the needs of the diverse families receiving services from CPS agencies
- Intervention in a family, particularly when involuntary, must be based on "the timely gathering of objective information . . . to determine if the child has been or is at risk of being abused or neglected" (1, p. 31)

III. Primary Functions of CPS Practice Today

1. Mandatory Reporting and the Acceptance of Reports

All states allow anyone, but require certain professionals, to report any incidents of suspected physical or sexual abuse, physical neglect, or emotional abuse of a child to the public CPS agency. These four forms of child abuse and neglect are cumulatively referred to as child maltreatment. The premise on which these laws are based is that the general public is not able to discern whether child abuse or neglect has occurred. Therefore any suspicions, even without evidence, can and should be presented to an agency specializing in determining whether maltreatment has occurred, whether a child is at risk of further maltreatment, and what intervention is needed to protect the child from (further) maltreatment.

The agency's taking of the child abuse report is simply collecting the information which the reporter is able to offer. Such information ordinarily includes the name of the child and other identifying information; the incident, behavior, or circumstances which caused the reporter to suspect maltreatment; the location of the child; the name, address, and phone number of the reporter; his or her relationship to the child; and any additional information which might be helpful.

State laws consistently protect the identity of persons reporting child maltreatment, except in the case of malicious reports, both to encourage persons suspecting abuse or neglect within families or social or professional groups to bring their suspicion to the attention of CPS for appropriate action and to facilitate the reporting process.

2. Screening

State laws differ on whether the CPS agency must thoroughly investigate every report submitted (4, pp. 51–52). The NAPCWA *Guidelines* recommend that CPS intake staff "should have the flexibility to screen [out certain reports] at the time a report is taken" (1, p. 30). The assumption underlying this recommendation is that many of the reports received will be describing situations of poor parenting rather than maltreatment; this is the inevitable consequence of the broadness of the reporting laws, which are explicitly intended to assure that any potentially abusive situation is reported for professionals to investigate. NAPCWA based the screening guidelines on the contention that CPS resources should be targeted on reports that relate parental behavior which, if substantiated, would present some danger to the child. However, some states require the investigation of all reports, on the assumption that even if the reported incident appears not to constitute child abuse or neglect, some other, unreported maltreatment might well be occurring within the family.

Some controversy exists about this component of the CPS process. Proponents of giving CPS agencies the discretion to screen cases emphasize the need to direct the limited financial resources of CPS to investigating reports of the most serious abuse. They urge that reported situations of poor parenting or families in need of social services be handled through prevention or early intervention programs rather than through CPS. The opponents of granting CPS staff the discretion to screen out—that is, not investigate—some reports fear that significant situations of child maltreatment might escape detection as a result.

3. Emergency Intervention

One of the key strengths of the child protection system, often questioned by critics, is its ability to intervene immediately to protect an endangered child. At any stage in the investigative process, CPS either on its own authority or using the authority of law enforcement (depending on state law) can take a child into protective custody on an emergency basis. When information available to CPS indicates that there is imminent danger that further abuse will be inflicted or that there may be recriminations directed against the child because of the CPS involvement, the child may be taken into protective custody for up to seventy-two hours without court action. During this time, the child may be placed in a shelter, a receiving center for children, or a short-term foster home. Ordinarily, at this point, the child undergoes a physical exam to identify any signs of abuse or need for medical attention.

During the seventy-two-hour emergency intervention period, the CPS staff are expected to conduct sufficient investigation to determine whether continued CPS custody of the child is necessary to protect him or her. At the end of this period, unless the parents voluntarily yield temporary custody to the CPS agency or the court awards temporary custody to CPS, the child must be returned to his or her parents.

The practice and policy dilemma surrounding this component of the CPS process stems from the "emergency" factor. By definition, the child's safety at home has been called radically into question; hence a determination must be made on the basis of whatever information is immediately available, the reliability of which may be questionable, given the crisis situation. Such uncertainty, combined with the potential of intrusive governmental action, can give rise to accusations both of unwarranted interference in private family life (when a child is removed from the home and maltreatment is ultimately determined not to have occurred) and of irresponsible inaction (when a child remains in the home and is further abused or even killed).

4. Investigation

During this step in the CPS process, information is systematically gathered; on the basis of the material collected, CPS will decide what further action will be taken on a case. During the early history of CPS, this one step was termed *assessment* and followed the social work model of studying and analyzing the family circumstances and level of functioning to determine whether the social worker had something to offer the family. Currently, "assessment" is applied to the full range of the first stage of the CPS process, while the term *investigation* accurately describes actual fieldwork practice of collecting data and reflects the introduction during the mid-1980s of the influence of law enforcement, the attention to criminal liability, and the concern for assembling the evidence needed for presenting a sound case in court.

Investigation procedures are prescribed in great detail in many state laws and regulations. Time lines are set, ordinarily requiring contact with the family within twenty-four hours of a serious report and seventy-two hours for other reports. The requirement that the investigator actually see the child has assumed major importance as the result of cases in which investigators were assured by parents of a child's well-being only to detect later that severe child abuse had ensued. Both parents are interviewed, as well as the child if he or she is old enough to participate. Other "collateral" persons—that is, other professionals who have contact with the child and/or the parents—also are interviewed to discover if they have any information which might help determine whether or not the child was maltreated. Whether or not relatives or neighbors are interviewed is often subject to local interpretation of data privacy laws, since some jurisdictions deem that conducting such interviews reveals that a family has been reported for abuse or neglect and therefore violates the parents' right to privacy.

As the complexity of child abuse increases and as more professional knowledge is gained about this abuse, the need for involving additional specialists in the investigative process grows. If the alleged maltreatment would constitute criminal behavior, law enforcement personnel should be brought into the investigation to assure that the criminal aspect of suspected maltreatment is thoroughly investigated and that the evidence necessary for criminal prosecution is adequately safeguarded.

When child abuse was first criminalized, the relationship of CPS and law enforcement was often adversarial. Child protection staff were often accused of contaminating the criminal investigation, either by precipitately warning the parents of the pending charges or by mishandling the physical evidence. Conversely, CPS staff often accused law enforcement personnel of caring more about prosecution than about the safety of children. Because these strained relationships were developing throughout the country, a number of efforts were initiated to establish guidelines for cooperation between law enforcement and child protective services (5). These guidelines led in many jurisdictions to the development of written interagency agreements delineating the respective roles of the two systems (6, pp. 55–58; 7) and to the formulation of strong recommendations for interdisciplinary training sessions to promote mutual understanding and respect.

The investigative process frequently requires the involvement of medical personnel, in particular to assess whether the child shows any physical symptoms indicative of abuse or to determine whether a parental failure to obtain medical treatment constitutes child neglect. This medical consultation is frequently obtained through the multidisciplinary child abuse teams discussed above.

The increased reporting of sexual abuse has led to the need for highly specialized investigative techniques because of the frequent lack of conclusive evidence and the frequent inability of the child to testify (see chapters 8 and 12, for example, especially on the use of anatomically correct dolls). The use of child advocacy centers provides specialized interviewing techniques in a child-friendly environment to minimize the trauma to the child and to avoid unduly influencing the child's memory of events. Often these child advocacy centers also possess the medical equipment and qualified personnel necessary to conduct detailed physical examinations which may be able to determine if a child has been sexually abused.

In a highly professional CPS agency, trained staff will respond quickly to child abuse reports. Their response will include structured collection of the information needed to establish whether child maltreatment occurred and what services the CPS agency specifically can offer to the child and family. Professionals from a variety of fields will be available for consultation to provide perspectives and consider information outside the scope of the CPS staff's expertise. Every member of the family will be seen by investigators, and those old enough will be interviewed, as will all other individuals who might have knowledge of the family's treatment of the child.

5. Risk Assessment

The risk assessment tools developed in the mid-1980s supply a structured protocol to assure that comprehensive information is gathered during the investigation and to determine the level of risk which a child is currently facing in his or her home. Professional standards assume that the assessment of risk is not a onetime event but, rather, an ongoing process while CPS is actively involved with a family's case (1, p. 31). The intent of these tools is to assure that the same factors will be consistently used in making decisions over time with each family assessed.

The NAPCWA *Guidelines* list eight factors which should be considered in a risk assessment:

- Impact of parental behavior
- Severity of abuse or neglect
- Age, physical and mental abilities of the child
- Frequency/recentness of the alleged abuse or neglect
- Credibility of the reporter
- Location, and access by the perpetrator to the child
- Parental willingness to protect the child and level of cooperation
- Parental ability to protect the child (1, pp. 28–30)

These factors correlate with child abuse and neglect within families but, like other human service diagnostic and assessment tools, cannot predict future behavior. Obviously, this limitation is a significant one. Risk assessment is a valuable method of assuring that each CPS decision is made in the context of consistent information, to assure that throughout the CPS involvement with a family the safety of the child is considered and to provide a structured basis for delivering services and setting priorities. However, when this tool is used as the primary basis for deciding whether a child will face risk in the future, it is being misused and will predictably lead both to overly intrusive action in some families and insufficient protection for children in other families.

Within a professionally sound CPS agency, risk assessment will be an ongoing process which systematically reviews the elements which contributed to the maltreatment of the child and seeks to identify the continued presence of factors which research indicates are highly correlated with maltreatment. This formal assessment of risk to the child will be performed when any major CPS decision is in the offing—for example, whether or not to remove a child from foster care and return him or her to the parental home. The resulting assessment will provide the basis for determining what aspects of the family life and functioning should be addressed in the service delivery plan.

6. Disposition

State laws and regulations governing the CPS process require that the CPS agency conclude the investigative process by arriving at a disposition, a formal finding on whether or not child abuse or neglect has occurred. The categories available to CPS are ordinarily specified in the legislation: most agencies use the categories of "confirmed," "founded," or "substantiated" to indicate that abuse or neglect occurred, and "unfounded" or "unsubstantiated" to indicate that "no credible evidence of abuse or neglect has been identified" (1, p. 31).

Prior to the publication of the NAPCWA *Guidelines,* a third major category, "unable to substantiate," was the conclusion most frequently reached. This signified that even though there was no clear indication of child abuse or neglect, the situation within the family was sufficiently ambiguous that the CPS staff was unwilling to state that abuse or neglect had not occurred. The problem with this category was that it left families without a firm closure to the CPS investigation; furthermore, this category's availability encouraged CPS staff to resort to it as a safe disposition. NAPCWA recommended eliminating the use of this disposition. Simultaneously, however, NAPCWA emphasized that "unsubstantiated" was not to be interpreted as a positive finding of no maltreatment (that is, it was not to be taken as a decree of "innocence") but, rather, as a finding of insufficient evidence to conclusively establish any incident of maltreatment (that is, more like a judgment of "not guilty").

Some states have begun using a two-part disposition. After determining whether there is evidence that child maltreatment has occurred, there is an additional determination about whether or not providing ongoing child protective services to the family is appropriate. Ordinarily, if there is a finding of "unsubstantiated," there will be no further action on the case by CPS. On the other hand, a finding of "substantiated" does not necessarily result in the assignment of ongoing protective services. For example, the parent who abused the child(ren) may have left the family's home in compliance with legal orders to do so or at the insistence of the other parent; similarly, the risk assessment may have classified the abuse as a onetime, uncharacteristic episode unlikely to recur.

Most agencies require the primary CPS staff person to consult with his or her supervisor before arriving at a disposition to ensure that a second opinion is entered and that law, regulation, and agency protocol have been followed. Often, when the facts emerging from the investigation do not clearly point to any single disposition, the CPS agency's child abuse team will conduct a review to obtain the advantages of other experts' opinions.

Most states require that families be formally notified of the disposition reached, and many states permit the child protection agency to send the initial reporter of the suspected maltreatment at least a brief summary of the disposition and the action which CPS will take.

State legislation will expect and permit the CPS agency to arrive at a clear determination at the end of its investigation of whether child maltreatment has occurred. This determination will be based on the professional standards of social work assessment and will be used to formulate the agency's course of action; these are to be distinguished from the standards of the legal profession used to prepare cases to present in court. Because of the crucial implications of this determination, it will not be made by a single individual but by the child abuse team, a CPS agency staff team, or at least by the CPS staff contact-person in consultation with his or her supervisor.

7. Formulating Case Plans

Historically, the case plan was the central tool of child protective services, emphasizing that the major role of CPS was to provide assistance to the family within the sphere of social work services. Early in the history of CPS, the content of a case plan would have detailed proposed action relating primarily to the child. More recently, particularly in view of the "reasonable efforts" requirement of Public Law 96-272, the emphasis has been on providing services for the entire family.

Most case plans include services for the families available directly from the CPS agency. However, since more and more CPS agencies are investing the greater part of their resources in the investigative process, fewer resources are available for making social services available to families who need them. Agency staff usually do not have much time for the provision of the social services once—historically—the core of CPS work. In addition, because many CPS staff members in many jurisdictions are not trained in social work or other human services, they have not acquired the expertise needed to assist families in making significant changes in their lives. The array of services available to CPS families in most communities is limited, although case plans often routinely require such standard components as parenting education and mental health services for all families rather than individually crafted responses reflecting the assessed needs and circumstances of the individual family.

The emphasis on preparing cases for a potential court appearance and the influence of attorneys on the case plans have shifted the content of case plans. Rather than describing the path which the family and the CPS staff person will take jointly to make the family safer for the child, the typical case plan today reflects the conditions which the family will have to fulfill to retain or regain custody of their child(ren). Because the conditions in the case plan will become the determining factors of whether or not the parents have custody of the child, the family's attorney or public defender must negotiate the conditions to get the "best deal" for that family. As a result, the case plan has come to resemble a property settlement more than a reasonable outline of the steps necessary to achieve child safety and well-being.

Ideally, the case plan will emerge from a thorough, competent assessment of the family's strengths as well as of its weaknesses—the risk factors present. The plan will reflect the changes all parties think must be made both to assure the child's safety and to improve family life. The family, including children and adolescents, will have played an active role in the development of the plan case and will accept it as a way for them to make the changes they desire in their family life. The case plan will, accordingly, reflect the expectations and responsibilities of family members, of the CPS agency, and of other community agencies whose services are included in the plan.

The CPS agency's role will be primarily that of a facilitator of change rather than that of a monitor of compliance or a judge of behavior. If the agency does not have the staff time to allocate to helping the family pursue the change, or if its staff members do not have the competence, then the staff will arrange for such assistance through the services of other community agencies. The CPS agency will either make the contact itself or provide the family whatever assistance it needs to get services; in addition, CPS will make sure that the community agency has enough information (with the appropriate permission from the family) to meet the family's expectations effectively.

The terms of the case plan will be mutually acceptable, both to the agencies involved and to the family, but will be clear enough and closely related enough to the child's safety to arouse concern if they are not being fulfilled. The CPS staff will follow the progress of the family in seeking the changes agreed upon in the case plan. If the progress is not being achieved, then sufficient revision must be made in the case plan to attain the desired changes through other methods.

8. Going to Court

Although many people's perception of child protection services is that most families end up in an adversarial juvenile court proceeding, statistics indicate that is not so. Only a small proportion of families involved with CPS end up in court. In some cases, this is so CPS can obtain the court's authority to take emergency action to protect a child.

Outside emergency situations, the court has traditionally been the source of the child protection agency's authority to intervene in a family without the parents' consent. Historically this meant that CPS would ask the court to grant temporary custody of the child to the CPS agency if it was not satisfied that the family would provide adequate and safe care for the child. CPS would then place the child in foster care.

Over the past fifteen years, the authority of the court has been invoked to rule on less serious interventions. CPS might ask the court to order the parents to participate in treatment programs or take other actions which were part of the case plan but were not being followed. Ordering such treatment is less desirable of course than voluntary participation by the parents, but it is much preferable to removal of parental custody; however, the effectiveness of this intermediate approach is limited because juvenile courts in most states cannot exercise authority over the parents. Since there are no legal sanctions on parents who do not follow court orders for participation in treatment programs, such parental noncompliance often escalates into loss of child custody.

Since 1980 and the passage of Public Law 96-272, the court has assumed another role, that of monitoring the compliance of the CPS agency with the law's requirement for "reasonable efforts" to keep children with their families. The federal law requires the juvenile court (1) to conclude affirmatively that the CPS agency has taken "reasonable efforts" to avoid the need for removing a child from his or her family home before using the authority of the court to approve an out-of-home placement for the child, and (2) to review periodically the action of the CPS agency to assure that "reasonable efforts" are being taken to return foster children to their birth families.

Professional best practice would urge the child protection agency to view the juvenile court as a neutral party with the authority to assure that both the family and the agency itself are actively fulfilling their responsibilities to protect the child. The agency should not take any steps simply for the sake of building a legally more solid case if court action occurs, and families should not be threatened with a court appearance simply because they are seen as uncooperative. Agencies should make clear what measures they think are essential to assure the child's safety and should likewise insist that if the family does not take these appropriate measures the agency will seek the court's authority to achieve what is necessary to protect the child. Similarly, the agency should inform the parents not only of their own recourse to the court in a dispute but also of the agency's accountability to that same court in fulfilling CPS responsibilities.

9. Provision of Social Services

Usually child protective services agencies are not thought of as family treatment agencies, particularly in light of today's emphasis on the investigative component of child protection. Most of the CPS agency's resources are consumed in responding to initial reports of child abuse or neglect and in court time spent pursuing public custody of the children. Little time remains for CPS staff to work with the family in implementing the case plan to change how the family cares for its children. In such situations, the CPS staff members often assume the role of monitoring the extent to which the family pursues social services on its own and makes the changes prescribed in the case plan.

In a child protection agency reflecting the best practice, the provision of social services to the family will be regarded as central to the role of the agency. The agency will look to its professionally trained staff to assist the families to make the changes necessary to ensure the safety of the children. Even when the CPS staff does not have the time or the training to provide this service personally, the agency should emphasize that assisting the family in making the changes necessary to protect the child(ren) and to improve family life is one of its core roles. In such agencies, the case plan will be implemented through the clients' participation in services offered by other public or private nonprofit social service agencies. Ideally, the CPS agency would assume enough responsibility for providing these services to guarantee their availability through purchase of service contracts that would pay for services to referred CPS client families.

There is no legally prescribed or professionally accepted set of services which make up an ideal continuum or array of services which should be available to a CPS agency, either within the CPS agency itself or within the local community. Public Law 96-272 requires that "reasonable efforts" be made to avoid the unnecessary recourse to foster care, which assumes the availability of alternative services, but this legislation does not identify what service mixture would be necessary to meet the criterion of "reasonable efforts." While numerous class action lawsuits have been filed against states for failure to comply with this requirement and the settlements of those suits have indicated which services will be offered in that jurisdiction, no legal precedent has been set regarding what services are deemed reasonable enough.

A large number of national commissions and task forces established during the late 1980s and early 1990s considered this same question and concluded that although there is no monolithic set of services which should be uniformly available throughout the country, there is consensus about the principles which should guide individual communities in establishing their array of services. This general consensus was articulated during the Leadership Policy Institute conducted by the American Humane Association during the summer of 1991. The participants in this institute agreed that each community should provide a network of services that is

- community based,
- culturally relevant,
- outcome-oriented,
- coordinated,
- accessible, and
- based on family needs (8, p. 21).

And even though many commissions and task forces concurred that no single prescriptive set of services will be appropriate for every community, many of their final reports recommended that the following set of services, similar to those identified by the American Public Welfare Association's National Commission on Child Welfare and Family Preservation, become the standard in most communities:

- Home visitor program
- Prenatal care
- Parenting education
- Early childhood screening and developmental services
- Child care, including special-needs care
- Literacy and employment programs
- Recreation programs
- Case management
- Homemaker and chore services
- Comprehensive mental health services
- Drug abuse treatment programs
- Emergency shelter
- Crisis nursery
- Family preservation
- Respite care
- Foster care
- Residential treatment
- Adoption (9, pp. 11–12, 18–19, 26)

10. Out-of-Home Placement

Currently, out-of-home placement of a maltreated child—in a foster home, a group home, or a residential treatment center—is only one of the options available to a CPS agency. Emphasis during the initial assessment and development of the case plan should be on identifying the least restrictive method of protecting the child and improving family inter- actions. When a variety of services are available within the CPS agency or the community, a number of alternatives less restrictive than foster care will correspondingly be available for use as "reasonable efforts." These less restrictive alternatives will be preferred as long as expectations are good that the child will be safe and that these other services will assist the family in making the desired changes. Only when a professional assessment indicates that the child would remain in danger or that the less restrictive alternatives would not adequately effect the family changes needed will foster care be employed.

In recent years, family preservation services have been established in many states in an attempt to avoid unnecessary foster placements. These services are modeled on the Homebuilders program developed by Behavioral Sciences Institute (BSI) of Federal Way, Washington. In this model, intensive home-based services are provided to families in which one or more children have been assessed as in imminent risk of being placed in foster care. While the BSI model is not limited to preventing out-of-home placements of children be- cause of abuse or neglect, I will limit this discussion to such placements.

Each therapist in the program will work with only two families at a time in order to provide intensive services, and the services will usually be provided in the family home. Because this is a crisis intervention service, the therapist will be available twenty-four hours a day, seven days a week, but the service will be offered only for a six-week period. The purpose of this time limit is to resolve whatever crisis precipitated the perceived need for out-of-home placement, as well as to connect the family with ongoing services in another community agency.

It must be emphasized that the assessment of risk to the child should be taken as seriously in family preservation services as it is throughout the rest of the child protection system. The intent of family preservation is to enable the child to remain home *safely*. If there is truly not a reasonable expectation that the intensive services will make enough difference in the family situation to ensure the child's protection, then a foster placement is appropriate.

A well-run CPS agency will have a diverse variety of licensed foster homes available to provide temporary care for children who cannot remain safely in their parental home and for whom appropriate caregivers cannot be found among extended family or other kin. Again, foster homes will be used *only after* the agency has taken "reasonable efforts" to maintain the child safely at home and will be treated as a temporary situation pending the child's safe return home. Foster parents, extended family members, or other kin will receive from CPS the support they need to provide nurturing care for the child(ren).

Because research conclusively indicates that a child visited by parents while he or she is in foster care is much more likely to return home, such visits will be encouraged and facilitated. The foster parents will be instructed to see their role as preparing the foster child to return home; accordingly, they will be asked to assist the birth parents in improving their parenting skills and will serve as models and mentors to them both during and after the child's stay in foster care.

It cannot be emphasized too often that the use of the foster home will not be an end in itself (that is, not necessarily a final refuge for the child) but one part of the child protection system's permanency effort (10).

11. Permanency and Reunification

The theme of permanency has emerged in professional debates as the opposite of "foster care drift," the image evoked when children are transferred from one foster home to another and ultimately grow to adulthood with no close familial ties. Public Law 96-272 recognized the importance not only of making efforts to avoid unnecessary foster care but also of attempting to reunify the child with his or her family of origin as quickly and safely as possible after foster care is begun.

The CPS and foster care system should vigorously encourage family reunification efforts. As I stated earlier, the focus of the CPS staff should be on effecting whatever changes within the family are necessary, according to the case plan, for the child to return home safely. However substantial the efforts needed to significantly improve the functioning of the child's family, the threshold for returning the child to the family home should not be higher than that for removing the child from it. Mothers and fathers should not be expected to exhibit ideal parenting conduct as a condition for winning the return of their child, and the CPS expectations on the family members' interaction should not grow incrementally during the foster care period. Since services for the family will continue to be provided after the return of the child(ren), additional progress in the family's care for the child(ren) can be promoted after reunification.

12. Termination of Parental Rights and Permanency

In a limited number of situations, it is either clear at the time of child protection's initial involvement with a family or it becomes clear after repeated efforts at seeking change within the family that no alternative can be identified which will enable the child(ren) to be safe in their home. In such situations, the CPS agency petitions the juvenile court to terminate the parental rights of the child's parents. This is one of the most intrusive acts the state can take. As one child protection worker remarked at a national conference,

> "Families might be afraid of the police, because the police might arrest them. But they are really afraid of CPS, because we can take their children."

Needless to say, this termination action must not be entered into lightly. However, in egregious situations such as those often reported in the media,[1] the actions of the parent(s) are so damaging and so unlikely to change for the better that the most appropriate action CPS can take is to expeditiously pursue termination of parental rights.

When termination is sought, another form of permanency planning must be initiated. It is not uncommon today for a termination proceeding to go on for three years in court. During this time, which might be substantially the length of the young child's life, the child is in limbo. Child development research consistently finds that the greater the uncertainty of remaining with a family and the greater the number of homes in which a child lives, the greater the risk to the child's emotional development. Consequently, when termination of parental rights is pursued, a substitute family for the child must be sought, a substitute family must be identified for the child, and the child must then be established there as quickly as possible.

Traditionally, the permanency option for children whose birth parents have lost their parental rights has been adoption. Because of growing recognition of the importance to children of being with their own kin, permanent placement with members of the child's extended family has become more frequent. In some cases, this placement is through legal adoption, and the legal permanence is assured. But many families, particularly families from ethnic minorities, find legal adoption by a member of the extended family redundant and offensive. While kinship placements (that is, placements with extended family members, including those not related by blood, or with significant familial adults who are not blood related) are increasingly common and guardianships by relatives are being explored, the extent to which these alternatives will provide true permanence for children permanently separated from their parents remains to be demonstrated.

13. Case Closing

Little research has been conducted on the circumstances under which a CPS case should best be closed. Unfortunately, too often CPS agencies terminate their relationship with families for extraneous reasons. Most disturbing is the phenomenon of CPS job attrition:

---

1. For example, see the PBS *Frontline* documentary "Who Killed Adam Mann?" (Carole Langer, producer), originally broadcast on 3 December 1991.

when a CPS staff person leaves the agency or moves to another position, the majority of that staff person's cases are sometimes simply closed rather than being transferred to another worker. Similarly disturbing is the closing of cases because the assigned CPS worker has ended up spending a diminishing amount of time with the family (presumably because other client families have demanded greater attention); when the direct service time is negligible, the case is often perfunctorily closed. This decision making by default highlights the lack of criteria for determining when it is appropriate for CPS to terminate involvement with a family.

It would be more appropriate for CPS to decide affirmatively to terminate its involvement when specific, positively stated conditions are met, such as:

- The child is living with the family, the family's care of the child meets community standards (that is, if the family came to the attention of CPS, CPS would not become involved), and a professional assessment of factors associated with risk to children concludes that the child is safe insofar as can be determined
- The family refuses to participate significantly in further services, and there is no current maltreatment or other basis on which to pursue court authority for further involvement
- Parental rights have been terminated, and provision for a permanent substitute family for the child has been made

14. Aftercare

Seldom do child protection programs make provision for families to receive services from community social service agencies after the CPS case has been closed. Perhaps this stems from an assumption that the CPS agency will be active with a family until all of the changes sought by both the family and the CPS agency have been made. In view of the minuscule resources available in most CPS agencies for providing effective social services for families even in the presence of significant levels of risk of child maltreatment, such an assumption is unrealistic. Whether such a role would be appropriate for CPS agencies if resources were available remains an open question. One opinion is that CPS agencies should most appropriately offer their direct services only as long as families are in crisis and are abusing their children or only while children who have been maltreated remain in families exhibiting a high risk for further maltreatment. Another opinion suggests that CPS agencies should not limit direct services just to de-escalating the level of crisis associated with a recent incident of abuse or neglect. In this latter scenario, the role of the CPS agency would extend to working with the family to make improvements in family functioning as long as the family is willing and significant improvements for the family and child are emerging.

Both the CPS agency and community social service agencies should recognize that simply de-escalating risk does not necessarily guarantee long-term well-being for the family and child. Moreover, if services are terminated as soon as the level of imminent risk is lowered, the family pressures which occasioned the original report of abuse or neglect can easily build up again. Professional CPS experience with abusive families suggests— although no research has yet been done to validate this hypothesis—that the high rate of former CPS clients who are reported once again for child maltreatment which is then substantiated is highly correlated to this lack of aftercare services. Until CPS agencies are appropriated sufficient resources to do more than investigate reports of maltreatment, intervene in emergency situations, and offer social services to de-escalate the imminent risk of child abuse or neglect, they must rely on other community agencies to meet the remaining needs of families leaving the CPS program. These other community social service agencies in turn must use the resources allocated to them by the community to offer needed services to families whether or not the families are or have recently been active with CPS.

The final responsibility of a CPS agency to its client families is to assure their effective involvement with these other community agencies.

IV. Policy Issues

Today's practice of child protective services emerges from many factors—its history, the expectations of the community, the professional practice methods which have developed, the limitation of financial resources, legislation requiring extensive investigations of all reports of child maltreatment which are received, and the influence of the courts and of the attorneys who represent the CPS agency in the court. The cumulative impact of these factors has resulted in the child protection services we have now.

These services are critical within our society not only because of their role in protecting abused and neglected children but because in many jurisdictions they are the only child welfare services available to families. In 1988, Sheila Kamerman and Alfred Kahn reported that:

> Child protective services . . . have emerged as the dominant public child and family service, in effect "driving" the public agency and often taking over child welfare entirely. . . . Child protective services today constitute the core public child and family service, the fulcrum and sometimes, in some places, the totality of the system. (11, pp. 9–10)

The National Commission on Child Welfare and Family Preservation researched all fifty states and identified CPS as one of only three family and children's services uniformly available in every state (12). These protective services address the needs of many families and children, save many children from further abuse and neglect, and meet the expectations of many sectors of society. However, today's practice of child protective services also raises many policy questions, which I will identify and briefly explore in this section.

1. Prominence of the Governmental Role

The CAPTA legislation of 1974 assigned to public child welfare agencies the role of exploring situations of child abuse and neglect; unfortunately, this has tended to diminish the role of the rest of the community in protecting children.

Individuals who might otherwise assume greater personal responsibility for protecting children may conclude that simply reporting suspected child maltreatment to CPS absolves them of any further responsibility, particularly if the impression is given that CPS can handle the situation unilaterally. Other social service agencies, respectful of the limited financial resources available to them, defer to CPS to handle families in which child maltreatment has been substantiated.

My discussion in the previous section of CPS's main functions today indicates, I hope, that CPS does not and cannot unilaterally satisfy the needs of these families and children. Whether the resources allocated by the community to CPS should be increased for that agency to significantly expand its services to families or whether individual members of the community and other community agencies should accept again an active role in protecting children is a policy question. The preponderance of professional opinion today about how individuals and families change would suggest that neither CPS nor any other single sector of society can by itself provide the support families need to avoid child maltreatment. What role the larger community can and should play, and what collaborative relationship other community agencies should develop with CPS to serve abused and neglected children and their families continues to be debated.

2. The CPS Promise to Protect Children

During the latter part of the 1980s, the increasingly limited public funds available for family and children's services were primarily allocated to CPS. Such budget decisions were premised on the contention that an expanding CPS system would reduce or eliminate child maltreatment. Conversely, human service agencies recognized then that the password for additional resources was "child protection." Expectations mounted, and promises, at least implicitly, were made that if more funds were given to CPS, fewer children would be maltreated or die at the hands of their parents.

The assumption operating here is that a well-funded and well-managed CPS agency can assure the community that child maltreatment tragedies will not occur. When the CPS agency's risk assessment procedure is portrayed as a good predictor of future parental behavior, this assumption is strengthened. When a maltreatment tragedy does occur, the community assumes, understandably, that CPS has failed, that someone must be blamed, and that additional funds must be allocated to CPS.

We must acknowledge that some of the most egregious child abuse tragedies that have been widely reported would most likely have been avoided had CPS staff—or other members of the community—indeed fulfilled reasonable expectations about protecting the victimized children. Such tragedies cannot be discounted as the "margin of error" inherent in organizations. However, the converse is not true. A well-run and well-funded CPS agency, while presumably reducing the incidence of child abuse and neglect, cannot eliminate all such tragedies. The policy questions remain open about what expectations of the CPS system actually are reasonable and what further provisions a caring community should make for its children.

3. Allocation of CPS Resources

Since the initiation of mandatory reporting of child abuse, the states uniformly have seen a geometric growth in the number of reports received. Particularly since 1985, the number of reports received has been escalating annually.

Because few states permit cases to be screened out on the basis of the content of the report itself, most of these cases are fully investigated, which consumes an increasingly large percentage of the resources available for CPS. It is interesting to review the policy and procedure manuals of a child protection agency and compare the specificity of the prescribed requirements for the early stages of the agency's process with those prescribed for the later stages. Detailed time lines, procedures, and criteria are prescribed for receiving reports, investigating, and for reaching dispositions. But little comparable detail is prescribed for providing ongoing services or for assuring that families receive the ongoing aftercare required when the CPS case is formally closed. Because the prescribed procedures are legislatively established or are under regulation, administrative sanctions can be imposed on agencies if the procedures are not followed strictly. If a maltreatment tragedy occurs in a case under CPS management and a statutory or regulatory requirement has not been fulfilled, the assigned CPS staff person faces the possibility of disciplinary personnel or legal action. These mandates attached to the early part of the CPS process assure that when the staff and financial resources available are insufficient for all CPS functions, the taking of reports and conducting of investigations will receive a substantially higher percentage of the resources.

The amount of time CPS staff members spend in court and on court-related activities also consumes a large percentage of CPS resources. CPS is forced to rely on the court because it may be the only source of the legal authority needed to protect the child. The legal procedures attendant on court action require large amounts of CPS staff time for case preparation and for consultation with legal staff. Court schedules are often so overloaded that CPS workers wait hours for their scheduled appearance. And, of course, the demands of court activities further reduce the time available for providing direct services to the families active with the CPS agency.

The cumulative impact is that few CPS resources are available to the very families in which child abuse or neglect has been substantiated and for which ongoing services are vitally necessary to protect the child.

This raises what is perhaps the major policy issue facing child protective services today. This system was created to protect children and emerged from the social work field with its emphasis on assisting families and individuals in seeking changes in their lives. Public Law 96-272 requires that CPS agencies make "reasonable efforts" to enable children to live safely with their families. The case plans that CPS develops with the families identify the services which are intended to precipitate the changes necessary for the child's well-being, including the CPS agency's obligations to actually provide those services. The public certainly expects that the CPS agency will provide social services to assist its client families. But with the intensive channeling of resources into receiving reports, investigating them, and going to court, few resources are committed to direct services for families and children.

Since 1990, yet another force has provided impetus to CPS's investing the bulk of its resources in receiving reports and investigating. Advocates for children have increasingly been employing the strategy of bringing class-action lawsuits against CPS agencies for failure to insure constitutional protections for children. The settlements of these suits usually include provisions to assure that the defendant agency will follow its own policies and procedures, and may even include increased funding to make this possible. Insofar as these suits focus on the prescribed actions of report taking and investigating—as contrasted with the providing of direct services and making "reasonable efforts" at avoiding unnecessary foster care—they further exacerbate this dilemma.

A major redirection of policy to resolve the biggest problems in today's practice would best include such changes as:

- The CPS agency would emphasize assessment of whether a child has been maltreated, whether indication exists that immediate protection from the parents is necessary, and whether any of the social services available can be of benefit in improving the family and child's well-being and in reducing the likelihood of further abuse.
- Reports received about parental behavior which would not be considered maltreatment would not be investigated, that is, the CPS agency would take the report at face value and would not search for unreported maltreatment.
- The collection of evidence for court appearances, particularly criminal court, would be left to law enforcement.
- Greater emphasis would be placed on allocating resources for services to assist families in making changes in how they raise their children.

4. Racial and Cultural Issues

A major issue which must be addressed within the entire child protection system is the overrepresentation of families of color among CPS clients. First, the system must consider why this overrepresentation is so prevalent throughout the country. Some critics of the child protection system would argue that CPS is another manifestation of society's institutional racism and is actively fostering the deterioration of the family in communities of color. Similarly, some critics charge that CPS agencies use a middle-class Eurocentric norm of raising children and contend that the high representation of children of color within CPS results from risk-assessment tools which do not recognize legitimate cultural child-rearing differences. A different line of thought suggests that the stresses of poverty lead to physical child abuse, that poverty contributes greatly to child neglect, and that it is the high correlation of poverty and families of color which leads to the high representation of these families within the general CPS population (see chapters 2 and 3).

In addition to addressing the overrepresentation of families of color entering the CPS system, agencies must seek to become increasingly culturally competent in their service delivery (see chapter 2). Cultural competence is not a yes-or-no issue; it is, rather, the process of an agency becoming increasingly better able to meet appropriately the needs of families from diverse cultural backgrounds. This includes making certain that CPS staff have the knowledge and appreciation of criteria needed to identify cultural differences among the many various families in communities and that CPS staff respect, value, and reinforce the positive traditional child-rearing practices of these communities. Provision must also be made for assuring that the assessment of family child-rearing practices is culturally appropriate; hence CPS agencies are increasingly turning to the elders and other leaders in these communities for such assistance. Finally, in working with families, CPS agencies must consider and treat as family all of the persons perceived by the child as family members. In efforts to support families' efforts to safely keep their children at home, services should accordingly be extended to individuals who broadly constitute "the family." This, of course, includes legally recognized members of the extended family but also persons with a familial relationship that is not by blood or by recognized legal ties.

The need for children to live with family and within their own cultural community has become an increasingly high priority within communities of color. In 1978, Congress passed the Indian Child Welfare Act, which gives tribes the prerogative to care for Native American Indian children who cannot live with their parents: this assures that these children have the opportunity to be raised within their tribal community. Some states have passed similar legislation assuring children certain rights of being raised within their racial or ethnic community if they cannot live with their parents.

5. Poverty-Related Neglect

The high representation in CPS agencies of children living in poverty must similarly be addressed as a policy issue. The CPS system was not developed as a societal response to poverty, but CPS is increasingly playing that role. CPS agencies (as well as other agencies that provide family support services to help families avoid foster placement of their children) often end up assisting families in obtaining safe and affordable housing, food, clothing, transportation, and/or medical care as elements necessary for the prevention of child abuse or neglect. While this activity is definitely preferable to placing the child in foster care because of the lack of these necessities in the child's own home, families should not have to access them through the CPS system. The CPS agency should be concentrating its resources on protecting children from maltreatment rather than from poverty.

Until welfare reform and other societal efforts aimed at income support are successful, the policy issue here remains whether community-based family support agencies will meet the poverty-related needs of families or whether low-income families will also be forced to be officially identified as neglectful of their children just to receive basic human needs.

V. Practice Issues

A review of today's practice of child protection services highlights the strengths, the shortcomings, and some thorny issues seeking resolution. In the section above, I presented a number of policy issues which must be addressed by elected officials responsible for the CPS system and by the executives responsible for setting policy within the system. A number of additional issues arise in the arena of social work practice that must be addressed by the clinical professionals who deliver child protective services.

1. Ability to Predict Risk

When risk assessment tools were first developed, they provided a methodology for systematically assuring that all aspects of a child's family situation were considered when a report of abuse or neglect was being investigated. Research continues to identify factors which correlate highly with child abuse and neglect.

Other professions—psychiatry, economics, law enforcement, for instance—recognize that they cannot predict the future, particularly human behavior. Similarly, CPS professionals must affirmatively state that they can neither predict the future nor guarantee the future safety of a child. CPS professionals must limit their use of risk assessment tools to their intended uses, that is, the systematic assurance of comprehensive assessments and the identification of aspects of family life which should be the focus of social services case plans.

2. Interaction with Other Systems

Child protection services is a specialized service (1, p. 23) which plays a significant role within our society. But, as is true with most other specialized professions, CPS cannot function effectively apart from other systems designed to support families and children. CPS alone cannot identify all of the children at risk of maltreatment, so reporting of suspected abuse and neglect by other professions is necessary. CPS alone cannot determine whether reported children have been the victims of maltreatment, so law enforcement personnel and psychologists are needed. CPS alone cannot provide the protections which abused and neglected children need, so the police and courts are necessary. CPS alone cannot improve family functioning to eliminate the factors associated with child maltreatment and to improve the well-being of children, so other family and children's social service agencies are needed.

All communities offer, at least at some level, some of these other systems. The best CPS staff have learned to work with these systems to serve their clients better, but often this cooperation and collaboration is not systematically reinforced within the CPS agency. The professional culture within a well-run CPS agency recognizes that CPS best fulfills its role when it functions as part of a community system of care designed to meet the needs of families comprehensively and effectively. The interrelationships within such a system are best identified through written interagency agreements which clarify mutual expectations and responsibilities.

To make this formal agreement operational, staff within each agency must understand the roles of staff in other agencies, view other staff with mutual respect, and be willing to negotiate legitimate professional differences to assure appropriate and effective services for families. Many communities have found that offering joint training for staff from different agencies on the implications of the interagency agreements is a productive method (5, p. 34) to assure mutual understanding of roles, to encourage the trust which comes from personal interaction, and to overcome the barriers which are often raised by formal and impersonal interactions between staffs.

3. Uniformity of Intervention in Various Kinds of Child Maltreatment

Child abuse reporting statutes ordinarily include a variety of intrafamilial child maltreatment—physical abuse, sexual abuse, neglect, and emotional maltreatment. Certain other forms of maltreatment, such as abuse by adults outside the family (1, pp. 23, 29, 24), should be dealt with by law enforcement or licensing agencies. While the four forms of intrafamilial maltreatment are consistently included within the responsibility of CPS and while most legislation and policy does not differentiate among them, practitioners are increasingly recognizing the differences which exist among these kinds of maltreatment.

For example, when emotional abuse was first treated as a CPS issue, agencies would take action based on the negative impact clinicians predicted such abuse would have on the child in the future. Because of the difficulty in determining what parental behavior might lead to children's future emotional problems, present-day CPS agencies ordinarily deal with cases of emotional abuse only when identifiable negative effects are already occurring in the child's life (13, pp. 45–49).

Similarly, as child sexual abuse became more prominent among the maltreatment reports to CPS agencies, specialized procedures as described above (see also chapter 12) were developed in response to this newly emerging practice issue.

Two additional contemporary examples can be identified of differences among the kinds of maltreatment which are within the purview of CPS but for which pertinent CPS practices have not yet been devised. The first example is child neglect within poor families in which the parents willingly accept—and may actually have sought—the assistance of CPS in obtaining the necessities the child needs. The dynamics of such families are very different from those of a wealthy family that denies a child basic needs. Perhaps such cases should not be handled within the CPS system at all (a point I raised earlier), but until that policy issue is resolved, these families will be clients of CPS. CPS practitioners might well explore whether the needs of these families are best met by the standard (and in many cases prescribed) CPS procedures or whether directly assisting the families in obtaining the basic necessities would not be a more appropriate and more effective response. If the latter alternative became the standard CPS response, families would have their needs met without the cost or intrusiveness of an investigation and a disposition of substantiated child maltreatment.

The second example is the broader issue of responding to any physical child abuse or neglect that occurs within a family living in poverty. Statistics indicate that these forms of maltreatment occur, or at least are reported, more frequently within poor families than more prosperous ones. Many researchers conclude therefore that it is the lack of necessities and the stress which comes with poverty which usually lead to these forms of child maltreatment. CPS practitioners might well explore whether a different service strategy or perhaps a totally separate response to poor families is appropriate. The community development efforts currently funded by some national foundations as a means of improving the well-being of children without reliance on the child protection system suggest the type of alternative practice which might be more effective.

VI. Today's CPS Dilemma

Today's child protection practice is a viable one, although significantly different from the early days of such practice. Although the CPS family situations most frequently brought to public attention reflect tragedy and often portray mismanagement and malpractice, many families are positively assisted and many children are protected by CPS agencies. However, the focus of CPS has been shifting from providing services to assist families in making changes to protect and improve the well-being of their children to the investigation of reports to determine what level of abuse the reported child may have experienced. If this trend continues, the provision of social services will be minimally practiced, despite the fact that the training of staff still reflects a social service tradition. Conversely, the concentration on determining what happened to the child will intensify, with investigations conducted by CPS staff, who do not have the professional background that trained investigators do. If this emphasis on investigation leads primarily to interventions which are punitive or sanctioning—as contrasted with assessments which lead to service plans to assist families in seeking changes which they also want—CPS will be an even less desirable option for families than it is now.

The dilemma which CPS faces today is whether to reemphasize its social work tradition and become a family service agency once again or to continue its current emphasis on investigation and become a public safety agent.

If the former option is followed, reports will be seen as indicators of families potentially in need of services to protect the children from abuse or neglect. The reports will be explored to determine whether the children need immediate protection, but the extensive assessment will mainly seek to identify aspects of family life which are problematic and will have to be resolved to protect the child(ren) and to increase their well-being. Staff time will be spent with the families themselves, assisting them in effecting the changes which staff and family mutually determined as appropriate and making connections between the family and other community supports which the family will need in parenting their children. The CPS agency will still seek court action in the rare instance in which the family cannot or will not provide a safe environment for the child, but even in such situations the focus of the CPS agency will be to assure that the child becomes a permanent member of a substitute family as quickly as possible.

If the dilemma of CPS is resolved in the direction of the latter option, reports will be analogous to accusations and will be investigated to establish whether or not wrongdoing occurred. If no wrongdoing is found, no intervention will be initiated. However, if wrongdoing is found, the CPS response will focus on determining the appropriate sanction, including temporary or permanent removal of the child. In consequence, court action to impose such sanction will be the primary intervention. The primary consideration for the child will be deciding where she or he should live, that is, with the parent(s) or with another caregiver, either temporarily or permanently.

If the latter scenario comes true, which is likely in the absence of conscious actions on the part of policy makers and practitioners to reverse current trends, CPS will be abandoning its historical role in society and shifting into the realm of public safety. Should this occur, the role of helping families to make changes to protect children and to improve their well-being and the role of assuring that children have the safest, most familial, most stable, and most nurturing environment feasible will have to be assigned to another sector of society.

An extremely promising resolution to this dilemma has been emerging in a number of states since 1993. In that year, the Florida legislature passed legislation (Florida Statutes, Part 3, Chapter 415) enabling the state's child protection program to launch a state Family Response System. This legislation recognizes that neither of the options presented above is appropriate for all reports received by the public agency; consequently, the legislation creates a multiple response system. Under such a system, the agency has the responsibility for creating the capacity to provide families with either of the above options (identified in the Florida legislation as either an "assessment" or an "investigation"), and the agency has the authority to determine which option is the most appropriate for each abuse or neglect report received.

This policy has been followed and enhanced by a number of states, including Missouri, Iowa, North Dakota, South Dakota, and Virginia, and additional states are considering such legislation. The most optimistic outcome of this emerging trend would be that each state's child protection program will have the capacity for multiple responses to the child abuse reports it receives. These responses should include at least:

1. *Diversion* to community agencies of reports which can best be handled by organizations other than the child protection agency. The situations included here would most often be inadequate housing, educational neglect, and single incidences of minor neglect which occurred within socially isolated or low-income families. Such diversions must be cooperative ventures between the child protection agency and the community organization.

2. *Preventive services* for families and children, which would begin with a full assessment of the family environment within which the reported abuse occurred and would lead to the provision of the services and supports which are expected to most effectively prevent any further abuse or neglect. This response correlates highly with the social work tradition of child protection.

3. *Authoritative intervention* emphasizing the immediate safety of children, including an intensive investigation of the reported incidents and usually including extensive involvement of law enforcement and the courts. This response correlates highly with the investigative trends developed over the past decade and a half and would be appropriate for the most egregious reports received.

As this recent policy trend toward multiple response systems unfolds, we can see the promise of states and communities being able to avoid trying to resolve the dilemma by choosing only one option, either of which would necessarily be appropriate for only some of the child abuse and neglect which is occurring. By establishing a child protection agency with the capacity to offer more than one response and to work in collaboration with other community agencies, this emerging policy trend has the promise of enabling each community to respond differentially to the wide variety of abuse and neglect reports being received, selecting the response with the greatest likelihood of protecting each child from future abuse or neglect. Insofar as this trend realizes its potential, the best aspects of the long-term history of child protection efforts and the most positive effects of the factors emerging during recent years will be brought together optimally to prevent child abuse.

References

1. National Association of Public Child Welfare Administrators, ed. 1988. *Guidelines for a Model System of Protective Services for Abused and Neglected Children and Their Families.* Washington, D.C.: NAPCWA.
2. Child Welfare League of America. 1989. *Standards for Service for Abused or Neglected Children and Their Families.* Washington, D.C.: Child Welfare League of America.
3. Council on the Accreditation of Services for Families and Children. 1994. *Standards for Agency Management and Service Delivery.* New York: Council on the Accreditation of Services for Families and Children.
4. Harris, Norma J. 1988. Child Protective Services Risk Assessment. In *Guidelines for a Model System of Protective Services for Abused and Neglected Children and Their Families,* ed. National Association of Public Child Welfare Administrators. Washington, D.C.: NAPCWA.
5. Besharov, D. J. 1990. *Combating Child Abuse: Guidelines for Cooperation between Law Enforcement and Child Protective Services.* Washington, D.C.: AEI Press.
6. Weber, M. W. 1988. Child Protective Services Protocol for Inter-Agency Relationships. In *Guidelines for a Model System of Protective Services for Abused and Neglected Children and Their Families,* ed. National Association of Public Child Welfare Administrators. Washington, D.C.: NAPCWA.
7. Motz, J. 1991. *Colorado Guidelines for Cooperation between Law Enforcement and Child Protective Services.* Denver: Colorado Department of Social Services.
8. Leadership Policy Institute. 1991. Working toward an Agenda for Change. *Protecting Children* 8(2):21.
9. National Commission on Child Welfare and Family Preservation. 1990. *A Commitment to Change.* Washington, D.C.: American Public Welfare Association.
10. National Commission on Foster Care. 1991. *A Blueprint for Fostering Infants, Children, and Youths in the 1990s.* Washington, D.C.: Child Welfare League of America.
11. Kamerman, S. B., and Kahn, A. J. 1989. *Social Services for Children, Youth, and Families in the United States.* Greenwich, Conn.: Annie E. Casey Foundation.
12. National Commission on Child Welfare and Family Preservation. 1990. *Factbook on Public Child Welfare Services and Staff.* Washington, D.C.: American Public Welfare Association.
13. Baily, W. H. 1988. Defining Emotional Maltreatment in Child Protective Services. In *Guidelines for a Model System of Protective Services for Abused and Neglected Children and Their Families,* ed. National Association of Public Child Welfare Administrators. Washington, D.C.: NAPCWA.

8

Family Assessment

ELIZABETH A. W. SEAGULL

The family assessment seeks information which will help to answer the following kinds of questions:

1. Was this child maltreated?
2. If so, by whom?
3. Did harm come to the child as a result of neglect or inadequate supervision?
4. Are parents or guardians capable of understanding and controlling the potentially harmful behavior of abusive persons (including themselves) in the child's environment?
5. Are the adults involved willing to take responsibility for making changes to provide a safe environment for the child?
6. What factors in the child, parents, family interaction, and social environment may have contributed to maltreatment?
7. Can the child's situation be improved by the implementation of a treatment plan targeted to these factors?
8. What is the likely prognosis for improvement within a reasonable period of time?
9. Does the child need to be temporarily placed outside the home?
10. Should a recommendation be made to petition the court for permanent termination of parental rights?

Benefits of a Team Approach

Professionals working in child protection must be aware of the limits of their knowledge and the benefits of coordinating their assessments with those of other professionals. In the most complex cases of child maltreatment, families may be referred to a multidisciplinary child protection team for assessment. This chapter presents the perspective of working with such a team.

When child maltreatment cases are complex, they may be too multifaceted for any one professional discipline to handle competently alone. Medical evaluation is critical for determining whether the nature of injuries is diagnostic of physical abuse. The child protec-

ELIZABETH A. W. SEAGULL, Ph.D., is a pediatric psychologist and professor in the Department of Pediatrics and Human Development, College of Human Medicine, Michigan State University.

tion worker's evaluation of the home is key for understanding the safety and adequacy of the environment. Psychological testing or psychiatric evaluation of parents may be of decisive importance in those cases in which a parent is significantly cognitively limited or has a major mental disorder. And the sensitive, nonleading interview of the child which results in disclosure of sexual maltreatment may be crucial in the absence of physical findings. Team members must maintain a high level of communication and develop a secure sense of trust in one another's skills and judgment.

Ideally, teams meet together on a regular basis both to consider new referrals and to discuss assessments in progress. With new referrals the focus of the discussion is on generating initial hypotheses and developing a plan for conducting the assessment, based on available information. Following a joint introductory meeting with the family, the team may separate family members and conduct several parts of the assessment simultaneously. The team then reconvenes to discuss findings while the assessment is still in progress, to refine hypotheses and to decide what further information is needed. With this approach, no two assessments are alike; each is tailored to the questions posed by the reasons for referral and the clinical findings in the case.

Mutual Support and Respect among Team Members

Dealing with severely dysfunctional families places a great deal of personal stress on the professionals involved in assessment teams (1). Such families frequently elicit anger, blame, and a sense of helplessness or hopelessness. Often they are uncannily successful in getting the "helpers" to fight with each other. Because of these families' provocative characteristics, team members must be alert to the possibility of "splitting" within the team and make a special effort to offer support, understanding, and acceptance to one another. Maintaining our self-awareness when families attempt to split the team can be diagnostically very helpful. How does it feel to be in the room with this family? What about them is making us feel so frustrated? How can understanding our own responses help us to understand the problems outlined by the referring professional? At its best, the team should not only offer competent professional help to the referring person and the family but also serve as a haven of trusted friends and colleagues amid the emotionally draining demands of work with abusive families.

When genuine respect for the competence of others pervades the team's interactions, asking for help, sharing feelings, and presenting work openly results in spontaneous teaching and learning which strengthens the expertise of the entire group. Mutual respect among team members also facilitates open discussion of overlapping roles. Over time, each team member should seek to learn some of the skills of the other members to increase individual skills and role flexibility on the team.

Acceptance of Families

In the context of child abuse and neglect, a discussion of acceptance may seem strange, since the main function of the assessment is to make judgments about the family. Professionals working in child protection make a clear and explicit value judgment that the protection of children is an overriding value which has greater weight than family privacy or people's right to rear their children according to their own philosophy. How can judgment be reconciled with acceptance?

Distinguishing between feelings and actions allows team members to accept even those parents who have treated their children in ways which provoke feelings of outrage, depression or disgust. This is analogous to what we ask of abusive parents in treatment: to learn that feelings are not the same as actions, and to accept feelings while changing actions (2, pp. 54–58). Professionals must learn to accept the imperfect adult as a person who, although troubled, is a valuable human being with potential for change. This open attitude is possible even when the abuser's potential for change is slight. The concept of "damaged parents"—human beings severely damaged by their childhood experiences—advanced by Polansky et al. (3) may help professionals to accept maltreating parents as valuable persons, in spite of strong negative feelings about their harmful actions.

Ethical Issues

Given the often adversarial circumstances surrounding the assessment of families referred for suspected child abuse or neglect, questions arise as to how the ethical professional should behave. Two of the foremost ethical principles of professional practice are the patient's right to give informed consent before participating either in research or in clinical activity and the patient's right to confidentiality (4, 5). Obtaining informed consent for the family assessment rarely presents a problem among those who appear for the evaluation. Families (or individual family members) who refuse consent do so simply by not showing up. If a family keeps the initial appointment, they usually cooperate with the assessment process and, within the limits of their capabilities, keep return appointments.

Teams should routinely provide information to families about the limits of confidentiality to ensure that it is not inadvertently overlooked. In addition, the referring person may be asked to come with the family to the first appointment. The team, the referring professional, and the entire family can then meet together to go over the purpose of the assessment, what the family can expect of the team, what the team expects from the family, how the assessment will be paid for, and with whom findings will be shared. At this meeting it is a good idea to ask the parents to give their children permission to tell team members the truth during the assessment. The family must be told explicitly that the findings of the team are *not* confidential but will be shared in a report, as well as verbally, with the referring person and, in some circumstances, with attorneys, court officials, and other professionals.

Family members should be encouraged to ask questions and to raise issues of concern to them. For example, if the parents believe that one of their children is "hyper," and therefore impossible to control without harsh physical discipline, the team may decide to include an evaluation of the child's hyperactivity in the assessment. This kind of exchange helps families feel that the assessment is going to meet their needs, which accordingly promotes their sense of active and committed involvement, or "ownership" of the process.

Occasionally, families are unsure about the legal ramifications of the assessment process. If this issue is raised, encourage them to contact their attorney before proceeding with the assessment. At the family's request, team members can speak with the family's attorney to explain the assessment process. Although most attorneys advise families to cooperate with the assessment team's efforts, openness with families from the outset conveys the team's respect for them and their needs. In addition, it enables some families to feel a greater sense of control and participation in the decision making.

At the conclusion of the assessment, the team, the referring person, and any other professionals involved with the family may meet to review the case. Data collected are shared and potential recommendations discussed. The goal of this meeting is to develop a consensus of all professionals working with the family as to what interventions are most appropriate. The family should be informed beforehand that such a meeting will take place, and their written consent should be sought if written documentation is to be exchanged between professionals. Although written consent is not a legal necessity in cases of suspected child maltreatment, asking the parents to give this consent is respectful of their rights as parents. Parents almost always give such consent quite willingly once the need for interprofessional communication has been explained to them.

The final step in the assessment process is the feedback session. Team members meet with the family once again and present their findings and recommendations. Although these sessions are often stressful for professionals as well as for the families, they represent the most ethical way to conclude the assessment process. The family has a right to hear the team's conclusions directly from team members rather than through a third party.

Feedback sessions allow families to vent their anger, to cry, to ask questions, to challenge findings, or to agree with the team's conclusions and begin to move toward treatment. Although I have worked with this violence-prone population for over twenty years, my team has never experienced a violent incident during or as a result of a feedback session. This strengthens our conviction that such direct feedback to families not only is ethically necessary but also is likely to reduce their violent reactions to painful information. When families can express their feelings in words to people who listen and understand, the need to express feelings through violent actions disappears.

The Co-Occurrence of Various Types of Maltreatment

Several types of maltreatment are often found within the same family (6). Physical abuse, for example, is common in neglectful families. In some families, one child may be sexually abused while another is physically abused. Spouse abuse often occurs and is witnessed by children in violent families. Many children are victims of multiple types of maltreatment, and all abused children have experienced emotional maltreatment as a component of their abuse (7). When one form of maltreatment is present in a family, the possibility that other forms exist within that family should be kept clearly in mind as the assessment proceeds.

Research studies often mix children with different types of maltreatment, particularly physical abuse and neglect, within the same sample. In the text which follows, categories of maltreatment are not neatly separated. I do, however, include a separate section on interviewing in cases of suspected sexual abuse.

Assessment of the Child

Team members who conduct the medical portion of the assessment have the greatest responsibility for determining whether physical abuse has occurred (see chapters 9–12, 16, and 18). In addition to considering whether or not a particular injury represents abuse, team members should also give great weight to the nature and severity of the child's injury and to the child's age in evaluating the child's level of safety in the home. Children with more severe injuries are less safe, because severe injuries indicate that the perpetrator was seriously out of control when the injuries were inflicted. Such a situation poses a grave risk for re-abuse that could cause permanent disability or death. Bizarre injuries may be indicative of a seriously mentally disturbed perpetrator whose future behavior toward the child may be dangerously unpredictable. Younger children are potentially less safe if they are returned home after an initial incident of abuse, because they are physically more fragile and developmentally less able to protect themselves by leaving a dangerous situation or asking for help.

The psychosocial assessments of the child and the family create a context within which the information gained from the medical assessment can be more fully comprehended. When medical findings are equivocal or absent, as happens most often in cases of suspected sexual abuse, the psychosocial assessments of the child and family assume even greater importance.

After first considering general issues in the assessment of children who have experienced all types of maltreatment, I will then present issues specific to the assessment of child sexual abuse.

Assessing Development

Maltreated children often manifest deficits in social, emotional, cognitive, and language development, most of which have resulted from, and some of which may have contributed to, their abuse (8, 9). A child with serious deficits in development may be less safe than a developmentally normal child of the same age, both because developmentally disabled children are less able to protect themselves (thus evoking the plight of younger children mentioned in the previous section) and because developmentally disabled children can be more difficult to care for, thus placing them at increased risk of abuse (10, 11). Consequently, assessing the child's development helps team members document the effects of maltreatment, particularly their range and severity, and formulate a treatment plan that will adequately address the child's needs. Siblings who live in the home should also be assessed, as part of the family assessment. Although in some cases one child is singled out as the "family scapegoat" (12), it is more often the case that if one child is mistreated, all are mistreated, though perhaps in different ways. This is especially true in neglectful families, as the standard of living of the entire family is often quite low (3).

For infants and young children, the latest revision of the Denver Developmental Screening Test (Denver II) is a useful tool for documenting the child's developmental level (13). This is a screening instrument, not a psychological test, and can be performed by the team's pediatrician or pediatric nurse-practitioner. If further assessment is indicated, the team's psychologist can follow up with more detailed testing. Deficits in language development are frequently found in children from abusive and neglectful environments and should be carefully documented (14–16).

Drawing materials can be used to put the school-age child at ease during the assessment interview. In addition to providing a rich source of data regarding affective issues, the child's drawings, combined with parental report and direct observation of the child's conversational level, enable an initial determination of the child's developmental level. A decision can then be made as to the need for a more formal cognitive assessment.

The school should be contacted as a part of the assessment of the school-age child, as it is an important source of information about the child's peer relationships and relationships to authority figures, as well as his or her academic performance. In addition to impaired cognitive performance (8), abused and neglected children tend to have more problematic peer relationships than nonmaltreated children. Heightened aggressiveness, lower prosocial behavior, less positive affect, and more social withdrawal have all been documented as occurring with increased frequency among maltreated children (8, 17–20).

An easily overlooked but quite helpful item of information from the school is the child's attendance record. Failure to send children to school on a consistent basis is a common feature of disorganized, neglectful families (21, 22). Abuse is sometimes another reason for poor school attendance. Some families hold a child out of school when episodes of physical abuse leave noticeable marks; most parents know the school will question the presence of unusual bruises or burns on a child.

The school is also an important source of information about an adolescent's cognitive and social development. Since sexual abuse is possibly the most common form of abuse suffered by adolescents, their social and emotional development is especially likely to be impaired (23–25). A drop in school achievement is sometimes seen following the onset of sexual abuse. School failure in maltreated adolescents may stem from problems in motivation and concentration or cumulative cognitive delays when severe or ongoing neglect and abuse has occurred.

Interviewing the Child

The interview of a possibly maltreated child must be tailored to the child's age and the questions which the assessment is intended to answer (in the following section I will discuss specific interviewing guidelines for suspected sexual abuse). Interviews should be conducted in a private setting, out of sight and hearing of parents, relatives, or uninvolved bystanders (such as hospital roommates) in order to increase the child's feelings of safety. In many cases, the child's behavior during the interview is just as or even more revealing than what the child says, so careful observation throughout is important. With preschool children, interviewers may need to devote a good deal of time to playing and building rapport before they can productively introduce more specific questions.

Open-ended questions which yield a general picture of the child's life and interests can be used to establish rapport and may elicit problem areas which need closer scrutiny. General questions also serve as a bridge to the specific referral problem. Asking how a typical day is spent is a useful way to begin. Younger children, however, are less able to respond to open-ended questions, which obviously limits their usefulness with children of preschool age (26). With younger children questions must be concrete: Who lives at your house? Who puts you to bed? What did you eat for breakfast today? Answers to such questions give important clues about the amount of supervision and care the child receives and the presence or absence of the necessities of daily living. Team members combine information from the child with other information (from parents, physical findings, and other sources) to get a picture of the nature and severity of the abuse or neglect.

Children should be questioned about methods of discipline used in their home. Most physically abusive parents view their actions as physical discipline, a necessary part of proper child rearing (27). Ask the child what rules the children must obey and what chores they are expected to perform at home. This gives an idea of whether the household is chaotic (no rules, no routine) or whether expectations are unrealistic (for example, a seven-year-old placed in complete charge of two younger siblings while her parents are away from home). Discussing household rules and routines leads naturally to asking about what happens when rules are broken or chores left undone. If the child does not mention physical punishment as a possible consequence, put the question directly (for instance, "What about spanking?"). This can in turn lead to inquiring about the specifics of the method of spanking (What objects are used to hit the child? What body parts are hit? and so forth). As the interviewer conveys an attitude of acceptance and understanding and listens openly to whatever the child says, most children are able to tell him or her about physical abuse, even if they are initially reluctant because they fear the consequences of telling. Keep in mind that children can be quite attached even to abusive parents; encourage the child to express his or her positive feelings about the parent while at the same time helping the child to own his or her negative feelings about the abuse (28, pp. 17–20).

Older school-age children and adolescents are often easier to interview than younger children. Once they feel safe, they may find it a relief to talk with a sympathetic, skilled interviewer.

With children and adolescents who find it too difficult to talk directly with the interviewer, we may find projective techniques useful for identifying major areas of concern in interpersonal relationships, affective themes, and positive and negative fantasies. Of special importance in the assessment of abuse is discerning whether the child sees any interpersonal relationships as positive and nonexploitative (that is, relationships in which the adult meets the child's needs, rather than vice versa) and whether the adolescent shows an understanding of effective strategies for solving interpersonal problems.

Interviewing for Suspected Sexual Abuse

When sexual abuse is suspected, the interview of the child assumes greater importance than in cases of physical abuse and neglect, in which medical evidence generally plays a more prominent role. Sexual abuse is often reported well after the abusive events have taken place and frequently consists of behaviors that leave no visible signs, such as fondling and oral-genital contact. Despite increasingly sophisticated methods of diagnosing sexual abuse on the basis of physical examination and laboratory findings, the history given by the child remains crucial in determining whether sexual abuse has occurred (29).

The importance of contact between professionals to coordinate the interview and minimize the need for repeated interviewing is emphasized in other chapters (see chapters 5–7, 12, 21, and 26). The use of two people allows one to serve as the main interviewer and the second to take notes. The second professional can also be invited to ask additional questions at the close of the interview. Professionals selected for the role of interviewer should be familiar enough with developmental differences in language and cognition so that they do not misinterpret children or use age-inappropriate language which will confuse the child (30). Video- or audio-taping the interview allows multiple professionals access to its contents.

In preparation for conducting the interview, it may be helpful to obtain a detailed history from the adults who know the child well. As with all cases of abuse, keep in mind that these adults may have a motive to fabricate, exaggerate, minimize, or otherwise distort some aspects of the history. In addition to obtaining information about the specific verbalizations and behaviors which have led to the suspicion of sexual abuse, the names and nicknames of members of the household—including pets, friends, and baby-sitters—should be obtained, as children often use names in giving narrative accounts without explaining who the people are. The child's names for private body parts should also be obtained from parents or others who know the child well. Maximum familiarity with the child's social context and verbal labels will improve the interviewer's ability to follow the child's account. Inquire extensively about what forms of sex education the child has had, if any—including abuse prevention programs in preschool or school and other sources of exposure to sexual information, such as explicit movies, pornographic print materials, and intimate sexual behavior between adults. Find out where everyone in the household sleeps.

Interviews of children in cases of suspected sexual abuse have been the object of increasing criticism in recent years; this has resulted in closer scrutiny of interviewing technique. Sophisticated research on the validity of children's testimony is now available and has led to the development of better interviewing techniques in cases of suspected child sexual abuse (26).

Even very young children are surprisingly accurate in the accounts they give of events which they have personally experienced, especially when they are instructed to tell only "what really happened." The younger the child, however, the briefer and less complete the account will be. Younger children need more support from the interviewer, in the form of specific questions, to increase the amount of information they provide. Specific questioning by an adult increases the accuracy of the child's account, since the great majority of errors children make in recalling events are errors of omission rather than commission (26). In a clinical situation this presents the challenge of questioning the child sufficiently to bring out all the pertinent information the child can recall without inadvertently contaminating the child's story by introducing material which may lead the child to fabricate an answer in order to satisfy the perceived demands of the adult interviewer.

The Step-Wise Interview technique has been developed to solve this problem. It combines current knowledge of child development with memory techniques to help the child, without being leading or suggestive, to recall a maximum amount of information (26). The interview begins with rapport-building activities, for example, drawing and discussing neutral topics (such as school). During this phase, the child is asked to describe two specific past experiences—such as a birthday party, school outing, or going trick-or-treating at Halloween—which are memorable but have nothing to do with the allegations of abuse; details of these experiences must be obtained in advance from the child's parents, for the purposes of later comparisons. The interviewer encourages detailed recall by asking non-leading, open-ended questions, followed by specific questions based on what the child says. This not only builds further rapport by showing an interest in the child's life but models the pattern of the sexual abuse portion of the interview to follow. If the child is particularly difficult to engage, the general rapport building and recall of two events may be all that can be accomplished in the first meeting.

The next step in the interview is to introduce the topic of truth telling and falsehood. Establish that the child does know the difference between the two, and obtain the child's agreement to tell only the truth during the interview. The purpose of the interview can then be raised in the most general way, by inviting the child to tell the interviewer about anything that has happened lately that he or she might want to talk about. If general questions (such as those discussed above) do not result in disclosure, the interviewer may introduce concerns that the parents or others have raised about the child's affect or behavior (for example, "Your mother said you were scared of going to bed lately; can you tell me about that?" or "You told your grandma your bottom was sore; do you know about anything that happened that might have made it sore?"). Be careful not to name a suspect or suggest that specific acts took place. If these general questions do not result in disclosure, the interviewer and the child can make an outline drawing of a body together. Ask the child to add all the body parts from head to toe, naming them and telling their function. When the breasts, genitals, and anus are described, ask if the child has seen this part of another person, and who has seen and/or touched this part of the child. When this detailing is completed for one gender, the process can be repeated with a drawing of the other gender.

If the child does open up the topic of sexual abuse, facilitate the child's efforts to tell about the experience in his or her own words, encouraging him or her to tell "as much as you can remember, without leaving anything out." The interviewer should listen patiently without interrupting, pressuring, or interrogating. Gentle prompts such as "What happened then?" may be used. After the child has told as much as he or she can independently, questions may be introduced, based on what the child has said. When there have been repeated instances of abuse, the child will most often give a general "script" of how the abuse usually happened. Follow-up questions can be used to elicit further details, for example, "You said one time it happened at the house in the woods; think back to that time and tell me everything you can remember about that time, starting from the beginning." Reversing the order of telling, from the end to the beginning, can sometimes lead to disclosure of additional details (26). Increasingly specific questions may be asked to obtain as much detail as the child can give, as long as the questions are based on the child's account. Corroborating particulars may be elicited, such as what the child and perpetrator were wearing, the time of day, and so forth. Care must be taken to ensure that questions are not phrased or inflected in such a way that the child feels his or her account is somehow inadequate or unbelievable. If the child becomes distressed during the interview, acknowledge it—"It's hard to talk about this"—and shift the focus until the child is able to return to the topic of the abuse.

The interviewer must convey an accepting attitude, making it clear that the child can say "I don't know" if he or she does not remember something. Avoid using multiple-choice questions as much as possible. If they are used, one of the choices should be that the child is not sure or doesn't remember. In asking the child to recall events, use expressions such as "think back" or "can you remember anything about . . . ," rather than "pretend" or "imagine." If additional detail is needed, the school-age or older child can be asked to take a different point of view—for example, "If there had been a TV camera on the ceiling, what would it have seen?"

Anatomically explicit dolls were first developed to aid in interviewing young children in cases of suspected sexual abuse because they often lack the language to clearly describe sexual body parts and acts. For example, young children often refer to the vaginal area, buttocks, and anus all as "bottom" (31). If the child is too young or developmentally delayed to give a clear account in words (or is older but has problems with expressive language), providing dolls and asking the child, "Show me what happened," can be extremely helpful. Like other aspects of the child sexual abuse interview, the use of anatomical dolls has been increasingly challenged, both in the professional literature and by defense attorneys (see 26 and 32 for a review). One result of the controversy has been that California courts have banned the introduction of information obtained through the use of anatomical dolls as interview aids. Despite the controversy, research evidence to date indicates that incorporating anatomically detailed dolls into the interview process does not traumatize or frighten children or entice nonabused children to enact sexual play. Although sexually explicit play with dolls cannot, *by itself,* be taken as definitive proof that a child has been sexually abused, demonstrations of explicit sexual acts by nonabused young children are quite uncommon.

When used appropriately by a trained interviewer, anatomically explicit dolls can be of great value as interview aids (see 33 for detailed interviewing guidelines). When these dolls are used, they should be introduced late in the interview process, after all other information has been elicited verbally. This allows sufficient time to form a judgment about whether or not they are actually needed in the particular case at hand. If the child's verbal description is clear, dolls need not be employed. Because testimony based on interviews using anatomically detailed dolls as aids is not always admissible in court, interviewers should check with the legal authorities in their local area before preparing an interview plan. One recent study has shown that very similar information can be obtained from children using regular—that is, nonanatomical—dolls during interviews (34).

At the conclusion of the interview, the child should be thanked for participating and told what will happen next. Care should be taken not to make promises which are outside the power of the interviewer to keep (for instance, "We'll make sure nothing like that will ever happen to you again"). Ask if the child has questions, and answer them if possible.

Children who have been sexually abused are frequently too afraid and ashamed to disclose the abuse in one or two interviews. When there is good reason to suspect sexual abuse, the child may be recommended for psychotherapeutic treatment, during which disclosure may eventually occur when the child feels safe enough to trust the therapist. If treatment is begun under these conditions, the therapist must take extra care to avoid introducing leading statements during the therapy (for more information on the assessment of child sexual abuse, see chapter 13).

Emotional Reactions in the Child Interview

During the course of the interview, the child may express a variety of emotional reactions. Guilt, fear, anger, and depression are particularly common in these circumstances.

Guilt. Sexually abused children often feel guilty about having told the "family secret" of incest. Physically abused children may feel responsible for the abuse. They may have been taught that the abuse was their fault because of some childish misbehavior or because of their failure to meet parental expectations. In children as young as four or five it is already possible to see the foundation being laid for the perpetuation of the cycle of abuse in the next generation: blaming the victim (8). Guilt in maltreated children may also serve as a defense against anxiety. Psychologically it may be more bearable to feel guilty than to face the terrifying reality that disaster is unpredictable and uncontrollable (35). Feelings of guilt are often revealed spontaneously during the course of the interview. To elicit further information in this area, questions about why the child thinks the abuse happened or what might make it stop may prompt him or her to divulge attributions of responsibility for abuse.

Fear. Children may have been told that if they report the abuse, they will be taken away to a horrible foster home where they will be severely mistreated. Sexually abused children may have been threatened that telling will result in the father's suicide or the breakup of the family. Since many children have difficulty in disclosing fears directly, the interviewer's use of projective questions (such as, "What are some things that make you happy?" "What are some things that make you mad?" "What would you wish for if a fairy godmother gave you three wishes?") can help open the topic of negative emotions.

Anger. Heightened aggressiveness is one of the most commonly reported findings in studies of maltreated (especially physically abused) children's interactions with peers (8, 17–20). In school-age children, such aggression may be labeled by the family or school as hyperactivity. In adolescents, it often takes the form of antisocial behavior, such as property destruction (9). During the assessment, the child can be helped to clarify what it is that makes him or her feel so angry. It is helpful to ask children what they think should happen to "make things better in the family." Sometimes their responses are quite straightforward: "We shouldn't get hit for nothing." Or, "Dad should stop getting drunk."

Depression. This complex emotional state appears to be both an antecedent and a consequence of maltreatment. Parents of maltreated children (mothers are most often studied) are often depressed, leading to emotional unavailability or hostility toward their children (3, 8, 36–38), and abused children are often depressed (39–41). One study of depressed children found that their parents were more likely to use corporal punishment and to hit them with objects than were the control group of matched, nondepressed children (42). Having been abused is a significant risk factor for adolescent suicide attempts (43, 44). Among neglected children, depression may be the outcome of the failure of primary attachment (45). Incest is frequently associated with depression both in mothers whose daughters are victimized (as an antecedent and consequence) and in victimized daughters themselves (as a consequence) (24, 25, 45).

Assessing a child for depression is usually not difficult. A depressed child is withdrawn, has poor eye contact, flat or sad affect, and motor lethargy. Self-esteem is low, and somatic complaints without an identifiable medical cause are common (particularly abdominal pain, headache, and fatigue). Disturbances of eating and sleeping are not as common for a depressed child as they are for a depressed adult. The child often lacks friends and does more poorly in school than would be predicted by intellectual capability (46). Among incest victims, a drop in school performance frequently corresponds to the onset of the incest. When these indicators are seen, it is important to evaluate the child for suicidal potential by asking directly whether "you have ever thought that life was just not worth living" or whether "you have ever thought about hurting yourself." If the child's reply is in the affirmative, the interviewer should respond with specific questions to determine if the child has ever considered acting upon this feeling and if he or she has thought about how it might be done. The more detailed and realistic the child's plans are for suicide (in that the means described are actually available to the child), the higher the risk. Although suicide among children continues to be rare, it has increased significantly in recent years, as has adolescent suicide, and hence must be considered as a possibility in the depressed young client (47, 48).

Assessment of the Parents

Once it has been determined that intrafamilial maltreatment has occurred, findings resulting from the assessment of parents are of singular importance in developing recommendations for intervention. It is the parents' ability to change, after all, that will determine whether their children are protected from further maltreatment. Since the most straightforward cases are usually handled by protective services workers, assessment of those parents who are referred to a multidisciplinary team is likely to be difficult. It is, therefore, quite useful to involve team members from all disciplines in interviewing the parents on different occasions, in different combinations. This accomplishes several objectives. First, the parents will be less likely to "split" the team that works together closely. Second, conducting interviews jointly helps team members sharpen their skills of observation and judgment, as the individual members can make comparisons of what they saw and heard in the interview. Third, involving several team members in interviews facilitates the development of a consensus about treatment recommendations.

Because no consistent psychological profile has been found for abusive or neglectful parents, this part of the family assessment is directed toward understanding parent characteristics which need to be addressed in designing interventions. Goals for assessing the parents include:

1. Understanding how the parents construe the assessment process, including learning their feelings and fantasies about it

2. Obtaining a detailed history of each adult's own childhood and family of origin, which enables the identification of strengths and vulnerabilities which each brings to the parenting role

3. Obtaining a history of each parent's adult development and life course, with a focus on issues of impulse control (including substance abuse) and problem solving

4. Determining each parents' view of their children and their relationship to the children in terms of both nurturance and socialization

5. Confirming or ruling out disorders associated with extremely poor prognoses for adequate parenting.

1. Reaction to Assessment

Parents' reactions to the assessment process may be used to gauge their functioning under stress and their ways of interacting with authority figures. Responses which indicate rigid "black-and-white" worldviews are often the first indication that one is dealing with a borderline parent, so frequently encountered in abusive and neglectful families (49). How do they handle anger? Do they project blame onto others? Or are they able to acknowledge their role in the abuse or neglect once their anger has been heard and accepted? Can they be realistic about what is likely to happen, or do they see either themselves or others as omnipotent? Do they have any friends or relatives to whom they can turn appropriately for support? One mother brought her pregnant fourteen-year-old cousin with her as the only significant support person who could be with her during a stressful feedback interview. This spoke eloquently of the lack of caring people in her life who were available to help her with parenting.

2. The Parent's Childhood History

The importance of obtaining the adult's own childhood history is well known (50, 51) (see also chapters 23, 24, and 26). The work of Fraiberg and her colleagues suggests that the feelings which adults express when recalling mistreatment in childhood is equally important (52). Can they identify with the child-self who was hurt, or are those emotions completely split off, preventing them from empathizing with their own children? In their own childhood was any adult in a positive relationship with them? If so, the chance of forming a positive therapeutic alliance is increased, a hopeful sign that the adult may be able to benefit from psychotherapy. Adults abused as children are significantly more likely to be able to break the cycle of abuse under any of the following conditions: (1) they had a positive, emotionally supportive relationship with a nonabusing adult during their own childhood; (2) as an adult they have a positive relationship with a supportive partner; (3) they participate in extensive psychotherapy (53, 54).

A history of violence in the parent's family of origin is significant, even if the violence was not specifically directed at the individual being interviewed. Witnessing abuse of other family members seems to be as damaging to future parenting as having been the target of abuse (55). Failure to obtain a history of abuse from the parent does not necessarily mean that abuse did not occur. Many adults suppress or repress memories of childhood abuse

(56). As with physical abuse, the possibility that the adult was sexually abused as a child, or that his or her siblings were, should be inquired about, as well as how the adult's parents handled their own sexuality in the family. Confining questions to whether parents were molested as children often misses a history of precocious exposure to inappropriate sexuality in childhood. Find out if there was incest among other family members, or if the children were inappropriately exposed to parental sexual activities (such as their having multiple lovers in the house or their having sex in front of the children). This history should be obtained separately from each parent (57). Asking parents about their sex education in childhood is a relatively nonthreatening way to begin this line of questioning.

Obtaining a parental history of neglect is more difficult than obtaining a history of abuse. As Polansky and his colleagues have pointed out, it is rare for an adult to cite outright the fact of having suffered neglect, both because people lack standards with which to compare their own childhoods and because of psychological defenses against remembering, for "who could bear to know he was being neglected?" (3, p. 7).

On the other hand, clues to neglect abound as the history unfolds. Tales of extreme poverty coupled with parental indifference are typical of the neglected. A history of juvenile delinquency either of the person being interviewed, or of siblings, is not uncommon. Some adults neglected in childhood experienced frequent or prolonged separations from their families as they were moved to relatives' homes or removed by authorities to foster care in the days when foster parents were discouraged from forming attachments to their foster children. Parents who grew up in multiple foster homes have good reason to have strong feelings about keeping their families together. The prognosis for change is more hopeful if the basis for these feelings is concern for the welfare of the child, rather than the parent's need for the child as a "bulwark against loneliness" (3, p. 35).

Depression is quite prevalent among parents of abused and neglected children, including nonabusive spouses of abusive parents (3, 36, 38, 53). Parental depression may be an indication that the adult is not cut off from feelings stemming from his or her own history of childhood mistreatment. Although depression may interfere significantly with the ability to parent, the presence of depression can be considered a hopeful sign, since depression is usually considered treatable.

3. Parental Impulse Control, Substance Abuse, and Problem Solving

Because physical and sexual abuse both occur when adults do not sufficiently control their impulses, assessing the level of any parental problems with impulse control is especially important in determining whether children are safe at home. Maintaining the continuity of the parent-child relationship while the family is being helped is in the best interests of the child's emotional development if the child is ultimately to remain in the family; therefore, removal to foster care should not be recommended unless the child is judged to be unsafe in the home. Parents who have a history of impulsive behavior provide an environment for the child which is riskier than that provided by parents who have other types of problems. For example, the impulsive parent may suddenly decide to leave the state or may seriously abuse the child in an outburst of rage. Less impulsive parents present less risk because they are more likely to use crisis intervention services when they need extra help in controlling their behavior while they are in the process of treatment.

Impulsive behavior should be assessed in all areas of functioning, such as economic and sexual functioning, and not confined solely to violent impulsive behavior. Questions about arrests for drunk driving and disciplinary offenses while in the military are often fruitful. Alcohol problems among impulsive adults are so common that alcohol use should be asked about routinely in these interviews. The association between alcohol and family violence is a strong one (58, 59). Ask also about other substance use, because untreated substance abuse is significantly associated with poor outcomes for parents in treatment for child abuse (60–62).

The interviewer must refrain from showing disapproval about this topic, as with other lines of questioning. Remaining neutral is extremely important when asking about substance abuse if an accurate history is to be obtained. Questions must be framed so that people can admit their substance use. Subtle cues to chemically impaired behavior must be followed up with appropriate questions.

Low levels of skill and judgment in solving problems are common in parents who maltreat their children. Questions about recent and current life stressors (for instance, financial problems, illness, difficulties in the extended family, problems at work) provide the opportunity for interviewers to assess the impact of stressors on the family's treatment of the child, as well as to hear how the parent conceptualizes problems and solutions, and how quickly decisions are acted upon. While stressful life events, in themselves, are not responsible for abuse, maltreating families often deteriorate in the face of stressful circumstances, allowing abuse or neglect to emerge (55, 63). Does poor judgment stem from intellectual limitations, simple lack of knowledge, or problems in the social-emotional area of functioning? If the last of these is the case, is the difficulty due to neurotic, characterological, or psychotic processes? Each of these requires a different approach in intervention, and each is associated with a different prognosis.

4. The Parents' Relationship with Their Children

The parents' view of their children and their relationship to them should be assessed both by taking a relationship history and by direct observation. Essential parenting functions can be conceptualized as subsumed under the headings of nurturance and socialization.

Nurturance   Nurturance includes (1) physical caretaking, such as providing food, shelter, and protection from harm; (2) emotional nurturance, such as providing appropriate physical closeness, eye contact, and expressions of pleasure in and approval of the child as a person; and (3) nurturance of the child's intellectual development, such as talking to the child, encouraging the child's verbalizations, providing interesting sensory experiences, and allowing exploration of the environment while setting safe boundaries. In normal parenting these nurturing functions take place simultaneously, as when a mother participates in playful mutual babbling with her infant while giving him or her a bath. Children who are appropriately and sensitively nurtured form secure attachments which enable them to feel safe, to explore the environment, and to see themselves as valuable and lovable people.

Parents who are rated most highly on this parenting dimension are often described as warm or supportive (64).

Dysfunction in the quality of the parent-child attachment is a frequent finding in mal-treating families (8, 52, 65). There may be a failure of bonding on the part of the parent, sometimes seen in cases of failure to thrive (see chapters 15 and 16), or there may be a distorted attachment, in which the child symbolizes someone else to the parent.

Failure to provide sufficient nurturance is part of the definition of neglect. Neglectful parents are frequently oblivious to what their child's needs might be due to their own in-tellectual deficits or preoccupation with self stemming from severe psychopathology. A schizophrenic mother of a young infant with deprivation failure to thrive, for example, explained that she did not feed him often because, "When I'm awake, he's asleep, and when he wakes up, I'm asleep." Asked if she did not hear the baby cry, she replied that she did, but since it was when she was sleeping, she saw no reason to get up. She remarked, "I guess we're just on different schedules." Other neglectful parents may recognize some of their children's needs but simply be unable to meet them consistently due to overwhelming situational problems for which they lack the personal and social resources to cope. Lack of positive supportive relationships is particularly characteristic of neglectful parents (3, 66, 67). When situational stress rather than parental inability to function is a major part of the picture, intervention with increased resources—day care, nutritional supplementation, and parent aide programs—is more likely to be of significant benefit to the children. In any case, such interventions must be tried in an attempt to improve the children's quality of life. Polansky refers to such interventions as "parental prostheses" (3, pp. 221–37), a term which acknowledges that even though such interventions do not represent a "cure" for neglect, they may provide significant support for neglected children.

Physically abusive parents are often also quite neglectful of their children's emotional needs. They tend to generate a large number of negative and coercive family interactions, creating an atmosphere which is low in warmth (68–71). Distorted ideas of children's in-tentions and motivations may interfere with the abusive parent's ability to nurture. For example, a three-month-old was brought to the pediatrician for a well-baby visit. When his diaper was removed, his mother commented, "Look at how he wiggles his ass at the nurse. He's just like his father."

Sexually abusive parents distort the nurturant function by using physical closeness with the child to meet the adult's needs. When sexual abuse has been intertwined with nurturance, children are quite confused about the difference between nurturance and sexu-ality. In some families the sexualized relationship will have been the child's only significant experience of warmth. Replacing such experiences with healthy loving relationships in the family must be carefully considered in the treatment of the incestuous family. Simply re-moving the offender does not solve this problem.

Assessing the child's attachment system is a helpful way to evaluate the issue of nur-turance. Pertinent questions include: To whom is this child attached? Is the child so needy that "instant attachments" are formed to any kind adult, such as the interviewer? Does the young child use the parent as a secure base when threatened, or is there role reversal, with the child caring for the parent? Is the child able to leave the parent to explore and play, or is the child anxious and clinging? Can the older child identify both positive and negative aspects of the relationship to the parents? A child who has nothing negative to say about a parent is fearful of telling the truth. Even very good parents are not perfect!

Questions regarding attachment are particularly salient in making recommendations for placing the child in foster care or for terminating parental rights (28). Some children are firmly attached to a sibling, though unattached to a parent. Such children should not be separated from the sibling to whom they are attached. When a complete lack of attachment to a parent is seen, it is usually in very young neglected children (age three and under), or in children who have spent very little time living with their parents, such as children who have spent most of their lives in foster homes or with relatives other than their parents. In rare instances, failure of attachment between a parent and an older child is so complete that the child flatly states, "I don't care if I never see her again." Problematic (insecure) attachments are more common. When some positive attachment exists, the family has a higher likelihood of success in treatment, as there is a foundation of caring upon which to build. When parent-child relationships are characterized by complete lack of caring, there is little hope that the family will ever be able to meet the child's needs. In such cases, swift and permanent termination of parental rights is in the child's best interests.

Socialization   When performing the socialization function of parenting, parents act as the agents of the larger society by taking primary responsibility for rearing children who will be able to meet cultural expectations for age-appropriate behavior. For younger children, this means learning self-care skills such as self-feeding and control of excretory functions. As children grow older, society demands more impulse control—for example, taking turns, sharing, and expressing feelings in words rather than acting them out in tantrums. Eventually, parents are expected to teach their children abstract values and attitudes which will govern their behavior. The style of parenting which results in successful child socialization is characterized by clear structure, rules, and expectations for children's behavior and by firmness and consistency.

In normal development, attachments between parents and children, which are formed and intensified in the context of nurturance, then provide the basis for socialization. Secure attachment enables parents to socialize their children in the context of continued nurturance. Parents who are both warm and firm are referred to as "authoritative," and their children are prosocial, competent, and have few behavior problems (64).

Neglectful parents are ineffective in socializing their children. As a result, the behavior of severely neglected children often has a feral quality. Neglecting families are frequently chaotic. Although children's needs are sometimes met in such chaotic families, parental response is so inconsistent that the children cannot develop the cognitive, affective, and social skills necessary for competent functioning, thus perpetuating the cycle of neglect into the next generation.

In contrast to the neglectful parent, the physically abusive parent is typically overzealous, bent on socializing the child to expectations that the society has only for older children, and oblivious to the high emotional and developmental costs of the methods employed. Both the goals and the means of socialization used are often inappropriate to the child's age. One mother of a four-year-old, for example, was observed giving her daughter a coin to put into a parking meter. She gave the child no instructions on using the elevator, finding the car, or properly working the meter, saying, instead, "Put this in the parking meter, and if I get a ticket it will be your fault, and you'll have to pay for it out of your own money!"

Sexual abuse distorts the socialization function of parenting, as incest violates a universal human taboo. Some parents involved in incest, like physically abusive parents, justify their actions as socialization. "I wanted her first sexual experience to be a good one. It was just sex education."

Evaluation of Parenting   Using the framework detailed above to assess the parents' relationships with their children will enable each major area of parenting to be evaluated. When deficits are identified in specific areas of parenting, the professional team can recommend interventions targeted to the deficits. A useful way to begin this portion of the assessment is to obtain a history of the parents' attachment to each child (for example, what the circumstances surrounding the pregnancies were, what the family's conditions were then, how the pregnancies were viewed, whether the baby met parental expectations, and so forth). Obtaining the health history of each child is especially important as it relates to the question of attachment. Some children may be protected from abuse because of their status as a "vulnerable child." Other children are put at increased risk of abuse or failure to thrive because their parents view them as defective or difficult to care for (72).

Parental values, beliefs, and expectations concerning children's needs, acceptable behavior, and appropriate disciplinary techniques should be elicited. This aspect of the history is usually quite easy to obtain. With the exception of perpetrators of sexual abuse, few parents try to conceal even those attitudes, values, and beliefs regarding their children that professionals would consider quite damaging. As Caldwell and Bradley have observed, "most mothers believe that what they do with and to their children is for the children's own good, and they often report with pride actions that you might expect them to try and conceal" (73, p. 90).

In assessing father-incest families, the strength of the mother's emotional tie to her children versus her tie to her husband is of crucial importance in deciding whether it is safe to recommend that the child(ren) remain in the home and the abusing father move out voluntarily for a period of time. If the mother's bond to the children is insufficiently strong, she cannot be counted upon to protect her children by enforcing the exclusion of her husband from the household (even if there is a court order against his incursion). When the team cannot be sure that his access to the children will be denied, temporary foster care for the children may be the only safe alternative—although, sadly, the children usually experience this option as a rejection and punishment for their disclosure of the incest.

5. Parental Mental Disorders

After gathering the above information, the team will have a reasonably clear picture of the adult's functioning, especially with regard to the parenting role. Though the interviews need not follow the format of a standard psychiatric interview, the information gathered from them can be used by the team to determine the presence of one of the five conditions associated with extremely poor prognosis for improved parenting: (1) antisocial personality disorder (formerly called sociopathic personality), (2) multiple personality disorder, (3) uncontrolled psychosis, (4) mental retardation, and (5) religious fanaticism. When the presence of any of these problems is suspected, the involvement of the psychologist or psychiatrist is particularly useful in making or confirming the diagnosis and estimating the prognosis.

Antisocial personality disorder is generally acknowledged to be virtually untreatable. Individuals with this disorder often spend significant portions of their lives in penal institutions. Many, but not all, individuals who have serious substance abuse problems qualify for this diagnosis.

For the other four conditions listed, the judgment of poor prognosis for improved parenting is made from the point of view of the child's sense of time (28). Multiple personality disorder, for example, is not untreatable, but successful treatment takes several years, during which parental functioning may be so unpredictable that adequate parenting is impossible (74, 75). Many professionals have never seen a case of this uncommon disorder, making it more likely that the diagnosis will be missed. A clue to such dissociative disorders is a history of "blackouts," time periods during which the individual can remember nothing, although others report continued functioning. Sometimes these blank periods last as long as several years. These experiences must be differentiated from blackouts resulting from alcohol or drug use. Suicide attempts, psychiatric hospitalizations, and conversion symptoms are common in the histories of individuals with multiple personality, as are early childhood experiences of sexual and physical abuse of unusual brutality. Almost all patients with the disorder are female (76–78).

The psychotic adult is a poor risk as a parent if the psychotic process has continued over time. Although a history of a single psychotic episode, such as a postpartum psychosis, is not necessarily an indication that the individual will be unable to function as a parent, a history of uncontrolled psychosis is indicative of a poor prognosis for parenting. Schizophrenic, maltreating parents pass on a legacy of double vulnerability to their children; genetic risk compounded by environmental insult.

In developing recommendations for families with parents who are severely psychiatrically impaired or mentally retarded, an important consideration is whether other adults are present in the household who can provide care and nurturance for the children and, if necessary, protect them from inappropriate actions of the impaired parent. Most parents with serious cognitive or emotional limitations are not violent, but these parents may be neglectful simply because they lack adequate ability to meet a child's needs; their children may also be vulnerable to abuse by others because the parents are ineffective in keeping their youngsters safe (79, 80). Some families with a severely impaired parent can care for their children at least marginally well, unless the higher-functioning parent dies or leaves the inadequately functioning parent in sole charge of the children (81).

Religious fanaticism has received little attention in the child abuse literature, probably because of its relative rarity. When it is a factor in child maltreatment, however, it presents special problems because it is defended as part of an elaborate belief system with the support of a religious cult community. Even if the parents who are members of such groups might otherwise be open to change, group support for inappropriate actions toward the children effectively blocks attempts at help. Members of the larger community are defined as the outgroup, whose beliefs the "true believer" must resist if group membership is to be retained (82, 83). Courts are often more reluctant to interfere with parental rights when parenting behavior is based upon beliefs which are defended as religious, even when such behavior is otherwise unacceptable by the standards of the larger community. In recent years there have been reports of children abused as part of "satanic" religious rituals; however, to date the evidence regarding this type of abuse is inconclusive (84).

Assessment of Family Interaction

Assessment of the interaction between family members is a particularly fruitful procedure with physically abusive and neglectful families who have been defensive in interviews. Observation of family interaction in incest families is less likely to be helpful. Compared with other families from the same social class who have children the same age, physically abusive and neglectful families demonstrate social behavior patterns in which fewer interactions between family members take place and in which many more negative and many fewer positive interactions between parents and children occur (68–71). In physically abusive families, parents are often hostile and controlling, competing with their children for play resources, playing more like a sibling than a parent.

Interaction between adults in the family can initially be observed during the joint interview of the parents. A playroom is especially useful for observing the interactions between sibling groups of young children. With older children, siblings can be interviewed jointly without their parents present. Finally, the whole family may be observed in interaction.

When observing siblings in the play setting, note the strength of the children's bonds to each other, especially if there is a question as to whether the children should be placed together in foster care. Note whether the children display age-appropriate social behavior in the interaction.

To assess family interaction, parents can be asked to play with their children in a room equipped with appropriate play materials. One procedure is to first ask the family to select an activity that they can do together, and then ask them to play. If videotape equipment is available, observers can leave the room and start the tape. If not, the observers sit quietly in the room, taking notes. When the free play session is over, parents are asked to have the children clean up (69). This simple procedure allows the team to observe parenting skills involved in making a cooperative choice and playing together as well as parenting skills involved in obtaining children's compliance in a task. The result is a sample of family interaction when parents are on their "best behavior."

Under these conditions, are the parents able to play with their children at all, or do they spend their time talking to other adults or sitting numbly in a corner? Do the children approach their parents? If so, how do the parents respond? Can family members agree on an activity? Do play activities in which parents and children engage together meet the adults' needs or the needs of the children? Can parents set appropriate limits, or are they overly harsh and restrictive—or, alternatively, completely laissez-faire? Do parents engage in any language stimulation or other simple "teaching" with their young children? These observations may yield powerful evidence of deficits in family interaction. It is heartrending to see a two-year-old, his broken leg in a cast, begin to cry because he has tripped and fallen down in play, only to hear his teenage mother react with, "Don't be a damn crybaby; I hate wimps!"

Termination of Parental Rights

Termination of parental rights is an extremely serious step. The lay public, faced with sensationalized news accounts, vacillates between impatience with "the system" which allows abuse to occur and fear that legal terminations can be accomplished too easily because of prejudice or disapproval of a family's lifestyle. No one wants to live in the kind of society where it is easy for the relationship between parents and children to be permanently legally severed. In addition to the psychological wounds involved, it is very expensive for a society to care for other people's children.

The assessment team's responsibility to the community requires not only professional competence but also sensitivity to the delicate balance between parents' rights and childrens' needs. In cases where interventions have failed, the team must address the question, "Did this family receive intervention which was appropriate to their problems?" If not, another treatment plan must be developed. If, on the other hand, community agencies have offered help to the family which was appropriate in quality and quantity only to see serious maltreatment of children continuing, then professionals have a responsibility to make clear recommendations to the court about termination of parental rights. If the best available treatment has been attempted and has failed, nothing further can be gained by postponing a decision which will give the children security and permanency.

In a few cases, after time and therapeutic work, when the parent-child relationship has been too destructive and change over time has been too slow to meet the children's needs, parents may decide that the interests of their children are best served by voluntarily relinquishing them for adoption. An excerpt from a mother's letter illustrates the team's role in the evolution of her decision to give up her children.

> I have been through a lot since I last saw you and I have done a lot of honest thinking and not as much running from facing the truth. I don't hate you no more, in my heart you are my friend now. I have reread the [team's report] again and I now know what I must do just for my own survival. I'm letting go of the kids and I am going to go on with life. [The children] are humans with feelings too I was just being selfish with wanting the kids with me no matter what the consequences were. I love my kids more than that I'm just so sorry I didn't face this decision sooner.

References

1. Killén, K. 1996. How Far Have We Come in Dealing with the Emotional Challenge of Abuse and Neglect? *Child Abuse and Neglect: International J.* 20:791–95.

2. Helfer, R. E. 1978. *Childhood Comes First: A Crash Course in Childhood for Adults.* East Lansing, Mich.: Helfer Publications.

3. Polansky, N. A.; Chalmers, M. A.; Buttenwieser E. W.; and Williams, D. P. 1981. *Damaged Parents: An Anatomy of Child Neglect.* Chicago: University of Chicago Press.

4. Beauchamp, T. L., and Childress, J. F. 1983. *Principles of Biomedical Ethics,* 2d ed. New York: Oxford University Press.

5. American Psychological Association. 1992. Ethical Principles of Psychologists and Code of Conduct. *Am. Psychologist* 47:1597–611.

6. McClosky, L. A.; Figueredo, A. J.; and Koss, M. P. 1995. The Effects of Systemic Family Violence on Children's Mental Health. *Child Development* 66:1239–61.

7. Claussen, A. H., and Crittenden, P. M. 1991. Physical and Psychological Maltreatment: Relations among Types of Maltreatment. *Child Abuse and Neglect: International J.* 15:5–18.

8. Cicchetti, D., and Carlson, V. 1989. *Child Maltreatment: Theory and Research on the Causes and Consequences of Child Abuse and Neglect.* New York: Cambridge University Press.

9. Starr, R. H., and Wolfe, D. A. 1991. *The Effects of Child Abuse and Neglect.* New York: Guilford.

10. Frodi, A. 1981. Contribution of Child Characteristics to Abuse. *Am. J. Mental Deficiency* 85:341–49.

11. White, R.; Benedict, M. I.; Wulff, L.; and Kelley, M. 1987. Physical Disabilities as Risk Factors for Child Maltreatment: A Selected Review. *Am. J. Orthopsychiatry* 57:93–101.

12. Bell, N., and Vogel, E. 1968. The Emotionally Disturbed Child as the Family Scapegoat. In *A Modern Introduction to the Family,* ed. N. Bell and E. Vogel, 382–97. New York: Free Press.

13. Frankenburg, W. K.; Dodds, J.; Archer, P.; Bresnick, B.; Maschka, P.; Edelman, N.; and Shapiro, H. 1990. *Denver II Screening Manual.* Denver: Denver Developmental Materials, Inc.

14. Blager, F., and Martin, H. P. 1976. Speech and Language of Abused Children. In *The Abused Child: A Multidisciplinary Approach to Developmental Issues and Treatment,* ed. H. P. Martin, 83–92. Cambridge, Mass.: Ballinger.

15. Ammerman, R. T.; Cassisi, J. E.; Hersen, M.; and Van Hasselt, V. B. 1986. Consequences of Physical Abuse and Neglect in Children. *Clinical Psychology Rev.* 6:291–310.

16. Oates, R. K.; Peacock, A.; and Forrest, D. 1985. Long-Term Effects of Nonorganic Failure to Thrive. *Pediatrics* 75:39–40.

17. Conaway, L. P., and Hansen, D. J. 1989. Social Behavior of Physically Abused and Neglected Children: A Critical Review. *Clinical Psychology Rev.* 9:627–52.

18. Salzinger, S.; Feldman, R. S.; Hammer, M.; and Rosario, M. 1993. The Effects of Physical Abuse on Children's Social Relationships. *Child Development* 64:169–87.

19. Weiss, B.; Dodge, K. A.; Bates, J. E.; and Pettit, G. S. 1992. Some Consequences of Early Harsh Discipline: Child Aggression and a Maladaptive Social Information Processing Style. *Child Development* 63:1321–35.

20. Prino, C. T., and Peyrot, M. 1994. *Child Abuse and Neglect: International J.* 18:871–84.

21. Galloway, D. 1982. A Study of Persistent Absentees and Their Families. *British J. Educational Psychology* 52:317–30.

22. Weitzman, M.; Klerman, L. V.; Lamb, G.; Menary, J.; and Alpert, J. J. 1982. School Absence: A Problem for the Pediatrician. *Pediatrics* 69:739–46.

23. Bagley, C., and Ramsey, R. 1986. Sexual Abuse in Childhood: Psychosocial Outcomes and Implications for Social Work Practice. *J. Social Work and Human Sexuality* 5:33–47.

24. Beitchman, J. H.; Zucker, K. J.; Hood, J. E.; DaCosta, G. A.; Ackman, D.; and Cassavia, E. 1992. A Review of the Long-Term Effects of Child Sexual Abuse. *Child Abuse and Neglect: International J.* 16:101–18.

25. Browne, A., and Finkelhor, D. 1986. Impact of Child Sexual Abuse: A Review of the Research. *Psychological Bulletin* 99:66–77.

26. Goodman, G. S., and Bottom, B. L. 1993. *Child Victims, Child Witnesses: Understanding and Improving Testimony.* New York: Guilford.

27. Williams, G. J. 1980. Social Sanctions for Child Abuse and Neglect: Editor's Introduction. In *Traumatic Abuse and Neglect of Children at Home,* ed. G. J. Williams and J. Money, 9–13. Baltimore: Johns Hopkins University Press.

28. Goldstein, J.; Freud, A.; and Solnit, A. J. 1973. *Beyond the Best Interests of the Child.* New York: Macmillan.

29. Bays, J., and Chadwick, D. 1993. Medical Diagnosis of the Sexually Abused Child. *Child Abuse and Neglect: International J.* 17:91–110.

30. Sivan, A. B. 1991. Preschool Child Development: Implications for Investigation of Child Abuse Allegations. *Child Abuse and Neglect: International J.* 15:485–93.

31. Schor, D. P., and Sivan, A. B. 1989. Interpreting Children's Labels for Sex-Related Body Parts of Anatomically Explicit Dolls. *Child Abuse and Neglect: International J.* 13:523–31.

32. Koocher, G. P.; Goodman, G. S.; White, C. S.; Friedrich, W. N.; Sivan, A. B.; and Reynolds, C. R. 1995. Psychological Science and the Use of Anatomically Detailed Dolls in Child Sexual Abuse Assessments. *Psychological Bulletin* 118:199–22.

33. Boat, B. W., and Everson, M. D. 1988. Interviewing Young Children with Anatomical Dolls. *Child Welfare* 67:337–52.

34. Britton, H. L., and O'Keefe, M. A. 1991. Use of Nonanatomical Dolls in the Sexual Abuse Interview. *Child Abuse and Neglect: International J.* 15:567–73.

35. Gardner, R. A. 1970. The Use of Guilt as a Defense against Anxiety. *Psychoanalytic Rev.* 57:124–36.

36. Kinard, E. M. 1982. Child Abuse and Depression: Cause or Consequence? *Child Welfare* 61:403–13.

37. Scott, D. 1992. Early Identification of Maternal Depression as a Strategy in the Prevention of Child Abuse. *Child Abuse and Neglect: International J.* 16:345–58.

38. Rodenburg, M. 1971. Child Murder by Depressed Parents. *Canadian Psychiatric Assoc. J.* 16:41–48.

39. Kazdin, A. E.; Moser, J.; Colbus, D.; and Bell, R. 1985. Depressive Symptoms among Physically Abused and Psychiatrically Disturbed Children. *J. Abnormal Psychology* 94:298–307.

40. Kinard, E. M. 1980. Emotional Development in Physically Abused Children. *Am. J. Orthopsychiatry* 50:686–96.

41. Oates, K. 1986. *Child Abuse and Neglect: What Happens Eventually?* New York: Brunner/Mazel.

42. Seagull, E. A. W., and Weinshank, A. B. 1984. Childhood Depression in a Selected Group of Low-Achieving Seventh-Graders. *J. Clinical Child Psychology* 13:134–40.

43. Pfander, S., and Seagull, E. A. 1992. The Effect of Pediatric Psychologic Consultations on the Management of Adolescent Suicide Attempts in the Pediatric Service of a General Hospital. *Am. J. Diseases of Children* 146:898–900.

44. Shaunesey, K.; Cohen, J. L.; Plummer, B.; and Berman, A. 1993. Suicidality in Hospitalized Adolescents: Relationship to Prior Abuse. *Am. J. Orthopsychiatry* 63:113–19.

45. Koverola, C., and Pound, J. 1993. Relationship of Child Sexual Abuse to Depression. *Child Abuse and Neglect: International J.* 17:393–400.

46. Seagull, E. A. 1990. Childhood Depression. *Current Problems in Pediatrics* 20:710–55.

47. Advance Report of Final Mortality Statistics, 1986. 1988. *Monthly Vital Statistics Report* 37:1–56.

48. Orbach, I. 1988. *Children Who Don't Want to Live.* San Francisco: Jossey-Bass.

49. Prodgers, A. 1984. Psychopathology of the Physically Abusing Parent: A Comparison with the Borderline Syndrome. *Child Abuse and Neglect: International J.* 89:411–24.

50. Widom, C. S. 1989. The Cycle of Violence. *Science* 244:160–66.

51. Gara, M. A.; Rosenberg, S.; and Herzog, E. P. 1996. The Abused Child as Parent. *Child Abuse and Neglect: International J.* 20:797–807.

52. Fraiberg, S.; Adelson, E.; and Shapiro, V. 1975. Ghosts in the Nursery. *J. Am. Acad. Child Psychiatry* 14:387–421.

53. Egeland, B.; Jacobvitz, D.; and Sroufe, L. A. 1988. Breaking the Cycle of Abuse. *Child Development* 59:1080–88.

54. Romans, S. E.; Martin, J. L.; Anderson, J. C.; O'Shea, M. L.; and Mullen, P. E. 1995. Factors that Mediate between Child Sexual Abuse and Adult Psychological Outcome. *Psychological Medicine* 25:127–42.

55. Strauss, M. A.; Gelles, R. J.; and Steinmetz, S. K. 1980. *Behind Closed Doors: Violence in the American Family.* Garden City, N.Y.: Anchor Books.

56. Femina, D. D.; Yeager, C. A.; and Lewis, D. O. 1990. Child Abuse: Adolescent Records vs. Adult Recall. *Child Abuse and Neglect: International J.* 14:227–31.

57. Cole, P. M.; Woolger, C.; Power, T. G.; and Smith, K. D. 1992. Parenting Difficulties among Adult Survivors of Father-Daughter Incest. *Child Abuse and Neglect: International J.* 16:239–49.

58. Famularo, R.; Stone, K.; Barnum, R.; and Wharton, R. 1986. Alcoholism and Severe Child Maltreatment. *Am. J. Orthopsychiatry* 56:481–85.

59. Yama, M. F.; Fogas, B. S.; Teegarden, L. A.; and Hastings, B. 1993. Childhood Sexual Abuse and Parental Alcoholism: Interactive Effects in Adult Women. *Am. J. Orthopsychiatry* 63:300–305.

60. Wolfner, G. D., and Gelles, R. J. 1993. A Profile of Violence toward Children: A National Study. *Child Abuse and Neglect: International J.* 17:197–212.

61. Famularo, R.; Kinscherff, R.; and Fenton, T. 1992. Parental Substance Abuse and the Nature of Child Maltreatment. *Child Abuse and Neglect: International J.* 16:475–83.

62. Murphy, J. M.; Jellinek, M.; Quinn, D.; Smith, G.; Poitrast, F. G.; and Goshko, M. 1991. Substance Abuse and Serious Child Mistreatment: Prevalence, Risk, and Outcome in a Court Sample. *Child Abuse and Neglect: International J.* 15:197–211.

63. Whipple, E. E., and Webster-Stratton, C. 1991. The Role of Parental Stress in Physically Abusive Families. *Child Abuse and Neglect: International J.* 15:279–91.

64. Lamborn, S. D.; Mounts, N. S.; Steinberg, L.; and Dornbusch, S. M. 1991. Patterns of Competence and Adjustment among Adolescents from Authoritative, Authoritarian, Indulgent, and Neglectful Families. *Child Development* 62:1049–65.

65. Cassidy, J., and Berlin, L. J. 1994. The Insecure/Ambivalent Pattern of Attachment: Theory and Research. *Child Development* 65:971–91.

66. Brayden, R. M.; Altemeier, W. A.; Tucker, D. D.; Dietrich, M. S.; and Vietze, P. 1992. Antecedents of Child Neglect in the First Two Years of Life. *J. Pediatrics* 120:426–29.

67. Seagull, E. A. W. 1987. Social Support and Child Maltreatment: A Review of the Evidence. *Child Abuse and Neglect: International J.* 11:41–52.

68. Burgess, R. L., and Conger, R. D. 1978. Family Interaction in Abusive, Neglectful, and Normal Families. *Child Development* 49:1163–73.

69. Fagot, B., and Kavanagh, K. 1991. Play as a Diagnostic Tool with Physically Abusive Parents and Their Children. In *Play Diagnosis and Assessment,* ed. C. E. Schaefer, K. Gitlin, and A. Sandgrund, 203–18. New York: Wiley.

70. Lahey, B. B.; Conger, R. D.; Atkeson, B. M.; and Treiber, F. A. 1984. Parenting Behavior and Emotional Status of Physically Abusive Mothers. *J. Consulting and Clinical Psychology* 52:1062–71.

71. Mash, E. J.; Johnston, C.; and Kovitz, K. 1983. A Comparison of the Mother-Child Interactions of Physically Abused and Non-abused Children during Play and Task Situations. *J. Clinical Child Psychology* 12:337–46.

72. Sherrod, K. B.; O'Connor, S.; Vietze, P. M.; and Altemeier, W. A. 1984. Child Health and Maltreatment. *Child Development* 55:1174–83.

73. Caldwell, B. M., and Bradley, R. H. 1984. Home Observation for Measurement of the Environment, rev. ed. University of Arkansas, Little Rock. Typescript.

74. Boor, M., and Coons, P. M. 1983. A Comprehensive Bibliography of Literature Pertaining to Multiple Personality. *Psychological Reports* 53:295–310.

75. Benjamin, L. R.; Benjamin, R.; and Rind, B. 1996. Dissociative Mothers' Subjective Experience of Parenting. *Child Abuse and Neglect: International J.* 20:933–42.

76. Buck, O. D. 1983. Multiple Personality as a Borderline State. *J. Nervous and Mental Disease* 171:62–65.

77. Putnam, F. W.; Guroff, J. J.; and Silberman, E. K. 1986. The Clinical Phenomenology of Multiple Personality Disorder: Review of One Hundred Cases. *J. Clinical Psychiatry* 47:285–93.

78. McElroy, L. 1992. Early Indicators of Pathological Dissociation in Sexually Abused Children. *Child Abuse and Neglect: International J.* 16:833–46.

79. Taylor, C. G.; Norman, D. K.; Murphy, J. M.; Jellinek, M.; Quinn, D.; Poitrast, F. G.; and Goshko, M. 1991. Diagnosed Intellectual and Emotional Impairment among Parents Who Seriously Mistreat Their Children: Prevalence, Type, and Outcome in a Court Sample. *Child Abuse and Neglect: International J.* 15:389–401.

80. Tymchuck, A. J. 1992. Predicting Adequacy of Parenting by People with Mental Retardation. *Child Abuse and Neglect: International J.* 16:165–78.

81. Seagull, E. A. W., and Scheurer, S. L. 1986. Neglected and Abused Children of Mentally Retarded Parents. *Child Abuse and Neglect: International J.* 10:493–500.

82. Hughes, R. A. 1990. Psychological Perspectives on Infanticide in a Faith Healing Sect. *Psychotherapy* 27:107–15.

83. Shinwell, E. D., and Gorodischer, R. 1982. Totally Vegetarian Diets and Infant Nutrition. *Pediatrics* 70:582–86.

84. Putnam, F. W. 1991. The Satanic Ritual Abuse Controversy. *Child Abuse and Neglect: International J.* 15:175–79.

9

Evaluation of Physical Abuse

KENNETH WAYNE FELDMAN

The diagnostic evaluation of suspected child abuse victims inevitably involves and directly impinges upon both the child and his or her family. The potential risks of further abusive injury to the child must be weighed against the prolonged effects of family distress and disruption. Although the diagnosis of abuse or accident will often be clear-cut, some cases will remain problematic. Our goal should be to minimize the number of these uncertain cases.

The pediatric diagnosis of abuse, more than diagnoses in most fields of medicine, is directly tied to the need to prevent future injury. This causes us, in addition to providing basic medical care, to consider the needs of the legal and child protection systems. Consequently, the scope of the diagnosis of abuse is greater (table 9.1). Careful physical, laboratory, and radiologic evaluation must be conducted to define *what* are the anatomic and physiologic injuries confronting us. Next, *how,* equivalent to medical etiology, must be sought. We would not be satisfied with the knowledge that a child has meningitis without identifying the causative organism. Similarly, a diagnosis of fractured femur that doesn't establish whether abuse or an automobile accident caused the break is incomplete.

How has both global and biomechanical components. Globally, is the injury caused by abuse? This indicates that an intentional act of a caretaker resulted in physical injury of the child. The injury itself need not have been intended. The caretaker's act may have been as spontaneous as a blow by a frustrated caretaker to the head of a crying infant. The resulting subdural hematoma is an unexpected and unwished consequence. On a biomechanical level, we attempt to define the type and degree of force necessary to cause the injuries. Since direct, controlled experimental data about childhood injury is unethical, we depend on inference from biomechanical models, animal studies, and studies of postmortem tissue for controlled information. These studies have the beauty of isolating individual mechanical events but, unfortunately, may not represent real-life injury scenarios. Thus, we supplement information from controlled studies with case series of unintentionally injured children. Such "unintentional injury" series, however, do not isolate individual mechanical events and may be contaminated by unrecognized cases of child abuse.

By defining *when* the injuries occurred, we can tell whether they resulted from a single

KENNETH WAYNE FELDMAN, M.D., is clinical professor of pediatrics in the General Pediatric Division, University of Washington School of Medicine, and at the Odessa Brown Children's Clinic, Children's Hospital and Medical Center, Seattle, Washington.

TABLE 9.1
The Diagnostic Questions of Child Abuse

• What?
Injury—anatomic
Injury—physiologic
• How? (Etiology)
Macro = Is it abuse?
Micro = What is the mechanism, type, and magnitude?
• When?
• Who?
• Why?

uncontrolled event or constitute a pattern of injury over time. Also, by combining knowledge of *when* with the history of who was caretaking the child, we can often identify *who* caused the injuries. Without this information, we don't know how to provide protection to the child and where to direct caretaker treatment efforts. *Why* also has global and incident-specific levels. Why did it happen to this particular child/caretaker dyad at this time? Further, as a society, why does abuse occur? These questions may lead us to primary prevention efforts.

General Diagnostic Principles

Much of the diagnosis of physical abuse is common sense. Beyond this, diagnosis is based on a more in-depth knowledge of unintentional and abusive injury patterns. The diagnosis rests on three basic questions: (1) What is the history? (2) What are the injuries? and (3) Does the history explain the injuries?

Medical caretakers—including emergency medical workers, nurses, social workers, and physicians—should each obtain as detailed a history as possible. Immediately obtained history should detail any events leading up to medical attention and trace the evolution of the child's symptoms. A history of past illnesses or injuries should be sought. Less emergently, the child's developmental abilities should be defined. A perinatal history should be obtained for infants and toddlers. A family medical history, including propensity to injury, is helpful. The child's environment should be documented. Social work often provides this part of the history, which covers household structure, identity of caretakers, caretaker employment, mental health and substance abuse problems, past abuse by caretakers, spouse abuse, and past protective services involvement. The timing of recent caretaker involvement with the victim and medical events should be documented. Past medical care providers should be identified and their records, including growth and neonatal data, sought. Child care workers, school personnel, and lay observers may also provide collateral history.

Occasionally, the history is definitive. An eyewitness account may be available or the child may be old and capable enough to provide his or her own history. Professional report of either type of account to the legal system would be considered "hearsay." Hearsay evidence is generally inadmissible in court; however, exceptions can be made when there is strong reason to believe the statements are trustworthy and necessary.

To be admissible, history should be obtained through nonleading questioning. Children should not be forced into yes/no responses. Specific responses should not be implied or solicited by the form of the question. It is helpful to document not only the child's responses but also the questions asked. Both the specific content and the emotion behind disclosures and responses should be recorded. Common exceptions that allow hearsay to be admissible include: (1) "excited utterances," which are spontaneous, emotion-laden disclosures felt to be truthful because they are unguarded emotional outbursts, and (2) history provided by the patient to a physician to obtain diagnosis and treatment—a child's identification of a perpetrator would be an example. These exceptions apply to both physical and sexual abuse. The law assumes that a person seeking medical treatment will be truthful in order to obtain appropriate treatment.

Often the history is incomplete or only suggestive of abuse. Vague or intangible descriptions may be given. The injuries may have been discovered de novo: "We found him like this when he woke from his nap." Alternatively, injuries may be attributed to uncertain events: "He may have fallen at day care yesterday." If medical professionals seem to view these claims askance, the child's caretakers may offer multiple alternative and evolving stories until an acceptable explanation seems to be reached. Frequently, the child is blamed for self-injury: "The baby hit his head with his rattle." Siblings and peers may also be blamed for causing injuries far beyond their physical ability. Caretakers sometimes provide partial histories. They may admit to feeling frustrated with the child and to employing some discipline but simply not acknowledge the full scope of the injuries they caused.

Even if the history is very clear and consistent, it may not explain the child's injuries. For example, the injuries must be within the developmental capability of the child. History of the child's premorbid development should be obtained. One can then assess whether the behavior described is too advanced for the child. Alternatively, an older child may have sufficient cognitive and motor skills to have avoided the injury as it is described. The child's behavior and development should additionally be weighed against normal child behavior (fig. 9.1). An attempt should be made to time the injuries. Frequently, injuries caused by abuse may have occurred at different times than claimed. Old, infected burns may be described as fresh. Careful evaluation may also reveal multiple injury ages implying multiple injury incidents (fig. 9.2). Injuries may occur in patterns that are incompatible with the history or with typical unintentional injuries. Looped-cord whip marks or epiphyseal/metaphyseal chip fractures are injuries that don't occur naturally. Certain injury locations are also highly suggestive of abuse. For example, a child rarely bruises the buttocks or genitalia by unintentional injury (an exception might be straddle injuries). Confronted with one injury, the examiner should look for others. An obvious bruise, for instance, may be the clue to multiple occult fractures. All of these considerations may allow the observer to discount lucid and coherent histories as fabrications.

The child's caretakers should finally be considered in the light of the "reasonable parent." Did they respond in a prudent and expeditious way to the child's injuries? Abusive

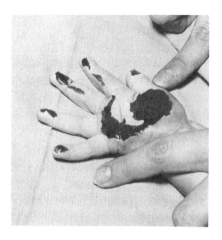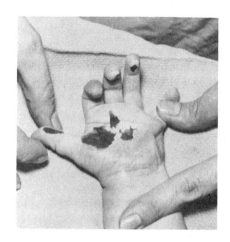

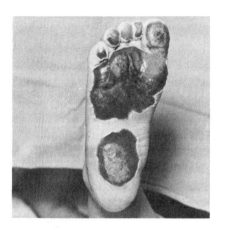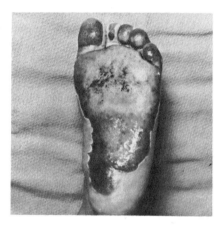

9.1 A twenty-month-old was said to have crawled onto a griddle, burning only his palms and soles. This is incompatible with normal toddler behavior.

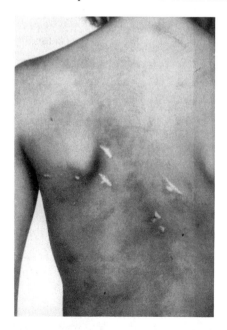

9.2 Multiple ages of injury are seen on a repeatedly beaten boy. Old hyperpigmentation is present on his right shoulder. As scabs from whipping slough, hypopigmented scars remain. A fresher bruise from whipping with a coiled cord angles down from his left shoulder.

caretakers frequently delay care in an attempt to hide the child's injuries. Thus, needed medical attention may be inappropriately postponed. The child may be brought for treatment only when complications develop. Alternatively, the injuring caretaker may keep the child from care. Another, innocent caretaker may later discover the child's injuries and promptly seek care. As an example, children with tap-water burns who were brought to medical care more than two hours after the injury or who were brought to medical attention by a caretaker other than the one with the child at the time of injury were victims of abuse 70% of the time (1).

"The battered child" was originally described as a syndrome including altered parent and child behavior, malnutrition, and multiple types and ages of inflicted injury (2). Individual children often exhibited many of the described abnormalities. Two factors seem to have changed this early pattern: (1) early recognition of and intervention in child abuse and (2) the changing pattern of child care. Child abuse has become widely publicized; as a result, many abusive injuries are now recognized even by lay observers. In the United States and several other countries, a universal reporting and protection system has been developed. Consequently, intervention is more likely to occur before repetitive injury has a chance to take place. As opposed to the 1950s, when mothers provided most child care alone at home, these days mothers are more likely to be single parents and/or work outside the home. The repetitive injury and malnurturing of children attributed to isolated, depressed mothers have often been replaced by a single or brief series of severe assaults (3). Many of these severe injuries are inflicted by new boyfriends who have coincidentally been recruited as child care providers (3, 4). In addition, children are more likely to be cared for by outside child care workers, who may then become perpetrators of abuse. As a consequence of these social changes, battered children are now more likely to have one or a few of the characteristics of the initially described syndrome rather than its full constellation.

Several triage decisions must be made at the initial evaluation. Are the child's injuries sufficient to require inpatient treatment? If so, hospitalization would place him or her in a protected environment. If not, will the child be safe in his or her own home or with a nonabusing caretaker from the family? This decision is often best made in consultation with social work and protective services. If the evaluator decides to send the child home with family members, a decision must also be made as to whether to tell the family about a protective services referral. This judgment is based on whether informing the caretakers would place the child at increased risk of injury. Disclosure might also allow the family to muzzle or alter an older child's history before protective services can intervene. If notification is unlikely to cause these problems, it is best to inform the family about protective services referrals.

Characteristics of Specific Injuries Caused by Abuse

Bruises

Normal childhood bruises are irregularly circular to amorphous injuries. They commonly occur over bony prominences and affect areas that the child leads with in activity (5). Further, these areas are age appropriate. Thus, fifteen-month-old children commonly have fore-

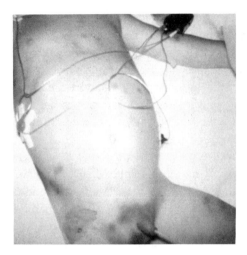
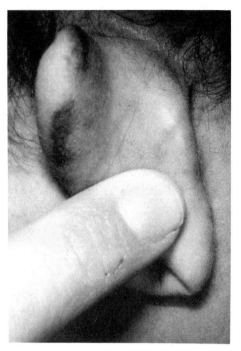

9.3 Genital bruising accompanies the distended abdomen of a boy with a fatal bowel perforation.

9.4 Bruises rim the pinna of a three-year-old girl who was struck by her foster brother. (Reproduced by permission of *Pediatrics*.)

head bruises and preschoolers have knee and shin injuries. Any bruises in the pre-cruising child should raise concern that the infant either has an undiagnosed illness associated with bruising or has been abused (6). Bruises resulting from abuse are more likely to involve well-padded areas of the body and areas protected from normal activity. Buttocks, thighs, genitalia (fig. 9.3), trunk, neck, cheek, and ear (fig. 9.4) injuries are more likely to be caused by abuse. As opposed to bruises, lacerations are more likely to result from accidental injury (5).

Although bruise coloration has been felt to undergo predictable evolution, the ability to accurately determine bruise age from coloration is limited (7). Bruises usually begin as a rosy pink to red-purple color. Acute injuries may have palpable induration and tenderness. On occasion, new bruises may develop while the child is under medical observation as blood continues to well up from recent deeper injuries. Damaged vessels also may continue to leak blood. The extent and spread of bleeding is determined, in addition, by the structure of the injured tissue. For example, the loose fatty tissue of the eyelid allows abundant, widely dispersed bleeding. The pace of bruise resolution depends on the bruise's depth within the skin and the quantity of bleeding. Smaller, superficial injuries (such as petechiae) resolve more quickly. Blood typically begins to break down in the thinner periphery, going from red-purple or black through green or yellow and brown hues. Yellow coloration may initially be seen at the margins of superficial bruises as early as eighteen hours after injury, and some red, purple, blue, and black hues may remain until bruise resolution (8). Although the pace of hemoglobin breakdown and bruise resolution is simi-

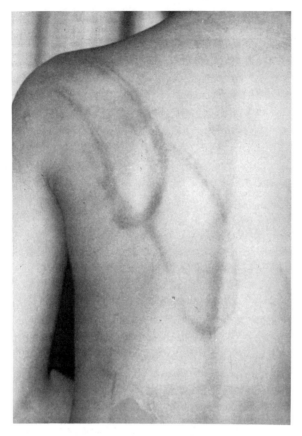

9.5 Whipping with a looped cord caused parallel bruising, outlining the cord over the child's left shoulder, and confluent bruising at the tip of the U-shaped bruise.

lar, the natural dark pigmentation of some children may make it difficult to see bruises and may alter the apparent color during resolution. Bruises ultimately resolve in two to four weeks, but postinflammatory hypo- or hyperpigmentation may persist for months to a year. These are often most notable in darkly pigmented children. At times, the pigment may be taken up by dermal macrophages, similar to what occurs with tattooing, resulting in permanent hyperpigmentation.

Patterned bruises often result from injuries of abuse (9). The bruise patterns commonly mimic the injuring objects. At the margin of a high-velocity injuring object, impact stretches capillaries sufficiently to tear them. This may occur even when the force does not crush directly impacted vessels. Thus, with high-velocity injuries, like whippings or slaps, an unbruised negative image of the cord or hand may be outlined by a fine rim of petechiae. Greater forces rupture directly impacted vessels, creating in addition a positive image bruise of the object. For example, looped-cord whippings commonly cause a negative image farthest from the U-shaped end of the loop (fig. 9.5). At the U, where impact force is

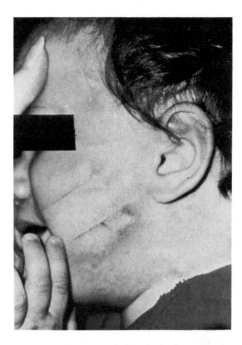

9.6 The pale image of a handprint is outlined
in petechiae. The assailant's fifth finger points
toward the child's ear lobe. (Photograph courtesy of Dr. Barton D. Schmitt.)

greatest, a positive image may be seen. These high-velocity injuries may also abrade or
lacerate the skin surface.

If severe forces are applied more slowly, the elastic limit of the capillaries at the margins will not be exceeded. Bruising underlying the site of injury, without a petechial outline, will result. On the other hand, shearing forces that are more slowly applied may well
leave an image of the injuring object outlined by petechiae. Grip injuries may be forceful
enough to leave a positive imprint of the thumb or fingertips. Alternatively, shearing may
be great enough to leave a petechial outline of the digit. Grip marks commonly appear on
the face, neck, and arm.

Typical patterned bruises include marks made by whipping, slapping, pinching, and
binding. Looped cords and linear objects like belts, switches, and rulers are commonly
used. Slap marks are most often seen on the face (fig. 9.6) or bare buttocks; the assailant's
handprint appears as a pale image outlined by petechiae. Pinch marks appear as fine, arcu-
ate bruises with concave sides facing each other. Ligatures used to restrain a child may
encircle the extremities, causing crisply delineated pressure necrosis injuries of the skin.
Gags may cause similar skin necrosis that droops down from the angles of the mouth.
Bruises or ligature marks may completely or partially encircle the neck, a sign of strangling
or throttling episodes.

Bite marks appear as partial or complete arcs of individual tooth prints (fig. 9.7). Children's primary maxillary canines (cuspids) are normally less than 3 cm apart; the adult span is greater. A mandibular intercuspid distance of 2.4 cm divides most primary and adult dentition. However, the intercuspid distance increases only 2.5 to 5 mm from childhood to adulthood. Most growth in the dental arch is in length. The greatest increase in arch width occurs posteriorly, where the permanent molars are developing (10, pp. 33–36). Thus, the primary dental arch has a relatively broader and shallower shape than the adult's. Primary upper central and lateral incisors are of equal width. Adult centrals are wider than laterals. A simple size measurement is not sufficient to identify specific perpetrators; the location and shape of individual teeth as well as the overall bite configuration are required. Suction produced bruises may be seen within the center of the bite. If the skin is broken by bites, dental impressions can be made. If the bites are fresh and unwashed, they can be swabbed with saline for perpetrator blood group, and/or DNA identification.

These patterned injuries all reflect the shape of the injuring object. Inflicted bruise patterns may also be determined by the anatomy of the injured part. Vertical gluteal cleft bruises can be caused by transverse paddling of the buttocks (fig. 9.8), and a line of petechiae may rim the top of the pinna of a boxed ear (9). Bruising also reflects the underlying bony anatomy. A blow to the side of the face may cause bruising only over the cheekbone.

Other, less patterned, bruises may also be seen with episodes of abuse. Eye bruising may occur with accidents or abuse (fig. 9.9). Bilateral black eyes may be caused by a single midline injury. In this case mid-forehead, glabella, or bridge of the nose injury should be evident. Midline injury may result from accidents. Alternatively, both orbits may be injured separately. It is rare, however, for both orbits to be separately injured accidentally at approximately the same time. Independent injuries involving opposite sides of convex surfaces—such as both sides of the face—or multiple body surfaces—like the back and front of the trunk—imply multiple injuries. Likewise, multiple bruises of differing ages imply multiple events and are highly suggestive of abuse. With accidental events, other skin changes such as concrete abrasions may confirm the history.

Intra- and perioral injuries may be seen with abuse. Blows to the lower face may contuse or lacerate the lips, tear the frenulum of the upper lip, and fracture or avulse teeth. The underside of the lips and the oral cavity should be carefully inspected. Tooth discoloration or dental abscesses may reveal earlier inflicted injury. Combined evaluation with dentists and with dental radiographs is helpful. Intraoral injuries may also result from forceful, frustrated feeding attempts. Tongue and palatal lacerations result from forcible spoon feeding. Soft palate petechiae may be caused by fellatio but also can result from natural events such as a child's repeated snuffling to clear postnasal mucous.

Care should be taken to recognize natural variations in skin coloration as well as illnesses that mimic abuse. Mongolian spots are frequently seen in darkly pigmented infants (blacks—95%, Asians and Native Americans—81%, Chicanos—70%, and whites—10%) (11). They may be mistaken for bruises by the unfamiliar. They are most frequent in the sacral region but can involve the entire back discontinuously. Less frequently, other body surfaces are also involved. Mongolian spots are present at birth and fade slowly over the

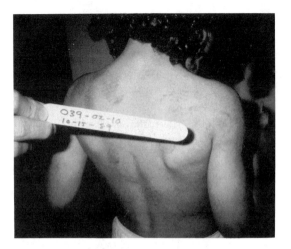

9.7 Multiple bite marks on the child's right shoulder accompany other patterned bruises.

9.8 Vertical gluteal cleft bruising accompanies outlines of fingers on the right buttock. The infant's bare bottom was spanked with an open hand.

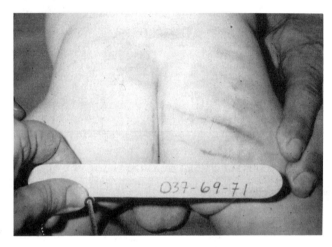

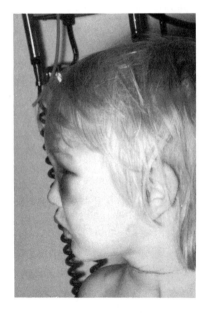

9.9 Ligature marks around the neck accompany a child's black eye.

first years of life. They appear similar to, but unique from, subacute bruises. Their color is a steely blue-black. As opposed to bruises, mongolian spots appear strikingly homogeneous, superficial, and thin. Bruises that involve similar large areas usually are, and appear to be, composed of multiple discrete or overlapping injuries.

Hereditary collagen disorders like Ehlers-Danlos syndrome and osteogenesis imperfecta are associated with increased skin fragility and bruising. Systemic disorders may result in easy bruising from either decreased coagulation ability (e.g., hemophilias and thrombocytopenias) or increased vascular fragility (e.g., meningococcemia and Henoch Schoenlein purpura). Similarly, medications may either reduce coagulation ability (e.g., aspirin's reduction of platelet function) or may reduce vascular integrity (e.g., as in chronic steroid therapy). Coughing, vomiting, or other causes of increased intrathoracic pressure may cause diffuse petechiae above the level of the nipples. Where clinical concern for an underlying disorder exists, appropriate tests of clotting ability, platelet function and number, or specific studies for underlying illnesses should be performed.

It should, however, be remembered that even children predisposed to bruising may be victims of abuse. Natural bruises in these children should, of course, follow natural patterns; specifically patterned or distributed injuries should not be ignored. If injuries occur only with a specific caretaker, this is strong evidence for unusual trauma.

Some inflicted injuries should not be considered to result from abuse. A number of folk-medicine practices result in unusual or patterned injuries. Southeast Asian coin rubbing, *Cao Gaio,* results in petechial bruising overlying ribs and paraspinal muscles (fig. 9.10) (12). Cupping results in circular suction mark bruises. These injuries should be viewed in the context of the family's cultural beliefs and the risk to the child of these practices (see chapter 2). Our Western culture also practices medical and cosmetic procedures that result in permanent injury and are of questionable therapeutic benefit (e.g., circumcision and ear piercing). Children may also inflict injuries such as "hickeys" on themselves or peers by suction on the arm or neck. Unusual patterns of skin injury may occur, such as the brown pigmentation of phytophotodermatitis. This results when a child's skin is coated with the juice of vegetables or citrus fruits, especially limes, and then exposed to the sun.

Skin injuries should be documented by written description, diagram, and photograph (13). The diagram and description should include location, size, shape, color, induration, and tenderness. Most state child protection laws allow photographic documentation of injuries of abuse without specific parental consent, but it is best to obtain such consent.

For identification, a distant photo of the child, including the face, should be taken. Injuries should be photographed at close enough range to render detail. Additional photographs need to be taken from sufficient distance to locate injuries on the body. To avoid angular distortion, detail shots should be taken with the camera/injury axis perpendicular to the surface of the injury. However, injuries with depth, such as bites, may best reveal their contours if photographed at, or with illumination at, a more tangential angle. In such cases, both angles of photos and lightings should be taken. The patient's identity, the date of the photo, and a centimeter scale should be included in the field of the photo. It is often helpful to take two exposures of each shot. One can then remain in the child's record while

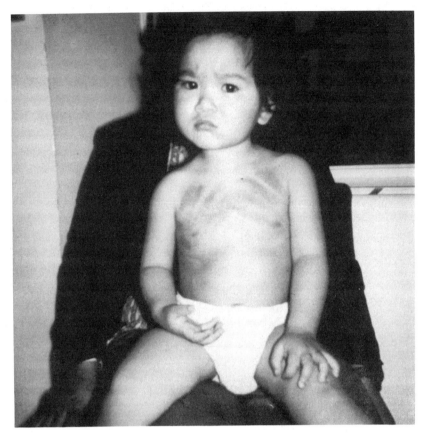

9.10 Coin rubbing, *Cao Gaio,* was used to treat a Southeast Asian child's chest congestion.

the other can be provided to the legal authorities. Although instant cameras allow the examiner to be certain that some photographic documentation has been obtained, the results are usually of poor quality and are difficult to reproduce.

Burns

Abuse has been recognized in 10% to 25% of childhood burn injuries (14). The two most common types of burns caused by abuse are contact burns and hot-liquid injuries. Several less frequent types may also be seen.

Contact burns often result in scarring but are rarely life threatening. Most commonly, they result from contact with hot metal or with smoldering objects. In both cases unintentional injuries are characterized by single, brief, glancing contacts of exposed body parts. Body surfaces burned are ones that the child normally presents in activity and are developmentally determined.

The commonest smoldering heat source used in abuse is the cigarette, but smoldering yarn, punks, or wood may also be used. Abusive cigarette burns are often multiple and inflicted to body parts that normally are clothed or protected (fig. 9.11). They are frequently deep, clear, circular imprints. They heal with cicatricial, circular scars resembling a small-pox vaccination. Although, when healed, they can be difficult to distinguish from healed chicken pox or excoriated, infected bug bites, their depth, size, discrete circular character, and sometimes patterned grouping may reveal their etiology. Since many of these injuries are used to discipline or torture older children, the child's history may corroborate the examiner's clinical impression.

Children clearly sustain unintentional cigarette burns, but these usually involve the face or exposed parts of the arms. A toddler who is sitting in the lap of a parent who is smoking may turn and contact the cigarette on the face. Walking or running children may also contact a cigarette held at the parent's side.

Folk-medicine therapy may mimic abuse from cigarette burns. The Chinese practice of moxibustion originally used smoldering moxa herb to inflict burns. Burning was to areas of symptoms or in a more representational pattern similar to acupuncture (fig. 9.12) (15). Typically these injuries are very patterned. I have not seen them inflicted by the child's family; instead, folk-medicine practitioners have caused the injuries with smoldering materials. Their therapeutic intent is evident from parental history of treatment for illness.

Hot metal objects may be used to inflict intentional contact burns. Like cigarette burns, these injuries tend to be forcefully and clearly inscribed. Thus, the identity of the injuring object is often visible in the burn pattern. Common objects used include metal floor heating grates, cigarette lighters, heated silverware, electric hair dryers, curling irons, and clothes irons. A barefoot, running toddler can step on a floor heating grate. It is less likely, although not impossible, that this toddler would plant and burn the second foot (fig. 9.13). If the injury is unintentional, the injury patterns tend to be blurred rather than sharply outlined. Similarly, curling irons and clothes irons may be left where toddlers can brush against them or pull them on themselves. Both unintentional injury scenarios result in smeared, generally shallow second-degree burns. Unintentional injuries from falling hot metal objects will commonly leave a V-shaped burn. The object glances away from and burns more shallowly at the lower margin of the injury. Inflicted burns are more likely to leave crisp images of the irons and cause deeper skin damage.

Hot-metal contact burns may also result from folk practices. Burn scarification is sometimes practiced traditionally for cosmetic purposes or as part of pubertal or initiation rites. This is seen in some central African and Oceanic cultures.

Patterned hot-metal contact burns have also occurred when children are seatbelted with sun-heated buckles (16). We should also keep in mind that some chemical hot packs and heating pads reach temperatures sufficient to burn insensate skin (17).

Hot-liquid burns caused by acts of abuse are generally inflicted with hot water. Although comprising only 7% to 17% of all childhood scalds requiring hospitalization, tap water accounts for 87% of those that are due to abuse (1). Hot-liquid injuries are also caused by foods. Foodstuffs tend to be more viscous and adherent than water; oils and foodstuffs also have a higher heat content. As a result of more prolonged exposure to greater reservoirs of heat, these substances burn more deeply than similar volumes of water.

Several principles underlie hot-liquid burn analysis. First, the depth of burning is

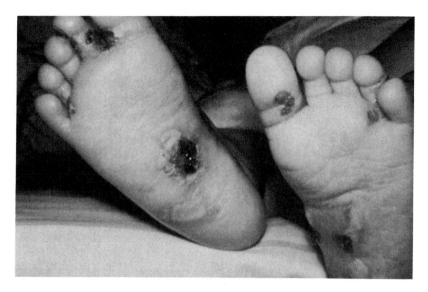

9.11 Multiple, inflicted cigarette burns of both soles of a toddler's feet create deep circular injuries. (Photograph courtesy of Dr. Barton D. Schmitt.)

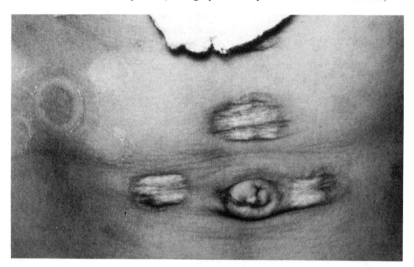

9.12 Patterned, cigarette-like, burn scars (moxibustion) encircle the umbilicus of a Southeast Asian child treated for abdominal symptoms.

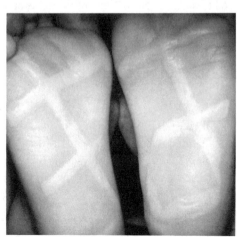

9.13 Deeply and clearly inscribed hot metal heating grate burns of both feet witness restraint.

related to both the temperature/heat content of the liquid and the duration of exposure. This relationship, as it applies to hot water, was studied in the 1940s (fig. 9.14) (18). The threshold for second-degree burn injury is 113° F. It takes about six hours to cause burns at this temperature. The pain threshold is variously noted to be 114–118° F. Water that is hot enough to burn will be painful to the touch. A history that a child who was left comfortably bathing was later found to have a peeling second-degree burn is fallacious. Extrapolation from adult data suggests that at 130° F it takes about ten seconds to cause deep second-degree burns of preschool children. At 140° F it takes about one second. Adult times at comparable temperatures are thirty-five and five seconds (19).

At lower water temperatures, the basal layers of the skin must be exposed to prolonged heat before irreversible injury occurs. Here the time for heat to reach the basal layers is proportionately short compared to the total burn time (fig. 9.15a). As a consequence, skin thickness does not significantly modify burn times below 130° F. This means that burn times for children and adults are similar (19, 20). However, above 130° F, the time for heat penetration to the basal layers becomes a much greater portion of the total exposure time. Thus, children, with their thinner skin, can burn more quickly than adults (fig. 9.15b). In a similar manner, regional differences in skin thickness modify burn times. Thinner skin, such as is found on the trunk, burns more rapidly than heavily keratinized palms and soles.

Normal infant and toddler bathing temperature is 101° F and hot tub temperatures run from 104° F to a maximum of 108° F. Bathwater hotter than 140° F will usually steam as it is drawn. Electric water heaters were commonly set at 150° F and gas water heaters at 140° F during the 1970s. Several jurisdictions now require, and the water-heater industry is moving toward, a preset standard of 120–125° F. This will increase the time of onset of deep second-degree burns of children from two seconds or less to five to ten minutes. Similar legislative changes have resulted in a decreased incidence of unintentional tap-water burn scalds, but the number of intentional scalds has been less affected. Accordingly, the percentage of tap-water burn scalds resulting from abuse has increased from 31% to 47% (21).

When a child sustains a tap-water burn injury, investigators should check the maximum water temperature at the involved tap to understand the degree of hazard. Although very hot water (and the very short burn times characteristic of children) may with brief, unintentional contact cause sharp demarcation of burned and unburned skin, unintentional injuries resulting from very hot water commonly are accompanied by splash mark burns. On the other hand, water that is less hot will not cause sharp, contour-line demarcations between burned and unburned skin to form unless the child is forcibly restrained during its contact with the water. Such cooler water is also unlikely to cause splash burns, because of its brief contact time and lower temperature.

Another principle of burn analysis is that flowing water follows the pull of gravity downhill. By observing the pattern of flowing-water injury, examiners can usually identify the initial point of contact, where burning is most intense (fig. 9.16). They can then follow the water as it thins, disperses, and cools on its downward course. The child's position relative to vertical can be discerned, and the direction of hot-water contact identified. Cups of hot water are commonly spilled upon children, or children pull filled cups down upon

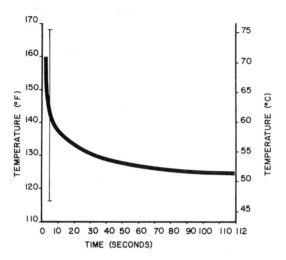

9.14 The mean ±2 standard deviations for Seattle-area home bathtub water temperatures are superimposed on the time-versus-temperature curve of hot water required to cause full-thickness scalds of adult skin (1). (Graph adapted from Moritz and Henriques [18].)

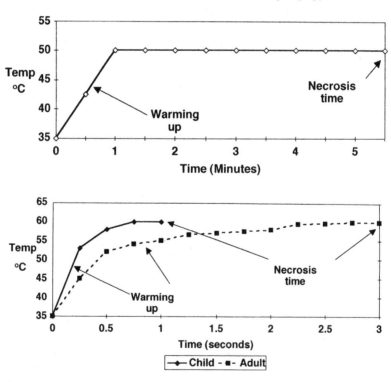

9.15 At low temperatures (water temperature 50°C [123°F]), the time it takes for heat to penetrate to the basal skin layers is short compared to the total burn time. Child and adult burn times are then equal (*a, above center*). At high temperatures (water temperature 60°C [140°F]), heat penetration time is a large part of the total burn time. Thicker adult skin insulates the basal skin layers, prolonging burn time (*b, above*). (Figures derived from data of Feldman [19] and Henriques [20].)

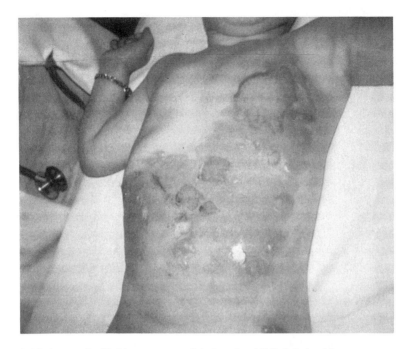

9.16 A cup of spilled hot water struck below the child's left shoulder.
It spread and cooled as it flowed downhill on the child's chest and abdomen.
A splash burn is present on the left pelvic brim.

themselves. If the child pulls down a cup or pot of water from above, he or she will usually be looking up at it. Burns under the chin are thus more likely to be unintentional, whereas water that is deliberately thrown on a child from above will usually spare the area under the child's chin. Unintentional flowing-water injuries from tub faucets or showers should exhibit appropriate distributions for the history. Evidence of restraint should not be seen. If a child's buttocks are rinsed under flowing hot water after a toileting accident, this implies adult restraint.

Finally, standing water seeks a level. If a child is forcibly immersed in a drawn container of hot water, a crisp contour line will divide uniformly burned from unburned skin. In its simplest form, hands or feet are immersed, causing "stocking" or "glove" burns (fig. 9.17). When children's bodies are restrained in hot water, crisply defined patches of unburned skin can often be seen within the burned areas. These occur where the body is forcibly flexed on itself so skin-to-skin contact prevents the incursion of hot water. The flexion creases of the groin and behind the knee are often spared (fig. 9.18a) (22). Sparing may also be seen where thighs are opposed to the abdominal wall and where a child is held sitting with a foot under its buttock. These spared areas imply that the child was unable to move in the hot water. Sparing may also be seen where the child's buttocks are forcibly held against the cooler tub bottom, creating a "hole in the doughnut" effect (figs. 9.18b, 9.18c). Finally, burn patterns can be used to reconstruct the child's position in the water.

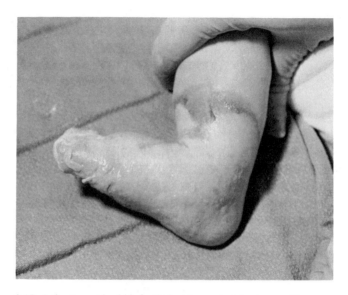

9.17 A three-month-old infant's foot has a stocking burn with a
sharp upper contour dividing burned and unburned skin. The
child's age, the sharp burn margin, and the lack of splashing burns
imply that the child's foot had been forcibly restrained in hot
water.

These often are not positions of stable balance or ones a child could maintain by his or her
own effort (figs. 9.18d, 9.18e). Many of these immersion burns involve the buttocks and
are frustrated caretaker responses to toileting accidents. Their greatest incidence is in the
toddler age. Purdue asserts that all buttock immersions are abusive (14). Other patterns of
forcible immersion, such as the headfirst pattern, have been observed. The key to recognition of abusive burns is burn-pattern evidence of restraint.

Rarer causes of abusive burns include fires, caustics, electrical cords, and microwave
or regular ovens. Electrical injuries frequently are deeply penetrating and may cause necrosis of underlying cartilage, muscle, and bone. Microwaves preferentially affect high-water-
content tissues. The skin and subcutaneous fat may be spared in the face of significant
muscle injury (23).

Bullous diseases including bullous impetigo, staphylococcal scalded skin disease,
toxic epidermal necrolysis, and epidermolysis bullosa may all be incorrectly thought to be
burn injury. The tendency for blisters to occur in response to trauma, Nikolsky's sign, may
augment this interpretation.

Sharply punched out erosions accompanying "ammoniacal" diaper rash may resemble cigarette burns. Photosensitive skin injury may cause alarmingly patterned pigment
changes and scarring but not betoken abuse. Some innocent pressure injuries cause second-
degree skin trauma that heals with patterned hyperpigmentation suggestive of burn injury.
For example, I have seen such injuries at the top of cowboy boots and at the back of the
thigh where skin was crimped between the seat and legrest of a high chair.

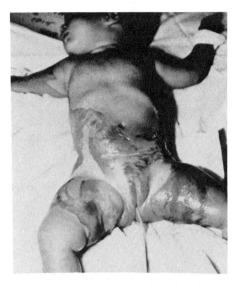

9.18 A ten-month-old girl was forcibly immersed in a tub of hot water. Flexion creases of the groin are spared burning where her legs were held flexed against her abdomen (*a*). A less-burned buttock "doughnut hole" is present where she was held against the cooler tub bottom (*b*). An artist's reconstruction delineates the burn margins (*c*). Burn contours can be used to reconstruct the child's position in the hot water (*d, e*). A child could not support herself in this position. (Reprinted by permission of Dr. K. A. Hunter and Williams and Wilkins, Inc. [22]).

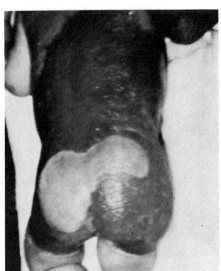

a

c

b

d   *e*

Head Injuries

Head injuries are the commonest cause of fatal or maiming physical abuse. Victims commonly present with altered consciousness, coma, seizures, vomiting, or irritability. Histories are either lacking, or they reflect minor events such as falls from couches.

Significant head injuries follow predictable time courses. Head trauma sufficient to cause subdural bleeding or parenchymal injury beyond focal impact contusions will render the child stunned or unconscious at the time of injury (24). With injuries of lesser force, consciousness may be regained, but such children usually exhibit lethargy, alternating with irritability, thereafter. Vomiting may be seen.

Delayed secondary loss of consciousness may result from evolving brain swelling, posttraumatic seizures, or space-occupying hemorrhage. The injury force required to cause these complications is significant. Snoek observed that only 4% of 967 children with historically minor head injury developed delayed deterioration of consciousness (25). One-third of these children who developed delayed deterioration of consciousness had posttraumatic seizures. The vast majority of these began within two hours after the injury. Although difficult to control acutely, posttraumatic seizures commonly resolve within one to two weeks after injury. Of the remaining two-thirds of children with minor head injury who later lost consciousness, 80% developed symptoms within one hour after injury. Only one of the six children without seizures had symptoms delayed more than two hours. Expanding hematomas were infrequent, and the three fatal cases were associated with acute brain swelling and brain dysfunction. More recently, Davis et al. studied children who sustained head injuries with brief loss of consciousness but subsequently regained a normal Glasgow Coma Scale of 15 (26). He found such children extremely unlikely to later develop surgically significant intracranial injuries.

Although most children with abusive head injuries present acutely with signs of brain dysfunction, some abusive head injuries are recognized much later, when older subdural bleeding has lysed. As the volume of the effusion increases, an enlarging head size or central nervous system symptoms of increased pressure develop.

Although many abusive head injuries have been recognized to result from blunt impacts, it has been postulated that whiplash shaking of infants may also cause injury. This assumption is based on several lines of evidence. Subdural hemorrhages have been observed in some adults who were involved in auto accidents but did not show evidence of head impact (27). Animals undergoing severe rotational acceleration/deceleration stresses in controlled biomechanical studies have developed similar patterns of injuries (28). Finally, some assailants have admitted shaking infants (29).

Controversy currently exists about whether whiplash shaking alone is sufficient to cause these injuries. Extrapolation from the biomechanical studies of animals, combined with observation of the forces generated when adults shake dummies, suggests that adults cannot shake infants with sufficient force to cause head injury (24). If, on the other hand, the dummy is struck against something, even a padded surface like a mattress, the predicted threshold for subdural bleeding is exceeded (fig. 9.19). One would not expect to see surface evidence of bruising with similar impacts of infants against resilient surfaces. Frequently, a child who has sustained impact injury to the head, even fatal impact, will lack surface bruising. However, if the body is autopsied, bruises are often found on the undersurface of the scalp (figs. 9.20a and 9.20b). The outer surface of the scalp is less vascular and thus more resistant to bleeding than its undersurface (the galeal side). Duhaime found that half of the children with fatal impact trauma to the head were not recognized to have been struck until autopsy (24).

Many physicians continue to feel that shaking alone is sufficient to cause these injuries (30, 31). Using physical examination, computed tomography (CT), and magnetic resonance imaging (MRI) scans, Alexander and his associates found that half of the children with inflicted head injuries lacked evidence of impact and that the presence of external impact evidence was not predictive of the severity of head injury (32). All of the sixteen children whom Green and associates recognized to have died of abusive head injury lacked evidence of cranial impact at autopsy (33). I have also observed infants who died with the typical intracranial and retinal bleeding of inflicted head injury who, at autopsy, lacked evidence of impact. These were rare, however, compared to infants with findings of impact.

This disagreement is unlikely to be resolved without testing an animal model closely similar to the human infant. Both potential scenarios involve severe rotational acceleration/deceleration of the infant's head on the axis of its neck (34). Both are abusive acts of distinctly greater force than any nurturing caretaker actions, including reviving an infant. In most instances it is appropriate to think of these children as shaken/impacted infants. One can reassure parents that normal play with infants, such as bouncing a child on the knee, will not cause shaking injury. But even if shaking alone does not cause these injuries, it is still wise to discourage shaking of infants in anger. During shaking, the child may be struck against something or the shaking event may terminate in the child being thrown down.

Rotational acceleration/deceleration events cause concussive loss of consciousness at a lower energy threshold than that required to cause subdural/subarachnoid bleeding or brain injury (fig. 9.19) (24). When some infants are brought into care, a history is given of a minor fall without loss of consciousness. If they have brain injury or intracranial bleeding, the history should immediately be suspect.

Children also sustain head injuries in linear decelerations such as falls from heights (35). Table 9.2 suggests that even very short falls onto unyielding surfaces like concrete may cause significant linear deceleration. The authors assert that linear decelerations as small as 50 Gs may result in head injury; however, the United States Consumer Product Safety Commission, which commissioned this study, has been unable to obtain the data on which these conclusions are based (36). Further, mechanical studies using solid objects are unlikely to model adequately the forces involved in cranial impacts. As a minimum confounder, the scalp has been estimated to absorb 35% of brief impacts (37). It is also simplistic to consider cranial impact tolerance as a function of G-force alone. The complex interaction of linear decelerative force and its time curve must be considered. Current standards for protective helmet design use a threshold of 300 Gs. This is based on study of helmets of adults involved in auto-racing crashes. Regardless of the source of the threshold, current bicycle helmets using the 300-G standard have been very effective in reducing the

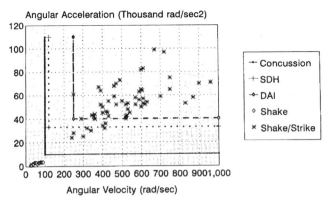

Angular Acceleration (Thousand rad/sec2)

Angular Velocity (rad/sec)

Legend:
- Concussion
- SDH
- DAI
- Shake
- Shake/Strike

9.19 Head injury threshold, angular acceleration versus angular velocity for shakes and strikes. Injury thresholds from primate experiments are scaled to an infant's 500gm brain weight. SDH = subdural hematoma; DAI = diffuse axonal injury. (Adapted by permission of Dr. Ann-Christine Duhaime [24].)

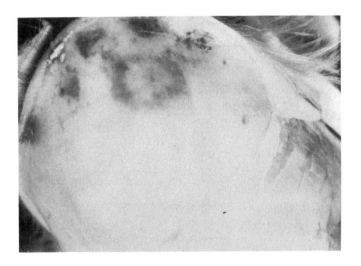

9.20 The underside of the scalp is bruised (*a, center above*) in the pattern of the brass knuckles used to inflict his head injury (*b, above*). The child's scalp surface was free of bruising.

TABLE 9.2
Linear Deceleration in Falls from Heights in G Forces of Fall

Surface Material	Drop Height (ft.)			
	0.25	1	4	8
Concrete	175	500		
Asphalt	42	150		
⅛" Mat	70	290		
Packed earth			200	
1⅛" Mat			4	47
12" Wood chips			22	32

Source: T. Reichelderfer, A. Overbach, and J. Greensher, "Unsafe Playgrounds," *Pediatrics* 64 (1979): 962–63.
Note: The threshold for head injury is a linear impact of 50 Gs.

head trauma of bicycle accidents (38). Common sense and experience belie the predicted forces and 50-G head injury threshold of table 9.2. If this threshold were true, every child who trips and hits his or her head on concrete should sustain a severe head injury.

A great number of observational studies of unintentional childhood falls have accumulated over the past twenty years (39–43). In most, severe intracranial injury similar to that seen with abuse is uncommon in falls of less than ten feet. However, simple skull fractures and epidural hemorrhage may occur with more minor unintentional falls (44). Complicated skull fractures, subdural and subarachnoid hemorrhage, and parenchymal brain injury are less likely (45, 46). Stairway falls follow a pattern of multiple short falls (47). They rarely result in significant head injury. Infants who fall down the stairway in a baby walker are an exception; they seem more susceptible to head injury (48).

Careful examination of the surface of an injured infant's head may reveal evidence of abuse. When a child's hair is pulled, clumps of hairs may be pulled out along with their roots. If the child is examined early enough, petechiae are frequently present at the base of the avulsed hairs. The scalp also may be pulled from the head, resulting in boggy subgaleal bleeding. The scalp should be carefully searched for bruises. Impact bruising may be seen on the outside, rim, and backside of the ear as well as on the underlying scalp (fig. 9.4) (9). In the "tin ear syndrome" these bruises are associated with subdural and retinal bleeding caused by rotational acceleration of the head after impact (49).

Simple skull fractures commonly result from normal infant falls of six feet or less (45, 46). They are rarely accompanied by significant intracranial injury other than occasional epidural bleeding (44). It is common for these infants to cry, then seem quite normal after the falls. The injury becomes apparent to caretakers when they observe boggy swelling of the child's head. Care is often delayed after the event but prompt after recognition of the swelling (45). The relatively thin parietal bone is fractured most often. More complex skull fractures (such as multiple independent fractures—ones involving multiple bones in the skull, crossing sutures, or accompanied by intracranial injury—and wide or growing fractures) are more likely to result from greater or more focused impact forces than those of normal infant falls. They are statistically associated with, but not pathognomonic for, abuse. Depressed fractures result from either greater force or moderate force against a focused object. Skull fractures do not exhibit healing patterns typical of other fractures, as I will discuss later in this section). However, acute skull fractures have been observed to have 4 mm or more (mean 8 mm) of soft-tissue thickness over the fracture than over the uninjured side on CT scan (50). This can aid differentiation of acute from old fractures. Bleeding external to the skull and beneath its periosteum will be bounded by the margins of individual fractured skull bones. This contrasts with subgaleal bleeding, which does not follow bony limits. Infants with severe intracranial injury may split their cranial sutures within a day of injury.

Subdural hemorrhage (SDH) is commonly seen in inflicted head injury of infants (fig. 9.21). Higher-strain injuries like assaults (that is, injuries resulting from rapid, brief acceleration) are more likely to result in subdural bleeding, while lower-strain events such as auto passenger injuries (that is, injuries resulting from prolonged, moderate acceleration) may result in brain injury (34). Acutely, the volume of SDHs is often not great enough to cause pressure symptoms. Instead, SDHs are visible markers on the CT scan of the associated, frequently severe, parenchymal injury. This brain injury may initially appear very bland on CT scan or at autopsy (fig. 9.22a). SDH often lies over the cortex or within the posterior falx (51).

Fresh blood is a very dense white on the CT scan. If bleeding continues to occur, merging into a preexisting intracranial hemorrhage, a swirl of varying density may be seen (52). As clot retraction develops, the density increases slightly. Thereafter, as the red cells lyse, the CT density of the intracranial blood decreases. It may be relatively isodense to brain tissue at one to two weeks and by several weeks appear similar to cerebrospinal fluid density (53).

As they age, SDHs may greatly increase in volume and then exhibit symptoms of mass effect (fig. 9.22b). Blood breaks down, new vessels invade the area, and membranes of scar tissue form (37). Effusion of fluid into the subdurals may be sufficient to require repeated needle drainage and eventual shunting. The new vessels seem more fragile than normal ones. Repeat fresh hemorrhage may develop within old effusions with more minor trauma. In many cases, though, new bleeding is seen in areas separate from the initial effusions and is accompanied by symptoms and signs of fresh parenchymal brain injury. Such findings document a second severe inflicted event.

Subarachnoid hemorrhage (SAH) is also commonly associated with head injury from abuse. Although usually multifocal, it is most easily recognized as a fine, white density extending the full length of the falx in the upper CT cuts (fig. 9.23) (54). It may also be seen layering along the tentorium. The increased falcine density of SAH may be subtle. High density becomes a normal finding as the falx calcifies in adults. Thus radiologists and clinicians unfamiliar with infant CTs may overlook the significance of this finding, considering it normal (55). On the other hand, the falx may appear artificially dense if old hypodense SDH or acutely edematous brain lies on either side of it. While the CT scan shows acute SAH, SAH is not imaged by the MRI scan until it is several days old (56). Even on the CT scan, SAH may become more evident in several days. It is very difficult to differentiate a very thin falcine SDH from SAH on CT scan.

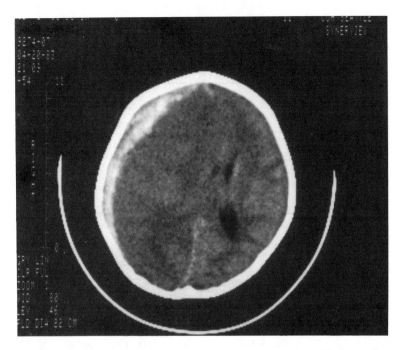

9.21 Fresh subdural bleeding is accompanied by severe ipsilateral brain swelling and midline shift.

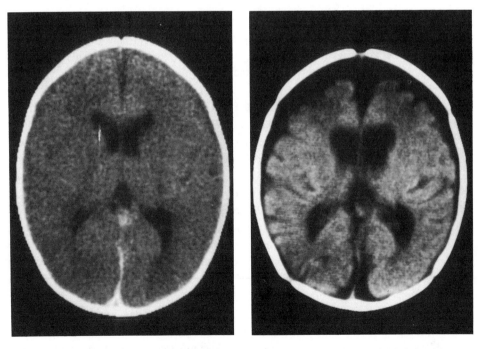

9.22 The initial CT scan of a five-month-old with seizures has subtle posterior falcine density and decreased gray matter–white matter distinction (*a, left*). Fourteen days later, large post-traumatic subdural effusions and brain atrophy are present (*b, right*).

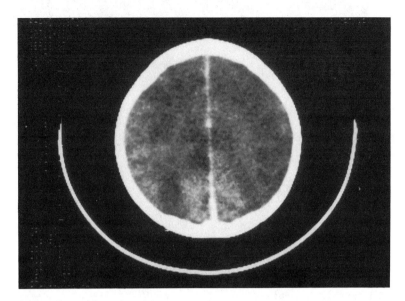

9.23 A fine, white stripe of fresh, high-density subarachnoid blood extends along the full length of the falx in the upper CT cuts. Patchy cortical hypodensity is also present.

It is not uncommon for children with a traumatic SAH to present with seizures, irritability and/or lethargy, fever, and a bulging fontanel. Physicians may initially respond to these children by performing a lumbar puncture for diagnosis of meningitis. Since the subarachnoid space communicates with the lumbar cerebrospinal fluid space, a lumbar puncture in an infant with SAH will yield bloody fluid. This can be differentiated from the acute bleeding of a "traumatic tap." SAH will yield nonclotting, nonclearing bloody fluid. If there is sufficient SAH to give the cerebrospinal fluid a pink tinge, an orange color will develop over time in the supernate of the centrifuged fluid. This xanthochromia initially appears two hours after SAH and should be visibly evident by twelve hours after bleeding (57). The centrifuged cerebrospinal fluid of a traumatic tap is not xanthochromic. Not all laboratories report both the presence and absence of xanthochromia in bloody cerebrospinal fluids; physicians should ask their lab to make this reporting routine.

Parenchymal brain damage may result from focal impact, tissue shearing of angular acceleration/deceleration, or secondary hypoxic/ischemic injury. Cortical brain contusion may be seen in a coup/contra-coup distribution. Parenchymal clefts and small hemorrhages are most often caused by severe rotational forces (58, 59). They lie within the white-matter radiations, and their presence is associated with immediate and ongoing unconsciousness.

Often, however, the child with severe brain injury or even death, may display a remarkably normal CT scan or autopsy if examined acutely (55, 60, 61). If the child survives one to two days, repeat scanning will frequently reveal loss of normal gray matter–white matter differentiation. Brain swelling and focal areas of ischemic hypodensity or hemorrhagic infarction hyperdensity commonly develop. The midbrain and basal brain structures and/or the posterior cerebral circulation may maintain normal density in the face of increasing cortical and white-matter hypodensity. This is a reversal of the normal pattern of brain density (fig. 9.24). Laminar cortical infarction appears as a band of increased subcortical density. Cortical hypodensity and laminar infarction are ominous signs of severe brain damage. In one to two weeks, edema resolves and hypodense or hemorrhagic brain may atrophy. Low density SDHs may develop and the overall brain size shrinks (51, 55).

In spite of these problems, the noncontrast CT scan remains the best acute diagnostic tool. The CT can produce images of bone revealing many skull fractures. It is sensitive to intracranial injuries that might benefit from surgery. Unlike the MRI scan, CT scan times are brief, limiting the need for patient sedation. In addition, metallic equipment may be taken into the CT scanner. The MRI is a good follow-up tool (54, 62). After two to three days it becomes more sensitive to small areas of bleeding than does the CT. It can follow injuries in multiple planes. It images the anterior temporal region and posterior fossa better than the CT scan can, and it can also highlight parenchymal edema and hemorrhage. Though it images soft tissue better than the CT scan does, it does not image bone. The MRI is helpful in determining whether collections of hypodense frontal fluid on CT scan are due to increased subarachnoid space or old subdural effusions (fig. 9.25). The sequence of evolution of blood density on the MRI scan complements that of the CT scan (table 9.3) (63).

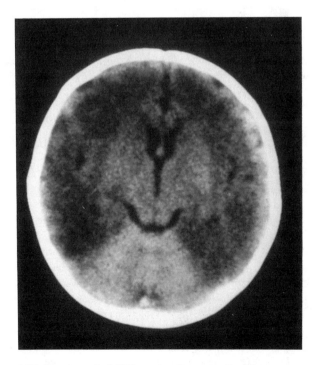

9.24 Severe cortical CT hypodensity contrasts with preservation of density in basal structures and the posterior circulation. This reflects brain infarction.

The MRI scan has been reported to image cervical spinal cord injury in child abuse (64), and it has proved sensitive to other causes of spinal cord damage as well.

Although intraventricular bleeding can accompany head injury, it is rarely seen as an isolated abusive central nervous system injury.

Cervical spinal cord injury may result from abusive events. Its symptoms are often obscured by associated brain injury in these abused children (30, 65). In symptomatic children, cord bleeding or edema is common, and vertebral ligamentous injuries may be present. However, vertebral fractures are seen in less than half of the children with cord injury and dysfunction.

Simple evaluation tools for abusive head injury should not be overlooked. Measure-

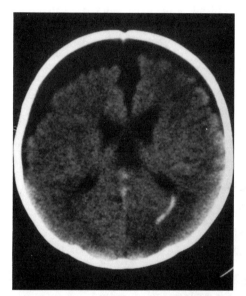

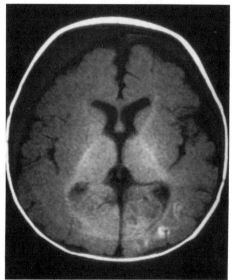

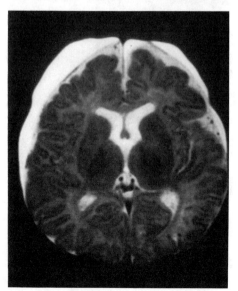

9.25 Dark bifrontal fluid, right frontal lobe atrophy, and acute left lateral ventricle bleeding accompany severe diarrhea with coagulopathy. On CT it is unclear if the frontal fluid is subdural fluid (*a, above left*). The MRI T$_1$ image shows contrasting densities of subdural fluid surrounding a normal subarachnoid space. Subdural fluid is grayer than intraventricular fluid (*b, above right*). The MRI T$_2$ image again contrasts subdural and subarachnoid spaces, but in this sequence subdural and intraventricular fluid densities look similar. The combination of densities implies a chronic subdural effusion (*c, left*).

TABLE 9.3
Evolution of MRI Density of Intracerebral Hematomas

Age	Location	Hemoglobin	T_1	T_2
Hyperacute (< 24 hrs.)	Intracellular	OxyHb	Isodense to Hypo	Isodense to Hyper
Acute (1–3 days)	Intracellular	DeoxyHb	Iso	Hypo
Subacute				
(Early: 3+ days)	Intracellular	MethHb	Hyper	Hyper
(Late: 7+ days)	Extracellular	MethHb	Hyper	Hyper
Chronic (14+ days)				
Center	Extracellular	Hemichromes	Iso to Hypo	Iso to Hyper
Rim	Intracellular	Hemosiderin	Hypo	Hypo

Source: W. G. Bradley, "Hemorrhage," in *MRI Atlas of the Brain,* ed. W. G. Bradley and G. Bydder (New York: Raven Press, 1990), 205.

ments of the circumference of the child's head taken before the injury can often be obtained from primary caretakers. A sudden increase in head growth may identify the timing of old SDHs. Infants with abusive head injury commonly develop anemia that seems disproportionately severe compared to the blood seen on CT scan. The hematocrit may fall rapidly after hospital admission. If this fall is followed by equilibration, this supports the acute nature of the head injuries. Polychromatophilia and reticulocytosis also help define the timing of injury. They usually become evident about two days after injury.

Children with severe brain injury or secondary acute illness may develop an acute coagulopathy. This is normally self-limited. On the other hand, intracranial bleeding similar to that of abuse may be seen in children with primary coagulopathies. It is appropriate to document vitamin K administration in the newborn nursery. Without it, breast-fed infants are more prone than bottle-fed infants to bleeding from late vitamin K deficiency. Coagulation studies should be done to evaluate primary clotting factor deficiencies, particularly factors VIII and IX. A blood count can document an adequate number of platelets. More sophisticated tests are required to evaluate for platelet dysfunction.

Ocular Injuries

Direct trauma to the eye can injure the surrounding soft tissue or bony orbit, leading to contusions and orbital fractures. Blows to the globe may result in corneal abrasion or laceration, anterior chamber bleeding (hyphema), traumatic iritis, and acute glaucoma. Subconjunctival hemorrhage may be caused by direct trauma, but it can also be a remote effect of strangulation, acute chest compression, or the increased intrathoracic pressure of an exuberant Valsalva maneuver.

Because of the strong association with abuse and the potential for causing blindness, retinal injury is of greatest significance. Hemorrhagic retinopathy is extremely common in child abuse (fig. 9.26). It can be found in 40% to 100% of carefully examined children following abusive intracranial trauma (66, 67). It is otherwise infrequent or caused by easily recognized illnesses. When present without evidence of these other illnesses, retinal hemorrhage is most likely to have resulted from abuse.

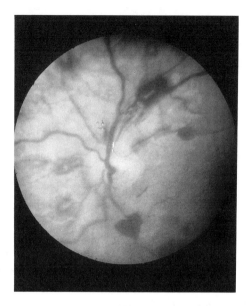

9.26 A flame-shaped retinal hemorrhage radiates out from the disk at twelve o'clock. A blot-shaped retinal bleed with a white center surrounds the superior temporal vessels. An arrowhead-shaped preretinal bleed obscures the inferior temporal vein. Other less prominent hemorrhages can also be seen.

Retinal hemorrhage has been described in children receiving cardiopulmonary resuscitation in whom abuse and other causes of bleeding have been excluded. The reported frequency has been low, 2% to 10% (68, 69). However, it should be noted that prolonged cardiopulmonary resuscitation in piglets has not resulted in retinal bleeding (70). Retinal hemorrhage can be seen as a result of a rapid increase in intrathoracic pressure in children who sustain severe closed chest injury (71). Nonspecific bleeding may be seen with carbon monoxide poisoning and coagulation disorders. SAH from vascular anomalies and severe systemic hypertension may be associated with retinal bleeding. Children with preexisting retinal disease are predisposed to retinal bleeds.

Retinal bleeding is a rare to nonexistent occurrence in well-studied series of sudden infant death syndrome (67, 72, 73). Although isolated anecdotes of retinal bleeding in victims of sudden infant death syndrome have been reported, abuse has not clearly been excluded in these cases.

At our current state of knowledge, we can say retinal bleeding is very common in abuse and rare in nonabusive trauma (74–76) or clinically and historically occult natural situations. It would be unwise to diagnose abuse on the basis of retinal bleeding alone. However, retinal hemorrhage is strongly suggestive of abuse and should be a clue to look for other evidence of trauma. The rarity of retinal hemorrhage with documented linear deceleration injuries and its frequency in abuse supports the role of a rotational acceleration/decelera-tion mechanism such as shaking in abusive head injury (33, 49, 67, 72, 76, 77). This asso-ciation, however, can not exclude a terminal decelerative impact as a necessary or usual event.

Hemorrhage into the nerve fiber layer of the superficial retina causes fine flame-shaped hemorrhages that radiate out from the disc. These are commonly associated with papille-dema and other evidence of increased intracranial pressure. Globular, blot hemorrhages arise from rupture of deeper retinal vessels. They may have white centers. Subretinal bleed-ing is partially obscured by the retinal tissue and is darker. Bright red globular hemorrhages lie between the retina and the vitreous or enter the vitreous. In the extreme, retinal schesis, traction folds, necrosis, or detachment may be associated (77). The severity of retinal injury increases in proportion to the severity of intracranial injury (33). It is important to involve an ophthalmologist in the care of these children, both to document ocular injury and to prevent visual sequelae. Some of the injuries mentioned above require acute treatment. Further, large hemorrhages may cover the macula, effectively patching the eye. This can lead to development of amblyopia. Healing of vitreal injuries may lead to scarring and late retinal detachment (66). Associated occipital lobe injury may cause cortical blindness.

Abdominal Injuries

After head injuries, abusive abdominal injuries are the most common cause of physical child abuse that is fatal. Abdominal injuries caused by abuse have a 40% to 50% case fatality rate (78, 79). These injuries usually result from a penetrating blow from a fist or a foot: the child's viscera are crushed between the striking object and his or her spine. The assailant may not appreciate the severity of injury or may attempt to hide it. Children are frequently not brought to care until they develop shock from peritonitis or hemorrhage. A nonabusing caretaker may discover the child in extremis and seek help. Comparable unin-tentional abdominal injuries result from high-velocity and/or penetrating trauma. Common situations include motor vehicle passenger injuries, auto and pedestrian accidents, bicycle handlebar penetrations, or falls from significant heights (79). Unintentional injury victims are, on the average, grade-school age; abuse victims are usually infants or toddlers.

These children commonly are brought to care with little clue given about the cause of their distress. Either the adult bringing the child to care is naive to the trauma, or the abuser continues to hide the incident. Although bruises may be found elsewhere on the child's body, the abdominal wall yields to forceful blows and most often escapes bruising (79). However, extra-abdominal trauma, such as bruising, fractures, or head injury, is usually seen. Vomiting, with or without bile, abdominal distension or pain, and signs of shock may be noted. The laboratory can be very helpful. Anemia suggests occult bleeding, while ele-vations of the white blood cell count, pancreatic enzymes, or hepatocellular enzymes sug-gest infection, pancreatic injury, or hepatic injury, respectively (80). The urine may be bloody due to direct renal trauma or may contain myoglobin from associated muscle trauma. Plain supine abdominal films can show the falciform ligament outlined by the air of a pneumoperitoneum or may reveal free abdominal fluid. Free air is easier to see in the upright or lateral decubitus views (fig. 9.27). If bleeding, liver injury, or pancreatic injury

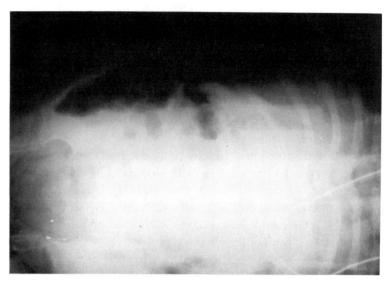

9.27 Free peritoneal air is seen on a lateral decubitus film.

is suggested, the CT scan is the best study to investigate the site and severity of injury (80). The abdominal ultrasound is also useful for evaluation of hepatic, pancreatic, splenic, and renal injury. It also can highlight an obstructing duodenal hematoma. Intravenous pyelography or scintigraphy may be needed to evaluate the functional integrity of the kidneys.

While serious unintentional intra-abdominal injury most often involves the spleen, abusive splenic trauma is not frequent (79). Abusive and unintentional abdominal trauma cause an equal percentage of hepatic, renal, and pancreatic injury. Hollow viscous injury, uncommon with unintentional injury, is frequent with abuse. Symptoms of pain and hemorrhagic shock predominate with hepatic and splenic trauma. Injury to the bowel can result in intramural or mesenteric bleeding. Symptoms result from bowel obstruction or blood loss. More severe bowel injury may cause immediate rupture or delayed perforation of necrotic bowel wall. The symptoms then become those of peritonitis. In addition to the bowel, a full stomach may rupture on impact.

As a rule, parents of unintentionally injured children respond quickly; in our study, 90% of unintentionally injured children were brought to care within three hours of the injury (79). On the other hand, care was delayed more than three hours for all abused children in that series. In another, the mean delay was thirteen hours (78). Death in these abused children is usually the direct result of septic or hemorrhagic shock secondary to the abdominal injury. However, death of children with unintentional abdominal trauma usually is due to multiple trauma—in particular, associated head injury (78, 79).

Skeletal Injury

Skeletal trauma played a large part in the original recognition of abuse as a cause of childhood injuries. In 1946, Caffey observed the striking association of unexplained fractures and head injury in infants (81). Currently, however, skeletal trauma is most likely to be recognized during a critical search for other trauma in children already suspected to be abused. Occult skeletal injury is most likely in the child less than a year old who shows other evidence of physical abuse. Merten studied abused children who had skeletal surveys performed. He found that 47% of these children under one year of age had fractures (82). In 67% of children, the fractures were clinically occult, and in 60% there were multiple fractures. For abused children one to two years old, fractures were still seen in 17%, but the frequency of occult injuries dropped to 16%. Of the two- to five-year-old children, 18% had fractures of which 4% were occult. Fractures were noted in children with other findings of impact trauma but were rare in children who had been burned, neglected, or sexually abused.

The skeletal survey is the best initial study for evaluation of infant bony trauma (fig. 9.28a) (30). A single "baby-gram" (a single x-ray film including the whole child in a single exposure) film is *not* an acceptable alternative. The skeletal survey identifies the location of injury and whether the problem is a fracture or some other bony pathology. One can often infer a specific mechanism of injury from the fracture pattern. Further, one can estimate the age of the injury (table 9.4) (83, p. 112).

Some fractures may be difficult to see acutely on the skeletal survey. These include rib fractures, nondisplaced fractures, unusually located fractures, and plastic bowing injuries. The presence of acute fractures sometimes can be inferred by careful examination of x rays for soft-tissue swelling and loss of normal soft-tissue planes. Skeletal scintigraphy is often more sensitive to these injuries (84, 85), but it is generally less available acutely and requires a great deal of skill and experience to interpret (fig. 9.28b). Scintigraphy identifies only increased metabolic activity; further evaluation is necessary to determine the cause. Since the epiphyseal regions of the long bones are normally metabolically active, it can be difficult to distinguish epiphyseal/metaphyseal chip fractures from normal radioactivity. If the cause of "hot" areas on the scintigraphy can not be acutely identified on standard radiographs, followup films in one-and-a-half to two weeks may reveal fracture line demineralization and early callus formation. Skeletal x rays and scintigraphy provide different types of information. Each can supplement, but not replace, the sensitivity, specificity, and clinical utility of the other.

TABLE 9.4
Timetable of Radiographic Changes in Children's Fractures

Category	Early	Peak	Late
1. Resolution of soft tissues	2–5 days	4–10 days	10–21 days
2. Periosteal new bone	4–10 days	10–14 days	14–21 days
3. Loss of fracture line definition	10–14 days	14–21 days	
4. Soft callus	10–14 days	14–21 days	
5. Hard callus	14–21 days	21–42 days	42–90 days
6. Remodeling epiphyseal closure	3 months	1 year	2 years and older

Source: Reprinted, by permission of Dr. Paul K. Kleinman, from *Diagnostic Imaging of Child Abuse* (Baltimore: Williams and Wilkins, 1987).
Note: Repetitive injuries may prolong categories 1, 2, 5, and 6.

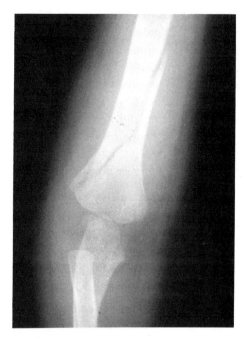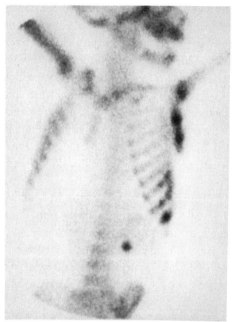

9.28 Older, yellowing arm bruising belied the parental history of a toddler tricycling off the porch the day before. An obvious spiral humerus fracture was found (*a, left*). Multiple other fractures were identified. Scintigraphy highlights the presenting fracture but also demonstrates three left lower lateral rib and two left lateral scapula margin fractures. The normal increased activity of the proximal growth plate of the left humerus is seen. This normal activity can hide epiphyseal/metaphyseal fractures (*b, right*).

Fracture patterns often provide important information about the mechanism of injury. The classic fracture of abuse is the epiphyseal/metaphyseal chip fracture (fig. 9.29a). In another x-ray projection, this appears as the "bucket handle" fracture at the end of the long bones. These injuries result from jerking or shaking of a child's limbs. The strong ligamentous attachments around the joint cause the ends of the bones to be sheared at their weakest point. Pathologically, transverse disruption is seen at the distal metaphysis just beneath the epiphyseal plate (30; 86, p. 17). Often the periosteum, the fibrous coat on the bone's surface, remains intact. This splints the injury, minimizing pain and loss of function. Such injuries may heal with little periosteal new bone. More often, fine to dramatic lines of periosteal reaction originating from the long bone ends are seen with healing (fig. 9.29b). This fine periosteal reaction needs to be differentiated from the normal, symmetrical midshaft periosteal layering associated with rapid infant skeletal growth. Consultation with an experienced pediatric radiologist may be useful in making this distinction (see chap. 10).

Children are usually not brought for care for these injuries; thus, the fractures are not immobilized. This may result in greater fracture instability and ongoing bony injury. In the extreme, the examiner sees exuberant callus cloaking the entire bone (fig. 9.30). Although the epiphyseal/metaphyseal fractures are specific for inflicted injury, they constitute only 19% of fractures caused by abuse (82).

Midshaft (diaphyseal) fractures may result from abuse or unintentional injury. Diaphyseal injury was found in 78% of children with abusive fractures (fig. 9.30) (82). The majority of midshaft humerus and femur fractures that occur in children less than one year old are caused by abuse (87–89). When these fractures result from unintentional injury, a history of severe trauma is elicited or evidence of bony weakness is found. The seeking of medical care for these injuries, if abusive, is commonly delayed.

With independent walking and running, unintentional midshaft femur fractures become more common (88). They may result from twisting, running, and falling. Unintentional humerus fractures also become more common with ambulation. They are usually supratrochanteric (89). Periosteal reaction or old bruises may belie acute histories. Spiral tibial fractures, "the toddler's fracture," commonly occur innocently in the toddler who has recently begun walking (90). The bone has not yet remodeled and strengthened itself to

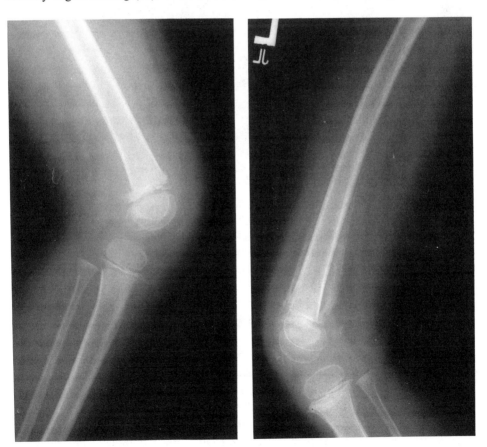

9.29 Subacute distal femur and proximal tibia fractures demonstrate "bucket handle" pattern (*a, left*). Ten days later, layered periosteal new bone is easily seen (*b, right*).

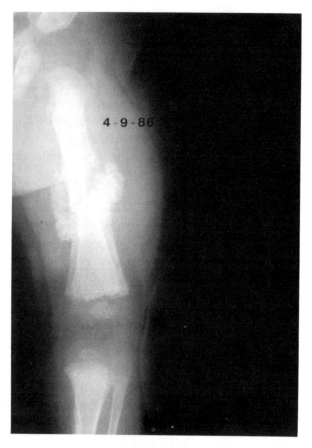

9.30 Dramatic callus is seen in an untreated transverse femur metaphysis fracture. Periosteal reaction of coexistent distal femur and proximal tibia injuries is also evident. (Photograph courtesy of Dr. Stephen Done.)

accommodate the force required to support the standing body. Minor twisting or jumping histories often accompany this injury. These toddlers usually present with histories of limping or of refusing to bear weight on the leg. Bruises are usually not seen. The fractures are usually not displaced and may be difficult to see on acute films. A fibula fracture rarely accompanies the toddler's fracture of the tibia.

Forearm fractures commonly result from spontaneous tripping or falling. Subtle distal cortical buckling (torus fractures) or dorsally angulated transverse fractures of the distal third of the radius and ulna are most often observed. Swelling and deformity with torus fractures are often minimal acutely, but careful exam is likely to reveal point tenderness. Transverse fractures of one forearm or lower-leg bone may be accompanied by plastic bowing injury of the adjacent bone (91).

Rib fractures are found in 15% of the battered infants who are x-rayed (92). Of abused infants who have fractures, 20% have rib fractures (82). In the absence of obvious unintentional trauma or abnormal bones, rib fracture should be considered to have resulted from abuse.

Rib fractures may be seen in the posterior neck of the rib or throughout the rest of the rib's arc. Injuries to the rib neck result from backward and inward bowing from severe squeezes of the rib cage. The rib neck is bent over the fulcrum of the transverse process of the vertebrae (83, pp. 67–77). This cracks open the inner cortex (fig. 9.31). Since their location is protected beneath the lateral vertebral processes and the paraspinal muscles, the rib neck alone can not be fractured by direct impact. Such fractures are rarely displaced and are very difficult to see acutely with plain x rays.

Severe front-to-back squeezes crack open the outer cortex or buckle the pleural cortex of the lateral rib arcs or the costochondral junctions. Also, more lateral or anterior rib fractures can be caused by either a direct impact or a severe focal squeeze that bends the ribs inward. In both cases, the inner cortex is again likely to break first, and displacement is not common. Although it is difficult to see the acute fractures, pleural thickening or fluid may underlie these injuries. If they result from impact injury, focal pulmonary contusion may also be present. This may be mistakenly interpreted as pneumonia. Groups of adjacent ribs are commonly seen to have a linear array of fractures. Some children with chest injury will come to care because of respiratory compromise from pleural effusions. These effusions may be either bloody or chylous. The rib fractures that often accompany these effusions may not be evident until after the effusion is drained and/or callus appears with rib healing. Infants can also sustain traumatic costochondral separation. This will not be seen acutely on x ray, but the junctions may expand beyond their normal size with healing.

Since rib fractures usually involve the inner cortex and are splinted by residual unbroken cortex and periosteum, they may not be accompanied by directive signs and symptoms. Infants may, however, have generalized irritability. Bruises often are not seen acutely and are rarely present by the time the fractures are recognized. Any parent who brings a infant to care voicing concerns of possible rib fractures is likely to have felt, heard, or observed the ribs being broken. Scintigraphy is most useful in identifying acute rib fractures, but an alternative is to repeat the rib film in one-and-a-half to two weeks, to look for callus.

The rib cage of the infant and child is quite pliable; thus, closed-chest cardiac massage does not cause rib fractures (92, 93). This is in contrast to adults, who commonly sustain rib fractures from cardiopulmonary resuscitation.

Abused children may have fractures of bones that are rarely injured with unintentional injury. Fractures of the plate of the scapula are rare without direct impact, as in a motor vehicle passenger or pedestrian injury or in deliberate abuse. Although midshaft clavicle fractures occur with falls on the shoulder, distal clavicle or scapular acromial process fractures usually result from abusive traction or shaking of the arm. Pelvic fractures result from direct impacts, like kicks. In unintentional injuries, they commonly result when children are run over by a motor vehicle. The small bones of the hands are abusively broken by bending or direct blows. Vertebral fractures are most common in the lumbar region,

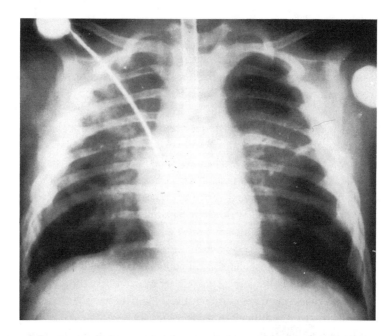

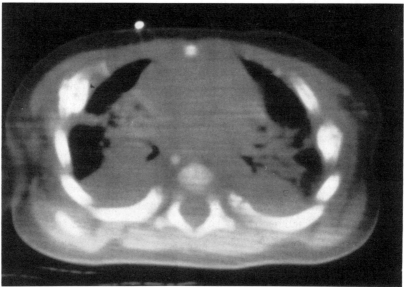

9.31 On plain chest film, multiple calluses are present along both lateral rib cages from old fractures. No posterior rib neck fractures are visible (*a, top*). Simultaneous chest CT scan demonstrates the lateral fracture callus. The inner cortex is also cracked open at the rib neck where it was bent over the fulcrum of the transverse vertebral process. Lack of callus there implies that the two injuries were inflicted at different times (*b, above*).

accompanying hyperflexion injuries of shaking: the anterior of the vertebral body is crushed, assuming a wedge shape. Tips of several vertebral spines may also be avulsed where they are joined by the intraspinal ligaments. Sternal fractures result from direct blows.

Bones have less tensile than compressive strength. Thus, if a bone is bent by a force perpendicular to its axis, it is likely to break open on the side opposite to where the force is applied. A cross section of children's bones breaks under less tensile force than a similar cross section of adults' but absorbs more energy in breaking (94). This lessens fracture propagation. It can lead to "greenstick" fractures, which break one cortex but do not completely cross the bone. Similarly, plastic bowing injuries may cause persistent deformation of the bone without any single, visible fracture line. The child's periosteum is relatively tough. Injuries, like the toddler's fracture, may be splinted in place by it and are difficult to see acutely. The ligaments in infants are also relatively stronger than the bones. This property leads to epiphyseal/metaphyseal fractures instead of sprains in infants.

Several inherited and acquired illnesses may simulate bony injuries of abuse (95). Congenital syphilis frequently presents as bony inflammation. Reduced mineralization and cystic erosions of the long bones with periosteal inflammation and reaction occur as a result (fig. 9.32). However, fractures are not common. Osteomyelitis, leukemia, and neuroblastoma can all cause bony destruction with periosteal reaction. They should be distinguishable from abuse by their radiologic appearance and other physical and laboratory findings.

Nutritional rickets may present with fractures secondary to reduced bone mineral content and strength. Generalized reduced calcification and a "moth-eaten" appearance at the zone of provisional calcification beneath the epiphyseal plates should be evident in such cases (fig. 9.33). The metaphyses of the long bones flare. Serum calcium is commonly reduced, and alkaline phosphate elevated. Nutritional rickets in the United States is currently most common among dark-skinned infants who are solely breast-fed past nine months of age. It also occurs secondary to kidney, liver, or gut disease or chronic anticonvulsant treatment. Elevated parathyroid function, as in renal rickets or pseudohypothyroidism results in rachitic changes. With excess parathyroid activity, however, more subperiosteal erosions of reabsorbed bone are seen than are evident with nutritional rickets. Reduced bone mineral content may also be seen in sick premature infants or children with reduced mobility secondary to neurologic disease. The abnormal bone density should be apparent on x ray.

Menke Kinky Hair syndrome includes metaphyseal spurring, which may resemble healing corner fractures. The seizures and brain atrophy of this syndrome may also initially suggest abuse. As the name implies, the hair has a peculiar kinky and fragile character. Scurvy can also result in subperiosteal bleeding with subsequent calcification.

Osteogenesis imperfecta (OI) is a disease with increased bony fragility. Children with this disorder may have fractures resulting from apparently minor trauma (96, 97). This inherited disorder is associated with more global problems of connective tissue. Joint hypermobility, increased skin distensibility, and bruising are common. The sclerae are often blue gray. Multiple wormian bones (skull sutural bones) may be seen. In addition, early

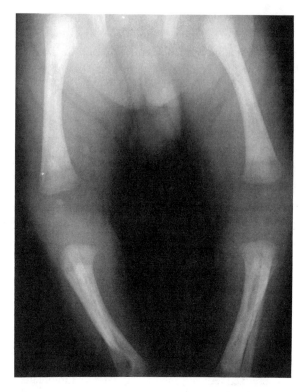

9.32 The ends of the long bones of an eight-day-old infant with congenital syphilis are undermineralized. Patchy meta-physeal hypodensity and diffuse periosteal reaction are evident.

hearing loss and dental maldevelopment are common. Several genetic types exist; of these, several dominant forms have variable expression and occasionally may be confused with abuse. OI type 1a is the most frequent form at 3.5 per 100,000 live births. Although some children have a mild fracture course, also present are blue sclerae, bony undermineraliza-tion, and wormian bones; consequently, diagnosis is usually apparent. OI type 4a has the greatest potential of confusion with abuse, but it accounts for only 5% of OI cases. Here, sclerae and teeth may be normal and osteoporosis subtle, making the diagnosis of OI more difficult. However, wormian bones are usually present in this form of OI. Rarely, mild OI type 3 can also cause confusion. OI types 2 and 3 usually cause severe disease from infancy and, hence, are unlikely to be confused with abuse.

Most children with OI have a positive family history, but fresh mutations and varia-tions in severity exist. Other physical findings of abuse and of the fractures characteristic of abuse (corner fractures, for instance) may aid in the differential diagnosis of abuse. With OI, fractures are unlikely to occur only in the household; instead, they will just as easily occur in other settings, the outcome of inappropriately minor injury. Biochemical studies are available to evaluate the rare, questionable cases (97) but are rarely more reliable than a history and examination by a physician knowledgeable about OI (98).

Abuse versus Unintentional Injury versus Neglect

The preceding discussion focuses on the differentiation of intentional injuries from those that are unintentional. However, in many cases an added dimension of etiologies that although unintentional are nonetheless neglectful must also be considered. As examiners, we commonly ask whether infant head injuries and toddlers' burns are signs of parental neglect.

Alter has observed that neglect is a sustained pattern of behavior in which parenting is inadequate by community norms of behavior (99). She found professionals using a variety of information to judge whether acts are neglectful. These criteria included concrete factors such as the child's age, the degree of injury, and the frequency of inadequate parental behavior. Qualitative judgments about the willfulness of the parental act, overall parental social deviance, quality of the parent-child interaction, and parental willingness to change also affected this evaluation. Reports of neglect may be more likely to be filed about lower-class families and nonwhite families. Parental substance abuse clearly increases the professional child care workers' concern about neglect.

Deciphering the circumstances of childhood drowning and near drowning also provides an example of this difficult differential triad: is the drowning the result of abuse, unintentional event, or neglect? The causes of drowning change as children age. At each

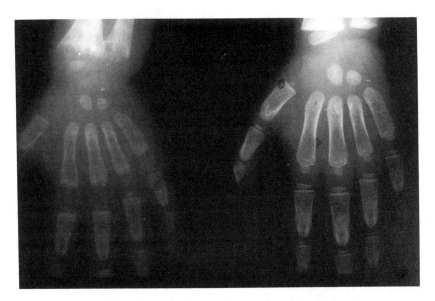

9.33 Before-and-after treatment films of an infant with nutritional rickets demonstrate the "moth-eaten" undermineralization of the growth region of the wrist.

developmental level, children are exposed to or expose themselves to different risks. Through maturation they learn ways to avoid those risks. Normal parenting tasks include fostering this learning of safety skills while recognizing and protecting children from hazards beyond their cognitive and motor abilities. Unintentional but neglectful injuries often occur when this balance of parental supervision and education goes awry.

Among drownings and near drownings, bathtub immersions of infants are most likely to be considered neglectful (100). Medical caretakers may get caught up in clinical care of and consolation of the families of victims. It is then easy to forget neglect as a possible contributor to the drowning event. It is helpful to utilize a team evaluation of these cases with social worker and public health nursing. If further investigation is needed, protective services should be involved. However, even when protective services are called, their initial role should be to assist in defining the ongoing risk to the injured child and any siblings. Once provided with appropriate services, many neglecting families will be able to become more competent caretakers.

Although the vast majority of drownings and near drownings are unintentional, some children are drowned by caretaker intent and action. These events are usually unwitnessed and more likely than unintentional drownings to occur in the home. Clues to abuse are family sociopathy, delay in seeking care, discrepancies between the event history and the child's developmental abilities, and physical and autopsy findings suggestive of inflicted trauma (101, 102). Foreign material in the lungs may belie histories of drowning in clear water, and pulmonary inflammation may be greater than expected from the history given by the caretaker of when the immersion occurred (101). Infants and toddlers are the most frequent victims of abusive drowning.

Summary

The diagnosis of abusive versus unintentional causes of childhood injuries can usually be made if the history is carefully compared with the observed injuries. Physicians should attempt to define and document their degree of confidence in the diagnosis. They should evaluate the timing and causal mechanism of injury. If the child sustains physical injury through abusive or neglectful events, the child's future safety must be considered and a plan developed to provide protection.

References

1. Feldman, K. W.; Schaller, R. T.; Feldman, J. A.; and McMillon, M. 1978. Tap Water Scald Burns in Children. *Pediatrics* 78:1–7.
2. Kempe C. H.; Silverman, F. N.; Steele, B. F.; Droegemueller, W.; and Silver, H. K. 1962. The Battered Child Syndrome. *JAMA* 181:17–24.
3. Bergman, A. B.; Larsen, R. M.; and Mueller, B. A. 1986. Changing Spectrum of Serious Child Abuse. *Pediatrics* 77:113–16.
4. Margolin, L. 1992. Child Abuse by Mothers' Boyfriends: Why the Overrepresentation? *Child Abuse and Neglect: International J.* 16:541–51.
5. Pascoe, J. M.; Hildebrandt, H. M.; Tarrier, A.; and Murphy, M. 1979. Patterns of Skin Injury in Nonaccidental and Accidental Injury. *Pediatrics* 64:245–47.

6. Wedgewood, J. 1990. Childhood Bruising. *Practitioner* 234:598–601.

7. Schwartz, A. J., and Ricci, L. R. 1996. How Accurately Can Bruises Be Aged in Abused Children? Literature Review and Synthesis. *Pediatrics* 97:254–56.

8. Langois, N. E. I., and Gresham, G. A. 1991. The Aging of Bruises: A Review and Study of Color Changes with Time. *Forensic Sciences International* 50:227–38.

9. Feldman, K. W. 1992. Patterned Abusive Bruises of the Buttocks and the Pinnae. *Pediatrics* 90:633–36.

10. Nanda, S. K. 1983. Age Related Changes in Dental Arches. In *The Developmental Basis of Occlusion and Malocclusion.* Chicago: Quintessence Books.

11. Jacobs, A. H., and Walton, R. G. 1976. Incidence of Birthmarks in the Neonate. *Pediatrics* 58:218–22.

12. Yeatman, G. W.; Shaw, C. S.; Barlow, M. J.; and Bartlett, G. 1976. Pseudobattering in Vietnamese Children. *Pediatrics* 58:616–18.

13. Ricci, L. R. 1991. Photographing the Physically Abused Child. *Am. J. Diseases of Children* 145:275–81.

14. Purdue, G. F.; Hunt, J. L.; and Prescott, P. R. 1988. Child Abuse by Burning—An Index of Suspicion. *J. Trauma* 28:221–24.

15. Feldman, K. W. 1984. Pseudoabusive Burns in Asian Refugees. *Am. J. Diseases of Children* 138:768–69.

16. Schmitt, B. D.; Gray, J. D.; and Britton, H. L. 1978. Car Seat Burns in Infants: Avoiding Confusion with Inflicted Burns. *Pediatrics* 62:607–9.

17. Feldman, K. W.; Morray, J. P.; and Schaller, R. T. 1985. Thermal Injury Caused by Hot Pack Application in the Hypothermic Child. *Am. J. Emergency Med.* 3:38–41.

18. Moritz, A. R., and Henriques, F. C. 1947. Studies of Thermal Injury: The Relative Importance of Time and Temperature in the Causation of Cutaneous Burns. *Am. J. Pathology* 23:695–720.

19. Feldman, K. W. 1983. Help Needed on Hot Water Burns. *Pediatrics* 71:145–46.

20. Henriques, F. C. 1947. Studies of Thermal Energy: The Predictability and the Significance of Thermally Induced Rate Processes Leading to Irreversible Epidermal Injury. *Archives of Pathology* 43:489–502.

21. Erdmann, T. C.; Feldman, K. W.; Rivara, F. P.; Heimbach, D. M.; and Wall, H. A. 1991. Tap Water Burn Prevention: The Effect of Legislation. *Pediatrics* 88:572–77.

22. Lenoski, E. F., and Hunter, K. A. 1977. Specific Patterns of Inflicted Burn Injuries. *J. Trauma* 17:842–46.

23. Surrell, J. A.; Alexander, R. C.; and Cohle, S. D. 1987. Microwave Oven Burns: An Unusual Manifestation of Child Abuse. *Pediatrics* 79:255–60.

24. Duhaime, A. C.; Gennarelli, T. A.; Thibault, L. E.; Bruce, D. A.; Marguiles, S. S.; and Wiser, R. 1987. The Shaken Baby Syndrome. *J. Neurosurgery* 66:409–15.

25. Snoek, J. W.; Minderhoud, J. M.; and Wilmink, J. T. 1984. Delayed Deterioration Following Mild Head Injury in Children. *Brain* 107:15–36.

26. Davis, R.; Mullen, N.; Kakela, M.; Taylor, J. A.; and Rivara, F. P. 1993. Cranial CT Scans in Children with Minimal Head Injury and Loss of Consciousness. *Am. J. Diseases of Children* 147:482.

27. Ommaya, A. K., and Yarnell, P. 1969. Subdural Hematoma after Whiplash Injury. *Lancet* 2:237–39.

28. Ommaya, A. K., and Hirsch, A. E. 1971. Tolerance for Cerebral Concussion from Head Impact and Whiplash in Primates. *J. Biomechanics* 4:13–23.

29. Caffey, J. 1972. On the Theory and Practice of Shaking Infants. *Am. J. Diseases of Children* 124:161–69.

30. Kleinman, P. K. 1990. Diagnostic Imaging in Child Abuse. *Am. J. Roentgenology* 155:703–12.

31. Hadley, M. N.; Sonntag, V. K.; Rekate, H. I.; and Murphy, A. 1989. The Infant Whiplash-Shake Injury Syndrome: A Clinical and Pathological Study. *Neurosurgery* 24:536–40.

32. Alexander, R.; Sato, Y.; Smith, W.; and Bennett, T. 1990. Incidence of Impact Trauma with Cranial Injuries Ascribed to Shaking. *Am. J. Diseases of Children* 144:724–26.

33. Green, M. A.; Lieberman, G.; Milroy, C. M.; and Parsons, M. A. 1996. Ocular and Cerebral Trauma in Non-accidental Injury in Infancy: Underlying Mechanisms and Implications for Paediatric Practice. *British J. Ophthalmology* 80:282–87.

34. Genarelli, T. A., and Thibault, L. E. 1985. Biomechanics of Head Injury. In *Neurosurgery,* ed. R. H. Wilkins and S. J. Rengaohary, 1531–36. New York: McGraw Hill.

35. Reichelderfer, T.; Overbach, A.; and Greensher, J. 1979. Unsafe Playgrounds. *Pediatrics* 64: 962–63.

36. Preston, J. 1993. United States Consumer Product Safety Commission. Personal communication.

37. Leestma, J. E., and Grcevic, N. 1988. Impact Injuries to the Brain and Head. In *Forensic Neuropathology,* ed. J. E. Leestma and J. B. Kirkpatrick, 184–216. New York: Raven Press.

38. Thompson, R. S.; Rivara, F. P.; and Thompson, D. C. 1989. A Case-Control Study of the Effectiveness of Bicycle Safety Helmets. *New England J. Med.* 320:1361–67.

39. Helfer, R. E.; Slovis, T. L.; and Black, M. 1977. Injuries Resulting When Small Children Fall Out of Bed. *Pediatrics* 60:533–35.

40. Nimityongskul, P., and Anderson, L. D. 1987. Likelihood of Injuries When Small Children Fall Out of Bed. *J. Pediatric Orthopedics* 7:184–86.

41. Chadwick, D. L.; Chin, S. C.; Salerno, C.; Landsverk, J.; and Kitchen, L. 1991. Deaths from Falls in Children. *J. Trauma* 31:1353–55.

42. Williams, R. A. 1991. Injuries in Infants and Small Children Resulting from Witnessed and Corroborated Free Falls. *J. Trauma* 31:1350–53.

43. Musemeche, C. A. 1991. Pediatric Falls from Heights. *J. Trauma* 31:1347–49.

44. Shugerman, R. P.; Paez, A.; Grossman, D. C.; Feldman, K. W.; and Grady, M. S. 1996. Epidural Hemorrhage: Is It Abusive? *Pediatrics* 97:664–68.

45. Hobbs, C. J. 1984. Skull Fractures and the Diagnosis of Abuse. *Archives of Diseases in Childhood* 59:246–52.

46. Meservy, C. J.; Towbin, R.; McLaurin, R. L.; Meyers, P. A.; and Ball, W. 1987. Radiographic Characteristics of Skull Fractures Resulting from Abuse. *Am. J. Roentgenology* 149:173–75.

47. Joffe, M., and Ludwig, S. 1988. Stairway Injuries in Children. *Pediatrics* 82:457–61.

48. Partington, M. D.; Swanson, J. A.; and Meyer, F. B. 1991. Head Injury and the Use of Baby Walkers: A Continuing Problem. *Annals of Emergency Med.* 20:652–54.

49. Hanigan, W. C.; Peterson, R. A.; and Njus, G. 1987. Tin Ear Syndrome: Rotational Acceleration in Pediatric Head Injuries. *Pediatrics* 80:618–22.

50. Kleinman, P. K., and Spevak, M. R. 1992. Soft Tissue Swelling and Acute Skull Fractures. *J. Pediatrics* 121:737–39.

51. Zimmerman, R. A.; Bilaniuk, L. T.; Bruce, D.; Scut, L.; Uzzell, B.; and Goldberg, H. I. 1979. Computed Tomography of Craniocerebral Injury in the Abused Child. *Radiology* 130:687–90.

52. Zimmerman, R. A., and Bilaniuk, L. T. 1982. Computed Tomographic Staging of Traumatic Epidural Bleeding. *Radiology* 144:809–12.

53. Bergstrom, M.; Ericson, K.; Levander, B.; Svendsen, P.; and Larsson, S. 1977. Variation with Time of the Attenuation Values of Intracranial Hematomas. *J. Computer Assisted Tomography* 1:57–63.

54. Dolinskas, C. A.; Zimmerman, R. A.; and Bilaniuk, L. T. 1978. A Sign of Subarachnoid Bleeding on Cranial Computed Tomograms of Pediatric Head Trauma Patients. *Radiology* 126:409–11.

55. Feldman, K. W., and Brewer, D. K. 1995. Evolution of the Cranial Computed Tomography Scan in Child Abuse. *Child Abuse and Neglect: International J.* 19:307–14.

56. Bradley, W. G., and Schmidt, P. G. 1985. Effect of Methemoglobin Formation on the MR Appearance of Subarachnoid Hemorrhage. *Radiology* 156:99–103.

57. Barrows, L. S.; Hunter, F. T.; and Barker, B. Q. 1955. The Nature and Clinical Significance of Pigments in the Cerebrospinal Fluid. *Brain* 78:59–80.

58. Genarelli, T. A. 1982. Cerebral Concussion and Diffuse Brain Injury. In *Head Injury,* ed. P. R. Cooper, 83–97. Baltimore: Williams and Wilkins.

59. Zimmerman, R. A.; Bilaniuk, L. T.; and Genarelli, T. 1978. Computed Tomography of Shearing Injuries of the Cerebral White Matter. *Radiology* 127:393–96.

60. Sinal, S. H., and Ball, M. R. 1977. Head Trauma Due to Child Abuse: Serial Computed Tomography in Diagnosis and Management. *Southern Med. J.* 80:1505–12.

61. Giangiacomo, J.; Jemshed, A. K.; Levine, C.; and Thompson, V. M. 1988. Sequential Cranial Computed Tomography in Infants with Retinal Hemorrhages. *Ophthalmology* 95:295–99.

62. Sato, Y.; Yuh, W. T. C.; Smith, W. L.; Alexander, R. C.; et al. 1989. Head Injury in Child Abuse: Evaluation with MR Imaging. *Radiology* 173:653–57.

63. Bradley, W. G. 1990. Hemorrhage. In *MRI Atlas of the Brain,* ed. W. G. Bradley and G. Bydder. New York: Raven Press.

64. Piatt, J., and Steinberg, M. 1995. Isolated Spinal Cord Injury as a Presentation of Child Abuse. *Pediatrics* 96:780–82.

65. Sneed, R. C., and Stover, S. L. 1988. Undiagnosed Spinal Cord Injuries in Brain-Injured Children. *Am. J. Diseases of Children* 142:965–67.

66. Harley, R. D. 1980. Ocular Manifestations of Child Abuse. *J. Pediatric Ophthalmology and Strabismus* 17:5–13.

67. Buys, Y. M.; Levin, A. V.; Enzenauer, R. W.; Elder, J. E.; Letourneau, M. A.; Humphreys, R. P.; Mian, M.; and Morin, J. D. 1992. Retinal Findings after Head Trauma in Infants and Young Children. *Ophthalmology* 99:1718–23.

68. Goetting, M. G., and Sowa, B. 1990. Retinal Hemorrhage after Cardiopulmonary Resuscitation in Children: An Etiologic Reevaluation. *Pediatrics* 85:585–88.

69. Kanter, R. K. 1986. Retinal Hemorrhage after Cardiopulmonary Resuscitation or Child Abuse. *J. Pediatrics* 108:430–31.

70. Falker, J. C.; Berkowitz, I. D.; and Green, W. R. 1992. Retinal Hemorrhages in Newborn Piglets Following Cardiopulmonary Resuscitation. *Am. J. Diseases of Children* 146:1294–96.

71. Tomasi, L. G., and Rosman, P. 1975. Purtscher Retinopathy in the Battered Child Syndrome. *Am. J. Diseases of Children* 129:1335–37.

72. Riffenburgh, R. S., and Sathyavagiswaran, L. 1991. Ocular Findings at Autopsy of Child Abuse Victims. *Ophthalmology* 98:1519–24.

73. Gilliland, M. G. F., and Lukenbach, M. W. 1991. Resuscitation and Retinal Hemorrhage. *Am. J. Forensic Med. Pathology* 12:354.

74. Elder, J. E.; Taylor, R. G.; and Klug, G. L. 1991. Retinal Hemorrhage in Accidental Head Trauma in Childhood. *J. Paediatric Child Health* 27:286–89.

75. Billmire, M. E., and Myers, P. A. 1985. Serious Head Injury in Infants: Accident or Abuse? *Pediatrics* 75:340–42.

76. Duhaime, A. C.; Alario, A. J.; Lewander, W. J.; Schut, L.; Sutton, L. N.; Seidl, T. S.; Nudelman, S.; Budenz, D.; Hertle, R.; Tsiaras, W.; and Loporchio, S. 1992. Head Injury in Very Young Children: Mechanisms, Injury Types, and Ophthalmologic Findings in One Hundred Hospitalized Patients Younger Than Two Years of Age. *Pediatrics* 90:179–85.

77. Greenwald, M. J.; Weiss, A.; Oesterle, C. S.; and Friendly, D. S. 1986. Traumatic Retinoschisis in Battered Babies. *Ophthalmology* 93:618–25.

78. Cooper, A.; Floyd, T.; Barlow, B.; Niemirska, M.; Ludwig, S.; Seidl, T.; O'Neill, J.; Templeton, J.; Ziegler, M.; Ross, A.; Gandhi, R.; and Catherman, R. 1988. Major Blunt Abdominal Trauma Due to Child Abuse. *J. Trauma* 28:1483–87.

79. Ledbetter, D. L.; Hatch, E. I.; Feldman, K. W.; Fligner, C. L.; and Tapper, D. 1988. Diagnostic and Surgical Implications of Child Abuse. *Archives of Surgery* 123:1101–5.

80. Oldham, K. T.; Guice, K. S.; Ryckman, F.; Kaufman, R. A.; et al. 1986. Blunt Liver Injury in Childhood: Evolution of Therapy and Current Perspective. *Surgery* 100:542–49.

81. Caffey, J. 1946. Multiple Fractures in the Long Bones of Infants Suffering from Subdural Hematoma. *Am. J. Roentgenology* 56:163–73.

82. Merten, D. F.; Radkowski, M. A.; and Leonidis, J. C. 1983. The Abused Child: A Radiological Reappraisal. *Radiology* 146:377–81.

83. O'Conner, J. F., and Cohen, J. 1987. Dating Fractures. In *Diagnostic Imaging of Child Abuse,* ed. P. K. Kleinman. Baltimore: Williams and Wilkins.

84. Jaudes, P. K. 1984. Comparison of Radiology and Radionucleotide Bone Scanning in the Detection of Child Abuse. *Pediatrics* 73:166–68.

85. Sty, J. R., and Starshak, R. J. 1983. The Role of Bone Scintigraphy in the Evaluation of the Suspected Abused Child. *Radiology* 146:369–75.

86. Kleinman, P. K. Skeletal Trauma: General Considerations. In *Diagnostic Imaging of Child Abuse,* ed. P. K. Kleinman. Baltimore: Williams and Wilkins.

87. Dalton, H. J.; Slovis, T.; Helfer, R. E.; Comstock, J.; Scheurer, S.; and Riolo, S. 1990. Undiagnosed Abuse in Children Younger Than Three Years with Femur Fracture. *Am. J. Diseases of Children* 144:875–78.

88. Thomas, S. A.; Rosenfield, N. S.; Leventhal, J. M.; and Markowitz, R. I. 1991. Long Bone Fractures in Young Children: Distinguishing Accidental Injuries from Child Abuse. *Pediatrics* 88:471–76.

89. Leventhal, J. M.; Thomas, S. A.; Rosenfield, N. S.; and Markowitz, R. I. 1993. Fractures in Young Children: Distinguishing Child Abuse from Unintentional Injuries. *Am. J. Diseases of Children* 147:87–92.

90. Tennebein, M.; Reed, M. N.; and Black, G. B. 1990. The Toddler's Fracture Revisited. *Am. J. Emergency Med.* 8:208–11.

91. Borden, S. 1974. Traumatic Bowing of the Forearm in Children. *J. Bone and Joint Surgery* 56-A:611–16.

92. Feldman, K. W., and Brewer, D. K. 1984. Child Abuse, Cardiopulmonary Resuscitation, and Rib Fractures. *Pediatrics* 73:339–42.

93. Spevak, M. R.; Kleinman, P. K.; Belanger, P. L.; Richmond, J. M.; Blackbourne, B. D.; and Primak, C. 1990. Does Cardiopulmonary Resuscitation Cause Rib Fractures in Infants? A Postmortem Radiologic-Pathologic Study. *Radiology* 177:162.

94. Currey, J. D., and Butler, G. 1975. The Mechanical Properties of Bone Tissue in Children. *J. Bone and Joint Surgery* 57-A:810–14.

95. Brill, P. A., and Winchester, P. 1987. Differential Diagnosis of Child Abuse. In *Diagnostic Imaging in Child Abuse,* ed. P. K. Kleinman, 221–41. Baltimore: Williams and Wilkins.

96. Ablin, D. S.; Greenspan, A.; Reinhart, M.; and Grix, A. 1990. Differentiation of Child Abuse from Osteogenesis Imperfecta. *Am. J. Roentgenology* 154:1035–46.

97. Gahagan, S., and Rimsza, M. E. 1991. Child Abuse or Osteogenesis Imperfecta: How Can We Tell? *Pediatrics* 88:987–92.

98. Steiner, R. D.; Pepin, M.; and Byers, P. H. 1996. Studies of Collagen Synthesis and Structure in the Differentiation of Child Abuse from Osteogenesis Imperfecta. *J. Pediatrics* 128:542–47.

99. Alter, C. F. 1985. Decision-Making Factors in Cases of Child Neglect. *Child Welfare* 64:99–111.

100. Feldman, K. W.; Monastersky, C.; and Feldman, G. K. 1993. When Is Childhood Drowning Neglect? *Child Abuse and Neglect: International J.* 17:329–36.

101. Greist, K. J., and Zumwalt, R. E. 1989. Child Abuse by Drowning. *Pediatrics* 83:41–46.

102. Gillenwater, J. M.; Quan, L.; and Feldman, K. W. 1996. *Archives of Pediatrics and Adolescent Medicine* 150:298–303.

10

Imaging in Child Abuse

Wilbur L. Smith

Child abuse is epidemic in our society. Estimates of the incidence of child abuse and neglect run from between five hundred thousand to one million cases every year. This incidence rate is much higher than that of most infectious diseases, including AIDS, and several magnitudes of order greater than that of childhood tumors. Despite its frequency, child abuse often fails to receive proportionate attention in curricula of medical instruction, and reports about its victims are occasionally viewed with some skepticism by the medical community as well as the lay press. This "silent epidemic" has been tolerated by society for a number of reasons, not the least of which is the concept of family privacy. As late as the early twentieth century the attitude prevalent throughout much of the world deemed children to be a form of private property. Parents, as holders of the property, were accordingly free to treat their children as they saw fit; thus, abusive behavior, except at its most extreme, was tolerated.

This attitude is changing; however, the change is slow, and regressive attitudes still prevail (to an alarming degree) in many social and cultural settings. Compounding the problems engendered by defensive attitudes about the relation of children to property and privacy rights are problems arising from the medical community's and the public's denial of the extent of abuse. Abusive behavior is so repulsive that many people either cannot or will not believe it occurs at all, let alone commonly. Instead, they look for alternative explanations to account for a child's suffering and will accept a diagnosis only remotely possible before they will countenance a diagnosis of child abuse even when an injury is considerably more likely the result of abuse.

Diagnostic imaging can play a strong role in countering some of the common mechanisms of this denial. When confronted with irrefutable documentation of fractures, professionals, caretakers, and the public at large find it difficult to deny that the fractures are real, that the injuries were inflicted, and that they were mild or appropriate for "disciplining" a child. Documenting and comparing these deliberate injuries with those occurring accidentally (for instance, in automobile accidents) enhance our perception of the severity of the forces that can be applied to the battered child's skeleton.

The history of the recognition and description of the effects of assaultive child abuse

Wilbur L. Smith, M.D., is a professor in the Department of Radiology and in the Department of Pediatrics, College of Medicine, University of Iowa.

is closely related to the evolution of diagnostic radiology. In the nineteenth century, Ambroise Tardieu, a pathologist, provided the initial eloquent descriptions of the pathologic findings of child abuse victims. Until the advent of radiology, however, it was difficult to document the skeletal, visceral, and central nervous manifestations of physical abuse in cases that did not result in death (1). The modern history of recognition of abusive injuries dates from 1946, when John Caffey issued a seminal report describing children manifesting a combination of long bone fractures and subdural hematomas (2). Caffey suggested inflicted trauma as a possible etiology for the unusual combination, principally owing to the likely traumatic origin of the subdural hematomas. In 1953 Fred Silverman reported the radiographic manifestations of unrecognized skeletal trauma in infants and included an instance in which the parents had confessed to injuring their child (3), thereby eliminating speculation as to the etiology of the injuries. For some time thereafter, the debate centered on whether the victims were "fragile" and more prone to trauma or whether in fact they were normal children who were the victims of excessive trauma. Echoes of this debate persist today. But in 1961 C. Henry Kempe, in a presentation at the Annual Meeting of the American Academy of Pediatrics, introduced the term "the battered child," calling to national attention the severe manifestations of nonaccidental trauma to children (4). The descriptive term "battered child" caught the public imagination, and within five years the medical literature on the subject more than doubled in volume. As a result of the heightened public and medical awareness, laws were passed throughout the United States recognizing the need for a special approach to child protection.

Despite this proliferation of knowledge and attention the epidemic continues unabated. If, from the perspective of public health, we look at child maltreatment as a societal disease, in the 1990s we are still very much in the descriptive phase. Effective treatment for this epidemic of domestic violence seems still a long way off. The reasons are complex, involving issues of economics, individual rights, social values, and history, but the results of treatment failure are generations of victims who perpetuate their suffering at enormous cost to society.

Radiographic Evaluation

Despite the many advances in imaging in recent years, conventional radiographs continue to be the mainstay of imaging in cases of suspected child abuse. Careful analysis of clinical data and association of these data with radiographic images have added much to diagnosing and understanding abusive injury. An absence of appropriate trauma history coupled with an unsuspected fracture detected on x rays taken for other reasons often leads to a diagnosis of abuse. Fractures cause intense pain in children though they lack adult ability to localize pain and to verbally express it. Rather than complaining, therefore, a patient with a fractured radius and ulna (fig. 10.1), must have manifested symptoms of inability to use the extremity, pain, fussiness, and probably local swelling. Any competent caretaker in prolonged contact with the child would have been able to note these obvious symptoms. The facts that the child was brought in to have another condition treated and that injury to the

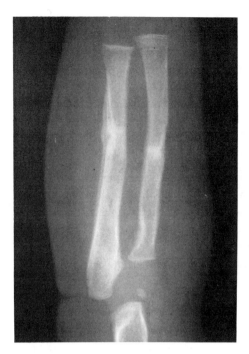

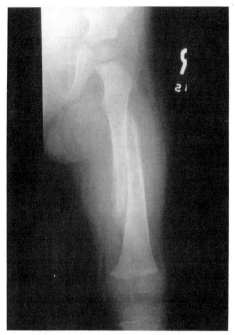

10.1 Healing fractures of the radius and ulna in a three-month-old child who also suffered a head injury. The parents reported the child to have been completely asymptomatic prior to the head injury. Subsequent skeletal radiographs confirmed other fractures.

10.2 Fractured femur in a six-month-old child. Allegations that this child was behaving normally—in particular, that it had been crawling about—with this fracture were false. The parent was convicted of wanton neglect of a minor.

forearm was never explained or even reported by the caretaker are clear-cut evidence that the child had been neglected at least and, more likely, abused. An additional example is in order. The child illustrated in figure 10.2 was picked up by its primary caretaker after it had stayed with a baby-sitter; both the caretaker and the baby-sitter agreed that before it was taken home the child had been crawling about at the sitter's. Hours later the child was brought to the emergency room with a fractured femur, and the allegation was made that the injury had occurred at the baby-sitter's. Clearly, a child with a fractured femur such as the one shown in this radiograph could not have crawled about and played happily. The injury must, therefore, have occurred after the child left the baby-sitter's home. Combining the clinical history with the radiographs improved precision in timing the injury and served a case-finding function as well.

When and under what circumstances we may best obtain the radiographs of the skeletal system is a central issue. Certainly, if there is evident pain, swelling, or deformity, radiographs are usually necessary. The more difficult issue is when to obtain radiographic skeletal surveys as a case-finding device or when to show additional injuries in a child in whom abuse is suspected. In their review of abusive skeletal trauma, Merton et al. documented that the major value of radiographs is for younger children, specifically those younger than two years of age (5). While he and his co-workers found some yields from radiographing asymptomatic areas in children aged two years or older, in most instances all fractures could be detected by radiographing only the parts of the body that were symptomatic.

Accordingly, at the University of Iowa we concur with the recommendations of the Section of Radiology of the American Academy of Pediatrics in advocating a policy of skeletal radiographs for any child younger than age two years or about whom there is suspicion of neglect or abuse (6). Skeletal radiographs of older children should be taken only in response to localized symptoms suggesting fracture. The minimum radiographic series is similar to that outlined by Kleinman (7), consisting of radiographs of the skull, long bones, hands, feet, ribs, pelvis, and spine. The radiographs should be of detail quality, preferably on single emulsion film, and should include, with particular attention, the metaphysis of the bones. The practice of obtaining all of these x rays on a single sheet of radiographic film, placing the baby on a large cassette and exposing the entire infant, is to be condemned. These x rays, often called "baby-grams," not only are generally of insufficient detail for delineating the fine metaphyseal fractures so frequently seen in abusive injury—they also result in excessive radiation to the child. We must hope that once we have better understanding of the mechanics of the injuries and the types of fractures that the x rays are expected to diagnose, this slovenly radiographic practice will be discontinued.

Some authorities recommend a repeat bone survey be taken on all child victims of abuse and neglect approximately seven to ten days after the initial survey. The stated rationale is that bony callus forms from between seven to ten days *after* the injury and, consequently, is often inconspicuous on the original study. I use this technique selectively and have found it of particular value for rib fractures. I do not, however, radiograph each infant a second time seven to ten days after the initial injury.

Bone scan has been advocated as a primary case-finding device (8); most frequently, however, the bone scan is supplementary to the conventional radiographs. It too is particularly valuable as a case-finding tool for rib fractures. Bone scans normally demonstrate considerable activity along the metaphysis of long bones: this is the area that overlaps the most frequent sites of the metaphyseal fractures of child abuse. Sophisticated methods for measuring differential intensity at each metaphysis may assist in distinguishing between normal and abnormal metaphyseal uptake of tracer, though this technique is rarely used for screening studies. Occasionally, bone scans yield false-negative results for up to two days after fracture in young children (9). In areas of practice where considerable experience with pediatric nuclear medicine is available, it is probably appropriate to consider using bone scanning as a screening device; however, in most practice climates, conventional radiography remains the gold standard.

In abused children older than two years, we radiograph all bones only if there is strong clinical suspicion of prior injury or definite evidence of current injury. In those instances in which the suspected abuse is believed to have occurred more than six months before the child is brought in for evaluation, we have gleaned a very low yield from skeletal radiographs. On the other hand, for children under the age of two years who have been subjected to the same caretakers as has a documented abused child, we advocate complete radiographic bone studies.

Special note should be made of the need for quality postmortem radiographs of any infant who dies under unexpected circumstances. In our practice it is policy that any infant under age two years who dies without known prior illness has postmortem skeletal radiographs. Radiation dosage is not a concern with this group; hence, detailed views of all of the joints and oblique rib films may be routinely obtained. Obviously this postmortem work has to be done with sensitivity for the grieving parents, but parental grief alone does not preclude the possibility of child abuse, for we have found a number of unsuspected fractures in cases of unexpected childhood death.

Bone and Soft Tissue Injuries

As we have seen, conventional radiographs are still the mainstay in the evaluation of abusive injuries. Although soft tissue injuries are usually evident on physical examination, careful inspection of the images of soft tissues on radiographs can occasionally substantiate the amount of swelling, detect penetrating foreign bodies, and reveal the depth of lacerations or burns. Abdominal radiographs are the first step in the imaging evaluation of children with visceral injuries owing to physical abuse and are often used in conjunction with computed tomography (CT) or ultrasound (10). The principal value of the plain radiograph is the detection of bowel perforation, as well as the documentation of mass or hemorrhage (fig. 10.3). Occasionally, in cases of starvation as a result of neglect, the abdominal radiograph can be predictive of severe gastric atony which may be life threatening. In these children ad lib feeding coupled with the gastric atony of chronic starvation may result in gastric rupture. The recommended treatment is simple, gradual feeding. The danger is in failure to recognize the gravity of the situation (fig. 10.4) (11).

The most commonly used conventional radiographic study in physical abuse is the bone survey, which is both a diagnostic tool and a guide to management. I have discussed technical aspects of the skeletal survey earlier in this chapter; however, the necessity of careful attention to the details of appropriate radiographic technique cannot be overemphasized. Gross fractures, such as the fracture of the femur shown in figure 10.2, are easily detected, and information pertaining to their imaging and management is available in standard textbooks.

Any fracture can occur as a result of child abuse, but there are certain types of fractures that occur only rarely except in cases of child abuse. Most prominent among these highly specific fractures are metaphyseal injuries. Metaphyseal fractures were thought to result from avulsion from a small fragment of bone from traction upon the soft tissues attached to the bone. In 1986, work by Kleinman et al. (12) documented that most of these fractures are instead a transmetaphyseal, Salter-Harris type fracture. In either event the etiology if not the mechanics is similar: a pulling or twisting force applied at or about

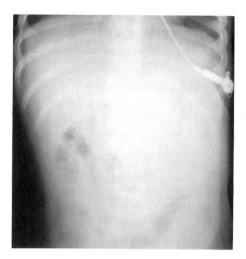

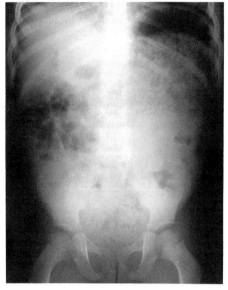

10.3 Free intraperitoneal air in a child with a
ruptured duodenum owing to repeated blows to
the abdomen by a caretaker.

10.4 Acute gastric distension after uncontrolled
initiation of feeding in a chronically starved
two-year-old. The child became so distended
that nasogastric tube decompression was
necessary.

the joint, with resulting fracture near or through the cartilaginous growth plate. Though
various configurations of these fractures are given descriptive names based on their radiographic appearance, the fundamental type of injury is the same.

The metaphyseal corner (chip) fracture is probably the best known. The "chip" represents the radiographically visible portion of the Salter-Harris fracture of the bone, while
the fracture through the nonradiopaque tissues abutting the epiphyseal plate can be seen
only by pathological examination (figs. 10.5 and 10.6). The so-called bucket handle fracture occurs when one whole edge of the metaphysis is torn loose, the fracture then extending through the epiphyseal plate (fig. 10.7). The loosened bony end of the metaphysis appears as a "bucket handle," or radiographically opaque arc projected over the radiolucent
cartilaginous epiphysis. Traumatic metaphysitis is yet another manifestation of an irregular,
serrated metaphyseal fracture that involves portions of the epiphysis as well (fig. 10.8).
This form of injury may be superficially confused with rickets; however, observation of the
remainder of the skeletal survey will eliminate any doubt, as rickets is a systemic disease
with manifestations throughout the skeleton. Failure to immobilize these metaphyseal fractures may lead to an exaggeration of any of these fracture patterns, occasionally presenting
as a severe pattern of bone destruction.

Periosteal injuries, although not strictly fractures, are common skeletal findings in
cases of child abuse. The periosteum is a vascular fibrous tissue layer attached directly to

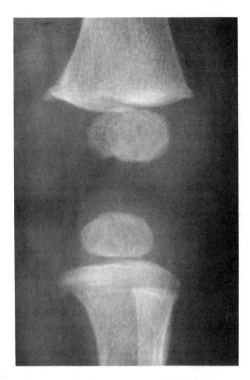

10.5 The knee of a seven-month-old demonstrates metaphyseal corner fractures of the distal femur and proximal tibia.

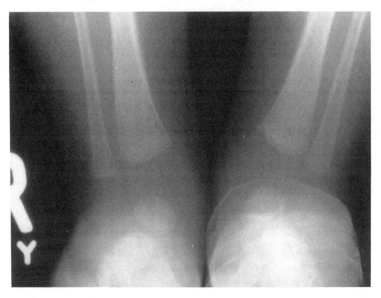

10.6 Autopsy-documented corner fractures of the left distal tibia of a two-month-old abuse victim.

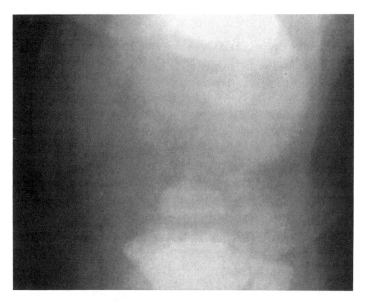

10.7 "Bucket handle" metaphyseal fracture of the proximal tibia in a six-month-old. The "bucket handle" deformity is actually a transmetaphyseal fracture, similar in genesis to a corner fracture.

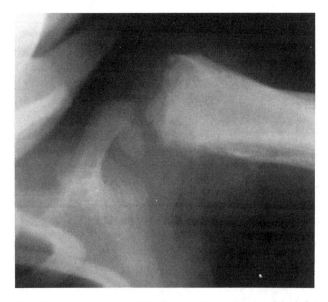

10.8 Traumatic metaphysitis owing to abusive injury of the left humerus. The irregularity of the metaphysis superficially resembles rickets. The differentiation can be made by examining other bones (rickets is a systemic disease), evaluating bone density, observing the changes over time, and testing biochemical parameters.

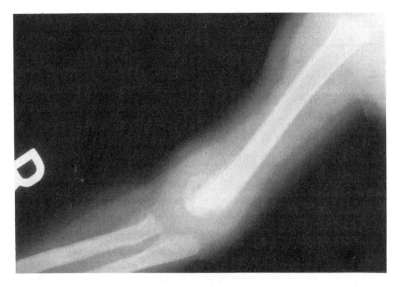

10.9 Diffusely layered periosteal reaction owing to repeated trauma applied to the legs of a nine-month-old abuse victim. The thickness of the periosteal reaction and the evident layering document repeated episodes of hemorrhage.

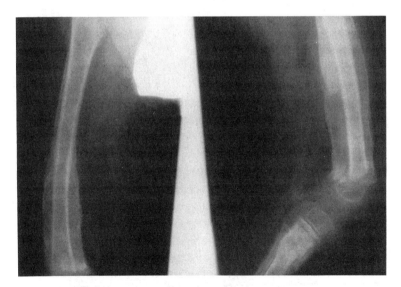

10.10 Thinner layer of periosteal elevation about the humerus of a child after abusive supracondylar fracture of humerus.

the bone surface. Repeated severe pulling or twisting of the extremity separates the peri-osteum from the surface of the bone. Periosteum is quite vascular, and hemorrhage located between the bone and the periosteum occurs subsequent to this periosteal separation. This hemorrhage usually becomes evident on radiographs taken seven to fourteen days after the injury, as a result of calcification of the breakdown products of the subperiosteal hemor-rhage (fig. 10.9) (13). Repeated trauma often leads to the appearance of multiple layers of calcified subperiosteal hemorrhage with so dramatic an appearance as to suggest a perios-teal tumor or mass (fig. 10.10). It is important to differentiate the abusive periosteal injury from the benign periosteal proliferation that is frequently seen on bone radiographs of pre-mature infants and occasionally in normal newborns. This latter condition is virtually al-ways symmetrical and presents as a thin single layer of periosteal elevation. Comparison of symmetry, both in thickness and in location of periosteal elevation, is usually sufficient to differentiate benign periosteal cloaking from the more dramatic periosteal cloaking of traumatic periostitis.

Epiphyseal separation in a child younger than two years of age is an infrequent but highly specific skeletal injury among abused children. Since it is very unusual to find epiphyseal separation in children younger than two years of age, its presence in this popu-lation is almost pathognomonic of abusive injury. The forces applied to cause the separa-tion are always severe torsion of the limb (fig. 10.11). The twisting separates the epiphysis

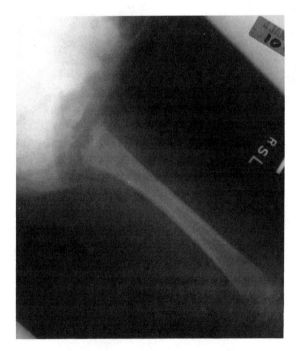

10.11 Epiphyseal separation fracture of the left femur in a six-month-old child. The leg was severely twisted by a frustrated caretaker.

by creating a fracture through the cartilage plate and, therefore, is mechanically similar to the various metaphyseal fractures discussed above.

In my experience, the majority of abusive long bone metaphyseal fractures occur in the lower extremities. This may be because the lower extremities are easily accessible to the perpetrator. The legs and ankles are often used as "handles" by which caretakers gain control of the child or lash out at it. One might speculate that diaper changing, a time often associated with frustration because children typically cry then, may also trigger a caretaker's tendency to fracture a child's lower extremities. Both lower- and upper-extremity metaphyseal fractures are identical in basic pathophysiology—only the frequency of incidence differs.

Rib fractures are commonly encountered among children suffering abusive skeletal injuries. The combination of acute and healing rib fractures in a child is practically pathognomonic of child abuse. Rib fractures are often difficult to detect clinically because they do not result in an obvious deformity or lack of function. The rib cage is splinted by muscles and soft tissues in such a way that rib fractures rarely demonstrate chest deformity. As anyone who has experienced one knows, a rib fracture is extremely painful; however, in a child too young to describe the pain, the symptoms apparent to a caretaker are usually nonspecific fussiness and irritability. A clinical physician asked to see a fussy child is unlikely, unless given a history of trauma for the patient, to detect rib fractures as the underlying etiology; therefore, rib fractures are often unanticipated markers of child abuse (fig. 10.12).

Fractures of posterior ribs are particularly noteworthy. The posterior ribs are well protected by paraspinous and intercostal muscles; consequently, they are rarely fractured except by severe squeezing and compression of the chest (fig. 10.13). This compression results in fracture of the rib both at its articulation to the vertebral body and at its articulation with the transverse process (fig. 10.14) (14). Since these fractures are often subtle, they are more easily demonstrated on two-week-delayed radiographs, as they become more conspicuous after healing callus has formed. The presence of posterior rib fractures, without an appropriate explanation, is virtually pathognomonic of child abuse.

Owing to the subtlety of these fractures, the thoracic cage is an area where nuclear medicine bone scintigraphy is occasionally of value in detecting additional occult fractures. From a practical standpoint, it may make little difference whether there are four rib fractures or ten rib fractures—nonetheless, judicious use of scintigraphy can be of great value in selected situations. In our practice we routinely request follow-up radiographs on infants below the age of two years who have rib fractures resulting from abuse; we reserve scintigraphy for selected difficult cases. In lethal cases, postmortem radiographs can be especially helpful in directing the medical examiner's attention to suspicious rib injuries.

Skull and Spine Injuries

Spinal fractures and spinal trauma are relatively infrequent in cases of child abuse, although some authors suggest that this low frequency may simply indicate failure to appreciate

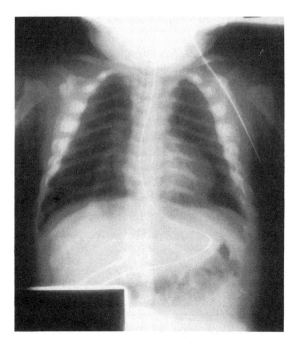

10.12 Multiple rib fractures, including many of varying ages, in a four-month-old abuse victim. The child had been seen by several different physicians for "fussiness" and other vague complaints, but the fractures were not detected until the child suffered a severe head injury.

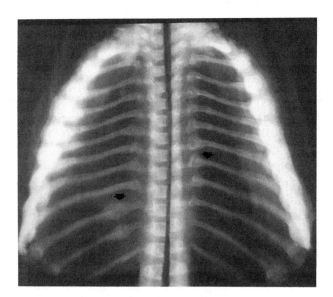

10.13 Autopsy radiograph of the thoracic cage of an abuse victim shows the multiple rib fractures in various stages of healing, including a number of posterior rib fractures (note arrows on some examples).

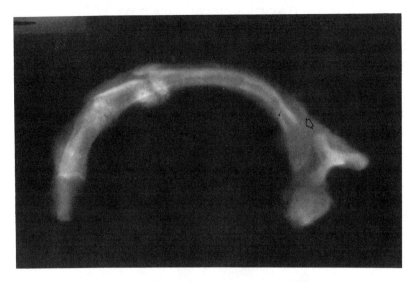

10.14 Excised rib of a child abuse victim demonstrates multiple fractures of the same rib. The fractures near the spine articulation (arrow) are often particularly difficult to image: detection may be enhanced by delayed films or by bone scintigraphy.

these lesions (15). When spinal fractures occur, they are usually some variant of a Chance fracture from marked hyperflexion resulting in fractures either of the spinous processes or of the vertebral bodies (fig. 10.15). Occasionally, direct trauma from severe blows to the anterior abdomen will result in fractures of the vertebral bodies. Secondary involvement of the vertebral body owing to fat necrosis associated with pancreatitis is an extremely unusual lesion; it has been reported to be caused by child abuse (16). Lesions involving the spinal cord itself without evident involvement of the bony supporting structures usually occur at the cervical medullary junction and are associated with shaking injuries (17). Lumbar cord contusions and epidural hematomas resulting from hyperflexion incurred during shaking are unusual.

Skull fractures are an important marker in judging the severity of cases of child abuse, since most of the fatal child abuse is secondary to head injury. The skull fracture itself rarely causes brain injury. Rather, the trauma, shearing effects, and ensuing cerebral edema are the major causes of morbidity and mortality. Thus, it is important to image the brain in cases of abusive skull fracture. If the patient is severely injured and exhibits significant neurological symptoms, we usually choose computed tomography (CT) as the first line of imaging. For the neurologically intact patient who is not critically ill, in whom the skull fracture is often an unexpected finding, magnetic resonance imaging (MRI) is recommended, as it has greater sensitivity and specificity for many of the subclinical lesions that are present in victims of child abuse.

Considerable significance can be ascribed to the correlation of the radiographic appearance of the skull fracture and the clinical history of the injury. Using physics measure-

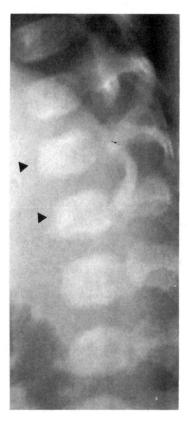

10.15 Subtle compression fractures
of T-11 and T-12 (arrows) caused
by hyperflexion on the child's torso
during abusive shaking episode.

ments and tensile strength of desiccated skulls, Root has shown that falls from as little as
twelve inches onto a hard surface can cause a skull fracture (18). Studies on traumatic
injuries demonstrate, however, that diastatic or stellate skull fractures do not result from
short falls (figs. 10.16 and 10.17). Helfer, Slovis, and Black (19) and Williams (20) have
studied children injured by documented accidental falls. In falls of three feet or less, children in the Helfer-Slovis-Black series had a 1% incidence of short, linear skull fractures.
None of these fractures were ever associated with neurologic injury. Chadwick (21) documented a number of accidental falls from substantial height. He showed that skull fractures
and intracranial injuries did not occur until the height of fall exceeded two stories. From
these studies it is reasonable to conclude that a short fall can cause short, linear skull fractures unassociated with neurologic injury in approximately 1% of the short-fall victims.
Fractures that are more extensive or associated with intracranial injuries require considerable more trauma than a short fall could produce. Stellate fractures, diastatic fractures, and

long parietal skull fractures are more characteristic of severe trauma and are very unlikely to be caused by a short fall.

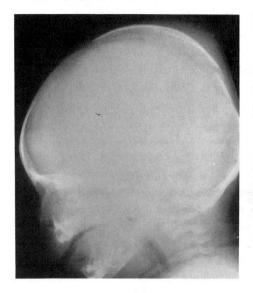 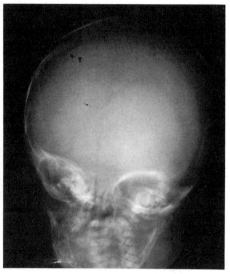

10.16 Diastatic skull fracture in a four-month-old child. Initial history given was of a fall from two feet onto concrete. Mother subsequently confessed to slamming the child's head into a doorframe during a shaking episode. Severe fractures with diastatic edges do not occur after minor trauma.

10.17 Anterior-posterior view of the skull in an abuse victim shows a two-limbed stellate skull fracture (arrows). Child also had long bone fractures and intracranial injuries.

Intracranial Injuries

Head injury is the leading cause of morbidity and mortality among children who are the victims of abuse. Abusive head injury is most common in young children, and the injury, if not lethal, frequently leaves serious and permanent sequelae, some of which may not be evident until years after the injury is inflicted. The precise anatomical and metabolic definition of brain injuries is still at a primitive descriptive stage. It is often possible, with current imaging techniques, to gauge the onset of symptoms and provide a gross estimate of outcome. Improved imaging techniques and functional imaging of the brain show promise in developing an understanding of the long-term morbidity of severe intracranial injury; however, the understanding of more subtle injuries and their impact upon behavior remains far off (22, 23). Considerable future research opportunities exist for defining the long-term morbidity and sequelae of abusive head injury.

The classic lesion of abusive head injury, and the one that was the first to be described, is the subdural hematoma (24). A subdural hematoma occurs secondary to forces that cause extravasation of venous blood beneath the dura mater after tearing of the bridging vessels from the surface of the brain (fig. 10.18). Most abusive subdural hematomas are small and do not cause major morbidity, but occasionally a subdural hematoma can be large enough to cause mass effect, compress critical areas of the brain, and require emergency evacuation. Despite this, in the large majority of instances the subdural is more an indicator of the severity of the trauma than a primary cause of morbidity.

Frequently, one finds both new *and* old subdural hematomas: this is invaluable in documenting the repetitive nature of abusive trauma. Documentation of differing ages of subdurals can be obtained either with CT scanning or magnetic resonance imaging (MRI) and is dependent upon the imaging characteristics of hemoglobin breakdown products (fig. 10.19). Windows of time for imaging identification of each state of hemoglobin breakdown are specific to the imaging modality used and may have overlap; hence, it is not always possible to document each separate episode of injury. A detailed discussion of the radiological timing of hemoglobin breakdown is beyond the scope of this chapter, but what is important to recognize is that explicit information on the imaging modality and consultation with a radiologist are needed for precise dating. In a large series of child abuse victims, it was documented that MRI showed approximately 50% more subdural hematomas than CT (25). Most of the hematomas shown by MRI were small or in areas parallel to the plane of CT scanning. CT is, therefore, the imaging modality of choice in the acutely ill child with neurologic symptoms where the unusual, large subdural hematoma might need rapid evacuation. I use MRI for those instances in which the diagnosis is in doubt or for those children who are seen in consultation beyond the acute period. After the acute period has passed, MRI will not only show small subdural lesions but will also give a better estimation of the degree of associated brain lesions.

Epidural hematoma is not a frequent lesion from child abuse. Most intracranial epidural hematomas occur after a blow that disrupts the meningeal artery, causing arterial hemorrhage (26). Epidural hemorrhage is distinguished from subdural hemorrhage both by the clinical course, which is usually more severe and rapid, and by the convex inner margin of the hemorrhage, which contrasts to the concave inner margin of subdural hemorrhage (fig. 10.20). The classic clinical picture of the epidural hematoma is that of the "lucid interval." The patient is stunned by the initial blow, then recovers briefly, only to suffer decreased levels of consciousness as the epidural hematoma progressively enlarges and causes mass effect upon the brain. Epidural hematoma is virtually always caused by impact trauma. In most instances, an epidural hematoma is a true emergency, requiring rapid surgical drainage. There are rare reports of venous epidural hematomas and delayed presentation of acute arterial hematomas, but these are clear exceptions to the usual behavior of the lesion (27).

Subarachnoid hemorrhage is, in our experience, the single most common imaging finding in abusive head injury. In subarachnoid hemorrhage the bleeding occurs beneath the arachnoid membrane, often filling the cerebral cisterns and flowing along the surface of the gyri (28). These blood collections have a characteristic location, opacifying the cisterns with high-CT-number blood, collecting over the tentorium cerbelli, and assuming a

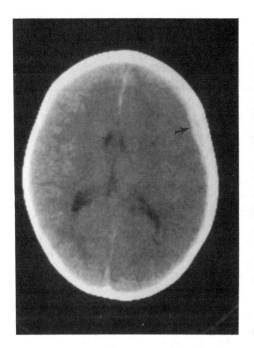 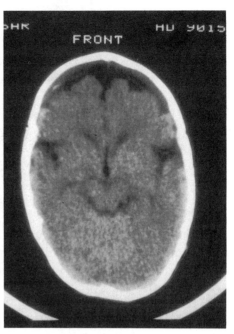

10.18 CT scan documents acute subdural hematoma (arrow) associated with severe brain
swelling. The subdural hematoma is a marker
of brain injury; the cerebral edema reflects the
severity of the injury.

10.19 CT scan documents acute and chronic
subdural hematomas with associated brain atrophy. The acute bleeding is white due to the presence of iron in the hemaglobin; the chronic
components are gray or black.

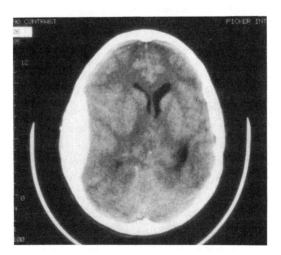

10.20 CT scan documenting an epidural hematoma in
a child injured in an automobile accident. The hematoma is convex from the inner table of the skull, as opposed to the concave subdural hematoma in
figure 10.18. Epidural hematomas almost always result
from direct external trauma.

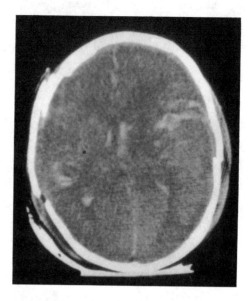

10.21 Diffuse subarachnoid bleeding along the gyral surfaces. The child also has a small acute subdural hematoma and severe cerebral edema. Subarachnoid blood appears as white linear or pooled collection along the gyral surfaces or in the subarachnoid cisterns. CT scan is generally better than MRI for detection of subarachnoid bleeding.

serpiginous gyriform pattern over the convexities of the cerebral cortex (fig. 10.21). There is some controversy in the imaging literature as to the accuracy of MRI and detection of subarachnoid hemorrhage. Conventional teaching has stressed CT as the primary diagnostic modality; however, in some instances subarachnoid hemorrhage is evident on MRI. The origin of the subarachnoid hemorrhage is similar to that of the subdural hemorrhage in that it usually is a vein that bleeds beneath the arachnoid membrane but external to the pia mater. In adults and older children, subarachnoid hemorrhage is almost invariably accompanied by severe headache. Although younger children cannot verbally express their discomfort, it seems logical to assume that they suffer similar symptoms. Younger children with subarachnoid hemorrhage exhibit irritability, fussiness, and sometimes vomiting. Identification of subarachnoid hemorrhage is time related: it is easier to detect the first few days after the trauma and becomes increasingly difficult over the course of the week (approximately) following the trauma. This timing and identification are considerably affected by the amount of subarachnoid blood present, since large hemorrhages are easier to identify than small ones are.

Cerebral edema ranks very closely with subarachnoid hemorrhage as the most common finding of abusive head injury. It is certainly the most common cause of permanent brain injury among abused children (23). CT scanning is relatively insensitive to cerebral edema: there have been well-documented cases of lethal cerebral edema undetected via normal CT scans (29). The key CT findings of cerebral edema include mass effect and obliteration of the normal architecture of the brain (fig. 10.22). With severe edema the basilar cisterns are filled by the expanding edematous brain, and the gray matter–white matter interfaces in the cerebrum are lost because of the extravasation of fluid into the brain parenchyma (30). Extreme cases of cerebral edema result in complete obliteration of all architecture of the normal brain, demonstrating the so-called reversal sign on CT scans, where the cerebral cortex appears hypodense relative to the brain stem and deep gray matter nuclei (fig. 10.23). The reversal sign is uniformly associated with a poor prognosis. Cerebral edema causes neurologic compromise in a number of ways, including inducing herniation in portions of the brain, disruption of neural transmission, and compromise of vascular supply to the brain.

The degree of cerebral edema varies with the severity of the insult. Massive cerebral edema usually renders the infant immediately comatose, while milder forms of cerebral edema may make the infant drowsy, cause vomiting, irritability, and hyperreflexia. If untreated after a traumatic event, brain swelling is progressive, and cerebral edema usually maximizes over forty-eight to seventy-two hours. Often it is possible to time injuries by comparing the images to the clinical history. Patients suffering acute severe cerebral edema are virtually always rendered unconscious immediately and rarely can survive more than a short period of time without artificial life support.

Parenchymal injuries of the brain are best revealed through MRI scanning (26, 20). CT scanning will show, as it does with other traumas, most lesions that need immediate surgical attention, but MRI is much more sensitive in detecting injuries to the brain parenchyma. Concussion and contusion are probably the most frequent parenchymal injuries and usually imply prior impact trauma. Concussion is manifest on MRI scanning as an injury with a base on the surface cortex and extensions a variable distance into the parenchyma of the brain (fig. 10.24). These lesions are particularly common in the rostral aspects of the frontal lobes just above the floor of the anterior cranial fossa and in the temporal areas, particularly in the rostral portion of the temporal lobe (31, 32). These two areas of the brain are in proximity to irregular bony surfaces, the floor of the anterior cranial fossa, and the posterior aspect of the sphenoid bone in the middle cranial fossa, against which the brain impacts upon deceleration.

Shearing injuries, or gray-white disassociation, are characteristic both of shaking injuries and deceleration injuries. These injuries may assume a pattern paralleling the gray matter–white matter interfaces of the gyri or may be manifest as a local blood collection at the gray-white junction. A typical site of shearing injury is the pericallosal area, or the basal ganglia; however, individual cortical gyri can also be involved (fig. 10.25) (33). This type of injury causes almost immediate symptomatology, usually unconsciousness. Residuals of these injuries are often more severe than one might expect from simply viewing the amount of tissue injured.

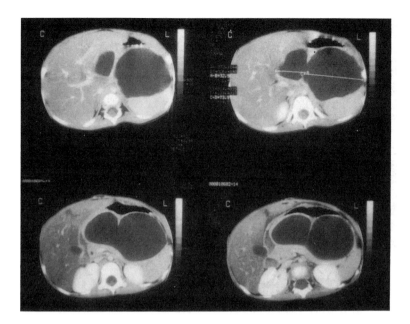

10.26 CT scan of the abdomen documents a huge, multilocular pancreatic pseudocyst. This two-year-old child was repeatedly struck in the abdomen by a caretaker who wanted to "toughen him up." The child had elevated serum amylase levels, severe pain, and pernicious emesis.

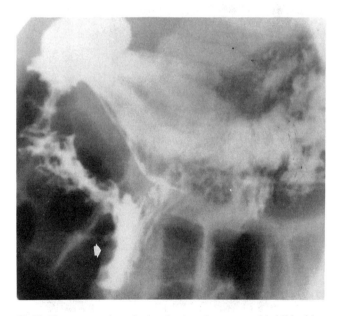

10.27 Upper gastrointestinal series in a three-year-old child with severe vomiting shows a deformed, partially obstructed duodenum. The undercut edge (arrow) is characteristic of an intramural mass.

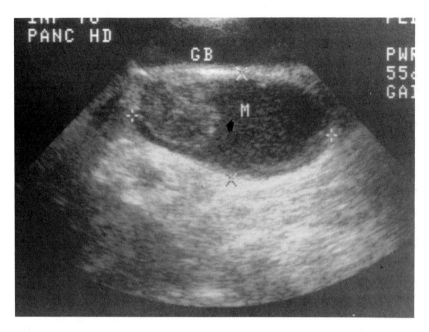

10.28 Ultrasound of the duodenum of the patient illustrated in figure 10.27 shows the hematoma mass (M) located around the duodenal mucosa (arrows). The gall bladder (GB) is located anterior to the mass.

this lesion, but ultrasound and CT scans have also been used for the diagnosis. Since the appearance of the periduodenal hematoma at surgery is often confusing, a precise radiographic diagnosis often prevents unnecessary surgical procedures.

Bowel perforation occasionally follows severe abusive blunt trauma. This type of perforation usually involves the jejunum or duodenum but can occasionally involve the colon. The signs and symptoms of peritonitis secondary to bowel perforation in an abuse victim are the same as those in children suffering peritonitis from other causes. The cardinal radiographic finding is that of free air in the peritoneal cavity; however, it is important to recognize that only 60% of children with a bowel perforation show free air. In the presence of an acute abdomen, the absence of free air should not exclude bowel perforation. The pathophysiology of the abusive bowel perforation involves a number of factors, including direct bowel entrapment, perforation by a blunt instrument, or creation of a venous hematoma that causes local bowel infarction. Occasionally, bowel perforation is seen in sexual abuse, particularly if instrumentation of the rectum takes place.

Differential Diagnosis of Child Abuse

In considering the differential diagnosis of child abuse, we must keep in mind that child abuse is extremely common. Using Bayesian reasoning to estimate prior probabilities, in general the odds are with us if we look for the uncommon manifestations of a common disease rather than the common manifestations of a rare disease. Since abusive injury is so common, readers can draw their own conclusions about the probability of occurrence of some of the unusual conditions proposed as alternative explanations. The principal differential is, of course, that of accidental trauma. Here the correlation with specific history is important. In actual cases of trauma, the caretaker: (1) recognizes the injury, (2) seeks aid promptly, (3) tells a consistent story, and (4) identifies an event consistent with the magnitude of the injury. If these four criteria are lacking, the likelihood of abuse increases substantially.

A number of infrequent metabolic conditions can superficially mimic the bony findings of abuse. Both rickets and scurvy can look somewhat like traumatic metaphysitis; however, scurvy is so rare as to be reportable, and rickets is generally a relatively easy diagnosis on clinical grounds. Infantile cortical hyperostoses (Caffey's disease) occasionally simulates the appearance of child abuse; however, the characteristic pattern of involvement (with high-frequency involvement of the mandible, the elevated erythrocyte sedimentation rate, the characteristic age, and the extremely thick periosteal reaction) should be sufficient to diagnose most cases of Caffey's disease. The prevalence of Caffey's disease is several thousand times less frequent than is child abuse. Wilson's disease can also superficially mimic an abusive injury; however, the clinical pattern of Wilson's disease (with characteristic hair changes, mental dysfunction, serum copper abnormalities, and uniform bone involvement) is so different from child abuse that it should not be difficult to make the diagnosis.

Osteogenesis imperfecta is probably the most difficult differential diagnosis. Most cases of osteogenesis imperfecta are diagnosable based upon radiographic appearance of the bones (36). Generally, the bones are demineralized, with thinned cortex and abnormal metacarpal cortical thickness. Osteogenesis imperfecta is caused by an error in collagen formation, and a large number of different variants of amino acids substitutions result in the variability of the phenotype of osteogenesis imperfecta (fig. 10.29). There are a few phenotypes of osteogenesis imperfecta that cannot be distinguished on conventional radiographs from abusive injury, and in these few instances fibroblast skin culture may be of assistance (37). Children with osteogenesis imperfecta, like any children with chronic disease, can also be child abuse victims—the presence of osteogenesis imperfecta does not exclude the possibility of child abuse. Careful consultation between radiologists, clinicians, dentists, and geneticists is sufficient to diagnose osteogenesis imperfecta in the vast majority of those cases in which the condition actually exists.

Occasionally, children with neuropathic conditions such as myelomeningocele may manifest fractures resulting from normal (that is, nonabusive) handling. These fractures often appear alarming because there is marked bony proliferation. In most instances, though, taking a careful social history and monitoring for recurrence of injury are sufficient to establish that the injury is secondary to neurotrophic bone weakening.

Subarachnoid hemorrhage and subdural hematoma can occasionally have etiologies other than trauma; these include major bleeding diathesis and intracranial vascular malformations. Usually both of these diagnoses can be made after further imaging or laboratory

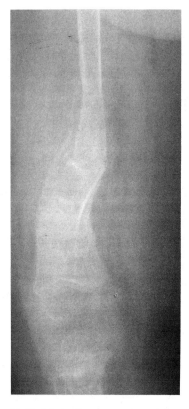

10.29 Markedly osteopenic and deformed femur of a two-year-old
child who has osteogenesis
imperfecta.

study. Any severe intracranial lesion that causes brain cell lysis will invariably be associated with a clotting abnormality, so minor clotting abnormalities in head-injured patients
are likely due to the trauma.

The many manifestations of abusive injury necessitate a team approach, with close
consultation between pediatricians, radiologists, social services workers, other allied health
workers, and often law enforcement officials. Many of the difficulties encountered in the
diagnosis of child abuse stem from these professionals' failure to coordinate their approaches, inquiries, and expertise. An incorrect clinical history is frequently all that is
provided, often making it necessary for those involved in a case to evaluate multiple faulty
explanations for the child's injuries before concluding that they in fact are the results of
abuse. To prevent deceptive clinical histories, all parties with information about the case
must have opportunities to participate in the diagnosis. With careful analysis and understanding of the roles of each professional, the diagnosis, causation, and timing of the injuries can usually be established accurately.

References

1. Silverman, F. N. 1972. Unrecognized Trauma in Infants, the Battered Child Syndrome, and the Syndrome of Ambroise Tardieu. Rigler Lecture. *Radiology* 104:337–53.
2. Caffey, J. 1946. Multiple Fractures in the Long Bones of Infants Suffering from Chronic Subdural Hematoma. *AJR* 56:163–73.
3. Silverman, F. N. 1953. The Roentgen Manifestations of Unrecognized Skeletal Trauma in Infants. *Am. J. Roentgenology* 69:413–26.
4. Kempe, C. H.; Silverman, F. N.; Steele, B. F.; Droegemueller, W.; and Silver, H. K. 1962. The Battered-Child Syndrome. *JAMA* 181:17–24.
5. Merton, D. F.; Radkowski, M. A.; and Leonidas, J. C. 1983. The Abused Child: A Radiological Reappraisal. *Radiology* 146:377–81.
6. Haller, J. O.; Kleinman, P. K.; Merton, D. F.; Cohen, M. D.; Hayden, P. W.; Keller, M.; Towbin, R.; and Sane, S. M. 1991. Diagnostic Imaging of Child Abuse. *Pediatrics* 87 (2):262–64.
7. Kleinman, P. K. 1990. Diagnostic Imaging in Infant Abuse. *AJR* 155:703–12.
8. Sty, J. R., and Starshak, R. J. 1983. The Role of Bone Scintigraphy in the Evaluation of the Suspected Abused Child. *Radiology* 146:369–75.
9. Matin, P. 1979. The Appearance of Bone Scans Following Fractures, Including Immediate and Long-Term Studies. *J. Nucl. Med.* 20:1227–31.
10. Sivit, C. J.; Taylor, G. A.; and Eichelberger, M. R. 1989. Visceral Injury in Battered Children: A Changing Perspective. *Radiology* 173:659–61.
11. Franken, E. A., Jr.; Fox, M.; Smith, J. A.; and Smith, W. L. 1978. Acute Gastric Dilatation in Neglected Children. *AJR* 130:297–99.
12. Kleinman, P. K.; Marks, S. C.; and Blackbourne, B. 1986. The Metaphyseal Lesion in Abused Infants: A Radiologic Histopathologic Study. *AJR* 146:895–905.
13. Chapman, S. 1992. The Radiological Dating of Injuries. *Arch. Dis. Childhood* 67:1063–65.
14. Kleinman, P. K.; Marks, S. C.; Spevak, M. R.; and Richmond, J. M. 1992. Fractures of the Rib Head in Abused Infants. *Radiology* 185:119–23.
15. Kleinman, P. K., and Marks, S. C. 1992. Vertebral Body Fractures in Child Abuse: Radiologic-Histopathologic Correlates. *Invest. Radiology* 27:715–22.
16. Neur, F.; Roberts, F. F.; and McCarthy, V. 1977. Osteolytic Lesions Following Traumatic Pancreatitis. *Am. J. Diseases of Children* 131:738–40.
17. Towbin, A. 1968. Spinal Injury Related to the Syndrome of Sudden Death ("Crib-Death") in Infants. *Am. J. Clinical Pathology* 49(4):562–67.
18. Root, I. 1992. Head Injuries from Short Distance Falls. *Am. J. Forensic Med. Pathology* 13 (1):85–87.
19. Helfer, R. E.; Slovis, T. L.; and Black, M. 1977. Injuries Resulting When Small Children Fall Out of Bed. *Pediatrics* 60:533–35.
20. Williams, R. A. 1991. Injuries in Infants and Small Children Resulting from Witnessed and Corroborated Free Falls. *J. Trauma* 31(10):1350–52.
21. Chadwick, D. L.; Chin, S.; Salerno, C.; Landsverk, J.; Kitchen, L. 1991. Deaths from Falls in Children: How Far Is Fatal? *J. Trauma* 31(10):1353–55.
22. Mendelsohn, D.; Levin, H. S.; Bruce, D.; Lilly, M.; Harward, H.; Culhane, K. A.; and Eisenberg, H. M. 1992. Late MRI after Head Injury in Children: Relationship to Clinical Features and Outcome. *Child's Nervous System* 8:445–52.
23. Pascucci, R. C. 1988. Head Trauma in the Child. *Intensive Care Med.* 14:185–95.
24. Zimmerman, R. A.; Bilaniuk, L. T.; Bruce, D.; et al. 1979. Computed Tomography of Craniocerebral Injury in the Abused Child. *Radiology* 130:687–90.
25. Sato, Y.; Yuh, W. T. C.; Smith, W. L.; et al. 1989. Head Injury in Child Abuse: Evaluation with MR Imaging. *Radiology* 173:653–57.

26. Lobato, R. D.; Rivas, J. J.; Cordobes, F.; Alted, E.; Perez, C.; Sarabia, R.; Cabrera, A.; Diez, I.; Gomez, P.; and Lamas, E. 1988. Acute Epidural Hematoma: An Analysis of Factors Influencing the Outcome of Patients Undergoing Surgery in Coma. *J. Neurosurgery* 68 (Jan.):48–57.

27. DiRocco, A.; Ellis, S. J.; and Landes, C. 1991. Delayed Epidural Hematoma. *Neuroradiology* 33:253–54.

28. Haymann, L. A.; Pagani, J. J.; Kirkpatrick, J. B.; and Hinck, V. C. 1989. Pathophysiology of Acute Intracerebral and Subarachnoid Hemorrhage: Applications to MR Imaging. *AJR* 153:135–39.

29. Gentry, L. R.; Godersky, J. C.; Thompson, B.; and Dunn, V. D. 1988. Prospective Comparative Study of Intermediate-Field MR and CT in the Evaluation of Closed Head Trauma. *AJNR* 9:91–100.

30. Zimmerman, R. A.; Bilaniuk, L. T.; Bruce, D.; Dolinskas, C.; Obrist, W.; and Kuhl, D. 1978. Computed Tomography of Pediatric Head Trauma: Acute General Cerebral Swelling. *Radiology* 126:403–8.

31. Gentry, L. R.; Godersky, J. C.; and Thompson, B. 1988. MR Imaging of Head Trauma: Review of the Distribution and Radiopathologic Features of Traumatic Lesions. *AJR* 150:663–72.

32. Hesselink, J. R.; Dowd, C. F.; Healy, M. E.; Hajek, P.; Baker, L. L.; and Luerssen, T. G. MR Imaging of Brain Contusions: A Comparative Study with CT. *AJR* 150:1133–42.

33. Mendelsohn, D. B.; Levin, H. S.; Harward, H.; and Bruce, D. 1992. Corpus Callosum Lesions after Closed Head Injury in Children: MRI, Clinical Features, and Outcome. *Neuroradiology* 34:384–88.

34. Bongiovi, J. J.; and Logosso, R. D. 1969. Pancreatic Pseudocyst Occurring in the Battered Child Syndrome. *J. Pediatric Surgery* 4:220–26.

35. Kleinman, P. K.; Brill, P. W.; and Winchester, P. 1986. Resolving Duodenal-Jejunal Hematoma in Abused Children. *Radiology* 160:747–50.

36. Ablin, D. S.; Greenspan, A.; Reinhart, M.; and Grix, A. 1990. Differentiation of Child Abuse from Osteogenesis Imperfecta. *AJR* 154:1035–46.

37. Gahagan, S., and Rimsza, M. E. 1991. Child Abuse or Osteogenesis Imperfecta: How Can We Tell? *Pediatrics* 88 (5):987–92.

11

The Pathology of Child Abuse

Robert H. Kirschner

Traditionally, discussions of the pathology of child abuse focus on the physical characteristics of injuries typical of the battered child. In this chapter, I present a somewhat different but integrated approach, discussing injuries within the context of the process of child death investigation. I emphasize those aspects of the investigation—including the autopsy, scene investigation, and record review—that are most important and/or most likely to cause the greatest diagnostic dilemmas for the pathologist. I also address those issues about which the pathologist is most likely to be challenged in court. The chapter concludes with a discussion of the rationale of medicolegal determination of cause of death and manner of death.

Deaths of infants and children from abuse and neglect affect all communities and social groups in the United States. Approximately two thousand such fatalities occur annually, 90% in children under the age of five, and 41% among infants (1). From the late 1960s to the late 1980s, the rate remained relatively stable (1, 2). Reports of a recent rise in abuse and abuse-related fatalities may reflect variations in survey technique (1) and an increasing awareness of the more subtle manifestations of abuse and neglect in living children (2, 3). Many such deaths that were previously misdiagnosed are now properly attributed to abuse, and the abuse perpetrators successfully prosecuted. There is strong evidence, however, of persistent underreporting due to inadequate death investigation (including failure to perform autopsies in children who die suddenly), lack of information sharing between agencies, and reporting systems that often fail to recognize abuse or neglect as contributing to a child's death (4).

The diagnostic features of the battered child syndrome are now easily recognized by the experienced clinician or forensic pathologist. Battered children, however, represent only a small proportion of abused children, and many deaths from child abuse occur without evidence of significant battering. What we see instead is a spectrum of fatal injuries whose causation often cannot be determined by autopsy or laboratory studies alone. These subtle forms of abuse are most common in infants, who are especially vulnerable because

Robert H. Kirschner, M.D., former deputy chief medical examiner, Cook County, Illinois, is clinical associate in the Department of Pathology and the Department of Pediatrics at the University of Chicago and at the LaRabida Children's Hospital and Research Center. He is also director of the International Forensic Program of Physicians for Human Rights.

of their relative isolation, small size, lack of verbal skills, and total dependence upon a caretaker.

Despite the growing recognition of various subtle forms of abuse, most sudden, unexpected deaths in infants will be due to natural causes, usually sudden infant death syndrome (SIDS). Within this context, a revised definition of SIDS has had important implications for the process of child death investigation. Part of a continuing effort to differentiate SIDS from accidental or intentional suffocation, genetic diseases, and other subtle metabolic or respiratory disorders, this new definition requires not only that a complete autopsy be performed but also that a death scene investigation and complete review of the child's clinical history be conducted in order for pathologists to establish a diagnosis of SIDS (5). These requirements are equally important in documenting deaths due to abuse or neglect. In consequence, pathologists are increasingly challenged in their efforts to correctly diagnose the cause of death in an infant or child who has died suddenly and unexpectedly.

The Autopsy

Autopsies involve a process of observation, documentation, and interpretation. The child death autopsy, more than any other, requires the maximum skills of the pathologist; moreover, wherever possible, a forensic pathologist with pediatric autopsy experience should perform the postmortem examination. Most general pathologists are less familiar with the special requirements of both the forensic autopsy and the pediatric autopsy than they are with the usual hospital autopsy, and they are accordingly often uncomfortable in interpreting the findings of a child death autopsy. Table 11.1 identifies the essential questions a pathologist may be expected to answer regarding the sudden death of an infant or child. These question often cannot be answered from the autopsy alone but require knowledge of the environment in which the child lived, the medical and family history of the child, and the circumstances of the fatal event.

TABLE 11.1
Sudden Death in Infants and Children: Questions to Be Answered by Pathologist

1. Was death due to injury, neglect, or complications of injury or neglect?
2. If related to injury, what was the mechanism of injury?
3. Was the injury consistent with the alleged history or circumstances of injury? If not, why not?
4. When did the injury occur in relation to the time of death?
5. Did a delay in seeking medical care contribute to death? If so, was this an "unreasonable" delay?
6. Did death result from a single episode of injury or as the result of multiple episodes of injury?
7. Were drugs or poisons involved in the death?
8. If neglect was involved, what form did it take?
9. If there is evidence of failure to thrive, was this due to metabolic disorder, other disease, or neglect?
10. To what extent did environmental, nutritional, and social factors contribute to death?

Photographic Documentation

It is important that documentation of the autopsy findings be thorough and accessible to review by other pathologists. In this regard, photography is an integral part of the child death autopsy. If a dead child has not been removed from the scene of death, it should first be photographed in that setting. Photographs should be used to document all injuries, congenital anomalies, and dysmorphic features. The body should be photographed prior to being undressed; prior to being cleansed if there is blood, dirt, or other foreign matter present; and then again after the cleansing. Individual lesions or groups of lesions should be photographed at close range using a macro lens and appropriate label and scale. The photographs must accurately portray the body and the injuries as they would appear to a layperson seeing the child in a nonmedical context. Photographs that show a background of extraneous blood, dirty instruments, or internal organs may be considered inflammatory or prejudicial by a judge and ruled to be inadmissible in court.

Technically, color transparency film is preferable to print film because it has better color balance, permits greater enlargement by projection, and is thus easier to interpret when viewed at a later date. High-quality prints can easily be made from these slides if necessary for courtroom purposes. Electronic flash provides the best lighting source. Because they lack necessary detail and color balance, Polaroid photographs are not a substitute for a 35 mm photography system (6).

Reflective ultraviolet photography in the near UV range (320 nm–400 nm) is used in some jurisdictions to enhance recent injury patterns on the skin and to detect older injuries that are no longer visible on the skin surface. The technique has been used particularly by forensic odontologists to enhance bite marks, but it has also been utilized to document older bruises in child abuse cases. Epidermal response to UV light has been documented as late as three months following injury, but there is great individual variability in the intensity and duration of this response (7). Further investigation of this technique under controlled laboratory conditions is needed to assess its reliability more fully.

Radiologic Documentation

Newer imaging techniques and improved diagnostic skills have revealed subtle injuries of the brain and skeletal system that previously escaped detection (8–10). These advances have important application to the autopsy. Small metaphyseal fractures, spinous process fractures, and digital fractures unlikely to be seen on the usual postmortem "baby-gram" can be identified when a complete skeletal survey with appropriate cone-down views is taken. The films serve as a guide to the pathologist, who should excise the involved bones or bone segments so that they can be separately radiographed, photographed, and submitted for histological evaluation after gross examination. This combination of techniques provides the best basis for establishing the age of injuries. Radiological examination does not relieve the pathologist of the responsibility of looking for fractures. Acute rib fractures and linear skull fractures may not be visible on x rays but they will be obvious upon careful gross examination.

Prolonged hospitalization, cerebral edema, neurosurgical intervention, and respirator brain changes may obscure traumatic lesions of the head and brain, and the findings at autopsy may be nondiagnostic. In such cases, hospital x rays and MRI and CT scans may provide the best graphic representation of the child's injuries.

Time-of-Death Determination

Estimating the child's time of death may be especially important when the child has had more than one caretaker or when a caretaker's story appears to contain discrepancies. Questions regarding the time of death are also frequently asked by parents who had placed their infants in bed for the night only to discover the child dead in the morning, an apparent victim of SIDS.

The pathologist must be cautious in any estimate that he or she makes regarding time of death. Body temperature and environmental conditions at the time of death exert significantly greater influence in infants and young children than in adults on the development of postmortem changes such as rigor mortis and lividity. It is difficult to generalize about the specific timing of these events. Estimating the time of death from body temperature is subject to sufficient error that it may lead investigators astray, and the pathologist should be cautious in using such measurements. The presence or absence of food in the stomach should be correlated with the child's feeding history and the reported time of the last meal. As with adults, infants' gastric emptying time depends on the type of meal and the quantity of food ingested, but is usually less than two hours. Time of death is most accurately determined by interviewing witnesses who can reliably state when the child was last seen alive and at what time he or she was found dead. There are so many variables involved that it is prudent to be circumspect in forming and announcing an opinion.

When an attempt has been made to conceal the death of a child—a not uncommon event when newborns die—discovery of the body may be delayed for days or even years, and the body will consequently be decomposed or skeletalized. In such instances, a forensic entomologist may provide valuable information regarding the time of death, based on examination of the life stages of flies and other insects found on and around the body (11). Whenever it is possible, the entomologist should visit the death scene prior to removal of the body to personally recover evidence.

Skeletalized remains should be examined by a forensic anthropologist to determine stature and age range using standardized anthropologic tables, dental developmental charts, and radiographic atlases. Unambiguous determination of sex in prepubertal skeletons is not possible (12). However, recent anthropological analysis by Snow et al (13) of the skeletal remains of 136 child victims (who ranged in age from one to twelve years, the average being six years of age) of the 1982 military massacre at El Mozote, El Salvador, was approximately 80% correct in sex assignment, based on comparison of the children's skeletons with their clothing, which is usually gender specific from infancy onward in that country. This corresponds to data cited by Krogman that presents a range of 73% to 81% accuracy of sex assignment in subjects from two to eight years of age (14).

Search for Trace Evidence

With rare exception, fatal abuse occurs in the child's usual environment, and the victim is normally in intimate contact with the suspected abuser (when there is a suspect). Under such circumstances, trace evidence may be of limited value. Furthermore, the body and the

death scene are usually "contaminated" by therapeutic intervention and by numerous outsiders at the scene. Paramedics, who are usually the first responders on the scene, will
institute appropriate cardiopulmonary resuscitation (CPR) unless there is clear evidence
that the child has been dead for a prolonged period of time. CPR is often continued in the
hospital emergency room, invasive procedures are often performed, and the body may be
partially washed, particularly if stool, vomitus, or other body fluids are present.

The child's diaper or underpants, clothing, covers, and associated paraphernalia are
likely to be displaced, left at home, or discarded in the hospital emergency room. These
items should be brought to the autopsy suite and examined for evidence of vomitus, urine,
feces, and blood stains. Medications, formula, milk, or other items that might have been
ingested should also be recovered. A search should be made for hairs, fibers, or other trace
evidence that may be found on the body and the clothing. Where indicated, appropriate
toxicological tests should be conducted on formula, milk, and other food items. When there
is evidence that a commercial product contaminated through spoilage or tampering may
have been involved in the death, the appropriate local and/or federal government agencies
and the manufacturer should be notified immediately.

Nutrition and Hygiene

A child's appearance can be assessed for state of personal hygiene by noting the level of
cleanliness of the skin, including the presence of stool, food, and secretions on skin surfaces. Poor hygiene may be manifested by severe chronic diaper rash, lichenification and
pigment changes of the perineal skin, chronic seborrhea of the scalp, and dirt in the skin
creases. Many experienced forensic pathologists have seen accusations of neglect leveled
at parents whose infants have died with a coincident moderate to severe acute diaper rash
but without any other sign of possible abuse or neglect. Such accusations are unfair and
only add to the parents' guilt feelings. Diaper rash can progress rapidly, particularly in the
presence of diarrhea or when caused by a yeast infection.

Determinants of appropriate growth and development such as weight, body length,
head circumference, and stature should be compared to standard growth charts as well as
to the child's previous growth measurements, including birth weight and length. If a child
was premature, corrections should be made for gestational age. Standard curves indicating
normal weight for height of a child are helpful in assessing failure to thrive, yet pathologists
underutilize these tools. Because the infant and childhood years are a period of rapid
growth, a plateau in a child's growth or a loss of weight prior to death must be viewed with
concern and an appropriate explanation sought at autopsy.

Cutaneous Manifestations of Abuse

Although accidental injuries are as much as fifteen times more common than abuse-related
injuries in infants and young children (15), the benign nature of almost all accidental injuries that occur in the home has been repeatedly demonstrated (16–18). Cutaneous manifestations of accidental falls are usually confined to the forehead, bony prominences of the
face and extremities, and the palms; abrasions of the face, palms, elbows, knees, and shins
are common in these circumstances, as are bruises and superficial lacerations of the fore-

head and chin. These injuries are age appropriate, often confirmed by independent witnesses, and are consistent with the reported circumstances. Serious injury is rare (19).

In contrast, injuries that are not in fact accidental but inflicted are inconsistent with the alleged circumstances, lack independent witnesses, and are usually not appropriate to the child's age. Such injuries may be scant or numerous, of different ages, produced by a variety of blunt trauma and other forms of assault, and involve any part of the body (20–23). Certain types of injuries are more commonly seen in particular age groups, and the abuse is often triggered by behavior patterns characteristic of that age group. In the infant of less than one year of age, persistent crying or crankiness may lead the parents to shake or suffocate the child in an attempt to quiet him or her; in the one-to-two-year-old, toilet training may become the focus of abuse, leading to beatings or scald burns as a form of punishment. In the older child, "misbehaving" may provoke a variety of punishments. As the infant matures, suffocation, occult head injury, and rib fractures become less common; severe beatings, burns, and abdominal injuries become more common.

Contusions caused by blows are the most common form of abuse in all age groups and are often clustered on the face (figs. 11.1a, 11.1b), chest, abdomen, or back. Even an apparently innocuous injury in a child who has died unexpectedly must be viewed with suspicion, and significant injury must be considered to be abuse until proven otherwise. While it is appropriate to estimate the age of bruises based on their color, this is an imprecise exercise (24, 25). Deep bruises may take days to appear, while superficial bruises may occur almost immediately and disappear within a few days. Anatomic location and skin complexion also influence the appearance of bruises. Accordingly, bruises inflicted on a child at the same time and by the same mechanism may nevertheless be of different color and resolve at different rates.

Although precise determination of the age of bruises may not be possible, the pathologist should compare all of the bruises to one another, both grossly and microscopically, to derive both their relative age and a time span during which injury can reasonably be assumed to have occurred. Burns and abrasions can be similarly compared. The presence of varying aged lesions establishes a pattern of continued abuse as opposed to a single episode of injury. Figure 11.2 shows ulcerated bite marks of the tongue in a chronically abused child. These injuries were judged microscopically to be at least one week old, were consistent with the age of several bruises noted on the face, and helped the pathologist to determine that a pattern of repeated beatings had led to the child's death.

If patterned injuries are apparent, scene investigation should include a search for an implement or implements that are consistent with the patterns on the body. It is unusual to find an injury with a unique pattern, so one should be cautious in specifically identifying an alleged weapon as responsible for an injury. A suspected weapon, however, may show evidence of trace elements of blood or tissue to link it to the assault. Loop marks caused by a belt, cord, or similar implement are probably the most common patterned injuries of child abuse (figs. 11.3a, 11.3b).

A two-and-a-half-year-old child who was developmentally delayed (the result of an unexplained apnea episode that occurred when the child was eleven months old) was admitted to hospital in

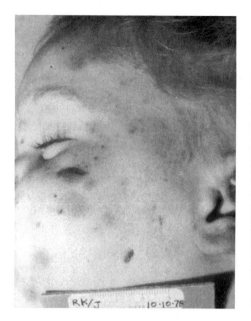
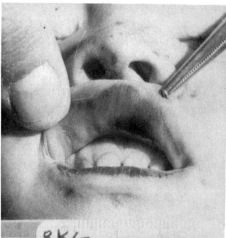

11.1 Eighteen-month-old child who had more than 120 bruises and abrasions of the body. Contusions of left side of face caused by blows with hand; abrasions caused by ring worn by perpetrator (*a, left*). Contusion of buccal mucosa due to blow to mouth (*b, right*).

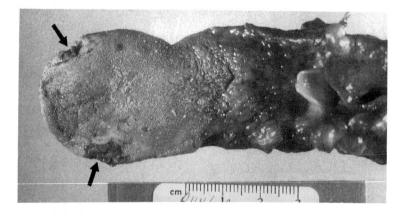

11.2 Ulcerated bite marks (arrows) of the tongue of at least one week of age in a chronically abused child.

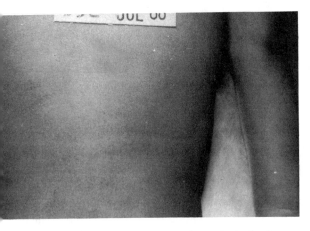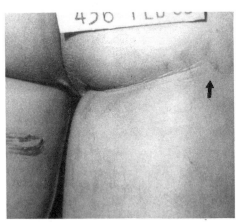

11.3 Patterned injuries: Loop marks on the back of a two-year-old, caused by beating with electric cord (*a, left*). Abraded loop mark injury on the thigh of a toddler; faint, patterned contusions (arrow) at margin of right buttock (*b, right*).

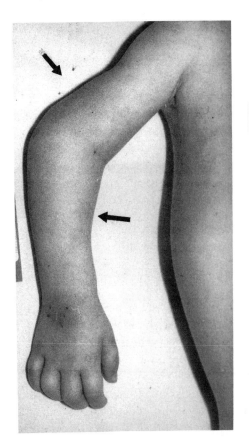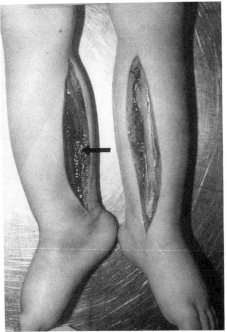

11.4 Two-and-a-half-year-old child with deformities of arms and legs due to multiple old and more recent skeletal fractures. Deformities (arrows) of right arm and forearm (*a, left*). Hemorrhage in subcutaneous tissues and muscles (arrow) of right leg, demonstrated by incision during autopsy (*b, right*).

a coma and died within hours. Multiple old and recent extremity fractures were noted, with deformity of the right arm and leg (figs. 11.4a, 11.4b). The parents claimed that the child was clumsy and frequently fell. At autopsy there were numerous bruises, skeletal fractures, and marked cerebral edema. Review of the hospital records revealed a serum sodium concentration of 200meq/L, diagnostic of exogenous hypernatremia.

When blunt trauma injuries are identified or suspected, it is appropriate for the pathologist to incise through the skin and subcutaneous tissues of the involved regions to determine the depth to which hemorrhage extends. This provides an indication of the severity of the blunt force used and may also reveal significant soft tissue injury not apparent from examination of the skin surfaces (fig. 11.4b). This is particularly true in children who die within twenty-four hours of injury, before deep bruises have had the opportunity to diffuse closer to the skin surface. Faint bruises and abrasions may also become more distinct after the autopsy, due to postmortem "aging" of the injury and drainage of blood from vessels. If the body is reexamined twenty-four hours later, bruises and abrasions that were difficult to distinguish at first examination may appear accentuated. Samples of representative lesions should be taken for histological evaluation.

Burns are a common form of abuse, and scald burns have a significant mortality (see also chapter 9). One prospective study found that four deaths resulted among thirty deliberately scalded children (mean age twenty-two and a half months) with burns of the buttocks. The infants who died had burns involving 32.3% of their total body surface area (26); sepsis from stool contamination of the burns was felt to be the significant factor leading to death. Inflicted scald burns tend to be symmetrical, often mark the child's hands or feet in a glove or stocking pattern, and have sharp margins. These injuries are inconsistent with the alleged "accidental" circumstances and often inappropriate for the infant's age (figs. 11.5a, 11.5b). During scene investigation, the caretaker should be asked to recreate the incident using a mannequin approximately the same size as the child. If the injury allegedly was related to hot tap water, water temperature at the same faucet should be measured.

Bite-Mark Injuries

Bite marks associated with child abuse may be found anywhere on the body, particularly in infants. Because the skin is an elastic substrate which is easily distorted by movement of the assailant or the victim, bite marks usually form imperfect and incomplete impressions. Depending on the amount of force that was used and where it was applied, bite marks may be missed by the untrained eye, particularly bite marks on regions such as the fingers or toes. If there are any lesions suspected to be bite marks, a forensic odontologist should be consulted at once, since the autopsy procedure is likely to distort these injuries. Failure to observe this rule may cause irretrievable loss of evidence. Body surfaces should not be washed before bite marks are examined, to preclude loss of serological evidence from the saliva of the perpetrator. Since bite marks are often found on victims who have sustained multiple cutaneous injuries, careful examination of the body is necessary to distinguish

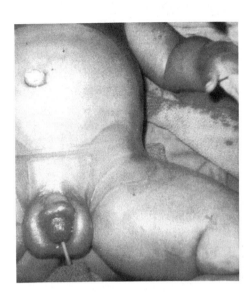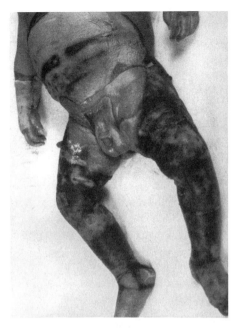

11.5 A two-year-old child with scald burns inflicted in a bathtub was admitted to the hospital;
he survived for ten days. Photograph taken at time of admission, showing sharp margins of the burn
and the sparing of the groin region (*a, left*). Autopsy photograph demonstrates change in appearance
of burn during hospitalization: injuries remain sharply demarcated; note glove pattern of burn to
right forearm (*b, right*).

possible bite marks from other abrasions and contusions. Photographs and impressions
should be made using accepted forensic techniques.

The forensic odontologist must evaluate the evidence and attempt to determine the
probability that a bite mark corresponds to or excludes the dentition of one or more suspects. A search warrant or court order is necessary to permit dental impressions to be taken
of the suspected abuser. Recognition and processing of such evidence may be a critical link
in identifying the perpetrator of the abuse. It must be remembered that retarded or disturbed
children may bite themselves and that children may be bitten by a sibling or other child.

Thoracic Injuries

Inflicted intrathoracic injuries are uncommon in infants—except for rib fractures
(fig. 11.6). Pulmonary contusions may result from abusive compression of the chest, usually in association with multiple rib fractures. Resuscitation efforts may produce contusions
of the anterior chest wall, but such efforts alone will not cause rib fractures (27, 28). Cardiac injury is rare. Cohle et al. (29) have reported six cases of abusive cardiac trauma in
children from nine months to two-and-a-half years of age. In five cases, the right atrium
was lacerated, and in the other, the left ventricle. All of their cases showed other evidence

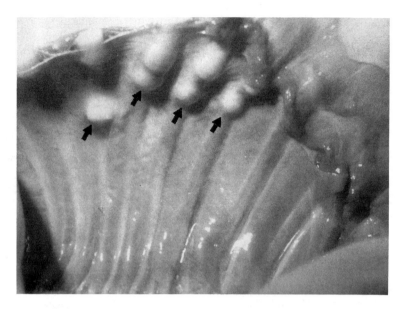

11.6. Healing rib fractures (arrows) in a six-month-old who died of abuse. Note advanced callus formation. The costochondral junctions are directly above the fracture sites.

of abusive trauma. Reardon et al. (30) reported successful repair of a laceration of the right atrium, allegedly following inexpert CPR in a four-year-old boy who suffered a seizure in association with a viral syndrome. The clinical history in this case is sketchy, however, and open to question.

I have seen two cases of right atrial laceration due to inflicted injury; in neither of these cases was there other evidence of abuse. The defense in each case claimed the cardiac injury was caused by inexpert cardiopulmonary resuscitation upon a child who just happened to collapse suddenly.

An eleven-month-old previously healthy infant became unresponsive while in the care of her baby-sitter, who called 911 after allegedly initiating CPR. The child was reportedly found unresponsive on the floor, having been seen alert and happy only moments earlier. At autopsy, there were scattered abrasions of the face and several small contusions of varying ages of the chest and abdomen inconsistent with accidental injuries. The right atrium was lacerated at its junction with the inferior vena cava and 80–100 ml of blood was present within the pericardial sac. Two other children in the care of this baby-sitter had suffered injuries of abuse, including the sister of the deceased, who had sustained skull and wrist fractures when she allegedly tripped while running. Three forensic pathologists and a pediatrician with extensive experience in child abuse cases testified as to the nonaccidental nature of the child's cutaneous and cardiac injuries. The defense retained a forensic pathologist who claimed that the child had died of a "viral" illness, although there was no evidence of such, clinically or at autopsy. He attributed the atrial laceration to CPR. The jury deadlocked and failed to bring a conviction.

This injury was most likely caused by the caretaker stepping on the child or by severe, prolonged compression of the chest with the hands. Several physicians testified that the force necessary to produce cardiac laceration was clearly beyond the limit of therapeutic chest compression. Furthermore, this child was afebrile and had no symptoms of viral illness. Even the presence of a mysterious viral disease would not explain sudden death in the absence of other findings.

Abdominal Injuries

Blunt trauma to the abdomen, usually seen in the older infant or young child, is the second leading cause of fatal abuse, exceeded only by head trauma (31). Three major types of injuries are common: (1) laceration of a solid organ, most commonly the liver (figs. 11.7a, 11.7b) and, less commonly, the spleen, pancreas, or kidney; (2) intramural hematoma or laceration of a segment of the gastrointestinal tract, particularly the small intestine; and (3) laceration of the bowel mesentery (fig. 11.8). The mechanism of injury is usually a sharp blow or kick to the abdomen producing displacement or compression of the affected organ. This leads to a shearing or crushing injury. Increased intra-abdominal pressure may also lead to a blowout injury of a distended stomach or loop of bowel. Less commonly, a child may suffer abdominal injury by being thrown against a wall, floor, or other hard surface. The mechanism of death is intra-abdominal hemorrhage or peritonitis, depending upon the type of injury and its severity. Such injuries do not occur as a result of the usual accidents within the home such as tripping while running, falling down stairs, or falling out of bed (16–19, 32).

Abdominal injuries are not always fatal. Figure 11.7b demonstrates a healed liver laceration from a previous episode of abuse in a child who subsequently died of other inflicted injuries. In a case from the Cook County [Illinois] Medical Examiner's Office, previous exploratory laparotomy of a young child with peritoneal signs revealed healing injury at the base of the mesentery which was misinterpreted at surgery and on biopsy as retroperitoneal fibromatosis. The child later died after further abuse, and review of earlier hospital records showed evidence of contusions of the abdomen that had been dismissed as usual childhood bruising.

The child with abdominal trauma may appear relatively symptom-free for several hours following injury. The onset of symptoms may be insidious, developing over a period of up to twenty-four hours. This is particularly true in the preverbal child, who cannot voice complaints, and is characteristic of injuries such as duodenal perforation or other retroperitoneal injury. Likewise, when there is a small liver or mesenteric laceration that bleeds slowly, a child may also appear relatively asymptomatic but collapse suddenly with massive accumulation of blood in the abdominal cavity. The blood volume of a young child is approximately 75 milliliters of blood per kilogram of body weight; the percentage of blood loss into the abdominal cavity may be calculated on this basis and may be as great as one-third of the total blood volume. In the child with untreated peritonitis, several days may elapse between injury and death.

When a child dies from inflicted abdominal trauma associated with a lacerated liver, there may be a claim that the injury was sustained during resuscitation. Even vigorous,

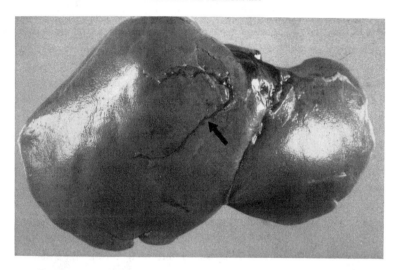

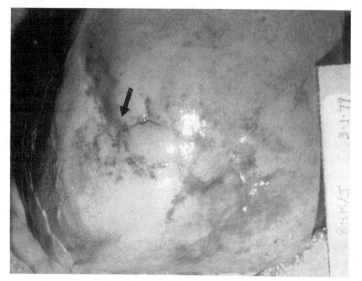

11.7 Acute laceration of the liver (arrow) in an infant who died of inflicted abdominal injury (*a, top*). Laceration of the liver that healed without treatment (arrow) in a chronically abused infant who later died of head injuries (*b, above*).

inexpert resuscitation in a young child will rarely, if ever, produce hepatic injury. If it does occur, the laceration will be superficial, located in the midline on the superior surface of the liver, and associated with only minimal hemorrhage as opposed to the significant hemorrhage characteristic of lethal inflicted injury. Similarly, attorneys for the defense in one case argued that a large mesenteric laceration in a seventeen-month-old child with multiple abdominal bruises was caused by overvigorous resuscitation efforts applied to the lower

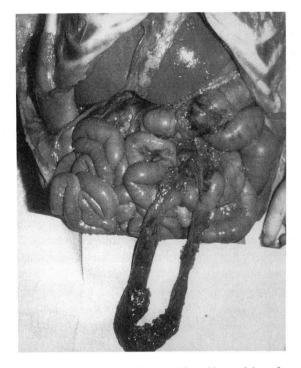

11.8 Severe abdominal injury manifested by avulsion of
a segment of small bowel from its mesentery and multiple contusions of other regions of the intestinal tract.

abdomen. The presence of significant intra-abdominal hemorrhage, in and of itself, was inconsistent with resuscitation injury.

The full extent of gastrointestinal trauma is often better appreciated after fixation of the bowel in formalin, and histological sampling is also best done after fixation. If the child has had surgery with partial bowel resection, the surgical specimen and associated histological slides should be retrieved and examined. Interpretation of the age of the injuries requires sampling for microscopy not only of the lesion itself but of inflamed peritoneal surfaces and other tissues secondarily involved by hemorrhage or infection.

Musculoskeletal Injuries

Skeletal fractures are a prominent component of child abuse injuries. Skull fractures are most common, followed by long-bone fractures. In one study of seventy-five abused children under the age of three with an average of two fractures per child, 77% of the fractures were acute and 23% old (33).

Toddlers and older children may fall and fracture limbs or sustain uncomplicated skull fractures in a fall from a moderate height; however, these age-appropriate accidental fractures conform to the clinical history and are clinically benign. At autopsy, any skeletal fracture in an infant or child should be considered to be abuse until proven otherwise—unless there is a confirmed history of motor vehicle accident or fall from an upper-story window. Fractured bone(s) should be excised by the pathologist for further gross and microscopic examination.

The need to differentiate between a diagnosis of abusive fractures and one of osteogenesis imperfecta (OI) rarely occurs at autopsy. However, this question may arise in living infants with one or more fractures (34; and see chapter 9) and may lead to extensive diagnostic testing. A full discussion of the topic is beyond the scope of this chapter; however, one does not expect OI to be associated with multiple bruises, subdural hematomas, cerebral injury, or damage to internal organs. Such findings indicate abuse, even in a child with proven OI. The concept of "temporary brittle-bone disease" (35), coincidentally characterized by fractures more typical of abuse (for example, rib and metaphyseal fractures) but lacking features common to OI, remains totally unsubstantiated. Unfortunately, this specious disorder is being raised as a defense in many child abuse cases. Thorough investigation, appropriate laboratory and radiological studies, and documentation of all injuries is necessary to deflect this hypothesis.

Significant injuries to muscle tissue are unusual even in fatal abuse associated with severe beatings. However, some children may die following such a beating, without evidence of internal injuries. I will consider the problem of fatal abuse without "fatal" injuries later in this chapter.

Sexual Abuse Injuries

Sexual abuse injuries are an uncommon component of fatal child abuse and may or may not be associated with the injuries related to death. When there is a suspicion of sexual abuse, the pathologist should take oral, rectal, and vaginal swabs for DNA analysis of sperm and antigenic typing of semen. There must be a careful search for trace evidence, particularly hairs and fibers. Pathologists in consultation with crime laboratory personnel should determine the techniques to be used; appropriate materials for the studies must be available when needed and not assembled on an ad hoc basis. Examination of the external genitalia, perineum, and anal region will establish whether there is evidence of acute or chronic injury, most commonly lacerations, due to sexual abuse. Injury to the genitalia may also be inflicted as a form of punishment during toilet training rather than as a direct sexual assault (fig. 11.9). Toluidine blue can be used to aid in the detection of recent perianal and anal trauma (36). A photographic record of the findings is essential for documentation since inflammatory, infectious, and congenital lesions may all be confused with lesions produced by sexual abuse (37–39).

Although external examination may reveal no evidence of sexual abuse, a further search should be made during internal examination both for foreign bodies or trauma within the vagina or rectum and for evidence of perforation into the peritoneal cavity. Press et al. reported a case of small-bowel evisceration in a four-year-old boy caused by forceful insertion of a long object, perhaps a toilet plunger, into the rectum with subsequent sigmoid perforation (40). When there is evidence of rectal trauma, the rectum, anus, and perianal tissues should be excised en bloc; in the female, the dissection should also include the

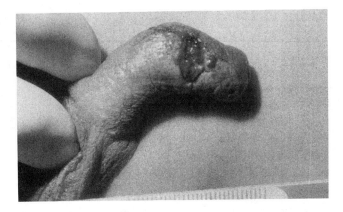

11.9 Laceration of the penis in a toddler who was fatally beaten for wetting his pants.

perineum, uterus, vagina, and vulva. The bladder and urethra are usually incorporated within this block. After removal, the anus (and vagina) should be opened, the injuries photographed, and the tissues fixed in formalin and subsequently sectioned for microscopic examination. The remaining pelvic tissues can be sewn together to leave little evidence of the exenteration.

A mistaken diagnosis of sexual abuse may arise from misinterpretation of postmortem changes in the perineal region.

A six-month-old infant was pronounced dead in a hospital emergency room and reported to the medical examiner's office as a probable victim of sexual abuse. Upon investigation, it was determined that a nurse had cleaned the infant's genital and perineal region of adherent stool. During the cleansing, the rectal sphincter relaxed, giving a false impression of recent anal penetration; congealing of subcutaneous fat produced a gaping of the vulvar tissues that suggested vaginal penetration (fig. 11.10a). In comparison, figure 11.10b shows the perineal region of a young child previously subjected to repeated rectal penetration.

Effects of Hospitalization and Therapy

Even brief hospitalization and therapy may alter the appearance of injuries, and after prolonged hospitalization, injuries heal or are markedly altered in appearance (see figs. 11.5a and 11.5b). A range of iatrogenic lesions may also develop and must be recognized as such. Common findings related to therapy include excoriations of the face related to prolonged intubation, tape marks, pressure purpura in the occipital region, and ecchymoses associated with cutaneous needle puncture sites.

Major surgery such as craniotomy or laparotomy may obscure cutaneous injuries or lead to removal of damaged internal organs. Review of operative reports is essential, and examination and histological sampling of surgical specimens is often helpful in reconstructing the original injuries. The greatest difficulty imposed by surgery is the later recognition of blunt trauma injury of the scalp in regions contiguous with a craniotomy. Ab-

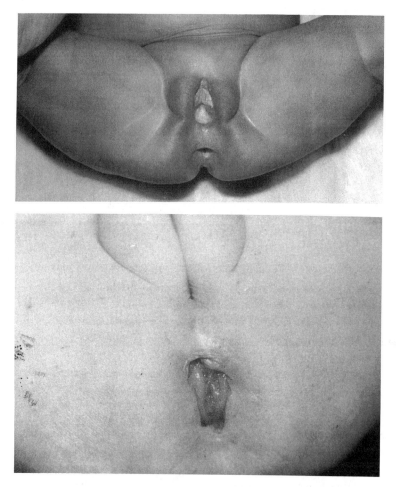

11.10 Postmortem gaping of the vulva and rectum, which was reported as child abuse but which was found to have resulted from the cleansing of the area by a nurse (*a, top*). Healed lacerations and incipient rectal prolapse in a sexually abused infant who suffered repeated rectal penetration (*b, above*).

dominal surgery does not usually interfere with identification of cutaneous injuries to the anterior abdominal wall.

A brain-dead child maintained on a respirator will develop a "respirator brain." The features include cerebral edema, progressive softening of the brain, clot formation within the dural sinuses, and occasional focal subarachnoid hemorrhage. Low-grade infection may develop within the middle or inner ears, which in an infant may normally show evidence of mild chronic inflammation. Similarly, bronchopneumonia can develop within hours when a comatose child is placed on a respirator; the pathologist must take care not to identify this secondary phenomenon as the cause of death.

The failure of a pathologist to differentiate respirator-associated phenomena from underlying injuries caused significant problems in the coroner's office of one city. The cause of death given by the pathologist was not only incorrect but implausible, and reflected lack of knowledge of pediatric medicine. This case also underscores the importance of pathologists' reviewing medical records and investigating circumstances of injury before reaching conclusions regarding cause of death.

A fifteen-month-old previously healthy infant male was brought into a hospital emergency room, seizing and then comatose, after an alleged fall from a couch at home. He had been in the care of his mother's paramour at the time of the incident. Treating physicians noted a small bruise on the right ear, cerebral edema (right greater than left), and retinal hemorrhages; tympanic membranes were judged normal by three examiners. The clinical diagnosis was blunt head trauma due to abuse. The child died after three days on a respirator. At autopsy, there was cerebral edema, a small subdural hematoma, clot within the transverse sinus misinterpreted as thrombosis, and mild inflammation of the middle ears. The pathologist listed the cause of death as transverse sinus thrombosis secondary to middle-ear infection, and the manner of death as natural. He failed to review the child's medical records or inquire as to the alleged circumstances of injury. The police were forced to release the assailant, who had been in custody since the day of the assault; he promptly fled to Mexico. Review of the case by other pathologists confirmed the clinical diagnosis of child abuse and identified the middle-ear "infection" and transverse sinus clot as components of respirator brain changes. The suspect later returned to the United States, was indicted, and convicted.

Microscopic Interpretation and Dating of Injuries

The normal histological appearance of neonatal and infant organs differs in important respects from that in older children and adults. This is particularly true in regard to development and maturation of the immune system. Pathologists unaccustomed to the normal exuberant appearance of lymphoid tissue in the lungs, gastrointestinal tract, and lymph nodes of infants may mistake this normal histological pattern for evidence of a viral reaction. The most common error is the misinterpretation of interstitial cellularity and peribronchiolar lymphoid aggregations within the lungs as evidence of pneumonia. Microvesicular fat within the liver is also a common finding in normal infants that may be misinterpreted as evidence of metabolic disease, nutritional deficiency, or toxicity (41). Children dying of these disorders invariably show far more fat within hepatocytes than is seen in healthy trauma victims or babies dying of SIDS.

Wound organization and healing in infants evolves more rapidly in young children than in adults, and this must be considered when dating the age of injuries. Although more accurate than gross examination, dating of injuries by microscopic examination remains imprecise; hence, the pathologist should not pinpoint a time but, rather, should estimate a time range during which the injuries could plausibly have occurred. This time window expands as the interval between injury and death increases. Special stains for collagen and hemosiderin may assist in refining the estimate, but age, nutrition, immune system status,

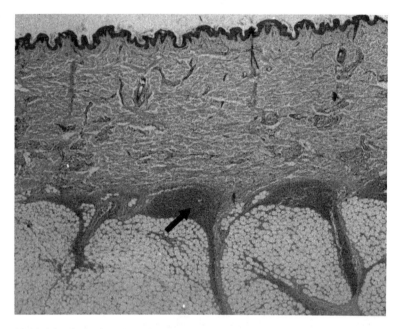

11.11 Histological section of a contusion from an abused infant hospitalized in a coma for four days prior to death. The subcutaneous hemorrhage (arrow) shows no evidence of the organization that would be expected in an injury of four days age.

and inherent individual differences are important variables that affect healing and should be kept in mind. Inflammatory response and wound healing in the severely injured (42, 43) or malnourished child may be markedly inhibited.

Children who are comatose also show impaired inflammatory response to systemic and cutaneous injury, such that wound healing is inhibited (fig. 11.11). The cause of the coma does not appear to be a factor in determining this altered time sequence, but pathologists must be aware that it does occur. When there is a time lag between injury and death, the outcome of an investigation may depend in part upon the ability of the pathologist to date the injuries. He or she must resist any pressure to adjust the injury time range derived through gross and microscopic examination to conform to theories of the police, prosecutors, or defense attorneys.

Laboratory Studies

Postmortem Chemistry

Postmortem chemistry is an important component of the child death autopsy. Normal vitreous electrolytes are a significant negative finding, and abnormalities may provide a clue to the cause of death. The relatively sequestered environment of the vitreous humor enhances its value as a fluid for postmortem electrolyte studies. Sodium, urea nitrogen, and creatinine values closely parallel antemortem serum values and remain stable after death in the absence of decomposition. Chloride levels are less predictable, having a normal range approximately 20 milliequivalents per liter (20 meq/L) greater than normal antemortem serum values. Vitreous potassium rises rapidly after death and does not reflect antemortem serum levels.

An elevated vitreous glucose concentration reflects antemortem hyperglycemia, but low vitreous glucose is of little diagnostic value, since glucose is rapidly utilized after death. Ethanol, ketones, and other volatiles are easily measured in the vitreous. If factitious hypoglycemia is suspected, serum total insulin and C-peptide concentrations can be determined by the usual radioimmunoassay methods. Under usual circumstances, these proteins as well as albumin, globulins, and hemoglobin remain stable in the body for at least twenty-four hours after death, permitting reliable postmortem analysis.

Hypernatremia as a form of abuse is probably more common than reported (44, 45); consequently, in the absence of an appropriate clinical history, hypernatremia must be regarded with suspicion. Vitreous sodium concentration greater than 155 meq/L and urea nitrogen greater than 30 mg/dl indicate a contracted intravascular compartment; severe clinical consequences can occur at a sodium concentration higher than 160 meq/L (46). Physicians should consider vitreous sodium concentration greater than 175 meq/L as diagnostic of abuse or neglect until proven otherwise.

Meadow (47) reviewed twelve cases of intentional salt poisoning, most of the victims were in the first six months of life. The mother was the perpetrator in ten of the twelve cases. I have investigated three cases of salt poisoning in toddlers from two to three years of age admitted to hospital with serum sodium concentrations in the range of 190 to 205 meq/L. One child died in the emergency room, after water intake had been restricted for several days while she was in the care of a baby-sitter; two others died as inpatients and, in addition, showed evidence of having been physically abused. All had been forced to eat salt or drink saltwater as a form of punishment. In one such case, in which the parents claimed the child had been playing with a saltshaker, the excess salt load was calculated to be thirty grams (fig. 11.12). In none of these children did the pediatric house staff or attending physicians suspect the true cause of the hypernatremia; rather, in all cases, they considered hypothalamic tumor high on the differential diagnosis list.

Nonfatal dilutional hyponatremia due to water intoxication has been reported in infants chronically fed diluted formula, which produces markedly low sodium and chloride concentrations (48). I am not aware, however of any deaths from this practice.

Intoxication and Poisoning

The yield from toxicological screening in infant deaths remains relatively low despite a marked increase in the birth of drug-intoxicated infants in recent years (49, 50). Cocaine or its major metabolite, benzoylecgonine, is the drug most frequently recovered, and Mirchandani et al. (51), in 1991, reported sixteen such cases in Philadelphia. This figure met with some skepticism at the time, but subsequent experience in other jurisdictions has been

11.12 Beaker containing 30 grams of salt, to demonstrate the excess salt load a two-year-old was forced to ingest as punishment for misbehaving; death caused by hypernatremia.

similar. The presence of any concentration of either cocaine or its metabolite benzoylecgonine should be considered sufficient to cause or contribute to the death of any live-born infant in whom an unrelated, obvious cause of death is not present.

Additional substances that are frequently part of routine screening include alcohol, opiates, acetaminophen, phencyclidine, and aspirin, but the yield for these drugs will be below that for cocaine. Clearly, the presence of any illicit drug, alcohol, prescription drug not prescribed for the child, or inappropriate over-the-counter medication is cause for concern. The presence of nonprescribed medications may represent innocent attempts at home doctoring, accidental ingestion, or intentional poisoning, often as a manifestation of Munchausen syndrome by proxy (see chapter 18). Careful review of a child's symptoms, when attempts to discover a medical etiology have failed, should provide a clue to unusual forms of poisoning (52). However, apparent toxic postmortem serum concentrations of certain prescribed drugs such as digoxin may reflect only postmortem artifact and not indicate antemortem toxicity (53).

Inaccurate laboratory procedures may lead to serious error and unnecessary grief for parents.

An eight-year-old boy drowned in a recreation center swimming pool in a northern Illinois county, and the boy's parents alleged negligence in the guarding of the pool. An autopsy was performed, and the county toxicology laboratory reported the presence of cocaine in the boy's blood. The examining pathologist, not experienced in forensic pathology, subsequently misinterpreted aspirated small food particles within bronchioles as intravascular foreign matter consistent with intravenous drug abuse. Cocaine intoxication was listed as the underlying cause of death. Review of the gas chromatograms by an experienced forensic toxicologist showed them to be virtually uninterpretable but demonstrating no evidence of cocaine or any other drug.

Both the toxicologist and the pathologist in this case failed to consider how unlikely it would be to find an eight-year-old intravenous drug abuser. The pathologist, biased by incorrect laboratory results, produced an incorrect microscopic evaluation of the lungs. A lawsuit brought by the parents of the dead child against the county was settled out of court.

Documentation of Infection

Microbiological studies without autopsy evidence of infection are unlikely to be positive except in the young infant, where sepsis or pneumonia may remain occult at autopsy. Even when a child has had a clinical history of febrile illness, the yield of positive cultures at autopsy, will be low, since most fevers will be of viral origin. Blood cultures taken more than twenty-four hours after death are almost certain to be contaminated by intestinal flora and are not worthwhile.

Postmortem testing for most sexually transmitted diseases will also be unreliable if not done in the immediate postmortem period. However, such tests should not be done by emergency department personnel, who first see the dead child, without the permission of the medical examiner or coroner's pathologist. Probing of the vaginal or rectal regions may produce artifactual injury or distort existing injuries.

When suggested by the child's history, stool cultures for *salmonella, shigella,* and other intestinal organisms should be obtained. Where viral disease is suspected, serum viral antibody titers are more likely than viral cultures to be positive, and at a fraction of the cost.

Special Problems in Child Autopsies

As I discussed earlier, certain types of injury to children pose particularly difficult diagnostic dilemmas to treating physicians and forensic pathologists, either because of perplexing physical findings, absence of physical findings, discordant histories, or failure of the physicians involved in these autopsies to understand mechanisms of injury in infants and children. Most significant in this last category is the disparity among physicians in their ability and willingness to identify head injuries as having been inflicted. Because child abuse accounts for approximately 95% of serious head injuries in children less than one year old (54) and head injuries are responsible for most of the fatalities in this age group, it is appropriate to begin with a discussion of this topic.

Fatal Head Injury

Differentiating accidental from intentional head injury is not usually a difficult process in older children and adults. The amount of force required to produce significant injury is such that contusions and/or lacerations of the scalp will mark the impact site(s). The number and location of these external injuries, and their relationship to the underlying injuries of the skull and brain, permit the forensic pathologist to distinguish between injuries caused by falls and those inflicted by blows. Typically, falls produce deceleration injury character-ized by cerebral contusions on the surface of the brain opposite the point of impact—that is, contre-coup injury. Inflicted traumas, on the other hand, is usually associated with cere-bral contusions directly below the impact site—that is, coup injuries. Skull fractures and/ or intracranial hemorrhage are a frequent component of both accidental and inflicted trauma in older children. Severe accidental trauma almost always occurs outside the home and is usually verifiable by independent witnesses; pathologists should bear these facts in mind when a child's death is alleged to have resulted from an accident in the home.

Clinically, an older child may appear to recover briefly following severe head impact and then become comatose some hours later due to an evolving subdural hematoma. This so-called lucid period, during which the signs of increasing intracranial pressure may not be obvious to the casual observer, occurs because the subdural space is large enough to accommodate moderate bleeding before intracranial pressure rises sufficiently to compro-mise cerebral function.

Several features differentiate the infant less than one year old from its older siblings in regard to lethal head injury. Unlike the older child, the infant may sustain significant head trauma without evidence of impact to the scalp. Furthermore, the thin pliable skull of the young infant transmits force more diffusely than the more rigid skull of the older child. Thus, cerebral contusions are less common, and one rarely sees a typical pattern of coup or contre-coup injuries. The subdural space in the young infant is narrower and thus less tolerant of space-occupying lesions; finally, the unmyelinated infant brain with its higher water content is more susceptible to rapid life-threatening diffuse brain swelling than iᶜ the brain of an older child. Between the ages of one and two years, as the skull and brain mature, a child's response to head injury shows a transition from the infantile to the more adult form.

Despite the seeming fragility of the infant head, it is highly resilient to accidental trauma, as has been documented in many studies (18, 32, 55, 56). For example, Chadwick et al., examined the outcome of head injuries—all supposedly due to fall—in 317 children brought to a children's trauma center in San Diego. Seven deaths occurred in 100 children who allegedly fell four feet or less, no deaths in 65 children who fell five feet to nine feet, and only one death among 117 children who fell ten feet to forty-five feet (18). The height of the fall was unknown in the cases of the other 34 children, all of whom survived. The histories in those children who died after short falls proved to be false: these children all died as a result of abuse. In another study, the medical records of 151 children who fell from buildings were reviewed, including 108 who fell two stories. There was significant morbidity in the latter group, but there were no fatalities (55). A prospective clinical study by Goldstein et al. (57) of forty children admitted to a pediatric intensive care unit con-firmed the results of these retrospective studies. They concluded that "severity of neuro-logical injury and neurologic outcome in cases of inflicted head injury [were] worse than in any other type of childhood head injury."

Were trivial falls of the type encountered within the home potentially lethal, the human race would not have survived. Hence, when a caretaker indicates that a child's severe head trauma has resulted from such a fall, or occurred without the knowledge of the caretaker, the story must be presumed to be false until proven otherwise. Despite this, inflicted head trauma deaths continue to be difficult to prosecute because there is often no external evidence of injury (this can lead to speculation about mysterious natural causes or trivial accidental injury) and because many clinicians and pathologists equivocate about the timing of the lethal event. It is useful to consider the following statements when evaluating head injuries in infants:

1. Falls within the home, down stairs, and so forth, are relatively trivial events and produce trivial (non-life-threatening) injuries. Blows, shaking, and forced impact are violent events and produce potentially lethal injuries.
2. There is no "lucid" or asymptomatic period in infants following serious or lethal head injury. Progressively more severe symptoms develop almost immediately.

Serious or lethal head injury may result from shaking, impact, or a combination of shaking and impact. External injuries in these cases are often minimal or absent; thus, the history given by the caretaker must be carefully recorded since the story is likely to change if inconsistencies are discovered in the relation of the circumstances of the "accident" to the child's symptoms.

In the most difficult clinical circumstances, a previously healthy, afebrile infant may present to the hospital with the rapid onset of unexplained coma, diffuse brain swelling, no external evidence of injury, and no evidence of subdural or retinal hemorrhages. The differential diagnosis must include infection, metabolic disease, drug intoxication, or, rarely, carbon monoxide poisoning. When studies for these disorders prove negative, the diagnosis should focus on near asphyxiation or blunt head trauma. Shaking may also produce diffuse brain swelling without other manifestations of the shaken baby syndrome, but this is unusual.

The autopsy in such a case may reveal only a swollen brain, with no evidence of subgaleal hemorrhage, retinal hemorrhage, skull fracture, or cerebral contusions. Absence of any such injury supports a diagnosis of asphyxiation. Small parenchymal tears or lacerations within the subcortical white matter of the brain indicate deceleration injury, such as might be caused by shaking the infant or by striking the head against a firm padded surface. Striking an infant's head against a surface or striking the head with a hand or other object will usually produce subgaleal hemorrhage even in the absence of external bruising (fig. 11.13). Careful documentation of these hemorrhages is important as they may represent the only markers of fatal injury other than diffuse brain swelling.

Shaken baby syndrome (SBS) is the result of a *violent shaking force* that causes a whiplash acceleration-deceleration motion of the relatively unstable infant's head upon its neck. It is not possible to quantitate the force, but it is the type of shaking that an *independent lay observer* would recognize as likely to cause serious harm. It is more common in younger infants. It may, however, be seen at any age if there is great enough disparity between the size of the victim and the size of the perpetrator.[1] Rapid deceleration occurs

1. A thirty-year-old, 45kg prisoner in a Middle Eastern country was violently shaken by two secret police agents while they were interrogating him. He suddenly collapsed, was admitted to hospital in a coma, and died

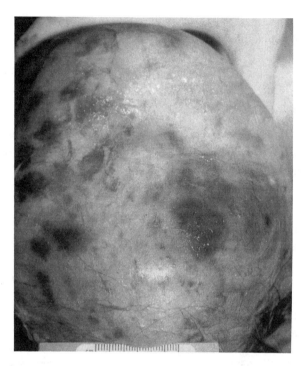

11.13 Multiple regions of subgaleal hemorrhage due to repeated blows to the head. No injuries were noted on the surface of the scalp; however, there was marked cerebral edema.

when the victim's chin strikes the chest and subsequently when the occiput strikes the interscapular region of the back at the base of the neck. This shaking often produces slight to moderate hemorrhage in the cervical paraspinous muscles. Epidural or subdural hemorrhage in the cervical canal is a variable feature; spinal cord injury is unusual. Shaken babies may show other evidence of injury, such as rib fractures or bruises of the chest, arms, or legs where the infant has been grabbed. There may also be an associated fracture of a clavicle, humerus, femur, or tibia.

A variation of SBS is the "tin ear" syndrome, in which the infant is struck on the side of the head, producing contusion of the ear and rotational acceleration of the head that produces ipsilateral cerebral swelling, subdural hemorrhage, and hemorrhagic retinopathy (58).

SBS usually produces a diagnostic triad of injuries that includes diffuse brain swelling, subdural hemorrhage, and retinal hemorrhages. This triad must be considered virtually

---

shortly thereafter. Autopsy revealed typical findings of SBS—subdural hemorrhage, cerebral edema, and retinal hemorrhages. There was no evidence of impact injury. Violent shaking without impact (to avoid leaving marks on the victim) had been reported as a common form of torture used in this particular country to extract information from prisoners.

pathognomonic of SBS in the absence of documented extraordinary blunt force such as an automobile accident. Blood dyscrasias, infections, ruptured intracranial vascular malformations, and other natural disease processes may rarely mimic SBS but are readily distinguished by appropriate diagnostic studies.

Fatal shaking events are, with rare exception, characterized clinically by almost immediate loss of consciousness, often with associated seizures and apnea. Irritability, inability to feed, vomiting, and lethargy are common components of less severe shaking episodes and may be mistaken for a viral illness.

While Duhaime et al. have claimed that shaking alone is insufficient to produce the observed injuries and that an impact component is necessary (59), others have proposed that shaking, in and of itself, is sufficient (60, 61). I concur in this latter opinion, based on my experience at the Cook County Medical Examiner's Office, where many autopsies of shaken babies both showed no evidence of blunt trauma injuries to the head and elicited caretakers' confessions that described shaking alone (see also footnote 1). Shaking a baby who has allegedly stopped breathing to start it breathing again, or shaking a baby that has allegedly aspirated food or some foreign object, does not cause the shaken baby syndrome.

Subdural hemorrhage is not usually a significant space-occupying lesion in young infants (fig. 11.14), but the torn bridging subdural veins that cause the bleeding are manifestations of the extreme forces involved. Death is caused by diffuse brain swelling secondary

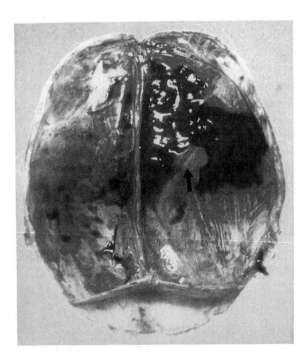

11.14 Subdural hematoma (arrow) in a shaken baby. Although this is not a significant space-occupying lesion, it is a marker for shaken baby syndrome.

to cerebral hypoxia, diffuse axonal injury and, in some cases, associated parenchymal tears or lacerations of the cortex. Unlike contusion injuries in older children and adults, contusion injuries in infants do not usually correspond to the point of impact on the cortical surface but extend as small tears along the lines of force through the brain.

The contribution of cerebral hypoxia to cerebral edema and ultimate outcome in SBS is being increasingly recognized. For example, Johnson et al. retrospectively studied twenty-eight children who suffered significant inflicted head injury. Their results strongly suggested that apnea induced by shaking, with or without impact, caused cerebral hypoxia and/or ischemia, and that this was more fundamental to outcome than diffuse axonal injury, contusions or parenchymal tears (62). Such a conclusion draws support from our common clinical experience that apnea and/or seizures is the most common presenting complaint in severely shaken infants.

Retinal hemorrhages are nearly pathognomonic of violent shaking and are frequently associated with retinal detachment and the formation of retinal folds (63, 64). They are characteristic of inflicted acceleration/deceleration injury, at least in part due to the susceptibility of the retinal vessels to these particular lines of force (65). A prospective study by Johnson et al. has documented that retinal hemorrhages occur rarely in accidental head injury and are associated with extraordinary force. Among 140 children who suffered accidental head trauma that included skull fractures and/or intracranial hemorrhage, including 52 children less than two years old, only 2 children both of whom were rear-set passengers in a motor vehicle collision, showed evidence of retinal hemorrhages (64).

Retinal hemorrhages have been reported following resuscitation, but not in children who had documented lack of hemorrhages prior to resuscitation. Except in children with blood dyscrasias or other risk factors for hemorrhage, retinal hemorrhages rarely, if ever, result from resuscitation rather than from the inflicted trauma that led to cardiopulmonary arrest (66, 67). Vaginal delivery may produce retinal hemorrhages in the neonate, but these will disappear within six to seven days. It is important to note that the extent of retinal hemorrhage in shaken babies may vary greatly from a few scattered intraretinal hemorrhages to extensive hemorrhage covering much of the retina (68). It is only the former type that have been reported in association with cardiopulmonary resuscitation, whereas extensive hemorrhage correlates with severe inflicted trauma.

Not all episodes of shaking are lethal. Autopsy will occasionally reveal evidence of previously undiagnosed, organized, or organizing subdural hemorrhage or old contusions. These should be evaluated histologically, but as Leestma has observed, the timetables for estimating resolution of these injuries in children are not well established (69).

It is important to state that there is no evidence to support the concept that re-bleeding of an organizing subdural hemorrhage can occur from a subsequent trivial injury and cause severe neurologic impairment or death. This is a frequent argument used in court by defense "experts" to explain how an infant with a previous, clinically unrecognized subdural hemorrhage could become comatose or die from a subsequent alleged trivial injury, such as a fall from a couch. As discussed above, the subdural bleeding is not clinically significant, but only a marker for severe shaking and/or impact. Therefore, even if re-bleeding could occur from a trivial injury, the infant should remain neurologically intact. Similarly, there is no evidence that trivial trauma will produce life-threatening brain injury in an infant who has been previously shaken. The presence of fresh subdural hemorrhage, diffuse brain swelling, and retinal hemorrhages is proof of another violent shaking episode. In my experience, in all cases in which these "re-bleed" arguments have been put forward, the circumstances of injury have been highly consistent with abuse. We must ask ourselves, why, if this "re-bleed" syndrome postulated in the courtroom really exists, it is not diagnosed under verifiably accidental circumstances.

Infants may die weeks or months after cerebral injury has been inflicted. Cerebral atrophy will be noted at autopsy, but the timing of the trauma and its cause will not be possible from postmortem examination alone. In such cases, it is important to review medical records, x rays, CT scans, and other documents relevant to the time of injury before reaching a conclusion as to cause and manner of death.

Simple linear skull fractures without significant neurological symptoms occasionally result when children are involved in falls around the home. Such falls can occur from upper bunk beds, from ladders, from trees, or from porch railings. These fractures are nondiastatic, usually parietal, and represent no danger to the child. There will be minimal to moderate associated subgaleal hemorrhage. Most significantly, these benign fractures are associated with age-appropriate activity.

In contrast, infants with skull fractures and significant brain injury will usually show extensive swelling overlying the fracture site due to hemorrhage and edema within soft tissues. Contusion of the scalp will be apparent, and the number of impact sites, in those children who die, can often best be gauged by examining the subgaleal region of the scalp. The force necessary to produce such injuries cannot occur from a simple fall at home but is comparable to injury that would be sustained in a motor vehicle accident or a fall from an upper-story window. When the parent or other caretaker indicates that severe head trauma has resulted from a fall in the home, his or her account of events must be presumed to be false until proven otherwise.

Timing of Head Injuries

As I discussed in the previous section, severe head trauma in infants produces immediate symptoms. This applies both to shaken babies and to infants with skull fractures and cerebral injuries. Since coma can mimic sleeping in the undisturbed child, the last time the child was awake and alert is an important marker. It should be noted, however, that if a comatose child is lifted from its bed, it should be immediately obvious that the usual reflexes, positioning, and breathing patterns are absent.

The father of a young infant retrieved his sleeping son from the apartment of a baby-sitter. It was agreed that the child appeared normal at that time. After returning home, the father changed the child's diaper, held it, and rocked the baby for several minutes when it cried. During this time, he noticed nothing unusual. More than one hour after returning home, he called 911 claiming that the child had stopped breathing. The infant died several hours later in hospital, and autopsy revealed two large subgaleal hemorrhages, subdural hemorrhage, cerebral edema, and retinal hemorrhages. The expert witnesses for the prosecution and one expert for the defense agreed that a layperson without special medical knowledge or skills would be able to distinguish between coma and sleep when actively handling an infant. One defense expert claimed that the baby's injuries had occurred earlier in the evening at the baby-sitter's and that the father had failed to recognize that his "sleeping" son was actually in a coma. The parent was convicted of first-degree murder.

In another case in which the injuries were more obvious treating physicians were reluctant to determine the time of injury.

A moribund three-month-old infant was admitted to hospital with a comminuted, depressed skull fracture, retinal hemorrhages, and fracture of the left femur due to abuse. During the eighteen hours prior to his admission, he had been in the care of several different relatives but had been reported as alert and acting normally until he suddenly became unresponsive while solely in the care of his father. None of the treating physicians was willing to narrow the injury time frame to less than eighteen hours, and the case remained unresolved for several months. The father confessed when faced with a forensic opinion that the onset of symptoms was necessarily concomitant with the time of injury.

I have seen numerous cases in which a so-called lucid interval is invoked to explain how an infant with massive head trauma can remain asymptomatic for hours following an injury that would quickly incapacitate an adult. At times, this explanation is used to avoid facing the reality that the perpetrator is someone who does not fit the appropriate abuser profile, often because of his or her socioeconomic status. Physicians in some hospitals refuse to recognize abuse by suburban parents. In other cases, there is a failure to prosecute abusers because of their social status, or prosecution has failed because juries refused to believe the perpetrator guilty of horrendous acts, despite the best persuasive efforts of the prosecutor.

A seventeen-month-old boy was dropped off by his mother at a baby-sitter's house at 7:20 A.M. in apparent good health. The mother had separated from her husband and had previously been accused of abusing her children. The baby-sitter was married and had a stable home environment. At 7:45, the child was seen by other parents to be sitting in the kitchen eating cereal. At 8:25, the baby-sitter called the mother to report that the child had fallen. The child was admitted to hospital with an extensive left parietal skull fracture and occipital fractures, cerebral contusions, and retinal hemorrhages. The baby-sitter claimed no knowledge of the parietal fracture but stated that the occipital fracture might have occurred when the child fell backward and struck a coffee table. She was indicted for murder. Medical evidence and eyewitness testimony ruled out the mother as the offender, but local newspapers attacked the district attorney for indicting the baby-sitter rather than the mother, claiming that the latter fit the profile of an abuser. All treating physicians and two forensic pathologists identified the injuries as occurring while the child was in the care of the sitter. A retired neurologist with no expertise in child abuse testified for the defense. He claimed that the infant might have suffered the first injury at home and had a prolonged lucid interval, which ended when he fell against the coffee table and suffered the second skull fracture. Unfortunately, this irresponsible testimony led to a hung jury and there was no conviction.

Responsibility for a child's injuries must be determined by coordinating the medical time frame derived from the medical records and autopsy findings, the circumstantial time frame based on who was with the victim at particular times, and the functional time limit— that time when the victim was last known to be well and eating, playing, and normally active for his or her age. With the rapid expansion of child abuse intervention teams around the country, the persistent myths about head injuries in infants should recede.

The Negative Autopsy: Suffocation or SIDS

A *negative autopsy* is defined as an autopsy in which there are no significant disease processes or injuries and in which the cause of death cannot be determined after the gross dissection, microscopical examination, and all laboratory tests have been completed.

Asphyxiation of the young infant usually produces no distinct pathological changes observable at autopsy. This is true of both accidental and homicidal suffocation. Punctate petechial hemorrhages may be observed on the head and neck, and in the sclerae and conjunctivae. This variable finding is suspicious of, but not diagnostic of, asphyxiation. The infant who has been febrile or septic may show similar petechial hemorrhages at postmortem examination. Some pathologists place emphasis on the presence of significant numbers of intrathoracic petechiae (on the thymus, epicardium, and pleural surfaces) as characteristic of SIDS, and few or absent petechiae as suspicious for suffocation (70, 71). In my experience, approximately 50% of documented SIDS cases will show only minimal to moderate intrathoracic petechiae, and their absence is not predictive of asphyxiation.

Cerebral edema, especially in the absence of prolonged resuscitation efforts, should suggest a diagnosis other than SIDS, such as direct trauma, severe anoxia, or some metabolic, toxic, or encephalopathic disorder.

Any previous family involvement with a child protective services department is cause for concern when a child dies suddenly or unexpectedly. A caretaker with a history of psychiatric disorders, marital difficulties of the child's parents, frequent visits of the child to emergency rooms, signs in the child of nonorganic failure to thrive, and reports of previous apneic episodes witnessed by only one parent are all warning signs of possible abuse. In most large metropolitan regions, the prevalence of SIDS within census tracts varies inversely with average income and other indicators of good quality of life. Most SIDS infants are born prematurely and are small for their age (almost all are below the twenty-fifth percentile, and many are below the third); approximately 30% have suffered prenatal and/or perinatal cocaine intoxication (72). Although the incidence of SIDS among black inner-city infants is nearly two to three times that of suburban infants of all races, there is no evidence that subtle infant homicide contributes to this difference.

A negative autopsy on an appropriately aged infant who is found dead in bed and who presumably died during sleep is consistent with a diagnosis of SIDS. Appropriate scene and circumstance investigation, negative medical history, family history, and social history will confirm this diagnosis. Approximately 75% to 80% of all sudden infant deaths in the two-to-four-month peak age range for SIDS will fall into this category. Given that SIDS is a diagnosis of exclusion, there is always concern that a subtle fatal injury, such as suffocation, or a rare or subtle metabolic disorder has been missed. Missing these kinds of vestiges is unlikely if careful attention is given to all aspects of the autopsy investigation.

SIDS occurs in young sleeping infants. Infants who die suddenly in a parent's arms, while in a high chair, or while being given a bath have not died of SIDS, and their deaths should not be labeled as such. If there are no substantive findings after autopsy and investigation, the death can be certified as due to natural causes. *Infantile apnea* is a term that can be used to indicate cause of death on the death certificate, with the recognition that this term is a euphemism for "undetermined." It is of some assistance, however, in counseling the bereaved family. Occasionally, an infant will be brought to hospital following an alleged episode of apnea with associated cyanosis, hypotonia, and choking or gagging. In the absence of a specific diagnosis, such infants were often labeled as "near miss" SIDS. It is preferable to avoid this term, to remain more noncommittal, and label these episodes as apparent life-threatening events (ALTEs). There is no evidence that these episodes bear any relationship to SIDS, and those that remain ill defined may be a manifestation of factitious apnea.

A negative autopsy following the sudden, unexpected death of an infant or child may raise the possibility that an "undiscovered" metabolic disorder, particularly medium-chain acyl-CoA dehydrogenase (MCAD) deficiency, was the cause of death. This idea may be proposed as an alternative diagnosis to suffocation when there have been multiple "SIDS" deaths among siblings. Indeed, inborn errors of fatty acid oxidation may occasionally cause death following minimal symptoms so as to mimic SIDS or following a clinical course similar to that of Reye syndrome (73, 74).

The frequency of the homozygous state for the gene mutation responsible for 80% to 90% of the cases of MCAD deficiency is about 1 in 18,500 births (74), based on data indicating that the frequency of the mutation in the general population is 1 in 68 (75). This indicates that MCAD deficiency might be implicated in approximately 5% of sudden, otherwise unexplained deaths. Others have found the frequency of gene mutation in SIDS cases not to be statistically different from that in controls (76).

Other inborn errors of metabolism, such as amino acidemias may also mimic SIDS or, in a rare case, be mistaken for child abuse. Shoemaker et al. (77) reported the case of a mother who was charged with the ethylene glycol poisoning of her infant. Reexamination of the postmortem serum showed that the gas chromatographic peak originally identified as ethylene glycol was actually propionic acid and that the child had died of methylmalonic acidemia, one of the inborn errors of branched-chain amino acid metabolism.

However, the absence of severe fatty change in the liver is evidence against a disorder of fatty acid oxidation, and the absence of organic acids on gas chromatography rules out a lethal amino acidemia. Less than one milliliter of blood is necessary to test for these disorders, and freezing samples of blood, urine, liver, and heart at $-70°C$ will permit testing at a later date, if necessary.

If a previous unexplained infant death, including SIDS, has occurred in a family and no further evidence of metabolic disorder is forthcoming, the unexplained death of a second infant should be classified as undetermined, as suggested by DiMaio (78). Should a third infant death without an obvious natural disease process occur in the same family, the cause of death should be identified as asphyxiation, and the manner of death classified as homicide. SIDS occurs in approximately 1 in 1,000 live births, and there is little evidence that the risk increases with subsequent births within a SIDS family. Even should the risk of subsequent SIDS deaths in a family increase tenfold, the likelihood of three such deaths in one family would be approximately 1 in 10,000,000. Given this extremely low probability of multiple incidents of SIDS, the diagnosis of Munchausen syndrome by proxy is appropriate. Careful investigation will invariably identify discrepancies in the alleged circumstances of the deaths. The differentiation of SIDS from suffocation is further addressed elsewhere by Reece (79).

The infant is more susceptible than older children to subtle fatal abuse that leaves no identifiable anatomic marker. However, a negative gross and microscopic examination can occur under a variety of circumstances, including cardiac arrhythmia, seizure disorder, gram-negative shock, drowning, and electrocution. At any age, a negative autopsy (including toxicology) most likely reflects a natural cause of death, and the circumstances beyond the SIDS age range usually indicate a cardiac arrhythmia. Sudden death may also occur in children with seizure disorders, even in the absence of a clinical seizure. When homicide is suspected, complete toxicologic studies are essential.

Fatal Abuse without "Fatal" Injury

Physical abuse may cause death in the absence of identifiable fatal injuries. This can occur in one of several ways:

1. Complications from failure to seek medical attention for a minor injury
2. Superimposed illness in a child whose immune responses are impaired by the stress of chronic abuse or severe neglect
3. Abuse of a child already impaired by acute or chronic illness
4. Stress from abusive injuries resulting in sudden death

An example of the first category is the child who dies of sepsis due to a caretaker's failure to seek medical attention for inflicted burns. In such a case, there is a direct relationship between the burn injuries, the subsequent infection, and the terminal sepsis. This example also involves medical neglect on the part of the caretaker, but such a finding is not necessary for making a determination of fatal abuse.

In the second group are children with multiple bruises, and often fractures, inflicted up to several days prior to death, who die of pneumonia or other infections. Many of these children have been chronically abused and will have healing and/or healed soft tissue and skeletal injuries. To the experienced forensic pathologist, the relationship of injury to superimposed "natural" disease is familiar although not anatomically demonstrable; repeated episodes of abuse produce sufficient physical and psychological stress to impair a child's immune system, lowering resistance to infection. This relationship has been well documented under a variety of circumstances (42, 43, 80), and these deaths are properly labeled as homicides. These children would not have contracted infections in the first place had they not been abused. It is neither coincidence nor "bad luck" that these children die: their deaths are a predictable, obvious result of chronic abuse.

Similarly, ill children who are subsequently abused are more likely to die as a result of the additional stress imposed by the abuse. There have been no studies to quantitate this increased risk, so each situation must be evaluated on its own merits. The pathologist must ask, given the child's underlying state of health, whether it is more likely than not that this child would have died at this particular time if he or she had not been subjected to abuse. In other words, is this a coincidental association of a natural disease process in a child who "just happens" to be abused, or did the abuse contribute to the death? Before answering that question, the pathologist must consider the usual risk of death from the particular infection or other disease process for a child of this particular age and state of health. The role of the inflicted injuries in causing death should be considered within that wider context. If the injuries aggravated the underlying disease or further impaired the child's health to any extent, the manner of death should be classified as homicide.

Occasionally, children who have been beaten may die suddenly, their autopsy revealing no anatomic cause of death. Most of these cases are characterized by significant bruising with extensive subcutaneous hemorrhage. The common feature in such cases is severe physical and psychological stress due to the pain produced by injuries that are repetitive, anticipated, and inflicted in sessions lasting from minutes to hours. This is unlike the pain of accidental injury, which is almost always sudden and unexpected, of short duration, nonrepetitive, and lacking in the emotional impact that accompanies abuse.

> A three-year-old girl was severely beaten by her mother on the arms, lower back, buttocks, and thighs, by hand and with a plastic wagon handle. There was no prior history of abuse. Approximately thirty minutes after the beating, the child collapsed and died. At autopsy, several small bruises consistent with pinch marks were noted on both arms. There was confluent bruising of the buttocks and thighs, and incision into the injured regions showed extensive subcutaneous hemorrhage and focal intramuscular hemorrhage. There were no internal injuries. There was no evidence of fat emboli or aspiration of gastric contents. Microscopic examination was unremarkable.

In the absence of an anatomic cause, the pathologist must establish a probable pathophysiological mechanism to explain the death. There is strong experimental and clinical evidence to support the concept of stress cardiomyopathy as the mechanism of death. The release of high levels of catecholamines induced by stress damages the myocardium and may be reflected microscopically by the development of focal myocardial cell necrosis (81). The absence of such foci does not negate the diagnosis.

Other mechanisms of death have also been proposed. Release of myoglobin, tissue lipases, or other enzymes into the bloodstream might similarly provoke sudden cardiovascular collapse. Extensive hemorrhage into areas of soft tissue injury has been reported to produce significant anemia or exsanguination and may play a role in some deaths (82). Fat emboli to the brain may cause death, but intrapulmonary fat is probably not fatal. Whatever cellular and molecular factors may be involved, the essential elements are pain, stress, shock, and collapse.

Dehydration and Failure to Thrive

Dehydration with metabolic derangements can cause unexpected death in an infant. Because gastroenteritis can cause rapid dehydration in a young infant, it is necessary to obtain a careful medical history from the parents regarding any illness the child may have had prior to death. Insufficient fluids, a hot environment, and neurological impairment are other frequent causes of dehydration. Elevated vitreous humor sodium and urea nitrogen are reliable criteria of dehydration, as I discussed in the "Postmortem Chemistry" section above. Recent body weight, if available, can provide information about acute weight loss secondary to dehydration. Sunken eyes, markedly depressed fontanel, and dry mucosal and serosal membranes are indicators of moderate to severe dehydration. Skin turgor is generally not a good indicator in the dead child: refrigerated bodies develop significant postmortem drying artifact, which may mimic dehydration, when a small infant is placed in a cooling unit in the morgue overnight. Dehydration usually reflects an acute condition, but severe dehydration is a common finding in the fatal outcome of chronic failure to thrive.

Failure to thrive (FTT) may be due to metabolic disorders, congenital anomalies, infections, acquired immune deficiency syndrome (AIDS), or other chronic diseases. FTT can also be a manifestation of chronic abuse, nutritional deprivation, or emotional neglect. Commonly, components of both organic and nonorganic FTT manifest in the same child (83). By consulting appropriate growth charts, the pathologist can gain objective measurements of nutritional status. For example, an infant whose weight for height is less than the fifth percentile or whose weight is less than the fifth percentile when the weight for height is less than the tenth percentile is probably suffering from nutritional wasting. An infant whose height is less than the fifth percentile is probably growth-retarded if its weight for height is less than the twenty-fifth percentile (84).

Cause and manner of death in FTT children is among the most difficult problems for the pathologist to solve. Review of previous medical records, scene investigation, and interview with the primary caretaker(s) are necessary. Frequently, the medical records will reflect uncertainty on the part of the child's physician as to the cause of FTT, even following hospitalization. There may be a lack of postnatal health care, or lack of continuity of care, characterized by visits to various emergency rooms or health clinics for acute care only. To establish nutritional neglect as the sole cause of FTT, it is necessary to rule out preexisting organic disease. Significant congenital and acquired disorders should be readily recognized by careful autopsy. HIV testing should be done if AIDS is suspected. In practice, autopsy rarely reveals a previously undiagnosed organic cause for failure to thrive.

The diagnosis of starvation is appropriate when the autopsy findings in a severely malnourished and growth-retarded child are otherwise negative and there is no documented medical history of significant disease. Autopsy clues to support this diagnosis include poor hygiene; dry, thin skin; loose skin folds; alopecia; and chronic rash with scabbing and scarring. There is also a lack of body fat and decreased muscle mass. The gastrointestinal tract is usually empty, and there may be evidence of marasmus or kwashiorkor. This is an end-stage process, and not at all subtle.

> A four-month-old infant was found unresponsive by his father, who offered inconsistent explanations for his child's condition. At autopsy, the infant was well below the third percentile for both height and weight and showed the usual medical and environmental stigmata of starvation (figs. 11.15a–11.15c).

Not surprisingly, this diagnosis is rarely made beyond infancy, since older children are able to forage for food and drink unless shackled in a locked room.

Mistaken Diagnosis of Child Abuse

Child abuse occurs throughout all levels of society, and it must be recognized as such in the suburbs as well as in the inner city. At the same time, false accusations of fatal child abuse must be avoided, lest parents suffer additional hurt beyond the loss of their child (85). Mistaken allegations of abuse are usually based on lack of knowledge rather than on malice, but allegations by a mother of physical or sexual abuse of her child or children may also be one of several manifestations of Munchausen syndrome by proxy in such children (86). Various dermatologic conditions, blood dyscrasias, osteogenesis imperfecta, accidental injuries, and the sequelae of folk treatments applied to the skin have all been mistaken for child abuse. The subject has been exhaustively reviewed by Bays (87).

When a dead child is taken to a hospital emergency room, physicians and nurses who are unfamiliar with usual postmortem changes—such as purging of fluids from the nose and mouth, dependent lividity, and congealing of subcutaneous fat due to a decrease in body temperature—may examine the child. These changes, Mongolian spots, and postmortem roach bites may be misinterpreted as evidence of injury. They represent the most common form of mistaken diagnosis of abuse seen by forensic pathologists (85). If these erroneous opinions are given to police officers, criminal charges may be pending against a caretaker before the pathologist has even begun an autopsy.

> A one-year-old child, clothed in infant pajamas, was brought dead on arrival to a hospital emergency room. The pediatrician-on-call noticed circumferential injuries of both wrists, which he interpreted to be rope burns (fig. 11.16). The police were notified and charges of abuse were filed against the parents. At autopsy, the injuries were identified as postmortem roach bites. Excursion of the roaches above the wrists was prevented by the elastic in the sleeves of the pajamas. The infant died of natural causes, but a juvenile court hearing proceeded because of the original charges.

This case, unfortunately, is not unique. When an infant or child has died, it is best to await the results of an autopsy before commenting upon the cause of death. Common disorders mistaken for child abuse are listed in table 11.2.

Perinatal Deaths

Perinatal deaths pose particular medical and legal issues for the forensic pathologist. Births may take place in a nonmedical setting following concealment or attempts at concealment

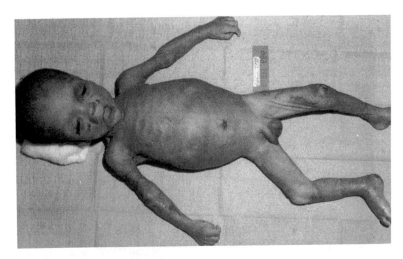

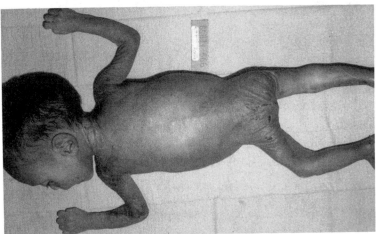

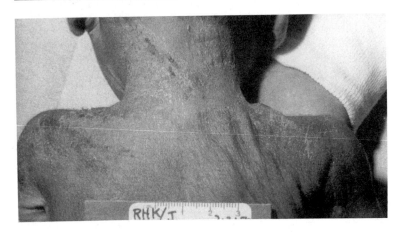

11.15 Starvation due to neglect in a four-month-old. Sunken eyes, lack of subcutaneous fat, spindly extremities, and loose skin folds are evident (*a, top*). Desquamative dermatitis of shoulders, arms, and buttocks and areas of excoriation of buttocks (*b, center*). Skin changes resulting from poor hygiene and probable vitamin deficiencies (*c, above*).

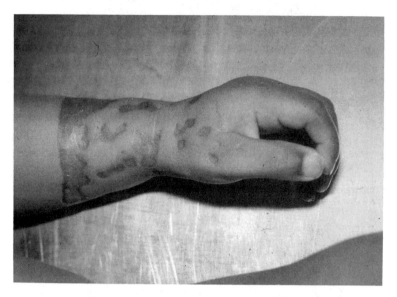

11.16 Postmortem roach bites of wrist and hand mistaken for rope burns. The infant's pajama sleeve protected the forearm from the insects.

TABLE 11.2
Common Disorders Mistaken for Child Abuse

Mistaken for Bruises or Abrasions

Mongolian spot	Disseminated intravascular coagulation
Erythema multiforme	Purpura fulminans
Folk remedies	Leukemia
Hemophilia	Henoch-Schonlein purpura
Vitamin K deficiency	Idiopathic thrombocytopenic purpura
Postmortem lividity	Postmortem roach bites

Mistaken for Burns

Epidermolysis bullosa	Diaper rash
Impetigo	Folk remedies

Mistaken for Inflicted Fractures

Osteogenesis imperfecta	Rickets
Congenital syphilis	Accidental fractures
Anomalous skull suture	Osteomyelitis

Mistaken for Sexual Abuse

Lichen sclerosis et atrophica	Impetigo
Congenital anomalies	Hemangioma
Crohn's disease	

Source: R. H. Kirschner and R. J. Stein, "The Mistaken Diagnosis of Child Abuse: A Form of Medical Abuse?" *Am. J. Diseases of Children* 139 (1985): 873–57; and J. Bays, "Conditions Mistaken for Child Abuse," in *Child Abuse: Medical Diagnosis and Management,* ed. R. M. Reece (Philadelphia: Lea and Febiger, 1993).

of a pregnancy, with subsequent concealment of neonatal death by secret disposal of the body. Some babies are born into toilets; many are drug-intoxicated at birth. The pregnant mother may have been assaulted or suffered accidental trauma alleged to have contributed to fetal or neonatal demise. In all of these cases, the pathologist is faced with the question of whether this was a live birth, and, if so, whether the death was due to natural causes, accidental or intentional injury, or abandonment.

The pathologist should start with the presumption of stillbirth and then attempt to establish sufficient evidence of live birth to reach that conclusion with a reasonable degree of medical and scientific certainty. In cases of alleged trauma to the pregnant mother, the specific maternal factors that contributed to fetal demise should be identified. When the identity of the infant is unknown, or parenthood disputed, blood and other tissues should be preserved for maternity/paternity testing.

The complete perinatal autopsy should include placental examination whenever possible. Evidence of trauma should be evaluated as in any other autopsy. Birth trauma such as cephalohematomas or fractures of the clavicle must be differentiated from postbirth trauma such as rib fractures and skull fractures. Clavicular fractures occur in approximately 3% of hospital deliveries (88), but other fractures are rare. Birth injuries that I have seen include two cases of fatal depressed skull fracture and a case of cervical spine dislocation due to incorrect application of forceps by inexperienced physicians.

A variety of injuries can be seen in neonatal homicides. Stab wounds of the infant may be alleged to have occurred during attempts to cut the umbilical cord, and there may be an effort to dismiss marks of strangulation as efforts to remove a nuchal cord. Skull fractures and other blunt trauma injuries are not uncommon. Asphyxiation by suffocation will rarely leave any telltale signs.

Signs of live birth must be evaluated. If the lungs or sections of lungs (in the absence of attempted resuscitation or decomposition) float in water, it is probable that the infant was live-born. If the lungs sink, this is indicative of, but does not prove, stillbirth. Lungs of live-born infants that are atelectatic or congested may not float. Milk or colostrum in the stomach is proof of live birth. Meconium or squamous alveolar debris does not indicate live birth, but lungs with alveolar hyaline membranes are characteristic of a living infant.

Newborns remain relatively hearty at moderate temperatures, as illustrated by the survival of forty-four newborns buried for seven to ten days without food or water in the debris of a collapsed hospital in the 1985 Mexico City earthquake (89). In another example of neonatal durability, a newborn baby girl survived for three hours after being placed in a home freezer following her birth. Body temperature was 50°F upon admission to a hospital emergency room. The mother claimed that she thought the baby had died at birth, but she was subsequently charged with attempted murder (90).

Infants may be live-born but die shortly after birth because they are lethally malformed, of previable gestational age, or septic. The child may be full term and live-born but be nonresuscitatable due to perinatal asphyxiation from a variety of causes, including placental anomalies, nuchal cord, and meconium aspiration. A diagnosis of neonaticide requires that the live-born infant would still be alive but for abandonment or neglect, purposeful asphyxiation, inflicted trauma, or intoxication or poisoning. Obviously, maceration of the fetus is diagnostic of intrauterine death, and precludes live birth. Such maceration usually becomes evident within twenty-four hours after intrauterine demise and is usually readily distinguishable from decomposition changes in the deceased live-born infant.

Investigation

The autopsy alone is often insufficient to provide the necessary answers to establish the cause and manner of death of an infant or child. Greater emphasis is now being placed upon the nonlaboratory aspects of the investigation, including the development of multidisciplinary multiagency death review teams. This places greater demands upon all involved, but it results in much improved diagnoses. The major components of child death investigation beyond the autopsy are described below.

Review of Records

Records that should be reviewed include investigative reports pertaining to the death, paramedic reports, police reports, hospital emergency room records, child protection agency records, and previous hospital and/or physician's records, including birth records. Birth records provide information regarding prematurity, maternal drug abuse, neonatal drug intoxication, and other medical and/or social problems that might increase the risk for sudden death or abuse.

Emergency Responders

The observations and reports of paramedics, often the first responders on the scene, can provide crucial information about the injured child, the surrounding environment, and verbal exchanges among family members, witnesses, and others. Knowing the type of treatment that was administered by paramedics during transport may be important to the pathologist in reaching a decision about the cause of the injuries. In particular, inquiry should be made as to whether or not prehospital resuscitation was attempted and, if so, by whom. The recorded body temperature of the infant at the time of transport is also important. Hypothermia may reflect cerebral dysfunction secondary to shaking (91) or cold-water immersion (92), although these are not often considered in the initial differential diagnosis of hypothermia. Because the paramedics' run sheet is unlikely to contain all of this information, a personal conversation with the paramedics soon after the event is often best.

When children die in hospital following an emergency admission, the medical record may be incomplete, particularly in regard to specific injuries noted on the child. Medical attention is primarily directed at treatment, and the description of bruises, abrasions, and other skin lesions may be sketchy. If the death occurs after some days in hospital, injuries present when the child was admitted may have healed or been obscured by subsequent treatment. It may be necessary to discuss with the attending physician his or her recollection of the injuries, the child's clinical status, medical history, and family situation.

Family History

Review of the child's personal and family history should include developmental, medical, and social history. In particular, inquiry should be made regarding illness or death of other siblings. Unexplained deaths of previous siblings or deaths due to SIDS should alert the pathologist to the possibility of serial suffocation or, less likely, a rare metabolic disorder.

Many medical examiners and coroners maintain an infant death file cross-indexed for the mother's maiden name, family name(s) of all her children, and fathers' names. Such an index is particularly useful to pathologists when they are searching for previous, undisclosed infant deaths within the same family. Unfortunately, when families move from one jurisdiction to another, there is no effective way of tracking these prior deaths. Attempts to form regional or national child death registries might involve a significant infringement of privacy rights and face court challenge (see chapter 7).

Scene and Circumstance Investigation

Scene investigation has long been recognized as important in establishing the cause and manner of infant deaths; an article by Bass et al. (93) in 1986 highlighted this issue. They conducted independent death scene investigations in twenty-six consecutive cases in New York City in which a presumptive diagnosis of SIDS had been made and discovered strong circumstantial evidence of accidental death in six cases, and various other possible causes of death, including abuse, in eighteen cases. Their findings are at variance with the experience of most other forensic pathologists, and the validity of their results have been questioned (94, 95). However, the impact of the study has been great, virtually mandating scene investigations in all infant death cases since the time of its publication.

The scene investigator should be someone trained to recognize the unique circumstances surrounding infant deaths—namely, sleep position, type of bedding, type of covers, and room temperature. The home environment may provide important information in making the determination of cause and manner of death, particularly when there is evidence that abuse or neglect may have contributed to the death. It is unusual, for example, when an infant is found dead in the home for the death scene to be undisturbed by evidence of attempted resuscitation by the caretaker. Such a scene, in and of itself, is suspicious, since it implies a relatively composed awareness—as opposed to shock and acute distress—in the face of the child's death.

Recent studies suggest that rebreathing of expired air in a restricted, but not occlusive, microenvironment may lead to suffocation in young infants (96, 97). Other studies, indicating a significant increase in SIDS in infants sleeping in the prone position, lend support to this concept (98, 99). Such findings require further investigation, but they do serve to emphasize that the differentiation of SIDS from accidental or intentional suffocation cannot be made by autopsy alone but is also dependent upon other aspects of the investigation.

When an infant has been on a home apnea monitor, the investigator must try to determine if the infant was attached to the monitor, if the monitor was functioning properly, and if the monitor's alarm sounded. If a discrepancy is noted between the caretaker's story and the apparent functional state of the monitor, the monitor should be retained as evidence and, if necessary, evaluated by an independent, qualified laboratory. It should be noted that noncompliance with proper monitoring occurs in a majority of families using such devices (100). Paradoxically, in families in which an infant's repeated apnea spells are later found to be due to Munchausen syndrome by proxy, home monitor compliance is high (101).

Investigators must be sensitive to socioeconomic factors that may place certain children at greater risk for accidental death in the home, such as toddler drownings in industrial buckets (102, 103), a phenomenon much more common in the inner city than in the suburbs, where swimming-pool drownings represent a significant hazard. The scene investigation is essential in determining whether situation neglect—that is, leaving an infant or child alone in a situation which is dangerous, considering the developmental age of the child—played a role in the death of the child. The scene investigation is also necessary to assess possible caretaker impairment due to age, intoxication, mental disorder, or retardation.

When a child has been battered, an attempt should be made to recover implements that might been used to inflict the fatal injuries or any previous injuries noted on the child. All objects, furniture, or places that a caretaker claims the child may have struck, fallen against, or fallen from should be photographed; a tape measure or yardstick should be included in the photographs. When the child has died as a result of bathtub scald burns, the dimensions of the tub, the height of the faucet, and the hot-water temperature should be measured.

All persons, including children, who were present during the hours preceding the infant's death and at the time of death itself should be interviewed individually as soon as possible after the death. The circumstances of alleged falls and bathtub injuries and other types of burns should be reconstructed by the involved caretaker. Accidental injuries can often be distinguished from inflicted injuries by such a reenactment; in fatal abuse, there is usually a clear lack of consistency, but at times the reported circumstances may be equivocal. The story may also change as the caretaker attempts to tailor the circumstances to fit the child's injuries when he or she is confronted with the extent of the injuries discovered at autopsy. Denial by all caretakers of any knowledge of how an injury occurred is of itself indicative of abuse by one or more persons. Often there is partial truth in the story provided by the caretaker, but facts are inverted, shaded, or omitted in an attempt to conceal the true circumstances of injury or death.

As I discussed earlier in this chapter, physicians hear a recurring litany of alleged trivial events that caretakers provide to explain children's lethal injuries, including falls from a couch, bed, or crib; a fall down stairs; alleged trauma at an earlier date; injury inflicted by siblings; unexplained seizure; or sudden death while in the caretaker's arms. Violent shaking of an infant is often explained as a response to an infant who has suddenly stopped breathing, an effort the caretaker supposedly made to resuscitate the child. It remains discouraging that physicians, other health care professionals, and child protective workers still so often accept these stories at face value.

Agency Investigation and Collaboration

The success of the investigative process is dependent upon good working relationships among agency personnel. However, such relationships among so many agencies do not come about easily—they require considerable effort. The medical examiner or coroner, police, child protective agencies, and prosecutor must keep one another informed, share data, and otherwise cooperate in various stages of the investigation as appropriate for each agency. Only by this means will the details surrounding an infant's or child's death become known. This collaboration will not succeed, however, if there are excessive restrictions on access to records, excessive scruples about confidentiality, investigative secrecy, or agency indifference to a child's death. We have found that, throughout the country, the development of child death review teams whose members are actively involved in child death investigation significantly promotes this collaborative effort (104).

Determination of Manner of Death

The determination of the manner of death—that is, ascertaining whether death is due to natural causes, is accidental, suicide, or homicide—is the responsibility of the medical examiner or coroner. Ultimately, if no decision can be reached, the manner of death is classified as undetermined. To reach his or her determination, the pathologist must first integrate the autopsy findings and results of the death investigation to determine the cause or causes of death. In doing so, the pathologist must consider to what extent, if any, injuries contributed to the death. This can often best be done by asking the question, Within a reasonable degree of medical and scientific certainty, is it probable (that is, more likely than not) that this child would have died on this day and at this time if he or she had not suffered the observed (inflicted) injuries? If the answer to this question is no, then the manner of death is homicide. When the death involves allegations of neglect, the infant shows evidence of failure to thrive, or the home environment is marginal, the determination of manner of death may remain unresolved, leading to an "undetermined" classification (105). The collective experience of the child death review team is often most helpful in these cases.

The influence of the investigative process on determining the manner of death is summarized in table 11.3. Autopsy results fall within one of four categories: (1) natural disease process with no evidence of injury, (2) a negative autopsy—no evidence of disease or injury, (3) "nonfatal" injuries with or without an associated disease process, (4) fatal injuries. The investigation may be negative, inconclusive, or positive for abuse or neglect.

When a child dies of a natural disease process, the manner of death is usually natural. However, investigation may reveal that the parents refused to seek medical care despite their child's obvious signs of severe illness or were induced to put their child in the care of an unqualified practitioner.

When the autopsy findings are entirely negative, then the results of the investigation are crucial in determining the manner of death. Similarly, in cases in which elements of injury, neglect, and/or natural disease are present at autopsy, thorough investigation is essential to arriving at an appropriate determination of the manner of death.

Injuries associated with fatal abuse are usually so characteristic as to be diagnostic in and of themselves. However, investigation of the circumstances surrounding injuries that are not of themselves diagnostic of abuse or neglect, such as death due to a fall from an upper-story window, will be needed to determine the manner of death because such cases are less clear-cut.

Those involved in child death investigation, including the pathologist and those who may assist him or her in arriving at a conclusion about the manner of death, must remain

TABLE 11.3
Determination of Manner of Death

Autopsy	Investigation	Manner
1. Natural disease process: no injury	a. Negative	a. Natural
	b. Inconclusive (e.g., FTT, impaired parent, possible neglect)	b. Undetermined or natural
	c. Positive (intentional neglect, MSBP)	c. Homicide
2. Negative autopsy: no disease, no injury	a. Negative	a. Natural
	b. Inconclusive (prior abuse or neglect, prior SIDS, or unexplained death)	b. Undetermined
	c. Positive (two or more prior SIDS or unexplained deaths), physical evidence, confession	c. Homicide
3. "Nonfatal" injury: with or without aggravating disease process	a. Confirmed accidental injury, medical complication	a. Accident
	b. Injury due to abuse, medical complication	b. Homicide
	c. Inconclusive investigation	c. Undetermined
	d. Injury due to abuse, no anatomic cause of death	d. Homicide or undetermined
4. Fatal Injury	a. Negative (circumstances documented, consistent with accident)	a. Accident
	b. Inconclusive investigation	b. Undetermined
	c. Positive (inconsistent with injuries)	c. Homicide

Source: R. H. Kirschner and H. Wilson, "Fatal Child Abuse: The Pathologist's Perspective," in *Child Abuse: Medical Diagnosis and Management,* ed. R. M. Reece (Philadelphia: Lea and Febiger, 1993).

cognizant of the significant social and economic difficulties faced by many families and strive to maintain a sense of balance, impartiality, and compassion. Every child has the right, however, to be shielded from harm and to receive the physical care and emotional support necessary to permit normal growth and development.

References

1. McClain, P. W.; Sacks, J.; Froehlke, R.; and Ewigman, B. 1993. Estimates of Fatal Child Abuse and Neglect, United States, 1979 through 1988. *Pediatrics* 91:338–43.
2. Leventhal, J.; Horwitz, S.; Rude, C; and Stier, D. 1993. Maltreatment of Children Born to Teenage Mothers: A Comparison between the 1960s and 1980s. *J. Pediatrics* 122:314–19.
3. Marshall, W. N.; Puls, T.; and Davidson, C. 1988. New Child Abuse Spectrum in an Era of Increased Awareness. *Am. J. Diseases of Children* 142:664–67.
4. Ewigman, B.; Kivlahan, C.; and Land, G. 1993. The Missouri Child Fatality Study: Underreporting of Maltreatment Fatalities among Children Younger than Five Years of Age, 1983 through 1986. *Pediatrics* 91:330–37.
5. Willinger, M.; James, L. S.; and Catz, C. 1991. Defining Sudden Infant Death Syndrome (SIDS): Deliberations of an Expert Panel Convened by the National Institute of Child Health and Human Development. *Pediatric Pathology* 11:677–84.
6. Ricci, L. R. 1991. Photographing the Physically Abused Child: Principles and Practice. *Am. J. Diseases of Children* 145:275–81.

7. Krauss, T. C. 1990. Close-Up Medical Photography: Forensic Considerations and Techniques. In *Legal Medicine, 1989,* ed. C. H. Wecht. Salem, N.H.: Butterworth Legal Publishers.

8. Kleinman, P. K.; Blackbourne, B. D.; Marks, S. C.; Karellas, A.; and Belanger, P. L. 1989. Radiologic Contributions to the Investigation and Prosecution of Cases of Fatal Infant Abuse. *New England J. Med.* 320:507–11.

9. Kleinman, P. K. 1990. Diagnostic Imaging in Child Abuse. *Am. J. Radiology* 155:703–12.

10. Alexander, R. C.; Schor, D. P.; and Smith, W. L. 1992. Magnetic Resonance Imaging of Intracranial Injuries from Child Abuse. *J. Pediatrics* 89:1068–71.

11. Greenberg, B. 1991. Flies as Forensic Indicators. *J. Med. Entomology* 28:565–77.

12. Bass, W. A. 1987. *Human Osteology: A Laboratory and Field Manuel,* 3d ed. Columbus, Mo.: Missouri Archeological Society.

13. Snow, C. C.; Kirschner, R. H.; Scott, D. D.; and Fitzpatrick, J. 1993. Report of Forensic Investigation, El Mozote, El Salvador. Appendix I in *Report of the Truth Commission on El Salvador.* New York: United Nations.

14. Krogman, W. M., 1962. *The Human Skeleton in Forensic Medicine.* Springfield, Ill.: Charles C. Thomas.

15. Rivara, F. P.; Kamitsuka, M.D.; and Quan, L. 1988. Injuries to Children Younger than One Year of Age. *Pediatrics* 81:93–97.

16. Helfer, R. E.; Slovis, T. L.; and Black, M. 1977. Injuries Resulting When Small Children Fall Out of Bed. *Pediatrics* 60:533–34.

17. Joffe, M., and Ludwig, S. Stairway Injuries in Children. *Am. J. Diseases of Children.* 141:383.

18. Chadwick, D. L.; Chin, S.; Salerno, C.; Landsverk, J.; and Kitchen, L. 1991. Deaths from Falls in Children: How Far Is Fatal? *J. Trauma* 31:1353–55.

19. Chiaveillo, C.; Christoph, R.; and Bond, R. 1994. Stairway-Related Injuries in Children. *Pediatrics* 94:679–81.

20. Ellerstein, N. S. 1979. The Cutaneous Manifestations of Child Abuse and Neglect. *Am. J. Diseases of Children* 133:906–9.

21. Ayoub, C., and Pfeifer, D. 1979. Burns as a Manifestation of Child Abuse and Neglect. *Am. J. Diseases of Children* 133:910–14.

22. Sterne, G. G.; Chadwick, D. V.; Krugman, R. D.; Pakter, J.; Porter, G. E.; Schor, E. L.; and Wagner, V. 1986. Oral and Dental Aspects of Child Abuse and Neglect. *Pediatrics* 78:537–39.

23. Feldman, K. W. 1992. Patterned Abusive Bruises of the Buttocks and Pinnae. *Pediatrics* 90:633–63.

24. Schwartz, A. J., and Ricci, L. 1996. How Accurately Can Bruises Be Aged in Abused Children? Literature Review and Synthesis. *Pediatrics* 97:254–56.

25. Stephenson, T., and Bialas, Y. 1996. Estimation of the Age of Bruising. *Archives of Diseases in Childhood.* 74:53–55.

26. Renz, B. M., and Sherman, R. 1993. Abusive Scald Burns in Infants and Children: A Prospective Study. *Am. Surgeon* 59:329–34.

27. Feldman, K. W., and Brewer, D. K. 1984. Child Abuse, Cardiopulmonary Resuscitation, and Rib Fractures. *Pediatrics* 73:339–42.

28. Spevak, M.; Kleinman, P.; Belanger, P.; Primack, C.; and Richmond, J. 1994. Cardiopulmonary Resuscitation and Rib Fractures in Infants: A Postmortem Radiologic-Pathologic Study. *JAMA* 272:617–18.

29. Cohle, S. D.; Hawley, D. A.; Berg, K. K.; Keisel, E. L.; and Pless, J. E. 1995. Homicidal Cardiac Lacerations in Children. *J. Forensic Science* 40:212–18.

30. Reardon, M. J.; Gross, D. M.; Vallone, A. M.; Weiland, A. P.; and Walker, W. E. 1987. Atrial Rupture in a Child from Cardiac Massage by His Parent. *Annals Thoracic Surgery* 43:557–58.

31. Cooper, A. 1992. Thoracoabdominal Trauma. In *Child Abuse: A Medical Reference,* 2d ed., ed. S. Ludwig and A. E. Kornberg. New York: Churchill Livingstone.

32. Lyons T. J., and Oates, R. K. 1993. Falling Out of Bed: A Relatively Benign Occurrence. *Pediatrics* 92:125–27.

33. Loder, R. T., and Bookout, C. 191. Fracture Patterns in Battered Children. *J. Orthopedic Trauma* 5:428–33.

34. Gahagan, S., and Rimsza, M. E. 1991. Child Abuse or Osteogenesis Imperfecta: How Can We Tell? *Pediatrics* 88:987–92.

35. Smith, R. 1995. Osteogenesis Imperfecta, Non-accidental Injury, and Temporary Brittle Bone Disease. *Archives Diseases in Childhood* 72:169–71.

36. Bays, J., and Lewman, L. V. 1992. Toluidine Blue in the Detection at Autopsy of Perianal and Anal Lacerations in Victims of Sexual Abuse. *Archives Pathology Laboratory Med.* 116:285–86.

37. Bays, J., and Jenny, C. 1990. Genital and Anal Conditions Confused with Child Sexual Abuse Trauma. *Am. J. Diseases of Children* 144:1319–22.

38. Loenig-Baucke, V. 1991. Lichen Sclerosis et Atrophicus in Children. *Am. J. Diseases of Children* 145:1058–61.

39. Hanks, J. W., and Venters, W. J. 1992. Nickel Allergy from a Bed-Wetting Alarm Confused with Herpes Genitalis and Child Abuse. *Pediatrics* 90:458–60.

40. Press, S.; Grant, P.; Thompson, V. T.; and Milles, K. L. 1991. Small Bowel Evisceration: Unusual Manifestation of Child Abuse. *Pediatrics* 88:807–9.

41. Bonnell, H. J., and Beckwith, J. B. 1986. Fatty Liver in Sudden Childhood Death: Implications for Reye's Syndrome? *Am. J. Diseases of Children* 140:30–33.

42. Wilson, N. W.; Ochs, H. D.; Peterson, B.; Hamburger, R. N.; and Bastian, J. F. 1989. Abnormal Primary Antibody Responses in Pediatric Trauma Patients. *J. Pediatrics* 115:424–27.

43. Krause, P. J.; Woronick, C. L.; Burke, G.; Slover, N.; Kosciol, C.; Kelly, T.; Spivak, B.; and Maderazo, E. G. 1994. Depressed Neutrophil Chemotaxis in Children Suffering Blunt Trauma. *Pediatrics* 93:807–9.

44. Pickel, S.; Anderson, C.; and Holliday, M. A. 1970. Thirsting and Hypernatremic Dehydration: A Form of Child Abuse. *Pediatrics* 45:54–59.

45. Chesney, R. W., and Brusilow, S. 1981. Extreme Hypernatremia as a Presenting Sign of Child Abuse and Psychosocial Dwarfism. *Johns Hopkins Med. J.* 148:11–13.

46. Conley, S. B. 1990. Hypernatremia. *Pediatric Clinics of N. America* 37:365–72.

47. Meadow, R. 1993. Non-accidental Salt Poisoning. *Archives Diseases in Childhood* 68:448–52.

48. Keating, J. P.; Schears, G. J.; and Dodge, P. R. 1991. Oral Water Intoxication in Infants: An American Epidemic. *Am. J. Diseases of Children* 145:985–90.

49. Fulroth, R.; Phillips, B.; and Durand, D. J. 1989. Perinatal Outcome of Infants Exposed to Cocaine and/or Heroin in Utero. *Am. J. Diseases of Children* 143:905–10.

50. Weathers, W. T.; Crane, M. M.; Sauvain, K. J.; and Blackhurst, D. W. 1993. Cocaine Use in Women from a Defined Population: Prevalence at Delivery and Effects on Growth in Infants. *Pediatrics* 91:35–54.

51. Mirchandani, J. G.; Mirchandani, I. H.; Hellman, F.; English-Rider, R.; Rosen, S.; and Laposata, E. A. 1991. Passive Inhalation of Free-Base Cocaine ("Crack") Smoke by Infants. *Archives Pathology Laboratory Med.* 115:494–98.

52. Sutphen, J. L., and Sulsbury, F. T. 1988. Intentional Ipecac Poisoning: Munchausen Syndrome by Proxy. *Pediatrics* 82:453–56.

53. Koren, G.; Beatie, D.; Soldin, S.; Einerson, T. R.; and MacLeod, S. 1989. Interpretation of Elevated Postmortem Serum Concentrations of Digoxin in Infants and Children. *Archives Pathology Laboratory Med.* 113:758–61.

54. Billmire, M. E., and Myers, P. A. 1985. Serious Head Injury in Infants: Accident or Abuse? *Pediatrics* 75:340–42.

55. Lehman, D., and Schonfeld, N. 1993. Falls from Heights: A Problem Not Just in the Northeast. *Pediatrics* 92:121–24.

56. Rivara, F. P.; Alexander, B.; Johnston, B.; and Soderberg, R. 1993. Population-Based Study of Fall Injuries in Children and Adolescents Resulting in Hospitalization or Death. *Pediatrics* 92:61–63.

57. Goldstein, B.; Kelly, M. M.; Bruton, D.; and Cox, C. 1993. Inflicted versus Accidental Head Injury in Critically Injured Children. *Critical Care Med.* 21:1328–32.

58. Hanigan, W. C.; Peterson, R. A.; and Njus, G. 1987. Tin Ear Syndrome: Rotational Acceleration in Pediatric Head Injuries. *Pediatrics* 80:618–22.

59. Duhaime, A. C.; Gennarelli, T. A.; Thibault, L. E.; Bruce, D. A.; Margulies, S. S.; and Wiser, R. 1987. The Shaken Baby Syndrome: A Clinical and Biomechanical Study. *J. Neurosurgery* 66:409–15.

60. Alexander, R.; Sato, Y.; Smith, W.; and Bennett, T. 1990. Incidence of Impact Trauma with Cranial Injuries Ascribed to Shaking. *Am. J. Diseases of Children* 144:724–26.

61. Nashelsky, M. B., and Dix. J. D. 1995. The Time Interval between Lethal Infant Shaking and Onset of Symptoms: A Review of the Shaken Baby Syndrome Literature. *Am. J. Forensic Med. Pathology* 16:154–57.

62. Johnson, D. L.; Boal, D.; and Baule, R. 1995. Role of Apnea in Nonaccidental Head Injury. *Pediatric Neurosurgery* 23:305–10.

63. Munger, C. E.; Peiffer, R. L.; Bouldin, T. W.; Kylstra, J. A.; and Thompson, R. L. 1993. Ocular and Associated Neuropathologic Observations in Suspected Whiplash Shaken Infant Syndrome. *Am. J. Forensic Med. Pathology* 14:193–200.

64. Johnson, D. L.; Braun, D.; and Friendly, D. 1993. Accidental Head Trauma and Retinal Hemorrhage. *Neurosurgery* 33:231–35.

65. Duhaime, A. C.; Alario, A. J.; Lewander, W. J.; Schut, L.; Sutton, L. N.; Seidl, T. S.; Nudelman, S.; Budenz, D.; Hertl, R.; Tsiaras, W.; and Loporchio, S. 1992. Head Injury in Very Young Children: Mechanisms, Injury Types, and Ophthalmologic Findings in One Hundred Hospitalized Patients Younger than Two Years of Age. *Pediatrics* 90:179–85.

66. Kanter, T. K. 1986. Retinal Hemorrhage after Cardiopulmonary Resuscitation or Child Abuse. *J. Pediatrics* 108:430–32.

67. Gilliland, M. G. F., and Luckenbach, M. W. 1993. Are Retinal Hemorrhages Found after Resuscitation Attempts? A Study of the Eyes of 169 Children. *Am J. Forensic Med. Pathology* 14:187–92.

68. Gayle, M. O.; Kissoon, N.; Hered, R. W.; and Harwood-Nuss, A. 1995. Retinal Hemorrhages in the Young Child: A Review of Etiology, Predisposed Conditions, and Clinical Implications. *J. Emergency Med.* 13:233–39.

69. Leestma, J. 1988. Neuropathology of Child Abuse. In *Forensic Neuropathology*. New York: Raven Press.

70. Valdes-Dapena, M. 1982. The Pathologist and the Sudden Infant Death Syndrome. *Am. J. Pathology* 106:118–31.

71. Knight, B. 1991. Sudden Death in Infancy. In *Forensic Pathology*. New York: Oxford University Press.

72. Ostrea, E. M.; Brady, M.; Gause, S.; Raymundo, A. L.; and Stevens, M. 1992. Drug Screening of Newborns by Neconium Analysis: A Large-Scale, Prospective, Epidemiologic Study. *Pediatrics* 89:107–13.

73. Roe, C. R.; Millington, D. S.; Maltby, D. A.; and Kinnebrew, P. 1986. Recognition of Medium-Chain Acyl-CoA Dehydrogenase Deficiency in Asymptomatic Siblings of Children Dying of Sudden Infant Death or Reye-like Syndromes. *J. Pediatrics* 108:13–18.

74. Hale, D. E., and Bennett, M. J. 1992. Fatty Acid Oxidation Disorders: A New Class of Metabolic Diseases. *J. Pediatrics* 121:1–11.

75. Blakemore, A. I. F.; Singleton, H.; Pollitt, R. J.; Engel, P. C.; Kolvraa, S.; Gregersen, N.; and Curtis, D. 1991. Frequency of the G985 MCAD Mutation in the General Population. *Lancet* 337:298–99.

76. Miller, M. E.; Brooks, J. G.; Forbes, N.; and Insel, R. 1992. Frequency of Medium-Chain Acyl-CoA Dehydrogenase Deficiency G-985 Mutation in Sudden Infant Death Syndrome. *Pediatric Research* 31:305–7.

77. Shoemaker, J. D.; Lynch, R. E.; Hoffman, J. W.; and Syy, W. S. 1992. Misidentification of Propionic Acid as Ethylene Glycol in a Patient with Methylmalonic Acidemia. *J. Pediatrics* 120:417–21.

78. DiMaio, V. J. M. 1993. Personal communication.

79. Reece, R. M. 1993. Fatal Child Abuse and Sudden Infant Death Syndrome: A Critical Diagnostic Decision. *Pediatrics* 91:423–29.

80. Weiner, H. 1992. New Concepts about the Organism and Its Perturbation by Stressful Experience. In *Perturbing the Organism: The Biology of Stressful Experience.* Chicago: University of Chicago Press.

81. Cebelin, M. S., and Hirsch, C. S. 1980. Human Stress Cardiomyopathy: Myocardial Lesions in Victims of Homicidal Assaults without Internal Injuries. *Human Pathology* 11:123–32.

82. Zumwalt, R. E., and Hirsch, C. S. 1987. Pathology of Fatal Child Abuse and Neglect. In *The Battered Child,* 4th ed., ed. R. E. Helfer and R. S. Kempe. Chicago: University of Chicago Press.

83. Homer, C., and Ludwig, S. 1981. Categorization of Etiology of Failure to Thrive. *Am. J. Diseases of Children* 135:848–51.

84. Task Force for the Study of Non-Accidental Injuries and Child Deaths. 1987. *Protocol for Child Death Autopsies.* Chicago: Illinois Department of Children and Family Services and Cook County Medical Examiner's Office.

85. Kirschner, R. H., and Stein, R. J. 1985. The Mistaken Diagnosis of Child Abuse: A Form of Medical Abuse? *Am. J. Diseases of Children* 139:873–57.

86. Meadow, R. 1993. False Allegations of Abuse and Munchausen Syndrome by Proxy. *Archives Diseases in Childhood* 68:444–47.

87. Bays, J. Conditions Mistaken for Child Abuse. 1993. In *Child Abuse: Medical Diagnosis and Management,* ed. R. M. Reece. Philadelphia: Lea and Febiger.

88. Joseph P. R., and Rosenfield, W. 1990. Clavicular Fractures in Neonates. *Am. J. Diseases of Children* 144:165–67.

89. DiMaio, D. J., and DiMaio, V. J. M. 1989. Neonaticide, Infanticide, and Child Homicide. In *Forensic Pathology.* New York: Elsevier Science Publishing Co.

90. *Chicago Tribune.* 1993. Sect. 2, 3 April.

91. Wahl, N., and Woodall, B. 1995. Hypothermia in Shaken Infant Syndrome. *Pediatric Emergency Care* 11:233–34.

92. Gustavson, E., and Levitt, C. 1996. Physical Abuse with Severe Hypothermia. *Archives Pediatric and Adolescent Med.* 150:111–12.

93. Bass, M.; Kravath, R. E.; and Glass, L. 1986. Death-Scene Investigation in Sudden Infant Death. *New England J. Med.* 315:100–105.

94. Gross, E. M., and Leffers, B. 1986. Investigation of SIDS [Letter]. *New England J. Med.* 315:1675.

95. Valdes-Dapena, M. A.; Mandell, F.; and Merritt, T. A. 1986. Investigation of SIDS. [Letter]. *New England J. Med.* 315:1675–76.

96. Kemp, J. S., and Thach, B. T. 1991. Sudden Death in Infants Sleeping on Polystyrene-Filled Cushions. *New England J. Med.* 324:1858–64.

97. Kemp, J. S.; Kowalski, R. M.; Burch, P. M.; Graham, M. A.; and Thach, B. T. 1993. Unintentional Suffocation by Rebreathing: A Death Scene and Physiological Investigation of a Possible Cause of Sudden Infant Death. *J. Pediatrics* 122:874–80.

98. Guntheroth, W. G., and Spiers, P. S. 1992. Sleeping Prone and the Risk of Sudden Infant Death Syndrome. *JAMA* 267:2359–62.

99. Ponsonby, A. L.; Dwyer, T.; Gibbons, L. E.; Cochrane, J. A.; and Wang, Y.-G. 1993. Factors Potentiating the Risk of Sudden Infant Death Syndrome Associated with the Prone Position. *New England J. Med.* 329:377–82.

100. Meny, R. G.; Blackman, L.; Fleischmann, D.; Gutberlet, R.; and Naumberg, E. 1988. Sudden Infant Death and Home Monitors. *Am. J. Diseases of Children* 142:1037–40.

101. Rosen, C. L.; Frost, J. D.; and Glaze, D. G. 1986. Child Abuse and Recurrent Infant Apnea. *J. Pediatrics* 109:1065–67.

102. Jumbelic, M. I., and Chambliss, M. 1990. Accidental Toddler Drowning in Five-Gallon Buckets. *JAMA* 263:1952–53.

103. Mann, N. C.; Weller, S. C.; and Rauchschwalbe, R. 1992. Bucket-Related Drownings in the United States, 1984 through 1990. *Pediatrics.*

104. Durfee, M. J.; Gellert, G. A.; and Tilton-Durfee, D. 1992. Origins and Clinical Relevance of Child Death Review Teams. *JAMA* 267:3172–75.

105. Kirschner, R. H., and Wilson, H. 1993. Fatal Child Abuse: The Pathologist's Perspective. In *Child Abuse: Medical Diagnosis and Management,* ed. R. M. Reece. Philadelphia: Lea and Febiger.

12

Assessment of Suspected Child Sexual Abuse

DAVID P. H. JONES

The sexual abuse of children has received increasing recognition over the course of the past fifteen years. Through studies of adult behavior in different periods of history, however, we learn that sexual abuse is an age-old problem. In the past, most victims remained silent for if they broke their silence, they were ignored or disbelieved, or disgraced.

We now know that a wide range of children are affected, all ages and both genders. Most abuse is committed by males, from boys to old men, but some females also abuse children sexually. The term *sexual abuse* describes a wide variety of sexually assaultive activities and circumstances. Furthermore, the majority of child victims already know their abuser before abusive sexual activities start. It is within this overall context that we will consider the question of assessment in cases of child sexual abuse. My general strategy in this chapter is to chart the territory of assessment, to enable the professional practitioner of each contributing discipline both to consider his or her own position within the community and to compare the principles and approaches expressed here with the procedures in place in his or her locality.

Assessment is a widely used yet ambiguous term in the field of child abuse and neglect. We will consider three ways in which this term is employed in relation to child sexual abuse:

1. Assessment of whether or not child sexual abuse has occurred
2. Assessment of the degree and extent of subsequent risk to the child
3. Assessment of requirements for, and response to, intervention and treatment

This chapter is primarily concerned with the first two items, broadly corresponding to the investigation stage of suspected sexual abuse. I will briefly discuss assessment in relation to intervention and treatment, but this theme is more fully developed in later chapters of this book (see, for example, chapters 14, 22, 24, and 26).

I define *child sexual abuse* very simply as "the actual or likely occurrence of a sexual act (or acts) perpetrated on a child by another person."[1] Children cannot give consent to

1. DIRECT SEXUAL ACTS
   - Contacting child's genital or anal area
   - Penetration—anal, vaginal, or oral

DAVID P. H. JONES, Mb.Ch.B., F.R.C. Psych., D.C.H., is consultant psychiatrist, Park Hospital for Children, Oxford, England, and senior clinical lecturer in child and family psychiatry at Oxford University.

such activities because of their dependent condition. However, consent may be more complex with older children or when there is only a small age gap between "abuser" and "abused." The key issue for the professional care provider in assessing whether sexual abuse has occurred in such situations is that of *exploitation.*[2]

Presentation

Cases of child sexual abuse come to light in various ways. In our study of the process of intervention when child sexual abuse was suspected, one-third of the cases reported were previously known to welfare agencies for other reasons prior to the investigation for sexual abuse (1). A substantial minority of cases came to light gradually, with suspicion slowly evolving.

Sexual abuse can come to public attention at various points in a victim's life. Summit has proposed five stages of a "child sexual abuse accommodation syndrome" (2). First, a child is engaged in a sexual relationship. Second, this makes the child feel helpless and entrapped. Third, the enforcement of the "secret," with overt or covert threats to the child or the child's family, leads the child to accommodate himself or herself to continuing sexual abuse. Fourth, at some point the child discloses that the sexual abuse has occurred. Fifth, and finally, the child may recant, depending upon the responses of the parents and professionals to his or her disclosure.

The way in which disclosure occurs is varied. Some children give an early warning, similar to Ounsted and Lynch's "open warning" in physical abuse (3), which may be a broad, ambiguous statement, for example:

One nine-year-old boy moved to Colorado with his parents from California. Within a week he announced to the neighbors, "There's a whole lot of raping and molesting going on in California." The neighbors did not realize he was trying to tell that his father was anally penetrating him. It was several months later before the incest secret was disclosed.

Early warning may consist of behavioral symptoms as well. For example, very young children may simulate sexual intercourse with friends or siblings; older children and adoles-

---

- Other acts in which the child is the object of the adult's gratification (for example, bondage, frotteurism, ejaculation onto child, fondling of postpubertal child's breasts)

INDIRECT SEXUAL ACTS
- Genital exposure
- Production of pornographic material
- Encouraging two children to have sex together
- Exposing children to pornographic material

2. By *exploitation* we mean the balance of power between the child and the other person, at the time when the sexual activity first occurred. Exploitation is considered to have occurred if the activity was unwanted when it first began and/or involved a misuse of conventional age, authority, or gender differentials. When the suspected perpetrator is five or more years older than the child, there will generally have been an exploitation of the age differential (adapted from Oxfordshire Area Child Protection Committee, *Child Protection Procedures* [Oxford: Oxfordshire Social Service Department, 1996]).

cents may suddenly run away, hoping that someone will ask them the reason for their distress.

Other children make direct statements to adults, or to their friends, about being sexually abused. These statements often comprise only a small part of their sexual abuse experience. They use brief direct statements to "test the waters." Since many children have been threatened that they will get in trouble if they discuss their sexual abuse, they carefully gauge the response of the listener. If the response is anger or admonition not to talk of such things, they may not disclose the issue for some time, if ever. Direct statements from young children often occur at quiet times, such as bedtime or bath time.

Another form of presentation is a marked change in behavior. In general, children tend to respond in a nonspecific way to specific stresses that are placed upon them. The behavioral consequences of sexual trauma may be neurotic disorders or disturbances of conduct, both of which may be relatively nonspecific. The behaviors may include temper tantrums, fears, anxiety, sleep disturbance, appetite disturbance, or inability to concentrate on schoolwork. Other children show signs of withdrawal, depression, guilt, or an increased expression of anger over and above what is usual for their character. Some children begin to lie, steal, or become aggressive with their friends. Sometimes children and young people demonstrate sexual acting-out behavior or unusual knowledge of or interest in sex out of character or out of keeping with their peer group. Older children and adolescents may act out their stress more dramatically. For example, they may become involved in drugs, make suicide attempts, run away, act out beyond the control of their parents or teachers, or become involved in prostitution.

For a minority of children, medical diseases or conditions may be the first indication of sexual abuse. The most obvious are venereal disease in prepubescent children and pregnancy in early adolescent children. A few children brought to medical attention immediately after an assault or rape manifest acute physical signs and symptoms. Infections by chlamydia, trichomonas, herpes virus, or lymphogranuloma venereum (venereal warts) may have other modes of transmission in prepubertal children, but the presence of these infections in the young distinctly raises the possibility of sexual abuse.

For other children, especially boys, the first indication of their sexual victimization occurs when they sexually abuse younger children. Many sexual abuse victims do not present until adult life, when they may exhibit a wide variety of symptoms, including sexual dysfunction, suicidal behavior, drug and alcohol abuse, prostitution, personality disorder, and psychiatric illness. On occasion, the manifestations in adults do not emerge until they themselves become parents. It is within this broad context that professionals have to assess potential cases of sexual abuse.

The Assessment Process

The principal aim of the assessment process is to find out whether or not sexual abuse has occurred and, if so, to develop a clear account of it. At the same time that we pursue these rather limited aims of the initial investigation, we need to develop an understanding of the whole child's state of health and development, as well as an understanding of the abuser and the family setting where the child lives. This information is required in order to make a more accurate initial assessment of the level of risk of further harm to which the child may be exposed if he or she continues to live at home. Such a risk assessment is also very helpful to those professionals involved in making decisions about child placement and making arrangements about the type and extent of child monitoring. Hence, the components of the assessment will include the child, the alleged abuser, and the child's family context.

If sexual abuse is confirmed and intervention is contemplated, this investigative part of the assessment will establish the basis for further comprehensive assessment. Adopting this approach, we do not consider assessment complete after the first investigation, however—rather, it continues, albeit with a changed form and focus, throughout the entire process, from initial disclosure of sexual abuse to intervention and treatment.

A Planned Approach to Investigation

The importance of a planned approach, coordinated between individuals and child services agencies, when suspected child sexual abuse is being investigated cannot be overemphasized. The local professionals who are primarily involved in investigating suspicions of sexual abuse will need to assume primary responsibility for designing these plans. Who does what depends on the laws and procedures of each country, local agreements and procedures, and the resources available for implementing plans. Local procedures should best be sensitive to issues of gender and should work out thoughtful responses to cases of suspected sexual abuse among the learning disabled, those with sensory impairment, and in situations of organized or institutional abuse (4–6).

A number of guidelines have been prepared for professional organizations (7–12), for the government (4, 13), and for inquiry reports (14): these can be extremely helpful to practitioners and are essential to those involved in frontline assessments.

Such guidelines often cover similar, but not identical, ground and in general illustrate a marked degree of consensus concerning assessment. However, areas of difference and emphasis do exist among them. For example, over the use of anatomically correct dolls, APSAC guidelines (12) generally are more permissive than those of the AACAP (9), although both advise caution and recommend that the dolls may be used only *after* a child has already indicated that abuse has occurred.

Partnership with Parents and Young People

Wherever possible, the practitioner should attempt to work in partnership with the abused child's parents. The approach should be as supportive as possible, recognizing the enormous trauma not only to the child but also to parents and other family members that occurs when sexual abuse is suspected. It is essential to maintain a nonaccusatory stance, although this is usually extremely hard for the practitioner when he or she is faced with the horror and tragedy of some sexual abuse cases. Indications are, however, that the family's openness to future work with practitioners depends crucially upon the professionalism and the quality of conduct they demonstrate during the initial investigation (15).

Partnership is not solely a matter of open communication and involvement of parents and children in the decisions which affect them; in addition, it must be firmly grounded in a vision shared by both professionals and clients on what constitutes the best interests of the child (15, 16). Through this shared perspective, the opposed views based on the rights of children and their parents to be informed and involved in the decisions which affect them, on the one hand, and the right of the child to have his or her safety from sexual assault assured, on the other, can be brought into focus simultaneously. Partnership fails when one aspect of this joint vision becomes blurred or overshadowed by the other.

Talking with Children

We have already discussed the fact that disclosures of child sexual abuse do not occur in a simple or predictable way. Hence it is likely that the subject will crop up unexpectedly in conversations between the child and professional caregivers or parents. Individuals who work with or care for children will need to be alert to the possibility that they could be approached at any time by a child who wants to communicate with them about some form of sexual mistreatment (17). Children may indicate their concern in some indirect manner, as we saw in the "Presentation" section above. Alternatively, the issue of sexual abuse may simply emerge during a conversation which anyone in a child care situation might initiate when a child appears distressed or upset in some way.

These sorts of discussions are quite separate from formal investigative interviews, which are deliberately set up for the purpose of assessing whether sexual abuse has occurred. My colleagues and I (18) have described four kinds of situations in which discussion with a child may reveal the possibility of sexual abuse. Each is perfectly legitimate in itself, but practitioners need to know which mode they are in. The four types of settings are:

1. Initial discussions with the child
2. Investigative interviews
3. Assessment interviews
4. Therapeutic interviews

Initial discussions are usually spontaneous conversations in which a child first starts to talk to a teacher, parent, or baby-sitter about sexual assault. *Investigative interviews* are those formal interviews which take place with a child, usually conducted by child protective services and/or police personnel, to determine whether abuse has occurred and, if so, the exact nature of the abuse. *Assessment interviews* have a broader scope and are usually undertaken by child care experts (perhaps child psychologists, or child psychiatrists, or those with expertise, for example, with learning-disabled children) who are making an assessment of a child's apparent distress or difficulties and keeping numerous possible causes in mind—including, but not limited to, child sexual abuse. *Therapeutic interviews* are those sessions conducted solely for therapeutic purposes, focused on helping the child with his or her emotional and/or behavior difficulties, either with children known to have been sexually abused or with children whose sexual abuse suddenly emerges during treatment originally undertaken for a different reason.

In the United Kingdom, a High Court ruling (19) has recognized this variety of types of discussions with children; the ruling made distinctions between investigative, assessment, and therapeutic interviews.

In initial discussions which may be held with the child, the person on the receiving end must listen and accept what the child is saying yet at the same time avoid slipping into an investigative interview mode without due preparation. In the United Kingdom, the official guide for practitioners investigating possible child sexual abuse with a view to the possibility of initiating criminal proceedings is the *Memorandum of Good Practice* (13). It recognizes that there will usually be an initial revelatory discussion with the child, and it emphasizes the following basic principles for practitioners in such a situation:

1. Listen to the child rather than directly question him or her
2. Never stop a child who is freely recalling significant events
3. Make a note of the discussion, taking care to record the timings, setting, and personnel present, as well as what was said
4. Record all events leading up to the investigative interview (13, para. 1.8)

Stages of the Investigative Process

The investigative process begins when concerns about a child are referred to a professional agency and ends when an appropriate plan for the welfare of that child has been worked out and put into practice. My colleagues and I (18) have identified the following stages of the process through which this end result can be achieved:

1. Referral
2. Immediate response
3. Consultation and planning
4. Information gathering and processing
5. Investigative interview
6. Child protection planning
7. Taking action to protect the child

With these stages in mind, I have illustrated in figure 12.1 the process of investigation of suspected sexual abuse from the point of referral through to either an endpoint of "No further action," or the outlining of a plan for responding to the child's needs, including any action necessary to protect the child from harm. Clearly, the primary weight of responsibility for managing referrals of suspected child sexual abuse falls upon whichever agencies are mandated in the local community. Very often these are the social services department and/or the police. Agency personnel then gather and sift information and plan further approaches, always considering the child's welfare as the paramount concern. However, other professionals can play a crucial role in the process (indicated on the right-hand side of figure 12.1). These professionals may be from the same agency as the primary investigators, but more commonly they are from other professional backgrounds and have a specific

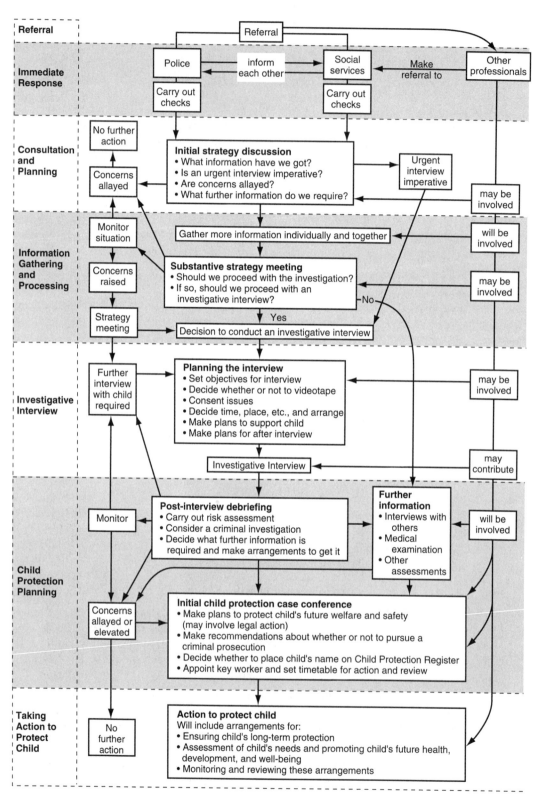

12.1 The investigative process.

expertise to contribute. Unfortunately, all too often such specialists are either excluded, or exclude themselves, from involvement in child sexual abuse investigations. If there is to be improved recognition of child sexual abuse, all those professionals who work with children, together with those who work with adult clients who take care of children, must accept an appropriate level of responsibility and be prepared to play their part. Child sexual abuse is not a phenomenon that can be relegated to one agency, uncomfortable and disturbing though the problem is.

Referral

Sometimes referrals are clear and relatively unambiguous—for example, when a specific, telling statement is made by a child or young person to a parent or teacher. Usually, however, referrals are much more vague—as when a child makes an ambiguous statement that he does not wish to go home but will not say why, or when unexplained yet suspicious behavior changes occur in a previously well-adjusted young student. It is in these latter situations that initial discussion between a child and either a parent or a professional working with children may well already have taken place by this point (see "Talking with Children," above).

In many senses, this early referral stage is a crucial test of the capacity of the local community of child care professionals to work together, as well as a test of local child protection procedures. No matter how extensive the investigative training is in a particular locality, there will always be—and, indeed, should be—room for doubt at this early referral stage; professionals need to be wary of becoming overzealous. It is here that an effective child protection service needs to incorporate a mechanism through which professionals can obtain expert advice about child protection concerns. This backup enables them to sift concerns and discuss suspicions, however vague and uncertain. Only after engaging in such a winnowing process should they decide how to proceed.

Immediate Response

When a referral is made to one of the mandated local agencies, what will normally follow immediately is a sharing of information with all other professionals and agencies in a need-to-know position. Each agency then carries out some initial checks to see if there are any other causes for concern about the child's health and welfare.

If the referral has been received by a professional outside the mandated agency (particularly in the United Kingdom and in the United States), he or she will generally make a another referral, to the social services department. Although this protocol varies from country to country, usually the "outside" professionals will need the backup and support of the mandated social services or welfare agency to ensure that an appropriate investigation occurs.

Consultation and Planning

Here, at this stage, core professionals confer to discuss the nature of the referral and the outcome of whatever initial checks were made. Basically, they must assess the urgency of the situation. In some cases, earlier concerns are fully allayed, and a decision can accordingly be made to take no further action. In other cases, referral may have been based on vague suspicion and initial checks discovered nothing to increase it, leading to a decision to monitor the situation further. In yet other cases, the decision will be made to actively gather more information.

In many cases, the initial strategy decision is simply to pursue the investigation with a core team of professionals, usually comprising a social worker and police officer with specific responsibilities for child protection investigation, although special circumstances may require the inclusion of another professional, for example, a specialist from the learning difficulties field. The core team decides what further information is required and how long it will take to get it and then sets a date to meet again. Throughout these discussions, the core team will be continually assessing the situation's level of urgency. Despite strong pressures on professionals to act quickly, we have found that immediate interviews with children are not normally necessary. However, sometimes children or young people are anxious to give an account as soon as possible or, similarly, may be receiving immediate external threats to their safety; in either case, the core team can move quickly to set up an investigative interview.

During this initial strategy phase, the core team will reach a decision about whether or not to draw in other professionals to supplement their own expertise. Examples of situations requiring such additional expertise include cases in which:

- The allegedly abused child is less than three years old, approximately
- The child has a learning disability, sensory impairment, or communication impairment
- The child is severely psychiatrically disturbed
- The child's first language is not the indigenous one
- Members of the team do not have sufficient knowledge and understanding of the child's racial, religious, or cultural background
- More than one child or more than one potential abuser may be involved
- Unusual or bizarre types of abuse have been alleged
- Abuse is alleged to have occurred in an institutional setting (for example, a residential school or children's home)

Information Gathering and Processing

In this phase, the core investigators obtain and process further information. They may interview the person who made the referral or obtain more detailed information about the child's health or development. Wherever possible, the investigators will work with the child's parents (see "Partnership with Parents and Young People," above); legal advice also may well be sought during this stage.

Once further data have been gathered, the team meets again to decide whether further action is indicated and, if so, what kind. Some situations will involve continual monitoring and setting a schedule for regular review. In these cases, professionals will need to articulate and agree upon the criteria for further action.

Investigative Interviews

The first step for investigators, regardless of the degree of urgency, is to plan any proposed interviews. This does not necessarily entail a face-to-face meeting of the core team members, but a number of key issues need to be decided on before the investigators interview the child. The primary objectives the interview is to accomplish must be defined; in addition, the time and location of the interview, the team member(s) who will conduct the interview, and the arrangements to record its content must be settled. The question of consent will need to be carefully considered, as well as the role the child's parents will take during the interview. The core team also must decide whether, and how, to obtain the child's agreement. It is also appropriate and important to detail possible further actions that might be necessary after the interview—for example, medical examinations and support and immediate protection for the child in the event that abuse is clearly disclosed during the interview.

The interview should take place only after the core team has established its objectives. The basic aim of the interview is to determine whether sexual abuse has occurred and, if so, to what extent. Specialist skills may be incorporated—perhaps, for example, by involving someone fluent in sign language, or possessing skills with augmentive communication, in an interview with a sensory-impaired child.

The most useful interviews are those which encourage the child to recall freely any abusive events that have occurred. Interviews which are leading, or which seem to be guided by the professional's agenda rather than the child's, not only have limited value but may be actively misleading and confusing to the child and family. Comprehensive protocols for interviewing children are available (20, 13, 21, 22), but the broad principles are described in outline below. It is of great interest that there is remarkable consensus among different authors about the best approach to investigative interviewing. Indeed, this consensus has been the guiding force behind the recent *Memorandum of Good Practice* in the United Kingdom (13).

All these interview protocols agree that interviews with children suspected of having been sexually abused should consist of a series of phases which aim, first of all, to encourage free recall from the child, followed later by progressively more focused or facilitated approaches to reach the more reluctant or fearful children. All the approaches also emphasize the importance of establishing good rapport with the child before starting, and most emphasize the importance of closing the session in a way appropriate for the child or young person. The following phases are suggested (though all these protocols warn against any overly regimented checklist, and stress flexibility):

1. Gaining rapport
2. Initial inquiry about sexual abuse
3. Facilitation
4. Gathering specific detail
5. Closing

The type or origin of the suspicion of sexual abuse will inform the interviewer's initial line of inquiry. For example, if the child has said something which has created suspicion of sexual abuse, the interviewer's initial line of inquiry will be different from the situation in which it is a physical disease or condition that has raised the suspicion of sexual abuse. In the former case, general prompts to encourage the child's free recall will contrast with the latter situation, in which the child may be asked if he or she knows how he or she became "sore" or "unwell." A child's behavior change may also lead to suspicion, as may an adult's suspicion on behalf of the child. In each of these two situations, the interviewer will be required to pursue a different line of inquiry.

It may not be effective to encourage the child to give a freely recalled account of the event; if suspicion is serious enough, the interviewer might wish to move to a more focused or facilitative phase. Here the aim will be to enable a reluctant child to talk but without the assumption on the interviewer's part that abuse is the only explanation for the child's presentation. These facilitative approaches involve a combination of modulated interview style, special types of questions, and, with younger children, the use of toys and play materials (20). There is also much scope for the use of various drawing materials and ordinary dolls, which, it has been shown, can help younger children to express themselves without any sacrifice to their accuracy.

Anatomically correct dolls are more controversial, and in many areas local regulations are very strict or even prohibitive about their use. Individual practitioners should take care to check local procedures and the attitude of local courts before using anatomically correct dolls on a routine basis in investigative interviews (see chapters 8 and 13).

These anatomically correct dolls may help children who, having previously described sexual abuse verbally or through other means, can make use of the dolls as a more graphic medium of expression, one that can either confirm abuse or provide greater detail. No compelling evidence exists that children frequently make false allegations as a consequence of using anatomically correct dolls. However, a minority of children, especially in the preschool years, do make erroneous replies in experimental situations when using anatomically correct dolls (see 23). In addition, there is much disagreement among professionals about the implications of particular types of doll play by children. One study has shown that the low socioeconomic status, black, nonabused preschoolers—as compared to other groups of children of approximately the same age—not infrequently demonstrated sexualized behaviors with the dolls (24). These findings do limit the usefulness of anatomical dolls, in this author's view.

If abuse is disclosed during the investigative interview, a phase of gathering further detail will be necessary. This will forestall subsequent requests for additional interviews arising from the court's need for specific facts (20). Examples here include exactly where and when the abuse occurred, the identity of the perpetrator, and the presence of blood or ejaculate.

The closing phase of the investigative interview is important because the child is likely to require reassurance and vindication of his or her participation in the session. The interviewer should confirm any emotional struggle which the child has been through during the interview but refrain from expressing congratulation or judgmental opinions about the rights and wrongs of sexual abuse. If possible, it will be helpful to provide the child with some information about what to expect next. However, it is important to avoid promising anything which cannot be delivered.

Child Protection Planning

The first step in this stage begins immediately after the investigative interviewing. The core professionals review the information gathered and decide what to do next. Further data may be required, and a medical examination may be deemed necessary (see chapter 13). Moreover, questions will need to be asked about the child's immediate future: Is the child safe to go home? Who can protect the child from further abuse? Is there a likelihood of any physical violence either to the child or another family member? Decisions about legal action—civil action to protect the child, and possibly criminal action to prosecute the abuser—need to be made. In many cases, earlier data gathering will enable the core team to reach an informed decision at this point about these risk factors. Risk will need to be assessed according to its potentiating factors, as well as according to those aspects of the child and family situation which may protect the child or ameliorate the risk of harm. Thus the search for more information should be as much to identify protective factors as to identify potential risks to the child of further abuse.

Following this immediate postinterview debriefing, some form of planning meeting is necessary, including all the professionals involved with the case of this particular child and family. Here the entire group will make plans to protect the child's future welfare and safety and will decide who among the group should take a central position to monitor the progress of the case (the key worker). It will be important at this stage to set a timetable for any action and review. The process will vary in different countries, but decisions will need to be made about whether or not to pursue a criminal prosecution and whether or not this child's name should appear on any form of register of abused children. In order to come to these kind of conclusions, further information may well be required: interviews with other children, parents or caregivers, alleged abusers, and other witnesses, as well as a thorough medical examination of the child, will contribute to effective decision making.

At this stage, the direction may change from child protection to child welfare, especially when an investigation has allayed fears about abuse but highlighted significant areas of the child's unmet needs. The focus of professional attention should then, in consequence, shift from protecting the child to responding to the child's need, yet the professional system may be sluggish or ill-suited to this challenge. From the perspective of children and their parents, this lack of responsiveness is a major deficit (1).

Taking Action to Protect the Child

The next stage is to act on the agreed plans, in order to protect the child and ensure his or her long-term welfare. This involves ensuring the child's protection, assessing the child's needs, and promoting his or her future health, development, and well-being. It also involves monitoring and reviewing these arrangements, following an appropriate timescale jointly agreed on by the various core professionals, so that cases do not "slip through the cracks."

The Whole Child

Up to now we have considered the investigative phase of assessment and concentrated on the investigative interview with the child to see if abuse has occurred. However, a broader-based assessment of the child's overall condition will also need to be made. Much of this will have to wait until a treatment planning stage (see chapter 24), but even at this early stage, a broader-based assessment of the child's situation should be conducted to inform risk assessment decisions and determine whether alternative, outside-the-home, placement is going to be necessary.

During the investigative process, the practitioner will need to make a preliminary assessment as to how well-adjusted the child is. A majority, but not all, sexually abused children do show short-term emotional or behavioral difficulty following disclosure of abuse. Emotionally, common responses consist of anxiety and fear, as well as guilt and shame. Fear may not be wholly unrealistic and may in itself relate to threats of reprisal which the child has received prior to disclosure. The syndrome of "post-traumatic stress disorder"—consisting of anxiety symptoms, fear of the recurrence of abuse, and sleep and appetite disturbances—will be evident in up to half of all sexually abused children. A significant number of children will be depressed, and this may be harder to detect. Any self-harming behavior, both through direct methods and indirectly through substance and alcohol abuse, should be noted and evaluated. Some children evidence significant behavior or conduct disturbance, which may escalate in the aftermath of disclosure.

The nature of the child's attachment to his or her parents and to others will help inform placement decisions. Information about the child's progress in school, or in other activities outside the home, should be used to complement any information gathered about the child's adjustment in the home setting. If there is doubt about the degree of the child's maladjustment, the help of other professionals—in particular, child mental health professionals—plays an important part. The needs of the learning disabled or sensory impaired, or children with communication difficulties, almost certainly involve the additional help of other professionals besides the core assessment team.

Assessment Interviews

These interviews fall in between investigative interviews, which are focused on detecting any possible sexual abuse, and the more broad-based therapeutic interviews of children. Assessment interviews may be undertaken for a wide variety of reasons when children are showing evidence of distress or disturbance. These interviews are usually conducted by professionals with special expertise on the type of problem which the child evidences and are not wholly focused on questions of abuse and neglect. Indeed, their primary purpose is to make a diagnostic assessment of a child or young person, with the broad aim of clarifying whatever etiological factors might be contributing to the child's state. Thus abuse becomes only one of several possibilities which might be impinging on the child. One of the most important objectives of such assessment interviews is to contribute to the understanding of the child in question, particularly through the formulation of appropriate diagnostic conclusions.

A variety of professionals might be enlisted to undertake assessment interviews with children and young people, including child psychiatrists, psychologists, and specialists in the field of learning and communication disability or sensory impairment. These assessment interviews are unlikely to be conducted along the same strict lines as those set out in interview protocols for the express purpose of discovering if a child has been abused. Their whole purpose and scope is different. Nevertheless, these assessment interviews do have a significant place in the broad picture of the early assessment of suspected sexual abuse.

The Assessment of the Alleged Abuser

This topic is a specialized one, and I refer the interested reader elsewhere for a comprehensive description (see chapter 14) (25). Many such interviews are conducted by the police, usually from specialist units, at least in the United Kingdom and the United States.

It is relatively easy to be taken in and convinced by a persuasive abuser—his or her forthright denial is very commonly encountered. Skillful interviewing will enable a minority of sexual abusers to acknowledge their actions and so will facilitate a much easier process of planning for the child's protection. Those who steadfastly deny abuse that they have in fact committed, unfortunately appear similar to those who deny and genuinely have not committed any wrongdoing. Thus an enormous weight is placed on the investigation of the child's account, because very rarely do abusers volunteer information about their crimes.

Assessment of the Family

This process comprises both assessment of individual family members from the index child's household and assessment of the functioning and interrelationships within the family. The interactions of sexually abusing families differ significantly from those in which a child is disturbed but not sexually abused (26). Such assessments can be carried out in the clinical setting and can assist treatment planning.

The assessment of significant individuals other than the child him- or herself will need to include all those within the household or family who are either caretakers or siblings of the index child. Siblings need to be assessed not only to see if they are at risk for abuse or have already been abused but also to see whether they can shed light on any abuse of the index child, family violence, or other relevant family dynamics. At this early assessment stage, the accent is on determining the family's strengths and weaknesses and, in particular, the family's capacity to provide a protective and safe environment for the index child if abuse is considered likely to have occurred.

During these assessments, a nonaccusatory stance by the core professionals will be crucial to eliciting the support and cooperation of any nonabusive adults within the child's family. The shock of realization and the throng of conflicting choices which the nonabusive parent will need to negotiate at the point of disclosure of abuse are particularly difficult, even though this is a dilemma with which some practitioners may find it hard to sympathize. The nonabusive parent's allegiance may be equally split between her partner and her child; in these circumstances, some mothers are quickly alienated by the intervention system and may prove extremely hard to engage thereafter. The task for the professional is a difficult one, combining tact and compassion with a clear focus on the abused child's welfare.

In the end, the professional is assessing the family's capacity to protect, the family members' acceptance that the index child needs protection, and their concomitant willingness to cooperate and comply with welfare agency requests. During early stages of an investigation practitioners do not know everything, and although they may suspect that the child has been abused by only one adult person, more details of the abuse may yet emerge. Nevertheless, assessments of the family and its individual members will be crucial to the assessment of risk and will inform decisions about how best to ensure the child's protection and immediate safety.

Validation

After the assessment interview with the child has been completed, the core professionals have to evaluate its contents, along with any other data gathered from the other assessments, in order to decide if the child is likely to have suffered sexual abuse. The issue here is whether the child's situation is sufficiently convincing to warrant further action. As there is no simple test of truth or falsehood, the following areas should be considered when assessing the credibility of cases of suspected abuse:

1. The child's account and behavior during interview(s)
2. The child's behavior and emotional state before and after the investigation
3. The way in which disclosure originally occurred
4. Any prior accounts or expressions of concern about sexual abuse
5. Witness by others
6. Information gathered from assessment of the family and family members
7. Assessment of the suspected abuser
8. Physical evidence, from medical and forensic examinations
9. Probability assessment

Within this broad framework, primary importance must be given to the child's statement itself. All the other sources of data may be considered as either supporting or detracting from the worth of the child's statement, but they rarely can substitute for it.

The Next Steps

We have concerned ourselves in this chapter with the early stages of the assessment of possible sexual abuse. When the investigation is conducted sympathetically, as far as all the participants are concerned, a firm basis is established for continuing successful work with the child and family members in the future. The process of assessment will then become increasingly concerned with determining the child's and family's capacity for intervention and their likely response to treatment efforts. Assessment and intervention become increasingly intertwined as the treatment process moves ahead. The early investigative assessments and the various other assessments undertaken to assist initial child protection decision making form the all-important foundation for this future work.

References

1. Jones, D. P. H.; Aldgate, J.; Sharland, E.; Seal, H.; and Croucher, M. 1994. The Impact of Investigation on Cases of Suspected Sexual Abuse in Oxfordshire. Summary Report to the Department of Health, London.

2. Summit, R. 1983. The Child Sexual Abuse Accommodation Syndrome. *Child Abuse and Neglect: International J.* 7:177–93.

3. Ounsted, C., and Lynch, M. 1976. Family Pathology as Seen in England. In *Child Abuse and Neglect: The Family and the Community,* ed. R. E. Helfer and C. H. Kempe. Cambridge, Mass.: Ballinger.

4. Department of Health. 1991. *Working Together under the Children Act of 1989: A Guide to Arrangements for Interagency Cooperation for the Protection of Children from Abuse.* London: Her Majesty's Stationery Office.

5. Oxfordshire Area Child Protection Committee. 1996. *Advisory Team: Guidelines for Dealing with Organized and Institutional Abuse.* Oxford: Oxfordshire Social Services Department.

6. Westcott, H. I. 1993. Investigative Interviewing with Disabled Children. In *Investigative Interviewing with Children,* ed. W. Stainton-Rogers and M. Worrel. Milton Keynes: Open University Press.

7. American Psychiatric Association. 1991. Position Statement on Child Abuse and Neglect by Adults. *Am. J. Psychiatry* 148:1626.

8. American Academy of Pediatrics. 1991. Guidelines for the Evaluation of Sexual Abuse of Children. *Pediatrics* 87:254–60.

9. American Academy of Child and Adolescent Psychiatry. 1988, modified 1990. *Guidelines for the Clinical Evaluation of Child and Adolescent Sexual Abuse.* Washington, D.C.: AACAP.

10. American Professional Society on the Abuse of Children. 1990. *Guidelines for Psychological Evaluation of Suspected Sexual Abuse in Young Children.* Chicago: ASPAC.

11. Royal College of Psychiatrists. 1988. *Child Psychiatric Perspectives on the Assessment and Management of Sexually Mistreated Children. Psychiatric Bull.* 12:534–40.

12. Royal College of Psychiatrists. 1993. Child Psychiatry and Child Sexual Abuse. Council Report, no. CR24. London: Royal College of Psychiatrists.

13. Home Office. 1992. *Memorandum of Good Practice on Video Recorded Interviews with Child Witnesses for Criminal Proceedings.* London: Her Majesty's Stationery Office.

14. Butler-Sloss, E. 1988. *Report of the Inquiry into Child Abuse in Cleveland in 1987.* London: Her Majesty's Stationery Office.

15. Jones, D. P. H. 1995. The Process of Investigating Suspect Abuse. In *A Festschrift for Professor Israel Kolvin,* 59–76. London: Tavistock and Postman NHS Trust.

16. Adcock, M. 1991. Significant Harm: Implications for the Exercise of Statutory Responsibilities. In *Significant Harm: Its Management and Outcome,* ed. M. Adcock, R. White, and A. Hollows. London: Significant Publications, Croydon.

17. Jones, D. P. H. 1990. Talking with Children. In *Understanding and Managing Child Sexual Abuse,* ed. R. K. Oates. London: Bailliere Tindall.

18. Jones, D. P. H.; Hopkins, C.; Godfrey, M.; and Glaser, D. 1993. The Investigative Process. In *Investigative Interviewing with Children,* ed. W. Stainton-Rogers and M. Worrel, 12–18. Milton Keynes: Open University Press.

19. Re M (Minors). 1993. *Family Law Reports* 1:822–31.
20. Jones, D. P. H. 1992. *Interviewing the Sexually Abused Child: Investigation of Suspected Abuse.* London: Gaskell.
21. Vizard, E. 1991. Interviewing Children Suspected of Being Sexually Abused: A Review of Theory and Practice. In *Clinical Approaches to Sex Offenders and Their Victims,* ed. C. Hillins and K. Howells. Chichester: Wiley.
22. Yuille, J.; Hunter, R.; Joffe, R.; and Zaparnink, J. 1993. Interviewing Children in Child Sexual Abuse Cases. In *Child Victims, Child Witnesses,* ed. G. Goodman and B. Bottoms. New York: Guilford.
23. Everson, M. D., and Boat, B. W. 1994. Putting Anatomical Doll Controversy in Perspective: An Examination of the Major Uses of the Dolls in Sexual Abuse Evaluations. *Child Abuse and Neglect: International J.* 18:113–29.
24. Boat, W. W., and Everson, M. D. 1994. Exploration of Anatomical Dolls by Nonreferred Preschool Aged Children: Comparisons by Age, Gender, Race, and Socioeconomic Status. *Child Abuse and Neglect: International J.* 18:139–53.
25. Becker, J., and Quinsey, V. 1993. Assessing Suspected Child Molesters. *Child Abuse and Neglect: International J.* 17:169–74.
26. Madonna, P.; Van Scoyk, S.; and Jones, D. P. H. 1991. Family Interactions in Incest and Nonincest Families. *Am. J. Psychiatry* 148:46–49.

13

Medical Evaluation of the Sexually Abused Child

SUSAN K. REICHERT

The recognition of sexual abuse of children is no longer the "hidden" problem C. H. Kempe exposed almost twenty years ago (1). The latest estimates (accurate data have never been collected, and *no* "official statistics" have been tabulated in the United States since 1986) suggest that approximately 0.5% to 1% of children experience sexual abuse annually in this country. For 1994, there were approximately 3.14 million reports of all forms of child abuse and neglect; nationally, 40% of these reports are "substantiated," and about 25% of these are sexual abuse cases (2). Retrospective surveys indicate that approximately 16% of all men and 27% of all women were sexually abused in childhood.

Pediatricians and other practitioners have an important role to play in the multidisciplinary approach to examining and evaluating child sexual abuse. This chapter is intended to assist primary care practitioners, rather than those specializing in the forensic evaluation of sexually abused children.

Recognition

It rings true that "recognition of sexual molestation in a child is entirely dependent on the individual's inherent willingness to entertain the possibility that the condition may exist" (3). Clinicians vary in their willingness to consider the diagnosis of child sexual abuse. Nonetheless, it is the responsibility of all pediatric care providers in the United States to report any suspicions of child sexual abuse.

There are many reasons why some practitioners avoid involvement with abuse cases. Dealing with the challenge of too little time, disruption of office routine, feelings of incompetence regarding assessment of findings, inadequate technical expertise, and lack of specific interviewing skills is difficult. Add to this the rigors of documentation, loss of control over outcome of the case, possible adversarial interactions with various agencies or individuals, court demands, and emotional stress, and any busy practitioner's enthusiasm will be taxed.

SUSAN K. REICHERT, M.D., is medical director of Kids Intervention and Diagnostic Service Center in Bend, Oregon.

The author wishes to express appreciation to Richard D. Krugman, M.D., for his assistance with the statistical information in this chapter and for his valued influence and inspiration.

TABLE 13.1
Possible Historical Indicators of Child Sexual Abuse

Unexplained burns, bruises, or scars
Torn, stained, or bloody clothing
Difficulty walking or sitting
Pain with diapering or when held
Bowel dysfunction, e.g., constipation, encopresis
Increased somatic complaints
Behavioral changes

In many areas, specialized abuse evaluation teams or centers have been developed, to which patients suspected of having been sexually abused may be referred. This is an appropriate option for any care provider who feels uncomfortable with these difficult cases, whatever the reason may be. Given the significant progress that has been made in assessing sexually abused children over the last few years, practicing clinicians who were not trained adequately during residency or who have not concentrated their continuing medical education efforts on enhancing their skills in this area may find such referral useful.

Regardless of whether a given practitioner chooses to refer a patient in need of a sexual abuse evaluation to the local expert(s) or opts to undertake it her- or himself, it is safe to say that all who provide health care for children will confront a sexual abuse case at one time or another. Because of the nature of the problem, patients come to medical attention by a variety of routes. Occasionally, concern about sexual abuse is the chief complaint. Parents may want help in confirming their suspicions and/or in deciding how to proceed when they fear that their child has been abused. A clinician may be called upon by social services, law enforcement, another health care provider, the child's therapist or teacher, or other concerned professionals to assist in determining whether a child has been victimized.

These direct presentations constitute the minority of sexual abuse cases that may confront the average practitioner. It is more likely that some degree of detective work will be required. The astute care provider must be aware of the historical, behavioral, and physical signs of child sexual abuse and be ready to respond appropriately when these signs are discovered during a routine health maintenance or illness visit (see tables 13.1–13.3).

A child's inadvertent, or even purposeful, disclosure of sexual abuse, the discovery of unusual bruises or other marks of trauma near the child's genitals or mouth, an abnormal genital or anal examination, lab results positive for sexually transmitted diseases (STDs) or pregnancy—these are but a few of the cues that should trigger a more extensive sexual abuse investigation. Some questions will have to be asked immediately, even if the discovering clinician intends to refer such cases to specialists for a more comprehensive evaluation.

It is critical to determine when the most recent abuse may have occurred, because the timing of the suspected abuse is relevant to the type of exam that should be performed. If the sexual abuse occurred within the prior seventy-two hours, skilled examination and collection of forensic evidence must be undertaken expeditiously. The patient should not be bathed, and the clothes worn at the time of the sexual contact should not be laundered but,

TABLE 13.2
Physical Symptoms That May Be Present in Sexual Abuse Victims

Nonspecific

Headaches
Recurrent abdominal pain
Frequent throat infections
Leg or hip pain
Chronic pelvic pain
Recurrent vaginal infections
Pain with defecation or urination

More Specific

Pain, redness, lesions or "rash," swelling, discharge, unusual odor, bruises, bites, scratches,
    or blood in genital or anal areas
Sexually transmitted diseases
Pregnancy

TABLE 13.3
Behavioral Indicators of Child Sexual Abuse

Mostly Nonspecific (but should raise a red flag
if present or if a change from normal)

Fear of certain people, places; general clinginess	Less pleasure in activities previously enjoyed
Difficulty eating or swallowing	Overly passive affect
New-onset enuresis, encopresis	Regression
Abnormally sexualized behavior	Unusual aggression
Social withdrawal, few friends	Sleep disturbances
Refusal to, or excessively afraid to, bathe or undress	Panic attacks
	Crying; depression
School phobia or increased absences	Secretive behavior
Decreased ability to concentrate; decline in school performance	Self-destructive acts
	Diminished self-esteem

Signs Especially Noted in Teens

Eating disorders	Delinquency
Sudden increase or decrease in weight	Substance abuse
Preoccupation with sexual activities	Running away
Hysteric symptoms	Prostitution
Pregnancy	Suicide attempts

rather, left on or taken along to the clinician who will perform the examination. However, if the child has been bathed and his or her clothing already washed, a forensic examination should still be ordered, nevertheless.

Clinicians who perform the medical assessment of acutely assaulted children should be aware of the particular capabilities of local law enforcement and/or forensic laboratories which will process the collected materials. Sophisticated forensic techniques are available in many jurisdictions or may be accessed by sending specimens to referral centers. These include tests for the presence of semen (for example, acid phosphatase analysis, p30 protein, and other biochemical markers) and a variety of perpetrator identification methods, such as hair analysis, blood group antigen typing, isoenzymes electrophoresis, and DNA typing. Contacting the laboratory that will process the specimens for instructions regarding evidence collection, handling, and storage is advisable.

Even in remote areas without specialized referral centers, examiners can aid the investigation by microscopically inspecting urine samples or wet mounts from vaginal swabs to detect the presence of sperm. Previously prepared "rape kits" can greatly aid the clinician in the organization and speed of evidence collection. A Wood's lamp, if available, may be used to aid in the detection of semen stains on a victim's skin, and application of toluidine blue may enhance the visualization of superficial abrasions of the perineal skin.

Referral of a child who has not been acutely sexually abused to the nearest emergency room for immediate examination should be avoided. The inherently chaotic nature of the emergency room setting is entirely inappropriate for this emotionally charged diagnosis. Nonacute exams should not be performed in the emergency department unless no other options for evaluation exist.

In locations where specialized consultants are available, a timely appointment should be made. In cases of past or chronic, but not current, abuse, a wait of even a few weeks for the calm, professionally conducted, comprehensive approach that can be offered by these skilled providers is well worth the delay. However, the referring practitioner must enlist the help of child protective services and/or law enforcement to determine that the abuse is not ongoing and that the child will be protected from the abuser(s) or the abusive environment in the interim.

Access to emotional support for the child and family should not be put on hold while the medical findings are yet forthcoming. The health care professional should report her or his suspicion of abuse, based on the presenting information or findings, to the proper agency without waiting for the consultant's examination. This allows for protective and investigative measures to be initiated promptly. If the referring care provider has not seen the patient and/or does not have adequate information to determine if a report to social services is warranted—as, for instance, when he or she is contacted by phone—it may be reasonable to defer the decision to report the suspected abuse to the abuse evaluation team. However, it is best to err on the side of safety and report any reasonable suspicion of child sexual abuse.

Knowledge of the parent's concern about the possibility that her or his child has been subjected to sexual abuse does confer a degree of responsibility onto the clinician. The care provider should advise the parent or other contacting party to notify the police or social services at once of their suspicions. Providers should also plan to follow up on the case within a reasonable period of time. If the family does not pursue the consultation or the reporting, the alerted professional should consider generating a report at that time so that the initial concern can be investigated more thoroughly.

If the alleged abuse occurred more than a few days before it is brought to medical attention, several options are available as to how best to conduct the evaluation. Limiting the total number of interviews and examinations to which the child will be subjected is paramount. Multidisciplinary participation of the necessary agencies by or at the time of the first extensive interview is desirable. If social services workers, or law enforcement personnel, or a specialist at a sexual abuse evaluation site interview the child first, those individuals can then share information with the clinician, who can direct the physical examination accordingly. On the other hand, an assessment may begin with the medical evaluation and then the alleged victim can be interviewed after the exam has been completed.

It is prudent, and certainly preferable, for care providers to "know their limits" and refer patients who may have been sexually abused to specialists or to colleagues who have more experience and proficiency with such cases. Lack of expertise, discomfort with the subject matter, or reluctance to become involved does not permit any health care professional to close his or her eyes to the diagnostic possibility of child sexual abuse when it arises in the course of patient care. Clinicians who do take on these cases must be sure that they are reasonably competent in this area. Courses in medical management of sexual abuse cases are regularly offered at many sites. And, though advances in such case management over the past several years are many and may seem overwhelming (for an excellent review of two decades of the literature in the area of medical diagnosis of child sexual abuse, see 4), there are a few easily learned pointers about the medical assessment of sexual abuse that, once acquired, can raise the practitioner's facility and level of competence in making this diagnosis.

Medical Interview

Knowing whether she or he will be the primary interviewer of the child suspected to have been sexually abused or whether social services professionals, law enforcement officers, or evaluation specialists will interview the child separately enables the health care professional to determine how extensively to question the patient. Nevertheless, even in those cases in which the main forensic interview is done elsewhere, the examining clinician should include some very specific questions about the suspected abuse while she or he is taking the patient's history.

In cases of suspected child sexual abuse, a careful, well-conducted interview is likely to be even more critical to making the diagnosis than is the physical examination. Before they make a decision about the disposition of a child who has disclosed sexual abuse, parents, caseworkers, police officers, attorneys, and judges often demand that the child undergo a physical examination. Health care providers must explain to them that intervention determinations should not be based on the medical findings alone. It must be stressed that a normal examination not only *does not refute* the possibility that a child has been abused—the absence of physical evidence of sexual abuse, especially in nonacute cases, is in fact the *expected* finding (5–8).

In addition to the usual routine of inquiring about the past medical history, the history of the present illness and the chief complaint, and the social and family history of the child, the clinician should also ask questions focused on physical and behavioral indicators of sexual abuse (see tables 13.1–13.3). The existence of previous abuse in the child and a history of abuse in parents or other family members should be identified. It is preferable that information pertaining to abuse, especially to the presenting situation, be gathered from the caretaker first and not be discussed in the presence of the child. It is furthermore advisable that the child then be interviewed alone, so that the caretaker's presence does not influence the information obtained. Separation from a support person should never be forced, as this may further traumatize these already vulnerable patients. If the child prefers, the physical examination may also be done with the supportive parent-figure present to comfort the patient. However, it is considered desirable that no one be present during the examination who might influence the child's statements to the examiner, since children often volunteer additional history as the examination proceeds.

When the practitioner has been consulted specifically to help investigate possible sexual abuse, it is often helpful to lay the foundation for the interview by asking the child why he or she has come to the clinic or office that day. If the child does not know or if the response is not related to the suspected abuse, the clinician may introduce the intent to do a complete physical examination to check the child from head to toe. Alternatively, the examiner may directly express to the child that he or she has been made aware of a concern about possible abuse to the child. A very general statement such as, "Your daddy told me that he's worried about something that has been happening to you," or, "I understand that you told your teacher that someone has been touching you," can give the child a frame of reference. This should be immediately followed with an invitation to the child to expound: "Can you please tell me more about that?"

At this point, or if the child initially mentions the abuse as the presenting problem, the clinician can assure the child that as a medical professional he or she has taken care of other children who have had the same kind of thing happen to them. The practitioner may wish to acknowledge that it is sometimes uncomfortable or embarrassing to discuss such matters. Establishing a rapport with the child may significantly ease the interview and examination experience, so these preliminary steps, while somewhat time-consuming, are worthwhile. Such conversation, as well as unrelated "icebreakers"—that is, asking questions about school or friends, or having a young child name colors—can also provide important data for the clinician's appraisal of the child's developmental level.

The health care provider may wish to become familiar with several sources in the literature which discuss the medical interview of abused children and the way that children tend to reveal information (9–12) (see also chapters 6, 8, and 12). The use of anatomic dolls and/or body drawings (a very inexpensive option) may be helpful to the clinician; providers who choose to employ these tools should be knowledgeable in their application and interpretation (13, 14). Estimating the child's developmental level, discovering the child's own terms for body parts and which ones he or she considers "private," talking about different forms of "touching" and assessing the child's opinion about the appropriateness of each are a few of the techniques that can be easily incorporated into the medical evaluation. In regard to information he or she shares, it may also be valuable to elucidate the child's understanding of the difference between "what really happened" and "what didn't really happen," or between "real" and "pretend" (these terms are less emotionally and morally charged than "truth" or "lie").

In many cases, including those of very young children or those who cannot generalize from their experience sufficiently to be able to use drawings or dolls effectively, the examiner's attention to the child's own body parts may trigger disclosures or additional details of the abuse. Questioning the child about *each* body part as it is examined, regarding function, symptoms ("Do you have any problems with your ears?" or "Does your tummy hurt?"), and action taken by others ("Has anyone ever hurt your mouth [chest, arms, bottom, private parts, and so forth] or touched it in a way that made you feel funny or uncomfortable?") conveys systematic progression through the entire body that makes sense to the child and does not focus excessively on the genitals. All positive answers should be explored—not just those related to the sexual abuse concerns. Asking the patient to tell more about someone touching or hurting them and following up with who and where and other simple descriptive questions will often allow the child to reveal a more complete story.

The examiner must begin with open-ended questions and avoid being leading or directive, particularly if future interviews by other professionals may occur. If the child does not respond to the nonfocused queries (this may be especially true in younger children whose developmental level may require that questions contain some concrete reference points), the clinician may choose to be somewhat more directive. The child's attention may be called either to a given individual reported to have been involved, to a previously disclosed event, or to a certain finding (for example, "Your mom said that you told her about someone named Bob," or "Has anything happened to your body at school that you didn't like," or, "I notice that you are very red around your pee-pee [use the child's word]. Do you know what might have caused that?"). These more pointed questions should again be followed with an open invitation to the child to explain further: "Tell me more about that."

The practitioner should gather as many details through nonsuggestive, nonleading, nonjudgmental questioning as the child will relate. As the encounter progresses, health care providers should consider asking for details about the nature of the sexual contact, whether drugs were used or given to the child, and if photographs or videotapes were taken. If the child has disclosed that a male exposed his genitals or touched the child with his penis, particularly convincing information may be obtained from questioning the child about whether the perpetrator ejaculated. The clinician may ask the child to describe the abuser's private parts and inquire whether the child saw or felt anything "come out of" the perpetrator's penis. By then urging the victim to describe what she or he can remember about it, idiosyncratic detail of an event with which children have no normal, natural experience may be revealed. This may prove to be very valuable evidence for court cases.

It is also important to ascertain the degree of force or coercion used by the abuser, whether the child experienced pain or bleeding, and whether or not threats were employed. Children who do not disclose to direct inquiries ("Did someone touch you?") may sometimes respond affirmatively when asked more indirectly ("Did someone touch you and tell you not to tell?").

All the information elicited during the encounter with the patient should be carefully documented, quoting the examiner's exact questions and the child's exact words whenever possible. A description of body language and emotional reactions displayed should be included, as these factors may assist in affirming the validity of the child's statements.

Physical Examination

A prerequisite for conducting an adequate physical examination of a girl suspected of having been sexually abused is a clear understanding of female genital anatomy. Some previously commonly used terms ("virginal exam," "marital introitus") and descriptions (characterizing the vaginal opening in relation to the ease of "admission" of the examiner's finger) are inappropriate. It is also not adequate to state "normal female," or "hymen intact," or "vaginal opening patent." More exact descriptors of the structures and of the location of findings are now recommended (fig. 13.1). It should be kept in mind that the need for an internal or speculum examination of the prepubertal female's genitalia or for a digital examination of any sexually abused patient's anus is quite rare. Almost all of the important findings related to sexual abuse are revealed via careful external inspection. In fact, routinely proceeding to invasive maneuvers can result in distortion or actual destruction of critical physical evidence.

The use of the colposcope, both with and without photographic capabilities, has come to enjoy widespread acceptance by specialists. The magnification can be very helpful in making determinations about the condition of the tissue examined. Some jurisdictions go so far as to *require* colposcopic documentation of the sexual abuse examination. However, Muram demonstrated that, in many cases, the instrument adds little to the capabilities of the trained examiner's naked eye (15).

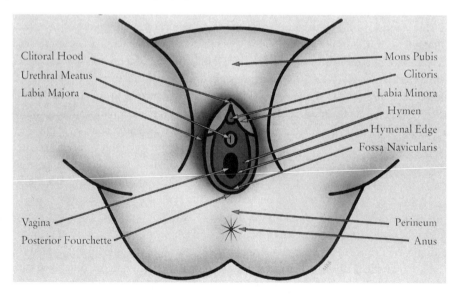

13.1 Female genital anatomy. (With thanks to Maya Bunik, M.D., for the original drawing, which was subsequently modified by computer.)

13.2 Supine frog-leg position for genital examination. (Reprinted from "Pre-pubertal Female Genitalia: Examination for Evidence of Sexual Abuse," in *Pediatrics* 80, no. 2 [1987]: 204–5, with permission of the author, Marcia Herman-Giddens, B.H.S., P.A., M.P.H., and the editors of *Pediatrics*.)

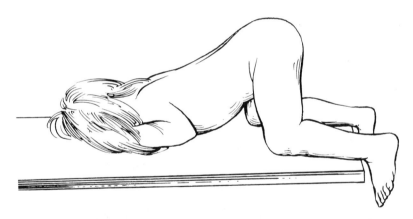

13.3 Knee-chest position for genital and anal examination. (Reprinted from "Prepubertal Female Genitalia: Examination for Evidence of Sexual Abuse," in *Pediatrics* 80, no. 2 [1987]: 204–5, with permission of the author, Marcia Herman-Giddens, B.H.S., P.A., M.P.H., and the editors of *Pediatrics*.)

Easily incorporated into the general medical examination routine are the positions and techniques suggested by McCann, Emans, Heger, and others (16–18). With the upper body clothed or gowned and with the pelvic area draped, the child can lie fairly comfortably in the supine frog-leg position. Most findings can be identified with the child in this position. However, the knee-chest position utilizes gravity to provide another view of the child's genitals. Confusing presentations noted with the child in supine position can become suddenly clarified when the child is reexamined in the knee-chest position (19) (figs. 13.2, 13.3).

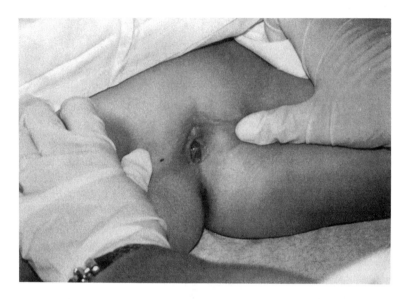

13.4 Demonstration of labial separation technique for female genital examination.

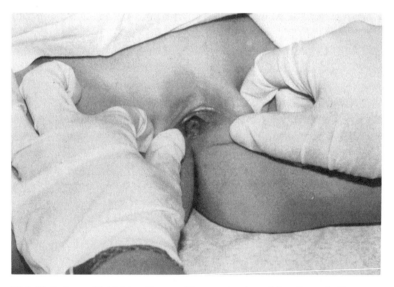

13.5 Technique of labial traction used in examination of female genitalia.

Although it has been routine for clinicians to use labial separation when examining a girl's genital area, the addition of the labial traction technique will greatly enhance the thorough inspection of genital structures. By gently grasping each side of the labia majora between a gloved thumb and index finger in a "pinch" posture and applying slight traction laterally and toward the examiner, the clinician can access a significantly larger field of vision (figs. 13.4, 13.5).

An awareness of the normal variants of hymenal configurations and of the developmental changes expected as the female child matures will greatly aid the clinician in interpreting each patient's anatomy (20–23). Similarly, the examiner must be familiar with the effects of muscle relaxation, traction of surrounding tissues, and body position on the appearance of the hymen and anus (16, 24).

Congenital absence of the hymen is no longer considered a plausible explanation for the lack of hymenal tissue noted on genital inspection of a female (23, 24). Another controversial concept, the significance of the size of the vaginal opening as a determinant of sexual abuse, has generated a great deal of critical review and attention. In her 1983 article, Cantwell gave examiners the first tangible criterion on which to base their opinions about subtle physical evidence of sexual abuse (27): her "4 mm rule" was widely quoted.

But other investigators have proposed broader ranges of "normal." Current thinking is that considerable variation exists in the size of vaginal openings in normal girls. Several factors, including the examination position in which the measurement is taken, the degree of relaxation achieved by the patient, the amount of traction applied to the surrounding tissue, estrogen effect on the hymen, and obesity can influence the measured size of the hymenal orifice. The tables compiled in McCann's studies of nonabused children attest to an upper limit of normal for transverse hymenal diameter, using the labial traction technique with the patient in the supine frog-leg position, as 8 mm for girls ages two to five years, 9 mm for five- to eight-year-olds, and 10.5 mm from age eight to Tanner stage 2 females (28).

It is perhaps of even greater significance that examiners have concluded in the past several years that the size of the opening, rather than being the only example of physical evidence we can measure, is just one characteristic of the hymen that can be described. The thickness and regularity of the hymenal edge, its vascular patterns, and the shape of the hymen—as well as the presence of embryological remnants (such as tags and bands) and possibly normal hymenal attributes (such as small "mounds" and anterior "clefts")—should be observed and commented upon. The width of the hymen from its attachment to supporting structures to its edge should be noted, as significant narrowing may be the result of past penetrating injury. The degree to which intravaginal contents are exposed can also be impacted by trauma to the hymen. Studies of nonabused females have helped immensely by increasing our knowledge of normal patterns that may be compared to findings that result from trauma (28–31).

Other abnormal findings—including tears and scars, bruises or petechiae, and other lesions—should be recognized and their location documented. By using the face of the clock to describe the location of the finding and by mentioning the position the child was assuming when the finding was noted, other examiners can confirm or follow the area of concern. An understanding of the effects of time on various types of injuries will aid the examiner who will be seeing patients at different intervals after their abuse occurred (18, 32).

The structures surrounding the hymen must also be examined and any abnormalities noted. The posterior fourchette and fossa navicularis are frequently damaged in the process of attempted vaginal or intracrural (between the legs or vulvar) intercourse. It is important to look for lacerations, abrasions, and bruising in those sites. Lesions (for example, warts and ulcers) and ecchymoses may also be found on the labia and the perineum; these areas should be carefully inspected.

Examiners should know that unintentional straddle injuries generally result in damage to anterior structures, due to the body's center of gravity and the usual body mechanics in these accidents. Lacerations between the folds of the labia, as well as clitoral and labial swelling and hematomas, are not uncommon. Conversely, the hymen, because of its recessed anatomic position, is well protected from impact other than that of penetrating forces and is not injured in most straddle accidents.

Discovery of varying degrees of labial fusion or adhesions is not uncommon in general pediatric practice. It is thought that the underlying cause for the development of this condition may be a chronic inflammatory process. Recurrent diaper rashes, poor hygiene, and frequent vaginal infections are possible culprits. Sexual abuse may also cause irritating manipulation of those delicate tissues; consequently, this etiology should be considered in patients discovered to have labial fusion (33).

Just as increased attention to the female genital exam has led to better descriptive capabilities and more precise diagnosis of abnormalities in that area, so the information presented in recent studies of normal and abnormal anal findings has improved the examiner's ability to assess the child suspected to have been anally abused (24, 34, 35). Examining clinicians must be familiar with normal anal findings and must recognize the abnormal or questionable observations which make the diagnosis of sexual abuse more likely. It is believed that digital examinations can be avoided, unless absolutely necessary to assess the full extent of damage or to further delineate a medical diagnosis. Even under those circumstances, the introduction of the examining finger should be delayed until careful visual inspection of the anus and perianal tissues is completed and documented. Assessment of the tone, dilatation, and shape of the anal opening may be distorted if made subsequent to digital intrusion by the examiner.

Examination of the anus may be done in the supine, knee-chest, or lateral recumbent position with one or both knees raised. The choice of a particular examination position should be made to maximize the individual's child's comfort, acknowledging his or her embarrassment and keeping in mind that resumption of the stance in which the abuse occurred may trigger significant anxiety or other emotional distress. The examination of boys should include thorough inspection of the penis and scrotum; the clinician should note any signs of trauma or infection and should proceed with laboratory studies and documentation accordingly.

Clinicians who care for sexually abused children must be familiar with current developments on sexually transmitted disease (STD). Broad recommendations for screening victims have been issued by the Centers for Disease Control (36). Knowing the incubation period of the various pathogens, the highest yield tests with which to recover the individual organisms, and the appropriate therapy for each disease can best help tailor the clinician's approach to the sexually abused patient at risk for STDs. Most pertinent for parent counseling—as well as for formulating diagnosis of abuse which can then be acted upon by child protective services and law enforcement agencies—may be the doctor's knowledge of the likelihood of sexual and nonsexual transmission of a particular STD. Tables such as the one published by the American Academy of Pediatrics in "Guidelines for the Evaluation of Sexual Abuse of Children" (37) can be very helpful in making these determinations.

Genital warts have been the topic of much controversy recently, especially regarding the proportion of sexual versus nonsexual etiologies. The discovery that the human papillomavirus is, perhaps, more ubiquitous than previously thought has made the origin of many cases of genital condylomata less clear. However, just as with cases of genital chlamydial infection, trichomoniasis, or herpes, the presence of genital or anal warts must prompt a complete sexual abuse assessment. Nonsexual transmission of these infections, particularly in children beyond infancy, appears to be uncommon. More definitively, when perinatal acquisition is ruled out, gonorrhea or syphilis infections may be considered to be diagnostic for sexual abuse. Likewise, HIV in children without perinatal or other known risk factors must be considered to be a sexually transmitted disease. It may be very helpful for the practitioner to have current references on hand to review when patients with possible STDs present (38–42). Liberal consultation with a specialist in infectious diseases, STDs, or child sexual abuse who keeps up with the rapid developments in the area of pediatric STDs is also recommended.

It is critical to remember that despite the medical profession's aggressive efforts to quantitate and standardize abnormal findings on these examinations, a very significant proportion of sexually abused patients will nonetheless have entirely normal examinations. Even those cases with solid historical evidence, including perpetrators' confessions of penetration, may have no physical findings diagnostic for sexual abuse (4–6).

Perhaps the most important single message for primary care providers is that the best way to assess a child's genital or anal examination is to compare it with other documented examinations performed on the same child. Brief—but adequate—genital inspection should be a routine part of every well-child physical examination. Such practice will provide a baseline documentation of the patient's normal state that may be followed over time. Should allegations of abuse arise or questionable findings be noted subsequently, referral to earlier, well-documented examinations will be invaluable.

At the close of the encounter, some recognition by the examiner of the impact of the examination on the patient is important. Praising or thanking the child for the good job she or he did in talking with the practitioner and cooperating with the exam is an option (however, reinforcement about specific content should be avoided). Informing the child about her or his physical findings and emphasizing normality may be very valuable, as children often fear that they have been permanently and recognizably marred. Some clinicians tell children that they did the right thing by coming forward with information about inappropriate touching. It can be reinforced to the child that any abuse that was disclosed was not his or her fault. It may also be helpful to ask the patient what she or he would do if such a thing ever happens again and then reinforce that the child should tell a trusted adult. With some older children and teens, issues of future voluntary sexual activity, as well as some of the labels which they may encounter (such as "ruined," "used goods," or no longer a "virgin"), may be compassionately addressed.

The practitioner may be tempted to reassure the child that she or he is safe now that she or he has come forward and to guarantee that the abuse will not recur. In reality, it is frustrating, but true, that health professionals have little or no control over the outcome in most cases of child sexual abuse. It is best not to make promises to the child victim that cannot be kept; the examiner can empathize with the patient and let him or her know both that the information gathered will be communicated to those who make determinations and that the clinician will advocate for protection of the child from further abuse. It is wise to leave a door open for further disclosures by letting the child know that if he or she thinks of anything else, or if something more happens in the future, the care provider is quite willing to talk with him or her again.

Discussing findings with the parents and offering support to them is also a necessary step in this process. It is important to let children know what will be communicated to the parents and to gain their permission, if possible. Any resistance to informing their caretakers should be noted and explored. In the circumstance in which a child names an accompanying adult as a possible perpetrator, emergency assistance from child protective services and/or law enforcement should be sought before confronting the adult or releasing the child into a potentially unsafe environment.

Parental permission for release of information should be obtained, as necessary, and copies of the medical report should be made available to all involved agencies. In addition, the practitioner should assess the child's and the family's emotional state and suggest therapy or other support measures for all who need it. The stress of sexual abuse, suspected or confirmed, may affect all family members—accordingly, the potential benefits of early counseling intervention cannot be overemphasized.

The health care provider who accepts the challenges of evaluating suspected victims of child sexual abuse plays a critical role in the child protection system. Relying upon the basic skills of history taking and observation, the clinician can access information unavailable to any of the other professionals involved. Also unique to the health care provider is the comprehensive approach to problem solving that is derived from the medical model. The consideration of historical, social, behavioral, and emotional aspects, as well as the physical findings on each patient, leads to the development of diagnostic opinions and recommendations. These routine "assessment" and "plan" components of the medical report form the basis of an "expert opinion," which can be very useful to professionals in other fields who make placement, therapeutic, and prosecutorial decisions. Pediatric medical practitioners doing what they do best can make significant contributions to the evaluation of sexually maltreated children.

References

1. Kempe, C. H. 1978. Sexual Abuse, Another Hidden Pediatric Problem. *Pediatrics* 62:382–89.
2. Wiese, D., and Daro, D. 1995. *Current Trends in Child Abuse Reporting and Fatalities: The Results of the 1994 Annual Fifty State Survey.* Chicago: National Committee to Prevent Child Abuse.
3. Sgroi, S. M. 1982. *Handbook of Clinical Intervention in Child Sexual Abuse.* Lexington, Mass.: Lexington Books.

4. Bays, J., and Chadwick, D. 1993. Medical Diagnosis of the Sexually Abused Child. *Child Abuse and Neglect: International J.* 17:91–110.

5. Muram, D. 1989. Child Sexual Abuse: Relationship between Sexual Acts and Genital Findings. *Child Abuse and Neglect: International J.* 13:211–16.

6. DeJong, A. R., and Rose, M. 1991. Legal Proof of Child Sexual Abuse in the Absence of Physical Evidence. *Pediatrics* 88 (3):506–11.

7. Kerns, D. L., and Ritter, M. L. 1992. Medical Findings in Child Sexual Abuse Cases with Perpetrator Confession (Abstract). *Am. J. Diseases of Children* 146:494.

8. Adams, J. A. 1994. Examination Findings in Legally Confirmed Child Sexual Abuse: It's Normal to Be Normal. *Pediatrics* 94 (3):310–17.

9. Jones, D. P. H. 1992. *Interviewing the Sexually Abused Child: Investigation of Suspected Abuse.* London: Gaskell.

10. Myers, J. E. 1986. The Role of the Physician in Preserving Verbal Evidence of Child Abuse. *J. Pediatrics* 109:409–11.

11. Sorensen, T., and Snow, B. How Children Tell: The Process of Disclosure in Child Sexual Abuse. *Child Welfare* 70 (1):3–14.

12. Walker, A. G. 1994. *Handbook on Questioning Children—A Linguistic Perspective.* Washington, D.C.: American Bar Association Center on Children and the Law.

13. Everson, M. D., and Boat, B. W. 1988. Use of Anatomic Dolls among Professionals in Sexual Abuse Evaluation. *Child Abuse and Neglect: International J.* 12:171–80.

14. Task Force on the Use of Anatomical Dolls in Child Sexual Abuse Assessments. 1995. *Practice Guidelines—Use of Anatomical Dolls in Child Sexual Abuse Assessment.* Chicago: APSAC.

15. Muram, D., and Elias, S. 1989. Child Sexual Abuse—Genital Findings in Prepubertal Girls, Part 2: Comparison of Colposcopic and Unaided Examination. *Am. J. Obstetrics and Gynecology* 160:333–35.

16. McCann, J.; Voris, J.; Simon, M.; and Wells, R. 1990. Comparison of Genital Examination Techniques in Prepubertal Girls. *Pediatrics* 85 (2):182–87.

17. Emans, S. J. H., and Goldstein, D. P. 1990. *Pediatric and Adolescent Gynecology,* 3d ed. Boston: Little, Brown.

18. Heger, A., and Emans, S. J. 1992. *Evaluation of the Sexually Abused Child,* ed. S. J. Emans. New York: Oxford University Press.

19. Herman-Giddens, M. E., and Frothingham, T. E. 1987. Prepubertal Female Genitalia: Examination for Evidence of Sexual Abuse. *Pediatrics* 80 (2):203–8.

20. Yordan, E. E., and Yordan, R. A. 1992. The Hymen and Tanner Staging of the Breast. *Adolescent and Pediatric Gynecology* 5:76–79.

21. Pokorny, S. F. 1987. Configuration of the Prepubertal Hymen. *Am. J. Obstetrics and Gynecology* 157 (4):950–56.

22. Berenson, A. B. 1993. Appearance of the Hymen at Birth and One Year of Age: A Longitudinal Study. *Pediatrics* 91 (4):820–25.

23. Berenson, A. B. 1995. A Longitudinal Study of Hymenal Morphology in the First Three Years of Life. *Pediatrics* 95 (4):490–96.

24. McCann, J.; Voris, J.; and Wells, S. M. 1989. Perianal Findings in Prepubertal Children Selected for Nonabuse: A Descriptive Study. *Child Abuse and Neglect: International J.* 13:179–93.

25. Jenny, C.; Kuhns, M. L. D.; and Arakawa, F. 1987. Hymens in Newborn Female Infants. *Pediatrics* 80:399–400.

26. Berenson, A. B.; Heger, A.; and Andrews, S. 1991. Appearance of the Hymen in Newborns. *Pediatrics* 87 (4):458–65.

27. Cantwell, H. B. 1983. Vaginal Inspection as It Relates to Child Sexual Abuse in Girls under Thirteen. *Child Abuse and Neglect: International J.* 7:171–76.

28. McCann, J.; Wells, R.; Simon, M.; and Voris, J. 1990. Genital Findings in Prepubertal Girls Selected for Nonabuse: A Descriptive Study. *Pediatrics* 86 (3):428–39.

29. Berenson, A. B.; Heger, A. H.; Hayes, J. M.; Bailey, R. K.; and Emans, S. J. 1992. Appearance of the Hymen in Prepubertal Girls. *Pediatrics* 89 (3):387–94.

30. Emans, S. J.; Woods, E. R.; Flagg, N. T.; and Freeman, A. 1987. Genital Findings in Sexually Abused, Symptomatic, and Asymptomatic Girls. *Pediatrics* 79 (5):778–85.

31. White, S. T., and Ingram, D. L. 1989. Vaginal Introital Diameter in the Evaluation of Sexual Abuse. *Child Abuse and Neglect: International J.* 13:217–24.

32. McCann, J.; Voris, J.; and Simon, M. 1992. Genital Injuries Resulting from Sexual Abuse: A Longitudinal Study. *Pediatrics* 89 (2):307–17.

33. McCann, J.; Voris, J.; and Simon, M. 1988. Labial Adhesions and Posterior Fourchette Injuries in Childhood Sexual Abuse. *Am. J. Diseases of Children* 142:659–63.

34. Hobbs, C. J., and Wynne, J. M. 1989. Sexual Abuse of English Boys and Girls: The Importance of Anal Examination. *Child Abuse and Neglect: International J.* 13:195–210.

35. Berenson, A. B.; Somma-Garcia, A.; and Barnett, S. 1993. Perianal Findings in Infants Eighteen Months of Age or Younger. *Pediatrics* 91 (4):838–40.

36. Centers for Disease Control. 1993. 1993 Sexually Transmitted Diseases Treatment Guidelines. *MMWR* 42:97–102.

37. American Academy of Pediatrics, Committee on Child Abuse and Neglect. 1991. Guidelines for the Evaluation of Sexual Abuse of Children. *Pediatrics* 87 (2):254–60.

38. DeJong, A. R., and Finkel, M. A. 1990. Sexual Abuse of Children. *Current Problems in Pediatrics* 20(9):495–567.

39. Hammerschlag, M. R. 1988. Sexually Transmitted Diseases in Sexually Abused Children. *Advances in Pediatric Infectious Disease* 3:1–18.

40. Jenny, C. 1992. Sexually Transmitted Diseases and Child Abuse. *Pediatric Annals* 21 (8): 497–503.

41. Paradise, J. E. 1990. The Medical Evaluation of the Sexually Abused Child. *Pediatric Clinics of North America* 37 (4):839–62.

42. Stewart, D. 1992. Sexually Transmitted Diseases. In *Evaluation of the Sexually Abused Child*, ed. S. J. Emans. New York: Oxford University Press.

14

The Sexual Abuser

GAIL RYAN

The perpetrators of the sexual abuse of children have much in common with abusers who batter, berate, and betray children in nonsexual ways. Victimization and trauma, parental loss and disrupted attachments, neglect and deprivation early in life are often apparent in the clinical descriptions of all types of child abusers. The sexual nature of child sexual abuse is perceived as different from physical or emotional abuse for a variety of reasons that have influenced both pervasive beliefs and particular interventions. This chapter will review relevant theories, the nature of the abusive behavior, motivation and deterrence, intervention, multidisciplinary roles, and research and prevention.

Theories of Sexually Abusive Behavior

Beliefs about the nature of child-molesting behaviors have evolved over several decades through a process of validation and correction of theories as clinical knowledge has increased and research has examined various aspects of such abusive behavior. The silence which followed the early discoveries of Tardieu (1) and Freud (2) in the late nineteenth century protected the secret of child molesters until the mid-1970s, when child molestation began to be described as yet another form of child abuse (3, 4). The work of the first therapists who endeavored to treat perpetrators of child sexual abuse described their characteristics in psychodynamic and psychoanalytic terms, which influenced treatment interventions. The earliest systematic differentiation of child sexual abusers viewed the incest perpetrator as a co-participant in a dysfunctional family system (5) and the extrafamilial child molester as a sexual deviant. These distinctions were based on variables such as where the abuse occurred and the relationship of the perpetrator to the victim and had little to do with the pathology of the individual perpetrator.

Groth and his colleagues (6) proposed one of the earliest typological schemes by suggesting the dichotomy of "fixated" and "regressed" pedophiles, recognizing that some individuals had a primary sexual attraction to children while others became sexually involved with children in reaction to some stress in their lives. The dynamic progression between such stressors and sexually abusive behavior began to be described by many cli-

GAIL RYAN, M.A., is senior instructor in the Department of Pediatrics, University of Colorado School of Medicine, and director of the Perpetration Prevention Project at the C. Henry Kempe National Center for the Prevention and Treatment of Child Abuse and Neglect.

nicians and theorists and is well defined today by the "sexual abuse cycle" (7), and the "relapse prevention model" (8–10), which are widely used in clinical work related to all types of sexually abusive behaviors and all ages of abusive individuals. These visual models depict the interaction and progression of situations, thoughts, feelings, and behaviors which commonly precede and follow abusive behaviors. The concept of a sexual assault "cycle" is generally attributed to Lane (11), and the application of relapse prevention concepts to sexual offenders is usually credited to Pithers et al. (12), although it is apparent in the early literature that others were noting similar patterns (13–16).

There is no evidence to suggest that sexual abusers are born abusive; however, there is a great deal of research indicating that sexually abusive behavior is the product of life experiences (see, for instance, 15, 17–22).

The sexual abuse cycle and the relapse prevention model describe precursors to the behavior as it manifests in the functioning of the individual. Other models describe the precursors in the life cycle which help us to understand conditions which may be related to how someone becomes a sexual abuser (see, for instance, 17, 23–28). Most influential in this regard has been Finkelhor and Araji's four-factor model (29), which explores

1. Emotional congruence (reasons why an adult might find it satisfying to relate sexually to a child)
2. Sexual arousal (to children)
3. "Blockage" (factors which prevent success in age-appropriate relationships)
4. Disinhibitors (conditions which interfere with normal inhibitions against sexual activity with a child—that is, stress, substance use, irrational thinking, and so forth)

Motivation

Many sexual abusers experienced victimization themselves as children (physical, sexual, and/or emotional). For those perpetrators who were sexually abused, early offenses sometimes appear to be reenactments of their own victimization. This may be related to defensive mechanisms which attempt to manage intrusive, overwhelming or unresolved memories and emotions from the past (8, 23, 17, 30). Other perpetrators learned the dysfunctional patterns for coping with stress that are evident in their sexual offending from troubled role models in their lives. Many of the compensatory and abusive beliefs which support such patterns are prevalent throughout our culture as well.

It has become clear over time that sexual abusers are first and foremost "abusive" and that their abusive behavior represents their imagined "solution" to a predominant personal dilemma. That dilemma is characterized by a sense of powerlessness, of being unable to manage successfully and control their lives in order to feel competent and safe. Theorists have described sexual offenses as related more to "power" than to sexuality (31–33). It is important to note, however, that it is not the "powerful" who commit such actions. The abuser is the product of vulnerability, of precisely the *lack* of power. The compensatory pattern represented by the abusive cycle (7) is a dysfunctional attempt to achieve a sense of control. The solution—abusive behavior—is dysfunctional because the control it offers is only transitory and is based on an external locus of control; in other words, although the behavior is temporarily fulfilling, it does not effectively resolve the internal issues which are the source of distress.

Perpetrators who from an early age rely exclusively on deviant or abusive sexual behaviors to achieve comfort or relief are at risk to develop a primary sexual interest in these behaviors. Others may have a larger repertoire of compensatory behaviors (for instance, violence and aggression, substance use, eating disorders, risk taking, or self-abuse), and sexually abusive behaviors may occur less frequently in a larger context of more normative sexual interests.

It is usually very apparent from his history how the abuser learned to be abusive. What may be less clear is: (1) why does an individual's abusive pattern take a sexual form? and (2) why do others who appear to have similar life experiences not become sexually abusive? The answers to these questions lie in the etiology of sexually abusive behavior. The search for understanding of the "causes" of this behavior has been conducted along two parallel paths: sexuality and abusiveness. Attempts to understand the developmental course of sexually abusive behavior are ongoing and continue to indicate new directions for both prevention efforts and treatment plans.

Deterrents

The bottom line for the prevention and treatment of child sexual abuse is deterrence. By conceptualizing a continuum of deterrents, a range of prevention and intervention strategies can be defined.

The lowest levels of deterrence are external restraints. For the identified perpetrator, jail is the most certain deterrent, though not often viewed as a permanent option. Variations of restraint are provided by such interventions as termination of familial relationships, "no contact" orders, supervised visitation and probation, and parole supervision, including electronic monitoring. Such interventions address the perpetrators' proximity to past or potential victims and limit access and opportunity. Pain and punishment are only slightly higher levels of deterrence, but although many behaviors are deterred by the threat or experience of pain or punishment, sexual behaviors which the perpetrator perceives as pleasurable and secret do not yield easily to the threatened consequences of discovery by the criminal justice system.

Negative consequences and the negative associations which arise from them may be perceptual or real. Shame and embarrassment; estrangement from family, friends, and past victims; arrest and legal action; and negative self-attributions may delay or deter some behavior, but they also ultimately support the poor self-image, negative expectations, and victim stance of the perpetrator, thus increasing rather than decreasing the drive for compensatory behaviors. Furthermore, such negative inhibitors are ultimately dependent upon judgments from outside the individual and do not represent any internalized sense of control. The taboo against sexually abusive behavior is a cultural value.

Positive associations and the rewards of avoiding abusive behaviors move into the higher range of deterrents. For identified abusers, the rewards of abstinence may result in reductions of the negative deterrents previously described: return to the community, reunification with family members, and increased freedom. Positive associations may come from improved esteem, within the family or community, the growth of pride in self and others, and an increased sense of control over the emotional triggers, cognitions, and sexual urges. Higher levels of positive associations may be the rewards of perceived morality or righteousness and increased self-esteem. The social taboo thereby becomes an internalized personal value.

All of these deterrents are related to the perpetrator's needs and concerns and, to a great extent, place the responsibility for deterrence on an external locus of control. The highest levels of deterrence will be altruistic and relational, focused on the harm done to the victim. The abuser's appreciation of the harm he has caused has been blocked by objectifying or depersonalizing the victim, by distortions and rationalizations, and by the perpetrator's concentration on his own needs, which have taken precedence over the needs of others. Sympathy may deter abusive behavior if the perpetrators perceive that they would not enjoy or would be distressed by their sexually abusive behavior if they themselves were in the victim's position. Sympathy breaks down, however, when the offender's distortions support the belief that the victim does in fact enjoy the behavior and is benefited by it or when the perpetrators' motivation is to recreate the pain of their own victimization in order to make another share that pain (that is, "misery loves company"). Sympathy is based on an assumption of sameness (34)—that others will perceive and experience situations and interactions the same as oneself.

A higher level of deterrence results from empathy, the ability to recognize the cues of others which indicate what they are needing or experiencing, even when those needs and experiences are different from one's own. The lack of empathy (failure to perceive harm to the victim) and lack of accountability (avoidance of accurate attributions of personal responsibility) are ultimately the most significant deficits of all abusers. Empathic foresight (the ability to imagine the impact of one's behavior on another before making a decision to act) and personal accountability are the highest deterrents to abusive actions. The individual who fantasizes an abusive behavior but perceives the harmfulness of that behavior and feels personally responsible for the behavior is deterred by internal processes.

Interventions

Finkelhor (35) also described four preconditions which must be met in order for child sexual abuse to occur at any point in time:

1. Sexual arousal to the child (or to children in general)
2. Ability to overcome internal inhibitions
3. Ability to overcome external obstacles
4. Ability to overcome the resistance or avoidance of the child

This model has guided development of strategies for prevention and intervention and has supported an integrated approach which draws on cognitive, behavioral, and developmental theories.

Behavioral theory has guided research and treatment interventions relevant to the first condition: sexual arousal. The sexual arousal associated with sexually abusive behavior poses a particularly troublesome risk, best understood in relation to theories of learning and behavioral conditioning. Because of the powerful reinforcers intrinsic to all sexual behavior (intimacy, arousal, orgasm, and/or tension reduction), sexual behaviors tend to progress over time and to resist abstinence or change. In this respect, sexually abusive patterns of behavior are learned and reinforced in the same manner as any other sexual behavior. Once learned and engaged in, the behavior is likely to continue.

Behavioral research, by using plethysmographic measurement of sexual arousal patterns, has enabled researchers to study sexual preference and changes in arousal patterns resulting from treatment interventions (see, for instance, 36–39). Covert sensitization, masturbatory conditioning, and arousal reconditioning are techniques designed to directly impact the arousal which reinforces the behavior. Treatment of the sexual aspects of the offender's abusive pattern is particularly intrusive: the psychological discomfort and embarrassment contribute to resistance to treatment.

Inspired by the work of Yochelson and Samenow (40), cognitive interventions address the thoughts and beliefs which enable and support offending. The cognitive aspects of the abuser's pattern of offending are referred to as "distortions" or "thinking errors" (41–44). The thoughts which allow the abuser to override internal inhibitions and to rationalize violation of the cultural taboos against his or her sexual involvement with children are products of the offender's unique "view of the world," created by defense mechanisms which attempt to integrate deviance into an acceptable self-image.

Cognitive restructuring draws on theories from rational-emotive therapies, which postulate that emotional responses are products of one's thoughts; it challenges sexual perpetrators to change their beliefs about themselves and their behavior, as well as their beliefs about the world and relationships. Any challenge to such beliefs is perceived by the abusers as an attack on themselves (and, actually, it is an affront to the defensive structures which protect their sense of self), and the vulnerability evoked in such interventions increases defensiveness and resistance in the treatment setting. Such resistance impedes the therapeutic relationship; consequently, therapists must move slowly and patiently toward change, inviting participation (45) and creating a sense of "psychological safety" (46) which will enable growth and change (47).

The affective aspects of the abusive pattern include the vulnerable emotions which trigger the perpetrator's abuse cycle and which may bring up a flood of unresolved issues associated with past experiences of abuse, trauma, loss, or other intolerable feelings (23). Clinical interventions which address these emotions include more traditional psychodynamic approaches to access, express, and validate emotions which have been overwhelming and which the compensatory pattern has defended against. Trauma processing (48, 49) revisits memories of overwhelming life experiences in order to resolve feelings of helplessness and achieve a sense of affective control. Anger management and anxiety reduction techniques address other emotional components.

As perpetrators become more able to tolerate and express vulnerable emotions, they begin to recognize physical, affective, and behavioral cues within themselves and thus become able to recognize the cues of others. This, in turn, enables them to apply empathy and empathic foresight in interactions. Also, the therapist's accurate attributions of responsibility in relation to the perpetrator's own childhood experiences and validation of harm increase the perpetrator's accountability to and empathy for the victims of his subsequent abusive behavior.

The perpetrator's sense of vulnerability is directly related to a lack of developmental competence; accordingly, the psychoeducational components of treatment work to develop the skills and knowledge which support more adequate functioning. Social skills training and relationship skills, sex education, parenting skills, and assertiveness training may all be covered, through a program of didactic modules.

Multidisciplinary Roles

A broad, multidisciplinary range of interventions is necessary to identify and treat the perpetrators of sexual abuse successfully. Identification requires training potential reporters and investigators to define clearly what constitutes sexual abuse and to recognize any signs which warrant suspicion that a child has been abused. Child protective services and law enforcement agencies respond to reports of child abuse in order to protect child victims, restrain the alleged perpetrator, and conduct an investigation of the situation, which may include the collecting of evidence for court proceedings. The involvement of law enforcement and the courts conveys a message to the perpetrator about the seriousness of abusive acts and the illegal nature of such offenses. The observance of accountability to the law conveys an important message to victims as well regarding the accurate attribution of responsibility to the perpetrator. In those cases in which a finding of guilt is reached by the court (whether by admission or in spite of denial), an evaluation of the perpetrator is performed in order to determine what disposition of the case should be recommended. An extensive clinical assessment evaluates the risk posed to the community, the perpetrator's amenability to treatment, and the treatment options available (50, 8, 51). At the same time, probation personnel make recommendations regarding their ability to provide community-based supervision, and child protective service workers evaluate the safety and needs of intrafamilial victims (52).

The clinical assessment gathers information from many sources and may utilize a wide variety of assessment tools. Many different models have been proposed for assessments of risk and of treatment needs. Salter (51) describes the use of a wide range of inventories and scales to measure the perpetrator's sexual attitudes and interests, degree of empathy, locus of control, social attitudes, and so forth. Carich and Adkerson (53) provide structure for a comprehensive clinical interview as well as forms for many of the measures described by Salter (51). Ross and Loss (54) and Gray and Wallace (55) similarly address the assessment of adolescent offenders.

Initial risk assessments consider factors such as history of abusive behaviors (that is, frequency; victim access, selection, and grooming; levels of coercion; intrusiveness of behavior), current stressors (for instance, social, familial, marital, economic), current inhibitors (that is, supervision and external restraints), and current disinhibitors (such as substance use or depression). Risk assessments at the end of treatment consider observable demonstrations of changed functioning as well as stressors and supportive relationships (56). In general, abusers are at the lowest risk of committing another offense during the period immediately following arrest due to the anxiety and aversive experience of the disclosure and the legal process. These risk-lowering effects diminish within months, and risk subsequently fluctuates in relation to internal and external management of risk factors. Supervision can impact access and opportunity for reoffense and can sometimes recognize and address lapses into the dysfunctional pattern.

Initial assessments provide recommendations to the court, to help it make informed decisions about placement and treatment prognosis, child protection, supervision, and risk to the community. The court orders may include punitive measures, such as incarceration or community service, as well as fines for victim restitution and/or orders mandating that the abuser participate in treatment. Davidson (57) speaks to the importance of the court's role in the management of these cases (see also chapter 22), and Wheeler (58) demonstrated significant improvements in treatment compliance when the legal system provided a consistent response.

Therapists appreciate the court's assumption of responsibility for coercing perpetrators' participation in treatment; when this coercion is the role of the court, it reduces the coercive aspect in the therapeutic relationship. Nonetheless, the unique conditions of the treatment relationship include:

1. The external mandate for treatment, which constitutes a "lack of consent"
2. The imbalance of power in the therapy relationship
3. The *coercion* associated with the threatened consequences of noncompliance

Since these conditions describe exactly those elements present in abusive interactions (59), it is not surprising that the perpetrator perceives the treatment process as abusive and feels victimized by the system.

The therapeutic relationship is further influenced by

1. The therapists' advocacy and concern for the safety of the victims, which takes precedence over the needs of their client
2. The lack of confidentiality, which enables the therapist to communicate openly with the court and others regarding the client's participation and progress in treatment
3. The lack of trust, which is rational and necessary, considering the circumstances, for both the therapist and the client
4. The directive and confrontive style, which is necessary for addressing issues that the client may not willingly pursue

All of these factors contribute to the client's resistance and reluctance during the treatment process.

Probation or parole orders include the conditions which the abuser must observe and comply with in the community. Intense monitoring and restrictions which reduce or prohibit access to past and potential victims are best enforced by specially trained probation officers who understand the abusers' patterns and risk factors. Relapse prevention models extend external sources of monitoring beyond the end of treatment to support the abusers' continued compliance with treatment goals and safety plans.

Program Design

Across the continuum of prevention and treatment strategies, "abusive" interactions are consistently defined by three factors: (1) lack of consent, (2) lack of equality, and (3) coercion (or pressure). The goal of treatment is, initially, to promote communication, empathy, and accountability. To successfully complete treatment, individuals must become able to:

1. Consistently define abusive behavior
2. Recognize and avoid patterns associated with the risk of abusive behaviors
3. Develop functional options or solutions for stress management
4. Resolve issues related to past victimization
5. Demonstrate empathic interaction and foresight
6. Demonstrate changed internal and interpersonal functioning

Individuals who achieve these goals in treatment at least have the option—attendant upon the skills they have acquired—to avoid further abusive behaviors if they so choose.

Treatment programs tend to be eclectic in design. Using the cycle of abuse and relapse as a framework for considering the cognitive, behavioral, and affective components of the abusive pattern (see fig. 14.1), treatment can address each component directly via the interventions described above. For example, the triggers—helplessness, anger, and anxiety—are emotional elements which benefit from the affective interventions. Defusing the emotional triggers reduces the risk of reoccurrence of abusive behavior by helping the abuser manage his emotions more effectively. The thoughts, distortions, and rationalizations which are characteristic of the hopelessness, the fantasized solution, and the decision to act on the plan are confronted by therapists and peers in group counseling. Isolative behaviors, angry control seeking, and abusive behaviors of all types are defined and addressed through aversive conditioning and behavior modification. Relapse prevention is based on the client's recognition of the pattern and attainment of competence and accountability in interrupting the chain of events by choosing more functional coping strategies.

Associating the parts of the cycle with the face of a clock, the pattern begins at 12:00 when some situation triggers the sensitive emotion. The individual's sense of safety is jeopardized by the stress, and his or her affective response is disproportionate to the realities of the situation: this contributes to a perception of helplessness. The hopelessness is a reflection of poor self-esteem, which is the product of repeated failures over the course of a lifetime. The individual's outrage at feeling victimized by his or her perception of life circumstances is defended against by angry defensive posturing. In a desperate search for some immediate solution which will gratify a personal sense of entitlement, the compensatory fantasies begin. As long as abusers are able to believe that sexual abuse is an acceptable solution, they remain at high risk for relapse. Successfully treated abusers should begin to experience an "abstinence violation effect" as soon as the thought of offending

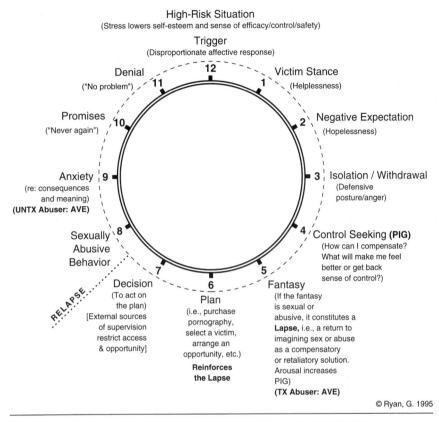

High-Risk Situation
(Stress lowers self-esteem and sense of efficacy/control/safety)

Trigger
(Disproportionate affective response)

Denial **12** Victim Stance
("No problem") **11** **1** (Helplessness)

Promises **10** **2** Negative Expectation
("Never again") (Hopelessness)

Anxiety **9** **3** Isolation / Withdrawal
(re: consequences (Defensive
and meaning) posture/anger)
(UNTX Abuser: AVE)

Sexually **8** **4** Control Seeking **(PIG)**
Abusive (How can I compensate?
Behavior What will make me feel
better or get back
7 **5** sense of control?)

Decision **6** Fantasy
(To act on Plan (If the fantasy
the plan) (i.e., purchase is sexual or
RELAPSE [External sources pornography, abusive, it constitutes a
of supervision select a victim, **Lapse,** i.e., a return to
restrict access arrange an imagining sex or abuse
& opportunity] opportunity, etc.) as a compensatory
or retaliatory solution.
Reinforces Arousal increases
the Lapse PIG)
(TX Abuser: AVE)

© Ryan, G. 1995

Note: Bold type refers to relapse-prevention terms (91, 12). Regular type refers to cycle terminology (7).
PIG: Problem of Immediate Gratification **AVE:** Abstinence Violation Effect **TX:** Treated **UNTX:** Untreated

14.1 Process represented by "cycle of abuse" and "relapse prevention" models.

occurs to them, because they have made a commitment to change and such thoughts are no longer congruent with their sense of self. The swirl of abusive fantasies has an aversive rather than gratifying effect—whereas prior to treatment, the abuser did not experience that anxiety and sense of dissonance until after the offense occurred. The successfully treated offender is able to recognize the danger of relapse and, in response, uses newly acquired skills to manage emotional stress more effectively.

Treatment is long-term, requiring one or more group sessions per week over many months (or sometimes years), facilitated by specialists experienced in the treatment of sexual abusers. Group treatment is the primary mode because it enables the therapists to observe patterns of interaction and allows the group members to challenge each other to change. Individual and/or family therapies are frequent adjuncts, addressing current and historical situations and relationships. Because the triggers occur in situations which are reminiscent of early life experiences, the client's history and family of origin are very relevant in the treatment process. Pharmacological interventions may be indicated when concurrent psychiatric disorders must be managed. Relapse prevention plans and after-care monitoring and support translate changes made during treatment into better future functioning.

In incest cases, issues relevant to decisions about family reunification, which may include redefinition of family relationships, are addressed and treated through marital counseling, victim/offender dyads, and family therapies. Some incest perpetrators become able to return home, others have only supervised contact with family members, and some require complete termination of those relationships.

With successful treatment, the individual's increased competency and self-esteem combine with a specific, personal recognition of the harmfulness of abusive behavior. The individual becomes less able to justify or rationalize abusive behavior, because it is no longer congruent with his or her self-image. Consequently, thoughts and fantasies of sexually abusive behavior become a threat to personal integrity—this is the abstinence violation effect referred to earlier in the discussion of figure 14.1.

The unusual conditions under which abusers arrive in treatment and the unique characteristics of the therapeutic relationship require particular patience from therapists if they are to overcome the abuser's distrust and facilitate real change. Heavy confrontation and shaming are counterproductive, increasing defensiveness and poor self-image. Jenkins (45) describes the therapist's role in inviting the abuser to become responsible, respecting the abuser's need for improved self-esteem. By acknowledging that the dysfunctional cycle has had some utility to the abuser in managing past experiences, the therapist both respects developmental realities and encourages the attainment of higher levels of personal competence (59). The difficulties of beginning a therapeutic relationship in the absence of trust (59) requires use of self (60) and the therapist's willingness to struggle with the clients to create a psychologically safe environment in the treatment setting. The abuser's experience of empathy and safety in a functional therapeutic relationship becomes the basis for better relationships and empathic interactions in the future.

Current Research

Research continues to explore and discover new insights into prevention and intervention. While early research focused a great deal on the "sexual" aspects of sexually abusive behavior and the stimuli and fantasies associated with deviant sexual arousal (41, 8), current research is demonstrating a much greater interest in the "abusive" aspects of the behavior and in risk factors related to the development of the abusive individual over the life span (61). Such research promises to bring new depth to our understanding and may inspire even more effective and lasting interventions.

The application of attachment disorder theories to the interpersonal dysfunction of the sexual abuser is one example (62) (see also chapter 5). Adult attachment styles affect intimacy and loneliness—important dynamics in the sexual perpetrator's relationships (28, 63). Attachment disorders in childhood development are the product of disrupted, abusive, or inconsistent caregiving relationships, which become the "internal working model" for future relationships (64). Several researchers are exploring differences in the patterns of offending associated with various disordered styles of attachment. These disordered styles significantly hamper an individual's ability to achieve and maintain the healthy relationships that provide the sense of intimacy and belongingness which human beings strive to achieve. Whereas competent and secure attachments create trust in oneself, other people, and the world in general, the absence of trust is recognized as a major issue for abusive individuals.

Empathy is another focus of current research, and it has become apparent that there is some confusion and controversy about the construct itself. Theorists suggest that empathy is both a cognitive construct and an affective one. Research by Beckett and Fisher (65) has prompted questions regarding the abuser's general empathic skills as opposed to object-specific empathy: Can an abuser appear empathic on systematic measures for empathy (such as the Davis Interpersonal Reactivity Index [66]) yet be unempathic toward a particular child or children with particular characteristics? "Victim empathy" enhancement exercises have been an almost universal component in specialized treatment programs, aimed at impressing upon the abuser the pain or distress of past victims of sexual abuse. Although the abuser's cognitive distortions, which inhibit recognition of expressions of distress in his victims, are challenged in treatment and the abuser's cognitive deficits in empathy are addressed in didactic interventions, it is unclear how much clinicians have concentrated on the active development of "empathic recognition" of the cues which enable any individual to interpret one's own and others' affective experiences in daily interactions.

Some of the confusion about the construct of empathy must be resolved by defining "empathic experience" (having one's cues validated by empathic responses), "empathic interaction" (two parties reading and responding to each other's cues in a reciprocal process), and "empathic foresight" (imagining what another's affective experience will be) (67). Cognitive measures of empathic skills may illuminate one aspect of empathy but not account for the situational and affective variables associated with the distortion or inhibition of empathic interaction and/or foresight.

The experience of "empathic care" in the first two years of life is the basis for the natural development of empathy (18, 26) (see also chapter 5). The growing appreciation of the critical role of early life experience and developmental competence has important implications for prevention research as well as remedial efforts. Fisher and Howells's research (68) has also suggested important distinctions between measuring social "skills" and the qualities of social "relationships." Such distinctions may lead to more meaningful assessment and treatment applications.

Neurological functioning has become an area of interest for researchers, especially since the publicizing of significant neurological findings relevant to "post-traumatic stress disorder" and other psychiatric symptomology. Discoveries that neurochemical levels and neurological pathways change after traumatic experiences (69) open intriguing new ways of understanding more deeply the relationship between victimization and subsequent neurological functioning (70, 71). Similarly, advances in knowledge about neurochemical interactions related to the biology of some affective disorders further illuminate the compensatory function that drives the abusive cycle (72). For example, the individual who is chronically anxious or depressed may be at an increased risk to seek compensatory solutions. Research which relates to the neurochemical reinforcement of sexual aggression may be as significant as the earlier research on physiological reinforcement of arousal patterns. Pharmacological interventions which affect chronic neurochemical imbalances and/or acute neurochemical responses may enhance treatment prognosis for a significant portion of abusers.

Research continues on methods of validating and improving risk assessments, such as Prentky et al. (73) "Taxonomic System for Classifying Child Molesters," the PHASE typology (74), and others. Whereas research efforts focused on single physiological or psychological factors have failed to predict adequately either the development or recidivism of sexually abusive behaviors, multifactor models appear very promising, particularly in terms of their specific applicability to decisions about prevention, risk management, and legal interventions.

Quinsey (56) describes an actuarial model which identifies several variables associated with higher rates of recidivism: various early life experiences, psychopathy (75), characteristics of past offending, and personality disorders. Although the "unchangeable" nature of these risk factors is discouraging in terms of treatment prognosis, community safety may be significantly improved by more well-informed decisions and by more realistic management and relapse prevention strategies for the most high-risk abusers and those most resistant to change. At the same time, however, it must be said that treatment resources may be more cost effectively invested in what *is* changeable.

Another promising development is the new Abel Assessment (76), which has been introduced as a screening process for identifying risk without relying on the inclusion of plethysmographic arousal assessments. The Abel Assessment utilizes self-report of sexual interest in response to 160 slides depicting 22 content areas. Particularly in relation to preemployment screening, this promises to enhance child protection and risk management significantly for child-serving organizations if preliminary findings can be replicated by other researchers.

Yet another area of current research involves the validation of interactional assessments as a means of identifying the abuser in cases of child sexual abuse that defy existing investigatory methods. Whereas the child protection field has invested heavily in research to validate the reliability of children's statements as a means of identifying and prosecuting the perpetrators of sexual abuse (77), The Kempe International Assessment (78) addresses the need to identify abusive relationships in those cases in which the child is unable to verbally describe his or her experience. The notion that the nature of the abuser's pattern is observable is congruent with current theory on the abuser's cycle (7) and predictive variables (76).

Research on the effectiveness of the treatment of sexual abusers is pursuing two avenues of interest: treatment integrity (Are treatment providers actually doing what is described as treatment interventions, and, if so, can the intervention and its immediate effects be measured?) and recidivism (Are abusers continuing to abuse after treatment, and, if so, are the rates of occurrences or the nature of the offenses changed by the treatment?). It must be recognized that abusers probably fall into three categories:

1. Some who may discontinue abusing either temporarily or permanently without external interventions
2. Many who can become less likely to continue to abuse because they benefit from treatment interventions
3. Some who are likely to continue indefinitely despite all interventions

However, although research has already contributed to this understanding, differential diagnosis does not yet adequately distinguish the three groups. Current research is addressing the need for differential diagnosis and treatment of abusers in order to improve prediction, prevention, intervention, and long-term management.

Perpetration Prevention

Sexual abuse prevention strategies have usually focused on preventing victimization. Children have been taught to "resist and report" when someone attempts to molest them, and adults have been taught to reduce the access and opportunity of child molesters by screening and monitoring people who are in positions of authority with children. These strategies have placed the responsibility for protecting children from sexual abuse on children themselves and on their caregivers. Such strategies are appropriate and necessary; however, they constitute secondary levels of prevention, based on the fact that children are "at risk" for sexual victimization. The primary prevention of sexual abuse lies in preventing individuals from attempting to molest children in the first place—perpetration prevention.

The prosecution and treatment of sexual abusers constitutes a tertiary level of perpetration prevention, attempting to prevent additional victimization. At this level, the maximum benefit lies in identifying abusers early in their "careers" so they will have fewer victims. This strategy has gained significant support in programs to identify and treat sexually abusive youth (79).

Clinicians and researchers have described the high rates of offending by perpetrators who began offending as juveniles and continued the behavior over several decades (21, 24, 30). If it is possible to identify such offenders when they first begin to be abusive, the potential for prevention is much greater than if they are not identified until they are adults. Clinically, the prognosis in treating younger perpetrators appears better as well, due to the developmental flexibility of children and adolescents and the less habituated nature of their sexually abusive behavior.

In only one decade, programs in the United States offering specialized treatment for sexually abusive adolescents increased from only twenty (80) to over seven hundred (81). Most recently, the definition of sexually abusive behavior among children has led to development of over three hundred treatment programs for prepubescent youth. The realization that even very young children may manifest sexually abusive behavior (82–84) initially met with some resistance and disbelief. However, clearer definitions of abusive interactions and the self-reports of older perpetrators in response to questions about their childhood sexual activities have increased awareness that sexually abusive behavior does not suddenly appear in older adolescents or adults but, rather, develops over time (15, 85, 86).

Many of the theories about the etiology of sexually abusive behavior point to early life experience as the source of deviant influences and developmental deficits and failures. By describing childhood risk factors, it becomes possible to identify some groups of children who may be at an increased risk of developing sexually abusive patterns of behavior. Children who experience sexual abuse constitute such an "at risk" group (87, 88), and children experiencing inconsistent, abusive, or unempathic care, parental loss or betrayal, and neurological or developmental dysfunctions may represent another "high risk" population. Such children are identified in mental health and victim counseling programs, as well as in special education and out-of-home care settings. By addressing the risk of dysfunctional defensive and/or compensatory patterns becoming abusive, it may be possible to decrease the development of offending. This constitutes a secondary level of perpetration prevention (23, 59, 89). By applying preventive and corrective concepts to the dynamics associated with the abusive pattern, it is possible that "at risk" children may be helped to avoid dysfunctional outcomes and that, as a result, a new generation of child molesters may be preempted.

Ultimately, the primary prevention of perpetration must address the risk that any child in the general population may learn and manifest sexually abusive behavior once or occasionally and, because of the powerful reinforcers associated with sexual behaviors, such behavior might continue. As in all areas of child development, adults must be prepared to validate and correct what the child is learning by clearly defining what constitutes "abusive" behavior and clarifying goals for nonabusive sexual development. Primary perpetration prevention training was introduced for educators and paraprofessional caregivers in 1988 (85); those concepts are now included in information about childhood sexuality for parents (90). If children can receive pertinent guidance and support in relation to their sexual development, the incidence and prevalence of child sexual abuse may begin to decline.

Conclusion

There is wide acceptance in the field of the belief that every individual who has been sexually abusive in the past must be viewed as "at risk" for abusive acts in the future. Treatment is *not* a "cure"—rather, it provides new understanding, options, and motivation for the individual to manage that risk and avoid further abusive behavior. For some, the risk remains high despite vigorous interventions, even when the individual is motivated to change, due to the habituated nature of the pattern and/or a persistent sexual arousal to children. For others, the risk may be significantly moderated by the treatment process and their own commitment to changes in lifestyle. Relapse prevention plans must consider the individual's level of risk in order to provide appropriate deterrents. Aftercare may include ongoing supervision and restrictions imposed by the family or the court, as well as continued therapeutic supports.

Treatment of abusers is not an act of compassion in and of itself, and yet its goal must be to model compassionate behavior (9). The community's abhorrence of sexually abusive behavior is fueling more punitive responses, and treatment is available for only a minority of adult sexual offenders. Effective interventions must be both therapeutic and correctional, the therapist and the court exercising both empathy and accountability. Even so, treatment is only a defensive strategy after victimization has occurred. Preventive intervention in the care of infants and children is the key to prevention for all types of abusive behavior.

References

1. Tardieu, A. 1878. *Etude médico-légale surges attentat aux Maoris.* Paris.
2. Freud, S. 1896. The Aetiology of Hysteria. Qtd. in *The Assault on Truth: Freud's Suppression of the Seduction Theory,* by J. M. Masson. (New York: Penguin Books, 1985).
3. Kempe, C. H. 1978. Sexual Abuse, Another Hidden Pediatric Problem. *Pediatrics* 62:382–89.
4. Meiselman, K. 1978. *Incest.* San Francisco: Jossey-Bass.
5. Giarretto, H. 1981. A Comprehensive Child Sexual Abuse Treatment Program. In *Sexually Abused Children and Their Families,* ed. P. Mrazek and C. H. Kempe. Oxford: Pergamon Press.
6. Groth, N., and Birnbaum, H. 1978. Adult Sexual Orientation and Attraction to Underage Persons. *Archives of Sexual Behavior* 7:175–81.
7. Lane, S. 1991. The Sexual Abuse Cycle. In *Juvenile Sexual Offending: Causes, Consequences, and Correction,* ed. G. Ryan and S. Lane. Lexington, Mass.: Lexington Books.
8. Marshall, W.; Laws, D.; and Barbaree, H. 1990. *Handbook of Sexual Assault.* New York: Plenum Press.
9. Freeman-Longo, R. E., and Bays, K. 1988–1990. Sex Offender Study Series. Orwell, Vt.: Safer Society Press.
10. Gray, A., and Pithers, W. 1994. Relapse Prevention with Sexually Aggressive Adolescents and Children: Expanding Treatment and Supervision. In *The Juvenile Sex Offender,* ed. W. Marshall and S. Hudson. New York: Guilford.
11. Lane, S., and Zamora, P. 1978. Training Syllabus for Staff. Denver: Closed Adolescent Treatment Center, Division of Youth Services.
12. Pithers, W.; Marques, J.; Gibat, C.; and Marlatt, A. 1983. Relapse Prevention with Sexual Aggression. In *The Sexual Aggressor,* ed. J. Greer and I. Stuart. New York: Van Nostrand Reinhold.
13. Wiessberg, M. 1982. *Dangerous Secrets: Maladaptive Responses to Stress.* New York: W. W. Norton.
14. Wolf, S. C. 1984. Evaluation and Treatment of the Sexual Offender. [Manuscript prepared as part of a manual developed by the Sexual Assault Center, Harborview Medical Center, 325 Ninth Avenue, Seattle, Washington 98104] Seattle: Sexual Assault Center.
15. Longo, R. E. 1982. Sexual Learning and Experience among Adolescent Offenders. *International J. Offender Therapy and Comparative Criminology* 26:235–41.
16. Carnes, P. 1983. *Out of the Shadows: Understanding Sexual Addiction.* Minneapolis: CompCare Publications.
17. Prentky, R.; Knight, R.; Straus, H.; Rokou, F.; Cerce, D.; and Sims-Knight, J. 1989. Developmental Antecedents of Sexual Aggression. *Development and Psychopathology* 1:153–69.
18. Peters, R.; McMahon, R.; and Quinsey, V. 1992. *Aggression and Violence throughout the Lifespan.* Newbury Park, Calif.: Sage.
19. Rivera, B., and Widom, C. 1990. Childhood Victimization and Violent Offending. *Violence and Victims* 5(1):19–36.
20. Denno, D. 1990. *Biology and Violence from Birth to Adulthood.* Cambridge: Cambridge University Press.
21. Marshall, W.; Barbaree, H.; and Eccles, A. 1991. Early Onset and Deviant Sexuality in Child Molesters. *J. Interpersonal Violence* 6(3):323–36.

22. Malamuth, N. 1986. Predictors of Naturalistic Sexual Aggression. *J. Personality and Social Psychology* 50:953–62.

23. Ryan, G. 1989. Victim to Victimizer: Rethinking Victim Treatment. *J. Interpersonal Violence* 4:325–41.

24. Longo, R., and McFadin, B. 1981. Sexually Inappropriate Behavior: Development of the Sexual-Offender. *Law and Order* 29(Dec.):21–23.

25. Steele, B. A. 1980. Generational Repetition of the Maltreatment of Children. In *Parental Influences in Health and Disease,* ed. E. J. Anthony and G. Pollack. Boston: Little, Brown.

26. Steele, B. F. 1987. Abuse and Neglect in the Earliest Years: Groundwork for Vulnerability. *Zero to Three* 7(4):14–15.

27. Haynes-Seman, C., and Krugman, R. 1989. Sexualized Attention: Normal Interaction or Precursor to Sexual Abuse. *Am. J. Orthopsychiatry* 59(2):238–45.

28. Gilgun, J. 1988. Factors Which Block the Development of Sexually Abusive Behavior in Adults Abused as Children. Paper presented at the National Conference on Male Victims and Offenders, Minneapolis.

29. Finkelhor, D., and Araji, S. 1987. Explanations of Pedophilia: A Four-Factor Model. In *Sourcebook on Child Sexual Abuse,* ed. D. Finkelhor. Beverly Hills, Calif.: Sage.

30. Groth, A. N. 1979. Sexual Trauma in the Life Histories of Rapists and Child Molesters. *Victimology: International J.* 4(1):10–16.

31. Sgroi, S. M. 1982. *Handbook of Clinical Intervention in Child Sexual Abuse.* Lexington, Mass.: Lexington Books.

32. Darke, J. 1990. Sexual Aggression: Achieving Power through Humiliation. In *Handbook of Sexual Assault,* ed. W. Marshall, D. Laws, and H. Barbaree. New York: Plenum Press.

33. Person, E. S. 1993. Male Sexuality and Power. In *Rage, Power, and Aggression,* ed. R. Glick and S. Roose. New Haven: Yale University Press.

34. Bennett, M. 1979. *Overcoming the Golden Rule: Sympathy and Empathy.* Vol. 3 of *Communication Yearbook,* ed. D. Nimmo. New Brunswick, N.J.: Transactional Books.

35. Finkelhor, D. 1984. Four Preconditions: A Model. In *Child Sexual Abuse: New Theory and Research,* ed. D. Finkelhor. New York: Free Press.

36. Abel, G.; Becker, J.; Cunningham-Rathner, J.; Kaplan, M.; and Reich, J. 1984. The Treatment of Child Molesters: A Manual. Unpublished manuscript.

37. Quinsey, V., and Earls, J. 1990. Modification of Sexual Preferences. In *Handbook of Sexual Assault,* ed. W. Marshall, D. Laws, and H. Barbaree. New York: Plenum Press.

38. Quinsey, V., and Marshall, W. 1983. Procedures for Reducing Inappropriate Sexual Arousal. In *The Sexual Aggressor,* ed. I. Stuart and J. Greer. New York: Van Nostrand Reinhold.

39. Hunter, J. A., and Becker, J. V. 1994. The Role of Deviant Arousal in Juvenile Sexual Offending: Etiology, Evaluation, and Treatment. *Criminal Justice and Behavior.*

40. Yochelson, S., and Samenow, S. 1977. *The Criminal Personality.* New York: Jason Aronson.

41. Abel, G.; Becker, J.; and Cunningham-Rathner, J. 1984. How a Molester Perceives the World. *International J. Law and Psychiatry.*

42. Berenson, D. 1987. Choice, Thinking, and Responsibility. *Interchange* [C. H. Kempe National Center for the Prevention and Treatment of Child Abuse and Neglect] (Jan.). NAPN.

43. Hunter, J. A., and Santos, D. R. 1990. The Use of Specialized Cognitive-Behavioral Therapies in the Treatment of Adolescent Sexual Offenders. *International J. Offender Therapy and Comparative Criminology* 34:239–48.

44. Watson, R., and Stermac, L. 1994. Cognitive Group Counseling for Sexual Offenders. *International J. Offender Therapy and Comparative Criminology* 38:259–70.

45. Jenkins. 1990. *Invitation to Responsibility.* New Zealand: Dulwich Centre Publications.

46. Briggs, D. O. 1975. *Your Child's Self-Esteem.* Garden City, N.Y.: Doubleday.

47. Ryan, G. 1993. Confrontation and Empathy: Creating a Therapeutic Relationship in the Absence of Trust. Presentation at the Ninth National Conference of NAPN, Lake Tahoe, Nev.

48. Cornell, W., and Olio, K. 1991. Integrating Affect in Treatment with Adult Survivors. *Am. J. Orthopsychiatry* 61(1): 59–69.
49. Spiegel, D., ed. 1993. *Dissociative Disorders: A Clinical Review.* Lutherville, Md.: Sidran Press.
50. McGrath, R. 1993. Preparing Psychosexual Evaluations of Sex Offenders: Strategies for Practitioners. *J. Offender Rehabilitation* 20: 139–58.
51. Salter, A. 1988. *Treating Child Sex Offenders and Victims.* Newbury Park, Calif.: Sage.
52. Booth, S. 1990. Interviewing Parents. In *Understanding and Managing Child Sexual Abuse,* ed. R. K. Oates. Marrickville, New South Wales: W. B. Saunders/Bailliere Tindal.
53. Carich, M., and Adkerson, D. 1995. *Adult Sexual Offender Assessment Packet.* Brandon, Vt.: Safer Society Press.
54. Ross, J., and Loss P. 1991. Assessment of the Juvenile Sex Offender. In *Juvenile Sexual Offending: Causes, Consequences, and Correction,* ed. G. Ryan and S. Lane. Lexington, Mass.: Lexington Books.
55. Gray, A. S., and Wallace, R. 1992. *Adolescent Sexual Offender Assessment Packet.* Orwell, Vt.: Safer Society Press.
56. Quinsey, V. 1994. Predicting Recidivism among Sex Offenders. Presentation at the Thirteenth Annual Research and Treatment Conference of Association for the Treatment of Sexual Abusers, San Francisco.
57. Davidson, H. A. 1988. Improving the Legal Response to Juvenile Sex Offenses. *Children's Legal Rights J.* 8(4): 15–20.
58. Wheeler, J. R. 1986. Final Evaluation of the Snohomish County Prosecutor's Juvenile Sex Offender Project. Olympia, Wash.: Juvenile Justice Section, Department of Social and Health Services.
59. Ryan, G., and Lane, S. (eds.). *Juvenile Sexual Offending: Causes, Consequences, and Correction.* Lexington, Mass.: Lexington Books.
60. Blanchard, G. 1995. *The Difficult Connection.* Orwell, Vt.: Safer Society Press.
61. Ryan, G.; Lindstrom, B.; Knight, L.; Arnold, L.; Yager, J.; Bilbrey, C.; and Steele, B. 1993. Treatment of Sexual Abuse in the Context of Whole Life Experience. Panel Presentation at Twenty-First Annual Child Abuse and Neglect Symposium, Keystone, Colo.
62. Marshall, W. L.; Hudson, S. M.; and Hodkinson, S. 1993. The Importance of Attachment Bonds in the Development of Juvenile Sexual Offending. In *The Juvenile Sex Offender,* ed. H. Barbaree, W. Marshall, and S. Hudson. New York: Guilford.
63. Marshall, W. L. 1989. Intimacy, Loneliness, and Sexual Offenders. *Behaviour Research and Therapy* 27: 491–503.
64. Main, M., and Goldwyn, R. 1984. Predicting Rejection of the Infant from Mother's Representation of Her Own Experience: Implications for the Abused-Abusing Intergenerational Cycle. *Child Abuse and Neglect: International J.* 8: 203–17.
65. Beckett, R., and Fisher, D. 1994. Assessing Victim Empathy. Presentation at the Thirteenth Annual Research and Treatment Conference of the Association for the Treatment of Sexual Abusers, San Francisco.
66. Davis, M. 1980. *Interpersonal Reactivity Index.* Washington, D.C.: American Psychological Association.
67. Ryan, G. 1995. Resistance or Temperament: Characteristics Which Will Not Change. Presentation at Eleventh National Conference of the National Adolescent Perpetrator Network, St. Louis, Mo.
68. Fisher, D., and Howells, K. 1993. Social Relationships in Sexual Offenders. *Sexual and Marital Therapy* 8(2): 123–36.
69. Van der Kolk, B., and Greenberg, M. 1987. The Psychology of the Trauma Response. In *Psychological Trauma,* ed. B. Van der Kolk. Washington, D.C.: American Psychiatric Press.
70. Lang, R. 1993. Neuropsychological Deficits in Sexual Offenders: Implications for Treatment. *Sexual and Marital Therapy* 8(2): 181–200.

71. Lewis, D. O.; Shanok, S. S.; and Pincus, J. H. 1981. Juvenile Male Sexual Assaulters: Psychiatric, Neurological, Psychoeducational, and Abuse Factors. In *Vulnerabilities to Delinquency,* ed. D. O. Lewis. Jamaica, N.Y.: Spectrum Publications.

72. Ryan, G. 1993. Concurrent Psychiatric Diagnoses in Sexually Abusive Youth. Presentation at the Ninth National Conference of the National Adolescent Perpetrator Network, Lake Tahoe, Nev.

73. Prentky, R.; Knight, R.; Rosenberg, D.; and Lee, A. 1986. A Path Analytic Approach to the Validation of a Taxonomic System for Classifying Child Molesters. *J. Quantitative Criminology* 6(3):231–57.

74. O'Brien, M., and Bera, W. 1992. The PHASE Typology. In *Sexual Offender Assessment,* ed. A. Gray and R. Wallace. Orwell, Vt.: Safer Society Press.

75. Hare, R. D. 1991. *The Hare Psychopathy Checklist,* rev. ed. Toronto: Multi-Health Systems.

76. Abel, G. 1994. *The Abel Assessment.* Atlanta: Behavioral Medicine Institute.

77. Jones, David P. H., and McGraw, J. M. 1987. Reliable and Fictitious Accounts of Sexual Abuse to Children. *J. Interpersonal Violence* 2:27–45.

78. Haynes-Seman, C., and Baumgarten, D. 1994. *Children Speak for Themselves.* New York: Brunner Mazel.

79. National Task Force on Juvenile Sexual Offending. 1993. Revised Report. *Juvenile and Family Court J.* 44(4):1–88.

80. Knopp, F. 1983. *Remedial Intervention in Adolescent Sex Offenses.* Orwell, Vt.: Safer Society Press.

81. Freeman-Longo, R.; Bird, S.; Stevenson, W.; and Fiske, J. 1995. *1994 Nationwide Survey of Treatment Programs and Models.* Brandon, Vt.: Safer Society Press.

82. Cantwell, H. B. 1988. Child Sexual Abuse. Very Young Perpetrators. *Child Abuse and Neglect: International J.* 12:579–82.

83. Cavanaugh-Johnson, T. 1988. Child Perpetrators—Children Who Molest Other Children: Preliminary Findings. *Child Abuse and Neglect: International J.* 12:219–29.

84. Friedrich, W. N. 1988. Young Sexually Aggressive Children. *Professional Psychology Research and Practice* 19:155–64.

85. Ryan, G.; Blum, J.; Law, S.; Christopher, D.; Weher, F.; Sundine, D.; Astler, J.; Teske, J.; and Dale, J. 1989 [rev. ed. 1993]. *Understanding and Responding to the Sexual Behavior of Children: Trainers' Manual.* Denver: C. H. Kempe National Center for the Prevention and Treatment of Child Abuse and Neglect.

86. Friedrich, W. N.; Grambsch, P., Broughton, D.; Kuiper, J.; and Beilke, R. L. 1991. Normative Sexual Behavior in Children. *Pediatrics* 88(3):456–64.

87. Friedrich, W. N.; Urquiza, A.; and Belke, R. 1986. Behavioral Problems in Sexually Abused Children. *J. Pediatric Psychology.*

88. Summit, R. 1978. The Child Sexual Abuse Accommodation Syndrome. *Child Abuse and Neglect: International J.* 7:177–93.

89. Ryan, G., and Blum, J. 1994. Creating a Therapeutic Environment for the Child Who Has Experienced Sexual Abuse. *Trainers' Manual.* Denver: C. H. Kempe National Center for the Prevention and Treatment of Child Abuse and Neglect.

90. Ryan, G., and Blum, J. 1995. *Childhood Sexuality: A Guide for Parents.* Denver: C. H. Kempe National Center for the Prevention and Treatment of Child Abuse and Neglect.

91. Marlatt, G., and Gordon, J. 1985. *Relapse Prevention: Maintenance Strategies in the Treatment of Addictive Behaviors.* New York: Guilford.

15

The Neglect of Child Neglect

Hendrika B. Cantwell

There are distinct differences between child abuse and child neglect. These differences need to be emphasized and clarified. The common phrase "child abuse and neglect" points to our professional tendency to see abuse and neglect as components of a single issue; in fact, they are separate. Although significant issues of child neglect are often entailed in serious child abuse cases, neglect itself is often not addressed directly, because the cases are so frequently categorized primarily as either sexual or physical abuse. Abuse issues carry more weight in court, partly because investigators can more easily define them and describe their effects, while neglect is less readily recognized and considered critical. The result of this neglect of child neglect may be a child's receiving treatment for physical or sexual abuse but receiving little or no attention for symptoms of neglect—symptoms which nevertheless portend longer lasting and more damaging consequences in the child's development.

It must be emphasized that more children in the United States die from neglect than from physical abuse. Many of the most serious long-term developmental disabilities in children are due to neglect rather than to abuse. Perhaps because of disproportionate media attention to cases of abuse, these facts are not generally recognized. The American Humane Association has maintained a statistical database which clearly reflects this nationwide trend. Even though neglect is usually underrecognized as producing hazardous effects, it has consistently been reported as a major form of child maltreatment. In 1994, a national survey conducted by the National Committee to Prevent Child Abuse (NCPCA) indicated that neglect represented the most common type of reported and substantiated form of child maltreatment. Of the 3.14 million instances of child maltreatment reported, 49% of the substantiated cases were due to neglect. Of an estimated 1,271 deaths from abuse and neglect reported in 1994, 42% were due to neglect alone, and 4% were due to a combination of abuse and neglect (1). Neglect seriously harms children, often causing lifelong impairment. In this chapter, I will define and discuss this harmful neglect, to make clearer delineation available for decision making and treatment.

HENDRIKA B. CANTWELL, M.D., is clinical professor emerita in the Department of Pediatrics, University of Colorado School of Medicine.

Forms of Child Neglect

Definitions

"Child neglect may be defined as a condition in which a caretaker responsible for the child either deliberately or by extraordinary inattentiveness permits a child to experience avoidable present suffering and/or fails to provide one or more of the ingredients generally deemed essential for developing a person's physical, intellectual or emotional capacities" (2). It is the *children* who are the victims, and they carry the signs and symptoms of the harm done by neglect. In the evaluation of neglect, it must be clearly shown how these symptoms relate to the omission of parental care.

Neglect: The child has the right to expect, and the adult caretaker has a duty to provide, food, clothing, shelter, safekeeping, physical and emotional nurturance, teaching, medical care, and schooling. Failure to provide these constitutes neglect (3).

Food: Food and liquids in adequate amounts must be made available throughout childhood. The consistency and nutritional value must be appropriate for age level of the child. The yardstick by which adequate nutrition is gauged is normal growth (in the absence of diseases which interfere with normal growth).

Clothing: Children must have clothing which is reasonably appropriate to prevailing weather conditions. Clothing must be sufficiently clean and intact so that the children are protected from weather and from being ostracized by school peers and teachers.

Shelter: Shelter must be provided which adequately protects the child from extreme weather, is safe, and affords the child a place in which to eat and sleep.

Safekeeping: The adult caretaker has a duty to prevent reasonably foreseeable and avoidable injuries to the child. A young child does not have the judgment to anticipate danger and needs constant supervision. An older child needs guidance to acquire the knowledge to maintain and improve personal safety and gain understanding of societal expectations and prohibitions.

Nurturance: Nurturance is attentive, responsive behavior which parents offer throughout their offspring's childhood and which promotes the child's attachment to a primary caregiver, positive self-image, and capacity for empathy. Nurturance helps to develop the child's developmental skills, it spurs curiosity and learning, and it sets attainable age-appropriate goals.

Teaching: The parent or adult caretaker is a child's first teacher and has a duty to teach the child social interaction skills and age-appropriate limits and goals, as well as acceptable language usage and comprehension.

Medical Care: Medical care is adequately provided for in "well-child care," which can be ascertained by the current state of the child's immunizations and by the caregiver's attention to the child's acute and/or chronic illnesses. Visits are made to the medical office or clinic when indicated by the child's condition, needed medications are given, and medications for any chronic condition are renewed and continued.

Schooling: At the recommended ages (even at a very early age if the child has a need to attend remedial or preventive education), the child must attend school regularly and must be allowed a space in which homework can be done. If home schooling has been chosen by the parents, they must keep up with the age-appropriate schoolwork (following the rules set by the school board), and also ensure appropriate peer interactions.

Prenatal Neglect, Perinatal Neglect, and Other Medical Neglect

The neglect of child neglect is particularly evident in prenatal and perinatal neglect. Prenatal neglect is the disregard for the welfare of the fetus after the mother has made the decision to carry the pregnancy to term. This frequently involves the mother's use of legal or illegal drugs known to harm fetuses and leave physical traces of drug or alcohol effects in their developing bodies. Bross (4) proposed that the mother's prenatal drug addiction, so manifested, is prima facie evidence of neglect. This problem is especially difficult to handle when alcohol is involved, because the harm caused by alcohol occurs very early in the pregnancy, when the mother often is unaware that she is pregnant. Alcohol abuse is not illegal. A most difficult differential diagnosis is between the developmental effects of fetal alcohol syndrome (FAS) or the more recently described fetal alcohol effect (FAE) and those of other forms of medical neglect. Histories of maternal habits in early pregnancy are usually unknown or unavailable to diagnosticians, as are details of neglect endured during the first years of a child's life. Impaired psychosocial and intellectual functioning, as well as problems with language acquisition and schooling delays, are very similar in children who are emotionally neglected, lacking in stimulation, or living in an unpredictable environment and those who are suffering from FAS or FAE. The children whose heads grow on a smaller percentile level than their bodily growth are more likely victims of FAS or FAE.

When illegal drugs are evident in an infant at birth, some law enforcement opinions can be very punitive toward the mother's drug usage, demanding that mother and infant be separated. Child protective services cannot support such punitive attitudes, especially considering the scarcity of foster homes. Thus child placement decisions have to be made on a case-by-case basis, determined by the mother's interest in her infant, her general functioning, her willingness to enter into drug therapy, and the availability of another nonaddicted adult in the home who would care for the newborn if the mother were impaired by her drug or alcohol use. If the mother's home is deemed unsuitable, babies usually are placed with relatives, less often in foster care.

The absence of adequate prenatal medical care constitutes neglect, but unless other indicators of neglect are present, it is seldom acted upon by any agency. Sometimes when no medical care has been sought, infants are born in unusual places, such as toilets or backyards, and mothers deny knowledge of their pregnancy. The denial of pregnancy is serious and raises concerns for the perinatal and postpartum periods, when the mother may show disinterest or even aversion to the newborn. These behaviors may also be observed in the hospital when a mother does not want to see, or is frankly rejecting of, her newborn. Under such circumstances, it is critical that a history be taken on the mother's other children, their whereabouts (such as in foster care or with other relatives), and any incidence of serious accidents or death.

Emotional and Developmental Neglect

The earliest years of a child's life are generally spent with a parent or caretaker, usually the mother, who profoundly influences that child's entire future. The psychiatrist Rene Spitz wrote, "There is a point under which the mother-child relationship cannot be restricted during the child's first year of life without inflicting irreparable damage" (5).

Emotional neglect is such an integral part of the other forms of child neglect defined above that it seems sensible to consider them together. Emotional neglect, by omission or commission, "seriously undermines the development of competence" (6). This involves the inability of the caregiver to bond adequately or normally with the child (see chapter 5); the punishment of a child's displays of self-esteem; ignoring or deprecating a child's self-esteem skills, which are important in nonfamily settings such as school and peer groups; and punishing, ignoring, or deprecating behaviors normal to childhood (6–8). Emotional abuse often coexists with and is difficult to separate from emotional neglect (see chapter 17). Similarly, the separation of developmental delays from emotional difficulties in neglected children is frequently an artificial distinction. Because these problems so often overlap and are contiguous in their effects, I will consider them in the following sections within the wider context of emotional *and* developmental neglect.

Stimulation Neglect

The environment which the baby experiences affects his or her emotional and neurological development. Animal studies appear to show that touch and movement quicken both pleasure and affection centers in addition to triggering the development of aggressive behaviors (9). The nerve tracts which carry touch and positional sense into the limbic system largely develop during the first year of life.

The infant whose bottle is always propped, for example, suffers emotionally and is effectively deprived of sensory stimulation, specifically touch and proprioception, which are thought to be at least as important as hearing and seeing for normal psychological development (10, 8). Holding a baby when feeding him or her presents opportunities for interaction, such as talking and smiling. Babies who regard intently the face of the adult who is feeding them will soon explore what they see, with a little hand reaching up to feel the big face above them. This lays the foundation for hand-eye coordination and the acquisition of perceptual skills. This important behavioral opportunity is available to all parents when they simply feed (by breast or bottle) and hold the baby in their arms; it also promotes parent-child bonding and reciprocal communication, laying the foundation for language as well.

The absence of interaction in early infancy is often neglected by professional observers. In contrast, I have emphasized the early months of baby's life here because it is so important that observers notice and plan intervention as early as possible to correct the deficits which the neglected baby experiences. Visitors in the home can note the chronically propped bottle in the baby's mouth. To convince a parent that holding a baby during feedings is important proves to be very difficult. Reasons given by such parents include seeing no need for it, having no time, and fear of spoiling the baby, using grandmother or a friend as the authority. Unfortunately, despite professional advice, the baby is often still not held and the bottle stays propped.

When parental inattention appears to be a permanent pattern, it demonstrates lack of attachment, causing the infant to suffer developmentally. The paucity of stimulation continues beyond infancy and expresses itself in the lack of simple everyday experiences, particularly in the lack of parent and child having fun together by going to the park, baking cookies, playing in the dirt, playing peekaboo, playing ball, or engaging in other enjoyable activities. Neglected children lack experiences which we take for granted as normal. Some parents are teachable, and professional intervention may prove to be an opportunity to separate the teachable parent from the one who cannot or will not change.

Language Neglect

Communication, or language use, is the child's single most important accomplishment before the age of five (11). Professionals coached to look for and recognize attachment and bonding need to heighten their awareness of very early language development, as shown by a baby's smiling and cooing before the age of four months and then babbling. Most observers are taught only that babies begin to learn complete words just before they are one year old. That may already be late for intervention if it means that the baby has to make up nine months of language delay. Yet how often do we teach any of our experts to be wary of the silent infant whose hearing is normal? Such silence bodes ill for future development.

The desire for speech grows out of a need to communicate in social relationships. When parents talk with their children, gradually babies and toddlers hear the sounds often enough to repeat them, first as syllables and then as whole words. Gradually, the words, by repetition, take on meaning and create for the child an image in the mind's eye which corresponds to an object and its name. Reading to children improves their language development and increases their vocabulary, eventually improving school performance. Additionally, books allow children to see objects represented in pictures, which are two-dimensional but correspond to the word for the three-dimensional object with which they are familiar. This leap from the object to a representation of it assists the child in learning the next step: written words still refer to that same object when children have learned to picture in their mind's eye. This is the internalization of language. When parents converse with their child, they take the first step in encouraging this internalization, which not only stimulates the development of language comprehension but also hastens the child's learning to read and write in school. Typically, neglectful parents speak in command sentences which do not invite children's responsiveness. Adams and Ramey (12) reported that mothers of children at high risk for developmental delays did not speak less often to their children but used more imperatives in their speech.

When adults think something over or try to decide about something, they are employing internalized language. Resourcefulness, problem solving, and thinking are closely dependent on language skills. These skills are impaired in the absence of a minimal set of language building blocks. Thus what Sacks said of deaf children who learn no language may be applicable to the plight of the language-neglected child: To be defective in language, for a human being, is one of the most serious of calamities, for it is only through language that we enter fully into our human estate and culture, communicate freely with our fellows, and acquire and share information. If we cannot do this, we will be bizarrely disabled and cut off—whatever our desires, or endeavors, or native capacities. And indeed, we may be so little able to realize our intellectual capacities as to appear mentally defective. (13).

Poor language development in the parents themselves is frustrating to professionals who are trying to deal with neglectful families. One has to speak in simple sentences to make sure that they know what is being said. They frequently misunderstand the meaning of words. When tested for intelligence quotients (IQ), many attain a score in the neighborhood of 75 to 80. This usually does not reflect a deficit at birth but is further evidence of the effects of neglect.

Gross Motor Neglect

Gross motor activity is a childhood need. Satisfying this need has become increasingly difficult for many whose families in the course of the past two generations have moved to cities and are living in apartments. Parks, streets, and playgrounds have sadly become too dangerous in many urban areas. Especially in the inner city, gross motor activity must be conducted in fenced school playgrounds, supervised by teachers, or developed in organized sports. It is no longer safe to just go out and play.

Young children need to run and jump and play, and play noisily. They do not need to hear no! incessantly when they are engaged in exploratory playing or in touching the beautiful things in their world. Inherent in this exploring is learning. When they are constantly reprimanded, some children draw the conclusion that learning is forbidden. They sit quietly. Other children respond to the wall of no!s with out-of-control behavior; they can look inattentive, purposeless, and erratic, leading professionals to misdiagnose them as hyperactive.

"Hyperactive" is an appellation commonly used by parents who, lacking knowledge of children's normal development, expect a young child to sit passively for hours in front of a television set. What is in fact unusual, however, is a normally developed twelve- to thirty-six-month-old child who does not move around a room and touch things. "She gets into everything" is a description of the normal child in a restrictive environment. This comment, voiced as a complaint, is the third important observational clue professionals should recognize if we are really trying to identify neglected children who are becoming developmentally delayed.

Fine Motor Neglect

Hand-eye coordination has its beginnings in the babe in arms who reaches to find mother's face, now trying to touch what she or he has observed while being nursed. It is important that access is given to children in play to encourage perfecting this skill, to move the hand where the eye directs it, to learn to fit things into each other, to scribble with a pencil, to cut with blunt scissors, to do puzzles, or to turn pages in old books or magazines.

Parents will do well to keep expensive, fragile items out of a child's reach, thus avoiding excessive no!s in reaction to the child's appropriate need to explore. Children also love beautiful objects, and with a little time and supervision, a child can be allowed to look at and inspect expensive or valued possessions, thereby learning to be careful and to appreciate beautiful things. Saying no does not encourage such appreciation.

Neglect of Limit Setting and of Teaching Self-Discipline

When parents say no and give other commands to very young children, there is perhaps some benefit in the repetition, but not much of the meaning can be internalized by the children. As long as an adult is in the room, the no is there—but when the adult leaves, the no leaves too. However, when children are between three and three-and-a-half years of age, they finally achieve the realization that they can say no to themselves and that this no applies even in the absence of an adult. Saying no to oneself is the first step in achieving some internalization of limits, or self-discipline, which optimally develops throughout childhood. Repetitive reminders gradually enlarge the child's self-discipline vocabulary. The absence of internalized discipline in the child manifests itself in adulthood as impulsiveness; at its worst, the adult individual shows no understanding that laws are to be obeyed by all.

The major problem in much child neglect is the caretaker's inability to comprehend what a child is all about, what she or he needs, what is important, and what is appropriate to the parental role. This incomprehension is manifested in limit setting for children which is erratic, inconsistent, unpredictable, and often dictated by a mother's or father's momentary whim, as opposed to a predictable pattern of directives which sets limits on unwanted behavior and encourages acceptable play. Neglectful parents give unclear directions and instructions both about approved activity and about disapproved conduct. In the absence of consistent messages about how to behave in a socially acceptable manner, age-appropriate behavior is not learned. It is within their own home that children can best learn, through the reciprocal relationship of love, the meaning of rules which exist for everyone's benefit. The understanding and gradual internalization of rules learned first in the family and then in school are eventually extended by the child to her or his interactions in society at large, ultimately producing what we call a law-abiding citizen.

Neglect of Supervision

Parenting is a constant process of learning and discovering. A young child daily develops new skills and requires adults to adjust. Neglectful parents insist that their child's behavior conform to a predetermined pattern, to what they consider to be "right." They thus ignore a baby's helplessness and dependence, the toddler's drive to explore and discover selfhood, a preschooler's burgeoning desire to gain independence and control, and the school-age child's continued need for nurturance and guidance.

Parenting is an art of balancing all the maternal and paternal protective impulses against the recognition that a child needs, through accumulated experience, to gain independence. Thus, a parent allows a child to learn to walk, knowing all the while that he will fall and may well hurt himself in a minor way. Of course, walking should not be allowed in circumstances which might lead to the child's serious injury. The same is true when he learns to ride a bicycle, go downtown on the bus, or drive a car. Although worried, parents must allow their children to learn, to fail, to fall, to get hurt a little.

When the child is hurt in the process, it is called an accident, and causes parents pain and regret. What, then, is different when we call such an injury the result of neglectful supervision?

After a baby's birth, we expect to see parents engaging in a specific learning process. Parents come to perceive what their baby can do and then anticipate the next developmental step that requires their supervision. A good example is the crawling baby who gets to the edge of the stairs—parents have to do something or he will tumble the length of the staircase. They may spend a day or two teaching the crawler to turn around and go down the steps on his tummy with continued supervision. Or perhaps they install a gate at the top of the stairs. Functioning parents will anticipate that even though the crawler's two- or three-year-old sibling may be able to open the gate, he or she may not remember to close it. In contrast, blaming a baby's falling accident on its two-year-old sibling who failed to close a baby-gate typifies the reaction of some neglectful parents.

Neglectful parents, unaware of normal child development, often have unrealistic expectations. Their poor judgment reveals itself from the beginning of their child's life. Although inexperienced parents occasionally misjudge their child's abilities, neglectful parents don't seem to learn; they leave their infant on a table, couch, or bed to fall off and perhaps get hurt not once but repeatedly. The crawler can stick small objects into electric sockets, the toddler can pull down hot pans from the stove, and the climber can fall off balconies. All children need to be protected from poisons under the sink and pills in the bathroom. In any case, neglectful parents do not seem to think of childproofing the house. They have the notion that the child was told what not to do and therefore should "mind" and know better than to get into danger.

For example, one mother brought a fourteen-month-old toddler with a burned back to the hospital and explained, "I told her that the water heater was hot and that she should stay away. She didn't, so she got burned." The mother was next to her little girl when the "accident" occurred yet did not think she should have removed her from the area near the heater. This parent's mind is set on the notion that the child, regardless of age-related developmental ability, should remember not to do what was forbidden once. Such parents seem to see their child as an equal. To teach them a more appropriate understanding of how a baby develops is difficult, because although we, as child care professionals can give examples of caregiving situations which require a specific response from the parent, the neglectful parent is unable to draw inductively a general guideline from such examples. It is as if each potential instance calling for supervision and intervention from the parent needs to be taught separately; when new situations arise that have not yet been discussed, the parental responses continue to be inappropriate and unprotective.

Our social values now pervasively emphasize self-care. The excuse that neglectful parents frequently offer for not providing supervision is that they intend to raise a child who will be "responsible, independent, mature, and self-reliant." All these adjectives obscure the fact that the child whom professionals see is actually often scared and lonely: *all* children need nurturance, guidance, and supervision.

In numerous families in which both parents work outside the home, the agenda is to save the money that child care would cost, in order to buy something fun, like a boat. For others, adequate child care is an expense they simply cannot afford. Children are neglected by all who accept a societal laxity which allows children from the age of five onward to spend a portion of each day alone. If parents cannot afford day care, then society must subsidize it. If day care is affordable, parents have a duty, when they themselves are not available, to provide supervision for their children.

Juvenile courts officers, police, social services workers, teachers, doctors, and other community leaders can establish and promote a meaningful standard of supervision only if day care is subsidized for those who cannot afford it. Clearly, when children reach school age, it would be most practical for them to stay at school, before and after school hours, under a supervisory staff hired as a community responsibility and available to the child at least through sixth grade. The sports, crafts, and art and music now available to some would thus be extended to all. Tutorial help and homework time could also be provided.

Undoubtedly, children less than twelve years old can be home alone sometimes. It is a mistake, however, to assume that it follows that they can be left unsupervised every day after school or left on their own for long periods such as vacations (14). Similarly, expecting older children to baby-sit their younger siblings day after day is inappropriate; it produces anger in the older children toward their younger brothers and sisters and deprives the older children of peer activities. This anger may be expressed directly as child abuse, or abuse may occur inadvertently when the oldest child attempts to control younger siblings to avoid blame for their out-of-control behavior.

The potential for neglect and abuse is further exacerbated as more women have joined the workforce, since there are fewer neighbors or relatives around to keep an eye on the children and lend a helping hand. Large cities also promote isolation, as does the neglectful family which tends to move frequently. Unsupervised children are significantly more socially isolated than those cared for by adults; these children report fewer opportunities to spend time with friends (15). Latchkey children look around for company: their loneliness may be dangerous when they are spotted by those who prey on children. In addition, the possibility increases for the eruption of other undesirable behaviors, including early alcohol, cigarette, and drug abuse (14), gang involvement, sexual encounters, and criminal activities. As the child grows older, he begins to reject parental limits—from an adolescent point of view, it makes sense to challenge such limits as "You may not stay out all night," by countering "You trusted me to take care of myself when I was nine years old, why the big change now?"

Neglect of supervision can also occur if the parent is in the home but is too impaired (as a result of drugs, alcohol, mental illness, physical illness, low intelligence, immaturity, or lack of empathy) to pay adequate attention to the children. It also occurs if the parent is not in the home and (*a*) his or her choice of baby-sitter is inappropriate (too old, too young, impaired, or known to be abusive), or (*b*) no instructions are left for the baby-sitter in case of emergency, or (c) the oldest child left in charge is not able adequately to supervise the other children, or (d) the parent refused acceptable alternative arrangements that were offered.

In summary, neglect of supervision is the failure to provide attendance, guidance, and protection to children who, lacking experience and knowledge, cannot comprehend or anticipate dangerous situations (16, 17). Proper supervision requires from the parent a sufficient attention span; a sense of responsibility; and the ability to empathize with a child's needs and level of comprehension—or failing that, the ability to learn about a child's developmental process.

Fatal Child Neglect

Three children, the eldest of whom was seven years old, were left home without an adult; when a house fire raged out of control and the children were killed, their death was classified as accidental. The legal issue involved here is "intent": the parents did not "intend" to have a fire kill their children. Furthermore, once the police classify such an event as accidental, no permanent record of the incident remains. Should these parents ever be charged with child neglect, it would also be immaterial to the court that the fire was started by the unsupervised children. Moreover, child protective services (CPS) agencies do not stay involved in such cases if there are no more children in the family, meaning that any future children the parents might have would be unprotected. If a criminal filing is made, a record that could be usable for protecting future children would be available. In cases where there are surviving children, CPS could bring a separate case in civil or juvenile court for their protection. However, if the court in the criminal case concluded that the deceased children's deaths were accidental, the CPS case—that remaining or future children are at risk for life-threatening "accidents" or neglect—would in consequence be more difficult to prove.

In groups of siblings, the oldest child may be too young to have any concept of the danger of playing with matches or may be unable to keep a younger child from playing with them. Determining how young is "too young" thus becomes a matter of legal dispute. The law has never defined a threshold age below which it is not suitable for children to be left home alone or placed in charge of siblings without an adult nearby.

Fatal drowning accidents sometimes result from child neglect. For instance, a mother may use the telephone next door, leaving a nine-month-old infant in the bathtub, unattended. When she returns, the baby is face down in the water. Similarly, a young child trying to entertain a baby in mother's absence decides that playing in the tub would be fun. While they are together in the tub, the baby drowns; the young sibling has no way of conceiving that such a thing could happen to the infant. Or, occasionally, an unattended child drowns in a bucketful of water or in the toilet bowl.

Children can inflict serious injury not only to themselves but also to siblings and playmates—for example, by setting clothes, furniture, a room, or a house on fire. An excuse child care professionals frequently encounter when listening to neglectful parents is that a baby's older sibling is responsible for harm to the baby. Such parents expect a young child to be capable of taking care of a baby; they have not learned that young children cannot anticipate danger and that, as a consequence, even what they do with the best of intentions may end up harming an infant.

Anticipating tragedy and averting it can reasonably be expected of an adult; in neglectful parents, however, such forethought is deficient. As a result, their neglected children are often in danger, even if the parents are in the house. These parents may be abusers of drugs or alcohol, making them inattentive. Others are absent emotionally; this may be related to intense self-absorption, which might be the case in "soap opera addiction," for instance. Not uncommon are parents whose depression renders them unable to attend to their children. Sometimes the parent works at night or is ill and thus sleeps all day, leaving the children unattended. A support system of adults who could help out during a parent's illness is conspicuously lacking in many neglectful families.

Medical neglect which ends in death is also fraught with controversy. Several religious groups prohibit their members from taking an ill child to a medical facility; instead, healing by prayer is held to be the appropriate way of dealing with medical problems. Jehovah's Witnesses, for example, prohibit blood transfusion. Some Buddhists from Vietnam believe one cannot go into the next life if one's body bears any surgical scars or if any of one's organs has been surgically removed. The medical profession has been too timid in responding to such prohibitions in some instances. Its recommendation is always to have such a controversy over medical treatment heard in court; meanwhile, the child's future welfare, and even his or her life, may be at stake. A recent change in federal guidelines specifies that medical intervention should be instigated when "*threatened harm to a child's health or welfare* means a substantial risk of harm to the child's health or welfare" (18; original emphasis). Religiously based refusal to provide medical treatment for a seriously ill child is not valid in court. Such court cases do require a health care professional, preferably a physician involved with the child, to appear in court: risk, both that of the physician-recommended medical care or procedure and that of the parents' refusal to allow medical treatment for the child, must be explained. The court expects to have any medical risk factors—such as risk of anaesthesia, a blood transfusion, or of an unexpected drug allergy—quantified with generally accepted percentages, to facilitate comparison with the level of risk that would be incurred if no medical treatment were provided to the child.

The medical literature and the news media have made us aware that suicide of teenagers and young adults is a significant public health problem, ranking as the second or third most common cause of death in these age groups. It is important to recognize that younger children can also plan and commit suicide, in response to an intolerable situation. We have known several children who at eight years old or younger had formulated detailed plans to kill themselves, and some who succeeded. Attempted or completed suicides may be misinterpreted as accidents, especially if the child ingests a poison, or falls from a familiar high place, or is struck by a car. In all childhood suicides, attempted or completed, we can reasonably assume that the child had suffered serious emotional neglect. We know that such neglect exists as a daily fact of life for many children.

The incidence of fatal child neglect is difficult to ascertain because parental behavior, no matter how neglectful it might appear to be to some observers, may never be evaluated by investigators from CPS or the police department. Alternatively, as I discussed above, the death that results from neglect may be classified by investigators as accidental. In consequence, this recommendation needs to be put forth strongly; *a death scene investigation must be conducted in all child deaths; the investigators should be professionals with a thorough understanding of the problems which expose children to the risk of nonaccidental injuries or death as a result of parental neglect.* Recent articles on sudden infant death syndrome (SIDS) also indicate this diagnosis should always be based on the results of an autopsy and a full investigation.

Neglect and Poverty

Some maintain that child neglect is merely a function of poverty. Indeed, if poverty is a serious problem, help should be offered to alleviate it, with food, clothing, and shelter. Even when the need for food is obvious, however, a neglectful parent may be too suspicious to accepted donated food. Similarly, a child's need for acceptance at school should take precedence over the parent's pride in accepting suitable clothes for the child. Housing in good repair must be offered to the family which lives without heat, functioning plumbing, or intact windows, banisters, and doors. If the parents fail to acknowledge that their housing is unsuitable and if they refuse to move to a safer, warmer place with their children, then we have evidence of a situation of child neglect, not poverty.

The parents who refuse offered help may suffer mental health problems, including mental illness, mental retardation, or excessive suspiciousness resulting from their own experiences of abuse in childhood. Nonetheless, professionals must keep in mind that the issue at hand is child protection and that the parents have a duty to provide at least minimally for their children's well-being. Ascertaining whether or not the neglect is deliberate is neither our main concern nor our primary responsibility. It is more immediately important to help the children than to understand the parents.

For example, CPS sometimes will arrange and pay for day care, allowing the parent(s) to work. In this case, we could justly consider the parents to be neglectful if such day care provisions were rejected, or if the mother leaves the children home alone because it is inconvenient to take them to day care before she goes to work, or if she does not wish to pay her share of the day care expenses as expected, once she is earning a paycheck.

Close identification of neglect with poverty has not helped to protect children or remedy child neglect. One assumes this identification came about partly because, as is often the case, statistics were turned around. While we know statistically that child neglect is associated with a higher rate of poverty than is child abuse, we should not leap to the conclusion that therefore neglect exists solely because of poverty (19). In working with poor families, child care professionals gain awareness that most poor parents are very adequate parents, providing their children with nurturance and protection (20). Emotionally neglectful rearing, in contrast, leaves children inadequately prepared to compete in our complex world; this neglect can cause them to fall into poverty, from which they do not have the tools to escape. Furthermore, such neglect does not necessarily improve with financial aid (21). Research has shown that economic hardship has no direct effect on the rate of delinquency or drug use in children; conversely, inconsistent parental attentiveness does have a direct effect on the incidence of delinquency (22, 14).

The assumption that neglect is merely a by-product of poverty and not inherently harmful to children has resulted in many courts' refusal to hear neglect cases. This assumption has likewise blinded CPS and police department investigators to the fact that children can be neglected in households above the poverty level. When neglected by his or her parents, the "poor little rich kid" is also in need of help. The economic circumstances of a family have no direct bearing on the level of care provided for their children. In Colorado, for instance, no clear course of action has been formulated for CPS to take when wealthy families supply their teenagers with money and leave them alone in a resort condominium, unsupervised for months at a time, while the parents travel. If this situation comes to the attention of the police, there will be intervention, but otherwise no legal sanction exists, although clearly these teenagers are deprived and neglected. In other well-to-do families, intelligent parents are so immersed in their careers and economic success that they rarely interact meaningfully with their children. The family may employ a housekeeper who cooks, cleans, and stays in the house, so the child is not technically left alone, but such a housekeeper is only rarely expected or instructed to "raise" the children. Such uncared for school-age or teenage children suffer from emotional, supervisional, nurturance, and disciplinary negligence, and they sometimes grow up exhibiting self-destructive or delinquent behaviors (3).

Documentation and Court Presentation of Child Neglect

Anyone who has dealt with neglectful parents knows that whether the presenting complaint is a dirty house, or the children's excessive absences from school, or negligence in medical care, child neglect is usually pervasive, a multidimensional rather than a unidimensional issue. Therefore, of utmost importance to all who deal with these families is learning how to recognize children who suffer from parental neglect. Neglect must be documented in a clear manner; concerns must be described fully and presented in a format that can be readily comprehended by others who will be dealing with the neglected children. For instance, a teacher or doctor should not simply report, "I think the children in this family are neglected." To be useful, a referral should describe the specific problems, in detail, indicate the time frame during which these problems were observed, and outline the treatment and compliance expectations of the agency which has been requested to intervene. The juvenile court must be involved if the family fails to recognize the harm to their children, refuses to cooperate with offered remediation, or by noncompliance with expected parental behavior continues to place the children at risk of serious harm. In this context, "serious harm" may mean anything from continued physical danger resulting from lack of parental supervision to continued mental danger resulting from lack of stimulation. Such a lack of stimulation can prevent the young child from becoming adequately prepared for school. The understimulated child may become a student who is chronically falling behind academically in the early school years, which may in turn lead to an assortment of other developmental difficulties as the child grows older.

In court, information must be conveyed with clarity, logic, and organization, supported by knowledge of child development and the literature on child neglect. It is time we saw ourselves as bringing knowledge to the court to show judges and lawyers that our quest for protection of children is not vague nor is child neglect harmless. Judges can render decisions only on the facts which are presented in their courtroom. They must rely on the testimony of witnesses who explain—the more clearly, the better—what harm neglect does to the children and how that harm relates to the way the parents have been raising them. Additionally, the court must be made aware of what continued threat exists to the children, how this will influence their development, what outcome is likely without intervention, what plan for treatment is proposed, and how the proposed treatment plan will benefit the children.

Judges rely on experts, but only if these expert witnesses present testimony which is well prepared and understandable. It is a mistake to be too technical; the court responds better to information presented in simple language, preferably descriptive. Thus, for example, let us consider the case of a child who does not get to school regularly in the first three grades—by the time he reaches fourth grade, he will be discouraged because the work is too hard and catching up too difficult. Such a child would benefit most from intervention while he is still in the first three grades; without such an intervention, the child may well begin to be a truant and a drop-out sometime around fourth grade. He is then a candidate for "hanging out" with other such children, who eventually join gangs or become adults who are chronically unqualified to support themselves. Explaining this sequence in court, and thus illustrating why intervention is crucial even if the boy is "only" in first or second grade, is far more effective than saying, "The boy is showing symptoms of cognitive deficiency because of inadequate attendance in school."

As child care professionals, we must define the family's problems and design appropriate remediation, very clearly outlining what is to be accomplished not only for the parents but particularly for each child. Children are our concern, our clients or patients, but the difficulty is that as much as neglected children need intervention, they also need and continue to need parents. While the best situation would be to have the child's parents provide adequate nurturance and care from the beginning, treatment often addresses only current deficiencies, ignoring the child's need for help to remediate effects of the preceding years of neglect. Even though a professional may note improvement in some areas of parental conduct, the children may still not be parented well enough to recover from previous damage and thus may continue on a downward path in their behavior, development, and mental health.

Evaluation of the Parents

The neglected child may have problems which would tax the most talented of parents; ideally, child care professionals should offer neglectful parents a structured means to improve their parenting skills sufficiently to cope with their needy children. Treatment plans must be specific about what improvement is to be accomplished. Outcome measures must be defined in terms of clearly understood criteria for determining success or failure of the parents' efforts within a specified period of time. This is particularly important when babies and young children are involved; because their lives are so rapidly unfolding, they are in most acute need of decent parenting (23).

Obtaining a history of the parents is advisable before any treatment plan addressing their neglectful behavior is attempted. Some issues which might easily be missed in taking the parents' history are unacknowledged neglect or abuse in their own childhood, which is best ascertained by in-depth questioning; frequent moves as a child; long-term placements with other relatives or in foster homes; lack of school attendance; and loss or death of other children in the current family. If a certain topic is painful or embarrassing, no one is altogether truthful when being interviewed by a stranger, and the neglectful family is no different. Thus, discussion of previous attempts to make family and personal life changes and recognition of potential strengths and supports are especially germane in encouraging openness. Special attention must also be given to recording such factual data as past counties of residence, schools the children attended, and medical facilities the adults and the children used, both in the past and in the present time.

Learning what the parents lives have been is tantamount to learning how best to assist the children. To deal with parents who are neglectful is to be impressed by personal inadequacies and disabilities which remain as bitter testimony of the neglect and/or abuse they suffered during their own childhood. Particularly characteristic is poor language comprehension and vocabulary, which in practice means they often don't understand what is said to them by social workers, doctors, and nurses. It is good practice if this incomprehension is suspected to ask the adults throughout the course of the interview to repeat, in their own words, what was said to them.

Successful investigation and treatment of neglect must be a multidisciplinary undertaking. The children's and the parent's needs can be met only by professionals who are willing to work together. Although concerns about confidentiality between agencies exists, the federal guidelines have been relaxed to allow communication between agencies and their representatives if all are involved in the treatment of the same family and child. Hence, the interviewer should try to obtain the parents' consent to release information to all agencies which are potential contacts.

Because so few studies of neglectful parents have been conducted, we may do well to consult studies of the parents of children with nonorganic failure to thrive. Although most neglectful parents are found in the lowest socioeconomic group and are less than well educated, I want to stress again that most poor parents do not neglect their children. It appears more likely that parental neglect, experienced in the childhood of neglectful parents, itself contributed significantly to landing them in the poverty most of them now endure.

A study directed by Polansky (24) looked at the problems of isolation and lack of support experienced by neglectful mothers and compared them to a control group of mothers in the same neighborhood and life circumstances. The neglect group's perception was of being isolated and lacking in helpful resources; the control-group mothers, on the other hand, were able to find and use supportive resources in the same neighborhood (24). Neglectful mothers may have increased difficulties in relating to and reaching out to others, a difference that fits with characteristics Polansky has found in his other studies of neglectful parents—lifelong patterns of immaturity, impulsivity, difficulty with verbal communication, and apathy (2). Thus it appears that neglectful parents carry through life precisely those characteristics that make it difficult for them to use help or to succeed without it, deficits acquired in their own childhood and subsequently passed on to their children.

A prospective study of mothers who later raised nonorganic-failure-to-thrive children indicated these women had had unhappy childhoods, felt unloved, and rejected their mothers as models for parenting. Thus, their preparation for parenting was poor, their current support in the family less available, and their children potentially more difficult.

If the neglectful mother is psychiatrically ill, her treating psychiatrist may not consider her to be a candidate for hospitalization, especially with the recent emphasis on outpatient care. Hence, his diagnostic concern may not include her children. A psychotic parent is considered a danger to the children only if the delusional system places the child in harm's way—for example, a mother who, in her delusional state, may feel compelled to "defend" herself against imagined attacks by her child. This is also the case when adults are discharged from a psychiatric setting: they may no longer be a danger to themselves or others; this does not, however, mean they are ready to be a capable parent. Indeed, the psychiatric services providing for a hospitalized mother seldom even notify CPS upon her discharge.

To assure that mentally retarded parents are able to provide adequate child care, we need to evaluate them. If they do not have a support system, we need to establish one to assist them. In some families, problems increase when the children become smarter than the parents and take advantage of the disparity. In others, the children become helpers. This is acceptable within limits, but it is not acceptable if children are prematurely burdened with adult responsibilities and begin to show signs of stress.

Similarly, parents of children with chronic medical problems need a lot of support. Baby-sitters may refuse to stay with a child with complex medical problems, so respite care should be arranged to give the parents occasional breaks. Other help in the home may be needed to allow parents time with their other children.

Sometimes it is the parents themselves who have a long-term illness. A parent with a chronic disease may require repeated hospitalization. These absences from home are very difficult for children. Arranging out-of-home placement for them each time in the same household with a reliable relative is best. In such arrangements, public agencies generally do not get involved, but it becomes a problem if CPS has to repeatedly find temporary foster care, sometimes for weeks or months at a stretch, for several children. The issues then have to be carefully evaluated: older children who are well attached and understand the illness generally can adjust to the mother's absences; the real problem arises with a baby, toddler, or preschooler who gets confused in trying to distinguish mother and home from a mother figure and another homelike place. Confusion and developmental delays plague these youngsters, because so much of their energy has to be focused on mourning the loss of one mother and adjusting, adapting, and reattaching to another mother. "Mother" to a young child is not the biological parent but the person who fits the job description. This sad situation is not uncommon and is becoming more frequent with HIV-infected mothers who become ill. Counseling gravely ill parents to relinquish young children for adoption may be an alternative if parents can clearly understand the difficulties their long absences create for very young children. Adults involved in helping, such as social workers, tend to focus on the hardship which the illness causes in the life of parents rather than on its effect on the children. Generous visitation after adoption could allow parents to keep in touch with the growth and development of their offspring without endangering the baby's emotional well-being by inconstant relationships.

Attachment: Normal versus Abnormal

Judging the quality of attachment observed between the parent and the child is not taught to many professionals who deal with babies. Babies attach (see chapter 5). That is their nature, as though they were covered with velcro. Devoted caregivers who become sensitive to baby's needs and attend to them appropriately engender their infant's trust that he will be attended. Gradually this trust in the environment becomes specifically connected to the person who satisfies the baby's basic needs. This leads to a strong reciprocal relationship in which the baby is free to observe and learn without fretting about basic necessities. In the absence of this original trust in the environment, the baby appears uninterested in the world around it. This can be observed even in babies only a month or so old and reflects on the general care which they receive.

When they encounter another person, neglectful adults often respond with withdrawal or anger, emotions which they cannot recognize in themselves (25; see also chapter 8). The antisocial responses of these adults, established in early childhood, make it hard for professionals to develop a communicative relationship with them. Neglectful parents are neglected children grown up and continuing to distrust their environment. Their attachment to an infant in the next generation will likely not be any better than their own parent's was to them, which explains why such parents do not understand the attachment problems that professionals see clearly.

A child's insecure attachment is a reliable predictor of his or her preschool behavior at four to five years (26), particularly of aggression in elementary school (27). There also seems to be a compelling correlation between the quality of the parent-child relationship and the child's level of cognition (28, 29). Because neglected children are more often insecurely attached to their parents than nonneglected children are to theirs, the poor quality of the parent-child relationship in neglectful families may have profound implications for the neglected child's cognitive development (30).

Empathy, normally an aspect of a child's emotional development, is not transmitted in the emotionally barren landscape of the neglectful family. Children develop feelings of empathy by following the example of their parents: children become sympathetic and understanding if their own needs have been met with sympathy and understanding. Without empathy, children cannot form lasting attachments to anyone and parenting has a high risk of becoming neglectful or abusive.

Guidelines for the Treatment of Neglectful Parents

There is no "standard" or "routine" for devising a treatment program for neglectful parents. The following items are suggestions on how to proceed.

1. Evaluation for the presence of drug and alcohol abuse is necessary in *all* neglectful families (31). A specific treatment facility must be recommended if substance abuse is indicated by the evaluation. If the court orders such treatment, it can also assure disclosure to CPS agencies of the progress made by the parents in the program, thus circumventing any strictures some programs impose to maintain their clients' confidentiality. Treatment for alcohol or drug addiction (or overuse) must precede or accompany any other treatment. Parents who remain addicted are especially unlikely to change neglectful behavior. Treatment must be ordered even if the parents deny that their use of these substances is interfering with child care. There should be no hesitation to have testimony heard in court from witnesses who have seen young children kept at a bar for hours while the parents drank or who have been in the home when children were unsupervised and uncared for because parents could not be aroused.

2. Evaluate for education and/or employment in *all* families. This may reveal illiteracy or another major deficit in the parents' education. They may be too embarrassed to tell anyone about it, but it undermines their self-esteem and often negatively affects their attitude toward their children's education. Parents in these circumstances may pass on the message that they found school a waste of time (a valid perception, since they were not taught what they most needed to learn). Specific goals for the parents should be set and, ideally, with professional help, attained, such as: (*a*) learning to read to a baby or toddler, starting with describing pictures and progressing to reading simple words; (*b*) improving reading skills, to enable parents to enjoy more books with their children (32); (*c*) learning basic arithmetic, to enable parents to budget for the household; (*d*) earning an equivalency degree from a secondary school, which might lead to acquiring more skills in a technical school; (*e*) finding employment in a sheltered workplace, which may be available in cities; in small towns or rural areas, this can and has been developed if a local industry will make available training positions for simple tasks at low wages (for instance, helper to a school custodian). One school encouraged a mother to become a first-grade teacher's aide to help her learn to read along with the children. Those who do well might graduate to more demanding and remunerative employment over time. Bringing home a paycheck improves the self-esteem of a person who has seen him- or herself as a failure since early school years. Additionally, work can improve a family's sense of time and organization, and parental pride gradually improves the family's self-image.

3. Volunteer work by parents can be arranged through a social worker who is available to give careful supervision. Neglectful parents usually have severe deficits in social skills; volunteer work can provide exposure to good role models in a day care setting, in a meals-on-wheels program, or in church volunteer groups. Because of the neglect they may have suffered as children, many parents are themselves deprived of what we generally think of as typical human experiences. Volunteer groups can engage deprived parents in such activities as baking cookies and pies, taking children to the zoo, picnicking in the park, or other outdoor activities. The modeling of these previously unknown activities may help parents learn and begin to teach and share social skills and new activities with their own children.

4. If a trained volunteer can be assigned to parents, she or he sometimes successfully

re-parents the neglectful/neglected parent. Homemakers trained and paid to teach homemaking and parenting may be useful if available—and, optimally, they can remain involved with the parents over a long period of time (33).

5. Psychological and psychiatric counseling may be indicated. For those parents who are seriously mentally ill, medication may be necessary. When a referral is made for psychiatric or psychological counseling, it is valuable to be specific about the perceived needs of the person being referred, specifically, that there are unresolved attachment issues or that these parents need help with their own childhood experience of neglect or abuse. However, because psychotherapy is a language-based intervention, many language-poor neglecting parents are quite uncomfortable with it. In such cases, it is helpful to remember that the parent is a neglected child grown into an adult body, having brought along all the deficits of the neglected child. The best therapy devised specifically for language-deficient parents would be something like play therapy, particularly if the parent cannot play with the children, sees them as rivals, is competitive with them, and actually takes over their play. Sometimes counseling may be deferred until other intervention strategies have had a chance to improve the parents' outlook and demonstrate to them the sincerity of the treatment plan, especially if they perceive a recommendation for therapy as an indication that they are thought to be "crazy." Parenting classes, for example, may help to prepare these parents for individual counseling.

6. Neglectful parents who are of low intelligence may benefit from instruction in child care and in techniques for stimulating children designed by special education teachers specifically for such parents. In cases of grave mental retardation, parenting without live-in help is usually impossible (34).

7. Parenting classes are a tool with both advantages and liabilities. One of the goals of such parenting classes should be to encourage the parents to realize that many other parents also need help, that they are not alone and have not been maliciously singled out, and that indeed some other parents are less competent than they. Through seeing other parents talk about their problems, they themselves begin to feel safe enough to talk, and by continually receiving messages about positive parenting, they may gradually be able to put into practice what they have learned in the class and to internalize new information. However, the most recalcitrant child neglect comes not as a result of the parents' deficient information. Parents do not respond primarily to the information-laden aspect of classes. Rather, it is the environment of the class—the pervasive sense that someone cares about them—that may be of greatest therapeutic importance. Those in attendance at a parenting class begin to feel more comfortable in talking because they are listened to—often a new experience for these parents. A liability to be guarded against is a treatment plan that equates mandatory attendance at a parenting class with the actual improvement of parenting skills: mere attendance does not guarantee that these classes will be effective. The treatment plan must establish expectations of concrete changes, observable in the children, that result from what the parents learn in class (23).

8. Consulting with parents about the treatment plan, identifying and encouraging the strengths in the family, is very helpful. If they feel involved in the decision making, they will do better. They also need to know precisely what is expected of them. Parents need to

attend to the most important problems first. When they succeed in improving some aspect of their children's lives, their response to praise and encouragement is dramatic. Having only one or two items to accomplish within a specific time span allows them to win praise for their achievement, which in turn encourages further improvement. Overloading neglect-ful families with too many demands, or too many treatment issues at once, is to be avoided.

9. Sometimes parents are helped by unconventional forms of therapy, such as church groups which choose to provide help, or nurturance, or even communal housing. Whether or not these therapies are ultimately helpful must be judged by the extent to which the children improve, not by the degree to which the parents' emotional well-being increases.

10. Weaning parents from the involvement with CPS and the court takes time. Parents may precipitate a crisis when they know that treatment is near an end. Neglectful families suffer from isolation; therefore, it is expected that part of the treatment plan includes their involvement with individuals or community organizations that can supply some sup-port. Encouraging and helping parents to learn how, when, and whom to ask for help is important.

11. A final option, when parents cannot become even minimally adequate in providing care for their children, is termination of the legal parent-child relationship (35, 36).

Termination of the Legal Parent-Child Relationship

Social workers are compelled by legal mandate, and often feel compelled by their own "family values," to attempt to reunite the family that has been subject to a CPS or court-ordered intervention. However, social workers are also charged by legal mandate to protect children from "imminent danger" of harm. Unfortunately, under pressure to reunify fami-lies, social workers may not define "imminent danger" to include neglect of supervision, at times life-threatening; or serious mental impairment from lack of stimulation; or lack of parental bonding, with its serious consequences. Children at risk from physical, intellectual or emotional neglect which causes serious harm deserve to have their problem defined in a way that offers them legal recourse. Such children have the right to a better outlook for the future than their parents are providing. Without help, they remain mired in the same disa-bilities their parents exhibit, which they in turn may repeat in the next generation. (37, 38, 24).

Any long-term caretakers of such children—especially relatives or foster parents to whom the child has bonded—must be heard if a legal termination proceeding goes to court, and they should also be evaluated if they are being considered for long-term placement of the child (see chapters 7, 8, 21, and 22). After a time, the natural parent may mean less to a young child, and the psychological parent, who fills the job description of mother or father, becomes far more important. Although it is not known at what age a child is too old to attach to a new caretaker, there is evidence that removing children from the psychologi-cal parent may lead to permanent mourning. Ultimately, what is most important is that children be permanently placed with people who will truly nurture and protect them.

The courts sometimes have a task set for them which seems incongruous: they are asked to terminate parental rights to custody of one or two children but not to custody of all the children in a family. The question invariably asked is, How can that be possible?

The answer lies in understanding that each child is a separate being who comes into a mother's life at a different time and that the experiences surrounding each child's birth and upbringing are therefore different. A teenaged mother may be too immature and self-centered to get involved with her first and second children, but when the third baby is born, she may (having reached her twenties) find herself interested in this new baby. She can parent now, but to try to force her to parent the two who came too early in her life will usually not work.

Children born to parents after their legal rights to their older children have been terminated are at high risk for neglect. Rather than waiting for the damage these parents inflict to again become apparent to the community, child care professionals should intervene with vigorous early prevention measures. Although currently not in existence, a tracking system is needed to monitor such seriously neglectful parents. Best would be the implementation of a universal home visitor program in which every newborn baby has an assigned home visitor, paid by the state—a highly effective solution, which exists in most western European countries and in New Zealand.

The courts have a duty to understand that neglect is not nebulous, that it can be defined and documented, that parents can comply with treatment programs and still reap no benefit that extends to the care of their children. To protect children means that the court must focus on and look for the childrens' healthy progress—the only thing that reliably indicates the parents' ability to parent.

Guidelines for the Treatment of Neglected Children

Treatment of neglected children must remediate existing deficits and prevent the outbreak of further problems which result from living with neglectful parents. Prevention is particularly urgent for young children, since they must have access to a normal environment to avoid becoming irreparably damaged by neglect (39). The following items sketch the most significant issues involved.

1. If medical care was neglected, it must be provided.

2. For babies and toddlers, good quality attachment, food, safety, and emotional care are paramount. For toddlers, speech, socialization, and learning to internalize limits are the additional important goals.

3. School is the first societal agency which encounters on a daily basis the consequences of child neglect. The neglected children often cannot behave, cannot learn, cannot listen; their behavior is disruptive, aggressive, inappropriate, and lacking in self-control. In remedial or special classrooms, neglected children are mixed with children who have learning problems of a different nature, and the process is usually not effective in overcoming these neglected childrens' deficits. Neglected children do not need to repeat kindergarten— they need to experience the missed nurturance and developmental opportunities most children gain during the first five years of life. Remedial education is not effective because it does not address that crucial problem; if it were effective, the neglected child's deficit would resolve as a matter of course. Unfortunately, this is rarely the case. The other interventions mentioned above must be accomplished before the child will be able to benefit from re-

medial programs at school. Family involvement—including more consistency, nurturance, and appropriate socialization—combined with educational instruction seems to have a most salutary effect upon the children's cognition.

4. If schooling is a problem, help must be arranged to make it more satisfactory; any assistance provided, of course, should have some demonstrated promise of success. In particular, causes for absences and tardiness must be identified (for example, no alarm clock in the house; going to bed too late; mother's inconsistent attitude about children's bedtime; children staying home to baby-sit siblings; children staying home to protect mother; mother working nights and not supervising children's waking up) and alleviated.

5. Older children's perception that chaos and filth in the home represent acceptable norms is problematic. A program in which the child is exposed to a homemaker or home aide who teaches the family better housekeeping (for instance, washing and putting away of clothes and dishes, even if only in grocery boxes), helps to improve the child's perception about the proper appearance of a home. Alternatively, part-time foster care may prove beneficial, whereby a family or an interested older person in the community takes the children after school until their bedtime each day. Such skills and habits as grocery shopping for preparation of balanced meals, personal cleanliness (including bathing, hair washing, and clothes washing and repairing), and dish washing are shared and learned. Exposed to a family with better human interaction, children may internalize better hygiene and housekeeping as the acceptable norm. Such household tasks are best taught with the supervision and help of a caring and patient adult, not with scolding and punishment of the children for not knowing how to do it right without ever having been taught.

6. Some communities have adult volunteers who may be a normalizing influence and engage the children in outings, playing, and having fun. This avenue would be particularly suitable for a child forced into an adult caretaker role. Often the oldest child is expected to look after younger siblings and is rarely allowed to play at his or her own level. Volunteers can also afford time to do homework with the child, to help with difficult subjects, and to discuss the applicability of school learning to daily life. Especially helpful are discussions about goals in adulthood and options previously beyond the child's scope.

7. Some children are placed with relatives or in foster care if the parental neglect is thought to place them in imminent danger. Many neglected children are difficult to care for because their needs, not having been met in the past, render them more demanding of attention in a desperate attempt to make up for what was denied them. Most are developmentally delayed and emotionally immature, again requiring more in the way of parenting skills than normal children of the same age do. It may not always be wise to place sibling groups in the same foster home, because of these extra needs which each one of the children has—this can tend to overload well-meaning foster parents. When children are placed out of the parental home, planning for the family's future must begin immediately. The guidelines for the parents' treatment must be clear, as described above, to delineate from the beginning what conditions they must meet for the return of their children. Furthermore, the guidelines for the foster parents' standards of child care must be clear as well. And all guidelines must contain time lines, since children's childhood cannot wait in the need for permanent parents.

8. Psychotherapy may be needed for these children (40). It must be emphasized that the neglected child is not mentally ill but has problems which are the result of a damaging or deficient emotional and social environment. Formal psychological counseling may address the child's relationships both with adults and with peers. Interpersonal skills are often impaired in neglected children. Language delays frequently relate particularly to an inability to express feelings and identify moods. Absent are words about being happy, sad, or angry about disappointments, worries, daydreams, hopes. In neglectful families, adults do not talk much with children in interactive give-and-take conversations. This is reflected in the paucity of their inner life: the acquisition of language implies that meaning becomes internalized and therefore produces images which we can explore together when we converse. Many neglected children grow up with poorly internalized language, and it creates deficits in their thinking life as well. It is a prerequisite that the therapist working with neglected children be aware of the language problems common to neglect; then she or he might be able to help the children.

9. The child whose parent is mentally ill needs help in sorting out the reality of his or her own experience from the distorted reality presented by a schizophrenic, manic, or severely depressed parent. This need for help may also apply to a child dealing with a significantly retarded parent whom the child has surpassed in intelligence. Therapeutic intervention may bring understanding and empathy over time.

Societal Consequences of Neglect

The laws which protect children describe the duty of parents to conform to a standard of caregiving that is reasonable and prudent. Because the law specifically requires family reunification if at all possible, as I have mentioned above, the "reasonable" parent in practice has come to mean the "minimally adequate" parent. Child protection professionals have tended to underestimate what is necessary for minimally adequate care. After several decades of research and experience, it is now clearer that children, while often resilient, are not invincible (41). Some long-term studies of what seemed to be mild neglect had outcomes that were delayed before the effects became apparent. To observe neglectful parents who were themselves neglected as children is to be impressed by the extent of the damage resulting from neglect.

Neglected children may be poor scholars. Children, neglected at home and undereducated, are likely to be delayed developmentally. Appearing to be mild mental retardation and common in neglected children who live in low socioeconomic groups, this is unlike moderate to profound mental retardation (42). It is not that poverty makes a child less capable but rather, that neglect, which occurs more commonly in lower-income groups, does. Buchanan and Oliver found that 24% of 140 children in "subnormality hospitals" were mentally retarded as a result of neglect (43). High rates of mental handicap, backwardness, and antisocial behavior were seen in children who were born into families with two or more generations of child maltreatment (44).

Teenage pregnancy is especially common in girls who are unsuccessful in school and find it unrewarding. Many come from households where having babies in the teen years is the norm. In this context, it must be noted that teen pregnancy is also highly associated with sexual abuse in a girl's earlier years. There is also a strong connection between neglectful parenting and child sexual abuse. The age of the parent is significant in the quality of care the baby will receive. Generally, teenagers are more self-absorbed and have more difficulty with the necessary consistency of child care—which, after all, requires full-time attention—than are older mothers. Low income is another disadvantage facing these young, undereducated parents (45).

Boys and girls who have dropped out of school will associate with others who are on the streets for similar reasons. The association with gangs is not surprising; the neglect these young people suffered at home makes them needy for attention, so identification with a group of peers is very welcome. The sense of power and strength drawn from gang activities gives young persons status, a reward which children would normally find at home, in success at school and sports, and eventually in successful careers.

Richardson et al. (14) found substance abuse (particularly, cigarettes, alcohol, and marijuana) occurred more frequently in eighth graders who took care of themselves every day after school and even more frequently in those who had been in self-care since grade school. "Harder" drugs such as cocaine, crack, and heroin seem to be more commonly associated with the children in the inner cities, where poverty and neglect meet.

Delinquency is sometimes the precursor to criminal behavior or a disordered life. At seven- to twelve-year follow-ups, female delinquents had frequently become suicidal, alcoholic, drug-addicted, enmeshed in violent relationships, and unable to care for children. Even so, they were less violent than male delinquents (46). Severe neglect in childhood, emotional abandonment while young, and suicide attempts were thematic in the histories of condemned murderers (47).

The relationship between neglect and psychopathology is complex. Certainly, it does not relate only to the mental illness in the parent but, rather, to the quality of the child's relationship with the primary parent and with additional adults in his or her life. Still, children with a mentally ill parent have an increased risk of suffering both neglect and psychopathology (48). Professionals who deal with children need to heighten their diagnostic skills for detecting psychological disorder in childhood. In one study, 11.8% of children aged seven to eleven years had psychopathology, but pediatricians missed 83% of them (49).

Long-term studies have shown that even when children were victims of mild neglect, they had poor outcomes (26, 16, 6).

Summary

In spite of all the negative data presented above, the outlook for neglected children is not uniformly grim. Some research indicates that the majority of neglected children do not become delinquent, criminal, or violent (50), and it is also true that many previously neglected children manage quite well. Of the factors which seem to mitigate the consequences of profound neglect, the most important seems to be the presence, at some time, of an attentive person who took a genuine interest in the child. This would give impetus to intervention from a volunteer, a homemaker, or a home visitor who could be that part-time, additional nonneglectful parental figure who would provide some of the empathetic nurturing the birth parents did not. The main difficulty is that such an adult would need to be available and stay involved throughout the years of childhood.

Child neglect is psychologically, socially, medically, and financially costly, increasingly so with each year of the neglected child's life. Fortunately, some early intervention programs are now being initiated (see chapter 25).

References

1. Daro, D., and Wiese, D. 1995. *NCPCA Annual Fifty-State Survey.* Chicago: National Committee to Prevent Child Abuse.
2. Polansky, N. A., and Hally, C. 1975. *Profile of Neglect.* Washington, D.C.: Public Services Administration; Department of Health, Education, and Welfare.
3. Cantwell, H. B. 1988. Neglect. In *The New Child Protection Team Handbook,* ed. D. C. Bross, R. D. Krugman, M. R. Lenherr, D. A. Rosenberg, and B. D. Schmitt, 102–12. New York: Garland.
4. Bross, D. 1988. Medical Diagnosis as a Gateway to the Child Welfare System: A Legal Review for Physicians, Lawyers, and Social Workers. *Denver Univ. Law Rev.* 65(2–3):213–58.
5. Spitz, R. A. 1945. Hospitalism: An Inquiry into the Genesis of Psychiatric Conditions in Early Childhood. *Psychoanalytic Study of the Child* 1:53–74.
6. Garbarino, J. 1986. The "Elusive Crime" of Emotional Abuse. *Child Abuse and Neglect: International J.* 2:89–99.
7. Garbarino, J. 1989. The Psychologically Battered Child: Toward a Definition. *Pediatric Annals* 18:502–4.
8. Steele, B. F. 1987. Psychodynamic Factors in Child Abuse. In *The Battered Child,* 4th ed., ed. R. E. Helfer and R. S. Kempe, 81–114. Chicago: University of Chicago Press.
9. Montagu, A. 1986. *Touching: The Human Significance of the Skin.* New York: Harper and Row.
10. Prescott, J. 1971. Early Somatosensory Deprivation as an Ontogenetic Process in the Abnormal Development of the Brain and Behavior. In *Medical Primatology,* ed. I. Goldsmith and J. Moor-Janowski. New York: S. Karger.
11. Thal, D., and Bates, E. 1989. Language and Communication in Early Childhood. *Pediatric Annals* 18:299–305.
12. Adams, J. L., and Ramey, C. T. 1980. Structural Aspects of Maternal Speech to Infants Reared in Poverty. *Child Development* 51:1280–84.
13. Sacks, O. 1989. *Seeing Voices: A Journey into the World of the Deaf.* Berkeley and Los Angeles: University of California Press.
14. Richardson, J. L.; Dwyer, K.; McGuigan, K.; Hansen, W. B.; Dent, C.; Anderson Johnson, C.; Sussman, S. Y.; Brannon, B.; and Flay, B. 1989. Substance Use among Eighth-Grade Students Who Take Care of Themselves after School. *Pediatrics* 84:556–66.
15. Berman, B. D. S.; Winleby, M.; Chesterman, E.; and Boyce, W. T. 1992. After-School Child Care and Self-Esteem in School-Age Children. *Pediatrics* 89:654–59.
16. Fosarelli, P. 1986. Children in Self-Care: A New Priority for Pediatricians. *Pediatrics* 77:548–49.
17. Garbarino, J. 1988. Preventing Childhood Injury: Developmental and Mental Health Issues. *Am. J. Orthopsychiatry* 58:25–45.
18. U.S. Advisory Board on Child Abuse and Neglect. 1990. *Child Abuse and Neglect: Critical First Steps in Response to a National Emergency.* Washington, D.C.: U.S. Government Printing Office.

19. American Humane Association. 1987. *Highlights of Official Child Abuse and Neglect Reporting.* Denver: American Humane Association.

20. Halpern, R. 1990. Poverty and Early Childhood Parenting: Toward a Framework for Intervention. *Am. J. Orthopsychiatry* 60:6–18.

21. Piuck, C. L. 1975. Child-Rearing Patterns of Poverty. *Am. J. Psychotherapy* 29:485–502.

22. Lempers, J. D.; Clark-Lempers, D.; and Simons, R. L. 1989. Economic Hardship, Parenting, and Distress in Adolescence. *Child Development* 60:25–39.

23. Cantwell, H. B. 1988. Parenting Classes in Denver (with Outcome Measured) Working paper, Department of Pediatrics, University of Colorado School of Medicine, Denver.

24. Polansky, N. A.; Chalmers, M. A.; Buttenwieser, E. W.; and Williams, D. P. 1981. *Damaged Parents: An Anatomy of Child Neglect.* Chicago: University of Chicago Press.

25. Crittenden, P. M. 1988. Family and Dyadic Patterns of Functioning and Maltreating Families. In *Early Prediction and Prevention of Child Abuse,* ed. K. Browne, C. Davies, and P. Stratton, 161–89. New York: Wiley.

26. Erickson, M. F.; Stroufe, L. A.; and Egeland, B. 1985. The Relationship between Quality of Attachment and Behavior Problems in Preschool in a High-Risk Sample. *Monographs of the Society for Research in Child Development* 50:147–66.

27. Renken, B.; Egeland, B.; Marvinney, D.; Mangelsdorf, S.; and Sroufe, L. A. 1989. Early Childhood Antecedents of Aggression and Passive-Withdrawal in Early Elementary School. *J. Personality* 57:257–81.

28. Schneider-Rosen, K., and Cicchetti, D. 1984. The Relationship between Affect and Cognition in Maltreated Infants: Quality of Attachment and the Development of Visual Self-Recognition. *Child Development* 55:648–58.

29. Rutter, M. 1987. The Role of Cognition in Child Development and Disorder. *British J. Medical Psychology* 60:1–16.

30. Egeland, B., and Stroufe, L. A. 1981. Attachment and Early Maltreatment. *Child Development* 52:44–52.

31. Murphy, J. M.; Jellinek, M.; Quinn, D.; Smith, G.; Poitrast, F. G.; and Goshko, M. 1991. Substance Abuse and Serious Child Maltreatment: Prevalence, Risk, and Outcome in a Court Sample. *Child Abuse and Neglect: International J.* 15:197–211.

32. Needlman, R.; Fried, L. E.; Morley, D. S.; Taylor, S.; and Zuckerman, B. 1991. Clinic-Based Intervention to Promote Literacy: A Pilot Study. *Am. J. Diseases of Children* 145:881–84.

33. Lutzker, J. R. 1990. Behavioral Treatment of Child Neglect. *Behavioral Modification* 14:301–15.

34. Accardo, P. J., and Whitman, B. Y. 1990. Children of Mentally Retarded Parents. *Am. J. Diseases of Children* 144:69–70.

35. Cantwell, H. B., and Rosenberg, D. 1990. *Child Neglect.* Denver: National Council of Family and Juvenile Court Judges.

36. Ramey, C. T.; Bryant, D. M.; and Suarez, T. M. 1990. Early Intervention: Why, for Whom, and at What Cost? *Clinics in Perinatology* 17:47–55.

37. Helfer, R. E. 1987. The Litany of the Smoldering Neglect of Children. In *The Battered Child,* 4th ed., ed. R. E. Helfer and R. S. Kempe, 301–11. Chicago: University of Chicago Press.

38. Kincannon, M. 1989. The Child Abuse That Doesn't Count: General and Emotional Neglect. *U. C. Davis Law Rev.* 22(3):1039–71.

39. Wasik, B. H.; Ramey, C. T.; Bryant, D. M.; and Sparling, J. J. 1990. A Longitudinal Study of Two Early Intervention Strategies: Project CARE. *Child Development* 61:1682–96.

40. Jones, D. P. H.; Kempe, R. S.; and Steele, B. F. 1988. The Psychiatric Evaluation and Treatment Plan. In *The New Child Protection Team Handbook,* ed. D. C. Bross, R. D. Krugman, M. R. Lenherr, D. A. Rosenberg, and B. D. Schmitt, 163–80. New York: Garland.

41. Garmezy, N. 1991. Resilience in Children's Adaptation to Negative Life Events and Stressed Environments. *Pediatric Annals* 20:459–66.

42. Martin, S. L.; Ramey, D. T.; and Ramey, S. 1990. The Prevention of Intellectual Impairment in Children of Impoverished Families: Findings of a Randomized Trial of Educational Day Care. *Am. J. Public Health* 80:844–47.

43. Buchanan, A., and Oliver, J. E. 1977. Abuse and Neglect as a Cause of Mental Retardation: A Study of 140 Children Admitted to Subnormality Hospitals in Wiltshire. *British J. Psychiatry* 131:1458–67.

44. Oliver, J. E. 1988. Successive Generations of Child Maltreatment: The Children. *British J. Psychiatry* 153:543–53.

45. Hewlett, S. A. 1991. *When the Bough Breaks: The Cost of Neglecting Our Children.* New York: HarperCollins.

46. Lewis, D. O.; Yeager, C. A.; Cobham-Portorreal, C. S.; Klein, N.; Showalter, C.; and Anthony, A. 1991. A Follow-up of Female Delinquents: Maternal Contributions to the Perpetration of Deviance. *J. Am. Acad. Child and Adolescent Psychiatry* 30:197–201.

47. Feldman, M.; Mallough, K.; and Lewis, D. O. 1986. Filicidal Abuse in the Histories of Fifteen Condemned Murderers. *Bull. Am. Acad. Psychiatry and the Law* 14:345–52.

48. Andrews, B.; Brown, G. W.; and Creassy, L. 1990. Intergenerational Links between Psychiatric Disorder in Mothers and Daughters: The Role of Parenting Experiences. *J. Child Psychology and Psychiatry* 31:1115–29.

49. Costello, E. J.; Edelbrock, C.; Costello, A. J.; Dulcan, M. K.; Burns, B. J.; and Brent, D. 1988. Psychopathology in Pediatric Primary Care: The New Hidden Morbidity. *Pediatrics* 82:415–24.

50. Widom, C. S. 1989. The Cycle of Violence. *Science* 244:160–66.

16

Growth Failure in Infants

R. KIM OATES AND RUTH S. KEMPE

Growth failure in infants can be a useful model for thinking about child neglect, as it can encompass neglect of the infant's physical, emotional, and sometimes medical needs. Growth failure also offers us an example of how parent-child interaction can contribute to these aspects of neglect (see chapter 5).

Growth failure in infants that results from the parent's failure to provide for an infant's nutritional and emotional needs is often referred to as "nonorganic failure to thrive"—an unsatisfactory term. Nonorganic failure to thrive is a description, not a diagnosis; invoking it is like saying that a child's diagnosis is "a cough" without giving the underlying cause of the cough. In fact, there is no widely accepted definition of "failure to thrive." A review by Wilcox et al. (1) in 1989 of twenty-two current reference texts and thirteen recent journal articles showed that they lacked consensus in their criteria for abnormality, making it difficult to compare studies. Estimates of children admitted to hospital with "failure to thrive" have ranged from 0.9% (2) to 5% (3), with between 15% and 58% of these infants evincing no organic cause for their growth failure (3, 4).

Inherent in the research which has attempted to clarify distinctions between "nonorganic" and "disease-based" failure to thrive is the vague implication that organic and psychosocial disorders are somehow mutually exclusive. This concept has been repeatedly disproved by clinical experience. While certain behavioral characteristics of infants and young children have been identified as hallmarks of emotional deprivation, malnutrition itself has effects on the emotional state and behavior of infants, children, and adults. It is also true that neglect leading to caloric deprivation may occur in the presence of an organic disease, making management more difficult and increasing the severity of the malnutrition. The fact that an infant is growing poorly and is malnourished is in itself an organic problem (5, 6).

A reasonable definition for the varieties of growth failure where the problem is primarily one of caretaking is:

R. KIM OATES, M.D., is the Douglas Burrows Professor of Paediatrics and Child Health at the University of Sydney and chair of the Division of Paediatrics at The Royal Alexandra Hospital for Children in Sydney, Australia.

RUTH S. KEMPE, M.D., is associate professor emerita of pediatrics and psychiatry at the University of Colorado School of Medicine.

failure to maintain a previously established growth pattern (including the in utero growth pattern as determined by the gestation and birth weight) which responds to a combination of providing for the infant's nutritional and emotional needs.

Schmitt and Mauro have described growth failure in infants as being accidental, neglectful, or deliberate (7). *Accidental* causes can stem from ignorance or lack of understanding of the infant's needs, manifesting, for example, in poor feeding technique or errors in formula preparation, and can usually be corrected with practical help and advice. *Deliberate* underfeeding is unusual and can sometimes masquerade as Munchausen syndrome by proxy (see chapter 18). In the *neglectful* cases, there may be a problem with parent-infant interaction, lack of responsiveness to the infant's needs, psychological disturbance in the parent, or overwhelming social stresses which prevent the mother from adequately meeting her infant's needs for nutritional and emotional nurture.

More and more, growth failure has come to be recognized as a complex problem in which environmental stresses on the family, minor medical problems in the infant which make feeding more stressful or ineffective, problems of attachment or in parenting capabilities which culminate in inadequate or neglectful care of the child, all play a part. These factors can lead in varying proportions to a final common pathway where the infant does not take or retain adequate amounts of food, resulting in growth failure, with malnutrition being the major physical insult.

As is the case in child physical abuse, where the physical injury is an outward sign requiring careful assessment of the family, growth failure in an infant who is not otherwise ill is an outward physical sign which points to the need for a careful assessment of the family, including the parent-child interactions, so that a realistic management plan can be formulated.

Deprivation Dwarfism

Deprivation dwarfism probably represents a distinct subgroup (8) of growth failure. The reported ages of children with deprivation dwarfism—from two to sixteen years—cover a quite different range from that seen in growth failure due to maternal-infant dysfunction—children under two years. The behavior of children with deprivation dwarfism is also different. They are reported to steal and hoard food; to gorge themselves; to eat large amounts of unusual foods, such as condiments; and at times to eat from garbage cans (9). The relationship of growth hormone production to deprivation dwarfism is not clear. Powell et al. (10, 11) found that six of the eight children they studied had low growth hormone levels and that all six had an increase in growth hormone production following improvement in their environment. Other researchers have found growth hormone to be low in a smaller proportion of children with deprivation dwarfism (9, 12) and growth hormone response to an improvement in the environment to be variable (13) or absent (14).

In addition to their bizarre eating behaviors, most children with deprivation dwarfism may show severe depression, often with social withdrawal and apathy. In a study of ten such children, Ferholt et al. (15) also found evidence of abnormal personality development. Although there was in some of the families evidence of occasional deviant parenting behavior, such as an abusive episode, the problem for the parents seemed primarily related to a "negative mental portrait" of the child and rejecting feelings. There was remarkable improvement of the child when he or she was separated from the parents. Psychotherapy for child and parents, and often placement of the child outside the family, were recommended.

Historical Background

In 1915, Henry Chapin reported that the death rate in children under two years of age living in institutions in the United States was 42%. He contrasted the high incidence of mortality in institutions with the much more satisfactory results achieved by the Speedwell Society, which took infants from institutions and fostered them with carefully selected families. Chapin reported that "the majority of them can be saved if a fairly good individual environment can be secured and careful oversight of feeding maintained" (16–18). He also recognized the significant contributive role of parents, including fathers.

Chapin's views did not receive a great deal of attention. It was not until 1945 that interest was rekindled by the observations of Spitz (19), who reported depression, malnutrition, and growth failure in young infants living in foundling homes. Spitz believed that lack of emotional stimulation and loss of maternal care were the main reasons for the growth failure.

Coleman and Provence (20), in 1957, were the first to contend that the syndrome of retarded growth development could also occur to children living in their own homes. The controversy as to whether growth failure was due to lack of calories or lack of affection was heightened in 1969 by Whitten et al. (21), who demonstrated that children emotionally deprived in a hospital setting could still achieve adequate weight gain as long as they received sufficient calories.

Pollitt and Eichler (22) used a control group to show that children with nonorganic failure to thrive displayed more behavioral abnormalities than the controls did. In 1983, Kotelchuck and Newberger (23), using a control group in their study of family characteristics, suggested that the somewhat simplistic concept of "inadequate mothering" should be reassessed. They concluded that minor illnesses in the child as well as isolation from extended family and neighborhood support were characteristics significantly differentiating families who had an infant with failure to thrive. Altemeier et al. (24) in a controlled prospective study suggested that poor nurturing experiences in the mother's own childhood, adverse perinatal effects, and conflicts between the child's parents were among the most important antecedents of nonorganic failure to thrive.

Medical Assessment

One approach to the problem of growth failure in infancy is an inclination to consider the growth failure a result of dysfunctional maternal-infant interaction only after all possible organic causes have been excluded. We do not recommend this approach. Because disorders of parent-infant interaction are a common cause of growth failure in infancy, these causes should be considered in tandem with the search for any organic cause.

Child's History

Taking a careful history is the major diagnostic tool in infants with growth failure and should include four areas: (1) the usual disease-based investigative medical history, (2) the feeding history, (3) a history of growth and development progress, and (4) a psychosocial history. If the parent and child are together while the history is being taken, this is an ideal opportunity to observe the parent-child interaction. In all four aspects of the history, the information should be obtained in a nonjudgmental fashion, so that the parent feels like a partner in trying to find the cause of the infant's growth problem.

Medical History   In particular, the usual medical history should note the gestation and birth weights, because this information will be valuable as a baseline for assessing subsequent growth. The physician should seek to obtain a history of family stature and growth problems in any of the infant's siblings or family members. Immunization history reveals the parents' interest in and ability to utilize medical services on behalf of the child. The physician should also ask about any unusual losses of calories the infant might have undergone through vomiting or diarrhea, as well as through any brief illnesses.

Feeding History   A careful history of food intake should be obtained, starting with the first feeding of the day and proceeding through the twenty-four hour period. Growth failure resulting from breast-feeding is not uncommon, either because of difficulty in achieving early success in breast feeding or because of the mother's failure to recognize the baby's need for increased caloric intake later in infancy (25). If the infant is formula-fed, the doctor should ask how the formula is prepared, to ensure that it is being diluted correctly; how many cubic centimeters of formula the bottle holds; how many cubic centimeters of formula are left at the end of the feeding; how long the feeding takes; what other food, if any, is given in addition to the formula; the technique of feeding; whether the infant is hungry and demands feeding or has to be awakened to feed; whether the feeding is enjoyable for the mother and the infant; and whether the infant is irritable before, during, or after the feeding. As part of the assessment, it is very helpful to observe the mother feeding the child. In taking the feeding history, it is important to obtain specific information and not to be satisfied with vague, generalized replies. Well-framed questions should be able to elicit specific details.

In growth failure due to deprivation, the history which the mother gives, and which she believes to be true, may or may not correspond to what the doctor can discern from direct observation. The mother may not recognize the significance of the growth failure and is often unaware of the infant's obvious emaciation. She may be concerned that her child is feeding poorly, but she may perceive the difficulty to be related only to vomiting, diarrhea, the wrong formula, or the child's disinterest in food.

It is helpful to gain an understanding of what the parent believes to be the problem and what the parent thinks is adequate for the infant's nourishment, as well as an understanding of the source for these beliefs. Sometimes the parents have unusual beliefs about what constitutes a normal diet for an infant (26). Sometimes parents are following bad advice from a well-meaning but misguided friend or relative, while at other times the parent may have an abnormal perception of the child's nutritional needs or his capability to feed himself.

Growth and Developmental History   Charting the infant's growth pattern can be of considerable help. Previous weight, height, and head circumference measurements should be sought from clinic records whenever available and plotted to show the curve of the infant's growth pattern in these three areas. The infant's weight is the parameter which will deviate most from normal. If linear growth has also been affected, it suggests that the general condition of growth failure has been present for some time, although linear growth is never affected as much as weight. It is unusual for head circumference to be affected, except in long-standing or severe cases. The usual pattern found when size percentiles are plotted is for the head circumference to be normal and for the weight to be low out of proportion to any reduction there may be in length. If the growth curve fluctuates—goes up and down— rather than marking a steady decline, details of the circumstances at each change should be obtained.

The developmental history should start by determining as much as possible about the development in utero, whether the pregnancy was planned, the parents' reaction to the pregnancy, the mother's health during the pregnancy, the condition of the child at birth, the reaction of the parents at the time of the birth, what the infant was like to care for in the neonatal period, and what help was available. Developmental milestones should be carefully checked and compared with the normal range; in particular, the infant's age at the first instances of social smiling, vocalization, participation in play activities, interest in toys and surroundings, response to the parents' voices, and reaction with the siblings should be requested. Parental lack of awareness of the infant's milestones or answers giving quite unrealistic dates for those milestones would constitute a cause for concern. It is very helpful for the physician and parent to go over a typical day, with the parent detailing when the infant wakes, who in the family does the feeding, who is responsible for sharing the care of the infant, what the mother's other responsibilities are, and so on. Ascertaining baby-sitting or day-care arrangements is also highly important, because sometimes they represent a major share of the infant's care.

Psychosocial History   It is often helpful to start off by acknowledging to the parent how time-consuming and sometimes worrying it can be to care for an infant. The professional needs to ask about how much rest the parents get, how much time the mother has to herself, whether there is a father or partner, and whether that person is supportive. These questions can usually be asked early on and are rarely threatening for parents. Observing the parents' demeanor and reactions will often yield additional useful information and insight.

Encouraging the mother and father to discuss whether they see the baby's problems in the same way can further the doctor's understanding of the parents' expectations of the child and one another, their child-rearing beliefs, and the way in which they were brought up. This leads naturally to eliciting the parents' own childhood histories; information about abuse, neglect, or parent loss in their early years; and their perception of their relationships with their parents. Obtaining some history about their school experiences and job adjustments will provide impressions of their coping styles, their ability to meet stress and to call on others for help. A discussion of their social activities and friendships may reveal isolation, lack of resources, and depression.

Judicious probing will uncover some stresses in almost all families, although physicians should be careful not to jump to conclusions about a cause-and-effect relation just because some stresses are found. However, garnering an appreciation of the parent's own personal experience of child rearing, their current stresses, their support systems, and their ability to meet their infant's physical and emotional needs will go a long way toward enabling a physician to establish the extent to which growth failure may be a result of problems in the parent-infant interaction.

Physical Examination

A careful physical examination should detect any evidence of disease. In addition, the physician should look for any bruising, burns, or other marks which might indicate physical abuse, recognizing that infants with this type of growth failure are at risk for concurrent physical abuse (27, 28).

Loss of muscle bulk and subcutaneous fat is a characteristic feature of growth failure. The buccal fat pad is lost, and the face looks thin and drawn in contrast to the chubby facial appearance of most infants. Muscle wasting is most evident in the large muscle groups. When the infant's legs are extended at the hips, marked buttock wasting becomes more obvious, with loose folds of skin clearly visible at the buttocks. Loose folds are also apparent at the inner aspects of the thighs if muscle wasting has progressed. Along with poor muscle tone, pallor and cold hands and feet may be noted. Also, because the infant's head circumference is usually normal, the head may look large in relation to the rest of the body.

In addition to manifesting obvious developmental delays, some children are withdrawn and unsmiling, either avoiding eye contact or continually watchful, often with decreased overall mobility. Other children are irritable, distressed, not easily comforted even by the parent. Some older children show an indiscriminate desire for attention and affection but seem to lapse into depressed behavior between contacts (29–32).

Feeding behaviors may vary from voracious hunger to listless acceptance. Some infants show difficulty in feeding, are irritable, easily disrupted, and hard to soothe. Some children over six months of age resist or refuse food, particularly if a battle about control has arisen; other children signal defeat in this control issue, accepting all food passively and without pleasure.

Weight, length, and head circumference should be accurately measured to assist in making the diagnosis, for comparison with previous weights, and as a baseline against which subsequent progress can be measured. Weight should be measured with the child undressed, and the same scales should be used to weigh the child in subsequent visits.

Clinical photographs should be taken. Throughout the whole process of the history taking and physical examination, the interactions and relationship between the parent and child should be observed and documented.

Laboratory Investigation

The history is the major diagnostic tool, supported by the physical and developmental examination. When the history and physical examination suggest the need for a laboratory investigation, it should of course be performed. There is, however, little reason for initiating laboratory investigations to "rule out" organic conditions if they have not already been indicated by the history and physical examination. This caution is supported by a research study which found that out of 2,067 laboratory investigations performed on 185 children with growth failure, only 36 investigations (1.4%) were of positive diagnostic assistance. No test was positive in the absence of a specific indication from the history and physical examination that would normally prompt additional investigation (33).

One exception to this advice concerns urinary tract infection in infants in the first few months of life: as this infection can present with growth failure and exhibit no other symptoms, it calls for laboratory investigation as a matter of course.

Management

Management of the growth failure condition begins with a thorough assessment of the child and family. Assessment of the child should thus include not only gauging his or her growth pattern but developmental and emotional level as well.

For the developmental diagnosis, administering a Brazelton Assessment (34) for the neonate, a Bayley Scales (35) for the young infant, a McCarthy Scales of Children's Abilities (36), or, at minimum, a Denver Developmental Screening Test (37) can help. The infants' most marked developmental delay is usually in their gross motor behaviors and social behaviors, especially speech.

Family Assessment

The procedure outlined above in the "Psychosocial History" section is the basis of the family assessment, leading to more in-depth assessment or referral if indicated. Although the documented descriptions of parents of malnourished and deprived babies vary (38–43), some common features do occur and can be summarized. In general, these parents do not differ from other parents in terms of age, marital status, number of children, or intelligence. Medical complications of pregnancy, delivery, and the neonatal period did not differentiate the parents in many studies, but minor perinatal difficulties or minor illnesses in these children appear more frequently in other recent studies (23, 24). Most parents in large-scale studies come from lower socioeconomic classes, and most suffer financial stress as well as social stress. These statistics may overrepresent poor patients because the review of a problem like infant growth failure (malnutrition due to deprivation) tends to utilize the large clinic populations readily available in a teaching hospital. Because these families that rely on clinics are more often in financial stress than those who consult physicians in private practice, concentrating on them may give a true idea of the malignant influence of poverty, but it de-emphasizes the role of interpersonal difficulties in parenting within these families (39, 44).

In addition to documenting financial distress, some studies describe deprivation or abuse in the parents' own childhoods; social isolation, anxiety, and depression also are frequently present. These characteristics alone do not necessarily distinguish neglectful parents from nurturing parents. To date, no definitive study has been conducted on what makes the difference. However, the one area where there does seem to be a real difference is in the interaction between the mother and the nonthriving child (45–51).

Analyzing videotaped play and feeding interactions and the mothers' complete histories, Haynes et al. (48) compared fifty mother-infant pairs whose infants were hospitalized with deprivation malnutrition to twenty-five matched mother-infant pairs whose infants were growing and developing normally. The mother-infant pairs were all registered for care at the same hospital and were matched for the child's age at intake; the child's sex and birth weight; and the mother's age, ethnicity, and number of living children. The differences Haynes found suggested that the relationship between mother and child is often the crux of the malnutrition problem.

In contrast to the mothers of the healthy babies, the mothers of malnourished infants either asserted that they had no childhood memories or described an unhappy, deprived childhood with a high frequency of sexual abuse, physical abuse, or neglect. Such histories are seen in mothers with difficulties in attachment (47, 50). Some of the mothers of the healthy babies also described experiences of trauma in their childhoods, but they had later found supportive relationships to help them.

The mothers of malnourished infants had real difficulty in recognizing their babies' malnutrition and need for medical help. In all cases there seemed to be a conflict between the needs of the mother and the needs of her malnourished infant, making the mother unavailable as an effective caretaker. Mothering skills were not a significant problem except in the most disturbed mother-infant pairs. Some mothers appeared primarily overwhelmed by current stress in the home or were depressed and therefore unable to respond. When they were made more aware of the feeding difficulties, they seemed unable to recognize how to respond or unable to mobilize themselves to care for their infants' needs. Another group of mothers seemed to be more ambivalent, seeing the growth failure as the baby's problem alone. These mothers were able to respond effectively whenever their own needs and those of the infants coincided, but they misinterpreted the infants' needs when they conflicted with the mothers' wishes. For example, these were mothers who would suddenly feel like playing with the baby early in the feeding, ignoring the child's hunger. A third group of mothers were more hostile and tended to see their babies as demanding or "bad"; this group denied any feeding problems or need for medical help. Their approach to their babies lacked empathy, and they seemed very unskilled in relating to their babies either physically or socially. Their care occasionally became aggressive or even abusive.

Similar problems were observed in play behavior, with most mothers of the malnourished babies showing little ability to play. If not avoiding play entirely, they appeared more often like a peer (sometimes a competitive, teasing, or hostile one) of their child than a nurturing and facilitating adult. Their infants often obviously changed their behavior in response to their mothers' care. A small infant might go to sleep in response to intrusive bottle-feeding; a four-month-old might become unresponsive and turn away from a toy thrust aggressively and noisily in his face. A child who was alternately ignored and handled aggressively might become passive and withdrawn, yet by twenty months show his underlying anger in self-injurious behavior, such as head banging.

An important aspect of the study Haynes reported was the evidence indicating a high degree of continuity in the patterns of interaction between mothers and infants during successive observations over a period of at least one year. Although the details of a pair's activities might vary somewhat with the age and developmental advances of the child, the essential character of the relationship tended to remain much the same over that period.

Hospital or Clinic Care

In the past, management of infant growth failure secondary to maternal-infant dysfunction was carried out in hospital, which offered the advantages of control over the feeding of the infant and easy monitoring of the growth rate. However, hospital environments—even those provided by children's hospitals—are not like home. The mothers of these infants sometimes felt inhibited by the hospital's atmosphere of professionalism and efficiency, although efforts were made to encourage the mother to feel part of the hospital team, to be the infant's main caretaker in hospital, and to accept the credit for the infant's weight gain in hospital (28). The high cost of hospitalization now means that hospital stays must be very short or reserved for serious illness; therefore, if the medical and developmental risks to the child allow, most growth failure cases are managed in the clinic or private pediatric office. The initial decisions about interventions can be conservative if malnutrition is not severe and parents show some degree of concern. The professional health care provider may elect to observe and treat the child through frequent and regular clinic or office visits while gathering further information and judging the effects of education and advice about feeding. These early visits need to be sufficiently frequent, especially for an infant under four months of age, to guarantee that there is little risk of acute deterioration or worsening of the malnutrition.

Because so many medical, social, and psychological issues can complicate the course in growth failure, intervention must be flexible but broad in scope and provide a multidisciplinary approach. Recently, many teaching and community hospitals or clinics have set up feeding and growth clinics (under various titles) which employ multidisciplinary groups of professionals to cope more efficiently with the complex treatment needs in growth failure. The evidence available thus far indicates that this approach achieves the hoped-for outcome more effectively and rapidly (52).

Growth failure can be fatal if malnutrition is not treated, if neglect continues until an accident occurs, or if severe physical abuse intrudes. A continuum between growth failure in infancy and later physical abuse has been described (27): two children out of a series of 24 with growth failure in infancy later died as a result of injuries inflicted by their parents or caretakers (28). Growth failure is not fatal, of course, as long as the infant receives good treatment—but unless the baby's developmental difficulties are also adequately addressed, they may lead to lifelong deficits in learning skills and social behavior. To prevent these unfortunate outcomes, the multidisciplinary team must follow these intervention directives:

- Improve nutrition rapidly, commencing catch-up growth.
- Assess the risk of serious neglect or abuse.
- Manage "minor" medical problems (such as recurrent infections and diarrhea) or physical feeding problems (such as chalasia).
- Provide, within a supportive professional relationship, information and encouragement for better parenting.
- Provide an atmosphere in which the infant's development can improve, appropriately using community resources to support the family environment.

During the initial phase of clinic management, fostering a good relationship between the mother, the doctor, and the nurse is especially important. Ideally, the same professionals should see mother and baby on each visit, creating an opportunity for the development of mutual trust and confidence.

In clinic or office management of growth failure, professionals must continually assess the degree of improvement versus the level of risk to the child, as well as regularly monitoring the child's weight, height, and developmental progress. If improvement stops or is reversed, more vigorous intervention through hospitalization and/or out-of-home placement of the child may be necessary.

Reporting   When growth failure seems clearly to be caused by neglect, the situation needs to be reported to the legally mandated agency for child protection.

The written report should include a description of the child's physical and developmental status, a history of treatment efforts, and a list of the indications and signs of neglect, and an account of the mother's and/or father's failure or inability to parent. Chronological details should be documented. The child protection agency can then elect either to investigate and intervene or to wait until further treatment proves successful or indicates the need for court action. Any report made to child protective services or to the court, along with the reasons for filing the report, should be discussed immediately and fully with the parents.

Even if parents have accepted the need for medical treatment, they may feel betrayed, become angry about the reporting, and wish to reject further treatment. In turn, the doctor and nurse, for their part, may be angry with the parents both for not trusting them and for treating their child so badly. These angry feelings need to be recognized by the professional sufficiently to enable him or her to regain understanding and empathy for the parent's difficulties. Professionals should acknowledge and accept the parents' feelings but motivate them to focus again on how to help their child and themselves.

Intervention   For those cases initially admitted to hospital, a trial of nutritional rehabilitation is necessary. These infants often make a rapid weight gain in hospital, providing that an adequate caloric intake, one based on the infant's expected weight rather than the actual weight, is provided. As we noted earlier, the infant's feeding style can also be observed in hospital. Although a rapid weight gain is usual, it is not invariable. Some infants do not make this rapid weight gain until the second or third week of hospitalization, often when their social behavior also improves.

The percentile chart should be used to see what the child's expected weight for age, based on the fiftieth percentile, should be; the caloric intake should be calculated on the daily needs for an infant of that weight. As this may be a larger volume than the infant can tolerate initially, it may take several days to work up to the full amount. Increasing the caloric density of feedings from the usual 20 kilocalories per 30 cubic centimeters to 24 kilocalories per 30 cubic centimeters of formula can also help achieve the required intake. The infant should be weighed regularly—with the infant unclothed and the same set of scales used each time—and the weight plotted on a graph to show the rate of increase. Initially, especially in hospital, weighing is done daily.

If the infant is being managed at home, the parents must bring the infant in for weekly hospital visits, at least initially, and, ideally, a public health nurse should also visit the family at home at least weekly. Once the goal of expected weight for age has been reached and satisfactory growth is continuing, visits may be scheduled less frequently, although it is important to emphasize that this is a long-term problem, requiring ongoing review.

The clinic's monitoring of the infant's growth must also be accompanied by good medical care. Any medical problems such as recurring respiratory infections, otitis media, or episodes of vomiting or diarrhea need to be treated vigorously. Feeding difficulties due to oral motor dysfunction or to chalasia call for additional intervention: the prompt management of feeding problems such as these in a situation so highly charged with anxiety about food intake can reduce later difficulties.

It is important even at this stage for professionals to be alert to those cases of growth failure which are due mainly to parents' misinformation about formula preparation, feeding techniques, or a baby's nutritional requirements, since a case may have been assessed incorrectly or precipitously. Either in the clinic or on a home visit, the mother should be asked to demonstrate how she prepares the formula and how she feeds the baby. This provides the best opportunity for the doctor or other child care professional to discover those misunderstandings or errors of belief which cause some cases of inadequate feeding. Observing feedings also helps to clarify the quality of the mother-infant interaction during this activity, which may be characteristic of the overall relationship between mother and child. Particular aspects of the feeding interaction which are worth noting are the degree of comfort and pleasure experienced by mother and child, the clarity with which the child gives mother cues about his or her readiness to eat, how comfortable the child's position and the way bottle or breast is offered are for him or her, the child's signals of his needs for pauses, and the way the child signals satiety. On the part of the mother, we look to her ability to recognize and to respond to her baby's cues, her ability to maintain a level of attention to the baby no matter whatever else she may be doing or, conversely, her tendency to become carried away by her own concerns and, in effect, to forget about the baby. If the baby is bottle-fed, it is always very instructive to check at the end of a feeding to see how much of the formula has actually been given. The satisfying nonverbal communication and the comfortable reciprocity which develops in a good mother-child interaction can be encouraged during observed feedings on clinic visits. When, however, the mother seems impervious to suggestions, indifferent or resistant to information about the baby's development capabilities, and blind to or resentful of the baby's bids for attention, we should begin to look for issues in mother's own history which may make it difficult or impossible for her to recognize her baby's needs.

When neglect is the primary issue in growth failure, intervention must focus on ways to support the parents' capabilities to care for the child and to recognize whatever interferes with their parenting potential. Parents who have comparatively good parenting capabilities may be temporarily overwhelmed by adverse circumstances and will need both emotional support and practical help in maintaining their child's care while recovering their ability to cope. Illness in the family, loss of either parent's job, and marital difficulties may each present a crisis which threatens the whole family, preempting the attention which would otherwise go to the baby. The multidisciplinary team members may help the family find medical, community, or financial resources and should provide emotional support while the parents think through any decisions the crisis requires. At the same time, the growth team must maintain a primary focus on the welfare of the malnourished infant, making sure that progress continues while the family as a whole recovers.

Other parents will show lifelong difficulties which have left them chronically deprived and depressed, immature and impulsive, or apathetic and helpless (see chapter 26) (42, 53).

In another group of neglectful parents, we see a more malignant aspect. For them, the child is held to be responsible for their current problems, is perceived as bad, uncooperative, somehow defective. Other evidence in the parents' lives of mistrustful relationships with others, perhaps featuring antisocial or violent behavior, plus their negative or punitive view of the child increase the possibility that these parents are potentially abusive as well as neglectful. They represent an especially high-risk group for failure in parenting.

Inadequate income or lack of support from an absent husband or boyfriend may lead to real economic need. Help with obtaining milk supplements, food stamps, Aid to Dependent Children, child support payments, and housing program help may be encouraged through the clinic personnel. Helping parents who have had trouble coping with social systems learn how to use available help may improve their self-esteem as well as their home situation. This also applies to providing encouragement and information about further education or job training for young, unskilled parents who want to become more independent. A less obvious but no less important concomitant of such supportive efforts is the teaching of problem assessment and problem-solving skills.

A different kind of parent support is the recognition of serious mental handicap, major depression, or psychosis which can render the parent unable to provide consistent child care. If the professional makes sure that psychiatric care is available, as well as making sure that there is a person in the environment who can recognize potential problems and provide or summon assistance, the child may be allowed to remain at home.

To help parents more specifically with the care of the malnourished child, the growth team should focus on the parents' perception of the child's needs as a first step. It is here that team members may find that education about feeding and child development is not enough. If increased information has not brought about any change in the mother's caretaking practices, the answer may lie in the mother's inability to understand because of her own experience (see chapter 5).

One way to forge an alliance is by helping both parents to understand the child better and to find him or her rewarding and responsive. Teaching a new mother to recognize her baby's interest in her face, and the baby's quieting when snuggled by her, will help to prepare the mother for the investment of time involved in holding her baby *en face* and talking to him or her, which will lead in turn to the reward of the baby smiling at her. The use of the baby's developing physical and social potential, paired with the encouragement of appropriate social behavior on the part of the mother or father, fosters attachment and a feeling of success. Recognizing her own importance to her baby and feeling successful in her baby's care are powerful inducements to continue good care and to make herself more skilled, especially if the baby shows pleasure in her company.

In trying to help parents with care of the baby, we must also continue to watch the baby's development. Even if the growth rate stabilizes and begins to improve, additional care may be needed if development does not keep pace. If parents do not exhibit interest in learning to care for the baby or resist efforts to help them, it may become necessary to provide at least some alternative care on a part-time basis.

Alternative Care

Day care for part or all of the day in a small facility or foster home which can provide individualized, consistent care and environmental stimulation for an infant may supplement the home care sufficiently to avoid the immediate necessity for full-time foster care. If, simultaneously, attachment issues and a better understanding of the infant's needs can be promoted for the parent, preferably in the same setting, progress may be sufficient that the child can safely remain at home and an out-of-home placement be avoided.

If full-time foster care seems necessary, it is important to continue treatment very actively with the parents and to facilitate frequent visiting in a setting which promotes a good relationship between parent and child. A one-hour-a-week visit in the crowded social services department is a poor way to encourage a good relationship. More frequent visits in the home and in the clinic—or in the foster home, if feasible—can be more supportive and enjoyable. The professional who supervises these visits can be of great help in making the mother more effective with her child, encouraging reciprocity and enjoyment and promoting parental involvement.

Only after the parents have received good outreach efforts to help them with their baby's care, only after the other therapeutic resources they might need have truly been made available to them, and only after they have refused to comply with treatment or have shown themselves clearly unable to do so should termination of parental rights be seen as the alternative of choice. A brief trial of a very good foster home which will allow or encourage visiting between parents and baby may demonstrate to everyone that the child is capable of responding to good care. Although the parents may be discouraged by and resentful of this demonstration, a clear statement of the growth team's renewed wish to help them care for the baby more effectively may tide them over the feelings of discouragement and resentment. Foster parents who are understanding and able to model good care without criticism can also be very helpful at this juncture. It takes a lot of support for parents to continue working for the return home of their baby, but this can reasonably be done for a time as long as the baby is safe. Making it clear to the parents that the nutritional and developmental safety of their baby is the prime consideration places the emphasis where it needs to be and grounds the expectations of what the parents and professionals need to accomplish together.

Long-Term Results

Growth

If treated adequately, most of these infants catch up in growth to some degree (38, 54). It is likely that as the children become older and less dependent on an adult to feed them, they start to fend for themselves. However catch-up growth is often not complete. Although on follow-up the children are usually within the normal range, they are smaller than control children of similar age and social class (55). A follow-up at four years of fifty-five children hospitalized for failure to thrive showed a suboptimal growth pattern, compared with controls (56). In most studies, from 25% to 30% continued to have weights and often height below the third percentile; a few other groups of children usually showed growth closer to the normal range after prolonged nutritional and psychosocial intervention (of up to two to three years). If growth failure is severe and prolonged enough to lead to decreased brain growth and smaller head circumference, this deficit may persist into adulthood unless intensive nutritional rescue occurs during the period of active brain growth in the first two years of life. However, growth itself is much less a problem for these children than is their emotional and intellectual development.

Emotional Development

A high incidence of emotional disorders has been found in these children on follow-up. Early studies by Glaser et al. (57) and Elmer et al. (58) of children hospitalized for failure to thrive did not use control groups but reported high rates of behavioral disturbance and psychological problems at follow-up intervals averaging three or more years. Hufton and Oates (28) studied the behavior of the siblings of children with growth failure as well as the behavior of the index children and found significantly fewer behavioral disorders in the siblings. When this group of children was next reviewed, at an average of 12.5 years after their initial hospital presentation with growth failure, they exhibited significantly lower social maturity and significantly more behavior problems than did a control group (55). A one-to-four-year follow-up study by Mitchell et al. (59) found no significant differences, although in that study, the follow-up rate was less than 50%, which may account for the discrepancy from other studies.

Intellectual Development

Most follow-up studies show a high proportion of developmental disorders (60, 61). The review by Glaser et al. of forty infants followed for an average of 3.75 years found that

15% were of borderline or retarded intelligence and that 30% of those who were by then of school age had significant school difficulties (57). Slow speech development and difficulty in conceptual thinking have also been reported (58). A 12.5 year follow-up study showed that compared with control children matched for social class, the children who had growth failure in infancy secondary to maternal dysfunction tested significantly lower on the verbal scale of the Wechsler Intelligence Scale for Children and significantly lower in verbal language development and reading skills (55). These problems were probably not caused simply by the initial malnutrition; rather, the depriving and disturbed environment in which these children were raised also contributed noticeably.

A study by Galler et al. (62) showed clear relation of lower IQ compared to controls, on testing via the Wechsler Intelligence Scale for Children, in children who had suffered moderate to severe malnutrition in the first year of life. A further study of the same group described differences in classroom behavior, with the early malnutrition group showing difficulties similar to those associated with attention deficit disorder in poor attention span, poor memory, distractibility, and restlessness. These formerly malnourished children initiated fewer social interactions, and some of the children were also emotionally less able to control impulses and delay gratification. Most clear was their greater difficulty in problem solving (62).

Thus far, the discouraging evidence of continued difficulty reported in follow-up studies of growth failure may reflect the sad fact that once adequate growth was measured in the infant, most families received no further treatment. The few children from situations in which some family intervention or supervision was prolonged for two to three years seem to have maintained their general gains adequately. The nature of the parent-child difficulties or of the neglect seen so often with growth failure indicates a need for more prolonged intervention directed at all dimensions of the problem and not just at initial growth recovery.

Summary

We now understand that nonorganic failure to thrive is a complex problem and, as such, does not have a simple answer. It is not just a matter of increasing the amount of food or stimulation, nor is it a matter of focusing exclusively on maternal factors. Each family should be assessed individually, in relation to their interdependent strengths as well as weaknesses that can be utilized and compensated for in management.

While common threads will emerge in these cases, each family will present a distinctive profile. In some cases, the child's behavior may be a major factor; in others, external stresses may be foremost. In some, it may be maternal skills which need enhancement, while in others, deep-seated problems in the parent's own past may need to be resolved. All of these family factors—parental background, personality, level of child-rearing knowledge, current stresses—and factors in the child interact with one another. In some families, simple, practical measures may be sufficient, while in others, removal of the child may be the option which is in the child's best interests.

What is important in many of these cases is that the family problems which led to the infant's growth failure are frequently long-term ones. Even though the child may recover from the growth problem, the underlying family problems may continue to affect the child's behavior and personality development. This is why many of these families need much more than a thorough initial assessment and a management plan. They also would definitely benefit from regular review and modification of the management plan as required, as well as from specific programs to assist the child in developing acceptable behavior and personality characteristics. Many of these children may not be developmentally ready for beginning schoolwork, and thus preparation for special or remedial work prior to enrollment in kindergarten may be needed. In consequence, professional intervention and follow-up for these families may well need to continue for several years rather than ceasing abruptly after only a few weeks or months.

References

1. Wilcox, W. C.; Nieburg, P.; and Miller, D. S. 1989. Failure to Thrive: A Continuing Problem of Definition. *Clinical Pediatrics* 28:391–94.
2. English, P. C. 1978. Failure to Thrive without Organic Reason. *Pediatric Annals* 7:774–81.
3. Shaheen, E.; Alexander, C.; Truskowsky, M.; and Barbero, G. J. 1968. Failure to Thrive: A Retrospective Profile. *Clinical Pediatrics* 7:255–61.
4. Frank, D. A.; Silva, M. S.; and Needlman, R. 1993. Failure to Thrive: Mystery, Myth, and Method. *Contemporary Pediatrics,* February, 114–33.
5. Goldbloom, R. B. 1982. Failure to Thrive. *Pediatric Clinics of North America* 29:151–66.
6. Hannaway, P. 1970. Failure to Thrive: A Study of One Hundred Infants and Children. *Clinical Pediatrics* 9:96–98.
7. Schmitt, B. C., and Mauro, R. D. 1989. Non-organic Failure to Thrive: An Outpatient Approach. *Child Abuse and Neglect: International J.* 13:235–48.
8. Oates, R. K. 1984. Similarities and Differences between Non-organic Failure to Thrive and Deprivation Dwarfism. *Child Abuse and Neglect: International J.* 8:439–45.
9. Hopwood, N. J., and Becker, D. J. 1979. Psychosocial Dwarfism: Detection, Evaluation, and Management. *Child Abuse and Neglect: International J.* 3:439–47.
10. Powell, G. F.; Brasel, J. A.; and Blizzard, R. M. 1967. Emotional Deprivation and Growth Retardation Simulating Idiopathic Hypopituitrism I: Clinical Evaluation of the Syndrome. *New England J. Med.* 276:1271–78.
11. Powell, G. F.; Brasel, J. A.; Raiti, S.; and Blizzard, R. M. 1967. Emotional Deprivation and Growth Retardation Simulating Idiopathic Hypopituitrism II: Endocrinologic Evaluation of the Syndrome. *New England J. Med.* 276:1279–83.
12. Apley, J.; Davies, D. R.; and Silk, B. 1971. Dwarfism without Apparent Physical Cause. *Proceedings of the Royal Society of Med.* 64:135–38.
13. Krieger, I., and Mellinger, R. C. 1971. Pituitary Function in the Deprivation Syndrome. *J. Pediatrics* 79:216–25.
14. Castells, S.; Reddy, C.; and Choo, S. 1975. Permanent Panhypopituitarism Associated with Maternal Deprivation. *Child Abuse and Neglect: International J.* 3:439–47.
15. Ferholt, J. B.; Rotnem, D.; Genel, M.; Leonard, M.; Carey, M.; and Hunter, D. 1985. A Psychodynamic Study of Psychosomatic Dwarfism: A Syndrome of Depression, Personality Disorder, and Impaired Growth. *J. Am. Acad. Child Psychiatry* 24:49–57.
16. Chapin, H. D. 1915. A Plea for Accurate Statistics in Infants' Institutions. *Archives of Pediatrics* 32:724–26.
17. Chapin, H. D. 1915. Are Institutions for Infants Necessary? *JAMA* 64:1–3.

18. Chapin, H. D. 1908. A Plan of Dealing with Atrophic Infants and Children. *Archives of Pediatrics* 25:491–96.
19. Spitz, R. 1945. Hospitalism: An Inquiry into the Genesis of Psychiatric Conditions in Early Childhood. *Psychoanalytic Study of the Child* 1:53–74.
20. Coleman, R. W., and Provence, S. 1957. Environmental Retardation (Hospitalism) in Infants Living in Families. *Pediatrics* 19:285–92.
21. Whitten, C. F.; Petit, M. G.; and Fischoff, J. 1969. Evidence That Growth Failure from Maternal Deprivation Is Secondary to Under-Eating. *JAMA* 209:1675–82.
22. Pollitt, E., and Eichler, A. 1976. Behavioral Disturbance among Failure to Thrive Children. *Am. J. Diseases of Children* 130:24–29.
23. Kotelchuck, M., and Newberger, E. 1983. Failure to Thrive: A Controlled Study of Familial Characteristics. *J. Am. Acad. Child Psychiatry* 22:322–28.
24. Altemeier, W. A.; O'Connor, S. M.; Sherrod, K. B.; and Veitze, P. M. 1985. Prospective Study of Antecedents for Non-organic Failure to Thrive. *J. Pediatrics* 106:360–65.
25. Pfeifer, D. R., and Ayoub, C. 1978. Non-organic Failure to Thrive in the Breast Feeding Dyad: Keeping Abreast. *J. Human Nurturing* 3/4:283–86.
26. Pugliese, M. T.; Weyman-Daum, M.; Moses, N.; and Lifshitz, F. 1987. Parental Health Beliefs as a Cause of Non-organic Failure to Thrive. *Pediatrics* 80:175–82.
27. Koel, B. S. 1969. Failure to Thrive and Fatal Injury as a Continuum. *Am. J. Diseases of Children* 118:565–67.
28. Hufton, I. W., and Oates, R. K. 1977. Non-organic Failure to Thrive: A Long-Term Follow-Up. *Pediatrics* 59:73–77.
29. Wolker, D.; Skuse, D.; and Mathisen, B. 1990. Behavioral Style in Failure-to-Thrive: A Preliminary Communication. *J. Pediatric Psychology* 15:237–54.
30. Singer, L. T. 1987. Long-Term Hospitalization of Non-organic Failure to Thrive Infants: Patient Characteristics and Hospital Course. *J. Developmental and Behavioral Pediatrics* 8:25–31.
31. Mathisen, B.; Skuse, D.; Wolke, D.; and Reilly S. 1989. Oral-Motor Dysfunction and Failure to Thrive among Inner-City Infants. *Developmental Medicine and Child Neurology* 31:293–302.
32. Dolan, H. J.; Deon, A.; Kaplan, M. D.; Kessler, D. B.; Stern, D. N.; and Ward, M. J. 1991. Disturbances of Affect Expression in Failure to Thrive. *J. Am. Acad. Child and Adolescent Psychiatry* 30:897–903.
33. Sills, R. H. 1978. Failure to Thrive: The Role of Clinical and Laboratory Evaluation. *Am. J. Diseases of Children* 132:967–69.
34. Brazelton, J. B. 1974. *Neonatal Behavioral Assessment Scale.* Clinics in Developmental Medicine, no. 50. Philadelphia: Lippincott.
35. Bayley, N. 1993. *Bayley Scales of Infant Development.* New York: Psychological Corporation.
36. McCarthy, D. 1972. *McCarthy Scales of Children's Abilities.* New York: Psychological Corporation.
37. Frankenberg, W. K.; Dodds, J.; Archer, P.; Breswick, B.; Maschka, P.; Edelman, N.; and Shapiro, H. 1990. *Denver II Training Manual.* Denver: Denver Developmental Materials.
38. Singer, L. T.; Song, L. Y.; Hill, B. P.; and Jaffe, A. C. 1990. Stress and Depression in Mothers of Failure-to-Thrive Children. *J. Pediatric Psychology* 15:711–20.
39. Jacobs, R., and Kent, J. 1977. Psychosocial Profiles of Failure to Thrive Infants: Preliminary Report. *Child Abuse and Neglect: International J.* 1:469–77.
40. Pollitt, E.; Eichler, A.; and Chan, G. K. 1975. Psychosocial Development and Behavior of Mothers of Failure to Thrive Children. *Am. J. Orthopsychiatry* 45:4.
41. Fishoff, J.; Whitter, C.; and Pettit, M. 1971. Psychiatric Study of Mothers of Infants with Growth Failure Secondary to Maternal Deprivation. *J. Pediatrics* 79:209.
42. Polansky, N. H.; Chalmers, M.; Buttenweiser, E.; and Williams, D. 1981. *Damaged Parents: An Anatomy of Child Neglect.* Chicago: University of Chicago Press.
43. Weston, J. A.; Coccoton, M.; Halsey, S.; Covington, S.; Gilbert, J.; Sorrentino-Kelly, L.; and

Kenoud, S. 1993. A Legacy of Violence in Nonorganic Failure to Thrive. *Child Abuse and Neglect: International J.* 17:709–14.

44. Polansky, N. H.; Gandin, J. M.; Ammous, P. W.; and Davis, K. B. 1985. The Psychological Ecology of the Neglectful Mother. *Child Abuse and Neglect: International J.* 9:265–75.

45. Chatoor, I.; Egan, J.; Jetson, P.; Meirelle, E.; and O'Donnell, R. 1988. Mother Infant Interactions in Infantile Anorexia Nervosa. *J. Am. Acad. Child and Adolescent Psychiatry* 27:535–40.

46. Drotar, D.; Eckerle, D.; Satola, J.; Pallotta, J.; and Wyatt, B. 1990. Maternal Interactional Behavior with Non-organic Failure to Thrive Infants: A Case Comparison. *Child Abuse and Neglect: International J.* 14:41–51.

47. Main, M.; and Goldwyn, R. 1984. Predicting Rejection of the Infant from Mother's Representation of Her Own Experience: Implications for the Abused-Abusing Intergenerational Cycle. *Child Abuse and Neglect: International J.* 8:203–17.

48. Haynes, C.; Cutler, C.; O'Keefe, K.; and Kempe, R. 1983. Non-organic Failure to Thrive: Decision for Placement and Videotaped Evaluations. *Child Abuse and Neglect: International J.* 7:309–19.

49. Haynes, C.; Cutler, C.; Gray, J.; and Kempe, R. S. 1984. Hospitalized Cases of Non-organic Failure to Thrive: The Scope of the Problem and Short-Term Lay Health Visitor Intervention. *Child Abuse and Neglect: International J.* 8:229–42.

50. Benoit, D., and Zeanah, C. H. 1992. Maternal Attachment Disturbances in Failure to Thrive. *Infant Mental Health J.* 10:185.

51. Erikson, M. F.; Egeland, B.; and Pianta, R. 1989. Effects of Maltreatment on the Development of Young Children. In *Child Maltreatment: Theory and Research on the Causes and Consequences of Child Abuse and Neglect,* ed., D. Cicchetti and V. Carlson, 647–84. New York: Cambridge View Press.

52. Bithoney, W. G.; McJunkin, J.; Michalek, J.; Snyder, J.; Egan, H.; and Epstein, D. 1991. The Effect of a Multidisciplinary Team Approach on Weight Gain in Non-organic Failure to Thrive Children. *J. Developmental and Behavioral Pediatrics* 12:254–58.

53. Frailberg, S., ed. 1980. *Clinical Studies in Infant Mental Health: The First Year of Life.* New York: Basic Books.

54. Grantham-McGregor, S.; Schofield, W.; and Powell, C. 1987. Development of Severely Malnourished Children Who Received Psychosocial Stimulation: Six Year Follow-Up. *Pediatrics* 79:247–54.

55. Oates, R. K.; Peacock, A.; and Forrest, D. (1985). Long-Term Effects of Non-organic Failure to Thrive. *Pediatrics* 75:36–40.

56. Kristiansson, B., and Failstrom, S. P. 1987. Growth at the Age of Four Years Subsequent to Early Failure to Thrive. *Child Abuse and Neglect: International J.* 11:35–40.

57. Glaser, H. H.; Heagarty, M. C.; Bullard, D. M.; and Pivchik, E. C. 1968. Physical and Psychological Development of Children with Early Failure to Thrive. *J. Pediatrics* 73:690–98.

58. Elmer, E.; Gregg, A.; and Ellison, P. 1969. Late Results of the Failure to Thrive Syndrome. *Clinical Pediatrics* 8:584–88.

59. Mitchell, W. G.; Gorrell, R. W.; and Greenberg, R. A. 1980. Failure to Thrive: A Study in a Primary Care Setting: Epidemiology and Follow-Up. *Pediatrics* 65:971–77.

60. Drotar, D., and Storm, L. 1992. Personality Development, Problem Solving, and Behavior Problems among Pre-school Children with Early Histories of Non-organic Failure to Thrive: A Controlled Study. *J. Developmental and Behavioral Pediatrics* 13:266–73.

61. Ramey, C. T.; Starr, R. H.; Pallas, J.; Whitten, C. F.; and Reed, V. 1975. Nutrition, Response-Contingent Stimulation, and the Maternal Deprivation Syndrome: Results of an Early Intervention Program. *Merrill Palmer Q.* 21:45–53.

62. Galler, J.; Ramsey, F.; Solimano, J.; Lowell, W.; and Mason, E. 1983. The Importance of Early Malnutrition on Subsequent Behavioral Development II: Classroom Behavior. *J. Am. Acad. Child Psychiatry* 22:16–22.

17

Psychological Maltreatment

MARLA R. BRASSARD AND DAVID B. HARDY

While the lack of concise, commonly accepted definitions for all types of child maltreatment has frustrated progress within the field and impeded communication between research, legal, and child welfare professionals, definitional problems have been most pronounced in the area of psychological maltreatment (1–5). In consequence, the need to develop operationalized definitions and standardized assessment techniques has been widely recognized as a priority (1, 5, 6).

Psychological maltreatment has proven difficult to define for a number of reasons. It can result from acts of commission (abuse) as well as from acts of omission (neglect). It can occur in acute instances (e.g., specific threats to children), or it can occur as a chronic pattern of interaction (e.g., constant criticism). It can also occur as very subtle behaviors (e.g., emotional unavailability) or as extreme, pronounced behaviors (e.g., verbal assault). Additional confusion has arisen from the controversy about what should receive more emphasis: the abusive parental behavior or the resulting mental injury of children (7, 5). And, lastly, the situation has been exacerbated by the development of multiple definitions of psychological maltreatment developed for different purposes, such as research, judicial decision making, and clinical intervention (6).

The first coordinated federal investigation of the problem of child abuse and neglect culminated in 1974 with the passage of the Child Abuse Prevention and Treatment Act (CAPTA). This act established the National Center on Child Abuse and Neglect and provided definitions to inform national, state, and community efforts to prevent, identify, and treat child abuse and neglect. Section 3 of the act defines child abuse and neglect as

> the physical and mental injury, sexual abuse, negligent treatment, or maltreatment of a child under the age of eighteen by a person who is responsible for the child's welfare under circumstances which indicate that the child's health or welfare is harmed or threatened. (8)

While CAPTA and its amendments (PL 95-266, PL 98-457, and PL 102-295) provide clear definitions and guidelines to support child welfare agencies and state courts in their efforts

MARLA R. BRASSARD, Ph.D., is associate professor in the Department of Developmental and Educational Psychology, Teachers College, Columbia University.

DAVID B. HARDY is a statistical consultant in private practice.

to deal with physical abuse, sexual abuse, and, to some extent, neglect, they have failed to provide further clarification or direction in dealing with the problems of mental injury. The result has been a child welfare system that is committed to the protection of children's physical well-being but slow to recognize and deal systemically with the mandate to protect their psychological well-being.

Inclusion of the concept of mental injury as relevant to the determination of child maltreatment was controversial from the start. In a dissenting opinion presented in Congress during the preparation of CAPTA, Representative Earl Landgrebe cautioned against including this term in the statute. He warned that the concept was difficult to define, that "clear-cut evidence" of mental injury would be difficult to establish, and that the vagueness of the term would lead to contestation between the rights of parents and the responsibilities of state agencies mandated to implement the law.

While credit must be given to Representative Landgrebe for anticipating the legal problems that were to follow inclusion of "mental injury" in the wording of CAPTA, we now have thirty years' worth of empirical research documenting the relevance of mental injury to child maltreatment issues and a decade-and-a-half's worth of work on definitional issues.

Psychological maltreatment, as defined in this chapter, means "a repeated pattern of caregiver behavior or extreme incident(s) that convey to children that they are worthless, flawed, unloved, unwanted, endangered, or of value only in meeting another's needs (9, 10). "Psychological" is used instead of "emotional" because it seems to better incorporate the cognitive, affective, and interpersonal conditions that are the primary components of this form of child abuse and neglect (11).

The forms of psychological maltreatment are described in table 17.1. Children's experience of maltreatment may fall into one or more of these forms. The six forms of psychological maltreatment are: (1) spurning, (2) terrorizing (threatening), (3) isolating, (4) exploiting/corrupting, (5) denying emotional responsiveness, and (6) unwarranted denial of mental health care, medical care, or education. The subtype definitions given here incorporate family violence under the category of terrorizing or threatening. Some systems (12) include family violence as a separate category of maltreatment, while others (see 13) include it under psychological or emotional maltreatment. The definitions in table 17.1 are outcomes of the theories and fieldwork of Hart and Brassard (2, 14, 15); these definitions are similar to the work of Garbarino and colleagues (4) and are consistent with the National Incidence Study (NIS) definitions (16, 11), the psychological abuse and neglect categories of the Record of Maltreatment Experiences (ROME) (12), the operational definitions of Bailey and Bailey (17), and the ordinal scales of Barnett and colleagues (18), which were themselves derived from the work of Giovannoni and Becerra (19). The level of support for these subtype definitions is such that they have been recommended for application in efforts to establish the state of knowledge and practice (3).

While there is general acceptance for these categories and definitions, they have not been universally adopted, and suggestions have been made for their improvement. For example, some see *threatening* as a better term than *terrorizing,* because "terrorizing" implies the response to a caregiver behavior rather than the act of maltreatment itself. In

TABLE 17.1
Psychological Maltreatment Forms

A repeated pattern or extreme incident(s) of the conditions described in this table constitute psychological maltreatment. Such conditions convey the message that the child is worthless, flawed, unloved, endangered, or valuable only in meeting someone else's needs.

Spurning (hostile rejecting/degrading) includes verbal and nonverbal caregiver acts that reject and degrade a child. Spurning includes:
- Belittling, degrading, and other nonphysical forms of overtly hostile or rejecting treatment
- Shaming and/or ridiculing the child for showing normal emotions such as affection, grief, or sorrow
- Consistently singling out one child to criticize and punish, to perform most of the household chores, or to receive fewer rewards
- Public humiliation

Exploiting/Corrupting includes caregiver acts that encourage the child to develop inappropriate behaviors (self-destructive, anti-social, criminal, deviant, or other maladaptive behaviors). Exploiting/corrupting includes:
- Modeling, permitting, or encouraging anti-social behavior (e.g., prostitution, performance in pornographic media, initiation of criminal activities, substance abuse, violence to or corruption of others)
- Modeling, permitting, or encouraging developmentally inappropriate behavior (e.g., parentification, infantilization, living the parent's unfulfilled dreams)
- Encouraging or coercing abandonment of developmentally appropriate autonomy through extreme overinvolvement, intrusiveness, and/or dominance (e.g., allowing little or no opportunity or support for child's views, feelings, and wishes; micromanaging child's life)
- Restricting or interfering with cognitive development

Terrorizing includes caregiver behavior that threatens or is likely to physically hurt, kill, abandon, or place the child or child's loved ones/objects in recognizably dangerous situations. Terrorizing includes:
- Placing a child in unpredictable or chaotic circumstances
- Placing a child in recognizably dangerous situations
- Setting rigid or unrealistic expectations with threat of loss, harm, or danger if they are not met
- Threatening or perpetrating violence against the child
- Threatening or perpetrating violence against a child's loved ones or objects

Denying Emotional Responsiveness (Ignoring) includes caregiver acts that ignore the child's attempts and needs to interact and show no emotion in interactions with the child. Denying emotional responsiveness includes:
- Being detached and uninvolved through either incapacity or lack of motivation
- Interacting only when absolutely necessary
- Failing to express affection, caring, and love for the child

(continues)

addition, the definitions do not include inconsistent parental behavior, and it has also been suggested that parentification, or role reversal, should be considered a specific subtype rather than listed under *exploiting/corrupting*.

Although still largely ignored in child welfare practice, a small body of research now exists that suggests that psychological maltreatment poses a more serious threat to children

TABLE 17.1 (*continued*)

Isolating includes caregiver acts that consistently deny the child opportunities to meet needs for interacting/communicating with peers or adults inside or outside the home. Isolating includes: • Confining the child or placing unreasonable limitations on the child's freedom of movement within his/her environment • Placing unreasonable limitations or restrictions on social interactions with peers or adults in the community	*Mental Health, Medical, and Educational Neglect* includes unwarranted caregiver acts that ignore, refuse to allow, or fail to provide the necessary treatment for the mental health, medical, and educational problems or needs of the child. Mental health, medical, and educational neglect include: • Ignoring the need for or failing or refusing to allow or provide treatment for serious emotional/behavioral problems or needs of the child • Ignoring the need for or failing or refusing to allow or provide treatment for serious physical health problems or needs of the child • Ignoring the need for or failing or refusing to allow or provide treatment for services for serious educational problems or needs of the child

Source: Office for the Study of the Psychological Rights of the Child, Indiana University–Purdue University at Indianapolis, 902 West New York Street, Indianapolis, Indiana 48202-5155.

than any other type of child abuse or neglect. This chapter will proceed by offering a review of that research, organized around two of the major findings: (1) psychological maltreatment appears to be the most frequent form of child maltreatment, and (2) the existent body of research on the sequelae of psychological maltreatment consistently finds that it is responsible for most of the mental injury and adverse developmental outcomes associated with all forms of child abuse and neglect. We follow with a review of the literature on the intervention and prevention of psychological maltreatment and conclude with a discussion of the importance of thorough assessments and suggestions for approaches and procedures to use in this task.

Incidence

In the published literature, estimates of the incidence of psychological maltreatment vary widely. For instance, a study published by the American Humane Association (AHA) (20) that reported an incidence of only .54 cases per 1,000 children can be contrasted with a study conducted by Bouchard and his colleagues (21), which estimates the incidence at close to 900 cases per 1,000 children. This discrepancy clearly bears witness to the conceptual confusion that surrounds the concept of psychological maltreatment and most likely results from a combination of factors.

The first factor is the absence in current research of an agreed upon definition for psychological maltreatment. Second, different populations are employed in different studies, and psychological maltreatment may well not be equally distributed within different populations. For example, the AHA study used a sample of cases that were reported to official child protection agencies, while the Bouchard study used a sample of the general population. And, third, the method which is used to gather the information differs from study to study. In the AHA study, official case records were reviewed, whereas in the Bouchard study parents were asked to report on the behavior of their partners, thus minimizing the effects of social desirability on responses.

A number of studies of the incidence of psychological maltreatment are based on the extent to which it has come to the attention of human services professionals or official child protection agencies (20, 22, 16). The 1986 national incidence study, sponsored by the National Center for Child Abuse and Neglect (NCCAN), collected information on all cases of child maltreatment known to community agencies serving children—not just official child protection agencies. The study identified 211,100 cases of emotional abuse and 223,100 cases of emotional neglect. Combined, these represent an annual incidence of 6.9 children per 1,000. In general, the incidence of psychological maltreatment seemed to increase with the age of the child, showed no gender differences, and was related to family income (16).

In interpreting the results of the NCCAN and AHA studies, we must keep in mind that only an estimated 5% to 7% of the cases of child maltreatment come to the attention of authorities (23). It is believed that psychological maltreatment goes unidentified even more often than other forms of child maltreatment (7, 24), that, if identified, it is less likely to get screened into the child protective system unless it co-occurs with other types of maltreatment, and that, if screened in, it is less likely to receive serious intervention or result in court involvement (25). For these reasons, it is contended that studies with samples drawn from the general population provide more accurate estimates of the incidence of psychological maltreatment.

Two studies using samples drawn from the general population have investigated the incidence of verbal/symbolic aggression (which crosses several of the identified subtypes of psychological maltreatment), using a set of items from the Conflict Tactics Scales) (CTS) (see 26), an instrument developed to measure interpersonal conflict within families. The first study (27) used data from the Second National Family Violence Survey (28, 29), in which 3,346 parents were interviewed by phone. Six CTS items (including behaviors such as insults, threats, and the "silent treatment") were used to develop a Verbal/Symbolic Aggression Index. Results indicate that 63.4% of children had experienced at least one incident of verbal/symbolic violence during the preceding year, with the average at 12.9 incidents. Since there are no accepted standards of how frequently verbal aggression needs to occur to be considered psychological maltreatment, incidence estimates vary depending on the criterion used. If the criterion is set at ten or more incidents of verbal/symbolic aggression, the incidence is 267 per 1,000—yet, if a more conservative estimate of more than twenty incidents is employed, the incidence drops to 113 per 1,000. Because the data in this study are based on the self-report of violent behavior, it is reasonable to conclude that this is a lower-bound estimate, because some parents will not accurately report the number of times that they have verbally attacked their children.

In order to correct for this social desirability bias, parents were asked, in a second study using the CTS (21), to report on the conflict tactics (including verbal/symbolic aggression) they had witnessed in their family during the last year. As expected, the estimates of verbal/symbolic violence were higher than in previous studies. Eighty-four percent of fathers and 90% of mothers acknowledged witnessing verbal/symbolic violence directed toward their children. These results are supported by retrospective studies that report rates of parental verbal abuse at close to 90% (30) and studies that document the co-occurrence of psychological maltreatment with other types of child abuse and neglect.

There is strong evidence that most abused children tend not to experience only one type of maltreatment but are usually subjected to a number of types of maltreatment (30, 31, 18, 32–35). It has been suggested that not only do different types of maltreatment result in different child outcomes (36, 33) but that different combinations of maltreatment are associated with different sequelae (13, 35, 37, 38).

Claussen and Crittenden (7) investigated the co-occurrence of physical maltreatment and psychological maltreatment in 175 families that had been referred to child protective services (CPS)—96% of these cases involved physical abuse—39 families which had a child receiving mental health services, and 175 control families recruited through community preschools. All of the families were visited between two and four times, and maltreatment was assessed through a combination of measures of child outcomes, parental behavior, and a record review for families involved with child protective services (CPS). Results of the study indicated that in the CPS-case sample, 91% of the cases with physical abuse and 89% of the cases of physical neglect also involved psychological maltreatment. In the community sample, 93% of the cases of physical abuse and 91% of the cases of neglect involved psychological maltreatment. However, in the community sample only 19% of the psychological maltreatment cases involved any physical abuse or neglect.

The results of this study document that psychological maltreatment almost always co-occurs with physical abuse and physical neglect. In fact, the co-occurrence was so common in the cases of maltreatment referred to CPS that the investigators recommend that assessments of psychological maltreatment be performed on all identified cases of physical abuse and neglect. Also of interest is the fact that psychological maltreatment exist at a rate of five times that of physical abuse in their community sample, suggesting that it may be far more common than other forms of maltreatment in the population at large.

Finally, a number of retrospective studies are particularly relevant. Studies of undergraduate women (30, 31) and of adult middle-class women (39) all document the high rates of co-occurrence of various forms of child maltreatment, with psychological maltreatment occurring more frequently that the other types of abuse investigated. In the Briere and Runtz study, 90% of the women reported experiences of psychological maltreatment, while in the Moeller study, 37% of the sample reported severe emotional distress in childhood, including an extreme level of tension in the household (79%), frequent fighting between parents (45%), repeated rejection (27%), and repeated life-threatening invective (16%). An additional 21% of this population reported other forms of emotional abuse, including parental suicide attempts, alcoholic parents, threatened abandonment, or mentally ill parents.

In conclusion, although it is hard to compare results across studies because of different operationalized definitions of psychological maltreatment, populations, and methods of data gathering, there seems to be a growing consensus that psychological maltreatment is the most frequent form of child maltreatment and that it co-occurs in most other cases of child abuse and neglect.

The Sequelae of Psychological Maltreatment

Although the empirical research is limited by the same definitional issues and methodological problems discussed above, an emerging body of literature attests to the destructive consequences of psychological maltreatment and points to its centrality in all forms of child abuse and neglect. This research suggests that it is the psychological concomitants, more than the severity of the acts themselves, that constitute the real trauma and are responsible for the damaging consequences of physical abuse (7, 27), sexual abuse (40–42), and neglect (43, 44).

In their longitudinal study of high-risk, first-time mothers, Egeland and Sroufe (24, 43, 44) found that other than physical injury resulting in death, psychological unavailability may be the most damaging form of child maltreatment, especially during the child's first year of life. Although the behaviors that were used to determine whether a parent was psychologically unavailable were extremely subtle, every one of the children of psychologically unavailable parents in their study were identified as "anxiously attached" by eighteen months of age (33). Many of their measures, such as infant temperament, maternal characteristics, and contextual factors, related to anxious attachment and the other developmental delays identified in these children, but none of these measures demonstrated the predictive power that psychological unavailability did (3). A retrospective study of 118 adult psychiatric inpatients (45) also found emotional neglect related to poor developmental indicators such as a history of psychiatric treatment, higher scores on a symptom checklist, and lower self-efficacy expectations.

Vissing and colleagues (27) in their analyses of the data from the Second National Family Violence Survey found that children who experience frequent verbal aggression from parents register elevated rates of physical aggression, delinquency, and interpersonal problems. These effects were consistent across all age groups and segments of the population. The findings showed that verbal aggression was more closely related to psychosocial problems than was physical abuse and that together they created an even greater risk factor.

Verbal abuse has been implicated in a number of studies on diverse populations as contributing to poor outcomes. In a long-term study of 167 children and adolescents, including psychiatric patients, juvenile offenders, and public school students (35), a history of verbal abuse was more predictive of low enjoyment in living and perception of poor chances of living to old age than a history of any other type of maltreatment. In a retrospective study of college-age women (31), the combination of psychological maltreatment and physical abuse correlated with problems with self-esteem, sexual behavior, and anger and aggression. In Engles and Moisan's retrospective study of inpatients (45), the psychological maltreatment measure of "hostile rejection" related to a history of psychiatric problems, Axis II diagnosis, and to elevated scores on the SCL-90 symptom checklist. Ney (46) has suggested that verbal violence is more likely to be transmitted intergenerationally than is physical violence; furthermore, her research suggests that verbal violence in fact does leave deeper scars (47).

Other research has provided some suggestive findings. Cross-cultural studies of rejection, using the Human Area Relations Files (48), have found that this form of psychological hostility and neglect related to adverse developmental outcomes in children in every culture investigated. Parental rejection was consistently related to deficits of self-esteem, emotional instability, and excessive aggression in children.

A study of young children (49) found that maternal rejection contributed to the child's development of difficulty in controlling aggression, inappropriate responses to distress in others, and self-isolating tendencies by the age of three years—all characteristics that have also been identified as traits of maltreating parents. These behaviors were related to maternal rejection independent of physical abuse; moreover, this research established an empirical link between the mothers' experience of rejection in their own childhood, the distortion of their own cognitive representations of relationships, and the rejection of their own children.

In his classic trilogy on attachment and loss (50), Bowlby provides clinical evidence on the devastating effects of threats of abandonment, and DeLozier (51), who investigated the childhood histories of physically abusive mothers, has provided empirical substantiation. DeLozier thought she would find a high incidence of separation from parents and physical abuse in the childhoods of physically abusive mothers. Instead of actual abandonment and violence, however, she found that abusive mothers had experienced significantly more repeated *threats* of abandonment, beating, and killing from caregivers than mothers in the control group had. Denied emotional responsiveness was also evident. While all of the control mothers reported that they could turn to their mothers for help when in need, only 39% of the abusing mothers reported they could.

In addition, some pertinent research on other types of maltreatment does not mention psychological maltreatment as such, but it does indicate that it is the psychological climate of the family or the quality of the abused child's relationship with the caregiver that determines the developmental course of the young victim. For example, a number of studies suggest that the negative psychological outcomes associated with child sexual abuse are not related to the sexual abuse per se but, rather, to aspects of the family environment, such as lack of parental affection, parental impulsivity, alcoholism, and negative or hostile patterns of interaction (40–42).

The long-term effects of child sexual abuse, both the development of disorders and the course of recovery, have been predicted more accurately by the psychological quality of the parent-child relationship than by the classic indicators—severity, duration, and age of the child at the onset of abuse (52, 53). Results from a study of seventy-seven maltreated adolescents (54) suggests that adolescents who had experienced less emotional abuse were more resilient in the aftermath of other traumas than those who had experienced higher levels of emotional abuse.

To summarize our review of this literature, we can conclude that the available evidence indicates that psychological maltreatment has a more extensive and destructive impact on the development of children than do other types of abuse and neglect, with the single exception of those that result in death. The results also indicate that a large part of the negative impact associated with these other types of maltreatment might be more clearly understood in the context of those abusive or neglectful behaviors within the family that constitute psychological maltreatment. Hence, the accurate assessment of psychological maltreatment may provide more valuable information than more traditional investigations of abuse.

Implications for Intervention

Maltreating families are challenging to treat, manifest significant resistances to change, and often continue to abuse and neglect their children both during and after treatment. Cohn and Daro (55) reviewed evaluation studies of nineteen demonstration projects funded by NCCAN. These were state-of-the-art projects providing a wide range of services to families, including intensive casework, family support, vocational training, and recreational activities, as well as traditional mental health services to parents and children. The authors offer discouraging conclusions: "Child abuse and neglect continue despite early, thoughtful and often costly intervention" (55, p. 440).

Although none of the nineteen projects in the National Clinical Evaluation Study were designed specifically to treat psychological maltreatment, it was identified as co-occurring with other types of maltreatment in 60% of the cases studied and occurring alone in 5% of them. Unfortunately, the results indicate that psychological maltreatment was the form of abuse most resistant to treatment. During the projects duration, the recidivism rate for sexual abuse was only 30%, and the recidivism for neglect was 66%, but psychological maltreatment demonstrated a recidivism rate of 75%. Participating clinicians reported not only that 75% of the families being treated for psychological maltreatment continued to abuse their children in this way while involved in treatment but that clinical ratings indicated such abuse was likely to continue in the future, that clients' compliance with treatment was only minimally related to treatment success, and that almost 10% of the clients actually became more abusive during the course of treatment. It is clear that more research is needed to improve the effectiveness of interventions in all types of maltreatment and, with treatment outcomes so poor, it might seem that our resources would be better invested in prevention programs.

However, despite extensive research on the etiology of maltreatment, a recent review of eleven prospective controlled evaluations of the effectiveness of primary prevention programs indicates that the primary prevention of child abuse and neglect is no more effective than its remediation (56). As with the intervention programs reviewed, none of the eleven programs were designed to address psychological maltreatment per se. The programs were targeted primarily toward the perinatal and young childhood period and included such services as home visitation, intensive pediatric care, parent training, and parent drop-in centers. Although extended home visitation showed some positive effects, most of the primary prevention efforts evidenced no reduction in the rates of physical abuse and neglect. While the conclusions of this review are unsettling, they are congruent with earlier reviews of the efficacy of primary prevention projects (57).

The discouraging picture presented by the evaluation of these intervention and prevention programs is offset by three factors. First, as we have mentioned, none of the programs evaluated were specifically designed to combat psychological maltreatment. A number of researchers have raised the issue that treatment effectiveness is limited by the practice of lumping together all maltreating families in need of services without adequately identifying the types of abuse and neglect present, other problematic parenting practices or child behaviors, and other very real differences or commonalities that exist among maltreating families (57, 38). Since psychological maltreatment has been identified as a core component in all forms of child abuse and neglect, it is only logical that it become one of the core components in the design of interventions. We suggest that treatments which focus directly on the common problem of psychological maltreatment and the related relationship disorders that exist in most maltreating families will prove more effective than treatments that do not, regardless of the type of maltreatment that has brought the family to the attention of community agencies or CPS.

Second, although there is little evidence that interventions or primary prevention efforts are effective at reducing the incidence of child abuse and neglect, there is an emerging body of research literature that indicates that some components of these programs—such as home visitor programs, parent education, and parent support groups—are effective at improving the quality of parenting and eliminating some aversive parenting practices (57).

Third, much evidence does suggest that if child maltreatment is identified and appropriate treatment is provided to victims, much of the associated emotional distress and socioemotional delays can be mitigated (55)—and that this may well also prevent maltreatment of future offspring (see 58, 49). For this reason and, in addition, for the gathering of further research data, we strongly advocate that psychological maltreatment receive thorough assessment when any type of child maltreatment is suspected.

Assessment of Psychological Maltreatment

APSAC Practice Guidelines

The practice guidelines recommended in 1995 by the APSAC (American Professional Society on the Abuse of Children)—*Guidelines for the Psychosocial Evaluation of Suspected Psychological Maltreatment in Children and Adolescents* (9)—offer professionals evaluating children a framework for determining whether or not they have been victims of psychological maltreatment. The guidelines were designed to assist in case planning, legal decision making, and treatment planning both for cases in which psychological maltreatment occurs in isolation and for cases in which psychological maltreatment occurs in conjunction with other forms of abuse and neglect. The guidelines note that psychological maltreatment is often accompanied by or embedded in other forms of child abuse and neglect and, accordingly, should be assessed when professionals are evaluating possible physical abuse, sexual abuse, or neglect. According to the laws of many states, officials are not permitted to make a case determination until evidence has been collected not only of acts of maltreatment that have occurred or are predicted to occur but also of demonstrable harm that has either occurred or is predicted to occur; consequently, the APSAC guidelines deal both with acts and with harm.

Child behavior often produces evidence of psychological maltreatment, but the presence of emotional and behavior problems are not necessarily indicative of psychological maltreatment. Assessors are cautioned about inferring causation from behavior, as there are multiple pathways to particular behaviors. Also, it is particularly important to understand that base rates affect the diagnostic value of specific behavior. For instance, some signs of trauma and distress in children, such as post-traumatic stress disorder, are more common in neighborhoods with high rates of crime; hence, the cause of such signs may be accumulated environmental influences rather than caregiver-perpetrated maltreatment. Thus, while close observation of child behaviors can certainly yield useful information, child behavior alone is not sufficient to determine whether psychological maltreatment has occurred; it is also true that some victims of psychological maltreatment show no discernable signs of distress.

The APSAC guidelines recommend that in any evaluation of a family for possible psychological maltreatment, assessors should carefully note the children's developmental levels. Assessment of a child's relationship with the caregiver should take into account the primary developmental tasks of the child and the related tasks that are placed upon the caregiver (see chapter 25). The APSAC guidelines illustrate the important developmental tasks of each age, and assessors are encouraged to consider the degree to which the caregiver-child relationship and the family environment are facilitating or frustrating the achievement of these important developmental tasks.

To determine the level of severity of psychological maltreatment, evaluators are advised to consider the intensity or extremeness, the frequency, and the chronicity of maltreatment. The degree to which the psychological maltreatment pervades the caregiver-child relationship; protective factors; the salience of the maltreatment, given the developmental periods in which it occurs; and the extent to which negative child development outcomes exist or are predicted should all be weighed in assessing the severity of psychological maltreatment.

Barnett, Manly, and Cicchetti (18) have developed a system for evaluating the severity of all different forms of maltreatment on an ordinal scale, based on the ratings of professionals. Interestingly, they found that mild forms of maltreatment exert a powerful affect on children's adjustment and argue that confining the definition of maltreatment to include only the extreme end of the continuum may result in the exclusion of a considerable number of maltreated children who are suffering from the psychological consequences of maltreatment (see also 7).

In order to assess level of harm, the APSAC guidelines recommend that assessors consider the Federal Individuals with Disabilities Education Act (59), which includes a definition of severe emotional disturbance, or consider the mental disorders described in the American Psychiatric Association's *Diagnostic and Statistical Manual of Mental Disorders (DSM-IV)* (60) to guide determinations of current or predicted harm as a result of psychological maltreatment. The Individuals with Disabilities Education Act defines serious emotional disturbance as including a condition in which a child exhibits over a long period of time one or more of the following characteristics to such a marked degree that his or her educational performance is adversely affected: an inability to learn that cannot be explained by intellectual, sensory, or health factors; an inability to build and maintain satisfactory interpersonal relationships with peers and teachers; inappropriate types of behavior or feelings under normal circumstances; a general pervasive mood of unhappiness or depression; or a tendency to develop physical symptoms or fears associated with personal or school problems.

We feel that the above definition of severe emotional disturbance coupled with the APSAC list of developmental tasks that are critical for each developmental period can be used as a guide to both diagnosing and identifying the areas in which children are expected to exhibit appropriate mastery at each age level. The presence of one or more of the signs of severe emotional disturbance or the absence or clear dysfunction of an age-appropriate task should alert the evaluator that a child shows demonstrable harm, especially should caregiver psychological maltreatment be confirmed by the evaluation.

Caregiver competencies and risk factors should be assessed because this information can help professionals more readily identify child maltreatment and the attendant issues relevant to family intervention. It is also important to assess the family's social context and economic circumstances, as the caregivers may not be able to handle the pressures of poverty, community violence, and/or homelessness, and should not be held accountable for events out of their control. Finally, assessors should be sensitive to and knowledgeable about the ethnic differences in caretaking styles and customs and seek consultation as needed.

Assessment Techniques and Sources of Information

Observation of the Child-Caregiver Relationship   Since psychological maltreatment consists, for the most part, of messages a child receives about him- or herself from important others in the social environment, professionals should, if at all possible, observe the child-caregiver relationship and the child's other important relationships as well. Repeated observations may be necessary to obtain a representative sample of behavior because of the chronicity of much psychological maltreatment. Two experimental scales have been developed that show some promise for eventual use as part of a battery to assess psychological maltreatment.

Psychological Maltreatment Rating Scales (PMRS)   The PMRS (14, 61) uses global rating scales of actual parent-child interaction relevant to psychological maltreatment. The instrument contains four scales that assess subclinical psychological abuse and neglect (spurning, terrorizing, corrupting/exploiting, denying emotional responsiveness) and nine scales that assess prosocial parenting (the absence of which indicates psychological neglect).

The PMRS was validated on a sample of forty-nine preschool and early-school-aged children between the ages of four and nine, half of whom were from families with substantiated histories of maternal physical abuse or neglect, and the other half of whom had neither any known history of maltreatment nor any observed maltreatment during the home visits. Psychological maltreatment was independently verified from case records using NIS criteria. Blind raters obtained interrater reliability for the scales ranging from .72 to .94. An exploratory factor analysis identified three highly consistent factors—quality of emotional support, psychological abuse, and facilitation of cognitive development—that accounted for 65% of the variance in PMRS scores. The factor solution was replicated on the sample of ten pairs of CPS-identified maltreating mothers and control-group mothers and their infant toddlers (61). Discriminant analysis correctly identified 81.63% of the maltreating mothers and the comparison mothers, with a sensitivity of .92 (proportion of maltreating mothers to children who are correctly identified), and a specificity of .71 (proportion of children not maltreated who are correctly excluded). The PMRS was also significantly related to peer acceptance of children regardless of group (62).

The authors recommend that the PMRS be used only in conjunction with collateral reports of psychological maltreatment from as many other sources as possible. If the scales are to be used for intervention and judicial decision making, further refinement is needed. The scales were developed on a small number of cases, the interrater reliability is not consistently in the acceptable range for clinical use, and the test/retest reliability is based on nonmaltreating, middle-class, mother-child dyads with corresponding child behavior problems.

The CARE Index   The CARE Index (63) is a fifty-two-item behavioral rating system designed to assess the quality of adult and child interaction during a three-minute videotaped play episode. The rated aspects of the encounter fall into seven categories of dyadic interaction: facial expression, vocal expression, position and bodily contact, expression of affection, pacing, control, and choice of activity. For each of these aspects, the quality of adult behavior is rated on its level of sensitiveness, controllingness, and unresponsiveness. Child behavior for each aspect is rated on four styles of conduct: cooperative, difficult, passive, and compulsively compliant. Items describing quality are summed, yielding three scale scores for adults and four for children. Blind raters obtained item-by-item agreement ranging from 81 to 89 per unit across three studies. The CARE index scores discriminate four caregiver styles: neglectful, physically abusive, marginally maltreating, and adequate; these dyads show corresponding child behavior patterns.

Although direct observation is desirable, it is not always necessary to form an opinion on whether or not psychological maltreatment has occurred. It is also possible that the caregiver-child interaction may not reflect typical behavior. Other methods for assessing the child-caregiver relationship include interviews with the caregiver and the child (if old enough), review of pertinent records, and consultation with other professionals; collateral reports from siblings, grandparents, school and day care personnel, neighbors, and others are also important. The measures described in the sections that follow could be used with parents, other knowledgeable adults, and older children to collect information on psychological maltreatment and make decisions as to its severity and chronicity.

Verbal/Symbolic Aggression Index of the Conflict Tactic Scales   The only nationally normed measure of psychological abuse is the six-item Verbal/Symbolic Aggression Index of the Conflict Tactic Scales (CTS). This self-report questionnaire measures verbal/symbolic aggression, reasoning, and physical violence that result from conflict and compares them with other measures of a family's interactions and of the functioning of children outside the home. The author defines *verbal/symbolic aggression* as "a communication intended to cause psychological pain to another person or a communication perceived as having that intent" (64). The current form in use is Form R; it takes three minutes to administer and provides data on the incidence, prevalence, and chronicity of physical and psychological maltreatment.

The CTS was originally developed for large-sample epidemiological studies conducted by telephone. It has been used very widely for research on spouse abuse and, to a lesser extent, by researchers and clinicians interested in investigating child abuse (64). Since then, this simple nineteen-item, seven-point measure has been used for diagnosis and assessment in clinical settings and for evaluating the effect of treatment and prevention programs on the rate of child abuse and spousal violence. Studies on child maltreatment using the measure have investigated national maltreatment rates, risk factors for child maltreatment, effects of physical maltreatment on children, and national trends in the incidence of physical maltreatment; the CTS has also been used in one national study on the psychological maltreatment of children (27).

Problems with CTS as a measure of psychological maltreatment include the small number of items available, the inappropriateness of these items for assessing infants and toddlers, the lack of concurrent validity studies, and the low level of internal consistency reliability (.62 to .77). The strengths of the CTS are that its questions are directed to conflict resolution as opposed to child abuse, which makes it much more acceptable to caregivers; it possesses concurrent validity for spouse abuse; its high rates of reporting by the public suggest that parents are willing to divulge abusive behavior to strangers; and it does not seem to be confounded with social desirability (65, 66). CTS norms of conflict tactics are available for parents and children, as reported by mothers and by fathers in the National Family Violence Resurvey in 1985. The use of the entire measure allows clinicians to screen for verbal/symbolic aggression as well as for physical abuse during the interview. The CTS manual (26) provides information on scoring both by hand and by computer (using SPSS commands). In addition, CTS is available in two Spanish translations.

The author of the measure and his colleagues have developed a new version of the CTS (CTS-2) as part of a coordinated package of instruments. Psychometric data on CTS-2 has yet to be published, but the instrument is obtainable from the senior author (26). CTS-2 orders the items randomly, as opposed to hierarchically, it asks parents to describe what they themselves have done as well as what the other parent has done, and it includes an additional four items. Furthermore, new supplemental scales examine weekly discipline, neglect, and sexual abuse. CTS-2, with the supplemental scales, would allow an evaluator to efficiently obtain self-report data on physical, psychological, and sexual abuse and neglect from both parental figures in the home, which may provide a much better idea of all of the maltreatment to which a child is subjected..

Systems for Rating Case Records and Integrating Other Data

Four research teams have developed measures that evaluate the degree of psychological maltreatment as well as other forms of abuse and neglect present in case records or that integrate data from case records and other sources. We will briefly review these different systems for classifying cases because they may be helpful to child protective services workers and researchers and because they can be (and have been) modified for use as interview tools.

Giovannoni and Becerra (19) did an excellent job of exhaustingly categorizing and ranking different forms of maltreatment present in almost one thousand investigated and open CPS cases in four California counties. Barnett, Manly, and Cicchetti (18) built their work to develop a system for examining and classifying CPS workers' case records. They looked at five subtypes of child maltreatment (physical abuse; sexual abuse; physical neglect; emotional maltreatment; and moral/legal/educational maltreatment, which they lumped together because of its low occurrence). Using one hundred social workers as raters, they ranked all forms of maltreatment in a range from one (being low) to five (being high), yielding an ordinal scale of severity. They assessed frequency and chronicity by looking at the number of CPS reports for frequency and the number of months of active CPS involvement for chronicity. They examined nine developmental periods, with a heavy focus on the early years. They also examined the number of separations and placements, and they categorized the different perpetrators.

Their system has done a particularly nice job of providing clear definitions, with inclusion and exclusion criteria and examples for each particular form of maltreatment. They have the most difficulty with the emotional maltreatment subtype, finally defining it as "those acts that were judged by Child Protective Services to be instances of maltreatment that involved thwarting of children's emotional needs. These needs included needs for psychological safety and security in the environment, for acceptance and positive regard, and for age-appropriate autonomy, or sufficient opportunities to exploit environment and extra familial relationships" (18, p. 36). The authors claim that this system works well with other records, has been tried as a social work interview, and has been used with court and mental health records successfully. Their system does not include positive parenting.

Record of Maltreatment Experiences (ROME)   The ROME (12, 67) is an eighty-seven-item instrument designed to catalog the complete victimization history of a child or adolescent. It is organized into five subscales that measure constructive parenting practices, psychological maltreatment, exposure to family violence, sexual abuse, and physical abuse. The constructive parenting items describe prosocial parental behavior, and the absence of these items is used to indicate psychological and physical neglect. Originally designed for caseworkers to complete, it was modified for use with CPS case records and interviews with adolescents about their experiences (34, 67).

On the ROME, *psychological abuse* was defined as "communicative acts that have the potential to damage psychological attributes of the child (e.g., self-esteem)" and *psychological neglect* was defined as "acts of omission that may result in negative psychological consequences for the child" (12, p. 169). Psychological neglect was assessed by the absence of items on the Constructive Parenting Practices Scale. The twenty-four items in the Psychological Maltreatment Scale start with a description of parent or caregiver behaviors such as "tells child s/he is a burden, was unwanted (e.g., I wish you were never born)." Raters are then asked to circle one of six possibilities for each of three age categories. The six possibilities are: (1) no information, (2) suspected problem, (3) never occurs or occurred, (4) occurs or occurred rarely, (5) occurred sometimes or on several occasions, and (6) occurs or occurred often or very often. The three age periods are birth to age six, seven to twelve years, and thirteen to sixteen years. The authors report that a rating via the ROME by trained research assistants using agency records takes about two hours to process.

The factor structure of the ROME for a total sample of adolescents identified seven factors (67). The largest factor was psychological abuse, which accounted for 23.2% of the total variance of the solution (56.7%); this solution consisted of nineteen variables that described denigrating and threatening behavior towards children. Partner abuse was the second factor, followed by child neglect and physical abuse. The fifth and sixth factors were labeled violence/destructive and serious threats/assaults. A simple additive scale was created on sexual abuse using sixteen items. This resulted in five derived scales that reflected the principal types of maltreatment: psychological abuse, partner abuse, physical abuse, neglect, and sexual abuse.

The authors of ROME found that severity ratings were not helpful in predicting the adjustment of children, which they felt was perhaps due, in part, to the tremendous difficulty of discriminating levels of severity using file data. They noted that the global ratings completed by CPS staff were just as predictive as was the full ROME of the youth's adjustment using the Child Behavior Checklist. And, most important, they noted that the global ratings made by adolescent victims were the most potently predictive of children's adjustment (34). As a result, the authors recommend that the global ratings on the ROME be used. The five major types of child abuse are listed on the global ratings form, and raters are asked to indicate whether these types occur not at all, mildly, moderately, or severely and whether the perpetrator was the mother, father, or other individual. This in turn is accompanied by another form, which requests family information on the amount of contact a child has with parents, degree of alcohol abuse, psychiatric problems, criminal behavior in the family, and the child's residential and legal history from birth to the present time. The authors obtained interrater agreement of .79 to .98 between other researchers and social workers in the global rating scale, with emotional maltreatment being the lowest and sexual abuse the highest.

Multiple Informants Rating System   Kaufman and her colleagues (13) developed a system for integrating information about children's maltreatment experiences from CPS worker reports, parent interviews, medical records, and clinical observations. Their system allows the synthesis of information provided by the different sources of data in order to derive a zero-to-four-point rating of four categories of maltreatment experiences: physical abuse, neglect, sexual abuse, and emotional maltreatment. The authors report Kappa reliability coefficients for these scales as .88, .73, .83, and .90, respectively. In an examination of this system using thirty-four families who were under CPS supervision, the authors discovered information from parent interviews and medical records that led them to classify twenty-eight children as having suffered additional types of maltreatment experiences not reported by CPS workers. In twenty-four cases, the authors obtained information indicating that specific types of abuse were more severe than those reported by CPS workers.

The authors' Emotional Maltreatment Scale includes marital violence and parental substance abuse as well as emotional unavailability and/or rejection. The scale is arranged as follows: 0 is no evidence of emotional maltreatment; 2 is exposure to parental substance abuse and/or marital violence, with no evidence of emotional unavailability or rejection; 3 is either exposure to parental drug or alcohol abuse and/or marital violence with evidence of mild emotional unavailability and/or rejection, or no evidence of parental substance abuse or marital violence but exposure to extreme parental rejection (for example, the child is called unworthy of love; the parent threatens to send the child away and/or leave the child); and 4 is exposure to parental drug or alcohol abuse and/or marital violence in addition to extreme parental rejection (child called unworthy of love, openly rejected, threatened with abandonment, or abandoned). Raters were instructed to increase emotional maltreatment by one point if marital violence occurred throughout most of the child's life or if parental drug or alcohol abuse occurred throughout most of a child's life. Likewise, they were to decrease emotional maltreatment by one point if marital violence and/or drug or alcohol abuse had occurred more than five years ago.

The validity of the maltreatment rating system was examined by comparing ratings on the scale with several independent measures of children's behavior. The Externalizing Scale of the Child Behavior Checklist was significantly correlated with ratings of physical abuse and emotional maltreatment, and a stepwise multiple aggression analysis indicated that the physical abuse rating accounted for 32% of the variance in children's acting-out behavior scores. In terms of depression, children were given a structured interview (the kiddie-SADS) designed to determine the presence or absence of mental disorders: emotional maltreatment and physical abuse accounted for 12% of the variance, with emotional maltreatment accounting for most of the unique variance. Neglect ratings were significantly correlated with intellectual functioning and accounted for 10% of the variance.

The authors found that parents were a particularly valuable source of data. Parents provided the majority of information about new incidents of maltreatment; however, the information they provided did not completely overlap with CPS reports—in consequence, both seem necessary for obtaining a complete picture. Medical records and observation identified no new cases, but they did add information on severity.

Summary

Child welfare policy and the resultant CPS practice do not develop in a rational and cumulative fashion. Policy develops in reaction to specific crises and in the context of social contestation in which the varying interests and values of parents, children, taxpayers, social agencies, and governmental bodies are mediated. As researchers and clinicians, we must recognize our limited role in the social and political process. Although we might like to influence the outcomes of this process directly, our most significant contribution can be to provide a context in which the conflicting interests and values can be synthesized with and informed by empirically based knowledge about child development (57). In addressing psychological maltreatment, operationalized definitions and psychometrically sound clinical assessments can go a long way toward clarifying criteria for intervention in families, determining relevant treatment goals, and providing a framework for the development of future maltreatment prevention and treatment policy efforts. Although our understanding of psychological maltreatment is still in its early stages, significant progress has been made, and continued support for research in this area is indicated.

References

1. Barnett, D.; Manly, J. T.; and Cicchetti, D. 1991. Continuing toward an Operational Definition of Psychological Maltreatment. *Development and Psychopathology* 3:19–29.
2. Brassard, M. R.; Germain, R.; and Hart, S. N., eds. 1987. *Psychological Maltreatment of Children and Youth.* New York: Pergamon Press.
3. Egeland, B. 1991. From Data to Definition. *Development and Psychopathology* 3:37–43.
4. Garbarino, J.; Guttman, E.; and Seeley, J. 1986.*The Psychologically Battered Child: Strategies for Identification, Assessment, and Intervention.* San Francisco: Jossey-Bass.
5. McGee, R. A., and Wolfe, D. A. 1991. Psychological Maltreatment. Toward an Operational Definition. *Development and Psychopathology* 3:3–18.
6. Panel on Research on Child Abuse and Neglect, National Research Council 1993. *Understanding Child Abuse and Neglect.* Washington, D.C.: National Academy Press.
7. Claussen, A. H., and Crittenden, P. M. 1991. Physical and Psychological Maltreatment: Relations among Types of Maltreatment. *Child Abuse and Neglect: International J.* 15:5–18.
8. Child Abuse Prevention and Treatment Act, 42 U.S.C. §5102 (1983).
9. American Professional Society on the Abuse of Children. 1995.*Guidelines for the Psychosocial Evaluation of Suspected Psychological Maltreatment in Children and Adolescents.* Chicago: APSAC.
10. Brassard, M. R.; Hart, S. N.; and Hardy, D. 1991. Psychological and Emotional Abuse of Children. In *Case Studies in Family Violence,* ed. R. T. Ammerman and M. Hersen, 255–70. New York: Plenum Press.
11. Hart, S. N., and Brassard, M. R. 1990. Psychological Maltreatment of Children. In *Treatment of Family Violence,* ed. R. T. Ammerman and M. Hersen, 77–112. New York: Wiley.
12. McGee, R. A.; Wolfe, D. A.; and Wilson, S. K. 1990. *A Record of Maltreatment Experiences.* Toronto: Institute for the Prevention of Child Abuse. Obtainable from D. A. Wolfe, Institute for the Prevention of Child Abuse, 25 Spadina Road, Toronto, Ontario, Canada, M5R259.
13. Kaufman, J.; Jones, B.; Stieglitz, E.; Vitulano, L.; and Mannarino, A. P. 1994. The Use of Multiple Informants to Assess Children's Maltreatment Experiences. *J. Family Violence* 9 (3):227–48.
14. Brassard, M. R.; Hart, S. N.; and Hardy, D. 1993. The Psychological Maltreatment Rating Scales. *Child Abuse and Neglect: International J.* 17:715–29.
15. Hart, S. N., and Brassard, M. R. 1987. A Major Threat to Children's Mental Health: Psychological Maltreatment. *Am. Psychologist* 42:160–65.
16. National Center on Child Abuse and Neglect. 1988. *Study Findings: Study of National Incidence and Prevalence of Child Abuse and Neglect.* Washington, D.C.: U.S. Department of Health and Human Services.
17. Bailey, F. T., and Bailey, W. H. 1986. *Operational Definitions of Child Emotional Maltreatment.* Augusta, Maine: Maine Department of Social Services.
18. Barnett, D.; Manly, J. T.; and Cicchetti, D. 1993. Defining Child Maltreatment: The Interface between Policy and Research. In *Child Abuse, Child Development, and Social Policy,* ed. D. Cicchetti and S. Toth, 7–74. Norwood, N.J.: Ablex.
19. Giovannoni, J. M., and Becerra, R. M. 1979. *Defining Child Abuse.* New York: Free Press.
20. American Humane Association. 1988. *Highlights of Official Child Abuse and Neglect Reporting, 1986.* Denver: American Humane Association.
21. Bouchard, C.; Tessier, R.; Fraser, A.; and Laganiere, J. In press. La Violence familiale envers les

enfants: Prevalence dans la Basse-ville et étude de validité de la mesure. In *Enfance et famille: Contextes de developement,* ed. R. Tessier, C. Bouchard, and G. M. Tarabulsy. Quebec: Presses de l'Université Laval.

22. National Center on Child Abuse and Neglect. 1981. *Study Findings: National Study of Incidence and Severity of Child Abuse and Neglect, 1980.* Washington, D.C.: U.S. Department of Health, Education, and Welfare.

23. Green, A. H. 1988. Child Maltreatment and Its Victims: A Comparison of Physical and Sexual Abuse. *Psychiatric Clinics of North America* 11:591–610.

24. Egeland, B., and Erickson, M. 1987. Psychologically Unavailable Caregiving. In *Psychological Maltreatment of Children and Youth,* ed. M. R. Brassard, R. Germain, and S. N. Hart, 110–20. New York: Pergamon Press.

25. Melton, G., and Davidson, H. 1987. Child Protection and Society: When Should the State Intervene. *Am. Psychologist* 42:172–75.

26. Strauss, M. 1995. *Manual for the Conflict Tactics Scales (CTS) and Test Forms for the Revised Conflict Tactics Scales.* Durham, N.H.: Family Research Laboratory, University of New Hampshire.

27. Vissing, Y. M.; Strauss, M. A.; Gelles, R. J.; and Harrop, J. W. 1991. Verbal Aggression by Parents and Psychosocial Problems of Children. *Child Abuse and Neglect: International J.* 15:223–38.

28. Straus, M., and Gelles, R. J. 1986. Societal Change and Change in Family Violence from 1975 to 1985 as Revealed by Two National Surveys. *J. Marriage and the Family* 48:465–79.

29. Straus, M., and Gelles, R. 1990. *Physical Violence in American Families: Risk Factors and Adaptations to Violence in 8,145 families.* New Brunswick, N.J.: Transaction.

30. Briere, J., and Runtz, M. 1988. Multivariate Correlates of Childhood Psychological and Physical Maltreatment among University Women. *Child Abuse and Neglect: International J.* 12:331–41.

31. Briere, J., and Runtz, M. 1990. Differential Adult Symptomology Associated with Three Types of Child Abuse Histories. *Child Abuse and Neglect: International J.* 14:357–64.

32. Cicchetti, D., and Rizley, R. 1981. Developmental Perspectives on the Etiology. Intergenerational Transmission and Sequelae of Child Maltreatment. *New Directions for Child Development* 11:31–55.

33. Egeland, B., and Sroufe, L. A. 1981. Attachment and Early Maltreatment. *Child Development* 52:44–52.

34. McGee, R. A.; Wolfe, D. A.; Yuen, S. A.; Wilson, S. K.; and Carnochan, J. 1995. The Measurement of Maltreatment: A Comparison of Approaches. *Child Abuse and Neglect: International J.* 12(2):233–49.

35. Ney, P. G.; Fung, T.; and Wickett, A. 1994. The Worst Combinations of Child Abuse and Neglect. *Child Abuse and Neglect: International J.* 18(9):705–14.

36. Crittenden, P. 1985. Maltreated Infants: Vulnerability and Resilience. *J. Child Psychology and Psychiatry* 26(1):85–96.

37. Schneider-Rosen, K.; Braunwald, K. G.; Carlson, V.; and Cicchetti, D. 1985. Current Perspectives in Attachment Theory: Illustration from the Study of Maltreated Infants. In *Growing Points in Attachment Theory and Research: Monographs of the Society for Research on Child Development,* ed. I. Bretherton and E. Waters, 194–210. Chicago: University of Chicago Press.

38. Youngblade, L., and Belsky, J. 1990. Social and Emotional Consequences of Child Maltreatment. In *Children at Risk,* ed. R. Ammerman and M. Hensen, 109–46. New York: Plenum Press.

39. Moeller, T.; Bachman, G.; and Moeller, J. 1993. The Combined Effect of Physical, Sexual, and Emotional Abuse during Childhood: Long-Term Health Consequences for Women. *Child Abuse and Neglect: International J.* 17:623–40.

40. Abramson, E., and Lucido, G. 1991. Childhood Sexual Experience and Bulimia. *Addictive Behaviors* 16:529–32.

41. Friedrich, W.; Bulke, R.; and Urguiza, A. 1987. Children from Sexually Abusive Families: A Behavioral Comparison. *J. Interpersonal Violence* 2:391–402.

42. Nash, M.; Hulsey, M.; Sexton, M.; Harralson, T.; and Lambert, W. 1993. Long-Term Sequelae of Childhood Sexual Abuse: Perceived Family Environment, Psychopathology, and Dissociation. *J. Consulting and Clinical Psychology* 61:276–83.

43. Erickson, M., and Egeland, B. 1987. A Developmental View of the Psychological Consequences of Maltreatment. *School Psychology Rev.* 16:156–68.

44. Egeland, B.; Sroufe, L. A.; and Erickson, M. 1983. The Developmental Consequences of Different Patterns of Maltreatment. *Child Abuse and Neglect: International J.* 7:459–69.

45. Engles, M., and Moisan, D. 1994. The Psychological Maltreatment Inventory: Development of a Measure of Psychological Maltreatment in Childhood for Use in Adult Clinical Settings. *Psychological Reports* 74:595–601.

46. Ney, P. G. 1989. Child Mistreatment: Possible Reasons for Its Transgenerational Transmission. *Canadian J. Psychiatry* 34(6):594–601.

47. Ney, P. G. 1987. Does Verbal Abuse Leave Deeper Scars: A Study of Children and Parents. *Canadian J. Psychiatry* 34:371–78.

48. Rohner, R. P., and Rohner, E. C. 1980. Antecedents and Consequences of Parental Rejection: A Theory of Emotional Abuse. *Child Abuse and Neglect: International J.* 4:189–98.

49. Main, M., and Goldwyn, R. 1984. Predicting Rejection of Her Infant from Mother's Representation of Her Own Experiences: Implications for the Abused-Abusing Intergenerational Cycle. *Child Abuse and Neglect: International J.* 8:203–17.

50. Bowlby, J. 1973. *Separation.* Vol. 2 of *Attachment and Loss.* New York: Basic Books.

51. DeLozier, P. P. 1982. Attachment Theory and Child Abuse. In *The Place of Attachment in Human Behavior,* ed. M. Parkes and J. Stevenson-Hinde, 95–117. New York: Basic Books.

52. Conte, J., and Schuerman, J. 1987. The Effects of Sexual Abuse on Children: A Multidimensional View. *J. Interpersonal Violence* 2:380–90.

53. Kendall-Tacket, K.; Meyer Williams, L.; and Finkelhor, D. 1993. Impact of Sexual Abuse on Children: A Review and Synthesis of Recent Empirical Studies. *Psychological Bulletin* 113:164–80.

54. Crittenden, P.; Claussen, A.; and Sugarman, D. 1994. Physical and Psychological Maltreatment in Middle Childhood and Adolescence. *Development and Psychopathology, Psychological Supervisor* 1:145–64.

55. Cohn, A., and Daro, D. 1987. Is Treatment Too Late: What Ten Years of Evaluation Research Tell Us. *Child Abuse and Neglect: International J.* 11:433–42.

56. MacMillan, H.; MacMillan, J.; Offord, D.; and Griffith, L. 1994. Primary Prevention of Child Physical Abuse and Neglect: A Critical Review. *J. Child Psychology and Psychiatry and Allied Disabilities* 35(5):835–56.

57. Daro, D. 1988. *Confronting Child Abuse: Research for Effective Program Design.* New York: Free Press.

58. Egeland, B.; Jacobvitz, J.; and Sroufe, L. A. 1988. Breaking the Cycle of Abuse. *Child Development* 59:1080–88.

59. Individuals with Disabilities Education Act, 34 C.F.R. 300.7 (9) (1990).

60. American Psychiatric Association. 1994. *Diagnostic and Statistical Manual of Mental Disorders,* 4th ed. Washington, D.C.: APA.

61. Hart, S. N., and Brassard, M. 1990. *Developing and Validating Operationally Defined Measures of Emotional Maltreatment: A Multimodal Study of the Relationships between Caretaker Behaviors and Child Characteristics across Three Developmental Levels* (Final Report [Stages 1 and 2], Grant No. DHHS 90CA1216). Washington, D.C.: Department of Health and Human Services and National Center on Child Abuse and Neglect.

62. Brassard, M. R.; Hart, S. N.; and Hardy, D. 1994. Psychological Maltreatment and Peer Accep-

tance in Young Children: Predicting from Mother-Child Interactions. Teachers' College, Columbia University. Photocopy.

63. Crittenden, P. 1988. Family and Dyadic Patterns of Functioning in Maltreating Families. In *Early Prediction and Prevention of Child Abuse,* ed. K. Brown, C. Davies, and P. Stratton, 161–89. New York: Wiley.

64. Straus, M. A. 1990. Conflict Tactics Scales (CTS). In *Handbook of Family Measurement Techniques,* ed. J. Touliatos, B. F. Perlmutter, and M. Straus. Newbury Park, Calif.: Sage.

65. Sounders, P. G. 1986. When Battered Women Use Violence: Husband Abuse or Self Defense? *Violence and Victims* 1:47–60.

66. Sounders, P. G., and Hanusa, D. 1986. Cognitive-Behavioral Treatment of Men Who Batter: The Short-Term Effects of Group Therapy. *J. Family Violence* 12:357–72.

67. Wolfe, D., and McGee, R. 1994. Dimensions of Child Maltreatment and Their Relationship to Adolescent Adjustment. *Development and Psychopathology* 6(1):165–82.

18

Munchausen Syndrome by Proxy: Currency in Counterfeit Illness

DONNA ANDREA ROSENBERG

Munchausen syndrome by proxy (MSBP) is an odd form of abuse in which the mother fabricates illness in her child and repeatedly presents the child for medical care, disclaiming any knowledge about the cause of the child's illness.[1] The child, in consequence, is often subjected to multiple medical investigations and procedures. The disorder was first described in 1977 by Dr. Roy Meadow, who aptly called it "the hinterland of child abuse" (1). MSBP was once thought to be exceedingly rare, and though it is still encountered infrequently compared with true childhood illness, hundreds of cases of MSBP have now been reported in the medical literature, and many more cases occur that are not presented for publication.

MSBP is not merely persistence, nor is it merely fabrication: it is persistent fabrication of a child's illness. Furthermore, it is the reported condition itself that is a fiction ("He has seizures"), not simply the account of what precipitated the condition ("He fell off the couch"). In other, more typical forms of child abuse, the history given by the parent may also be false, but the child's injury is not faked. With MSBP, not only is the history an invention but so is the malady itself. What is presented is thus a double duplicity.

Some commentary has appeared in the medical literature concerning the diagnostic confines, the utility, and the misuse of the term "Munchausen syndrome by proxy" (2–6), chiefly because it has been applied questionably in some cases and because it has, bizarrely, been used to describe the condition of the mother (as in, "She has Munchausen syndrome by proxy") rather than the type of abuse to the child. Though Dr. Meadow advocates reserving the term for "abuse in which the perpetrator is motivated by the need to assume either the sick role by proxy or another form of attention seeking behavior," his additional recommendation that the term be limited to "describ[ing] a form of abuse, rather than . . . be[ing] applied to a perpetrator" (5) is the more practical usage. Abuse can be either documented or excluded though various diagnostic strategies (which I will discuss later in this chapter), whereas ascertaining the motivation of the perpetrator is largely a matter of specu-

---

1. Perpetrators of MSBP who have another relationship to the child—such as father, other relative, babysitter, or health care worker—have occasionally been reported. However, mothers are cited throughout this chapter as the perpetrators, both to facilitate reading and because they constitute the vast majority.

DONNA ANDREA ROSENBERG, M.D., is assistant professor in the Department of Pediatrics, University of Colorado School of Medicine, and forensic pediatrician with the Colorado Child Fatality Review Team.

lation. Worse yet, confirmation of those speculations rests precariously upon that very perpetrator's unreliable insights or unlikely confession.

Presentation

Illness in a child may be counterfeited in several ways. It may be simulated, it may be produced, or it may be both simulated and produced. Simulated illness involves lying about the child but does not involve actually doing something to the child. For example, a mother may repeatedly bring her child to the doctor, describing in vivid detail the seizures which she claims the child suffers, but the history she reports is later discovered to be a fiction. Produced illness, on the other hand, involves creating illness in the child. A mother may repeatedly suffocate her baby and claim that the baby spontaneously stops breathing.

Mothers may simultaneously, alternatively, or progressively simulate and produce illness. Because simulators may graduate into producers, we should not be reassured that a child is "safe enough" with such a mother. Furthermore, both simulators and producers frequently continue their activities while the child is hospitalized—which means that the child may be safe in hospital only if the MSBP diagnosis is suspected and the patient carefully monitored, with a strategy in place for documenting any falsification of illness.

The catalog of symptoms and signs with which victims of MSBP present is enormous. Also, the siblings of MSBP victims are often similarly victimized, and scrutiny of their medical histories reveals high rates of inexplicable, persistent illness and astonishing death rates (7).

Because of the extremes to which mothers are known to go in their fabrications, no list can ever be considered inclusive, but some presentations are considerably more common. Among the more common are apnea (stopping breathing) (8), seizures, bleeding, diarrhea, vomiting, fever, central nervous system depression (decreased level of consciousness), and rash. Any of these may be simulated or produced. For example, apnea may be counterfeited by manual suffocation, administration of various drugs, or lying (9). Diarrhea may be produced by administering various drugs, laxatives, or salt, or a fictional history of diarrhea may be given. Vomiting may be induced by administering substances or drugs with emetic effects or may be reported fallaciously. Seizures and central nervous system depression may be feigned by lying, poisoning with various drugs or salt, or by suffocating that causes hypoxia-induced stupor or seizures but is not yet lethal. Even complex disorders such as inborn errors of metabolism or immunodeficiency have been fabricated. All of these may result in injury or death.

Though some mothers actually research pediatric illnesses, many more learn about medical symptoms and signs from the questions that doctors, nurses, and others ask them; subsequently, the children tend to "develop" those problems that had been inquired about at a previous health care visit. Since a 1987 cataloging of the sixty-eight different presentations of MSBP that had been reported to date (10), at least twenty-one more have been described (11–15). Apart from the somatic ones, some of the more recently described presentations include psychiatric illness (16, 17), developmental delays (18), and false allegations of child abuse (19, 20). Munchausen syndrome by proxy may also present as fabricated compliance with treatment for a child's genuine underlying illness, with the specific goal of exacerbating that illness (21). This must be distinguished from the far more common occurrence of medical care neglect (6, 22, 23).

The child victims are typically under five years of age, but many cases of MSBP involving older children have been described. Older children sometimes adopt the symptoms as their own, believing themselves to be genuinely ill.

Almost by definition, MSBP entails a lengthy amount of time from onset of the child's symptoms until correct diagnosis: the average span is about fifteen months, but this varies widely (10). Perhaps this time lag in diagnosis will decrease as doctors become more attuned to this disorder and, consequently, include MSBP sooner on their differential diagnosis (list of possibilities) when a child presents with a persistent, inexplicable illness.

In the effort to treat their fabricated, but believable, disorders, surgeries typically performed on victims of MSBP are gastrostomy with fundoplication and installation of a central venous catheter. Many other surgeries, such as installation of a cardiac pacemaker and bone curettage, have also been performed on these children.

The harm that produced illness can do to a child is painfully obvious, but it is a fallacy to think of simulated illness as relatively benign. In the course of multiple medical investigations and therapeutic interventions, the children are exposed to a wide range of harm. The harm includes those effects, side effects, and complications associated with medical tests, prescribed medications, procedures, and surgeries. Harm certainly includes the fear, discomfort, and pain experienced by the child who has been subjected to multiple investigative and therapeutic procedures. Finally, the omission of tender, protective maternal care must be factored into the harm equation: the time that would otherwise be devoted to nurturance and teaching, and all that that means for developmental outcome, is lost to the child.

Although the risk of death to an individual victim of Munchausen syndrome by proxy cannot be precisely calculated, there is clearly an unacceptable death rate associated overall with this syndrome. Children who die as a result of MSBP are usually killed by the mother, but death may also follow from a complication of a medical intervention. Even when the immediate cause of death is a medical complication, however, the proximate (underlying) cause is the mother's fabrication, and the death therefore a homicide.

Since the spectrum of presentation of MSBP is so vast, the reader who is searching for information on a particular presentation is advised to use an on-line information service (such as Paperchase or Ovid) that simultaneously searches several computer databases (such as Medline, Health, Aidsline, Cancerlit, Psychinfo, Bioethicsline). These databases store medical articles published since 1966 or later. A reference librarian at a medical library, especially one associated with a university hospital, medical school, community hospital, or a medical society, can help. Most of these databases include, at least, the author, title, reference source, and abstract of the article; desired articles may then be found on the library's periodical shelves or ordered. Full-text databases will likely be available before much longer, allowing the searcher to download entire articles directly from the database.

Perpetrators

Mothers who perpetrate MSBP are commonly described as even-tempered, engaging, middle-class, and educated in some aspect of medicine or nursing. However, these characteristics by no means inevitably prevail. Perpetrators may also be wealthy, poor, cranky, temperamental, or uneducated.

Some mothers have fabricated medical symptoms in themselves, and some have florid Munchausen syndrome.[2] A review of their medical records may be very revealing for its medical detail about the mothers and for what they may have reported about their children to their own doctors.

While few of these mothers have a criminal record, I have seen, over the past fifteen years, that some have been involved in undetected or unreported criminal activity. Embezzling, defrauding various organizations that provide money, goods, or services (for instance, community groups, church groups, wish-fulfillment foundations), arson and staged thefts of their own homes, or staged compensable accidents are some of the crimes. Some MSBP perpetrators are also litigious, and while the targets of their lawsuits generally are doctors or medical institutions (for wrongful death or malpractice when the MSBP has not yet been uncovered, for malicious reporting of child abuse when it has), they may sue any entity, casting themselves as grievously wronged and entitled to monetary restitution. By definition, mothers who perpetrate MSBP have defrauded their medical insurance carriers. These women may also fabricate illness in pets, stage nonmedical events that bring them pity, attention, or respect, or eventually involve other agencies in their medical, and other, fabrications. They may occasionally have received some laudatory media coverage and, indeed, may reengage the media upon revelation of the MSBP. Thus, their fabrications may extend to many realms and consume much of their time.

As to motive, it appears that the most common are the desire to be the center of attention, respect, drama, awe, or caring; the need to belong somewhere; and the need to be connected to doctors or nurses. It must by rights be pointed out that however many mothers may desire these things, very few go on to perpetrate MSBP. Therefore, while these desires share the name of many other peoples' desires, the form and substance hugely differ.

Other motives include dislike or hatred for the child; repeated fury at something the child does (for example, crying); desire to outwit the doctors; tangible rewards such as money, charitable donations, life insurance, and access to special people, privileges, and institutions (though this is not generally the primary motive, it becomes an increasingly attractive perquisite of the fabrication); the desire to bring their husbands to their sides, literally or figuratively; and the desire to escape an unexciting or malignant mate. Additional motives are possible. Looking back through the medical histories of some MSBP victims, we can see that the child may have started out with a bona fide medical problem, usually transient or minor, but that in the course of exposure to medical care, the mother

---

2. Munchausen syndrome refers to a psychiatric disorder wherein adults—or, very occasionally, juveniles—repeatedly present fictitious medical histories in order to gain medical attention.

found something which suited her and which she elected to then pursue through spurious disease. Why some mothers choose this particular form of abuse over others is not well understood, but it is the only form of child abuse that permits the mother to abuse the child and simultaneously garner admiration. And unlike mothers who abuse their children impulsively, MSBP perpetrators deliberate, thus minimizing their own jeopardy while maximizing their peculiar gains.

So far this discussion has centered on what the mothers do. But, it is often asked, who are they? To some extent, the response to this question depends upon who is answering. The same mother may appear to the pediatrician to be needy, lonely, and desperate; to the psychiatrist, afflicted with a personality disorder; and to the police investigator, a criminal. However, because it is usually the psychiatrist or psychologist who is given the responsibility for understanding and describing the mother, much of the admittedly meager literature on this subject is, accordingly, in terms familiar to mental health professionals. Whether the language of psychiatric diagnosis is equal to the rendering of these mothers in all their macabre dimensions is, perhaps, questionable.

MSBP perpetrators are not, in the main, psychotic, mentally retarded, or delusional. Some claims have been made about their suffering from multiple personality disorder or a dissociative state, diagnoses fashionable at this point in psychiatric history, but it is not clear whether these labels enhance our understanding of these mothers or, rather, merely improperly reassure us that we grasp the problem. The fact that the mother has been able to replicate the moves, facial expressions, postures, and words of a loving parent—in short, that she has fabricated not only illness but also empathy—speaks more compellingly to a vigilant awareness than it does to "dissociation." She has learned, by astute observation, how a worried, grieving, frightened, loving mother behaves. She has been able to perceive what we, the doctors, expect, down to the subtlest nuance.

It is true that sometimes mothers have been noted to have some type of personality disorder (histrionic or borderline, most commonly); other problems, such as self-harming behavior, substance abuse, eating disorder, and depression, have also been described (24). Because these diagnoses have assignable codes (25), an inference may be made that the psychiatric condition divides the mother from responsibility for her actions, as if she were simply the hapless conduit for an irresistible psychopathology. This type of inference is almost always mistaken and would be valid only in the very rare instance where the mother was floridly psychotic or suffered from a similar psychiatric illness.

Psychiatric diagnoses are descriptive of the mother's own personality, feelings, or self-reported behaviors, but they are necessarily silent about whether or not the mother perpetrated MSBP. Psychological tests may reflect certain of a mother's personality traits, psychopathological tendencies, and capacities for particular acts, but they cannot determine if, in fact, she did or did not actually do something. Unless the mother confesses, no psychiatric interview technique or protocol, and no psychological test, can definitively either include or exclude the past perpetration of MSBP.

Sometimes, mothers who have perpetrated MSBP have been labeled psychiatrically "normal." The absence of a psychiatric diagnosis is not the same as the presence of a protective mother. It is no more astonishing for a psychiatrically "normal" mother to have perpetrated MSBP than it is for a psychiatrically "normal" person to have committed murder, been a con artist, or lied.

Occasionally a study appears in the medical literature that documents maltreatment in the backgrounds of MSBP perpetrators (26). Maltreatment during their own childhood would certainly help explain these mothers' marked disorder of empathy. Schreier and Libow emphasize "the profound impact upon these women of their early experiences of undervaluation and emotional neglect, within a society that reflects this devaluation of women on a larger scale" (26, pp. 184–85). But the fact that almost all women in this same society do *not* perpetrate MSBP emphasizes that the perpetration of MSBP is related not to grievous *harm from gender discrimination* but to individual and cynical *misuse of gender opportunity.*

Once MSBP has been exposed, many people assume that the mother must have had to overcome moral scruples, and her love for the child, in order to do something so heinous. No evidence generally supports this, and few mothers confess, much less exhibit remorse. Nonetheless, the question on everyone's lips (everyone except law enforcement agents, that is) seems to be, "How could such a nice mother do something so dreadful?" Perhaps the more apt question—the one discarding the assumption of the mother's fine character—is, "How could such a dreadful mother appear to be so nice?" There is very little discussion in the professional literature of such maternal drives as hate for the child, or homicidal self-interest, perhaps because such descriptions are considered indelicate, excessively explicit, or harsh. But, occasionally, such descriptions appear to be the most accurate ones. The drive to persistently fabricate illness in one's child may be ignited by many things, but in all cases the final common maneuvers are fueled by the grotesque misuse of power, and the assertion of the mother's will, whatever the cost.

While the mother's capacity for deception should never be underestimated, it is not true that these mothers are geniuses at medical fabrication. Though these perpetrators are generally persistent and often industrious, a careful review of medical records and a check with other sources to corroborate episodes (Did you see the child start to seize? Stop breathing? Did your hospital really lose those records?) will often reveal one or more events that could not have been the result of miscommunication or other confounders and are attributable only to the mother's unabashed and rather brazen lying.

Where, and with what power, empathy resides in most parents, in perpetrators of Munchausen syndrome by proxy something else dwells. The dimension of the perpetrator's aberration may be measured, at least figuratively, by grasping the enormity of its equal and opposite: the visceral pain experienced by the parent of a *genuinely* ill child *for the child.* Without pageantry, but with a precision that lances, such a father writes:

> My daughter has cancer. As some of you know, she is 8. In all the world I never conceived of all the sorrow I would feel at learning this, all the horror at watching her suffer so stoically through test after test. There is not a lot of hope, just a lot of medicine. We are preparing ourselves for the worst, which her doctor has hinted is what we should expect. . . . She asked me this morning, "Dad, does it get better? It does, doesn't it?" My mouth moved up and down, but nothing came out of it. (27)

Diagnosis

When a parent persistently presents a child for medical care, we must always bear in mind that genuine organic illness is the most common reason parents have for bringing a child for medical care. Therefore, organic diagnosis must always be pursued with appropriate vigor. Once organic possibilities have been excluded in our effort to account for the full range of the child's medical problems, nonorganic possibilities warrant consideration. MSBP is only one among several nonorganic possibilities (28).

Psychogenic illness, for instance, is a medical complaint having emotional origins. For example, the child may complain of, and actually experience, abdominal pain, but the pain is eventually determined to be caused by the child's avoidance of a relative or school (sometimes for good reason). Psychogenic illness occurs in children who have achieved some proficiency with speech and there is no maternal fabrication of illness. When the underlying cause of the child's complaint is remediable, the prognosis is excellent.

Distinguishing among parental concern, worry, and anxiety is something of an exercise in semantics for doctors, but these emotional states are all degrees of genuine caring and none involve fabrication. Cases of symptom overemphasis are similar. In these cases, a parent, despite detailed reassurances from health care professionals (because there are usually minor, if any, findings on physical exam or laboratory investigation), dwells upon symptoms which would not occasion much notice in most families. It does not, however, involve fabrication on the parent's part. Sometimes, though, it does involve traveling from doctor to doctor ("doctor shopping"). The "overemphasis" may take different forms. It may manifest as frequent medical visits and telephone calls but not as an extreme distortion of the medical complaint—for example, five medical visits for a child's runny nose, but not a complaint of bloody, thick nasal discharge with five minutes of breathing cessation. It may also appear as some common amplification or distortion of the observed problem— "my baby stopped breathing for two minutes"—but without the frequent medical visits. Especially with respect to the latter, there is no substitute for careful and thorough history taking. The history must include those open-ended questions whose answers help validate or refute the mother's observation and narrow the diagnostic possibilities. For example, the doctor might ask, "How did the baby appear just before she started breathing again? What was the baby doing just before she started breathing again? You say the baby was wheezing just before she stopped breathing—can you tell me what you saw? Felt? Heard?" Doctors sometimes hasten history taking by asking exclusively closed-ended questions—for example, "Was the baby blue?"—or, worse, questions with answers implicit in them—"How dark blue was the baby?" The history's accuracy is thereby diminished because of the inexperience, inattentiveness, or haste of the doctor. Because the differential diagnosis rests so much upon the history, it too may be incomplete or wrong as a result.

In symptom overemphasis, the complaint, if not grounded in accurate observation by the mother, is most likely to be driven by such benign circumstances as poor observation, terror, inexperience, or the mismeasure of time ("it seemed like forever") which commonly accompany fear and which are largely penetrable with a careful history. One type of symptom overemphasis, the so-called vulnerable child syndrome, can occur with a child whose health has been genuinely threatened in the past—but in such occurrences there is no fabrication of the child's symptoms or signs, nor fabrication of parental concern (29).

Extreme illness exaggeration is distinguished from symptom overemphasis because it involves fabrication. It is essentially the same as Munchausen syndrome by proxy.

Finally, malingering involves genuine illness which is elaborated for some gain, usually financial; it also involves fabrication. There is some common ground between malingering and MSBP, because certain mothers who perpetrate MSBP do thrive in various fiscal ways, consequent upon their fabrication of illness in their child.

Doctors often suspect Munchausen syndrome by proxy before they can definitively include or exclude the diagnosis. A protective order, frequently requested at this point, is based upon the *provisional diagnosis*. Provisional diagnosis is the most likely diagnosis to account for the child's problems, but it is a diagnosis not yet unequivocally confirmed. It generally leads the list of medical possibilities (differential diagnosis). Provisional diagnosis must be distinguished from the actual diagnosis, which implies unequivocal confirmation.

Provisional diagnosis may be made in several ways. A test or event may be presumptively positive for tampering, with no other explanation probable. The child may manifest a condition that cannot be medically explained, is therefore suspected to be faked, and for which only a trial of separation of the child from the parents would be diagnostically definitive. Similarly, a child may exhibit a condition unlikely to be explained by anything except MSBP but for which a remote possibility still exists of a true, minimally compromising condition; however, the diagnosis in such a case could be sought only via an especially dangerous or invasive procedure, or one unlikely to prove definitive. In this instance, a trial of separation of the child from the parents presents a significantly lesser risk and would likely prove diagnostically definitive.

A definitive diagnosis of Munchausen syndrome by proxy may be a diagnosis of inclusion—that is, based upon evidence of commission—or a diagnosis of exclusion—that is, based upon the definitive exclusion of all other contending diagnoses. Epidemiological data, which either support or epitomize the diagnosis, may also be available.

A *diagnosis of inclusion* is based upon incontrovertible evidence of commission, such as a videotape showing a mother smothering her baby or, under certain circumstances, a positive toxicological test. However, obtaining this type of diagnostic information is often problematic. Since collection of this type of evidence is generally devised once a diagnosis of MSBP is suspected, it obviously means that doctors must weigh the value of collecting the data against the risk to the child of being subjected to further assault. Before any such diagnostic procedures are initiated, the social services bureau responsible for child protection may be alerted, along with the police and/or the district attorney's office, in case these agencies would want to secure a protective hold, or to station an officer at the hospital to stand by with an arrest warrant. Contingency plans must be clear, coordinated, and in place. Most hospital risk-management offices prefer to be fully informed about these procedures before they are implemented. Nursing and medical staff who are closely involved in the case should also be informed of the diagnostic procedure, but we must be aware of the possibility that, within that corps of professionals, a disbelieving ally of the mother may independently decide to discuss it with her.

Other data of commission include assays for drugs, poisons, or their metabolic products on samples taken from various body fluids and tissues, or from bottles, foods, drinks, IVs, or syringes with which the child has had contact. Most hospital toxicology laboratories do not routinely test for many of the substances one might suspect the mothers are covertly administering to the child. In addition, the laboratory equipment may not be able to handle such specimens due to their consistency. Therefore, not only should routine toxicology be done, but the specific assays for suspected substances must be planned for, in terms of fluid or tissue collected, chain of evidence, storage, and transportation to another laboratory. This sometimes means arranging assistance from other laboratories around the country or holding specimens in a way that preserves their biologic integrity and the chain of evidence while a search for a suitable assay is being conducted. Attention to biologic integrity and chain of evidence is also important during transport of any specimens to outside laboratories.

A *diagnosis of exclusion* may be the most precise and least risk-laden route. In most cases, children are still alive when the diagnosis of Munchausen syndrome by proxy is first suspected, and a diagnosis of exclusion, fortunately, is not without a diagnostic test. This diagnostic test is the trial separation between the child and the alleged perpetrator of Munchausen syndrome by proxy. Inasmuch as all diagnostic tests entail the potential of liabilities, a trial separation may be the least harmful of the diagnostic tests available. Certainly it is preferable to the potential harm of leaving the provisional diagnosis neither confirmed nor excluded. We must make sure, however, that the only important factor at variance between the two settings—the child's home and his or her environment during the trial separation—is indeed the presence of the mother. If a dramatic difference in the child's health emerges during the separation, could it *reasonably* be attributed to some environmental change (levels of smoke or carbon monoxide; type of food), the absence of another significant individual (nurse, grandmother, baby-sitter), the natural history of a medical disorder running its course, or some other factor? In other words, as with every other aspect of the diagnostic process, logical and inclusive thinking is critical. And since no evidence suggests that parents abide by the terms of a voluntary intervention, the trial of separation must be under civil court supervision.

As the length of the separation must allow a reasonable amount of time for making an accurate diagnosis, it must reflect the frequency of the child's ill events and the severity of the child's condition. For example, if a child allegedly has had seizures for three months, three times a day, on an average of four days a week, and the longest period of time without seizures has been five days, then a reasonable diagnostic trial separation would be about four weeks. If the child's illness occurs less frequently and the "well" periods last longer, then the diagnostic separation must accordingly be lengthened. If the child has a true underlying illness that is suspected of being exacerbated by the deliberate withholding of medicine, the exposure of the child to illness precipitants, or the superimposition of fabricated illness, then the diagnostic period will be able to determine whether or not the child

about the child's diagnosis but whose accuracy, upon review, is seriously questioned; (2) age at death significantly outside the two to four months of age, with cause of death listed as SIDS; (3) a prior or subsequent instance of SIDS in the decedent's sibling or in an unrelated child in the same home, especially if the other child died significantly outside two to four months of age; (4) a sibling of the decedent with chronic, ill-defined medical problems; (5) a sibling of the decedent who previously or subsequently died, without a clear explanation, especially following an ill-defined or chronic illness, with (5*a*) cause of death allegedly an illness which overwhelmingly is nonfatal in childhood, *or* (5*b*) with cause of death related to intoxication or a highly unusual accident, *or* (5*c*) with death following a presumed illness which was either unsubstantiated or excluded at autopsy; (6) a mother with chronic, ill-defined medical problems.

These are historical flags which should spur further investigation, but they are not diagnostic criteria for MSBP. Given the facts of the case, contending causes of death apart from inflicted ones, and manners of death apart from homicidal ones, may bear consideration.

Review of Medical Records

Complete review of medical records may be conducted before, or during, civil court intervention or a criminal inquiry. Though it is optimal to complete a records review before civil court intervention, it is usually not possible because of the large volume and various locations of the records. Consequently, temporary protective orders are usually necessary, based upon the provisional diagnosis of MSBP. The court must allow sufficient time for a proper review, which may be very time-consuming.

Because of the typical mass of the records, it is important to have a system in place at the outset. The doctor must decide upon two main points: What questions am I asking? Which records do I analyze? These questions themselves shape the decision about which records to analyze first. For example, if one of the questions is, "Who saw the child start to seize?" the minimal data set for each seizure event might include the date, the time, the location, the person who saw the child start to seize, the names of other persons who saw the child seize, and whether that history was obtained directly from them or from the mother. If the information provided by the mother about the child is taken at face value and included in the data analysis, the conclusions may be incorrect. Whenever possible, all medical records should be reviewed, as should the records of siblings, and even those of the mother.

It is certainly possible to do this record review manually, using filing cards, for example, but it is more efficient to do it with a computer database management system. The latter has the advantage of being able not only to record data but also to organize it (this is especially helpful since the logistics of consulting records from several institutions would otherwise make it almost impossible to review all of the records together in chronological order). Once entered, even vast amounts of data in such a system are searchable and can be charted. Interpretation of data, which remains within the province of individual human beings, is facilitated by well-organized comprehensive data. It is best to use a system with which one is familiar, even if it is a little simpler than a state-of-the-art setup. A flat-file database system is sufficient, a relational system not generally being necessary. Pages of the medical records should be numbered and incorporated as a field for each event entered into the database. This allows the original medical notes to be located later, and is especially helpful when the records run to hundreds or thousands of pages. In addition, for effective analysis, someone who intimately understands the language and meaning of medical records must be involved in the review.

Intervention

In cases in which Munchausen syndrome by proxy is suspected, the most important first steps are to collect and document the diagnostic evidence and to protect the child. When data collection and child protection appear to conflict, child protection is always paramount—though we must nonetheless recognize that jettisoning the possibility of collecting data of commission may actually jeopardize the child's long-term protection if the court inappropriately devalues a properly made diagnosis of exclusion.

Confrontation of the mother does not inevitably stop the assaultive behavior. Leaving aside the obvious problem that "confrontation" has no universal meaning, the chronic nature of the mother's assault and the cruelty that allowed her to cause, and then ignore or enjoy, her child's pain, indicate an abiding, profound problem, not fixable by a conversation.

Given the complexity and chronicity of the abuse in MSBP, a well-coordinated multidisciplinary child protection team, even an ad hoc one, must be convened as soon as MSBP is suspected in a case. The child's doctor and nurse, social services representatives (caseworker, supervisor, and attorney representing the agency), and the police are necessary participants. Other team members may include a psychiatrist or psychologist, an epidemiologist, a prosecutor, visiting nurse, coroner, or the hospital attorney. Experienced team members are, obviously, desirable but, just as obviously, not always available. At least as important as experience, however, are team members with the capacities for logical and inclusive thinking, for appreciating their own limitations, for seeking help from those more knowledgeable, for making a long-term commitment to the case, and for vigor. Because these cases usually have such long lives, personnel turnover during the course of them often leaves the team with a replacement person hard-pressed to absorb the full array of case details. If team members, especially the county social worker and attorney, cannot work in paired sets (for example, two caseworkers, two attorneys), an understudy system, which works well for stage performances, would likely work well here too. Because multidisciplinary teams sometimes value consensus over reasoned assessment, or mistake consensus for accuracy, it may be helpful if team members rotate in taking on the role of devil's advocate. Finally, there is little point of multidisciplinary meetings in which the medical data are chronically unavailable, pivotally incomplete, or misrepresented.

Children who are victims of Munchausen syndrome by proxy should be placed outside of the home. Doing otherwise is an act of wishful thinking, and is not based upon any data which reassures us about the child's safety. There is no risk assessment instrument which can select, with any validity, those children who will be at low risk in their own homes. The high morbidity and mortality rates of child victims of MSBP and their siblings, and the chronicity of the maternal behavior, speak to the danger for the child. Siblings should likewise be protected.

Monitoring and documenting the child's health status, especially with respect to the medical problems allegedly fabricated by the mother, must be scrupulous. Every attempt must be made to secure for the child the care he or she needs for any problems consequent upon the abuse that are reversible. Reintegration of the child into school, play activities, and other regular parts of life is desirable. Generous contact with relatives other than the perpetrator should be encouraged, if considered safe. Siblings should be separated only if there is an extremely compelling reason for it. All visits with the suspected perpetrator must, of course, be supervised.

If a firm diagnosis of MSBP is made, treatment of the family must be attempted while the child is under protection. No proven method of effective intervention exists, and while some kind of talk therapy (rather than pharmacologic, biologic, or psychosurgical therapy) is the only method currently employed, the literature suggests MSBP perpetrators are particularly recalcitrant to psychotherapeutic intervention. Perpetrators are "masterful at evoking the sympathy, doubt, and narcissism of their caretakers," including the therapist, and "[u]nfortunately, their skill at imposturing and in fabricating believable stories can be utilized to consistently deny their actual harming behavior and/or to falsely convince therapists of their motivation for change" (26, pp. 162–63).

Specifically, the doctor must find out from the therapist if the mother has fulfilled the criteria for having the child returned home. Does the mother acknowledge having perpetrated MSBP? Has she sufficiently changed? If so, how, why, how much, and according to what evidence? The current system of "confidentiality" may neglect or endanger the child victim. Citing professional ethics and the need to gain the patient's trust, some therapists will not discuss the content of the mother's therapy. The fact that a mother appears for therapy, or "complies with the treatment plan," does not mean that she has benefited from it. Consequently, statements from the therapist that address only the mother's attendance, or that are oblique or incomplete, are not helpful. Without clear, inclusive information from the therapist, assessing safety for the child is a matter of pure speculation. If this information is not forthcoming, or is unsatisfactory, then the child cannot safely be returned home, and alternative long-term arrangements must be made.

Testimony

Many guidelines have been written for individuals who must appear as expert witnesses in court, either civil or criminal, and the reader will do well to consult a couple of these works (36, 37). A few points are particularly pertinent to Munchausen syndrome by proxy cases, so will be discussed at some length.

In cases of MSBP, the expert witness usually ends up teaching a lawyer unfamiliar with the syndrome. This is not simply a matter of providing literature. Given the volume of medical information peculiar to MSBP cases, what is involved is designing a logical sequence of questions for the lawyer to use in the direct examination of oneself as the expert witness. It also involves telling the lawyer how to defuse one's own cross-examination, both by preemptively addressing during the direct examination those matters one expects will be distorted or incorrectly recast by the mother's attorney and by suggesting the points that will probably need to be articulated during the redirect examination.

The expert witness must also help the lawyer to prepare effective cross-examination of the mother's witnesses. This involves outlining the usually predictable explanations that the mother will provide the court, customarily: (1) the child has a real illness that the doctors cannot, or did not, diagnose, so they are blaming me; (2) the child's illnesses and my presence are coincidentally related; (3) someone else is making the child ill; (4) I am simply a concerned mother, at worst highly anxious, trying to get help for my child and following doctor's orders; (5) this is all a big misunderstanding; (6) my confession was coerced, manipulated, misunderstood, or faultily recorded and is therefore inadmissible; (7) the doctors, or others, misconstrued a benign deed as a malignant one; (8) the doctor, lawyer, or someone else, is taking legal action for reasons of revenge, career advancement, or for some other venal reason.

If the lawyer is experienced with other types of child abuse and neglect cases, he or she may assume that the narrative testimony sufficient in those cases will also serve in a MSBP case. This is not true. The sheer volume of medical information, when delivered exclusively in narrative form, is enough to confuse even attentive triers of fact. Visual displays (such as charts, tables, lists, or graphs) based upon the narrative testimony are excellent supplements and reinforce the major points of the legal case. These visual displays may even be planned for and then put together, point by point, during the narrative testimony and in front of the triers of fact, so that they are left, literally, with a picture of the case. The visual displays should be large, easily readable, and not too complicated (not much more complex than those graphs which appear in popular magazines and newspapers to illustrate quantitative data).

The potential that cases of Munchausen syndrome by proxy have to rupture professional relationships is impressive (38). The involved professionals will almost certainly have different opinions about the case, sometimes diametrically opposite. We must even expect this. The role of the expert witness is to present an opinion founded on facts and to articulate how that conclusion was logically reached. It is not to the expert witness's advantage to become adversarial, entangled in the recruiting to "sides," or embroiled in the development of enduring professional antipathies. When one professional cannot agree with other involved professionals on a diagnosis, a better strategy is to agree to disagree but nevertheless maintain an intact professional relationship.

Since the diagnosis of MSBP is a pediatric one, the medical expert must be prepared to explain all other diagnostic possibilities that were considered, and why and how they were excluded from the differential diagnosis. Expert witnesses will have to explain a good deal of medicine in lay language; time should be allowed for preparing a coherent presentation, because all necessary concepts must be fully and clearly articulated.

Sometimes, professionals do agree about the behavior of the perpetrator but cannot agree about her intent. These are always futile discussions, as there is no practical way, without a confession, to penetrate intent. For the purposes of child protection, intent is immaterial. The civil court should take the point of view of the child, to whom it hardly matters whether his mother injected feces into his IV line to get attention, out of hate and revenge, or because she "dissociated." Intent is a more a matter for the criminal court to consider.

Outcomes

Few studies have assessed longer-term outcomes in child victims of MSBP. There is some risk of homicide to MSBP victims. Larger case series have noted mortality rates ranging from 9% to 33% (10, 24, 39), but quantification of death risk for an individual patient is no more possible in MSBP than it is in other forms of child abuse. Those children who survive may have serious lifelong physical or psychiatric sequelae (10, 40), and being a victim of MSBP may lead to manifesting Munchausen syndrome as an adult (41). Though the perpetrating mothers are unlikely to confess to their deeds even in the face of compelling evidence (42), some anecdotal evidence suggests that the occasional perpetrator of MSBP, with intensive psychotherapy, can become a functional mother (43).

Summary

When a diagnosis of MSBP is made, the discovery that the mother's deep concern for the child was actually an illusion—a sort of behavioral trompe d'oeil—may be especially shocking, or even ungraspable, to those who have known the mother for a long time. Some cannot imagine that this particular mother could be so deceptive; others cannot imagine that they themselves were so deceivable.

The child victim of MSBP faces the possibility of permanent impairment during every moment spent alone with his or her mother. Since there are tremendous disincentives to confessing to her deeds—loss of prestige and public persona; loss of husband, family, and friends; loss of her prop (the child); possibility of humiliation, financial loss, criminal prosecution—the mother is highly unlikely to confess, especially immediately. However, strategies for police interviewing of suspects, designed to increase the likelihood of confession, have recently been articulated (44, pp. 670–82).

The various people and agencies that intervene in behalf of the child may have rather different charges: the prosecutor wants to criminally convict the mother; the department of social services is attempting both to protect the child and reunify the family (daunting propositions, often mutually exclusive); the pediatrician and foster parents are striving to document any status changes in the child's health. Meanwhile, other doctors and nurses are being solicited by the mother for testimony. The possibilities for miscommunication, working at cross-purposes, and even undermining other professionals' charges are considerable. Caution, consideration, and compulsive communication go a long way toward reducing these problems. The expectation of an enormous investment of time on a case of alleged MSBP and the pairing of professionals in child protection teams may themselves be strategies sufficient to mitigate professional enervation and, consequently, to avert those ill-conceived decisions born of it.

The rigors of medical diagnosis must be brought fully to bear upon cases where Munchausen syndrome by proxy is suspected. Correct elimination of Munchausen syndrome by proxy as the diagnosis is entirely as vital to a child's welfare as is the diagnostic confirmation of this dangerous form of abuse.

References

1. Meadow, R. 1977. Munchausen Syndrome by Proxy: The Hinterland of Child Abuse. *Lancet* 2: 343–45.
2. Morley, C. J. 1995. Practical Concerns about the Diagnosis of Munchausen Syndrome by Proxy. *Arch. Disease in Childhood* 72:528–29.
3. Milner, A. D. 1995. Practical Concerns about the Diagnosis of Munchausen Syndrome by Proxy: Commentary. *Arch. Disease in Childhood* 72:529–30.
4. Fisher, G. C., and Mitchell, I. 1995. Is Munchausen Syndrome by Proxy Really a Syndrome? *Arch. Disease in Childhood* 72:530–34.
5. Meadow, R. 1995. What Is, and What Is Not, "Munchausen Syndrome by Proxy"? *Arch. Disease in Childhood* 72:534–38.
6. Rosenberg, D. A. 1995. From Lying to Homicide: The Spectrum of Munchausen Syndrome by Proxy. In *Munchausen Syndrome by Proxy,* ed. A. Levin and M. Sheridan, 13–37. New York: Lexington Books.
7. Bools, C. N.; Neale, B. A.; and Meadow, C. R. 1992. Co-morbidity Associated with Fabricated Illness (Munchausen Syndrome by Proxy). *Arch. Disease in Childhood* 67:77–79.
8. Rosen, C. L.; Frost, J. D., Jr.; and Glaze, D. G. 1986. Child Abuse and Recurrent Infant Apnea. *J. Pediatrics* 109:1065–67.
9. Byard, R. W., and Beal, S. M. 1993. Munchausen Syndrome by Proxy: Repetitive Infantile Apnea and Homicide. *J. Paediatric Child Health* 29:77–79.
10. Rosenberg, D. A. 1987. Web of Deceit: A Literature Review of Munchausen Syndrome by Proxy. *Child Abuse and Neglect: International J.* 11:547–63.
11. Rosenberg, D. A. 1994. Munchausen Syndrome by Proxy. In *Child Abuse: Medical Diagnosis and Management,* ed. Robert Reece, 266–68. Philadelphia: Lea and Febiger.
12. Aideyan, U. O., and Smith, W. L. 1995. Radiologic Features in a Case of Munchausen Syndrome by Proxy. *Pediatric Radiology* 25(1):70–71.
13. Porter, G. E.; Heitsch, G. M.; and Miller, M. D. 1994. Munchausen Syndrome by Proxy: Unusual Manifestations and Disturbing Sequelae. *Child Abuse and Neglect: International J.* 18(9): 789–94.
14. Magnay, A. R.; Debelle, G.; Proops, D. W.; and Booth, I. W. 1994. Munchausen Syndrome by Proxy Unmasked by Nasal Signs. *J. Laryngology and Otology* 108(4):336–38.
15. Schneider, D. J.; Perez, A.; Knilans, T. E.; and Daniels, S. R. 1996. Clinical and Pathological Aspects of Cardiomyopathy from Ipecac Administration in Munchausen's Syndrome by Proxy. *Pediatrics* 97(6):902–6.
16. Fischer, G. C.; Mitchell, I.; and Murdoch, D. 1993. Munchausen's Syndrome by Proxy. The Question of Psychiatric Illness in a Child. *British J. Psychiatry* 162:701–3.
17. Marcus, A.; Ammermann, C.; Bahro, M.; and Schmidt, M. H. 1995. Benzodiazepine Administration Induces Exogenic Psychosis: A Case of Child Abuse. *Child Abuse and Neglect: International J.* 19(7):833–36.
18. Stevenson, R. D., and Alexander, R. 1990. Munchausen Syndrome by Proxy Presenting as a Developmental Disability. *J. Developmental and Behavioral Pediatrics* 11:262–64.
19. Meadow, R. 1993. False Allegations of Abuse and Munchausen Syndrome by Proxy. *Arch. Disease in Childhood* 68:444–47.

20. Barker, L. H., and Howell, R. J. 1994. Munchausen Syndrome by Proxy in False Allegations of Child Sexual Abuse: Legal Implications. *Bull. Am. Acad. Psychiatry and the Law* 22(4): 499–510.

21. Godding, V., and Kruth, M. 1991. Compliance with Treatment in Asthma and Munchausen Syndrome by Proxy. *Arch. Disease in Childhood* 66: 956–60.

22. Rosenberg, D. A. 1994. Fatal Neglect. *APSAC Advisor* 7(4): 38–40.

23. Rosenberg, D. A., and Cantwell, H. 1993. Consequences of Neglect: Individual and Societal. In *Balliere's Clinical Pediatrics,* ed. C. J. Hobbs and J. M. Wynne, 1(1): 185–210. London: Balliere Tindall.

24. Bools, C. 1996. Factitious Illness by Proxy. *British J. Psychiatry* (forthcoming).

25. American Psychiatric Association. 1994. *Diagnostic and Statistical Manual of Mental Disorders,* 4th ed. (*DSM IV*). Washington, D.C.: APA.

26. Schreier, H. A., and Libow, J. A. 1993. *Hurting for Love: Munchausen Syndrome by Proxy.* New York: Guilford.

27. Katz, J. 1994. The Tales They Tell in Cyber-Space Are a Whole Other Story. *New York Times,* 23 January, sec. 2.

28. Waring, W. W. 1992. The Persistent Parent. *Am. J. Diseases of Children* 146: 753–56.

29. Boyce, W. T. 1992. The Vulnerable Child: New Evidence, New Approaches. *Adv. Pediatrics* 39: 1–33.

30. Halsey, N. A.; Tucker, T. W.; Redding, J.; Frentz, J. M.; Sproles, T.; and Daum, R. S. 1983. Recurrent Nosocomial Polymicrobial Sepsis Secondary to Child Abuse. *Lancet* 2: 558–60.

31. Willinger, M.; James, L. S.; and Catz, C. 1991. Defining the Sudden Infant Death Syndrome (SIDS): Deliberation of an Expert Panel Convened by the National Institute of Child Health and Human Development. *Pediatric Pathology* 11: 677–84.

32. Emery, J. L. 1993. Child Abuse, Sudden Infant Death Syndrome, and Unexpected Infant Death. *Am. J. Diseases of Children* 147: 1097–1100.

33. DiMaio, V., and DiMaio, D. 1988. *Forensic Pathology.* New York: Elsevier.

34. Centers for Disease Control and Prevention. 1996. Guidelines for Death Scene Investigation of Sudden, Unexplained Infant Deaths: Recommendations of the Interagency Panel on Sudden Infant Death Syndrome. *Morbidity and Mortality Weekly Report* 45 (RR-10): 1–23.

35. Pinholster, G. 1995. Multiple SIDS Case Ruled Murder. *Science* 268: 494.

36. Brodsky, S. 1991. *Testifying in Court: Guidelines and Maxims for the Expert Witness.* Washington, D.C.: American Psychological Association.

37. Haralambie, A., and Rosenberg, D. 1988. The Expert Witness: Social Work, Medical, Psychiatric. In *The New Child Protection Team Handbook,* ed. D. Bross, R. D. Krugman, M. R. Lenherr, D. A. Rosenberg, and B. D. Schmitt. New York: Garland Press.

38. Klebes, C., and Fay, S. 1995. Munchausen Syndrome by Proxy: A Review, Case Study, and Nursing Implications. *J. Pediatric Nursing* 10(2): 93–98.

39. Meadow, R. 1990. Suffocation, Recurrent Apnea, and Sudden Infant Death. *J. Pediatrics* 117: 351–57.

40. Libow, J. A. 1995. Munchausen By Proxy Victims in Adulthood: A First Look. *Child Abuse and Neglect: International J.* 19(9): 1131–42.

41. Conway, S. P., and Pond, M. N. 1995. Munchausen Syndrome by Proxy: A Foundation for Adult Munchausen Syndrome. *Australian and New Zealand J. Psychiatry* 29(3): 504–7.

42. Feldman, M. D. 1994. Denial in Munchausen Syndrome by Proxy: The Consulting Psychiatrist's Dilemma. *International J. Psychiatry and Medicine* 24(2): 121–28.

43. Parnell, K., and Day, D. *Munchausen Syndrome by Proxy: Misunderstood Child Abuse.* Thousand Oaks, Calif.: Sage Publications, in press.

44. Geberth, V. J. 1996. *Practical Homicide Investigation,* 3d ed. New York: CRC Press.

19

Unusual Forms of Child Abuse

Donna Andrea Rosenberg

This chapter discusses some of the less common forms of child abuse, but, unhappily, it cannot be exhaustive. As a species, humans have shown such a capacity for innovation that our brutalities defy comprehensive tabulation. Thus, in this short chapter, the omission of any particular form of child abuse should not be understood to imply that it has never previously been encountered or, indeed, that it is beyond the scope of human savagery. Furthermore, the brevity of this chapter and its various subsections should not be understood to prescribe a proportionally limited approach to any child who is discovered to have been the victim of one of these types of maltreatment.

It would obviously be helpful to provide prevalence rates for each of these forms of abuse, but, unfortunately, accurately determining the prevalence of unmonitored, secret, or illegal activities is virtually impossible. Most of the forms of child abuse discussed here are included because they are only infrequently encountered—meaning that, at this point, we cannot distinguish between their actually being rare, their being common but well-concealed, or their being common, ill-concealed, but poorly scrutinized. In other forms that I survey, such as technological and biotechnological means of abuse, the potential for misuse of children is still mostly latent but is nonetheless large.

The topics I address pertain primarily to developed countries. However, a few problems I describe, such as child labor and child prostitution, are enormously more common in some developing countries, where children suffer in numbers and in ways not seen in the United States and other advanced industrial nations.

Technology and Child Abuse

Child abuse does not usually involve technological weapons or means. As technologies develop, however, some are enlisted, predictably and tragically, in the abuse of children. While it is tempting to place the blame for these events at the feet of "technology" or "science" run amok, doing so improperly ascribes to them a volition they do not possess.

DONNA ANDREA ROSENBERG, M.D., is assistant professor in the Department of Pediatrics, University of Colorado School of Medicine, and forensic pediatrician with the Colorado Child Fatality Review Team.

For their time and help, the author thanks Jack O'Malley and Donald Huycke, senior special agents, U.S. Customs Service; Kenneth V. Lanning, supervisory special agent, Behavioral Sciences Unit, Federal Bureau of Investigation; Rita Swan; and Andrew H. Vachss.

Science and technology do not have moral lives, nor are they capable of judgments about their own usage independent of the people who develop and operate them.

Of the three general, admittedly overlapping, ways that technologies may be abusively subverted—that is, misuse, overuse, and underuse—the first is probably the most well known. Misuse of technology involves illegal applications, applications which are illegal but widely practiced and tacitly condoned, and immoral applications which the law, perversely, permits.

Illegal, abusive applications of technologies abound. It is something of a universal phenomenon that technologies are employed in child abuse almost from the moment they become available. Children are assaulted with a variety of objects, instruments, and devices that are, quite literally, limitless. Children are burned with matches, lighters, candles, scalding water, chemicals, all manner of heating devices, on stovetops, over open fires, and by conflagration. They are electrocuted, drugged, frozen, drilled, incinerated, gassed, shot, microwaved, dismembered, and exploded.

But sleeker and subtler strategies may prevail, utilizing, for example, latter-day leisure and office equipment. These devices are used to contact or induce a child; they are used to record the abuse, for personal or commercial reasons; they are used to seek or communicate information. Videotaping technology was quickly adopted by child sex abusers and pornographers. More recently, computer database management systems have been used to catalog the occasional pedophile's exploits, often in minute detail. Such readily available equipment as desktop publishing software, scanners, and quality printers have allowed the entrepreneurial pedophile affordable publishing capability. Computer bulletin boards, and the vast Internet, along with communications software, modems, and facsimile machines help pedophiles keep in touch. CD-ROM has branched into the child pornography business; the exploitative uses for interactive CD-ROM and videoconferencing technology are obvious. How virtual reality technology, and other burgeoning technologies, may be harnessed remains to be seen.

Not only are these uses of technologies illegal, they may also be deliberately overlooked. Those who overlook these crimes may be anyone from a neighbor or relative, to law enforcement personnel, prosecutors, judges, or government officials. The reasons that these crimes are overlooked obviously vary but are usually related to inexperience, indifference, or fear or self-interest of some kind.

Sometimes the law permits abusive applications of technological developments. Even before the Second World War, all manner of handicapped children were killed ("euthanized") in Germany, because they were the embodiment of "life unworthy of life." The "medical experimentation" which was performed in the concentration camps upon about three thousand children, many of them twins, was supported by government medical research funds and involved at least one highly prestigious medical institution (1, p. 20). The experiments involved inoculation of the children with various pathogens, with subsequent murder and autopsy of the children to assess the effects; the injection of dye into brown-eyed children's eyes in an attempt to make them blue-eyed; sterilization by castration, surgical removal of ovaries, or radiation; and the murder of children by direct injection of chloroform into their hearts so that their organs could be harvested and studied (1; 2, pp. 15–16; 3, pp. 362, 269–84, 283). A few of the involved doctors, though not those most involved with the experiments upon children, were tried and convicted after the war ended.

Apart from pronouncing verdicts and sentences upon the defendants, the 1947 Nuremberg court's final judgment on the German medical experimenters also articulated guidelines for medical experimentation with humans. These principles are known as the Nuremberg Code and are the basis for U.S. Public Law 99-158, which addresses the protection of human subjects in medical experimentation. The U.S. Department of Health and Human Services, as required by this law, publishes the specific regulations, which require review of any research on humans by an Internal Review Board (IRB), which itself is governed by federal law (4). The final section of these regulations provides additional protections for child research subjects.

The Nazi doctors' experimentation on children is by no means history's only evidence of research scientists' zealotry, ambition, immorality, and *conformity*. The fact that Public Law 99-158 also mandates the establishment of a formal process for assessing alleged violations of these regulations indicates that there is no expectation of full compliance without the institution of ongoing oversight. This is realistic. The Nuremberg Code is the basis for similar regulations in many countries around the world and is one of the few meaningful (when enforceable) correctives in place to prevent the misuse of children via technological tools.

Overuse of technology involves application that grossly exceeds the best interests of the child, resulting in harm. The medical care arena generates a good deal of controversy about technological overuse.

It is often said that physicians' ability to make ethical choices has not kept pace with the rapid development of technology, but this is a simplified view, implying that we just haven't moved quickly enough to catch up to the right answers and ignoring the possibility that the inevitable existence of right choices is an illusion. While the machine is predictable, the human response is, of course, maddeningly individual, even idiosyncratic. Indeed, whether technology is "overused" (that is, the child is harmed) or "appropriate" (that is, the child is helped); whether physicians are required or permitted to treat a child with an extremely poor prognosis or constrained from providing treatment; whether the parental refusal of such technology on behalf of a child is criminally actionable; whether the unwanted intrusion of such technology renders a hospital liable are all matters of recent legal disputes (5–8). It is a legal arena in which state child protection laws, criminal statutes, federal regulations concerning handicapped children and sundry other laws collide with parental wishes, physicians' recommendations, and the child's particular circumstances.

Underuse of technology is the withholding of readily available technological means, including medications or other treatment, which, if used, would almost certainly spare a child severe illness or death, would restore or maintain general health, and would likely cause little or no harm. This means an active withholding of care, by medical professionals and/or their employers, in cases where care was necessary and should have been considered but instead was deliberately omitted or denied. Underuse of technology, in this sense, is to be distinguished from nonavailability or poor availability of the technology, poor or mistaken medical judgment, failure to seek medical care, or other factors which would affect the availability of the technology or the willingness or accessibility of the patient. Children who are in some way less able to assert their needs may be most vulnerable. Predisposing factors may include poverty; some kind of deformation or disability that renders the child unappealing; institutionalization; a parent or guardian who, for any reason, does not adequately represent the child's needs; or an age, race, ethnic, or social affiliation, religion, or gender which, for any reason, is the focus of discrimination. In addition, the limitations on health care which have accompanied the restructuring and "management" of medicine in the United States may affect some children even more seriously than any of these factors do.

The withholding of medical-technological care from disabled newborns is addressed by law. The federal Child Abuse Prevention and Treatment Act, as amended in 1984 and modified in 1986, requires that all states implement a response system for reports of medical neglect, including the withholding of care from a disabled infant—the so-called Baby Doe regulations (9, 10). The withholding of medically indicated treatment means "the failure to respond to the infant's life threatening conditions by providing treatment (including nutrition, hydration and medication) which, in the treating physician's reasonable medical judgment will be most likely to be effective in ameliorating or correcting all such conditions" (9). The Baby Doe regulations describe three classes of infants whose conditions are effectively futile and who are therefore excluded from these legal protections.

Biotechnology and Child Abuse

Biotechnology is the use, manipulation, and engineering of biological materials, including human body parts and substances. Many biotechnology companies and genomic companies are in business worldwide. Genomic companies find, analyze, and commercially develop genetic information and use bioinformatic technologies. *Bioinformatics* refers to the use of proprietary computer methods for collecting, editing, analyzing, and storing DNA-sequence information. The activities of biotechnology companies are broad but should be followed closely, as should those of federally funded researchers and others working with biological materials, to determine their impact on children. Overall, at this time, we should be carefully monitoring how children are being used for the harvesting of biological material both in this country and abroad, and if they are sufficiently safe when they become either the recommended recipients of biopharmaceuticals or the target consumers of other bioengineered products.

Withholding Medical Care for Religious Reasons

As child protection statutes in every state appropriately include medical care neglect as a form of child abuse, all parents are legally held to provide necessary medical care for their children. Nevertheless, certain parents, who withhold medical care from their children in accordance with religious beliefs, are exempt from this legal duty. This means our society has not only two standards of care but two classes of children: those who are legally protected and those who are not. As children cannot assert rights for themselves, the religious exemption from child abuse statutes effectively allows some parents to leave their children suffering with, and dying of, treatable illnesses.

Churches that eschew medical treatment include the Church of the First Born, Faith Tabernacle, Believers Fellowship, Church of God Chapel, Faith Temple Doctoral Church of Christ in God, the Church of God of the Union Assembly, Jesus through Jon and Judy (presumably now defunct), and others. Christian Scientists also withhold medical care from their children and rely, instead, on spiritual treatments from church healers.

The American Academy of Pediatrics' Committee on Bioethics has issued a strong statement condemning these exemptions and reinforcing the academy's belief that no child should be permitted to suffer from, or die of, a treatable illness because the parents have certain religious beliefs which prohibit effective medical care (11).

Very few morbidity and mortality studies exist in the medical literature on children whose parents do not seek care for them, for the obvious reason that such children do not come to medical attention very frequently when they are alive. When they die, their deaths are likely to be signed out as due to natural manner and, therefore, are unlikely to be called to the attention of the child death review team (if one exists). The organization of child death review teams are a recent public health development, aimed at creating an inventory of child death cases, and devising primary prevention strategies for preventable causes of death in childhood. While most U.S. states have local teams in operation at the time of this writing (1997), the percentage of childrens' deaths under review is still small.

Child death review teams may heighten their "rate of capture" of child deaths associated with the withholding of medical care through various strategies that identify those cases requiring further inquiry:

1. *All* childhood deaths should be reviewed, not only deaths preselected for manner, cause, or another criterion. Only a review of all deaths will open the possibility of identifying those deaths which might be misclassified as to manner or cause or identify those deaths in which cause and manner are correctly recorded but the association with withheld medical care might be missed. Of course, this is not the only reason for universal review of all cases of child death. Each of these cases is individually important—the truth about each of them should be known—and they may also be significant for such reasons as public health maintenance, genetic counseling, protection of surviving siblings, and identification of consumer product hazards.

2. Childhood deaths associated with withholding of medical care for religious reasons are usually signed out as natural manner, with various causes, depending upon what was found at autopsy. In reviewing children's deaths, positive answers to the following questions should alert the reviewer to the necessity for further inquiry: Is the cause of death rarely seen to be fatal in a child of that age? Is the cause of death as listed on the death certificate unsupported by the autopsy findings? Are there findings at autopsy that are not explained by the listed cause of death? Are there signs of a chronically untended condition that would have caused obvious symptoms or signs while the child was alive? Have there been other natural but unusual deaths in that family, neighborhood, or church group? Withholding of medical care is only one of several possibilities that should be considered in each of these scenarios.

3. Obtaining antemortem medical records, if any exist, is useful. Ideally, child death review teams can obtain access to antemortem medical records when they are pivotally necessary for final determination of cause or manner of death. The more specific the question, the more useful they tend to be (for example, if the immediate cause of death is listed as a seizure, the purpose of the review of antemortem medical records might be to determine if the child actually had a documented seizure disorder and, if so, what was diagnosed as the cause of the seizure disorder). In religiously motivated withholding of medical care, the children usually have no locatable medical records. However, not all such religions forbid visits to all types of doctors; consequently, some children will have dental, optometric, or orthopedic records, or records involving those medical specialists that the church permits its members to consult. Sometimes the child has had medical records generated during visits to a doctor while the child was staying with other relatives or with the other parent if the parents are separated; a concerted effort should be made to find and assemble these records. Because prenatal and birth records may exist in some cases, they should be sought. If the decedent child or a sibling is school-aged, the parent may have signed a form entitling them to waive immunizations, depending upon the state. These situations are unlike those of chronically medically neglected children of nonreligious parents (see chapter 15); neglected children often have incomplete, scattered records; histories of visits to various clinics without appointments at odd hours; and immunizations that are delinquent by months or years.

4. In states that are mostly rural, certain churches tend to settle in one area, and are well-known. Inquiries made to local officials may be informative.

5. All children who die unexpectedly should be autopsied.

As of this writing, only four states, (South Dakota, Hawaii, Massachusetts, and Maryland) have removed these religious exemptions from both civil and criminal codes. The other forty-six states and two districts have not. This deplorable situation for children in the United States needs resolution.

Food Fadism

Occasionally, parents become enamored of a type of highly restrictive diet or vitamin regimen which they impose upon their children and which causes nutritional problems in them. Kwashiorkor; marasmus; rickets; iron, vitamin B-12, and zinc deficiency; multiple infections; and hypervitaminoses have all been reported as a result of parental food fadism (12, 13).

Parents have a duty both to understand whether or not the food they are feeding their children is adequate to their nutritional needs and to adjust their children's diet accordingly. While some parents cannot fulfill this obligation because of poverty, mental retardation, immaturity, or isolation, food faddist parents typically value the diet more than they appreciate the nutritional welfare of their child. Some of these parents are quite confrontational and highly suspicious of any medical diagnosis. Those who refuse to change the affected child's diet despite evidence of the presence, or risk of, significant harm to the child should be relieved of their parental custodial rights, at least until they can nourish the child properly. A child's somatic, developmental, and brain growth depends upon his or her receiving adequate nutrition, and prolonged, profoundly aberrant nutrition may place a child at great risk of suffering irreversibly damaging effects.

Bizarre Diets

Bizarre diets, as distinct from food faddist diets, are more likely to involve parental psychosis rather than misdirected, but not psychotic, parental beliefs. For example, a psychotic mother of a three-month-old infant presented her starved-looking baby at the clinic, saying that the child would eat nothing but beer and coffee. Most psychotic parents have a past history of this disorder, but occasionally a mother with severe, complicated postpartum depression develops psychosis. A parent who is clinically psychotic should not be tending children alone, or at all. The children may be harmed as the result of the parent's severely impaired judgment.

Water Deprivation and Water Intoxication

Water deprivation usually occurs when a child is being punished for toileting accidents or when a child is taken on a long trip through arid country and his or her hydration is neglected. Water-deprived children usually present to the emergency room in a state of profound dehydration that occasionally causes permanent damage or death. Other causes for dehydration, such as gastroenteritis, or any condition causing significant vomiting or diarrhea, are much more common than water deprivation and must obviously be excluded.

Other children may be water-intoxicated rather than water-deprived. They may have been forced to ingest a massive quantity of water, such as from a garden hose. One might rightly wonder why parents would do this to a child. Some parents attack the child's body part that most infuriates them at that moment—for example, the heads of crying babies or the bottoms of incontinent toddlers. When children have been forcibly water-intoxicated, it is possible that something had come out of the child's mouth (forbidden words; spit; food) or gone into it (prohibited food; drugs; excrement) that especially incensed the parent. These children may present to the emergency room with metabolic abnormalities, such as low serum sodium, or seizures. Again, other causes of total body water overload, such as various kidney, liver, or cardiac disorders, are more common and must be ruled out.

Psychosocial Obesity of Childhood

Psychosocial obesity of childhood is the constellation of severe obesity and family dysfunction in early childhood. The child's weight must exceed the standard weight for height (same gender, same age) by at least 20%, but often closer to at least 50%, and the obesity must demonstrably be the consequence of family dysfunction, not merely coexistent with it. This causal relationship is, and should be, challenging to prove. An overweight condition is not that uncommon: its mere presence should not invite social services intervention, nor should the effects of a family's problems be overstated. Most families can be found wanting in one way or another, but their weaknesses must not be distorted, pathologized, or spuriously amplified to prove a point. Obviously, when children do have psychosocial obesity of childhood, it is important to address not only the nutritional improvement of the morbid obesity but also the family's dysfunction. These children sometimes suffer from concomitant abuse and neglect, especially neglect of limit setting (13) (see chapter 15).

In all obese children, organic causes for the obesity must be ruled out. In general, intervention in childhood obesity is increasingly a medical concern, because of the respiratory, cardiac, orthopedic, ophthalmologic, and psychological complications which may be associated with it and because of increasing evidence of long-term, adverse health consequences.

Child Labor

Over 4 million children younger than sixteen years of age are employed in the United States (14). Health risks and developmental risks are the major hazards for these children (15–17).

Health risks include acute injury, impairment (temporary or permanent), exposures, occupational hazards, and death. Young workers are more likely than older workers to incur injury on the job, and such injuries—especially large lacerations, fractures, and burns—are sometimes serious. The National Safe Workplace Institute estimates that three hundred children are killed and seventy thousand injured on the job each year (18). Sixteen- and seventeen-year-olds are at higher risk than adults for occupational death by electrocution, suffocation, drowning, poisoning, and natural and environmental factors (19). However, occupational deaths overall in childhood, and adolescent injuries in particular, are underreported in official statistics, including those of the Department of Labor (20–22). Researchers at the University of Texas pointedly write that "the magnitude and severity of occupational illnesses in working children are unknown" (23). Additional risks for children of all ages include stalled or aberrant development: this results simply from the child's missing necessary developmental time because he or she is often too tired to learn at school or because he or she has no time or energy left for homework. The American Academy of Pediatrics has articulated its conclusions about the hazards of child labor (24). The Academy emphasizes that legal exemptions allowing young children to work with pesticides and heavy machinery on farms must be stricken; that parents and the business community, among others, must be educated about occupational hazards to children; and that the systems in place for issuing and monitoring work permits, as well as those for collecting data on work-related morbidity and mortality, must be revamped.

The process which led to the passing of federal standards for child labor was a long and arduous one. To document the extent and wretchedness of child labor, a quiet schoolteacher, Lewis Hine, quit his job in 1908 and accepted an assignment with the National Child Labor Committee to travel around the United States and photograph children at work. His photographs, taken over the next ten years, slowly but impressively became known to the American public, whose awareness eventually resulted in the first nationwide protections for children who work. Between the establishment of the United States Bureau for

Children in 1912 and the first federal child labor protections in 1938, there occurred various political and legal absurdities by no means extinct today. For example, beginning in 1924, and for the next ten years, the constitutional amendment passed by Congress to authorize a national child labor law was the focus of intense lobbying by groups opposed to any increase in federal authority in matters that pertained to children. They were eventually successful at having the amendment killed. Even before that, in both 1916 and 1918, Congress passed child labor laws that would protect all American children, but the Supreme Court held them to be unconstitutional because they infringed on states' rights and "denied children the freedom to contract work" (25). These historical events should actually hearten those who, today, venture into the political arena on behalf of children. It may help present-day activists to realize not just that others confronted comparably energetic and preposterous opposition to basic rights for children but that dogged persistence eventually carried the day.

Child labor laws (originally the Fair Labor Standards Act of 1938) limit the use of children in the workforce by defining and requiring restrictions such as minimum ages, maximum number of hours, adequate supervision, and reduced exposure to hazards. Nonetheless, children are still worked illegally in North America (and to a shocking extent in other countries).

In 1992, the U.S. Department of Labor recorded 19,443 violations of child labor laws, twice that of 1980. Even major American corporations have been fined by the Labor Department for wide-scale violations of child labor laws.

Poor American children, as young as seven years old, are being recruited into door-to-door selling schemes. They sell products after school until well after dark, are almost always unsupervised, and are taught to misrepresent the purpose of the sales as charitable. Poor children are also those most vulnerable to being recruited into selling illegal drugs.

Middle-class parents who do not need the extra income may believe that children need to work to "learn the value of a dollar." But not all children have the same amount of energy or resilience for work, even that which falls within legal limits. Homework and schoolwork may suffer, and some of the children are especially vulnerable to unsavory but persuasive people they meet on the job.

Illegal child labor appears to be a resurging problem. More immigrant children live in the United States, and they are sometimes made to work to supplement family income. By 1996, the problem had reached significant proportions in New York City, where large numbers of immigrant children were working very long hours, in dreadful conditions, for wages significantly less than the minimum wage or for wages promised but never delivered. These children are sent to New York to work and are often without family or supervision (26). Elsewhere, migrant laborers, unable to afford child care and paid by the box, may leave the children unattended or bring their children with them to the fields, where they have at least some supervision but are subject to occupational hazards.

The likelihood of significantly increasing the number of labor investigators is low, because of budgetary constraints. Instead, industries that are known to be frequent offenders and that are the most dangerous should be targeted first. Curtailing the illegal child labor practices of some businesses will not, however, solve the problems of poor children who are working illegally to supplement family income. Nor will tired rhetoric about children being our most valuable resource, or this nation's future, solve these families' troubles. In the short run, after-school and summer programs which offer courses, tutorial help, and perhaps some supervised paid duties are educational and safe. In the long run, a redoubled effort toward assisting them to complete their education or secure vocational training will result in a far greater probability that the children will grow up to be employable at a decent wage. This will reduce the number of children exposed in the next generation to hazards at jobs they would hold to help their families survive.

Children Used in Pornography and Prostituted Children

Child pornography and child prostitution are not only sexual abuses of children—they are also egregious forms of emotional neglect and physical abuse. The child's home situation, which precipitates or accompanies the descent into pornography or prostitution, is often cruel, violent, exploitative, emotionally desolate, or sexually or physically abusive (27). Hence, the child victims of these combined assaults exhibit complex disturbances, which may include such varied problems as a deficit of empathy and all its consequences (including criminal behavior), abuse and neglect of their own and other children, psychiatric disorders, and intractable substance abuse (28, 29). The array of physical consequences from assaults, poor nutrition, and infectious diseases is vast and includes serious bodily injury and death.

In general, children are recruited into child pornography and prostitution by their parents or caretakers, or by a person (usually known to the child) who deliberately insinuates himself or herself into a vulnerable child's affections, or by someone he or she meets while trying to survive on the streets. Predators have quite workable schemes for spotting vulnerable children (30): when a child runs away from home, that child may be forced to liquidate the only capital available—his or her body—in order to survive. This is the supply side of the equation, with children as the commodity. Inasmuch as we are currently unlikely to diminish the demand side of the equation, we must focus attention on the primary prevention of the supply side, that is, reducing the volume of children available to predators. However, emotional neglect and abuse, the most common causes of the children's vulnerability, are the ones least likely to be addressed by the existing child protection system.

Child pornography and child prostitution are considered separately in this chapter, but the reader should not understand from this that these enterprises do not overlap. They do.

Child Pornography

Child pornography is currently, though illegally, available in several formats: print media, videotape, audiotape, computer bulletin boards systems (BBS), and CD-ROM (compact disc read-only memory—a computer program which is usually multimedia). Comic book depictions of child pornography, which are largely produced in the Far East and include rape and sodomy, are not illegal unless they involve real child models in their production. Other formats, such as interactive CD-ROM programs, are available with adult subjects but no child pornography in this medium has yet been seized by federal agents.

It is illegal to produce, transport, distribute, or possess child pornography. According to the FBI and the U.S. Customs Service, most child pornography is produced overseas and is mainly produced by pedophiles themselves, without the involvement of nonpedophilic organized business. Most of the equipment necessary to produce the various forms of child pornography is readily available commercially. Federal seizures of child pornography were high in the early 1980s but have lately been lower. No one believes that this is because there is less of a market for it. Rather, explanations include the possibilities that fewer attempts are being made to smuggle in child pornography, that it is being transmitted via undiscovered means, or that other seizure priorities among U.S. agencies have taken precedence. Nonetheless, seizures are certainly still being made, as evidenced by the U.S. Postal Service's involvement in the May 1996 bust of a national child pornography ring, when 130 warrants were issued in thirty-six states.

Plenty of adults who sexually abuse children also have their own homemade child pornography collections—videotapes, instant photographs which do not require outside developing, and scrapbooks stuffed with such things as photographs, clipped from department store catalogs, of children modeling underwear. The pornography is used to induce other children to also comply, to instruct and blackmail the children, and for the adult's satisfaction.

Various organizations, such as the North American Man-Boy Love Association (NAMBLA), promote sexual abuse of children under the guise of advocacy for children's sexual liberty. Concerning child pornography, a spokesman for NAMBLA stated, "We do not believe that sex is a bad thing, therefore we don't believe that visual depictions of sex is a bad thing." Such is the level of self-absorption among these individuals that, even though he added, "We are opposed to any form of exploitation and wish that the privacy rights of individuals be respected," he also noted that it is perfectly acceptable to fondle a three-year-old boy who seems to enjoy it, that a child has "the right to say yes," and that if a "child perceives a problem [with sexual contact] he could leave home, go to a shelter, and then not be required to go back until the situation had been adjusted to his satisfaction . . ." (31).

Children as young as infants and as old as teenagers are depicted in child pornography. It is often impossible to locate these children in order to help them, because tracing the material to the production point is extremely difficult (32). Certain photographs, for example, may be reprinted in various publications and distributed around the world over several years. In the case of teenagers, child protection investigators can only estimate, by Tanner staging, their chronological age from the photographs. Since the age of majority is as young as fifteen in some pornography-producing European countries, the use of young models may not even qualify as child pornography there, though it would be qualified that way in the United States, where the age of majority is eighteen. Since establishing the illegality depends upon being able to prove that the child depicted is fifteen or sixteen, rather than eighteen, and because it is virtually impossible to distinguish an eighteen-year-old from a minor close to the age of majority, such proof is not likely to be established.

Much social debate centers around the definition of pornography, the definition of obscenity, and the issues of privacy rights and censorship, as if resolution of these matters will in any way enhance the protection of children. They will not. Our goal should be simply to prevent children from being recruited into pornography in the first place with the usual inducements and/or terrorizing, and, for those children who are already involved, to help disengage them with a realistic, nonabusive alternative.

Child Prostitution

Precursors in the backgrounds of child prostitutes commonly feature pervasive neglect, emotional abuse, and physical and sexual abuse. Sometimes parents themselves act as pimps for their children. It is extremely uncommon for a child to be abducted and forced into prostitution. On the other hand, children may be sold into prostitution by their parents, most commonly in Southeast Asia, where the clientele is diverse and includes Western businessmen, diplomats, and development workers. At the time of this writing, eleven countries, including New Zealand, Australia, and France, have passed extraterritorial legislation that permits prosecution of their own citizens for criminal sexual offenses committed elsewhere (33).

Very conservative estimates put the number of child prostitutes under sixteen years of age at four hundred thousand worldwide. The number in North America is unknown. In North America, many child prostitutes were victims of sexual assault in childhood. The sexual abuse is thus also a proxy measure of the extreme degree of emotional abuse. There is a high prevalence of drug and alcohol abuse in prostitutes' families of origin and among the people who raped and molested them as children.

Child prostitutes are male and female. They are usually school-age and above, though adults who prostitute infants are known. Since these babies are orally copulated, they are at risk of suffocation. Evidence of death from suffocation during fellatio has also occasionally been seen in young children.

Child prostitutes are at increased risk of sexually transmitted diseases and their complications, including death—from customers, drugs, pimps, or Acquired Immunodeficiency Syndrome (AIDS). In a sample of 235 male prostitutes in Atlanta, 29.4% were positive for human immunodeficiency virus (HIV), 25.1% for syphilis, and 58.3% for hepatitis B. A significant risk factor for HIV seropositivity was a history of childhood physical abuse (34).

Most of the recent research on child prostitution, contained in the National Library of Medicine's database, concerns transmission of sexually transmitted disease or HIV (at the time of this writing, twenty-five of thirty-seven articles published in the past two years). While obviously important, it is something of a secondary matter, as the risk would not exist for these children if they were not prostitutes in the first instance. The overwhelming predominance of research on infectious diseases reflects research funding priorities. Priorities translate fluidly into research dollars. Low priority is given to research into the more fundamental matters of prevention of, and intervention into, child prostitution. Although we might expect that publications in fields other than medicine would contain more research, this is really not the case, apart from a few notable exceptions, such as material published by the National Center for Missing and Exploited Children (35).

For children who are already ensnared in prostitution or pornography, what seems to be the most helpful option so far is street social work—that is, going out and finding the children and offering them an alternative—combined with transitional housing.

The absurdity of the notion that sexual predators can readily be "treated," and the titanic weight of damage to the child, once recruited, are captured in this dialogue between an investigative reporter and a pederast as they walked through a kiddie porn district in New York City:

> CHICKENHAWK: "I know that boy. I made it with him once—but never again because he embarrassed me."
>
> LLOYD: "How do you mean—he embarrassed you? You mean he told someone about you?"
>
> CHICKENHAWK: "No, it wasn't that. He was recommended by another young friend of mine—Steve. And Steve was right about one thing. That kid does everything in bed . . . and I mean everything. But while we were lying there and I was doing the work, I heard this strange whimpering sound like a lost puppy. I looked up and his eyes were closed tight. He was sucking his thumb like a baby and making this whimpering sound. It completely turned me off and left me with such a guilty feeling I didn't come down to the street for three days." (36)

Child Sexual Abuse within the Context of Other Abuses

When sexual abuse of a child also involves abusive ceremonies, rites, or practices, the child may be further or even more strangely traumatized. Because the time devoted to these practices replaces that which the child needs to sleep, learn, eat properly, play, make friends, or be protected by an adult, the child's growth and development may be aberrant.

Some forms of these sexually abusive practices have been labeled "ritualistic" or "satanic." The utility of adding these words to the classification "child sexual abuse" must be weighed against the liability. Words stand for things. Unless a word universally stands for much the same thing, it obscures rather than clarifies, and is ill-used. The words *ritualistic* or *satanic* have been defined too variably to be useful shorthand terms. The terms may themselves insidiously shape our understanding of a child's experience, causing us to incorrectly infer, surmise, or interpret a child's history instead of generating a complete list of hypotheses which could explain it. This leads in turn to underdiagnosis, overdiagnosis, and misdiagnosis. If and when a distinct subtype of child sexual abuse is both identified and uniformly defined, we should add another adjective. Until then, it makes more sense to "dispense with the term ritualistic or satanic abuse and instead consider the extent to which other types of abuse or multiple victims occur in any individual case" (37).

The types of activities which may accompany child sexual abuse include torture, killing, sadism, terrorization, emotional degradation, and forced drug use. They may involve one child or several. Claims have been made, but never substantiated, that "mind-altering" techniques (meaning drugs, not psychological methods) frequently accompany child sexual abuse. While it is known that some perpetrators of child sexual abuse do give their victims drugs and alcohol, overtly or covertly, it is also possible that a sexually abused child will describe the abuse in such a way that drugging of the child is incorrectly inferred by the interviewer.

The fact that I include this topic in this chapter on unusual forms of child abuse reflects the data currently available on prevalence. Claims of widespread torture, murder, and mind-control of children as the context for sexual abuse are not substantiated (38), though clearly there have been isolated incidents, as there has been with every other atrocity mentioned above. Law enforcement studies indicate that, to date, no evidence to support these claims of massively prevalent activity has been uncovered, despite vigorous investigations. Reviews of seized child pornography for evidence of such practices, searches for the trace evidence almost always associated with events involving sex, blood, murder, or mutilation, and major excavations of alleged sites (39) have failed to uncover any relevant evidence; hence, it does not appear that bona fide evidence has been systematically overlooked or discounted by the law enforcement community. Evidence in these alleged cases is held to a standard no higher than that in other criminal investigations. However, since no one disputes the idea that human beings are capable of organized evil, all allegations must be considered individually and explored thoroughly but not suggestively. It is certainly known that sexual abuse involving multiple children exists (40) and that the ringleaders often employ cruel and terrorizing practices. It no more behooves us to dismiss bizarre claims categorically than to embrace them unquestioningly.

Sexual Sadism

Children are sometimes the victims of sexual sadists. Children so victimized are usually abducted by strangers, and the sadism may involve beating; restraining; holding children captive; sexual bondage; forced anal, oral, or vaginal rape; assault with foreign objects; mutilation; murder; or cannibalism (41). The estimated number of children kidnapped and murdered in the United States each year is between 52 and 158, with adolescents from fourteen to seventeen years of age accounting for about two-thirds of these victims (39).[1]

Snuff films present a live-action documentation of a person being killed as the ultimate sexual event. Both the U.S. Customs Service and the FBI deny ever having seen or seized a genuine snuff film involving a child victim, though agents from both organizations have reported seeing films that, through special effects, generate the impression of it. No one disputes the possibility either that genuine snuff films involving the actual murder of a child may be available but not yet seized or that they will be made. There is clearly a market for snuff films. For example, in 1987, a plastic surgeon in Florida pled guilty to twenty-two counts in a federal drug and child pornography case. Among other activities, the doctor had responded to a pornographic newsletter that ran the following item: "Will pay generously for Lolita, Gold Showers, Animal or Snuff" ["Lolita" refers to sexual acts involving preteen girls; "gold showers" to urination; and "animal" to sex with animals]" (42). In 1991, a man in Virginia pled guilty for his role in a plot to kidnap, molest, and slay a boy for a snuff film (43).

1. The abduction and murder rates were misprinted in *Out of Darkness* (39); the rates shown above are correct and were verified in a telephone conversation in July 1995 with Kenneth V. Lanning, the author of the referenced chapter.

Some publications specialize in photographs and articles on spanking. In these publications, the spanking of children is depicted in the context of adult sexual arousal. Additionally, some adults exchange audiotapes of children being spanked.

Occasionally, the sexual sadist is not a stranger but is close to, or a member of, the victimized child's family. Sexual sadism in the home can be mutilatory and chronic. If a child shows evidence of body trauma or mutilation and claims that the damage was self-inflicted, the possibility that it was inflicted by someone whom the children sees frequently or with whom the child lives should also be considered.

Case example: B. K., a twelve-year-old boy, lived with his mother, younger brother, and stepfather. The stepfather had been a member of the family for many years and had assaulted both boys repeatedly, not only by forcing anal and oral sex with them but also by slamming the door while holding the younger boy's testicles in the door frame. Once, when the stepfather was performing fellatio upon B. K., the child urinated in his mouth. In retaliation, the stepfather told the child that he was "setting the date for your nuts to come off." The stepfather postponed the date by a week because the grandparents were coming to visit. Then, when the mother and younger brother were out of the home, the stepfather told B. K. to lie on the kitchen floor, where he bound his hands and feet. With a kitchen knife, the stepfather cut through one of B. K.'s scrotal sacs, chopped out the child's testicle and asked the child if he wanted to throw out the testicle, save it in a jar. or eat it. The child was then unbound, but because he was bleeding profusely, the stepfather called 911, ordering the child to tell the medical team that he had done it to himself. Emergency surgical treatment saved the child but could not replace the testicle. The child, understanding from the stepfather that he would cut off the other testicle if he told the truth, informed the psychologist that he had cut out his own testicle because his brother got more attention than he. The child was misdiagnosed as having had an acute psychotic episode. He remained in outpatient therapy for a few weeks, was then lost to follow-up until seven years later, when he appeared in a police station in another state, no longer a minor, and told his story. The perpetrator was apprehended, convicted, and served ten years. A few weeks before his discharge from the penitentiary, without parole time, exquisitely hand-done drawings were discovered in his cell. They portrayed a naked, prepubescent boy in four-point restraints on a table. Along one margin of the drawings was a list of the various medical and vernacular terms for the surgical removal of testicles. Along the other margin, drawn with particular patience and skill, was a series of surgical instruments. The boy depicted in the drawing has a small, erect penis and no testicles. He is smiling.

Conclusion

It is a horrifying measure of our species' behavioral repertoire that no inventory of cruelty to our young can ever be complete. Undoubtedly, in future editions of *The Battered Child,* sections of this chapter will warrant entire chapters of their own. One hopes that others may not even deserve mention.

References

1. Proctor, R. N. 1992. Nazi Doctors, Racial Medicine, and Human Experimentation. In *The Nazi Doctors and the Nuremberg Code,* ed. G. J. Annas and M. A. Grodin, 17–31. New York: Oxford University Press.

2. Annas, G. J., and Grodin, M. A., eds. 1992. The Nazi Doctors and the Medical Experiments. In *The Nazi Doctors and the Nuremberg Code.* New York: Oxford University Press.

3. Lifton, R. J. 1986. *The Nazi Doctors.* New York: Basic Books.

4. Department of Health and Human Services. 1991. *Protection of Human Subjects.* OPRR Reports, 18 June. Washington, D.C.: DHHS.

5. Clark, F. I. 1996. Making Sense of State v. Messenger. *Pediatrics* 97(4):579–83.

6. *State v. Messenger,* file 94-67694-FY. Clerk of the Circuit Court, County of Ingham, Michigan.

7. Lewin, T. 1996. Ignoring "Right to Die" Directives, Medical Community Is Being Sued. *New York Times,* 2 June.

8. Flannery, E. J. 1995. One Advocate's Viewpoint: Conflicts and Tensions in the Baby K Case. *J. Law, Medicine, and Ethics* 23:7–12.

9. U.S. Child Abuse Prevention and Treatment Amendments of 1984, Public Law No 98-457, Title I §101 (98 Stat. 1749); 1986 Amendment, Public Law 99-401, Title I §101–207 (100 Stat. 906), 42 USC 5101).

10. *Bowen v. American Hospital Association,* 476 US. 610/90 L. Ed. 2d 584.

11. American Academy of Pediatrics Committee on Bioethics. 1997. Religious Objections to Medical Care. *Pediatrics* 99:279–81.

12. Shinwell, E. D., and Gorodischer, R. 1982. Totally Vegetarian Diets and Infant Nutrition. *Pediatrics* 70:582–86.

13. Christoffel, K. K., and Forsyth, B. W. C. 1989. Mirror Image of Environmental Deprivation: Severe Childhood Obesity of Psychosocial Origin. *Child Abuse and Neglect: International J.* 13:249–56.

14. Dunn, K. A., and Runyan, C. W. 1993. Death's at Work among Children and Adolescents. *Am. J. Diseases of Children* 147:1044–47.

15. Lemen, R. A.; Layne, L. A.; Castillo, D. N.; and Lancashire, J. H. 1993. Children at Work: Prevention of Occupational Injury and Disease. *Am. J. Industrial Med.* 24:325–30.

16. Pollack, S. H.; Landrigan, P. J.; and Mallino, D. L. 1990. Child Labor in 1990: Prevalence and Health Hazards. *Annual Rev. Public Health* 11:359–75.

17. World Health Organization [WHO Study Group]. 1987. Children at Work: Special Health Risks. *WHO Tech. Rept.,* no. 756:1–49.

18. Duhaime, B. 1993. Illegal Child Labor Comes Back. *Fortune,* 5 April, 86–93.

19. Castillo, D. N.; Landon, D. D.; and Layne, L. A. 1994. Occupational Injury Deaths of Sixteen- and Seventeen-Year Olds in the United States. *Am. J. Public Health* 84(4):646–49.

20. Hayden, G. J.; Gerberich, S. G.; and Maldonado, G. 1994. Fatal Farm Injuries: a Five-Year Study Utilizing a Unique Surveillance Approach to Investigate the Concordance of Reporting Between Two Data Sources. *J. Occupational and Environmental Med.* 37(5):571–77.

21. Runyan, C. W.; Loomis, D.; and Butts, J. 1994. Practices of County Medical Examiners in Classifying Deaths as on the Job. *J. Occupational Med.* 36(1):36–41.

22. Parker, D. L.; Carl, W. R.; French, L. R.; and Martin, F. B. 1994. Characteristics of Adolescent Work Injuries Reported to the Minnesota Department of Labor and Industry. *Am. J. Public Health* 84(4):606–11.

23. Cooper, S. P., and Rothstein, M. A. 1995. Health Hazards among Working Children in Texas. *Southern Med. J.* 88(5):550–54.

24. American Academy of Pediatrics, Committee on Environmental Health. The Hazards of Child Labor. *Pediatrics* 95(2):311–13.

25. Freedman, R. 1994. *Kids at Work: Lewis Hine and the Crusade against Child Labor.* New York: Scholastic Inc.
26. National Public Radio. 1996. Immigrant Children Working in New York City. On *All Things Considered.* 2 June. Washington D.C.
27. Tyler, R. P., and Stone, L. E. 1985. Child Pornography: Perpetuating the Sexual Victimization of Children. *Child Abuse and Neglect: International J.* 9:313–18.
28. Paperny, D. M., and Deisher, R. W. 1983. Maltreatment of Adolescents: The Relationship to a Predisposition toward Violent Behavior and Delinquency. *Adolescence* 18:499–506.
29. Silbert, M. H.; Pines, A. M.; and Lynch, T. 1982. Substance Abuse and Prostitution. *J. Psychoactive Drugs* 14:193–97.
30. Conte, J. R.; Wolf, S.; and Smith, T. 1989. What Sexual Offenders Tell Us about Prevention Strategies. *Child Abuse and Neglect: International J.* 13:293–301.
31. Hechler, D. 1988. *The Battle and the Backlash: The Child Sexual Abuse War.* Lexington, Mass.: Lexington Books.
32. Pierce, R. L. 1984. Child Pornography: A Hidden Dimension of Child Abuse. *Child Abuse and Neglect: International J.* 8:483–93.
33. Canadian Press. 1996. Law Would Bar Sex Overseas with Children. Printed in the *Globe and Mail* (Toronto, Canada), 21 February, sect. A3.
34. Elifson, K. W.; Boles, J.; and Sweat, M. 1993. Risk Factors Associated with HIV Infection among Male Prostitutes. *Am. J. Public Health* 83:79–83.
35. National Center for Missing and Exploited Children. 1992. *Female Juvenile Prostitution.* Arlington, Va.: National Center for Missing and Exploited Children.
36. Lloyd, R. 1976. *For Money or Love: Boy Prostitution in America.* New York: Vanguard Press.
37. Jones, D. P. H. 1991. Ritualism and Child Sexual Abuse. *Child Abuse and Neglect: International J.* 15:163–70.
38. Putnam, F. W. 1991. The Satanic Ritual Abuse Controversy. *Child Abuse and Neglect: International J.* 15:175–79.
39. Lanning, K. V. 1992. A Law-Enforcement Perspective on Allegations of Ritual Abuse. In *Out of Darkness: Exploring Satanism and Ritual Abuse,* ed. D. K. Sakheim and S. E. Devine, 109–46. New York: MacMillan.
40. Burgess, A. W.; Harman, C. R.; McCausland, M. P.; and Powers, P. 1984. Response Patterns in Children and Adolescents Exploited through Sex Rings and Pornography. *Am. J. Psychiatry* 141:656–62.
41. Dietz, P. E.; Hazelwood, R. R.; and Warren, J. 1990. The Sexually Sadistic Criminal and His Offenses. *Bulletin Am. Acad. Psychiatry and Law* 18:163–78.
42. *Tampa Tribune.* 1987. Dubin Says He's Guilty in Drug, Child-Porn Case. 16 January, sect. 1B.
43. *Richmond Times-Dispatch.* 1991. Panel Agrees "Snuff" Film Figure Can't Change His Plea. 20 November, sect. B3.

PART

3

Intervention and Treatment

Part 3: Editors' Comments

Recognizing, investigating, and assessing the sheer existence and incidence of child abuse is not enough, although in many parts of the United States this is as far as the process gets. Part of the reason that treatment lags behind assessment in both knowledge base and implementation of programs is that it is expensive and it is hard. It takes skill, patience, and can rarely be done in a short period of time if our goal is the successful healing of children and families, whether they are suffering from intrafamilial abuse or recovering from extrafamilial abuse.

We have intuitively known for years that not all abused children have needed professional help. Therapy—or, more precisely, being treated therapeutically—is something that must have gone on through the ages; otherwise, every abused and neglected child .would have repeated the intergenerational cycle described by Brandt Steele in chapter 5. However, more than a sympathetic appreciation of the past, we need a much better understanding of what actual changes lead to a positive treatment outcome for children who have been abused. Longitudinal studies of the natural history of formally treated and not treated children would help—but to accomplish that, we would need to see a lot more treatment conducted under controlled study conditions than we have now. Maybe this will be accomplished by the time the next edition of this book appears. In the meanwhile, this section will provide a discipline-by-discipline review of intervention and treatment.

It is a measure of how dependent the child protection system is in most countries (and certainly in the United States) that we include three chapters in this book dealing with some aspect of the legal system. Each is different in its approach. Donald Bross has earlier, in part 1, given the legal framework for our assumption that children have legal rights. The two chapters in this section look at the role of lawyers (chapter 21, by Donald Duquette) and the child protection system (chapter 22, by Howard Davidson).

Treatment of the child, the parents, and the abusers is covered in the chapters in part 3. Of particular interest, and well worth studying, is chapter 23, by Catherine Marneffe, which presents the approach used in Belgium and some other European countries to deal with child abuse and neglect. Unlike the system in the United States, the United Kingdom, and Australia, this Belgian approach utilizes the health system as the "primary caregiver" through "confidential doctors." Marneffe and her colleagues who employ this system are passionate about the correctness of their approach and very disdainful of systems that focus on punishment rather than treatment of the abuser. It is an important debate. Regrettably, it is one that is informed mainly by nothing more than opinion on both sides and not by published data on outcomes which would let us, as professionals and societies, decide how best to deal with the problem of healing.

20

The Role of Law Enforcement in the Investigation of Child Abuse and Neglect

JACK R. SHEPHERD

This chapter will examine the role of the police in handling child abuse and neglect cases. By surveying the most pressing issues confronting law enforcement in this field and by providing an overview both of recent progress and future directions, I will demonstrate how law enforcement can improve its role in child abuse investigations. I will also discuss the trend in professional police work toward improving its ability to cooperate and coordinate with other community resources.

Current Approaches

The law enforcement profession has gradually come to be appreciated as a community resource which is readily available during times of crisis and which brings significant authority as well as a unique perspective to child abuse and neglect investigations. The law enforcement profession shares the responsibility for the protection of children with other child-serving agencies within the community. Its primary responsibilities include basic investigation and arrest and prosecution of perpetrators (1). A majority of states (thirty-four) have legislatively mandated law enforcement's role in child abuse cases to include maintenance of reporting standards, assistance to child protective agencies, and participation in investigations (2, pp. 149–56).

The role of the police in child abuse and neglect cases can be multiple and complex (see table 20.1). It is the police officer who has the authority to remove a child immediately from an environment or situation which is considered dangerous. Law enforcement agents are uniquely qualified by their training and skills to collect, handle, and preserve various forms of evidence for use in both civil and criminal proceedings. In addition, the police investigator is the community professional with the ready knowledge of state and federal statutes necessary to determine if an act of child abuse meets the criteria for a crime which would warrant arrest.

The primary mission of law enforcement as an institution is the protection of the community it serves. Perhaps the foremost reason law enforcement is expected to provide a leadership role in child abuse cases involves the public's view of the police as the community's most identifiable resource. This perception is based on the simple fact that law en-

JACK R. SHEPHERD is an inspector with the Michigan Department of State Police and the executive assistant in the department's Investigative Services Bureau.

TABLE 20.1
Situations Requiring Law Enforcement Involvement

When someone other than a parent has abused the child

When the case appears serious enough to warrant the consideration of an arrest or criminal prosecution, as established by state law, child protective services and law enforcement protocol, or local prosecutor's policy

When the child protective agency cannot be reached (such as at night and on weekends and holidays) and an immediate response is needed

When speed is essential and the proximity of the police to the child gives the police faster access than the child protective agency

When a child seems to be in immediate danger and the child protective worker cannot enter the home or the place where the child is located or the parents otherwise make the child inaccessible

When a child must be placed in protective custody against parental wishes

When it appears that the suspected perpetrator may flee

When police assistance is needed to preserve evidence

When police assistance is needed to protect the person reporting or the child protective worker or to otherwise maintain order (when the parent, for example, becomes belligerent or physically threatening)

Source: Derived from Douglas J. Besharov, *Recognizing Child Abuse* (New York: Free Press, 1990).

forcement officers are normally available on a twenty-four-hour-a-day basis. When this accessibility is combined with the other traditional areas of authority associated with this profession, it is logical to see why law enforcement has been given the responsibilities to report, investigate, and provide emergency services for victims of child abuse throughout this country (3, pp. 28–42).

At a secondary level, law enforcement's involvement with the issue of child abuse can assume a preventive role. While prevention here is of an auxiliary nature, the potential for its development in any given case can be greatly increased by the skills of individual officers. The investigator's ability to interact effectively with family members during an inquiry, as well as his or her interviewing skills, knowledge of applicable community services, and genuine empathy for the family's situation all can serve to influence the positive direction of a case (4).

Child Neglect

Although child neglect constitute the largest percentage of reported child maltreatment in any given community, with instances often totaling to numbers higher than physical abuse and sexual abuse cases combined, law enforcement is not usually involved in this type of case (5, pp. 1–15). This is true largely because neglect cases either do not get resolved within the legal system or, if they do, they are processed at the juvenile court level. Neglect cases usually do not make their way into criminal courts, which somewhat diminishes the police investigator's role. Even with the present trend toward multijurisdictional protocols, most states charge their child protective services with a separate legal obligation to investigate and treat child neglect.

The standard professional team approach to intervention has a greater tendency to break down when child neglect is the focus of attention. This is unfortunate, as the criminal investigator—if properly utilized—could bring the same skills to neglect cases that are frequently required in physical and sexual abuse investigations. These skills consist of evidence collection and preservation, interviewing and processing of adult suspects, and (to some extent) proper case management. Another compelling rationale for law enforcement involvement in child neglect cases is the police's understanding of and access to forensic laboratories.

Obvious as the need appears to be for joint investigations, however, the police investigator is often absent from this type of case for an equally appropriate reason: a large number of these cases handled by child protective services are intentionally resolved entirely outside the judicial process.

Nevertheless, law enforcement should reevaluate its lack of participation in child neglect investigations. Greater involvement would not only foster a more consistent level of service but might also, between these two principal investigative agencies, ensure better overall adherence to protocol procedure. Even apart from such basic issues as the police's ability to provide necessary forensic resources (photographic and recording equipment, for example), child neglect cases would be better served if the law enforcement investigator were able to work in concert with his or her protective services counterpart. A final consideration in support of law enforcement involvement is the potential for other forms of child abuse to be jointly discovered and investigated in the course of pursuing the original allegation of neglect. Considering what is currently known about the prevalence of overlapping abuses occurring within dysfunctional families, it would seem wise to explore the possibility of physical, sexual, and emotional abuse accompanying the reported neglect. This inquiry could be better accomplished through the combined efforts of law enforcement and child protective services.

Critical Issues

Recently, law enforcement agencies and child protective services have both been dramatically affected by large reductions in their budgets. With smaller staffing levels, the caseloads which face the typical professional in these fields are high. In addition to the downsizing of its services, the law enforcement profession is also confronted with other issues which must be addressed if it is to succeed as a significant resource in child abuse and neglect cases. A recent Police Foundation study (4) outlined these issues and recommended necessary action steps:

- Eliminate duplication of effort and ensure improved investigations
- Make available more trained investigative personnel
- Improve training and recognition of appropriate handling of child abuse cases by patrol officers

- Increase the number of agencies which have written child abuse and neglect policies (33% do not)
- Provide better services and treatment for victims and their families throughout the investigative process
- Improve policies and procedures dealing with abuse, with an emphasis on difficult cases

In addition to these areas, there is consensus among law enforcement professionals that to be more successful in child abuse investigations, their profession must improve the quality of the investigative process at the initial stages of inquiry. Specifically, at the time the allegations are first reported, the response must be timely and effective. This is not only a training issue—it also reflects the need to better integrate law enforcement's response with that of the other principal agencies responsible for child abuse investigations within the community (6, pp. 39–41).

Improving Investigations

There are a number of ways in which law enforcement agencies can improve their response to child abuse and neglect cases. However, little can be accomplished or sustained if the highest level of administration within a given agency does not support the effort. Strategic planning and setting priorities are the responsibility of administrators. If policy makers do not provide the leadership to establish child abuse as an important issue, the agency's response will be less successful and less effective.

Police administrators should have access to training on how to manage the issue of child abuse. The average law enforcement administrator is routinely faced with issues which compete for his or her attention. Given the number and variety of concerns the community desires to have addressed, the issue of child abuse can all too easily become only one of many priorities demanding attention. A promising solution to this problem is a training program for police administrators known as POLICY 1 (Police Operations Leading to Improved Children and Youth Services). The training was developed by the federal Office of Juvenile Justice and Delinquency Prevention (OJJDP) in 1982 and has been conducted for several thousand law enforcement managers throughout the country.

The three-day curriculum emphasizes better understanding and administration of juvenile justice issues, and the course includes a half-day session on the management of child abuse issues. The response to the training has been encouraging, as the experience has prompted a number of administrators to update their policies and guidelines for handling child abuse cases. It has additionally led to more advanced training for investigators as well as to improved cooperation between child-serving agencies within individual communities.

The OJJDP followed up in 1983 with a forty-hour course for child abuse investigators, which has been responsible for training thousands of law enforcement personnel and has reached professionals in all fifty states. The course addresses the major issues in child abuse investigations and also includes sessions on missing children and on legal considerations. This type of leadership from the federal government has been instrumental in providing police administrators and investigators with the knowledge and skills to perform more professionally with respect to this important issue.

In law enforcement agencies that are strongly committed to dealing with the problems of child abuse, we frequently find a higher degree of specialization and a larger number of personnel assigned to investigating these cases. In such agencies, basic training in the issue is more regularly available for departmental personnel and leads to a higher degree of motivation. Officers who believe they represent an organization which supports and places a high priority on their work are more likely to perform more effectively. This work ethic in turn tends to promote better cooperation with other community professionals. Only when there is widespread, strong, and consistent advocacy within the law enforcement profession for addressing this issue of child maltreatment will investigative improvements result or traditional denials yield to new solutions.

Policy Development

As the law enforcement profession continues to respond to the issue of child abuse and neglect in the 1990s, a larger number of police departments than ever before have developed written policies and guidelines pertaining to child abuse cases. These departmental rules vary in detail from the step-by-step process expected in a quality investigation to a summary of the state's child abuse and neglect reporting law. While the more sophisticated policy statements tend to be found in agencies with 250 or more officers, it is clear that some form of written guidelines are more readily available today in this profession than at any time previously.

Some of the impetus for this trend is the realization on the part of law enforcement leaders that written policy statements assist in establishing professional standards, which in turn raise the norm for conducting certain types of investigation. Law enforcement executives are also gradually accepting the premise that child abuse is an important community problem. Media attention directed toward this issue has been constant since 1980 and has added to the pressure for devising a better "game plan" in handling allegations involving child abuse (7).

An overview of the specific areas in which formulating formal policy statements is essential would begin with the role of the patrol officer. Patrol officers are frequently not the representatives of the law enforcement agency who will actually investigate the entire case. At this level, the responsibility of the first responders primarily consists of crisis intervention and assessment of the situation. Under model federal guidelines developed by the United States Justice Department (8, pp. 84–90), patrol officers would be responsible for answering the following five questions:

1. Does the child need to be removed from the home for his or her protection or for immediate medical attention?
2. Does the child need a medical examination to determine the nature of the injury or the need for further medical examination and treatment?
3. Can this examination be performed in the home, or must the child be brought to a hospital?
4. If emergency treatment or a medical examination in the home or in a hospital is necessary, is the parent willing to cooperate?
5. Is there reasonable cause to believe that a civil or criminal law has been violated?

At the investigative stage, at least four rationales are cited for law enforcement's involvement in child abuse cases, as I have discussed above. They include: (1) the traditional role police agencies hold in the protection of people and property, (2) the twenty-four-hour availability of law enforcement personnel, which makes them more capable of providing immediate protection to children than any other community agency, (3) police officers' legal authority to remove or arrest an abusive parent when necessary, and (4) the extensive training police officers receive in criminal investigative procedures. Policy statements intended to provide guidance and direction in child abuse investigation should include sufficient detail to address adequately most, if not all, situations which will be encountered by the investigator. They include the following:

- Distinguishing between emergency and nonemergency cases
- Interpreting legal mandates of the state child abuse reporting laws
- Photographing the scene
- Interviewing victims, suspects, and potential witnesses
- Collecting and processing of evidence
- Removing children from the scene, if necessary
- Understanding and interpreting standards for reporting children's injuries
- Arranging for children's medical examinations
- Establishing contacts with prosecutors
- Securing interagency cooperation
- Coping with child and infant deaths

The most successful written policies will be those which are developed jointly by law enforcement managers, investigators, and line officers. This approach fosters a greater sense of "ownership"—responsibility and pride—in the work product. More important, the outcome will reflect a comprehensive view of the issues being examined. When policy development is not adequately addressed, it can lead to inconsistent handling of cases.

Interagency Protocols

One promising solution to the issue of improving cooperation as well as coordination between law enforcement agencies and other child protective services is the establishment of written interagency protocols. Most protocols focus on three principal agencies within the community: the prosecutor's office, child protective services, and law enforcement constitute the leadership components within this type of agreement. A review of state and local approaches to protocol development can provide valuable insight.

The state of Georgia has encouraged the creation of interagency protocols in each of its counties. Citing a need for a more unified approach to investigations, professionals in Georgia have sought to eliminate the fragmented and ineffective handling of child abuse cases. As in other areas around the country, this need for better coordination between agencies is based on increasing caseloads. A task force in Michigan has recently followed Georgia's lead by recommending the development of interagency protocols within each of its eighty-three counties partly in response to a 52% increase in substantiated child sexual abuse cases over the past decade.

Law enforcement's key role in interagency child abuse protocols is clearly defined in the guidelines developed by the San Diego Regional Child Victim-Witness Task Force. This community's protocol clearly spells out the responsibilities of law enforcement, from the patrol officer's initial point of contact with a victim to the detective's follow-up work. Trumbell County, Ohio, has established a similar policy for processing physical and sexual abuse cases, through the leadership of the county prosecutor's office and its Child Assault Prosecution Unit.

Formal protocols have been developed for responding to all forms of child abuse in Cook County, Illinois, as well as by Nebraska's Commission for Protection of Children. The commission's model protocol is intended for use by legislatively mandated teams throughout the state. The Nebraska model also outlines the responsibilities of law enforcement in joint and independent investigations. In the community of Ketchikan, located in the southern end of Alaska, an interagency child abuse protocol clearly establishes law enforcement as the lead agency in child abuse cases along with the district attorney's office. This policy statement also establishes goals, definitions, reporting requirements, and procedures for agencies involved in child abuse investigations.

Recurring concerns in the rationales for the development of a child abuse protocol are expressed in the following eight points:

1. Avoidance of duplication of effort
2. Definition of roles and responsibilities
3. Avoidance of interagency procedural, legal, and regulatory conflict
4. Reduction of potential traumatic impact of prosecution on the victim
5. Maximization of available resources
6. Coordination of the civil and criminal process
7. Facilitation of interagency planning
8. Identification of legislative changes

However, the most compelling reason for interagency child abuse protocols is that they simply make sense. This approach to managing child abuse investigations enables a number of agencies to formally structure their work together toward a common goal. An effectively written protocol allows professionals the opportunity to work "smarter" and more efficiently. A viable set of guidelines also leads to a greater sense of community cohesiveness. This in turn maintains the critical momentum necessary to successfully face the many challenges associated with the field of child abuse and neglect.

As well-intended as interagency protocols have been, they are still merely words on paper unless every agency, and its representatives, agree to the terms of these documents. Experience has also shown that the leadership and active involvement of prosecutors or district attorneys is essential for an interagency protocol to succeed. The chief law enforcement official within the community should not only be available to consider or consult about legal issues relative to child abuse cases but must also assist in mediation involving conflict between agencies. While this approach requires a great deal of hard work, the results often include improved integration of services and increased cooperation between community agencies.

Conclusion

In 1987, during the fifteenth anniversary of the founding of the C. Henry Kempe National Center for the Prevention and Treatment of Child Abuse and Neglect, Dr. Ray E. Helfer delivered a paper written from the perspective he imagined he might have in the year 2007 (9). His presentation included a "retrospective" analysis of ten impediments to our existing treatment, protection, and prevention system. He summarized them into the following categories:

1. Confused organizational structure at the local, state, and federal levels
2. Movement from holistic child welfare services to narrow child protection services
3. Changes in civil (family) court procedures to more closely resemble the criminal court model.
4. Lack of standards/criteria for state services programs, including professional education, training, caseload limits, checks and balances of decisions made, and follow-up
5. Limited ability and opportunity for various professionals to problem-solve together
6. Resurgence of territoriality
7. Lack of a national priority or policy for children and families
8. Inconsistency and limited availability of treatment programs
9. Search for the "quick fix"
10. Minimal support for consistency in prevention programs

Dr. Helfer concluded that as a result of these impediments, the entire service and treatment delivery system needed to be revamped. His wise and insightful commentary is as appropriate today as it was when he offered his observations in 1987.

The law enforcement profession will continue to play a pivotal role in the response to child abuse and neglect cases. However, shared roles in the investigative process for both law enforcement and child protective services must be advanced to provide and improve a truly multidisciplinary team approach and to avoid duplication of effort. The best interests of the child should always guide our response; consequently, any differences between law enforcement and other community service agencies need to be constantly addressed and resolved.

It is a sad commentary that the problems associated with child abuse and neglect will not be alleviated within the foreseeable future. Only when we as a society make a commitment to developing and implementing more efficient, effective prevention programs will future generations begin to realize more positive outcomes. Until then, we must accept the premise that preventing child abuse and neglect is a responsibility which belongs to each of us. The question that every individual should ask is, "How can I help?" Only then will we begin to contribute effectively to the solution.

References

1. Kean, R., and Rodgers, E., Jr. 1988. The Law Enforcement Officer as a Member of the Child Protection Team. In *The New Child Protection Team Handbook,* ed. D. Bross, R. D. Krugman, M. R. Lenherr, D. A. Rosenberg, and B. D. Schmitt, 199–212. New York: Garland.

2. Whitcomb, D. 1992. *When the Victim Is a Child,* 2d ed. Washington, D.C.: U.S. Department of Justice.

3. Brow, J. A.; Unsinger, P. C.; and More, H. W., eds. 1990. *Law Enforcement and Social Welfare: The Emergency Response.* Springfield, Ill.: Charles C. Thomas.

4. Martin, M., and Hamilton, E. 1990. Police Handling of Child Abuse Cases: Policies, Procedures, and Issues. *Am. J. Police* 9(1):1–24.

5. Sedlak, A. 1989. *Supplementary Analysis of Data on the National Incidence of Child Abuse and Neglect.* Bethesda, Md.: National Institute of Justice.

6. Besharov, D. J. 1990. *Combating Child Abuse: Guidelines for Cooperation between Law Enforcement and Child Protective Agencies.* Washington, D.C.: AEI Press.

7. Webster, S. 1990. The Role of Law Enforcement Agencies in the Reporting of Family Mistreatment. *J. Crime and Justice* 12–13:1–31.

8. Schuchter, A. 1976. *Child Abuse Intervention.* Washington, D.C.: U.S. Department of Justice.

9. Helfer, R. 1991. Child Abuse and Neglect Assessment, Treatment, and Prevention, October 21, 2007. *Child Abuse and Neglect: International J.* 15 (suppl. 1):5–15.

21

Lawyers' Roles in Child Protection

Donald N. Duquette

What roles and responsibilities do lawyers assume in civil child protection cases? As distinguished from other legal proceedings which may grow from a case of child maltreatment, civil child protection proceedings focus on the child and the child's needs. These civil cases are not concerned with punishing an offender, recovering money damages from a person or institution who may have harmed a child, or suspending someone from a professional license. The focus here is on the proper care and custody of the child.

Nearly all aspects of interdisciplinary intervention in families to assist children who may be maltreated is governed by some type of law—from rules guiding professional ethics to statutes governing confidentiality and reporting of suspected child abuse and neglect, from criminal penalties for child maltreatment to state and federal constitutional protections of the family relationship. Yet, despite the fact that legal issues related to child abuse and neglect may be raised in forums as diverse as administrative hearings regarding professional licensure, criminal prosecutions, and the U.S. Supreme Court, the court most professionals think of first in connection with child abuse or neglect within the family is the local family or juvenile court. Juvenile or family courts are created by state statutes and are responsible for child protection and foster care. It is the juvenile or family court that receives (and oversees) the work of the physicians, social workers, psychologists, and other members of a community's multidisciplinary child protection network. It is the juvenile or family court that decides whether a child should be removed from a parent's custody, what rehabilitation program should be followed by the parent and the child welfare agency, and, ultimately, whether a child in foster care or other alternative care should be returned to a parent's custody or whether termination of parental rights is the appropriate course in the best interests of the child.

When society at large, through child protective services, attempts to intervene in the private life of a family on behalf of a child, the court must assure that the rights of the parents, the rights of the child, and the rights of society are protected. If any of these rights are to be abridged, this is decided only after full and fair and objective court process. Except in emergency situations, only the court can abridge these personal rights. Only the court can compel unwilling parents (or children) to submit to the authority of the state. The court,

Donald N. Duquette, J.D., is clinical professor of law and director of the Child Advocacy Law Clinic at the University of Michigan Law School.

then, controls the *coercive* elements of our society and allows those coercive elements to be unleashed only after due process of law.

The personal rights at stake for both parents and children in child protection have been recognized in our law as fundamentally important constitutional rights (1). The rights of parents to the care and custody of their children and the rights of children to live with their parents without government interference can be infringed only after due process of law.

Due process of law in our American system of justice generally means, among other things, that a parent and child facing child protection proceedings are represented by a lawyer. The child protection agency also has a lawyer acting on its behalf. What is the proper role of these attorneys? What can the nonlawyers involved in child abuse and neglect cases expect from the lawyers? In this chapter I will examine the three major roles of lawyers in child protection civil proceedings: representing the sometimes overlapping and sometimes conflicting individual interests of the child, the agency, and the parent.

The Adversarial Process

The lawyers' roles in child protection cases are defined in the context of an adversarial process—the traditional basis of all American jurisprudence. For good or ill, the legal system in the United States relies on an adversarial process to evaluate competing legal interests.

As in other areas of legal contest, lawyers in child protection act as advocates for one side or another or for one set of interests or another. Lawyers need not pursue the solution best for all concerned and need not even ascertain what is generally best in the circumstances; rather, they owe primary allegiance to their own client, whose particular position they must determine and then advocate for zealously. According to our legal traditions, the adversarial presentation of competing points of view should result in a fair and just resolution.

Most physicians, psychologists, and social workers come from professional backgrounds encouraging trust and cooperation and find the adversarial court process discomforting, foreign, nonproductive, or counterproductive in terms of the "real problems" faced by a family involved in child maltreatment proceedings. The influence of these "helping" professions, the growth of alternative forms of dispute resolution in the law today, and a problem-solving ethic long held by judges and lawyers experienced in child maltreatment cases all contribute to a muting of the adversarial tone in child protection cases. Instead, we see an emphasis on negotiation and mediation to work these matters out. Several communities have experimented extensively with mediation approaches to child abuse and neglect cases (2). Attorneys accustomed only to the adversarial system are well advised to adjust their thinking in juvenile court to a less confrontational approach and to greater reliance on negotiation and mediation.

There are times, however, when the adversarial process is important and must be relied upon. When negotiation cannot resolve the dispute, when the parties seriously differ about the right of the state to intervene in a family or profoundly disagree about the appropriateness of the action proposed (which could be as fundamental as foster care or termination of parental rights), some means to resolve these conflicts must be available—and enforceable. That is when the adversarial process has its place. Despite the important movement toward more cooperation and conciliation in family and juvenile court, the legal process remains ultimately adversarial when other means of conflict resolution fail. Participants in the court process must learn to function within the adversarial system, to appreciate its advantages and minimize its many disadvantages.

The Child's Advocate

Once a matter alleging child maltreatment is brought to a family or juvenile court, an independent advocate, nearly always an attorney, is appointed to represent that child. The Federal Child Abuse Prevention and Treatment Act (3) requires that guardians *ad litem* be appointed to represent children in civil abuse and neglect cases as a condition of states' eligibility to receive federal funding for child protection and foster care activities. Consequently, statutes in all states require or permit the appointment of an advocate for the child in child protection cases (4–6). Neither the federal law nor its implementing regulations,[1] however, define the roles or responsibilities of the child's representative once appointed. The duties and responsibilities of the appointed representative of the child are generally not clearly defined in state statutes either (4, par. 2.1).

Some see the child's representative as an extraneous figure and argue that the interests of the child are adequately protected by the child welfare agency, by the parents, or by the judge (5, p. 10; 7, p. 5). Others may see the child's representative as having limited value in a given case since the representative usually has had no special training or background preparing him or her for this nontraditional role (7, p. 13; 8; 9). The influential commentators Joseph Goldstein, Anna Freud, and Albert Solnit, in deference to parental autonomy, would reserve the power to appoint a legal representative for the child only to the parents, unless the parents are displaced as the legal protectors of the child by emergency out-of-home placement or formal court adjudication (10, pp. 111–29).

The prevailing view across the country today, however, is that children should be independently represented in civil child protection proceedings (5, 8, 11, 12). At least one court has held that the child's right to effective representation is based not only on statute but on the constitution as well. The Supreme Court of New York, Appellate Division, held in *In the Matter of Jamie "TT"* that the child has a right, in protection proceedings, to effective assistance of counsel not only based on state statute but also guaranteed by her (or his) constitutionally protected liberty interest in the outcome of the proceeding as it affects her personal safety and integrity (13).

Nonetheless, dissatisfaction about the representation and advocacy provided children in child abuse and neglect cases remains widespread. Many doubt that attorney represen-

---

1. "In every case involving an abused or neglected child which results in a judicial proceeding, the state must insure the appointment of a guardian ad litem or other individual whom the state recognizes as fulfilling the same functions as a guardian ad litem, to represent and protect the best interests of the child" (45 C.F.R. §1340.14[g]).

tation can really make a difference to the outcome of the case when attorneys generally receive little or no special training in the needs of children or in specific strategies of advocating for them in the complex child welfare system.

The search for the best way to advocate for children has taken many forms. The National Center on Child Abuse and Neglect has funded demonstration projects around the country since 1981 in which children are represented by volunteer lawyers, law students, multidisciplinary child advocate offices, and lay volunteers (5). Communities have experimented with trained volunteers to either represent the child or assist a lawyer in representing the child (14, 15). Seattle began a guardian *ad litem* program in 1977, using the acronymic title CASA (court appointed special advocate) to designate the lay volunteer who represents children in child protection cases (12). The National Council of Family and Juvenile Court Judges has encouraged CASA program development in many ways, including sponsoring a national CASA seminar.[2] The CASA movement is growing and spreading fast. When the fourth edition of *The Battered Child* went to press in 1987, there were 173 such programs, in thirty-nine states (16). As of summer 1996, there are 641 CASA programs, in all fifty states, coordinating approximately 38,000 volunteers (17, p. 20). In 1995 these men and women spoke for an estimated 129,000 abused and neglected children in court (17). An active national CASA association publishes a national newsletter, organizes an annual meeting, and provides other services.[3]

The question of whether someone other than a lawyer should represent children has been raised in several quarters (18, 19). The American Bar Association itself, in its 1979 Juvenile Justice Standards Project, comments:

> While independent representation for a child may be important in protective and custodial proceedings, a representative trained wholly in law may not be the appropriate choice for this function. . . .
>
> Accordingly it would not seem irresponsible to suggest that a professional trained in psychology, psychiatry, social psychology or social welfare be assigned the initial responsibility for protecting children under these circumstances. There is, however, no evidence that this alternative is presently available, either in terms of numbers of competent personnel or in terms of occupational independence from official and interested agencies. . . . [U]ntil there are sufficient numbers of independent, competent personnel trained in other disciplines who will undertake to ascertain and guard the child's interests in these proceedings, continued reliance on legal representation for the child is necessary. (8, pp. 73–74)

Empirical and anecdotal support for the current unhappiness with the legal representation children receive is close at hand. In 1994 the U.S. Department of Health and Human Ser-

2. For information on CASA programs, contact the Court Appointed Special Advocates Committee, National Council of Family and Juvenile Court Judges, Judicial College Building, University of Nevada, Reno, Nevada 89507.

3. Information on current programs can be obtained from the National Association of Court Appointed Special Advocates, 100 West Harrison Street, North Tower, Suite 500, Seattle, Washington 98119-4123 (the telephone number is 800-628-3233).

vices released the most ambitious national empirical study yet of the representation of children in protection cases (4).[4] This important study, conducted by CSR, Inc., of Washington, D.C. (hereafter referred to as the *Study of Legal Representation*), presents a sobering and somewhat disappointing portrait of child representation as currently practiced in the United States. In one remarkable finding, almost 30% of private attorneys had no type of contact with their clients, the children. Only 94.5% of the private attorneys attended all the court hearings in new cases affecting the child; 80% attended all hearings in review cases. Would an adult agree to be represented by an attorney who did not appear at all relevant court hearings?

The children themselves were rarely involved in the court process. The private attorneys reported that in only 18.6% of the cases did the child appear before the judge in court. CASAs reported that the child appeared in 12.3% of their cases, and staff attorneys reported that the child appeared before the judge in court in 9.8% of the cases.

Monitoring the progress of a case is considered by many as an extremely important aspect of advocacy for the child, yet more than 25% of the private attorneys in the study said that monitoring activities were inapplicable to their professional role. Over 50% of the private lawyers had no contact with the child between hearings, and only 36% of caseworkers reported being contacted by the private attorneys.

Dissatisfaction with the present system of attorney representation has provided an impetus for clarifying the duties and responsibilities of the child's representative and for searching out alternative means of representing children. Even though there is no consensus on the child advocate role, some common approaches are emerging. In 1988, the New York State Bar Association published standards for law guardians representing children in child protection proceedings (20, p. 11). The Colorado State Bar Association did the same in 1992 (20, p. 13). In February 1996, the American Bar Association adopted *Standards of Practice for Lawyers Who Represent Children in Abuse and Neglect Cases*. These standards are likely to be very influential and will provide the needed consensus on the child advocate role: "All children subject to court proceedings involving allegations of child abuse and neglect should have legal representation as long as the court jurisdiction continues" (11, p. 1301).

In *Advocating for the Child in Protection Proceedings* (21, p. 36), I set out ten dimensions of child advocacy for the child's representative to address at each procedural stage of the proceedings:

1. Investigation
2. Consultation
3. Assessment
4. Identifying the child's interest
5. Permanency planning
6. Client counseling

---

4. The complete study is available through the National Clearinghouse on Child Abuse and Neglect Information, U.S. Department of Health and Human Services, P.O. Box 1182, Washington, D.C. 20013-1182; by fax at 703-385-3206; or by telephone at 800-FYI-3366.

7. Decision making
8. Problem solving and mediation
9. Identifying action steps
10. Follow-up

Reflecting this emerging consensus on the child advocate role, the national CASA association has developed a very important statement of the roles and responsibilities of guardians *ad litem* applicable to whomever represents the best interests of the child in that capacity—attorney, CASA, or some other person (22). The guardian *ad litem* (GAL) must:

1. Act as an independent gatherer of information whose task it is to review all relevant records and interview the child, parents, social workers, teacher, and other persons to ascertain the facts and circumstances of the child's situation.
2. Ascertain the interests of the child, taking into account the child's age, maturity, culture and ethnicity, consistent with providing the child with a safe home, taking into account the need for family preservation and permanency planning.
3. Seek cooperative solutions to the child's situation within the scope of the child's interest and welfare.
4. Provide written reports of findings and recommendations to the court at each hearing to assure that all the relevant facts are before the court and ensure that appropriate motions are filed seeking child centered relief.
5. Appear at all hearings to represent the child's interests, providing testimony or ensuring that appropriate witnesses are called and examined.
6. Explain the court proceedings and the role of GAL to the child, when appropriate, in language and terms that the child can understand.
7. Ask that clear and specific orders are entered for the evaluation, assessment, services, placement, and treatment of the child and the child's family.
8. Monitor implementation of service plans and dispositional orders to determine whether services ordered by the court are actually provided in a timely manner, and are accomplishing their desired goal. Monitor the progress of a case through the court process and advocate for timely hearings.
9. Inform the court promptly if services are not being made available to the child and/or family, if the family fails to take advantage of such services, if services are not achieving their purpose, and bring to the court's attention any violation of orders, new developments, or changes in the child's circumstances.
10. Advocate for the child's interests in mental health, educational, and other community systems. (22, pp. 6–7)

The 1994 *Study of Legal Representation* included a "technical expert group" of academics, attorneys, judges, and lay volunteers which identified a core set of five functions that the child advocate should perform in order to be effective.

1. The representative should *advocate for the child* both within and outside the confines of the courtroom. The advocate should pursue the best interests of the child much as a reasonably concerned parent would for his/her own child.

2. The advocate should be *child centered,* that is, be aware of the child's age-specific, developmental, and cultural needs.

3. Since *continuity of representation* is especially important to a child, the same representative should act for the child from the initial emergency hearing to the time when the court no longer has jurisdiction over the child.

4. A mechanism for *accountability* should monitor and evaluate the performance of the child advocate.

5. The child advocate should act *independently,* as administratively and politically separate from the child welfare agency and the court. (4, pp. 5.2–5.3)

The *Study* encourages the use of CASAs but recommends that an attorney be present at all hearings.

Thus, whether the child is represented by a lawyer or a team of lawyer and lay volunteer, the child advocate's role should be aggressive, ambitious, and encompass both legal and nonlegal interests of the child. This definition of the child representative's role, consistent with that of most major commentators (8, 12, 19), rejects a passive, purely procedure-oriented approach. In child protection proceedings, the children need more than a technician to ensure legal precision; they need more than a passive observer and adviser to the court—they need an active advocate for their interests. Advocacy for children includes traditional courtroom advocacy but also emphasizes out-of-court advocacy in informal meetings with the social agencies and telephone contacts with other service deliverers. That advocate is generally a lawyer and is charged both with representing the "best interests" of the child and with making an independent judgment of what those "best interests" might be. The statute in Michigan is illustrative:

> The court, in every case filed under this act in which judicial proceedings are necessary, shall appoint legal counsel to represent the child. The legal counsel, in general, shall be charged with the representation of the child's best interests. To that end, the attorney shall make further investigation as he deems necessary to ascertain the facts, interview witnesses, examine witnesses in both the adjudicatory and dispositional hearings, make recommendations to the court, and participate in the proceedings to competently represent the child. (23)

But what are the child's "best interests"? What goals are child representatives obliged to pursue on behalf of the child? In most settings, a lawyer's client is an adult and is able to articulate what he or she wants, which essentially determines the position the lawyer will take. In child protection, however, the position to be taken by the advocate may be quite unclear. The child is frequently unable to express a view. And even when a child (sometimes a very young child) does express a view, the advocate charged with representing that child's "best interests" may disagree with the youthful client and advocate a different position (11, pp. 1308–14; 24, rule 1.14; 25; 26; 27, pp. 296–99).

The child's best interests are not susceptible to objective definition but remain wreathed in personal values. Robert Mnookin writes:

> Deciding what is best for a child often poses a question no less ultimate than the purposes and values of life itself. Should the decision maker be primarily concerned with the child's happiness

or with the child's spiritual and religious training? Is the primary goal long-term economic productivity when the child grows up? Or are the most important values of life found in warm relationships? In discipline and self-sacrifice? Are stability and security for a child more desirable than intellectual stimulation? These questions could be elaborated endlessly. And yet, where is one to look for the set of values that should guide decisions concerning what is best for the child? . . . [I]f one looks to our society at large, one finds neither a clear consensus as to the best child-rearing strategies, nor an appropriate hierarchy of ultimate values. (28, p. 18)

Describing the child representative as the advocate for the best interests of the child, moreover, does little to distinguish the child representative's role from that of the other participants in the child protection process. The child protection agency generally considers that achieving the best interests of the child is its primary goal and purpose. The parents' attorney will also argue for what his clients see as the best interests of the child (which is generally to be at home with his or her parents free of government interference). The judge makes the ultimate ruling of what is in the best interests of the child, and judicial opinions consistently reinforce the paramount importance of the child's best interests in court decision making.

The child's representative faced with deciding what is in the child's best interests only rarely has received law school training that equips him or her to assess parental conduct, to appraise the harms to a child presented by a particular environment, to recognize strengths in the parent-child relationship, or to evaluate the soundness of an intervention strategy proposed by the social agency.[5] The child's representative, to perform responsibly, must synthesize the results of the protective services investigation; the child's psychological, developmental, and physical needs; the child's articulated wishes; and the representative's own assessment of the facts and of the treatment resources available. Many of the child's best interests are ordinarily addressed by the various professionals involved in the child protection process, but others may be easily overlooked by all but the child's representative.

Despite the ambiguity of determining a child's interest (or "best interests"), there are many interests of most children, most of the time, that are quite clear and that a skilled advocate can help realize for the child. Certainly, the child is to be protected from physical and emotional harm and provided with minimally adequate food, clothing, shelter, guidance, and supervision. But other interests are more subtle. The state intervention itself presents additional risks to the child of which the child advocate must be wary. The interests of an individual child are not always consistent with those of the state agency. If it has high caseloads, the agency may not be willing or able to meet each child's individual needs (for example, for frequent visitation). An overburdened caseworker may not be as sensitive, as careful, or as skilled in judgment as he or she would under less taxing circumstances. Consequently, the caseworker may precipitately recommend separation of the child from fa-

5. The Child Advocacy Law Clinic at the University of Michigan Law School, founded in 1976, may be the longest-running clinic in the United States continuously providing live client-student experience in child protection and foster care. The Michigan clinic is interdisciplinary in approach. There are now approximately twenty American law schools that offer clinical programs in which student lawyers learn about representation of children and parents in child protection and related cases.

miliar surroundings or may inadequately assess the child's home situation and prescribe remedies that are inappropriate, inadequate, or too late. The child runs the risk of being placed in multiple foster homes, of being placed in inappropriate surroundings, of being abused in foster care, or of not being permitted frequent enough visits with his or her parents and family. Reasonable case plans may be developed by social agencies but not implemented properly, or implemented too slowly, thus adding to the length of time the child is out of his or her home and lessening the child's chances of ever returning home.

Although family preservation efforts may be in the interests of most children most of the time, an individual child's interests may not be served by preservation efforts. The child's advocate must be careful that his or her client is not sacrificed on the altar of family preservation. It is the *child,* not the *family,* who is this advocate's client.

In formulating a defensible position for the child, the child's advocate must ascertain the facts of the case as clearly as possible by relying on the protective services investigation in some cases and by interviewing family members, neighbors, and others as necessary. The child's advocate should meet his or her client in *every* case, even if it is simply for the purpose of getting a "feel" for the child as a real person facing a serious personal dilemma. The advocate should always keep the child in mind in the midst of all the paperwork of court petitions and social work reports.

The child's representative ought not to accept social work recommendations without analyzing them first. While maintaining a cooperative spirit, he or she should question the social worker closely and extract the underlying basis for the caseworker's positions and recommendations. The advocate should reach his or her conclusions independently.

The advocate should strive to identify what the determinants of the family's problems are. Once the underlying determinants are discerned, the advocate can help discover ways to address and ease them. Thus, I would encourage a child advocate to take a broad view of the child's interests, to avoid a piecemeal approach to the child's and the family's problems, and to see the child in the context of his or her family.

Having identified the needs and interests of the child, the representative should advocate vigorously for those interests. The advocacy for the child ought to begin with the social agency that filed the petition. The child's representative should advocate for a careful assessment of the family situation, for adequate and specific case plans, and for timely implementation of case plans. The child's interests include preserving his or her placement with a parent (or parents) if at all possible, when consistent with the child's own well-being and safety. The child generally has an interest in maintaining contact with the family through regular visits. If removal from the family is necessary, separation should be for the shortest time possible, and placement should generally be to a familiar setting (the least restrictive, most family-like setting).[6] If services to the child or the family are needed before the child can be allowed to return home, those services should be identified accurately and provided promptly.

6. Other authorities advocate for the "least intrusive form of intervention" (8, p. 82), or the "least detrimental alternative" (10, pp. 53–64). The Federal Adoption Assistance and Child Welfare Act of 1980 (P.L. 96-272, 42 U.S.C.A. §675[5][A]) requires the use of the least restrictive (or most family-like) setting available in close proximity to the parents' home, consistent with the best interest and special needs of the child.

The child's advocate can play a significant role in facilitating negotiation and mediation. Resolution of the legal dispute that is swift, as cooperative and as nonadversarial as possible, and efficient in providing needed protection and services to the child is nearly always in the child's best interests. Representatives of children should be trained to encourage negotiation and to assume the role of mediator and conciliator between the social agency and the parents.

In the court hearing, the child's representative ensures that all the relevant facts are brought before the judge and advocates for a resolution of the case most likely to achieve the identified interests of the child.

The role of the child's representative after adjudication should remain vigorous and active. The child advocate can press and persuade the responsible social agencies for services and attention which the child client (and perhaps the family) needs. Preferably, such nudging can be done in a collegial, nonaccusatory manner—but if social workers or agencies are not fulfilling their responsibilities to a particular child (or to the parents), the child's representative may insist on a higher standard of service either by entering a direct request to supervisors in the agency or by formally raising the issue before the court.

Thus the child advocate's role covers not only the traditional legal representation of the case but also the social, psychological, and service delivery aspects of the case so important to the child. In an empirical study, advocates trained to represent children in the manner I have described here provided improved representation for children and achieved better outcomes for their young clients (14, 15).

It is often in the interests of children for the child's representative to advocate for the child's interests in the mental health, educational, and juvenile justice systems, as well as in other community systems, if these play a part in the circumstances that caused the child to come within the child abuse and neglect jurisdiction of the juvenile or family court. The legal system may carve a child up into nice, neat categories of problems—but it is still one child after all, and an aggressive advocate can help coordinate the various legal proceedings and help the youngster get treated as a whole person. The advocate can pursue the child's legal rights and secure needed services in those other community systems.

The national *Study of Legal Representation* makes some recommendations about organizing the delivery of advocacy services to children. An optimal approach may involve a child advocate office in which the child is independently represented by an interdisciplinary team of lawyers, social workers, and lay volunteers. In additional to enhancing the advocacy of individual children, such offices may actually achieve some systemic economies by shortening the time spent in court, requiring few court hearings, and reducing the time a youngster spends in temporary foster care.

In any case, the ambitious child advocate role suggested here and by other commentators (29) is sorely limited in practice by the lack of specific training for the role and by the low fees paid in many communities to private attorneys representing children. The ABA report *America's Children at Risk* recommends that "[e]very law school should offer its students the opportunity to learn about children's issues (including related topics such as poverty and disability law) as part of their substantive studies and to represent children and families as part of clinical training programs during their law school years" (30, p. 8). The report also encourages the organized bar to organize a Lawyers' Committee for Children and Their Families, to promote adequate training programs for lawyers representing children, and to improve the quality of child advocacy lawyers through the creation of guidelines and mentoring programs and the enforcement of practice standards.

The Protective Services Attorney

For many years, and continuing today in some jurisdictions, no attorney appeared on behalf of the social agency or the individual that filed the petition alleging child abuse or neglect and seeking to protect a particular child from harm. In the recent past, if an attorney did appear in child protection cases, he or she was likely to be a young assistant prosecutor or assistant county corporation counsel with little preparation time, limited experience in such cases, and little familiarity with either the juvenile court or child protection law. The child neglect attorney, if there was one, was often the staff member most recently hired by the county prosecutor's office. And the juvenile court was seen in those days mainly as a good place for lawyers to get experience before moving up to bigger and more important cases in other courts.

Attorneys assigned to child protection often complained about the lack of specificity with which their social worker clients presented their cases and about the "murkiness" and lack of legal standards in the juvenile court generally. Juvenile court, and especially child abuse and neglect cases, often received low priority among members of the bar.

In recent years, concurrent with the due process revolution in juvenile court, the role and functioning of all attorneys in child protection have gained importance and more precise definition. The need for competent legal advice for petitioning agencies in child protection cases has been increasingly recognized. Proving child abuse or neglect in child protection cases is often very difficult. Furthermore, since the parents are generally represented by an attorney and the child in question must be independently represented, a petitioning protective services worker is at a distinct disadvantage in an adversarial court if he or she is charged with the burden of proof without benefit of legal counsel. In fulfilling their responsibilities to children and to families, child protection agencies need consistent and reliable legal assistance.

David Herring of the University of Pittsburgh Law School has produced a guidebook, *Agency Attorney Training Manual,* which details the important attorney–social worker collaboration necessary for successful child protection and termination-of-parental-rights actions.[7] The role of the petitioner's attorney in child protection cases includes conventional attorney duties but differs from the traditional lawyerly tasks in several respects.

---

7. D. J. Herring's *Agency Attorney Training Manual: Achieving Timely Permanency for Children by Implementing the Private Model of Legal Representation for the State Agency in Child Abuse and Neglect Matters* is available from Professor Herring at the University of Pittsburgh School of Law, Pittsburgh, Pennsylvania 15260. The phone number of the Child Abuse and Neglect Clinic there is 412-648-2656. An empirical study of agency representation done while Herring was at the University of Michigan Law School is reported in Herring, "Legal Representation for the State Child Welfare Agency in Civil Child Protection Proceedings: A Comparative Study," *Toledo Law Rev.* 24:603–87.

Lawyers who represent banks learn the banking business very well. Lawyers who represent labor become acquainted with labor unions and labor organizing from top to bottom. Likewise, lawyers who represent child welfare agencies must get to know both social work as a profession and the child welfare system. The child welfare lawyer must understand and appreciate the emphasis on nonjudicial (yet fair) handling of child protection cases. In addition to traditional legal skills, acquiring a solid background in juvenile court proceedings and family law and philosophy is essential for a protective services attorney. The attorney should comprehend and respect the functions, the capabilities, and the limitations of social workers and other behavioral scientists. The foster care system—its limitations and strengths, its advantages and disadvantages, the benefits and risks to children—must also be carefully studied. Concepts of family preservation, family reunification, and permanency planning should be very familiar to the agency lawyer.

What is the nature of the attorney-client relationship between the child protection agency and its lawyer? The legal agency which assumes responsibility for legal representation of the child protection petitioners in the juvenile or family court varies from state to state or sometimes even from county to county. The duties may be assumed by the local prosecuting attorney, the state attorney general's office, the county corporation (civil) counsel, or at times by lawyers who are actually employees of the child protection agency. Some legal agencies representing protective services assume a quasi-judicial role and will initiate legal action as requested by the social agency only if they personally agree that such action is warranted. Such lawyers exercise a sort of prosecutors discretion about which child protection cases are brought to court.

In contrast, I would recommend that the legal representatives of the agency see themselves in a traditional attorney-client relationship. In invoking the court system, child protection service workers should have access to a lawyer whom they can trust and who will act as the advocate of their point of view as necessary. Consistent with the ABA *Model Rules of Professional Conduct,* "[a] lawyer shall seek the lawful objectives of a client through reasonably available means permitted by law and these rules" (24, rule 1.2).

The lawyer and the agency personnel may not share all points of view and judgments about strategy, but such differences are certainly not unusual between lawyer and client and are rather common in both personal and corporate practice. When such disagreements occur, the lawyer should rely on the traditional counselor function of the lawyer: matters can be discussed in-house and recommendations for actions negotiated. If some differences cannot be resolved in this manner, the lawyer should then defer to his or her social agency clients in matters within the scope of their expertise (namely, in social and psychological judgments and in assessments of the needs of the child and family), while the agency should defer to the lawyer in matters of trial strategy and legal judgment. Unfortunately, in this context the boundaries between legal and social spheres of expertise are often not clear and distinct. Almost every judgment in child abuse and neglect cases reflects a value judgment that certain kinds of parental behavior constitutes legal neglect. Normative judgments of fact are made at every step of the child protection process: by the reporting person, by the social worker, by the social work supervisor, by the lawyers, and finally—and most importantly—by the judge. What is the minimum community standard of child care to which every child is entitled? What is the threshold of child care below which the state may and should intervene, even coercively, on behalf of the child (and for the good of the family unit)? These questions, addressed in every child protection case consciously or not, blur the distinctions between legal and social spheres of expertise.

With the understanding that their respective spheres of competence are not always clear and distinct, the attorney and the client agency ought to arrive at in-house positions, each deferring to the other's expertise where appropriate, with the lawyer acting as advocate for the final position much as a corporate attorney would adopt the direction of his corporate client.

The interface between the child protection agency and the court system must be explored and understood by the attorney representing the agency. The role of the court must be placed in context for the agency by their lawyer. The court acts as arbiter between the individual citizens and the social agency regarding the agency's right to intervene in the privacy of the family. when the family does not voluntarily agree to the agency's intervention, the court must decide whether or not the circumstances justify coercive, authoritative state intervention on behalf of the child.

Delivery of remedial services to the dysfunctional family remains the duty of the child protection agency whether or not court action is taken. The social workers have the responsibility, the skills, and the expertise to provide assistance to the children and their families. The court's role is to authorize the agency to act in cases in which parents will not voluntarily accept such services. The court order authorizes and facilitates the agency intervention. The court itself, however, has no treatment expertise, nor should it be relied upon to develop a treatment plan. The social worker may not recognize that the role of the court is limited to judicial decisions and that the social agency itself bears the responsibility to develop and implement a treatment plan for the children and family. The agency lawyer must in that case make clear to the social worker clients that the court itself can neither administer treatment nor engage in social planning for a family. The court's role is strictly to prevent unwarranted interferences with their private lives and to approve and monitor the agency intervention.

The agency lawyer must understand the role and functioning of protective services well enough to identify the long-term social objectives of the agency as separate and distinct from the generally shorter-term, more immediate legal objectives. The more thoroughly the lawyer understands the agency goals, the more creative he or she can be in the use of the court process. The agency lawyer should not define the client's goals only in terms of legal objectives—for instance, to acquire temporary jurisdiction, to prove probable cause, or to obtain emergency detention. With the help of the social worker, the attorney must identify the *social goals* of the agency as specifically as possible. Thereafter, by creative use both of the court process and of negotiation, the lawyer may be able to help accomplish the social goals whether or not the specific legal goals prove to be attainable.

To this end, the attorney should work closely with the protective services agency. In the initial interview with an agency social worker, the lawyer must ask: "What do you want to result from the legal action?" "What are your professional (that is, social work) goals for the client family?" The lawyer should test the social work strategy in a collegial but "devil's advocate" way: "Will court action facilitate the social work intervention strategy?" "How will it do so?" "Can each of the elements of the intervention plan be justified by facts presentable to the court?"

The social worker, with his or her experts and team members, must be able to articulate the social objectives of court action. The lawyer may wish to attend multidisciplinary team meetings concerning treatment plans for cases on which he or she is or may be active. The lawyer needs to know the behavioral science reasoning behind a particular intervention strategy, and he or she may be able to contribute knowledge to the team about the legal process available to facilitate the strategy. Knowing the plan and its basis, the lawyer is better able to support it in court through expert and material witnesses.

Attorneys should bear in mind that the legal process itself may add to the family dysfunction. Sometimes the trauma of adversary litigation cannot be avoided. But often, when the social objectives of the agency are clearly defined, an attorney can accomplish the goals of the agency without going to trial, through strategies of negotiation, mediation, and pacing the litigation.

It is a challenge for the lawyer to achieve the social results in an efficient, effective, and direct way which avoids or minimizes the negative effects of the adversary process. A process of mediation or negotiation may avoid the adversary system in which family members must testify against family members, and helpers (such as social workers and physicians) must testify against the parents they are trying to help. Skills and tactics in negotiations and mediation are especially important to the child protection attorney.

Thus far, I have identified two separate aspects of the protective services attorney's role: first, to prove and present the client's case in the most persuasive fashion possible; second, to understand and embrace the social goals of the client agency and to further those goals by nonadversarial means if possible.

We now come to a third aspect of the agency attorney's role: preparing the client agency for ongoing court review of a treatment plan ordered by the court. Certainly, as we have seen already, the preparation of the treatment plan remains in the sphere of the social worker. The lawyer, however, understands the degree of specificity and prompt action required by the court for such plans and serves the client agency well by encouraging the client to efficiently and clearly state the goals and specific details of the plan. The lawyer understands the legal significance of the treatment plan and the ramifications that noncompliance by the agency or the parents may have in subsequent court proceedings.

The court retains ultimate responsibility for the well-being of children under its jurisdiction. It cannot abrogate that responsibility. Federal legislation and several recommended model statutes contain procedures that formalize legal standards for the review of continuing intervention in a family under court authority (31, 32).

At a review hearing, the child protection agency is in a position to give an account of its stewardship. Before such a hearing, the court will have taken jurisdiction over a child and ordered certain interventions, which may have included placement of the child outside the home and counseling or other treatment for the family. At a review, the agency must report to the court about what services have been provided and what progress has been made by the family. The agency attorney can aid his or her client by not allowing matters to drift between the initial court order and the review hearing. Correlatively, the parents must give an account of themselves and show what progress they have made in correcting the problems that brought their child to the attention of the court.

The agency, in essence, is asking that the court extend its authorization to intervene in the family, perhaps including continued foster placement or termination of parental rights. Agencies must demonstrate that a treatment plan has been followed and that the legal and social intervention in the family's life is justified by tangible benefits, either realized or nearing realization, to the child and the family.

If the agency cannot justify its continued involvement with the family by demonstrating good faith efforts to rehabilitate the family, the court may revoke the agency's authority to act, that is, terminate the court's jurisdiction, place the child with another agency, or return a child to his or her home despite agency requests to the contrary. Admittedly, a return of the child to his or her home against the agency recommendation is a rare thing for a judge to authorize without some expert opinion to counter the agency recommendation or without additional resources to alleviate the family's troubles. A court whose orders are not followed may also use its contempt power and levy fines or even impose jail time.

The agency attorney must also recognize the importance to the child and the family of other legal proceedings which may be going on concurrently but not in conjunction with the local jurisdiction. At the same time that the child protection action is under way, a child custody dispute may be pending before another judge as part of a divorce or postdivorce action, or a guardianship action may be pending. It is not unusual for a criminal action also to be pending in which the child is a victim and/or a witness. These cases are all likely to affect the child protection case. The agency attorney should accept the responsibility of coordinating the response to these actions to the full extent possible; minimally, he or she should at least be fully informed about them, so he or she can keep the child protection court up-to-date on the status of these other proceedings.

The agency attorney's role demands well-developed traditional legal skills. However, the attorney must also know the "business" of his or her clients very well. Ultimately, a successful intervention in a family requires close collegial cooperation between the lawyer, the child protection agency, and the psychiatric, psychological, and medical consultants to the agency.

The Attorney for the Parents

The attorney for the parents is charged with representing the interests of his or her clients zealously within the bounds of the law.[8] Advocacy for the parents usually takes the form of minimizing the effects of state intervention on the family and may include diplomatic attempts to persuade the agency to withdraw petitions, in-court advocacy for dismissal, insistence that the charges brought by the state be legally proven in court, and negotiation for dispositions that are most acceptable to the parents.

---

8. "A lawyer shall seek the lawful objectives of a client through reasonably available means permitted by law and these rules" (24, rule 1.2).

A danger exists in child protection cases that the personal rights of parents and children will be infringed in the well-intentioned zeal to help children and parents. Even before an attorney is appointed to represent the parents, government intervention in the family may have been initiated that has not been reviewed by any court or magistrate. The good intentions of the child protection system do not alter the need to recognize and respect the personal integrity and autonomy of parents. Mr. Justice Brandeis warned about the dangers to liberty presented by the benevolently intended state:

> Experience should teach us to be most on our guard to protect liberty when the Government's purposes are beneficent. Men born to freedom are naturally alert to repel invasion of their liberty by evil-minded rulers. The greatest dangers to liberty lurk in insidious encroachment by men of zeal, well-meaning but without understanding. (33)

The U.S. Supreme Court in *In re Gault* held that benevolent state intentions do not justify any relaxation of legal safeguards or procedural protections for parents or children (34).

Child protective services is an area of state control over individuals and families rarely visible to most members of the community. Social workers and other helping professionals involved in child protection activities intend no harm to client families but aspire, instead, to stabilize the family as a unit, to protect the child, and to impart skills of child rearing where they are lacking. In spite of the benevolent motives of child protective services, however, significant intrusions by government into personal and family life is possible without the safeguards of due process of law. Government intrusions in family life by extensive child welfare services may not be warranted in some cases.

Children's services workers and supervisors should recognize that the clients often attribute considerably more power and authority to them than they and their agencies may actually possess. Child welfare clients are often poor and powerless. They may agree to accept intervention into their family privacy out of fear of agency authority or fear of a court petition. Overestimating the power of the department, the family may believe that a petition to the court is tantamount to removal of their children, not understanding that parents have rights in the legal process too. The exaggerated perception of protective services authority and the fear of the court process may intimidate clients into acquiescing to "voluntary" plans for services or for placement of their children outside the family home. Such "voluntary" and nonjudicial arrangements provide neither safeguards for the rights of the parents and the children nor checks on a possibly overzealous agency or social worker. Parents may well feel betrayed by the agencies ostensibly providing services to the family. A good part of any legal case brought on behalf of children (and against their parents, as the parents may see it) often comes from the parents' own solicited statements and candid admissions. Parents can, as a result, find themselves "condemned out of their own mouths."

Therefore, the risk of arbitrary social work action, of agency coercion, and of overreaching in violation of personal liberty and personal integrity looms large indeed. How should personal freedoms of parents and children be preserved in child welfare? Should procedural safeguards be established within the administrative structure of children's services to protect the privacy and personal liberties of clients? Federal law (35, 36) already requires "fair hearings" for recipients of services to appeal the "denial of or exclusions from a service program, failure to take account of recipient choice of service *or a determination that the individuals must participate in the service program*" (37, p. 3, emphasis added; 38, pt. 8, pp. 66–76).[9]

Some have suggested not only that all child welfare clients be given a warning upon first contact that anything they say can be used against them in court but also that a warrant be required prior to any protective services investigation (39). Such warnings and warrants are not now required by law. Basic fairness and good social work practice and ethics require that clients be fully advised of the protective services role and the limits of agency authority from the very first contact. Because child abuse and neglect cause such great societal concern and because the child protection network has generally been seen as benevolently motivated, society has, up to now, been willing to run the risk of occasional coerced and perhaps unwarranted invasions of family privacy in exchange for swift identification of and response to child abuse and neglect and related ills. The law has not required that notice and hearing be provided before child protective services is allowed to become involved with the family. Child welfare professionals, however, ought to be aware of the personal liberty issue and be responsive to it in their every dealing with potential clients—but they sometimes are not. The attorney consulted on behalf of parents who are the subjects of a child abuse and neglect investigation or of family reunification services should determine if the investigation has violated any state and federal standards and be prepared to invoke fair hearing provisions regarding reunification services. Each state has provision for expunging reports of child abuse and neglect; the parent's attorney may wish to pursue these provisions, to protect the reputation and good name of the clients.

Once a child protection action is actually filed, the attorney for the parents should know the applicable law and the local court procedures and practices. He or she should understand the particular family and thoroughly investigate the facts of this particular case (40). He or she should also become well acquainted with the common dynamics of child abuse and neglect and with the treatment programs in the local community that deal with such problems. Considerable information can be obtained from reading, but the lawyer should also be apprised of and familiar with the local scene. One of the best ways to achieve this is to spend time with local social workers, physicians, psychologists, and other lawyers with experience in child abuse and neglect cases.

Representation of parents in cases of alleged child abuse and neglect requires unique skills and resources in addition to those of traditional advocacy. Lawyers must first deal with their negative feelings toward the parent accused of child abuse or neglect. The feelings toward a client, unless dealt with deliberately from the beginning, can sabotage a lawyer's advocacy, either consciously or unconsciously. One means of working through personal feelings toward allegedly abusive or neglectful parents is to understand the dynamics behind child abuse and neglect. Accused parents often have difficulty trusting others, forming relationships (including relationships with their lawyers), and deferring gratification.

9. Not all states have implemented this federally mandated fair hearing system for child welfare services.

Lawyers are counselors-at-law as well as advocates. In the agency attorney's role, the lawyer may advise a client social worker to pursue nonlegal avenues in a case before taking legal action or to consult other professionals about treatment strategy before initiating court action. Similar advice may be given to parents.

The lawyer as counselor to parents must feel comfortable engaging each parent as a person, must evaluate the parents' difficulties and their legal and social situation, and should only then provide legal counsel as to how to accomplish their goals. The lawyer may explore the parents' perspective both on whether or not particular personal and family problems exist and on whether or not the social agencies can help them. He or she may counsel parents to accept certain services, seeking postponement of the court process in the interim. As a result, the parents may be willing to accept some limited assistance from an agency voluntarily. The parents may even be advised to forego immediate legal advantage in order to benefit from a social intervention that is calculated to prevent recurrence of abuse or neglect.

The parent's attorney can sometimes perform valuable functions for the parents by encouraging nonjudicial resolutions of the case. A voluntary plan of treatment may avoid formal court jurisdiction and still protect the child and address the problems which may have been identified by protective services. Nonjudicial resolutions reached in concert with legal representation of the parents avoid the danger of improper invasion of personal liberties without due process. A lawyer representing parents should make a point of ensuring that whatever agreement they enter into really is done voluntarily and knowingly, that is, with their full awareness of possible consequences.

Where the parents are willing to accept some services under the shadow of court action, the parents' lawyer should obtain from the social worker a detailed treatment plan for the family. The social worker should also make a contract with the parents defining in concrete terms the problems that are to be worked on, the obligations of the parents and of the agency, and the expectations of what is to be achieved by the parents before the child can be returned or the intervention by the agency terminated.[10]

The counselor's role is quite consistent with traditional lawyerly functioning and is similarly based on building trust and treating clients as important individuals. However, these nonadversarial tasks of the lawyer may be even more important in child protection cases than in other areas of the law. In exercising the counselor function, the lawyer must be careful to establish and encourage whatever trust he or she can with the clients. When the lawyer recommends cooperation with social agencies, he or she should do so carefully, to help the clients understand that even if the suggestions of the lawyer are not accepted, the lawyer will nevertheless stand by the clients as a vigorous advocate of their position. The lawyer's obligation is to advocate for what the client wants—so long as those objectives are legal. The client must clearly understand that duty of loyalty.

After exercising the counselor function, the lawyer may decide that vigorous advocacy of his or her clients' goals is necessary. This decision may be based on an appraisal that the case against the parents is weak or unfounded or that the agency response is unduly harsh

10. See elements of case plans required by P.L. 96-272, 42 U.S.C.A. §675(5)(A).

or drastic in light of the family problems identified. The attorney or parents may feel that the agency is offering no better alternative for the child: the tenuousness of foster care may be less desirable than attempting to protect the child in his own home and provide necessary family services. Federal law in fact requires that a child be placed in the "least restrictive alternative placement" and that "reasonable efforts" be taken to prevent or eliminate the need for out-of-home placement of the child (31). The client may also firmly deny the allegations in the petition and instruct the lawyer to contest the case. The lawyer is then duty bound to advocate zealously for his or her client. As one commentator notes:

> It is imperative that the attorney *not* be concerned with the best interests of the child. That is the initial task of the caseworkers and the ultimate task for the court. (40, p. 229)

Certainly, the lawyer begins his or her advocacy for the client through negotiation and conciliation efforts with the protection agency itself. Some discussion and negotiation may lead to a resolution of the conflict between parents and agency. Lawyers must learn the important art of persuading a large bureaucracy convinced of the inherent rightness of its position to modify that very position. In spite of the desirability of nonjudicial resolutions of disputes between the parents and the social agency, however, it is often necessary to proceed to trial.

The responsibility of a parent for injuries to or possible neglect of a child may be a contested issue. The lawyer has a duty to vigorously and resourcefully stand as the ardent protector of his or her clients' constitutional and personal rights. The lawyer must bring to the task the usual tools of the advocate—familiarity with the applicable law, ability to logically present the pertinent facts, and facility for forceful and persuasive exposition of the parents' cause. A few jurisdictions have developed resources for parents' attorneys which can be very helpful (41, 42).

Many nonlawyers find the lawyer's role as the zealous advocate for the parents in serious child abuse cases disquieting and difficult to understand. Lawyers are committed to the principle that all accused persons are entitled to a defense. The agency may, after all, be wrong or overly zealous. The injuries may be "apparently inflicted injuries" and not child abuse after all. This issue is one raised regularly in interdisciplinary groups concerned with child abuse and neglect.

In the dispositional phase of a case, the parents' lawyer may serve several different functions:

1. The lawyer can ensure impartiality by acting as a counterbalance to pressure exerted on the court by the emotionally charged nature of the issues.
2. He or she can assure that the basic elements of due process are preserved, such as the right to be heard and the right to test the facts upon which the disposition is to be made.
3. He or she can make certain that the disposition is based upon complete and accurate facts and that all the circumstances which shed light upon the conduct of his or her client are fully developed.
4. The lawyer can test expert opinion to make certain that it is not based on mistakes arising from either erroneous factual premises or limited expertise.

5. He or she can give the frequently inarticulate parents a voice in the proceeding by acting as their spokesperson.

6. The attorney's relationship with the parents may even enable him or her to give the protective services or court staff new and meaningful insights into the family situation.

7. Finally, the parents' attorney can interpret the court and its processes to the clients and thus assist the parents in genuinely accepting the actions of the court (43).

Conclusion

Attorneys in child protection, whether representing the child, the parents, or the protective services agencies, face unique challenges for which traditional law school education has probably not prepared them. In a recent report on the unmet legal needs of children and their families, the American Bar Association has recommended that the quality of counsel be improved, that Lawyers Committees for Children be established, and that training for attorneys who represent children be developed (30).

To function effectively in any of the lawyer roles, the attorney needs advice and consultation from social work and mental health professionals. This interdisciplinary collaboration is most beneficial when it goes both ways. Nonlawyers in child protection services need to know what to expect of the lawyers they meet in the court system. Interdisciplinary knowledge is as important to effective legal proceedings as it is to other aspects of state intervention on behalf of children.

References

1. *Meyer v. Nebraska,* 262 U.S. 390 (1963); *Pierce v. Society of Sisters,* 268 U.S. 510 (1925); *Griswold v. Connecticut,* 381 U.S. 479 (1965); *Stanley v. Illinois,* 405 U.S. 645 (1972); *Roe v. Wade,* 410 U.S. 113 (1973); *Moore v. City of East Cleveland,* 431 U.S. 494 (1977); *Smith v. Organization of Foster Families for Equality and Reform,* 431 U.S. 816 (1977); *Quilloin v. Walcott,* 434 U.S. 494 (1978); *Lassiter v. Dept of Social Services,* 452 U.S. 18 (1981); *Santosky v. Kramer,* 455 U.S. 745 (1980); *Michael H. v. Gerald D.,* 491 U.S. 110 (1989).

2. Palmer, S. E. 1989. Mediation in Child Protection Cases: An Alternative to the Adversary System. *Child Welfare* 68 (Jan.–Feb.):21–30.

3. 42 U.S.C. §5106a(b)(6).

4. CSR, Inc. 1994. *Final Report on the Validation and Effectiveness Study of Legal Representation through Guardian ad Litem.* Contract No. 105-89-1727, 30 November 1993 [released August 1994]. Washington, D.C.: U.S. Department of Health and Human Services.

5. National Center on Child Abuse and Neglect. 1980. *Representation for the Abused and Neglected Child: The Guardian ad Litem and Legal Counsel.* U.S. Department of Health and Human Services pub. no. (OHDS) 80-30272. Washington, D.C.: U.S. Government Printing Office.

6. Kelly, R., and Ramsey, S. 1983. Do Attorneys for Children Protection Proceedings Make a Difference? A Study of the Impact of Representation under Conditions of High Judicial Intervention. *J. Family Law* 21:405–8.

7. Davidson, H. A. 1980. *Representing Children and Parents in Abuse and Neglect Cases.* Washington, D.C.: American Bar Association, National Resource Center on Child Advocacy and Protection [now ABA Center on Children and the Law].

8. American Bar Association, Institute of Judicial Administration. 1980. *Juvenile Justice Standards Project: Standards Relating to Counsel for Private Parties.* Cambridge, Mass.: Ballinger.

9. Knitzer, J., and Sobie, M. 1984. *Law Guardians in New York State: A Study of the Legal Representation of Children.* Albany, N.Y.: New York State Bar Association.

10. Goldstein, J.; Freud, A.; and Solnit, A. 1979. *Before the Best Interests of the Child.* New York: Free Press.

11. *Standards of Practice for Lawyers Who Represent Children in Abuse and Neglect Cases* [approved by the ABA House of Delegates, 5 Feb.]. 1996. In Recommendations of the Conference on Ethical Issues in Legal Representation of Children. *Fordham Law Rev.* 64 (Mar.): 1301–14. And, as Proposed Standards, in *Family Law Q.* 29 (fall 1995): 375.

12. Note. 1983. The Non-lawyer Guardian ad Litem in Child Abuse and Neglect Proceedings: The King County, Washington, Experience. *Washington Law Rev.* 58: 853.

13. *In the Matter of Jamie "TT," Alleged to Be an Abused Child,* 191 A.D.2d 132, 599 N.Y.S.2d 892 (1993) N.Y. App. Div.

14. Duquette, D., and Ramsey, S. 1986. Using Lay Volunteers to Represent Children in Child Protection Court Proceedings. *Child Abuse and Neglect: International J.* 10: 293.

15. Duquette, D., and Ramsey, S. 1987. Representation of Children in Child Abuse and Neglect Cases: An Empirical Look at What Constitutes Effective Representation. *Michigan J. Law Reform* 20: 341.

16. National Association of Court Appointed Special Advocates, Seattle, Washington. March 1986. Personal communication.

17. *The Connection* [newsletter of the National Association of Court Appointed Special Advocates]. 1996. 12(2): 20.

18. Johnson, C. L. 1979. *Much More to Do about Something: The Guardian ad Litem in Child Abuse and Neglect Judicial Proceedings.* Athens, Ga.: Regional Institute of Social Welfare Research.

19. Johnson, C. L.; Thomas, G.; and Turem, E. 1980. Implementing the Guardian ad Litem Mandate: Toward the Development of a Feasible Model. *Juvenile and Family Court J.* 3: 3–16.

20. *ABA Juvenile and Child Welfare Law Reporter.* 1993. Vol. 12.

21. Duquette, D. N. 1990. *Advocating for the Child in Protection Proceedings: A Handbook for Court Appointed Special Advocates.* Lexington, Mass.: Lexington Books.

22. National Association of Court Appointed Special Advocates. 1992. *Roles and Responsibilities of Guardians ad Litem.* Seattle: CASA.

23. Michigan Compiled Laws Annotated §722.630.

24. *Model Rules of Professional Conduct.* 1983. Washington, D.C.: ABA.

25. Ramsey, S. 1983. Representation of the Child in Protection Proceedings: The Determination of Decision Making Capacity. Family Law Q. 17: 287.

26. Long, L. 1983. When the Client Is a Child: Dilemmas in the Lawyer's Role. *J. Family Law* 21: 611.

27. Horowitz, R. M., and Davidson, H. A., eds. 1984. *Legal Rights of Children.* Colorado Springs, Colo.: Shepards/McGraw-Hill.

28. Mnookin, R. 1985. *In the Interest of Children: Advocacy, Law Reform, and Public Policy.* New York: W. H. Freeman.

29. Haralambie, A. M. 1993. *The Child's Attorney: A Guide to Representing Children in Custody, Adoption, and Protection Cases.* [An excellent resource.] Washington, D.C.: ABA Family Law Section.

30. American Bar Association, *Presidential Working Group on the Unmet Legal Needs of Children and Their Families.* 1993. *America's Children at Risk: A National Agenda for Legal Action.* Washington, D.C.: ABA.

31. Federal Adoption Assistance and Child Welfare Act of 1980. P.L. 96-272, 42 U.S.C.A. §671(a)(15), 672(a)(11).

32. American Bar Association, Institute of Judicial Administration. 1981. *Juvenile Justice Standards Project: Standards Relating to Abuse and Neglect.* Cambridge, Mass.: Ballinger.
33. *Olmstead v. United States,* 277 U.S. 438, 479 (1928) (Brandeis, J., dissenting).
34. *In re Gault,* 387 U.S. 1 (1967).
35. 42 U.S.C. §671(12).
36. 45 C.F.R. 1355.21(b), 205.10.
37. U.S. Department of Health and Human Services; Administration for Children, Youth, and Families; Children's Bureau. 1983. Policy Interpretation Question 83–4, 26 October. Washington, D.C.: U.S. Government Printing Office.
38. Hardin, M. 1992. *Establishing a Core of Services for Families Subject to State Intervention: A Blueprint for Statutory and Regulatory Action.* Washington, D.C.: ABA Center on Children and the Law.
39. Levine, R. S. 1973. *Caveat Parens:* A Demystification of the Child Protection System. *Univ. Pittsburgh Law Rev.* 35:1.
40. Hewitt, C. 1983. Defending a Termination of Parental Rights Case. In *Foster Children in the Courts,* ed. M. Hardin. Boston: Butterworth Legal Publishers.
41. Besharov, D. J. 1987. *Defending Child Abuse and Neglect Cases: Representing Parents in Civil Proceedings.* Prepared for Counsel for Child Abuse and Neglect, District of Columbia Superior Court.
42. Davenport. 1990. *Representing Parents in Vermont Child Protection Proceedings: A Basic Introduction for New Attorneys.* Vermont State Bar Association.
43. Isaacs, J. L. 1972. The Role of the Lawyer in Child Abuse Cases. In *Helping the Battered Child and His Family,* ed. C. H. Kempe and R. E. Helfer. Philadelphia: Lippincott.

22

The Courts and Child Maltreatment

Howard A. Davidson

Since the beginning of recorded history of child protection in America, the courts have
played a key role in the response to child abuse and neglect. Reports of criminal action
taken against parents for mistreating their children date back to the seventeenth century.
Special juvenile court proceedings for abuse, neglect, and abandonment of children were
an integral part of that jurisdiction from the formative years of the juvenile court movement
in the early 1900s (1).

Today, child maltreatment cases are pervasive throughout the nation's court systems.
In the past two decades, their increase in volume and the number of hearings associated
with them have far surpassed juvenile delinquency proceedings despite the rise in violent
crime committed by young people. Child abuse and neglect court jurisdiction has both
peaked and been virtually transformed in a little over ten years, in large part because of
both the dramatic rise in the number of child sexual abuse matters reaching the courts and
new requirements imposed upon courts by federal and state law in foster care proceedings.

Some children's advocates believe there has been too much reliance on the courts, and
their inherent adversarial approach, in child protection matters. Others contend that the
judiciary plays a critical role in safeguarding the legal rights and welfare of maltreated
children. These tensions are readily apparent in many of the conflicts I will be exploring here.

This chapter describes the various categories of, and basis for instituting, child abuse
and neglect judicial actions. It further details various aspects of the two most prevalent
forms of proceedings related to child maltreatment and examines the emergence of proposals for reform—including alternatives to the traditional methods of involvement by the
courts and expansion of the presumed rights of children affected by judicial action or
inaction.

Types of Judicial Involvement

As soon as a report or complaint of child maltreatment is received by social services or law
enforcement authorities, those handling the case generally begin to think about the legal
consequences of the allegations. Such allegations always raise the possibility that one or

---

Howard A. Davidson, J.D., is the director of the American Bar Association Center on Children and the Law.

more judicial actions may have to be initiated and evidence of any child abuse or neglect properly preserved for court.

When abuse appears to have been inflicted by a parent or guardian, when a child is endangered by the behavior of negligence of any person in the home who has responsibility for the child's care, or when a parent/guardian's actions or gross disregard for the welfare of the child may have facilitated his or her maltreatment outside of the home, a *civil child protection* court action may ensue. Such an action is almost inevitable if the child is removed from home by child protective services or the police under their emergency powers. If maltreatment results in death or serious injury to a child, including severe physical or sexual abuse, the perpetrator of the harm upon the child—and, increasingly, a parent who failed to act reasonably in protecting the child from that harm—may face criminal charges.

A civil child protection action—also commonly referred to as a *care, protection, endangerment, dependency, abuse,* or *neglect proceeding*—is the most frequent judicial response to child maltreatment. These cases have grown increasingly complex as more actions have been brought on the basis of parental substance abuse or mental disability (2). In many communities, child protection actions are initiated in a court of general trial jurisdiction, one that hears all types of judicial proceedings, both adult and juvenile, and may not have any judges who either limit their work to, or specialize in, child-related cases. In urban areas, and in many states on a statewide basis, such actions are brought in a specialized court (or division of a larger court) called the juvenile court or family court, where the judges are more likely to be specially assigned and undergo special training related to child maltreatment cases. In this chapter, these cases will often be called *juvenile court child protection proceedings.*

Criminal actions related to child maltreatment will typically be heard in a court of general trial jurisdiction. Serious crimes involving child maltreatment, if characterized as felonies, may be handled far differently—probably in an elevated level of court—than offenses considered less serious (namely, those classified as misdemeanors). It should be noted that some states still classify certain parental behaviors related to child abuse, and especially neglect, as criminal misdemeanors (such as physical assaults that inflict neither life-threatening injury nor permanent harm and some acts that constitute child endangerment, neglect, or abandonment).

Sometimes child abuse and neglect issues emerge in other types of judicial proceedings. Parents in the midst of legal separation or divorce, involved in actions to modify custody or visitation orders previously granted in connection with a divorce, or responding to complaints of custodial interference or parental child abduction, may ask a judge in a specialized domestic relations court to take child protective action based on evidence of child maltreatment. Parents who have experienced domestic violence inflicted against them, often asserting that their children are also victims of assaultive behavior by a spouse or lover or have been traumatized by living in that abusive environment, may seek civil protective orders to help keep an alleged abuser away from themselves and their children.

Finally, child maltreatment issues have begun to emerge more regularly in civil damage actions brought against the perpetrator of abuse on behalf of children by a nonabusive parent or, more commonly, on behalf of themselves, by adults allegedly abused when they were children. These personal injury cases, or *tort actions,* are brought to obtain a judicial finding that harm was done to the child and that the person(s) responsible should be made to pay for those injuries with both compensatory and possibly punitive damages.

One barrier to lawsuits brought by adults for childhood abuse is the law known as the statute of limitations, which traditionally limited the filing of actions to a certain number of years after commission of the wrongful acts. States are, however, increasingly changing those laws in recognition of the difficulty children have in safely speaking out about their abuse, the legal handicap of being a minor, and the fact that victims may have a "delayed discovery" (awareness) of their abuse due to years of psychological suppression.

Addressing this last impediment to civil actions by survivors of childhood abuse has been controversial, although incest survivors have viewed it as an essential legal reform. Laws and court decisions have given legal recognition to the delayed discovery concept, and in some cases of delayed discovery, independent evidence has corroborated the abuse assertions. Yet it is claimed that some alleged childhood abuse victims who have spontaneously recalled "hidden" memories of abuse only during or after psychological therapy sessions may simply be summoning up "false memories" in response to a therapist's suggestion. Clearly, this is an area where increased research and litigation may provide much-needed enlightenment.

Almost all child abuse and neglect matters handled judicially are heard exclusively in state courts. Federal court jurisdiction over child abuse and neglect is strictly limited to cases in which children are maltreated on federal lands, including military posts, or in which there are purported violations of such federal laws as the Protection of Children Against Sexual Exploitation Act, which addresses interstate and intercountry child pornography, prostitution, and transportation of children for purposes of an unlawful sexual offense (3). Under the federal Indian Child Welfare Act, Native American tribal courts may assume jurisdiction over civil child protection judicial proceedings affecting Native American children (4). Occasionally, judicial decisions from state courts regarding child maltreatment will be appealed into the federal court system. In such cases, violations of constitutional rights or federal laws are most likely to have been alleged.

How and Why Court Actions May Ensue

In order for any court to hear a child abuse or neglect proceeding, a court action must be initiated by a legally authorized person. In the juvenile court, that person is usually a child protective services agency worker, an attorney for the agency, or a lawyer representing the agency (for example, a lawyer from the office of the county or municipal counsel, attorney general, or district or state's attorney), who files a petition beginning the action. Many state laws also permit other individuals, such as hospital personnel, physicians, legal custodians or guardians of children, or any other interested adults, to file juvenile court child protection petitions.

One area of increasing litigation concerns the legal authority of minor children to file petitions on their own behalf (or otherwise formally intervene, as parties, in ongoing court actions affecting their interests) without approval from parents, guardians, or adult "next friends" (adults acting for the benefit of a child in a legal matter). Some advocates suggest that this right arises under the language of state constitutions and other laws which recognize that children, as "persons," have the same right of "access to the courts" as other citizens. This argument first received public attention in Florida in 1992 during the case of "Gregory K."

A criminal proceeding can generally be commenced only by a local prosecutor (for example, a district attorney or state's attorney) at the request of an adult complainant, such as a nonabusing parent, or as a result of the direct disclosures of the child. In some jurisdictions, even though a complainant or victim may not have come forward, evidence of criminal wrongdoing may be presented by a prosecutor to a grand jury, which then determines whether criminal action will be initiated.

In a divorce-related custody or visitation dispute, abuse/neglect allegations may be raised by either party or a guardian *ad litem* for the child, or such allegations may first emerge through a report to the court on a social or mental health evaluation of the child and parents (5). In all such situations, domestic relations judges may decide to address the maltreatment allegations as part of their deliberations, or they may refer the case to a juvenile court—where those judges and other court personnel may be better prepared to resolve such allegations and make appropriate dispositional orders. The same case transfer approach may occur when a judge hearing a civil protection order request brought by a battered woman learns that her children may also have been victims of abuse and that she may not be able to protect them from further harm in the home.

There are also instances in which judges or attorneys involved in other types of child-related cases (for instances, delinquency and status offender cases, charges of contributing to the delinquency of a minor, and arrest of a sole caretaker) have caused a child protection proceeding to be initiated. This is most likely to happen when they become aware of facts related to child maltreatment when family members are before the court for some entirely different reason. Sometimes this will result in the postponement or dismissal of the original proceeding because the child abuse or neglect is considered to be the more basic problem; accordingly, a judge will conclude that the family's other problems should first be addressed by a court in that context.

After any report of child maltreatment is investigated and confirmed, a child protective services (CPS) agency must decide (*a*) whether or not the subject-child and other children in the home are in any immediate danger, and (*b*) whether the parents are capable of and amenable to working with the agency in a cooperative manner to eradicate that danger. In many situations where removal from the home is deemed necessary, parents are willing, often anxious, to have their child placed in out-of-home care without CPS instituting a child protective court proceeding. This is more likely when there is a safe placement for the child available in the home of a relative (called "kinship care"), godmother, good friend, or other suitable person close to the family.

If the answer to question (*a*) above is no, then the CPS caseworker will likely follow his or her discretion or agency policy guidelines and avoid court action altogether. If the child has been placed in foster care without parental consent, the CPS worker will have no choice but to initiate court proceedings—unless the child is quickly returned home, as would occur, for instance, if a missing parent were immediately located. In many states, a large proportion of children in agency-supervised foster, kinship, or residential group care initially come into care through a "voluntary placement." The placement is considered voluntary because prior parental consent for the removal of the child from home is obtained by CPS, even though the parent may feel pressure to consent to such placement in order to avoid more intrusive court intervention.

In voluntary placement cases, it is possible that no court will ever establish that the children were in fact victims of parental abuse or neglect. The lack of a court adjudication or written judicial findings of the facts of a child's maltreatment may, after a lengthy period of placement, become a serious impediment to executing a family reunification plan or making available for adoption an abused/neglected child who in reality has been abandoned. One of the primary reasons for court delays and judicial indecisiveness in formulating "permanency planning" orders for children has been the failure of earlier court proceedings to "establish a record" that makes it impossible for parents to deny their history of maltreatment, its impact on the child, and their lack of cooperation with treatment and service agencies. A full and complete court record is absolutely vital to laying the legal groundwork for timely, definitive rulings affecting the lives of abused and neglected children.

It has been estimated that, nationally, only a small percentage of confirmed cases of child maltreatment result in *any* type of court proceeding. The majority of cases in which there is no court action involve child neglect, lack of adequate parental care and supervision, emotional maltreatment, or minor physical abuse. Quite appropriately, these cases are rarely considered for criminal prosecution, and the families may actually be more effectively assisted, and the children more adequately protected, through the careful supervision and nonadversarial support of child welfare, mental health, and other community services without the necessity of costly and time-consuming judicial system oversight. Child protection authorities realize that children who have been mistreated, as well as their families, can often be better served without reliance on an accusatory system that is essentially driven by "allegations" of unlawful behavior by parents.

Nevertheless, there are places in this country where it has been common practice to petition the juvenile court in every, or almost every, substantiated case of child abuse and neglect, even if removal of the child from the home is not necessary. One rationale for this has been that some CPS personnel view the court as a necessary "hammer" to be held over the heads of parents who have mistreated their children, so as to assure parental cooperation in family treatment. Another reason for use of the courts may be to provide an independent review, by a judge, of the facts of every case; this, presumably, would exempt agency caseworkers from any charge of having acted improperly (for example, if CPS permits a child to remain at home and abuse later reoccurs).

In our increasingly litigious age—one of enhanced risk of liability for social workers and agencies—CPS may use the courts to protect itself, even though this option can appear unnecessarily costly to taxpayers, not to mention families forced unnecessarily into a coercive judicial process. Unfortunately, not enough research has been conducted to tell us the full effects of overuse of the courts. Although observers of the judicial system know that CPS caseworkers, and other professionals, are having to spend inordinate amounts of time preparing court-related documents and waiting in courthouses, it is not clear whether agency practices may actually be improved, and families better served, through more frequent court involvement and oversight.

The need that public social service agencies have for federal funds to offset foster care system costs may also precipitate these agencies to initiate court proceedings in cases where judicial intervention might not otherwise be considered essential. Under federal law, those funds can not be used to subsidize a state's costs for any voluntary placement of eligible foster children unless there is a timely review (within 180 days) by a court that the placement is in "the child's best interests" (6). However, most states rarely seek such findings. Rather, if the child(ren) cannot be safely returned home, CPS agencies will generally, within days or weeks of the voluntary placement, file a conventional juvenile court child protective abuse/neglect petition. Pursuant to this petition, a judge will be required to find that "reasonable efforts" have been made to avoid the need for continued placement; once that finding is made, the state will qualify for federal funds, assuming the child comes from a family meeting certain low-income requirements.

Federal law also requires that to receive funds for foster care placements, states must institute (a) a case review by a court or administrative body (for example, a CPS agency or citizen foster care review board) at least once every six months, and (b) a "dispositional" (permanency planning) hearing conducted by a court or court-approved body within eighteen months of the placement and periodically thereafter (7). These legislative reforms and their state law analogues have helped the number of court hearings to skyrocket since the early 1980s, since nearly all the mandated hearings are conducted by courts.

Principles Governing Court Involvement with Families

The most important legal theory supporting juvenile court child protective action is called *parens patriae*. Under that doctrine, courts are invested with the authority to intervene in the lives of family members and, by principle, may limit a parent or guardian's authority to deal with their children when a child's physical or mental health is jeopardized. Once a child is found to have been the victim of abuse, neglect, or abandonment, or is considered to be in imminent danger of such maltreatment, courts with clear child protection responsibility (that is, juvenile and domestic relations courts) will be guided by a second principle: the best interests of the child.

Under American law, it is initially assumed that the best interests of a child are served by preserving the integrity of the family unit, without any judicial interference. There is a strong legal presumption for parental autonomy in child rearing. However, once a child is brought within the juvenile court's jurisdiction because he or she has been found to have been abused or neglected (in other words, once the statutory grounds for court intervention have been proven), decisions concerning placement of the child, court-approved parental visitation with the child after placement, return of the child home, or court-ordered services to any family member may be guided by the court's application of the "best interests of the child" principle. Even that, nonetheless, can be tempered by a statutorily imposed priority of family reunification. But in my opinion and in the opinion of most child advocates, where it can be shown that separation from parents or continued absence from the home is necessary to assure the child's safety, the child's best interests should generally prevail over any claims of parental rights or policy-related goal of family reunification.

Sometimes, however, the law recognizes that removal of a child, and prolonged foster care placement, are not at all in his or her best interests. Under federal and most state laws, there is a standard, known as "reasonable efforts," designed to help courts assure that actions are taken and family services provided by public child welfare agencies to avoid unnecessary and unnecessarily prolonged out-of-home placement of children. Although courts are required to evaluate the CPS agency's reasonable efforts at the time of the child's removal, it should be noted that children can lawfully be removed from home without *any* efforts to avoid the placement when such action is deemed necessary for the child's safety. Legislatures have increasingly amended child protection laws to give children's safety interests special attention in the process of government intervention in the family. For example, in its 1996 reauthorization of the federal Child Abuse Prevention and Treatment Act, Congress added requirements that states receiving funds under this legislation assure procedures by CPS for an immediate child safety assessment upon receipt of a child maltreatment report. Furthermore, Congress required that immediate steps be taken "to ensure and protect the safety of the abused or neglected child and of any other children under the same care who may also be in danger of abuse or neglect and ensuring their placement in a safe environment" (8). With or without new legislative direction, judges are likely to also pay greater attention to the issue of child safety in their deliberations.

The issue of "reasonable efforts" to reunify maltreated children with their parents generally arises again in termination of parental rights cases, although that precise term may not be used in the laws addressing parental rights termination. In most but not all termination cases, the crux of the case may hinge on whether the agency responsible for services to the child and family provided all the help that could be reasonably expected and thus need not further work for family reunification due to the parents' failure to improve within a reasonable period of time (9, §9.18).

It is important to recognize that a court's action to terminate parental rights against the wishes of a parent usually will require more than assertions that it is in the child's best interests to do so—although, again, a best-interests "test" is still likely to be an important consideration in termination actions. Grounds for termination of parental rights included in state laws generally require courts to make findings of parental unfitness, based on a parent's behavior or condition, before permanently severing parent-child ties. Stated differently, where termination of parental rights is possible as a disposition of a child protection case or where a separate termination proceeding has been initiated, parental behavior, unfitness, and incapacity will be central elements of most cases.

Varying Court Standards and Approaches

The most important difference in how juvenile courts and criminal courts approach child maltreatment is that in juvenile court the focus ideally is on the child—the question of whether he or she has been subjected to abuse or neglect and, if so, what intervention is needed not only to protect the child but also, unless contraindicated, to strengthen the child's family. A criminal court proceeding, on the other hand, is centered on the alleged adult offender, the perpetrator of abuse or neglect. If convicted, the offender will face a variety of possible sanctions to be selected by the judge, but meeting the needs of the maltreated child, siblings, and other family members is not a core responsibility of the criminal court.

To look at this another way, in a civil child protection case brought by a CPS agency to obtain protective jurisdiction over a child, *it may not be legally necessary* to formally prove or even assert that a child's injuries or present endangerment has been caused by a specific parent, caretaker, or other person in the child's home. In fact, there is often a legal presumption that if the child has been maltreated in the home, the parents or legal guardians must be responsible. A common exception would be cases in which a third party, such as a baby-sitter, has abused the child. But *the child,* and the child's safety, are what the primary subjects of this type of court proceeding should be, and the evidence presented should generally focus on whether the child has been abused, neglected, endangered, or in need of care, assistance, and/or protection.

However, even if it is not an absolute prerequisite to court jurisdiction that the perpe-trator of child maltreatment in a given case be legally established, it is still very important to do so whenever possible. Such a finding of responsibility can be essential in the devel-opment of an appropriate case plan that focuses on specific parental behaviors that need to change.

The juvenile court child protection action will have a standard of proof far lower than that required for conviction in a criminal court. In the majority of states, proof by a simple "preponderance of the evidence" of the child's maltreatment will suffice to give the court jurisdiction, while in some states the burden is a higher "clear and convincing evidence" standard. Because of an important U.S. Supreme Court decision (10–13), courts cannot terminate a parent's rights without proving their case by the "clear and convincing" stan-dard. Criminal convictions, of course, require proof of guilt "beyond a reasonable doubt."

The practical impact of all this on child protection professionals is the recognition that evidence of injury in some cases may not be sufficient to convict a specific perpetrator of abuse since there may be no way to pinpoint who actually inflicted the injury. This is particularly true with physical abuse. However, evidence in the same case may be more than sufficient to give the juvenile court protective jurisdiction over the child. In such situ-ations, a decision not to file criminal charges may be a good CPS strategy, based in part on a wish to spare the child the trauma of living through or testifying in a lengthy criminal case that results in acquittal. Those who work with abusing families also know that a find-ing of "not guilty" resulting simply from insufficient evidence to sustain a conviction may promote continued denial from family members and, consequently, impede treatment and rehabilitation.

Without a prosecution drawn out over many months (during which defendant parents may become increasingly resentful and uncooperative) and without the criminal stigma that follows conviction, some families may experience a more rapidly enhanced ability to get fully involved in the rehabilitative process. On the other hand, the threat of prosecution or criminal conviction and the risk of incarceration may be exactly what it takes in some cases to get, and keep, a parent or caretaker in treatment. A criminal conviction for child abuse also sends a message to the affected child, other potential abusers, and the entire community, that such behavior will be treated as a serious penal offense and that the child's pain has not gone unheeded. Courts and CPS agencies need to be sensitive to whether an aggressive criminal prosecution approach is in the best interests of the *specific* children and families involved in a given case.

Also, in juvenile court child protection proceedings, children will be assured, in most cases, of receiving the help of some type of independent advocate. That person, appointed by the court, may be called a guardian *ad litem,* legal counsel, or court appointed special advocate (CASA). Ideally, the child's advocate should actively assist the child and vigorously protect his or her interests throughout the entire length of the proceeding or as long as the court has jurisdiction over the child (14, 15). Conversely, in criminal cases resulting from child abuse, special representation for the child is seldom arranged. The same is true, to a lesser extent, in custody or visitation actions in domestic relations court; however, state laws or appellate court decisions are increasingly directing judges to appoint a guardian *ad litem* for the child in such cases where abuse is alleged. Unfortunately, the quality of this court-appointed child advocacy is too often inadequate—but resources are now more and more available to courts, bar associations, and individual advocates to enhance the skills of those who represent abused and neglected children.

The Juvenile Court Process

Child protective judicial proceedings begin with the filing of a petition, often because a child has been removed from home by police or CPS. State laws require that after an emergency removal (that is, one without parental consent), a court action must begin within a short period of time, generally from twenty-four to seventy-two hours, if the child remains in placement. The first hearing in the process, typically referred to as a "preliminary," "shelter care" or "detention hearing," or as a "temporary custody hearing" (an inappropriate term), may be held immediately after that twenty-four-to-seventy-two-hour period if the child has been removed. If the child remains at home, the first hearing may not take place so quickly. The primary issue at this hearing will be the need for continued, or initial, placement of the child (pending the adjudicatory hearing at which evidence is presented to determine if the child has been mistreated in violation of law). The court at this time may also have authority to issue other types of protective orders against individuals alleged to be responsible for the child's maltreatment, such as orders for those individuals to vacate the home and have no contact with the child or other family members.

In addition to determining the immediate need for alternative custodial arrangements or protective orders, this first hearing will accomplish several other things. Parents, both custodial and noncustodial, should have been notified well in advance of the time and place for their court appearance, and they also should have received a copy of the court petition. Similarly, active CPS agency efforts should have been taken to assure the parents' presence at the initial hearing. Once the hearing begins—or, ideally, before—the court should appoint a fully independent representative or advocate for the child. If the parents do not have their own counsel, a determination should be made whether they will be provided with a court-appointed lawyer due to their indigency. Depending upon the state and locality, the presiding officer at this hearing may be a judge or may have the title of referee, master, commissioner, or magistrate. If removal of the child from home is an issue at the hearing, the court should also determine whether "reasonable efforts" have been taken to avoid the need for initial or continued placement; such efforts include the exploration of agency use of "family preservation and support services" (16).[1] If the child would remain at extreme risk despite provision of appropriate intensive services to the family, then the court can properly find that agency efforts have been reasonable.

Sometimes, at this initial stage of the case, the parents will admit that the allegations in the petition are true or that some modified version of the allegations are correct and will promptly accept the court's jurisdiction. Otherwise, the case will generally be continued to another date, optimally within a few weeks, for the adjudicatory hearing.

During this time—even on the day set for the hearing—there may be one or more meetings of the principals in the case (for example, the CPS agency attorney, the caseworker, the parents' attorney, and the guardian *ad litem*). These may be court-mandated case resolution conferences or informal attempts at negotiating a case settlement. Some courts may go so far as to employ a mediator, who works with the parties to facilitate a fair and prompt case resolution and obviate the need for formal adversarial hearings.

The danger inherent in negotiated resolutions is that courts may improperly permit an admission of parental responsibility that inadequately reflects the true nature of the harm inflicted upon, or the risk faced by, the child. For example, the case may contain evidence of severe physical abuse or sexual molestation, but parents may seek to limit the adjudication to one of general child neglect. To avoid this, there should always be, as a permanent part of the court record, a written account of the material facts associated with the specific types of child maltreatment that took place. Furthermore, no court should permit a clear case of child abuse to be settled through the parents' simple admission of unspecified child neglect.

If no case settlement is negotiated, a formal hearing will likely ensue, where witnesses and other evidence are presented to prove the abuse/neglect (although, unlike criminal court, it is rare that the maltreated child will have to testify). Increasingly, laws require this hearing to begin or conclude within a set time from the date of the petition or original placement of the child. Prior to the hearing, the parties may make efforts at pretrial "discovery," in which access to CPS, hospital, and other records are sought. Some information, such as the identity of child abuse reporters and sensitive mental health records, may not be accessible unless they are directly related to proof (or disproof) of the maltreatment.

---

1. In the 1993 federal Omnibus Budget Reconciliation Act (P.L. 103-66), Congress passed "Family Preservation and Family Support Services" funding provisions designed to make $885 million over five years available to the states for these services (§§13711–16).

The adjudicatory hearing resembles most trials, but instead of only two parties presenting and cross-examining witnesses, the child's attorney or guardian *ad litem* can also actively participate. Also, in these hearings, unlike in criminal proceedings, parents can be called to testify by any of the parties and, if given "use immunity" by the court, cannot refuse to testify on Fifth Amendment protection against self-incrimination grounds. If the court finds that the abuse or neglect is not proven, the case should be dismissed. Otherwise, the case next proceeds to disposition.

Once an adjudication is reached, the court has authority to order parents to accept treatment and to otherwise cooperate with the CPS agency's program for case resolution. The court's disposition hearing will often include testimony about recommended actions; admission of predispositional studies, evaluations, and reports; a renewed consideration of "reasonable efforts" that might safely lead to family reunification; and the submission of an agency case plan. This plan should address the educational, health, and psychological needs of the child, as well as social services needed by the family and foster parents. During the disposition hearing, hearsay evidence is typically admitted, whereas it would not have been at the adjudicatory hearing.

One of the key issues at this disposition hearing may be the amount of parental visitation to be allowed if the child remains in foster care. Even if the child remains at home in the custody of a nonabusing parent, the court should address the issue of contact between the child and the abusive parent, including the manner in which visitation will be supervised. In severe cases, some states permit termination of parental rights as a disposition immediately after the initial adjudication. Other postadjudication options that may be selected by the court are long-term kinship care with relatives or "extended family" members; placement of the child in the legal custody of the state or county child welfare agency; a change in custody to another parent, relative, or friend; or a change in legal guardianship.

Following initial case disposition, if the child remains in foster care—and often when the child remains at home under the agency's protective supervision—the court should hold a series of periodic review hearings (for example, at three- or six-month intervals). For children in lengthy foster care, federal law requires (simply as a condition for state eligibility for matching federal payments, as we have previously seen) that no later than eighteen months after the child's entry in placement there be a separate "dispositional hearing" to establish a firm permanent plan for the child. This may be quickly followed by a termination of parental rights proceeding, although in appropriate situations (namely, babies abandoned at birth, or parents whose abuse or neglect of a child is extremely severe) termination actions may be permitted immediately after a child's initial placement.

The Criminal Court Process

Thanks to television, most people have acquired a basic understanding of the main steps in a criminal prosecution. Accordingly, we need explore that system only briefly, through focusing on several decision points in criminal actions related to child abuse. All sexual abuse and unlawful sexual conduct or contact with a child, as defined by state statute, as well as severe physical abuse (for instance, inflicted brain injuries and burns) are criminal acts (17). When children are severely injured or die as a consequence of parental neglect, criminal prosecution may well ensue. Prosecution may also result when very young children are discovered by the police to have been left "home alone" in a potentially dangerous situation. However, the numbers of neglect-related prosecutions are very small in comparison to the volume of child sexual abuse cases.

Following police investigation of an abuse or neglect report, a referral from a hospital, or a child's direct disclosure of abuse, the decision to arrest a suspected perpetrator may be made without prior court approval. Law enforcement officials, however, often exercise discretion not to make a precipitous arrest in child maltreatment cases but, instead, to prepare their case through search warrants, forensic investigation, and questioning of parents and others. The case may then be presented to a grand jury, which can, if it finds that the case has merit, issue an indictment. The presentation of a case to a grand jury permits prosecutors to test their available evidence, including statements from the child, with a group of citizens in a closed setting without defense presence. In some states, prosecution for a felony must be preceded by a grand jury indictment, while other states require that evidence first be presented at an adversarial "preliminary hearing." At the grand jury or preliminary hearing, the evidentiary standard that the prosecutor must meet will be "probable cause" that an offense took place.

Many factors affect a prosecutor's decision to charge a defendant formally or seek a grand jury indictment in a child abuse case. First and foremost, prosecutors must be fully aware of the scope and seriousness of the specific acts of child maltreatment in the case and the effect prosecution may have on the child and family. In that regard, consultation, especially at the stage at which charges are preferred, with caseworkers, pediatricians, and mental health professionals is essential. One way of accomplishing this is by organizing an ongoing multidisciplinary team or "children's advocacy center" process in which the prosecutor's office participates.

Also, when prosecutors become aware of a serious child maltreatment situation in a case in which there is insufficient evidence to sustain a conviction, they can through team analysis of the case encourage CPS to institute child protective action leading to supervisory authority over the family. Another consideration requiring multidisciplinary input, often applied in intrafamilial abuse cases involving first-time offenders, is the use of criminal "diversion," in which charges may be kept on hold pending, or dismissed following, successful participation of the perpetrator in a treatment program. If prosecutors make decisions on any of these topics without consulting and coordinating with a team of child welfare professionals, children may be exposed to greater risk of continuing maltreatment.

Once a prosecutor decides to try an adult for abuse/neglect of a child, another important prosecutorial decision will be whether to ask the court, after bail has been set, to issue protective orders that limit the defendant's contact with and access to the child as well as to other children or significant adults. Because, at about this point, a child protective proceeding may be occurring in juvenile court simultaneously with the related criminal court action, it is essential that the attorneys responsible for the juvenile case and the criminal case coordinate closely on such issues as bail, conditions of release, evaluation and treatment of the alleged perpetrator, child and family visitation, timing of the two potential trials, and disposition and sentencing options.

In criminal proceedings, far more than in the juvenile child protection case, the defendant's attorney may vigorously pursue discovery of case records, therapy notes, and other sensitive documents. This is another reason why the attorney prosecuting the criminal case should closely coordinate with the attorney representing the CPS agency—that agency is often the repository of this material. If any question arises about the defendant's right of access to certain records, a judge has discretion to review them in private to determine whether any part is so materially relevant to the defense that it must be provided for inspection.

Plea bargaining is common in child maltreatment prosecutions, and the same cautions I expressed in the previous section about parents seeking to dilute the record to obscure the severity of their abusive act apply here. This is a particular concern, given recently enacted criminal history record screening laws, which may help identify only those convicted specifically of child abuse or crimes that are clearly child-related. Thus, an agreement to drop a charge of "unlawful sexual conduct with a child" in exchange for a plea to "indecent assault," or to permit a charge of felony child endangerment based on severe physical abuse of a child to be plea-bargained down to simple battery, places future children at risk.

Allowing a plea-bargained conviction for a crime that does not clearly reflect a parent's unsuitability to care for a child may also inhibit subsequent termination of the offender's parental rights, as well as provide a chance for the offender to later secure inappropriate visitation or custodial rights. In reference to the issue of properly labeling offenders, it should be noted that in recent years some laws have permitted judges to make a special finding of "sexual motivation" for offenders who are convicted of a nonsexual offense such as criminal abduction, manslaughter, or murder.

Laws related to the sentencing of child abuse offenders increasingly recognize the severity of their crimes by enhancing penalties, based on the age of the victim, the relationship of the offender to the child, the extent of the child's injuries (both physical and emotional), any special vulnerability of the child, and other aggravating circumstances. Some laws give judges authority to order convicted offenders to pay the costs of the child victim's therapy, as well as the offender's own treatment. Other laws specifically include appropriate treatment-related conditions of incarceration and/or probation that judges may impose— although community-based treatment is likely to be ineffective, and risky to children, so long as offenders deny their guilt.

Repeat child abuse offenders are increasingly likely to receive harsh punitive (for example, mandatory minimum) sentences. They also face newer sanctions under habitual criminal laws; the risk, for violent sex offenders, of indeterminate civil commitment, or lifetime or extended probation and parole; and, for sexual offenders, the requirement of registering with a law enforcement agency wherever they move. One unintended consequence of these tougher, mandatory criminal penalties for child abusers is that offenders may end up putting added pressures on victims to keep silent. Another undesirable consequence is that in intrafamilial abuse cases, family members may shield the perpetrator for fear of losing the family's breadwinner for a lengthy period. On the other hand, stronger penalties simply reflect society's growing view that child abuse must be treated as a very serious offense and our shared hope that such penalties will serve as a deterrence.

Enhancing the Justice System

Commentators on the court system in child abuse and neglect cases have urged that the courts be improved on a number of different fronts. The *first,* and possibly most important, is the necessity of elevating the status and enhancing the resources of all courts that hear civil child protection cases. Juvenile court judges in many communities are often just as, or even more, overburdened than CPS workers. One widely supported approach to refining the judicial system is restructuring the courts hearing child protection and other youth-related matters into "unified family courts" with encompassing jurisdiction over child and family cases.

In its first report (1990), the U.S. Advisory Board on Child Abuse and Neglect recommended government assurance that courts handling all forms of child maltreatment cases are accorded the requisite funding and status to resolve such cases promptly and fairly. In addition, the board stated that courts must have the following resources:

(a) Adequate numbers of well-trained judges, lawyers, and court support staff, as well as manageable caseloads that take into account the complex and demanding nature of child abuse and neglect litigation;

(b) Specialized judicial procedures that are sensitive to the needs of children and families;

(c) Improved court-based diagnostic and evaluation services; and

(d) Greater educational opportunities for all professional personnel involved in such proceedings. (18, p. 89)

The year after this report was issued, the board urged greater federal efforts to focus on probation, parole, and correctional agency involvement with child abuse offenders, including treatment for and monitoring of both juvenile and adult offenders in community and correctional settings (19, p. 95).

The federal Children's Justice Act[2] and the state Children's Justice Task Forces (statewide multidisciplinary, interagency committees found in most states), can be used to help assure that all these concerns are addressed. In addition, since its inception in federal fiscal year 1995, an unprecedented and substantial ($35 million over four years) program, sponsored by the U.S. Department of Health and Human Services, has been in operation to support state court system evaluation and improvement focused on child abuse and neglect proceedings.[3] This provides funding to help courts systematically study their operations in civil child protection cases and plan for appropriate reform.

In its 1993 report, the U.S. Advisory Board on Child Abuse and Neglect issued its most sweeping proposals for comprehensive judicial system reform in abuse and neglect cases. They included support for new dispute resolution mechanisms (as alternatives to the traditional adversarial court process) that could, as with programs in Scotland and New

2. This program is also called Grants to States for Programs Relating to the Investigation and Prosecution of Child Abuse and Neglect Cases (42 U.S.C. §5106c).

3. This program is called Entitlement Funding for State Courts to Assess and Improve Handling of Proceedings Relating to Foster Care and Adoption (§13712 of the Omnibus Budget Reconciliation Act of 1993; see n. 1 above).

Zealand, stimulate or enhance family and neighborhood responsibility for the protection of children. The board further called for studies that would increase understanding of the way children experience the legal process and help find ways of enhancing their satisfaction with it. This was called making children "partners in the pursuit of justice." In that regard, the board also supported the concept that children, instead of having to wait for government to initiate protective proceedings on their behalf, should have independent legal standing to file actions or appeal decisions, including disposition orders, pertaining to their protection and care (20, p. 40).

A related area of court improvement is directing sufficient judicial resources to the special needs of children who give testimony in cases related to their abuse (21–23). More writing and research has been done on the topic of child witness trauma than on any other court system reform issue of the last decade. No subject associated with abused children has received as much attention by judicial and prosecutorial educators. Yet, the child witness reforms that constituted a large part of the court-related child protection legislation of the 1980s, and led to several U.S. Supreme Court decisions, require still more refinement and enhanced resource support.

The *second* major theme of court reform related to child maltreatment has been the need to enhance the quality and accessibility of attorneys for children, attorneys for CPS agencies and parents in child protection cases, and specially trained criminal prosecutors of child abuse offenders. The 1993 U.S. Advisory Board report made a recommendation for relevant research, training, and financial support, as well as for model court rules and standards of practice (20, pp. 39–40). There has long been widespread recognition among active child advocates that the responsibilities of all attorneys involved in child abuse and neglect cases, as well as those guardians *ad litem* who are not attorneys, should be clearly delineated in writing, and that all parties, including the child, to civil child protection actions should be represented by competent counsel.

A *third* area of effort leading to reform in child protection cases lies in the use of mechanisms of administrative accountability that can help assure that both child welfare agencies and courts do their jobs more effectively. Despite laws mandating time limits for placements and hearings, and despite the legal requirement of "reasonable efforts" from CPS to keep families together, children too often face intolerable delays in case resolution, and their parents frequently don't receive the services they need to preserve and strengthen the family. In such situations, system oversight can be provided, and accountability (including permanency for children) enhanced, through volunteer CASA (court-appointed special advocate) advocacy and *pro bono* lawyer representation for the child, by such programs as citizen foster review boards, and through the creation of strong child welfare ombudsman offices (24). Although almost all states have CASA programs, many states have neither of the other programs, or have underfunded programs with inadequate authority to properly investigate problems or complaints about system breakdown or to get their recommendations heard by high-level policy makers and courts.

The common difficulty of the judicial system in achieving permanent placement for children in foster care within a reasonable amount of time presents a *fourth* reform challenge. In my view, all voluntary parental placements of children, except in emergency, short-term situations, should receive a periodic and on-time review by the court and trigger the appointment of a CASA for the child. To prevent "dumping" of children into foster care, all voluntary parental placements of older children should require special prescreening by a child welfare agency adolescent services unit. That unit, or the court, should provide a program to mediate parent-child disputes or should offer free family counseling services, so as to avoid unnecessary intrusive intervention by the judicial system. There should also be timely and definitive judicial permanent placement orders, prompted by a "permanency hearing" to be scheduled no later than twelve (rather than the present eighteen) months after a child has been in continuous foster care. In addition, we should put into effect a new legal presumption that either a child will be returned home at that time if it is safe to do so or a termination of parental rights process will be begun then, unless the court states in writing substantial reasons why both of these options are inappropriate.

Finally, the *fifth* and most complex issue that we must face in child protection legal system change is achieving the proper balance between a child-centered and a family-focused framework of laws. Although federal legislation on family preservation and support services was vitally needed, and should be implemented with the involvement of all child protection advocates, we must do a better job of keeping children out of dangerous and cruel homes. Family preservation and reunification is a well-supported policy. Yet, the goal of keeping families together and the responsibility of the courts to fulfill that goal can lead to terrible injustices, including death, to children after they have already been, at least once, seriously harmed by their parents. The legal requirement to make "reasonable efforts" to preserve families should not be construed to require heroic, futile, or unrealistic efforts.

Once a court has found a parent to have inflicted harm directly upon a child by severe neglect, severe physical or sexual abuse, or through gross negligence allowed such serious harm to be inflicted by another, and once the child or the perpetrator has been removed from that home, the burden of proof should shift to the parent seeking full restoration of the parent-child relationship. The law should also establish the presumption that the child will not be returned to, or remain in, that home unless there is a judicial finding that it is safe to do so. Additionally, there should be a child-centered ground for termination of parental rights in cases when the child has been in foster care for a long period of time (for example, several years), when there may be adults wishing to adopt, and when the child is strongly adverse to being returned due to past severe abuse, neglect, or abandonment.

Conclusion

In 1992 the nation was briefly transfixed by the case of a twelve-year-old Florida boy known only as "Gregory K." Unlike highly publicized child abuse homicides about which the public could only agonize and rue the failure of the system to protect children, this case gave citizens all over the country the opportunity to watch an actual child protective judicial process in which the affected child himself sought justice. Cameras were allowed into the otherwise private realm of the juvenile court, broadcasting Gregory's trial live all over the world. In many ways, this boy was representative of the thousands of faceless abused or neglected children identified annually for whom the primary public agency response is removal from home, who languish in the limbo of foster care, and whose parents are never criminally charged in connection with their maltreatment. Although child homicide and sexual abuse cases get the most attention from the media, most child maltreatment cases that enter the judicial arena are similar to Gregory's.

Gregory's case got so much attention because it was, erroneously, styled as a landmark case of a boy "divorcing" his parents. In reality, Gregory's legal action simply sought a commonplace judicial response to protracted child maltreatment. The press completely overlooked the fact that there had been a significant amount of court intervention in Gregory's family long before he filed through his own attorney a petition to terminate parental rights. The issue of whether, in such cases, children should be given the "keys to the courthouse door" to initiate a court action related to their own care and protection will likely remain unresolved for some time. But Gregory's need as a "neglected child" to approach the court on his own behalf, or else suffer continued neglect by the state, illustrates how far child advocates of all professions have yet to go in making the judicial system fully responsive to maltreated children.

References

1. Mason, T. P. 1972. Child Abuse and Neglect, Part 1: Historical Overview, Legal Matrix, and Social Perspectives. *North Carolina Law Rev.* 50:293–302.
2. Larsen, J., and Horowitz, R. M. 1991. *Judicial Primer of Drug and Alcohol Issues in Family Cases.* Washington, D.C.: American Bar Association, Center on Children and the Law, with the National Association for Perinatal Addiction Research and Education.
3. 18 U.S.C. §§2251 et seq.
4. 25 U.S.C. §§1901 et seq.
5. Nicholson, E. B., and Bulkley, J., eds. 1988. *Sexual Abuse Allegations in Custody and Visitation Cases: A Resource Book for Judges and Court Personnel.* Washington, D.C.: ABA Center on Children and the Law.
6. 42 U.S.C. §672(e).
7. 42 U.S.C. §§675(5)(B), 675(5)(C).
8. Amendment to section 107 of the Child Abuse Prevention and Treatment Act, 42 U.S.C. §5106a, in the amendments of 1996, P.L. 104-235.
9. Hardin, M. 1984. Children Living Apart from Their Parents. In *Legal Rights of Children,* ed. R. M. Horowitz and H. A. Davidson. Colorado Springs, Colo.: Shepard's/McGraw-Hill.
10. Haralambie, A. M. 1993. *The Child's Attorney: A Guide to Representing Children in Custody, Adoption, and Protection Cases.* Washington, D.C.: ABA Family Law Section.
11. Duquette, D. 1990. *Advocating for the Child in Protection Proceedings: A Handbook for Court Appointed Special Advocates.* Lexington, Mass.: Lexington Books.
12. ABA Center on Children and the Law. 1990. *Lawyers for Children.* Washington, D.C.: ABA.
13. Whitcomb, D. 1987. *Guardians Ad Litem in Criminal Courts.* Washington, D.C.: U.S. Department of Justice, National Institute of Justice.
14. American Bar Association, Presidential Working Group on the Unmet Legal Needs of Children and Their Families. 1993. *America's Children at Risk: A National Agenda for Legal Action.* Washington, D.C.: ABA.
15. American Bar Association. 1996. *Standards of Practice for Lawyers Who Represent Children in Abuse and Neglect Cases.* Chicago: ABA.

16. National Council of Juvenile and Family Court Judges; Child Welfare League of America; Youth Law Center; and National Center for Youth Law. 1987. *Making Reasonable Efforts: Steps for Keeping Families Together.* San Francisco: Youth Law Center.

17. Trost, T., and Bulkley, J. 1993. *Child Maltreatment: A Summary and Analysis of Criminal Statutes.* Washington, D.C.: ABA Center on Children and the Law.

18. U.S. Advisory Board on Child Abuse and Neglect. 1990. *Child Abuse and Neglect: Critical First Steps in Response to a National Emergency,* recommendation no. 28. Washington, D.C.: U.S. Government Printing Office.

19. U.S. Advisory Board on Child Abuse and Neglect. 1991. *Creating Caring Communities: Blueprint for an Effective Federal Policy on Child Abuse and Neglect,* recommendation D-6. Washington, D.C.: U.S. Department of Health and Human Services, Administration for Children, Youth, and Families.

20. U.S. Advisory Board on Child Abuse and Neglect. 1993. *Neighbors Helping Neighbors: A New National Strategy for the Protection of Children,* recommendations 17–19. Washington, D.C.: U.S. Government Printing Office.

21. Feller, J. N.; Davidson, H. A.; Hardin, M.; and Horowitz, R. M. 1992. *Working with the Courts in Child Protection.* Washington, D.C.: U.S. Government Printing Office.

22. Whitcomb, D. 1992. *When the Victim Is a Child.* 2d ed. Washington, D.C.: U.S. Department of Justice, National Institute of Justice.

23. Myers, J. E., and Perry, N. W. 1987. *Child Witness: Law and Practice.* New York: Wiley.

24. Davidson, H. A.; Cohen, C. P.; and Girdner, L. K. 1993. *Establishing Ombudsman Programs for Children and Youth: How Government's Responsiveness to Its Young Citizens Can Be Improved.* Washington, D.C.: ABA Center on Children and the Law.

23

Alternative Forms of Intervention

CATHERINE MARNEFFE

I have looked closely at who is guilty of child
abuse and have discovered it is I.

EDWARD ZIGLER, *Child Abuse and Violence*

From the earliest attempts to deal with the issue of child maltreatment, differences in concept and philosophy have arisen between the judicial approach to child rescue and the social work approach to child protection and protective services. Although these fundamental conflicts regarding the correct approach to caring for the maltreated child are now more present than ever, ideological controversy on this issue of child abuse is not really being addressed.

Analyzing the broader social context in which child protection in our modern societies is organized has not received enough emphasis. Evidently it is not easy to think about the larger context of child protection work in the day-to-day practice because there are so many overwhelming practical problems to be solved. This probably explains why destigmatizing and decriminalizing child maltreatment is not yet possible, why controlling responses are implemented so easily, and why the usual intervention is still, at least in regard to sexual abuse, a legal one. Mandatory reporting of abused and neglected children, thereby using a strategy of legal or social coercion against the perpetrators, is still considered as *the way* society will overcome this difficult problem.

Many authors in the United States have critically analyzed the crusade against child abuse and neglect, revealing both that professionals face a double mandate to help and to socially control and that families needing help hesitate to consult professional services (1–4). Accordingly, the conclusive report of the U.S. Advisory Board on Child Abuse and Neglect proposes "comprehensive, multidisciplinary child abuse and neglect treatment programs to all who need them . . . increasing efforts to support and strengthen families" (4). Practical initiatives such as the "homebuilders" in New York and Washington states are already functioning in this spirit, emphasizing the importance of family therapy to achieve protection of the child by his or her own parents rather than by the state (5).

Alternative forms of intervention are thus to be understood as alternatives to traditional child protection work and based on a new concept and practice of child protection work.

CATHERINE MARNEFFE, M.D., Ph.D., is a child psychiatrist and child and family therapist, specializing in the treatment of child abuse and neglect. She is the founder of the Confidential Doctor Center at the Vrije Universiteit of Brussels.

Comprehension and compassion, the offer of noncoercive services and voluntary support for those who fail in their familial relationships, are extended instead of stigmatization and reporting and the obligation to visit a specific agency for those who are labeled child abusers (6). This nonpunitive response to child abuse and neglect developed simultaneously in several western European countries in the early 1970s. The Confidential Doctor Bureau, created in 1972 in the Netherlands, was the first of these alternative agencies (7), followed by the Kind in Nood (Child in distress) Confidential Doctor Center in Belgium (8), and the Fifth Province in Ireland (9), reflecting the same background philosophy that had been introduced by Reinhart Wolff in the Berlin Child Protection Center in 1975 (6). Other initiative declarations (as yet unpublished) have led to the creation of similar nonpunitive alternative agencies in Austria, Italy, and Switzerland.

The Confidential Doctor Bureau was inaugurated without legal statute. Although the central figures, the doctors, are attached to a judicial structure of protection (the Raad voor Kinderbescherming [Council of child protection]), they can work independently with the support of a multidisciplinary team. Doctors are required to register reports, encourage intervention, advise other doctors or professionals with cases of abuse, and monitor each situation. This model was created to encourage private physicians to report cases of child abuse without breaking their confidentiality.

The Kind in Nood Confidential Doctor Center in Belgium was revamped in 1986 in reaction to the failures of its previous therapeutic framework. This framework, although embedded in a well-organized national public welfare system, contained the possibility of unintended coercion in professional acts of helping. The physician who lead the Center along with the other team members behaved as therapists, but they also acted as policemen or judges whenever they could not handle the parents' abuse of a child. This confusion of roles put the helpers as well as the families in a no-win situation, which prompted the team to examine itself and to implement an alternative, nonpunitive model. It is this evolution from the traditional to a new child protection paradigm that I will analyze in this chapter, in three parts:

1. an examination of the functions and philosophy of the Confidential Doctor Center;
2. a review of the effects on abusive families of traditional judicial and medico-psycho-social models of intervention;
3. a study of the influence on the treatment of abused children of the broader socioeconomic and political context in which child protection work is implemented.

The Confidential Doctor Center: An Alternative Model of Child Protection Work

The Kind in Nood Confidential Doctor Center is one of the seventeen multidisciplinary child- and family-oriented centers subsidized since 1983 by the Belgian Department of Social Welfare for the nation's population of 10 million people. The total annual cost is BEF 200 million ($7 million), and the funds are spent to provide direct help to abused children and their families. A total of 6,550 abused children visited the centers in 1993, from a total population of 1,800,000 children ranging from newborn infants to sixteen-year-olds (10).

The Belgian government has followed the Dutch example in deciding explicitly against mandatory reporting of child abuse (8). Cases of child abuse and neglect may be reported to the centers, but there is no legal obligation to do so. However, these child protection centers are not exclusively in charge: child abuse cases may be reported to the legal authorities when individual citizens do not trust health workers or when team members from these centers estimate that they cannot offer a therapeutic solution in a particular abusive family situation.

The Belgian government chooses to consider child abuse and neglect as social deviance and, as such, to keep it as much as possible outside the judicial sphere. This decision was based on data from previous research (conducted between 1979 and 1983) which showed that 80% of the abused children whose families completed family therapy returned home afterward with no further incidence of injury (11–13). Enough room has been made available now for doctors and other health professionals to respect confidentiality and to develop the helping relationship with abusive parents considered as basic for effective child protection. The state, after all, does not really provide environments better for children in the long run than their own family home.

Analysis of the Weaknesses

Before 1986, Kind in Nood used to work in an ambiguous spirit, outside the judicial system but unintentionally behaving like a punitive system anyway. This situation led the center's team to become aggressive, depressed, and tired. Parents were violent and too often kidnapped their children out of hospital or residential care against medical advice. The same abusive relationships that parents were having with their children were reproduced by the professionals in their dealings with the "bad" parents. Threat of sanctions, removal of the child as punishment for parental behavior, judgments instead of offers of help and services in answer to the parents' needs were wielded by the team without self-reflection or question. These tensions resulted in failures with dramatic consequences for the children—reinjuries, and even death. Between 1979 and 1986, 1 child was killed and 58 were reabused among 374 children followed in a prenatal primary prevention program sponsored by the center (12). Gradually, analysis of the tensions brought to light the duality of what is expected of professionals, the conflict between their role as therapists helping the individual family and their role as social controllers enforcing conventional behavior. Under further scrutiny, several aspects of the team's poor functioning also came to light.

1. Professionals' collaboration with the judicial authorities provoked confusion and a lack of credibility and trust, resulting in many parents' understandable hesitation to consult the centers.

2. The team's wish to control the situation often resulted in the imposition of authoritarian measures on the family, provoking conflicts between professionals and the abusive parents, who did not feel supported by proposed attitudes but, rather, frankly scared.

3. The energy spent in control, repression, and scandalizing could not be used for comprehending the underlying broad psychological and social factors, for therapy or for support.

4. The resulting tensions provoked conflicts within the team and burnout reactions in its individual members.
5. Most important, the team's threats of sanctions against the family, removal of the child, and
   belief that fear of repression would dissuade parents from harming their children set up a
   relationship to the families in fact not really different from the abusive relationships within
   the families that the team was ostensibly trying to treat.

It became clear that it was not possible to affect violent relationships other than by offering
another type of relationship, one based on openness, understanding, and trust in the hidden
possibilities of each family. It appeared that it was not enough simply to implement these
centers, even when relying on a full-fledged welfare system of services; it was just as essential to clearly differentiate therapeutic work from judicial work, not only as a system but
also in daily practice.

These outcomes brought the Kind in Nood Confidential Doctor Center to question
such traditional approaches as prosecution and close collaboration between therapeutic and
legal systems. The real question they faced, as we should today, is not How do we control
violence? but Is there a therapeutic response to destructive family relationships? Is the
primary responsibility of professionals to help children or to support the legal system?
Consequences such as incarceration for the perpetrator and loss often of both mother and
father, as well as school and friends, for the victim are more than unsatisfactory solutions.
Child abuse is a *conflict* in the parent-child relationship; separation of the child and parent
by out-placement of child or parent is a *rupture* of that relationship, corresponding to the
underlying (naive) wish or idea that separation will cure the conflict. Family disruption is
thereby created and reinforced; this cannot really be called therapeutic. Indeed, it often
results in strong denial from each person involved. Moreover, data show that 60% of
abusive parents themselves had experiences with juvenile courts and institutions for child
care during their childhood (14). To repeat the cycle of out-of-home placements cannot
be called therapeutic either. Additionally, we have to recognize that the judicial system—
already reluctant to condemn the paterfamilias and requiring clear, full forensic evidence—
is often unable or at times unwilling to take any legal measures against the parents, leaving
both the children and the parents alone with their unsolved problems.

Confronted with the risks of interventions more detrimental than beneficial to the child
and family, the Kind in Nood Confidential Doctor Center developed an alternative approach to child abuse in general, including child sexual abuse, largely influenced by Reinhart Wolff's model of child protection work introduced in Berlin in 1975 (6, 15).

Developing New Strengths

The philosophy underlying Wolff's effective work with abused children and their parents
consists of offering help instead of punishment, respecting confidentiality instead of implementing control, showing solidarity instead of making reports, mobilizing the family's own
resources instead of maintaining their passivity, and finally, collaborating with other professionals instead of competing against them.

Attractive, free, preventive and therapeutic mental and physical health services and social services, available at one location, are conveniently provided to the family (6, 15–17). Services offered include crisis intervention and telephone counseling; child, couple, and family therapy; a high-quality residential structure attached to the ambulatory unit; professional training and supervision; and research activities and teaching. These services are offered without control or sanctions: police and criminal court actions are not being sought. Consolidation of strength in families and children can be achieved only by means of a broad-minded approach aiming at voluntary participation of the family, not at its submission under the threat of court action.

Psychotherapy can be successful only if the patient is provided with an assurance of privacy and a sense of trust permitting the most open and intimate expression of thoughts and feelings. Confidentiality is an essential aspect of the therapeutic interaction (18, 19). Therefore, parents with difficulties or those who have endangered their children should be able to come spontaneously and of their free choice to places where they know they will get help without the risk of social or judicial control. To diminish their fear of being depreciated or judged, services have to be offered without delay, free of charge, and with a guarantee of anonymity.

The aims of this new child protective care are to relieve the family immediately of an actual crisis situation, to guarantee the well-being and security of an abused or neglected child, and to offer the child educational and therapeutic help. Additional aims are to work through the conflicts that led to the abuse and any actual separation from the family and, finally, to develop a sound perspective for the child and the family.

Coercive interventions that breach the privacy of the family should be permitted only on specific grounds, when there is an urgent necessity to implement a policy of decisive or emergency life-saving intervention in cases of serious bodily injury or abandonment. Moreover, these grounds for coercive intervention should be well known in order to provide advance warning to parents and to set the boundaries of restraint on the state's power to inquire and intervene into the affairs of the family (17).

This does not mean that judicial authorities have no role to play in the legal protection of children, especially when parents do not see the utility of treatment. Instead of reporting these abusive parents to the attorney, often behind their back, the social worker should, when necessary, accompany and support the parents in their contacts with the legal authorities. Although this situation is rare, it does pertain to "untreatable" parents or parents who are not willing or able to question themselves about their children's upbringing. They often live lives too difficult to enable them to take care of their children. These parents may be drug addicts, mentally handicapped, or psychotic. They are often too damaged and too destructive to be helped enough to be able to care for their children. In these cases, the professional should assist the parents in taking the necessary legal steps for finding other psychological parents, as urged by Goldstein et al. (20). In fact, police or other law enforcement agencies do not have to be involved very often. In 1992, only 167 cases of child abuse and neglect (out of a population of 1,800,000 children) were followed by judicial authorities in Belgium (21). A total of 6,550 cases, including cases of child sexual abuse, came to the attention of the centers in 1993 without any police involvement (10).

Even if judicial intervention is rarely required and rarely necessary, the helping system needs to be organized in a more responsible manner. Wolff's model thus proposes a multi-professional team approach instead of a disunited, hierarchical, bureaucratic social service approach. A meeting is organized by the professional team of the center for all of the professionals involved in, or worried by, the child's situation (teachers, family doctor, social worker, etc.), only if the parents and child agree that such a meeting should be held. The aim of these meetings is often to coordinate the helping efforts of these professionals even though they work in such different contexts. Fragmentation of responsibilities, competition between professionals, and identification with mother, father, or child that ends up reproducing family conflicts by proxy can be avoided by involving all of the professionals in the decision making concerning the family. Again, the family must be willing to agree to the team's involvement; families are not coerced into accepting this approach.

This model aims at providing universal services based on the principle of need, with services accessible to everybody. A special setup like the multidisciplinary Child Protection Centers in Germany and the Confidential Doctor Centers in Holland or in Belgium can be successful only if they can rely on a welfare state system with services ranging from general health insurance to low-cost public and private day care and schools, from low-cost counseling to free infant-and-mother health care, and from social assistance for people in need to family services and family aids. As Wolff puts it: "This social welfare structure greatly reduces the chance of having environments with a large amount of poverty and deprivation and thus contributes to having fewer and less severe cases of child maltreatment" (6, p. 5).

The Work of the Confidential Doctor Center

The daily work of Kind in Nood is practically organized around three functions.

1. The center offers direct assistance to and management of abused children and their families. This means that children are protected in the family and remain with the family whenever possible. Even if a safe place has to be found for them outside the family, the parents are involved in the decision making.
2. The center offers support, supervision, and counseling for professionals confronted with child abuse. Help for the families necessitates help for those who work with them.
3. A more general function of the center is prevention. The focus here is more on changing public opinion through education and public awareness than on trying to change the family, because child abuse and neglect cannot be reduced to a simple problem of bad or pathological parents.

Direct Assistance to and Management of Abused Children and Their Families This function covers four major steps:

1. Direct or indirect contact between the abusive family and the center
2. Assessment of the abused child and arrangement for protective measures to be taken if necessary
3. Offer of help to the child and his or her family
4. Continued protection of the child or return of the child to his or her family

The *first step* concerns the first contact between the abusive family and the center. Parents are encouraged through the media and through the distribution of leaflets to come in when something goes wrong with their child, when they are worried about their child's development, when they often quarrel about their child, when the child upsets them, when they think only hitting the child can help, when their child has been ill-treated in the past, or when they themselves were abused in childhood. Kind in Nood does not support reporting campaigns: citizens should not function as the "eye of the state." Instead of reporting a neighbor, individuals are encouraged to think of what they can do to help; the act of reporting is thus transformed into an act of solidarity. Accordingly, information concerning high-quality treatment programs is provided for all families in difficulties, motivating them to ask for help in confidentiality rather than goading them to hide from the surveillance of massive reporting campaigns.

Professional services have to be as accessible as possible for abusive parents and their children. Kind in Nood was reorganized to increase its accessibility through:

- the provision of an attractive, high-quality multidisciplinary facility, offering immediate mental and physical therapeutic services and social services (all these services are available without payment, twenty-four hours a day, seven days a week at each center);
- the guarantee of anonymity without judicial intervention (police and criminal court action are not sought by the center, although individuals are supported if they wish to consult the legal authorities);
- the offer of a real personal relationship to the parents in order to help them understand first themselves and then their child without threat or sanctions.

To respect anonymity and provide a large range of high-quality services available twenty-four hours a day, the center was located within the Children's Hospital of the Vrije Universiteit (Free University) in Brussels. Nobody can tell if parents are in the waiting room because their child is suffering from pneumonia or because they abuse their child.

When the safety of the child is jeopardized, the child can stay in the pediatric ward, which has a school, a garden, and a playroom, as well as rooming-in facilities for the parents, available without charge. The support of the hospital administration is of course indispensable, not only for evident financial reasons but also for moral reasons.

From 1986 to 1994, the center received referrals of 3,858 abused children, of which 997 were sexually abused. Half were referred by hospital services (like the pediatric and psychiatric outpatient departments) or external professionals; the other half were referred by family members. Self-referrals for all kinds of abuse by the abusive parents themselves occur now in 36.5% of the cases. However, this was not the case in the beginning. Before 1986, when collaboration with judicial authorities was the norm, only 3% of the parents came to the center on their own initiative.

Once the parents and the child have arrived at the center, the *second step* of direct assistance provided to them consists of the diagnosis of evaluation of risk. The first interview always includes the child with both parents, mother *and* father. Because fathers play a significant role in the family, we cannot expect to have a positive impact on the family problems without recognizing and addressing their part in the occurrence of child abuse.

The first interview is essential for two reasons. *First*, the interviewer needs to be able to examine the child and gather as much information as necessary to correctly evaluate the situation: How is the child? Does the child need to be protected immediately? Are the parents willing to think and talk about themselves? How do they live? What do they have or want to offer? *Second*, the first interview has an immediate therapeutic value: a confidential relationship can be established from the start if the interviewer concentrates on the parents' difficulties, on their previous life history, and on the intrafamilial emotional climate rather than on aggressively interrogating them about the abuse or neglect itself. This does not mean that the interviewer cannot be very firm about the fact that the child has been abused or that the parents at least have great difficulties regarding his or her upbringing. Instead of trying to reconstruct exactly *what* has happened, it seems more relevant to try to understand *how* it happened and how it can be prevented in the future. The guiding principle is to establish a trusting relationship with the mother and father from the start. Consequently, the first interview should not be focused primarily on the child and his injuries—yet neither should it lose sight of necessary treatments for the child. The interviewer's observation of the child's attitude, play, and relationship with his or her parents (as well as with the interviewer) are essential for evaluating the degree of further danger.

Another goal of the first interview is to convince the parents of the usefulness of a thorough assessment. I cannot emphasize enough how important it is to refrain from making a diagnosis of child abuse and neglect until after completion of a full assessment, which consists of a physical and psychological examination of the child, an interview of the parents, an interview of the parents and the child together, and a meeting of all the professionals involved, always with the consent of the child and his or her parents. The assessment's main aim is to gain more insight into the best way to help the child and his parents, not to find more evidence proving the abuse.

A thorough examination of the abused child, without danger for the child, sometimes requires a temporary hospitalization. Indeed time is needed to evaluate the entire situation seriously without putting the child at further risks. Hospitalization in high-quality conditions appears better than out-of-home placement for protecting the child for a short period without compromising the prospect of long-term protection within the child's own family. At Kind in Nood, hospitalization is always available immediately, which offers round-the-clock protection of the child, anonymity for the parents, and the status of a "child needing care" rather than that of "a difficult or bad child." Hospitalization provides not only high-quality assessment for the children and parents but also the opportunity of having more incisive therapeutic sessions with the parents without imperiling the child. Of the children referred to Kind in Nood, 27% were hospitalized during the first three weeks after the abuse was mentioned, discovered, or reported.

It is also important to be able to interview and see all the siblings. Sometimes they are much better off, but it often happens that they also show signs of neglect and/or abuse. They deserve their share of explanation, attention, and care.

The *third step* consists of the offer of help to the child and his or her family. Practically, therapeutic sessions include all family members, which does not mean that each person cannot also be seen individually. The adult needs help for the same things as the child does, and, to a certain extent, the therapy of the adult is similar to that of the child, being basically a "reparenting process" (11, 18). Abused children especially need to have their separate therapist, whom they can trust, before they can be brought to trust their parents again. The aim of therapeutic work is to enable the abused child to express his or her feelings of sadness, fear, shame, anger, guilt, and loneliness within a supportive setting distinct from the family but constantly sensitive to the family relationships. But even when the child is protected from harm by being separated from the family (for example, by being hospitalized or placed in a foster home), this separation should never be considered as therapeutic in itself. The question of the child's bonds with his or her parents always remains, whatever happens. The evolution of these bonds and the capacity of the child to live with them and to elaborate them will determine his or her openness to happiness, his or her capacity to be, to prevail—or, on the contrary, his or her predilection to sadness, his or her tendency not to be, not to thrive. Even if these bonds become chains, as they will when certain parents find themselves incapable of freeing their children from the weight of their own past or their imaginary projections, therapy still has to include the parents in the child's therapeutic process and in any decisions leading to out-of-home placement or to curtailing parental contact. The best way to help children is always through their parents.

Successful therapy therefore can come only from the different actors in the family drama confronting one another, so that each can understand the underlying mechanisms leading to the violent acts. Therapy for the children needs to provide enough scope to treat the consequences of abuse and to help them develop more self-esteem, more confidence, and some trust. However, child psychotherapy will always be more successful if parents are involved from the start. This involvement should not be limited to the parents' own therapeutic process, which will enable them to become more aware of their own difficulties, but should also extend to their child's psychotherapy, as well as to the global process. A family therapy approach will help each family member to confront his or her own life history and to exorcise his or her past so as to break old patterns of interaction within the family. Meanwhile, parents are encouraged in their individual therapy sessions with another practitioner to think about themselves, about their own childhood, about their sorrow as children, and about the sorrow they have provoked within their own children. Children as well as parents are brought to recognize, first, their anger toward their abusive parents, then their sadness, and finally their hopes. Only then does the possibility exist for a new type of relationship, following the model of the open professional relationship offered to the family at the center.

Psychotherapeutic work should thus adapt to the needs of the abused child and the family, not vice versa. If nothing but threats, aggression, contempt, and indifference are offered to abusive parents, professionals should not be surprised if their clients respond in kind. Despite the parents' outward objections and great resistance to therapeutic involvement, they often have a deeper feeling of desperation and loneliness and a stronger need of help than at first appears. Most abusive parents are aware of what they have done, but they are afraid of the depreciative and accusatory responses they might receive from the caretaking personnel. They thus react with indifference or, worse, with aggression. Although professionals usually expect patients to be motivated for treatment, to be pleasant, friendly, and trustful, and not to miss appointments, most abusive parents will disappoint professionals holding these expectations. Counselors and therapists therefore have to adapt their expectations to fit their clients as they are. Abusive parents cannot be forced to change by moralistic judgmental pseudoprofessional attitudes. Professionals, especially those with a theoretical background, should encourage change by offering a safe environment and ideas that parents can accept, use to grow, and use to develop their own thinking processes and self-esteem.

It must be clear that a positive attitude to abusive parents does not mean that decisions cannot be made against parents on the behalf of their children if they are in danger. But even if the family has to go through a process of separation, it is most important for the child and his or her parents to do it in close and continuous contact with one another whether or not they reject professional help.

Reporting to or collaborating with the judicial authorities is unthinkable if therapists are to establish a trusting relationship with families, for confidentiality is an essential aspect of the therapeutic intervention. When judicial authorities are necessary—judicial intervention was needed in 7% of the cases reported to Kind in Nood, when abuse was severe and no agreement was possible with the parents—a referral can be made to the juvenile court in consultation with the parents and never behind their backs. These cases mostly concern psychotic, mentally handicapped, or drug-addicted parents, or parents who are not prepared or inclined to care for a child. Their child is not wanted, something that is often not heard by professionals, who then try to persuade the parents to accept their parental duties rather than help them relinquish their parental role and look for a more satisfactory solution.

Therapeutic interventions are sometimes long and difficult. To be successful, three conditions must be met:

1. The therapeutic agency must have the financial backing of the government: an open, free, and high-quality service with twenty-four-hour coverage is expensive ($500,000 per year for eight full-time professionals, supported by the infrastructure of a public hospital, serving a population of 180,000 children, for the center in Brussels at which I worked).

2. Professionals must be open and honest with their clients if parents are to be more aware of their children's needs and to put this awareness into practice.

3. Parents must be able to understand who they were as children themselves before they should be asked to understand their own children. Only when abusive parents recognize the child in themselves will they be able to differentiate their own suffering from their child's sorrow and pain.

The *fourth step,* the center's final step in providing direct assistance to abused children, consists of the reintegration of the child in the family. There are no overall rules: each case needs an individual approach, and decisions about the child are taken progressively and together with the parents. This can avoid poor and hasty decisions regarding the child's future. To quote Dr. Brandt Steele, any improvement should be "explored to determine whether it is the real improvement which *can* happen quickly in a relatively less damaged personality, or whether it is evidence of a lifelong ability to deny the self and adapt very quickly to the expectations of the environment without any real internal change taking place" (22, p. 389) (and see chapter 26). When the child is in protective care, professionals need to ascertain if the therapy has produced real change in the parents' attitudes, or if the improvement has resulted merely from the removal of the problem child from the family.

So far, 81% of the 3,858 children referred to the center between 1986 and 1994 were returned into their families. One child died under guidance, and 26 (0.7%) were reinjured and brought back to the center by their parents. Follow-up of families is facilitated in Belgium because it is a small and crowded country, supported by a well-organized public welfare structure in permanent contact with nearly all families with children.

Support and Counseling for Professionals Confronted with Child Abuse   The center tries to disseminate its knowledge about and approach to nonviolent child protection work. It distributes information to professionals and students and also engages in training programs. Information is provided through leaflets, conferences, published writings, and public debates appearing in the print and broadcast media. Most important, however, is the center's promoting of new projects in the field.

Training of professionals is based on the center's experience with many practitioners involved in cases of child abuse. These practitioners' lack of an intellectual approach and a theoretical framework are often impressive. Usually this lack of knowledge does not concern child abuse itself so much as child development and general human conflicts. What is most striking is the fact that professionals' feelings of isolation, anxiety, anger, and indignation are responsible for alarmingly hasty decision making or, conversely, for minimization of problems and refusal of responsibility. Consequently, training has been centered not only on theory and technique but, more essentially, on the acquisition of increased understanding and control of their own feelings of anger and despair through role-play and fantasy games. Professionals are encouraged "to become" abusive parents and abused children in order to understand better the complexities of such situations.

Case conferences are organized for each child that enters the center. The Confidential Doctor Center invites all professionals involved to exchange information and develop a better working plan, after permission of the parents has been given. (The parents are always kept informed of what conclusions these meetings reach, particularly when a very concrete treatment program is proposed.) These discussions not only serve to support the professionals involved but also make them think about themselves.

Most professionals feel paralyzed by family violence and do not know how to handle such a difficult problem. Especially in cases of sexual abuse, professionals often either hesitate to intervene or else they react with a repressive attitude. By the time an abused child is referred to the center, that child has come into contact with a mean number of five professionals. These professionals know the child's family is having difficulties, and they try to help; frequently, though, they do not realize that child abuse is occurring and they are not able to consider analytically or compassionately the conflicts which are causing difficulty. This center's pragmatic form of training makes professionals more familiar with the most effective type of help to offer to abused children and their parents. The main goal is to help professionals feel enough at ease to be able, when they are confronted with violence toward children, to take the initiative toward abusive families.

Prevention of Child Abuse Prevention of child abuse starts with adequate information about the problem. The center challenges society's responsibility for child maltreatment by stressing the link between interpersonal and intrafamilial violence, which are issues involving everyone. The center refuses to be identified as the specialized structure responsible for the solutions to all the problems of abusive families. Medical and legal solutions to the problem of child abuse are not the center's purview. In addition, research is organized to introduce new insights in therapy, to enlarge general views on the problem, and to provide up-to-date information in order to offer better treatment to problem families.

Analyzing the Effect of Current Interventions on Abusive Families: Judicial versus Medico-Psycho-Social Models of Intervention

Whether child abuse is considered to be a crime or deemed to be a result of family dysfunction determines the way that society responds to it. At the core of the controversy about the proper role of the judicial system in dealing with an incidence of family violence is the question, To what extent does child abuse represent a violation of criminal law? By 1874, for example, the New York Society for the Prevention of Cruelty to Children, which was organized as a result of the famous Mary Ellen Wilson case, was given police powers, still in effect to this day (23). Perhaps this explains why the Massachusetts Society for the Prevention of Cruelty to Children, established in 1878, became known as "the Cruelty," suggesting eloquently the recognition and fear of its function, mainly centered on the removal of children from their families via judicial intervention.

In the *judicial model,* abuse and neglect of the child by his or her parents may be considered a criminal offense, and the first solution is to punish and penalize the abuser. This corresponds with a violent disapproval of deviant attitude and assumes that not to punish these parents amounts to giving them the right to martyrize their children. Although sanction hits the perpetrator, it does not heal the victim's wounds—the recognition of this appears as a leitmotiv throughout the professional literature (6, 11, 24, 25). The reputed benefits of prosecution for all offenses, including child abuse, is currently met with considerable skepticism. We can find ample illustration of penalty's feeble powers of dissuasion in the Susan Auckland case. This little girl was killed in Great Britain in 1974 by her father, who had previously been convicted for the murder of another of his children (26). Moreover, the punitive approach to the child's situation is often disastrous. The child is separated from his (or her) family, which he considers as a punishment, blaming himself for what happens to his parents. His parents, who were already marked by life—by their own past family lives and by social inequalities and injustice—are now exposed to yet more familial and social stigmatization. The results will be more isolation, more tensions, more reasons to feel bad about themselves, and thus more risk that they lose control and attack their children without seeking help, their distrust in society having been confirmed by its repressive intervention (7).

All parents who abuse their children were abused, although many do not remember or cannot put words on what was done to them. If they could, they would not be abusive: violence to children is always the enactment of a violent past. If you are not the victim of injustice, familial or social, you do not become violent and you do not abuse your own flesh and blood, your own child.

Judicial repression has today resulted in the development of judicial protective interventions that recognize the social importance of the family unit. In this context, abusive parents are no longer seen as guilty but, rather, as deficient and susceptible to being helped in their parental role by an action of judicial control with a socioeducative character.

Other forms of judicial interventions have thus emerged, more aimed at protecting children and supporting the family as a whole than at sanctioning the parents' inadequate behavior. Judicial protection has become the mainstream way to set up guidance or to promote counseling for the abused child and/or abusive family. Some authors in the field have gone even further, contending that threatening abusive parents with prosecution brings them into brutal contact with the reality of their situation and thus encourages them to accept treatment (27; 28, p. 70; 29–31).

In most countries (Norway, France, Great Britain, Canada, the United States) where mandatory reporting of suspected child abuse to child protective agencies has been introduced, professionals face civil and criminal penalties if they fail to report suspected cases (32). These agencies are charged with supervising the application of criminal and civil laws on child abuse and neglect to individual cases as well as with following up on families to whom guidance is proposed. Such agencies' reports may lead to administrative or court-ordered investigations, which can result in the filing of a formal petition or complaint against a parent and, in effect, a trial on the allegations of abuse and neglect (33).

The *medico-psycho-social model* assumes that child abuse and neglect are best understood as the result of a family dysfunction. Both abuser and child are perceived as victims influenced by broad sociological and psychological factors beyond their control (1). Accordingly, the parents have to be helped to normalize the relationships with each other and with their children. Protection of the abused child is also deemed a priority, but the child is more often maintained in his family and the parents provided with services to support them and help them cope with their child (11).

In this model, the child protection practitioners' approach to the abuse issue is frequently subjective or intuitive; attorneys, on the contrary, are unwilling to accept conclusions or impressions lacking empirical corroboration. For practitioners, the clinical "feeling" that a family is under stress or needs help, or that a child is "at risk," is enough to prompt intervention; lawyers, on the other hand, demand "hard" evidence (34). However, even when therapy seems advisable and possible, that does not necessarily mean the parents will consent to proposed interventions. As a result, it often happens that professional interventions become like judicial inquiries—inquisitive, moralizing, sometimes stigmatizing—even though they are supposed to be free of any judgment and based on the offer of help and counseling to families with difficulties (35). Such attitudes can culminate in threats to report the parents to the judicial or administrative authorities—more social control, and without the safeguards, guarantees, and rights offered by the justice system (26).

Many professionals have questioned the wisdom of their being cast as both the agent of social control and the helper of families in extremis (15, 35, 36). Although child welfare agencies should offer their assistance to violent families, they are in fact too often functioning as the disguised emanation of justice (26). Professionals' dependence on administrative or judicial authorities provokes a certain confusion and results in a lack of credibility and trust, not to mention an understandable hesitation of the parents to consult these services (34).

Both models, the judicial and the medico-psycho-social, are thus difficult to differentiate, since judicial authorities, responsible for implementing social control, are often proposing therapeutic solutions, while medical, psychological, and social services responsible for providing therapy, are often too controlling and not therapeutic enough. There is, consequently, a confusion of roles, since practitioners often use justice as "a stick behind the door," taking the place of the judge, while magistrates sometimes hesitate to make their own decisions, substituting a chorus of therapists of varying ability.

Moreover, findings in three American studies (16, 32, 35) show that in a majority of cases of child abuse, therapeutic services are not provided because of the urgency of investigation, regardless of the model in operation. Besharov (32) recognizes that mandatory reporting results in too many reports, too many unsubstantiated reports, too many intrusive investigations with deleterious consequences for children and parents, without comparable help being given to the children who really are in danger. However, Besharov does not question the reporting system itself. Currently, because of the urgency of investigating functions, social workers are forced to spend the majority of their time conducting investigations and completing the accompanying forms. The result is of course that little time is left for the therapeutic role and that many children are not better off for having had their cases reported.

Out-of-home placement is the most frequently provided service, but only one-third of the children who are placed receive any clinical services (16, 37). On the other hand, therapy in itself often presents retributive aspects, as pointed out by Illich (38). The less "curable" the abuser—that is, the more vindictive and independent the abuser—the less treatment will be offered and the more punitive will society's response appear (34). Socially marginal individuals are more likely to be defined as deviant than others are, since characteristics frequently identified with the "battered child syndrome" are associated with poverty (11). Professionals thus engage in an intricate process of selection, finding facts to fit the label that has been applied and becoming agents of social control, in defining aberrant behavior as a medical problem or a legal problem and in recommending treatment or court action.

In consequence, the "helping" services that can actually be offered are inadequate in most communities. The standard of professional action is so low, and so distressing are the consequences of incompetent intervention for the family, that a new philosophy in child protection work has to be conceptualized. It is not the medico-psycho-social model in itself that is inappropriate: the conceptual bases of medical and social practice need to be broadened and the intellectual and scientific repertory of the practitioner expanded (3, 39). Physicians and social workers need to become more aware of the complexity of human life, especially its social and psychological dimensions. Indeed, the strong emphasis on child abuse as a problem of individuals means that other equally severe problems of childhood can be ignored and the unequal distribution of social and economic resources in society can be masked. It seems that unless a diagnosis of abuse is made, such services as high-quality counseling, child care, and homemaker services are not available to many families in need (24).

Moreover, there are not enough therapists willing to handle all cases, since many therapists believe that abusers lack the introspective and conceptual abilities necessary for successful psychotherapy. Nor do most abusive parents have the time, money, or disposition for long-term therapeutic involvement. Under these conditions, less adequate treatment strategies or even clearly punitive alternatives, such as court action and foster placement, may be implemented.

As Solnit pointed out in the early 1980s: "The community is increasingly read to observe and report on suspected instances of child abuse and neglect and decreasingly ready to be tolerant, accepting, and supportive" (17). Such an attitude of course results in a control-oriented approach to child maltreatment, which is characteristic of traditional child protection work. Almost no systematic attempts are made to prevent family violence (40, p. 284): action is taken only when "a case" has been established. The main aim is to identify perpetrators or offenders who have to be prosecuted and punished in order to protect their children from them. The causes of child abuse and neglect are mainly seen as located in the personality of the abuser. In this framework, interventions, always done "in the best interest of the child," look more like fights against the parents than like real attempts to help the family.

The ambulatory and residential services that are offered are underdeveloped and accessible only to the designated victims. In most cases, fathers and the larger family and environment are not included in the helping process (40). Also professional teamwork is rare, resulting in poor exchange of information and, therefore, even more need for control. The mandatory reporting system reinforces the view of clients as targets and deprives the majority of people in need of services of the right to freely choose their helpers—a right professionals would not tolerate losing.

The Influence of the Socioeconomic and Political Context on Child Protection

It is crucially important to situate child protection work in the broader social, economic, and political context, to understand that professionals and clients are equal and that the crusade against child abuse is the result of a social construction.

Child maltreatment is not yet generally understood to be a socio-psychological, cultural, political, and gender problem. That is, most people do not see that anybody could become a child abuser, depending on their specific relational and societal circumstances (6). Child abuse and neglect differ only in quantity, and not in quality, from the usual attitudes of adults toward children. Furthermore, child abuse and neglect do not differ much from violent behavioral patterns that are obvious and even highly praised on other levels in our society but suddenly no longer tolerable when enacted in the home. On the one hand, our Western economy emphasizes freedom of the individual, opportunities of the individual, and responsibilities of the individual. On the other hand, the same society expects parents not to behave in the family as competing individuals using their power to dominate their weaker children but as compassionate nurturers moved by their children's well-being and preoccupied by the fate of the smallest. People who have suffered financial, social, or moral problems are blamed for their failures, but it becomes suddenly intolerable when parents blame their children for their failures (41–43). This does not mean that parents should be allowed to exploit their children. It means that behavioral patterns in abusive families are the mirror image of societal attitudes. This is well illustrated by the actual ongoing tendency to cut welfare budgets in the United States and in the European community. Governments refuse to support the "undeserving poor" but expect these same families to support, nurture, and understand their "undeserving" children (as we all sometimes experience our offspring).

As Gelles (44) pointed out almost thirty years ago, child abuse and neglect amount to a social construction. Of course, children were injured, abandoned, or tyrannized before people began to call these problems "child maltreatment"; the particular descriptive terms in use indicate the social construction in process. Today child abuse is most often described as a pathology or a crime—in other words, as an individual qualitative problem—but we will never get to the roots of the problem without analyzing the social context in which it is generated and enhanced. Child abuse is more fundamentally a social than an individual problem: it is not a fact of nature; it is a discourse.

This approach may sound irresponsible, since children experience a very real problem when they are hit, burned, yelled at, or ignored. This approach does not contend that there is no violent behavior on the part of parents toward their children, that there are no families in need of services or no abused and neglected children. It does contend that objective statements are impossible, because any statement arises from the same social context in which these problems of family violence arise. The areas of medicine, law, social work, and psychotherapy have generated different responses to these problems and various "constructions of reality." A similar approach should also be undertaken by the family: Each family member will have to understand his or her own particular construction of the reality to be able to change it, to adapt a new behavior, and to eliminate or at least diminish dysfunctional patterns underlying the child abuse and/or neglect. Is hitting a child a form of abuse, a way to educate him, the expression of rage or powerlessness? Is it necessary for the child's upbringing, or is it the result of parental failure? Do the parents share their ways of seeing the same facts? How does the child experience what occurs to him or her—as a cruel act from his or her parents or as a well-deserved reaction to his or her bad behavior? Parents indeed have to be encouraged to talk about why they want to destroy each other, they have to acknowledge their involvement in the family disputes, and they have to be brought to develop a new understanding of their children and their relationship with them: in other words, they have to reconstruct their perception of reality (6). The same is true for professionals: they have to include themselves in the problem they are defining. This means that they should question themselves, their knowledge, and their attitudes if they are to provide coping strategies less destructive than the ones used by parents who abuse their children.

A positive change in families can be only achieved when the problem that has to be changed is viewed in a broader context. Families without social or extended-family support, families with little prestige, money, and power suffer frustration and bitterness all the greater and thus will resort to more violence. The same can be said about social policies that provide insufficient means, insufficient staff, poor services, and correspondingly inadequate solutions (like mandatory reporting and deprecating and controlling attitudes in social work and medical practice): the result is to decrease the likelihood of adequate change, development, and growth in the families.

Child abuse cannot be isolated from the larger social and cultural institutions that unwittingly encourage it (45). Most public settings (day care centers, schools, courts, child care agencies, welfare departments, and social service institutions) generally promote negative and hostile attitudes toward children (46). What about our hospitals, which provide excellent technical care, only to abandon the most needy young families at the hospital door because psychological help is not reimbursed by health insurance? Worse, though, is the legally sanctioned, massive abuse of children who cannot profit from the policies and practices of comprehensive welfare systems or of the children living in foster homes or institutions (24, 45). Indeed, how many professionals would leave their own children for more than one day in the care of the institutions they so warmly recommend? Not to mention the political and economic violence of the developed countries against children in the developing countries, victims of systems the West condemns but activates at the same time: wars, child labor, and child prostitution.

Many authors famous in the field of child protection have discouraged fragmentary efforts aimed at one or another cause of child abuse (6, 45, 47–49). Instead they propose fundamental changes in social philosophy and value premises, in societal institutions and in human relations. They advocate changes centered on eliminating such social inequalities as poverty, unemployment, and bad housing instead of on holding abusive and neglecting parents accountable in a disproportionate manner. Although this model does not offer specific practical advice, critics of it are rare in the literature. This does not reflect a general approval but, rather, its marginal status, the fact that it is considered to be the position of a minority. Today, more than ever, it is clear that these types of basic changes are not going to come about immediately. Even in western Europe, where comprehensive public welfare seemed to be an achieved value and a guarantee of at least some equality, this fundamental right is, alarmingly enough, threatened daily by the increasing economic crisis.

However, by recognizing this major social evolution toward a truly comprehensive public welfare, we cannot afford to lose sight of the reality of damage in children, the misery of their parents, and the isolation of many professionals. Appropriate care that answers the needs of violent families instead of controlling them should thus be organized within a comprehensive welfare system. This was clearly noted by the U.S. Advisory Board on Child Abuse and Neglect: "The most serious shortcoming of the nation's system of intervention on behalf of children is that it depends upon a reporting and response process that has punitive connotations, and involves massive resources dedicated to the investigation of allegations. State and County child welfare programs have not been designed to get immediate help to families based on voluntary requests for assistance" (50, p. 80).

Conclusion

Violence is not the exclusive province of some marginal parents but is part of our society and culture—it is a daily lifestyle and a customary way of thinking. Preventing and treating child abuse and neglect thus requires overcoming repressive and punitive attitudes not only in families but in the wider societal context. Perhaps, to start with, professional controlling attitudes based on indifference and denial or, on the contrary, on reporting and scandalizing should be thoroughly examined and not simply projected onto abusive parents. Are the actual child protection agencies philosophically and materially ready to approach this delicate issue without provoking more misery than already exists in these families? Are clinics and services really equipped to offer a safe environment and ideas that the abusive families can use to develop their own understanding and self-esteem? The answers have been given by the four reports of the U.S. Advisory Board on Child Abuse and Neglect stressing the need for nonpunitive access to comprehensive care (4, 50–52). Even when child protection is embedded in public welfare it can still harbor the possibility of unintended coercion in professional acts of helping. It is not enough for professionals to situate their work in a broader social and political context: professionals questioning the problem of family violence should also question their own violent or neglecting attitudes. If they wish to help, they must not only engage both in humble tasks and in more complex negotiation with organizations on behalf of their clients, they must also regard their clients as fellow and equal citizens.

Although excessive medicalization is certainly not to be encouraged, it is nevertheless a reality that most distressed parents turn to their private doctor or to a hospital-based service when they are concerned about their children's health or strange behavior. Doctors, pediatricians, psychiatrists, and social workers thus have to create places within their practices or hospitals where people who harm their children would not be afraid to come, where parents and children would be able to talk about what happened, to show the darkest parts of their souls without threat or fear of sanction, and where, especially, doctors would not react to them the way many abusive parents react to their children, by ignoring, rejecting, threatening, or moralizing, without asking for their opinions or eliciting their best hopes.

Successful therapeutic responses to child abuse and neglect are possible if a new model of child protection is offered—one based on empathy, trust, and encouragement for those who fail in raising their children—in place of the traditional approaches based on mandatory reporting, control, judgment, and sanctions. This new system should provide high-quality treatment instead of high-intensity control, including more options of support for professionals, teamwork training, and a manageable caseload for the field-workers (instead of scapegoating them and giving them more and more work until they are burned out).

The difficulties facing practitioners dealing with child abuse cases are increased by daily interactions with regressive political, societal, and individual constructions of reality, shown more than twenty-five years ago by Gelles (44) and Gil (45) and reaffirmed by a new national survey on American parental attitudes toward children (53). Despite these previous efforts to unravel the social and economic context of child maltreatment, the problem of intrafamilial violence has become a widely debated political issue with little attention paid to its interrelation with public violence.

Evidently, we have to recognize that despite the tremendous amounts of energy and money that have been spent for the prevention and treatment of child abuse and neglect, the results that have been obtained are sadly disappointing. This is not because alternative forms of intervention have yet to be tried. It is because the alternative forms of new child protection work are still not the framework of majority.

References

1. Kagan, R., and Scholsberg, S. 1989. *Families in Perpetual Crisis.* New York: Norton.
2. Pittman, F. S. 1987. *Turning Points: Treating Families in Crisis and Transition.* New York: Norton.
3. Bush, M. 1988. *Families in Distress: Public, Private, and Civic Responses.* Berkeley and Los Angeles: University of California Press.
4. U.S. Advisory Board on Child Abuse and Neglect. 1993. *Neighbors Helping Neighbors: A New National Strategy for the Protection of Children.* Washington, D.C.: U.S. Government Printing Office.
5. Kinney, J.; Haapala, D.; and Booth, C. 1991. *Keeping Families Together.* New York: Aldine de Gruyter.
6. Wolff, R. 1991. Child Protection in Germany. *Violence Update* 2 (3):4–6.
7. Koers, A. 1981. *Kindermishandeling,* ed. Uitg, 8–9. Rotterdam: Ad. Donker.
8. Marneffe, C.; Lampo, A.; Proost, G.; and Boermans, E. 1987. *It Shouldn't Hurt to Be a Child.* Brussels: Confidential Doctor Center, Vrije Universiteit.
9. McCarthy, I. C., and Byrne, N. 1988. Mistaken Love: Conversations on the Problem of Incest in an Irish Context. *Family Process* 27:181–99.
10. Marneffe, C. *Jaaverslag Kind en Gezin* [annual report of the Belgian government public health agency for children and families]. 1992. Brussels: Kind en Gezin.
11. Kempe, R. S., and Kempe, C. H. 1978. *Child Abuse.* London: Fontana Open Books.
12. Marneffe, C. 1990. The Use of Psychotherapy during Pregnancy as a Means to Prevent Child Abuse and Neglect. Ph.D. diss., Vrije Universiteit, Faculty of Medicine, Brussels.
13. Clara, R. 1983. Kindermishandeling en Kinderverwaarlozing. *Tijdschrift voor Kindergeneeskunde* 39 (9):543–53.
14. Katz, M. H.; Hampton, R. L.; Newberger, E. H.; Bowles, R. T.; and Snijder, J. C. 1986. Returning Children Home: Clinical Decision Making in Cases of Child Abuse and Neglect. *Am. J. Orthopsychiatry* 56 (2):253–62.
15. Wolff, R. 1983. Child Abuse and Neglect: Dynamics and Underlying Pattern. *Victimology: International J.* 8:105–12.
16. Meddin, B. J., and Hansen, I. 1985. The Services Provided during Child Abuse and/or Neglect:

Case Investigation and the Barriers That Exist to Service Provision. *Child Abuse and Neglect: International J.* 9:175–82.

17. Solnit, A. J. 1980. Child Abuse: Least Harmful, Most Protective Intervention. *Pediatrics* 65 (1):170–71.

18. Green, A. H. 1979. Expanding Psychiatry's Role in Child Abuse Treatment. *Hospital and Community Psychiatry* 17:356–71.

19. Steele, B. F. 1986. Notes on the Lasting Effects of Early Child Abuse. *Child Abuse and Neglect: International J.* 10:283–91.

20. Goldstein, J.; Freud, A.; and Solnit, A. J. 1973. *Beyond the Best Interests of the Child.* New York: Free Press.

21. Dupont, Ms. [contact person], Nationaal Instituut voor de Statistiek [Brussels]. 1992. Personal communication.

22. Steele, B. 1987. Reflections on the Therapy of Those Who Maltreat Children. In *The Battered Child,* 4th ed., ed. R. E. Helfer and R. S. Kempe, 382–91. Chicago: University of Chicago Press.

23. Shepherd, J. R. 1987. Law Enforcement's Role in the Investigation of Family Violence. In *The Battered Child,* 4th ed, ed. R. E. Helfer and R. S. Kempe, 392–401. Chicago: University of Chicago Press.

24. Gil, D. G. 1978. *Violence against Children: Physical Child Abuse in the United States.* Cambridge, Mass.: Harvard University Press.

25. Eisenberg, L. 1981. Cross-Cultural and Historical Perspectives on Child Abuse and Neglect. *Child Abuse and Neglect: International J.* 5:299–308.

26. Somerhausen, C. 1979. Les Reactions: Controle social, formel et informel. In *Aspects crimologiques des mauvais traitements des enfants dans la famille,* 87–134. [Paris]: Publication du Quatrième Colloque Criminologique du Conseil de l'Europe.

27. Wolfe, D. A.; Aragona, D.; Kaufman, K.; and Sandler, J. 1980. The Importance of Adjudication in the Treatment of Child Abusers: Some Preliminary Findings. *Child Abuse and Neglect: International J.* 4:127–35.

28. Deltaglia, L. 1976. *Les Enfants maltraites: Depistage et interventions sociales.* Paris: Editions E.S.F.

29. Larter, D. 1979. Social Work in Child Abuse: An Emerging Mode of Practice. *Child Abuse and Neglect: International J.* 3:889–96.

30. Rosenfeld, A. A., and Newberger, E. H. 1977. Compassion versus Control: Conceptual and Practical Pitfalls in the Broader Definition of Child Abuse. *JAMA* 237 (19):2086–88.

31. Criville, A. 1983. Role mobilisateur du mondat d'autorité et du placement dans l'intervention sociale pour les enfants maltraites. *Child Abuse and Neglect: International J.* 7:451–58.

32. Besharov, D. J. 1985. An Overdose of Concern—Child Abuse and the Over-reporting Problem. *AEI J. Government and Society* (Nov.–Dec.):25–28.

33. Guyer, M. D. 1982. Child Abuse and Neglect Statutes: Legal and Clinical Implications. *Am. J. Orthopsychiatry* 52 (1):73–81.

34. Newberger, E. H., and Bourne, R. 1978. The Medicalization and Legalization of Child Abuse. *Am. J. Orthopsychiatry* 48 (4):593–607.

35. Drew, K. 1980. The Role Conflict of the Child Protective Service Worker: Investigator-Helper. *Child Abuse and Neglect: International J.* 4:247–57.

36. Pelton, L. J. 1989. *For Reasons of Poverty: A Critical Analysis of the Public Child Welfare System in the United States.* Westport, Conn.: Greenwood.

37. Cohn, A. H. 1986. *An Approach to Preventing Child Abuse.* Chicago: National Committee for Prevention of Child Abuse.

38. Illich, I. 1976. *Medical Nemesis: The Expropriation of Health.* New York: Pantheon.

39. Engel, G. 1977. The Need for a New Medical Model: A Challenge for Biomedicine. *Science* 196 (14):129–36.

40. Wolfe, D. A. 1994. The Role of Intervention and Treatment Services in the Prevention of Child Abuse and Neglect. In *Protecting Children from Abuse and Neglect: Foundations for a New National Strategy,* ed. G. B. Melton and F. D. Barry. New York: Guilford Press.

41. Muller, R. T.; Caldwell, R. A.; and Hunter, J. E. 1993. Child Provocativeness and Gender as Factors Contributing to the Blaming of Victims of Physical Child Abuse. *Child Abuse and Neglect: International J.* 17:249–61.

42. Keniston, K. 1979. Do Americans Really Like Children? In *Child Abuse and Violence,* ed. D. G. Gil, 274–85. New York: AMS Press.

43. Katz, M. B. 1989. *The Undeserving Poor: From the War on Poverty to the War on Welfare.* New York: Pantheon.

44. Gelles, R. J. 1979. The Social Construction of Child Abuse. In *Child Abuse and Violence,* ed. D. G. Gil, 145–57. New York: AMS Press.

45. Gil, D. G. 1975. Unraveling Child Abuse. *Am. J. Orthopsychiatry* 45:345–56.

46. Dubanoski, R.; Inaba, M.; and Gerkewics, K. 1983. Corporal Punishment in Schools: Myths, Problems, and Alternatives. *Child Abuse and Neglect: International J.* 7:271–78.

47. Garbarino, J. 1977. The Human Ecology of Child Maltreatment. *J. Marriage and the Family* 39:721–35.

48. Pelton, L. H. 1978. Child Abuse and Neglect: The Myth of Classlessness. *Am. J. Orthopsychiatry* 48:608–17.

49. Pelton, L. H. 1990. Resolving the Crisis in Child Welfare. *Public Welfare* 48:19–25.

50. U.S. Advisory Board on Child Abuse and Neglect. 1990. *Child Abuse and Neglect: Critical First Steps in Response to a National Emergency.* Washington, D.C.: U.S. Government Printing Office.

51. U.S. Advisory Board on Child Abuse and Neglect. 1991. *Creating Caring Communities: Blueprint for an Effective Federal Policy on Child Abuse and Neglect.* Washington, D.C.: U.S. Government Printing Office.

52. U.S. Advisory Board on Child Abuse and Neglect. 1992. *The Continuing Child Abuse Emergency: A Challenge to the Nation.* Washington, D.C.: U.S. Government Printing Office.

53. Wolfner, G. D., and Gelles, R. J. 1993. A Profile of Violence toward Children: A National Study. *Child Abuse and Neglect: International J.* 17:197–213.

24

Treatment of the Child and the Family Where Child Abuse or Neglect Has Occurred

DAVID P. H. JONES

In this chapter our topic is treatment for the abused child and her or his caregivers. Treatment is considered here in its widest sense, including the process of enhancing change in the child or parent or both. It includes a wide variety of activities and is not restricted to psychological or psychiatric treatment. Rather, we will be concerned with all the activities that aim to produce change. Although my emphasis in this chapter is on treatment of intrafamilial maltreatment—maltreatment that has occurred within the family—I will also refer to extrafamilial abuse and to the treatment of abusers. The chapter describes a practitioner approach to the treatment task, which the reader can supplement with reviews of treatment outcome studies (e.g., 1. 2).

Treatment itself is intimately bound up with assessment, relying on it as a house relies on its foundation. Consequently, assessment continues throughout the treatment process, despite a change in focus during its course.

A Developmental Perspective on Child Abuse and Its Treatment

The approach to treatment I describe here is grounded in a child developmental perspective on the phenomena of child abuse and neglect. This approach emphasizes the changes in individuals over time, both quantitatively and qualitatively. It stresses that the developing child simultaneously becomes increasingly differentiated and integrated, moving toward states of greater complexity and organization as his or her life unfolds. Although this approach centers upon the individual, it also recognizes that the child's development is multidetermined, ranging from genetic and constitutional influences, via physical and psychological factors, to influences emanating from the family, neighborhood, and cultural spheres of life. One key principle in developmental theory is that the individual is continually adapting to the environment in which he or she lives. The overall purpose of such adaptation is to maintain an integrity of basic biological functions, including the physical, psychological, and social. This theory places particular emphasis on the interplay between these different aspects of development. Further, once the individual achieves a degree of competence, or a higher level of organization in any one area, this paves the way for further increases in competence in that particular sphere of life, as well as in other areas of development.

DAVID P. H. JONES, Mb.Ch.B , F.R.C.Psych., D.C.H., is consultant psychiatrist, Park Hospital for Children, Oxford, England, and senior clinical lecturer in child and family psychiatry at Oxford University.

.rast to this overview of normal development, pathological development is con-
a lack of integration of the individual's competence in social, emotional and/or
fields of functioning. When significant disruption occurs in one of these fields,
y at an early age, not only is that particular ability or area of competence potentially damaged, but the basis for the next developmental achievement can also become
derailed, producing a cumulative effect with relatively greater levels of disturbance as the
individual grows. At the same time, subsequent influences following early trauma or disruption can tend to further potentiate earlier damage—although, alternatively, they can also
be ameliorating.

The developmental approach allows us to develop a model that illustrates the multifaceted nature of the key influences upon a child's development. At the same time, we
can consider the potential etiology, occurrence, and consequences of child maltreatment,
which will then put us in a better position to plan treatment efforts. For this purpose, I have
chosen to integrate the ecological perspective advanced by Belsky (3) with Cicchetti and
Rizley's conception (4), which emphasized subsequent factors that could potentiate or
compensate for early childhood trauma. Such an integrative model can incorporate individual mechanisms alongside the broader social influences which bear upon the child; in
this way, a broad range of influences can be covered. Figure 24.1 illustrates these influences
diagrammatically.

At the center of the diagram is the context within which child abuse or neglect is first
discovered. Although the initial focus of investigation will be the child and his or her parenting, this soon expands to encompass other relationships and influences upon the child.
The first to consider are the immediate family influences in the child's home, then the
extended family's effect, moving outward to include school factors, the quality of the
child's neighborhood, his or her social contacts, and the family's degree of isolation. This
is the ecological perspective on the maltreated child's situation, taking into account individual as well as family and social network influences.

However, this is a snapshot in time, and, as Belsky's model emphasizes, child and
parents all bring their entire histories to bear upon the situation in which maltreatment
occurs. It is well known that the parents' individual childhood experiences significantly
influence both their personality and their level of sociability. The residual influences of
these childhood experiences do not operate automatically, or all abused children would
grow to be abusive or victimizing adults—which clearly does not happen. The proposed
mechanism for processing these experiences is via the parents' internal working models
and subsequent assimilation of their childhood memories (see reviews by Main [5] and by
George [6]). Healthy as well as unhealthy adaptations to early childhood trauma are possible, offering hope to survivors of maltreatment.

Children also vary in temperament and in the extent to which they represent an added
stress factor for the parents. For example, a child's gender may be of great importance,
positively or negatively, as far as a parent is concerned. Some children are perceived as, or
may actually be, different from others so far as the parent is concerned, making them more
vulnerable to their parent's disappointed expectations.

Once maltreatment has taken place, and before we can consider the possible outcomes

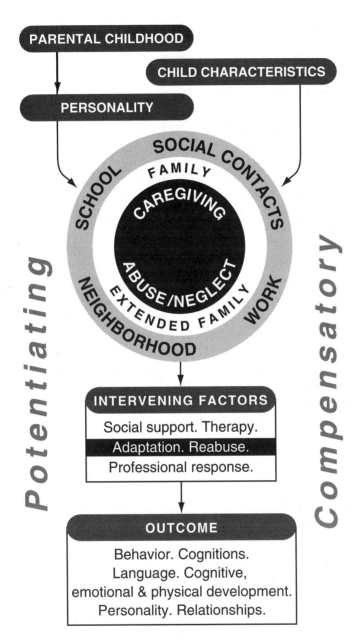

24.1 Child abuse from the perspective of developmental psychopathology.

for the child, we need to take into account a range of intervening variables. These can extend from influences at work within the individual child to familial and broader social influences. An important individual aspect is the manner in which the child adapts to any abuse or neglect, as well as whether he or she suffers reabuse. The diversity and quality of subsequent close intimate relationships with caregivers, friends, and family is also important. In addition, broader social support and influences, including therapeutic efforts, may have significant positive or negative effects upon the child. The nature of the professional response—all of the professionals involved and the expertise and energy they contribute—of course also informs the way the case is conducted.

Finally, at the bottom of the diagram, we consider outcome for the child. We can consider outcome in terms of the child's or adult's behavior and emotional life, but we must also keep in mind important outcomes in terms of cognitive patterns, personality, and relationships with significant others.

When child maltreatment is regarded in this way, we can see that the form maltreatment takes may not be the decisive factor affecting outcome; contextual elements and subsequent events become equally, if not more, salient to the eventual outcome. The more recent studies of the impact of child sexual abuse have clearly demonstrated the multifaceted pathways through which abuse and its surrounding context influence outcome (7). Claussen and Crittenden (8), for example, found that the degree and extent of accompanying psychological maltreatment were more important than the severity of physical abuse so far as eventual outcome for the child was concerned. Not all studies have found severity of abuse to be less significant than the quality of caregiving, but even these studies lend weight and pertinence to the multifaceted view of the occurrence and outcome of maltreatment by the very design of their investigative approach.

Aims of Treatment

The aims of treatment ideally are to help the child and his or her family and to ameliorate the child's social context by:

1. Stopping abuse or reversing neglect
2. Ensuring adequate caretaking
3. Improving the capacity for positive interpersonal relationships, in both child and family members
4. Addressing any symptoms of psychological disorder
5. Managing any sexually aggressive, violent, or exploitative behavior that is directed toward the child

The first priority is to create safety for the child and to prevent the recurrence of maltreatment. This will almost inevitably first require protecting the child through separation of abuser and abused or through a verifiable agreement with the child's primary caregiver that contact between the two will be controlled. In some instances, particularly those involving neglect or psychological maltreatment, it may be more appropriate to focus on promoting the child's welfare through the provision of extra services to child and parents, particularly in cases where the problem involves acts of omission rather than commission. A major aim of treatment is to ensure adequate care, in terms of offering affection and psychological responsiveness, meeting the emotional needs of the child and supplying physical needs and protection. Discipline that is appropriate, direction of the child's behavior, and guidance for the child's moral development also constitute important components of adequate caretaking that must be promoted. One of the most devastating outcomes of abuse and neglect is the effect on the children's future capacity to enjoy close personal relationships, or even to become adequate parents themselves in years to come. Improving this area of functioning is a particularly important treatment aim. Young abused children, when compared with matched controls, already evidence less capacity for empathy with their peers. However, the focus on encouraging positive interpersonal relationships is just as important for the other family members as it is for the child. This aim, from the child's perspective, lies at the root of the prevention of intergenerational continuity of patterns of maltreatment. It seems that the key change which is required, so far as the child is concerned, is in the capacity to form friendships and warm relationships with trusted adults—no mean task for the child who has been abused by a parent or close family member.

Treatment approaches aim to reduce symptoms, both within the child and family members. Management of any parental alcohol or substance misuse must be an early priority in the treatment program, before genuine improvement in caretaking and family functioning can be expected. Violence and sexual aggression among the child's caretakers are another major focus of treatment efforts, as the best work we can do with the child may be undone by a parent's continuing contact with a violent partner. Although initially the threat of violence will be managed through a child protection response, in many cases direct work with the abuser will be a necessary part of the overall treatment approach.

The Treatment Process

The treatment process itself can be considered as a three-stage sequence. This perspective is not meant to be rigidly applied; rather, I offer it as a means of analyzing the process of change into more manageable proportions and to introduce a sense of developmental progression to treatment. I argue that in order for the second and third stages to be negotiated, the first will have been addressed. However, the model is not intended to be implemented in a purely linear, unidirectional fashion. As cases progress in treatment there may well be a need to return to earlier phases in order to renegotiate them in greater detail or sophistication. The phases of the treatment process that I am proposing are:

1. Acknowledgment of abuse and its effects
2. The development of increased parental competence and sensitivity to the child
3. Resolution

Before detailing these phases of change in treatment, we will consider some general principles which are relevant throughout the treatment process.

Some General Issues

In previous work, I have emphasized the value of developing and maintaining a "child's-eye view" during all stages of treatment (9). This does not equate with advocacy; rather, it implies a need for therapists deliberately to adopt a view of life as though from the perspective of the child. The therapist might then consider what it must have been like to grow up in the family in question and live there day by day and, similarly, what it must have been like to sleep there each night and wake up each morning as a member of that family. Such a perspective can be of great value to adult-oriented therapists, since many adult and family therapists do not have training or expertise in child development.

A further issue is that the provision of therapy may be divided between several different therapists or agencies. Those who provide treatment for the adults may be unaware of the child's needs. For example, a therapist working with a maltreated child's parents may consider that his or her clients have made substantial progress and that more access contact with their child would be of benefit to them. Adopting a child's-eye view will raise the equally important question of whether the proposed increase in contact would be of benefit to the child.

Risk assessment permeates all stages of the treatment process, with the focus altering at different points. For example, risk assessment might initially center on whether the child is safe staying in the home, whereas later on the assessment could shift to whether an abuser can safely return. In any case, the assessment of risk will take into account child, parental, family, and wider social influences. Entering into the matrix will also be the seriousness of the abuse. Each domain can be considered in terms of factors which add further to existing risk or in terms of those factors which ameliorate or compensate for other elements of the total picture (10).

Integration of the services provided by different practitioners or agencies is crucial if risk is to be effectively managed, let alone an effective service delivered. This will mean that professionals will have to spend a considerable amount of time meeting and communicating with one another and ironing out any differences. It is here that written agreements, jointly signed by professionals and parents, can be of value, combined with regular review with professionals and, wherever possible, involvement of parents and older children.

The aim of integrated services should be the achievement of a partnership between the parents and the professionals. This partnership is not free-floating but firmly yoked to the common goal of the child's welfare (see chapter 12). If partnership is conceived in this way rather than simply as an attempt to form positive alliances between professionals and parents, the difficulties encountered when an alliance with the parents compromises the safety of the child can be avoided.

Denial of the maltreatment—by the abused child or the abusive parent—can prove a real impediment to any genuine progress. Denial by the perpetrator of maltreatment is not infrequent and sometimes is resolved only by removing the child from the dangerous situation or by the nonabusive caretaker separating from the abusive, denying one. Furniss (11) has provided a clinical perspective on the management of denial in cases of child sexual abuse. He emphasizes exploring in an empathic and safe way the full tragedy and disaster of disclosures of sexual abuse within a family, and he recommends the use of various techniques to reduce the family members' anxieties so that the consequences of disclosure can be gradually converted into potential solutions. Such approaches can also be useful in cases of physical abuse and neglect. The key to treating some parents in denial will lie in avoiding unproductive confrontations with them as to whether the abuse did or did not happen while simultaneously avoiding collusion in any way with parental denial. Sometimes this proves an impossible task, and the parents simply cannot trust professional support sufficiently in order to start to take responsibility for the maltreatment which has occurred.

In studies of consecutive cases of identified child abuse and neglect, a large proportion of abusers either refuse any form of intervention or persistently deny that any problem exists. In such a situation, do court orders from civil child protection courts help or hinder? Do they motivate reluctant parents into treatment when child abuse has been fully substantiated in the courts? Several studies have attempted to answer these questions; in general, the findings support the view that civil court orders can help to motivate some reluctant parents to accept help and assistance.

Treatment Planning

Plans for treatment should be firmly anchored in assessment, as I have been stressing throughout this chapter. Professionals' expectations for change in the child's situation need to be framed as explicit criteria for success or failure. This is necessary not only for the purposes of partnership with the parents (and, where appropriate, the child) but also for the requirements of the civil child protection court. The criteria can best be framed according to the factors that constitute the risk matrix, which I outline below in table 24.1. It will probably be necessary to review the treatment plan from time to time, especially in the more complex cases.

The following elements are necessary in any treatment plan:

1. Statement of problem(s), with specification of domains, with positive and negative features of each (I am using the word *domain* for groups of factors which are related to risk; I intend these domains to help the reader conceptualize the different compartments of the child's world and experience)
2. Proposed process whereby change is to occur
3. Criteria for success and failure
4. Timescale for change

The problems facing the child and family can be analyzed along the lines of the matrix outlined in table 24.1. The positive and negative features for factors within each of these domains can then be clearly identified. This is the essence of a risk management approach in which the elements of the problem are broken down into separate domains that can then be assessed in relation to one another.

TABLE 24.1
Factors Involved in Success or Failure

Domains	Rehabilitation More Likely to Fail	Rehabilitation More Likely to Succeed

Parental	Lack of compliance
	Denial of problems
	
	Personality disorder
	• Borderline
	• Antisocial
	• Aggressive (inc. sadism)
	Substance abuse/alcoholism
	Paranoid psychosis
	Learning difficulties accompanied
	   by mental illness
	Abuse in childhood—not recog-
	   nized as a problem
		Compliance
		Acceptance of problem
		Responsibility for maltreatment
		Mental illness or personality disorder, respon-
		   sive to treatment
		
		More healthy adaptation to childhood abuse

Parenting and
parent-child
interaction
	Disordered attachment
	Lack of empathy for child
	Own needs before child
	Poor competence in several
	   domains (neglect and physical
	   abuse/neglect)
		Normal attachment
		Empathy for child
		
		Competence in some domains

Abuse factors	Severe abuse and/or neglect
	Premeditated, sadistic abuse, e.g.,
	   burns, scalds
	Mixed abuse
	Penetrative child sexual abuse
	   and/or long duration
	Munchausen syndrome by proxy
		If severe, yet compliance and lack of denial, suc-
		   cess still possible
		
		Less severe forms of abuse

Child factors	Developmental delay with special
	   needs
	Very young child, requiring rapid
	   parental change
		Healthy child attributions (in child sexual abuse)
		
		Later age of onset
		
		One good ameliorating relationship with an adult

Professional factors	Lack of resources Ineptitude	Therapeutic relationship with child Outreach to family Partnership with parents
Social setting	Social isolation	More local child care facilities Volunteer networks

Family	Pervasive, diverse family violence
	
	Pervasive, continuing problems
	   with power, poor negotiation,
	   autonomy, and expression of
	   affect
		Absence of other forms of family violence
		
		Nonabusive and/or protective partner
		Negative interactions yet capable of change
		
		Supportive extended family
		Family members who accept that abuse has oc-
		   curred and will reveal recurrence

Based on an appropriate assessment, the process whereby change is expected to occur can then be formulated, at least in broad terms. This might include a range of provisions, from attendance at a self-help group to more specific forms of therapy. It is important to include all the activities which are expected to contribute to the process of change. Most cases will require a mixture of therapeutic approaches. The crucial factor is to make the aims and objectives of the treatment process explicit, following a thorough assessment of the overall predicament of the child.

Having set out the expected process of change, professionals should specify the criteria through which the intervention is to be judged successful or not. It is important to define these criteria as specifically as we can, right at the start of the treatment process, once an assessment has been completed. In this way, the tasks for the professionals and parents are made explicit. This can be of great value in all negotiations with the parents; in addition, these criteria can form the basis for an interprofessional review and, of course, a presentation of progress to the child protection court.

Lastly, the timescale for intervention should be estimated at the start. Once again, this makes expectations explicit to all involved and will help, when combined with the stated criteria for success, to inform decisions about the adequacy of process and whether to pursue a course toward relinquishment of the abusive parents' custodial rights or reunification of the family. The timescale will depend upon the age and developmental requirements of the individual child. In general, infants cannot wait as long as older children, and every effort has to be made to prevent unnecessary and harmful delay.

The outcome of treatment in the field of child abuse and neglect is a complex area, one in which it is hard to make definitive statements (12). In part, the reason for this is the broad nature and variety of predicaments which fall under the overall umbrella of child abuse. I have reviewed elsewhere (10) the effectiveness of intervention strategies and concluded that existing studies (despite their methodological difficulties) do help the practitioner to plan treatment. It is sobering to note that reabuse rates are significantly high. Even if there is no reabuse, the process of encouraging change after abuse and neglect have occurred does present significant difficulties for professionals and families alike. Research findings can be schematized into a matrix (see table 24.1) of those characteristics of cases which have been associated with a more positive outcome in contrast to those characteristics associated with a more negative outcome. While stressing that no single factor should be taken as a definite indicator that a particular child or parent will or will not be amenable to treatment, the matrix can alert practitioners to positive or negative features about their individual case, which might aid the process of treatment planning.

The difficulty for both practitioners and courts is the relative weighing of different factors within each of the domains outlined. In some situations it will not be either possible or safe to calmly weigh one factor against another as though each were of equal relative significance. For, as Gelles (13) has aptly stated, in some situations one blow may be quite enough and family reunification would accordingly be wholly inappropriate to pursue as a goal.

The Three Phases of the Treatment Process

Phase 1: Acknowledgment

This phase of treatment is not merely concerned with confession or admission but, rather, with the parents' taking responsibility for abuse and neglect as well as developing a full and genuine appreciation of any effects the maltreatment may have had on the child(ren). Is it possible to treat a family that denies abuse? Most therapists do not think so. Some families never progress beyond this initial stage and proceed, despite the best professional efforts, to relinquish their children (see "Phase 3: Resolution," below). However, it is always best to start treatment by attempting to find some point of agreement between abuser and professional about some aspect of the abuse or its impact upon the child. Sometimes, after the abuser feels safer with and more trusting of those providing treatment, he or she will be able to face the full reality of the maltreatment. There is a fine line to be drawn between, on the one hand, attempting to form an alliance and shift the process of denial and, on the other hand, entering into a collusion with the abuser that abuse either has not occurred or is of less significance than it really is. Since the acknowledgment phase is an essential prerequisite for later work, we must set adequate time aside for this complex process and provide every opportunity to help family members in their attempts to come to terms with extremely painful emotions.

Acknowledgment will mean different things for each family member: the child acknowledging the memory of his or her victimization, the abuser(s) taking responsibility, and any other nonabusive caretakers acknowledging that abuse to the child has occurred along with acknowledging whatever implications this may have for their own parenting competence.

During this early phase, assessments will have to be made to determine if it is safe for the child to remain with the current caretakers. If the abuse is within the home, it will sometimes be possible to arrange for the child to remain and for the suspected abuser to agree to move out temporarily while further assessment of risk proceeds.

Acknowledgment of the abuse itself by the abuser is a process rather than a single, cathartic admission of guilt. The aim is not simply to have the abuser dramatically confess and then to proceed with the remainder of his or her treatment. Rather, what is needed is a more gradual unfolding of the various elements involved in the abuse. Some abusers make a hasty admission and then request the return of their children. Therapeutic work in such a case would be aimed at expanding the abuser's awareness of the acts of commission or omission for which he or she needs to take responsibility.

In his first session with his daughter in which he was to take responsibility for having sexually abused her, one father said, "Remember when we were in bed together, I touched your pee . . . hurt you . . . shouldn't have . . . all my fault. It is not right for daddies and little girls to touch like that. Daddy wants to get better and never do that again." Later that week, in her individual therapy session, and to her foster parents, the daughter said, "He said it was an accident and was sorry, but he hurt me, and he was awake. . . . It happened lots of times. I shouldn't have let him."

This example illustrates the capacity of even a five-year-old child to appreciate that the acknowledgment made by her father was insufficient. She perceived that he had described an "accident." She was also able to indicate that she knew he was fully conscious and responsible: "He was awake." Furthermore, the father had implied that there was mutual consent when he sexually abused his daughter ("not right for daddies and little girls to touch like that") and had tried to share his guilt with the five-year-old child. Sadly, she took on this burden and guiltily expressed the feeling that she "shouldn't have let him." The session reveals the ease with which the abuser's distorted thinking about consent and sexual activity between adults and children could be transmitted to his daughter. It then became a focus of therapeutic work to help unburden her of this responsibility and to help her understand that it was her father, not she, who had a problem which required attention and assistance.

While under pressure to acknowledge abuse, a family might well split into pairs or dyads and exclude other family members. It appears that the family does this in order to defend itself against the overwhelming anxiety induced by the disclosure of maltreatment within the family. For example, a father and mother may become closer than they have been for many years, overcoming disharmony and even violence to unite and blame the child for being badly behaved (in cases involving physical abuse) or seductive (in instances of child sexual abuse). The child then becomes perceived by the marital pair as being bad, or perhaps a liar, or disturbed. Similarly, a mother and child may collude and align themselves together against the father, despite the fact that the two of them may have their own significant differences or disharmonies. The father is then seen as the source of all the family's ills. Some of these splits and alignments can be seen as a defense against the pain of taking responsibility for abuse or neglect.

The initial aspect of acknowledgment—namely, admitting to the fact of abuse and taking responsibility for it—may be encouraged by various techniques. In selected cases, video- or audiotape of the child's statement, direct quotes, or description of injuries may be used to facilitate the parents' acknowledgment. The therapeutic interview with the child can be helpful in sexual, physical, or emotional abuse cases when used to give feedback to the parents about what has occurred, and the nature and basis for concern. However, we need to exercise caution in exposing the child to further pressure or risk when using this kind of technique. If different therapists are assigned to the abuser or other adult caretaker(s), they will need to keep the exact nature of the abuse clearly in mind in their work in order to counter the abuser's natural tendency toward minimization and denial of the seriousness of the maltreatment.

Sometimes a face-to-face session between abuser and abused can be of great assistance to both parties. Normally, such a session will first involve a selected dyad (such as mother and daughter, or father and daughter); then, if this goes well, the whole family can be involved in further sessions. Siblings are often left out of the initial process, yet they do need to be seen by the family therapist. Joint sessions will also need to be arranged, so that minialliances or collusions, often rooted in secrecy, do not develop anew. The family's task will be to develop an appropriate explanation, or shared script, for the events that is acceptable to each family member. This does not necessarily mean that younger siblings must be informed of all the specific details if they had no prior knowledge of them, but it is recommended that they do need to know what has happened, whether the abuse occurred within or outside the family. It is likely that the siblings will know much more than their parents or the therapist expect them to know. We have found siblings to be genuine therapeutic allies, facilitating family therapy work. Through such processes the therapists can model and facilitate the communication of clear messages and explanations during sessions with the whole family.

From the child's point of view, the experience of being maltreated may have several interrelated components. In addition to any sexual assault, there may be other types of further violence, for example, physically or through threat, which may constitute a significant component of the experience from the child's perspective. In cases of intrafamilial sexual abuse, for example, this component may be as problematic as the sexual assault itself. We have encountered threats of bodily harm or even of death to a child should he or she disclose maltreatment. Threat of violence may not always be so overt, however, and may primarily consist of a misuse of the authority and power bestowed upon parents and caregivers through social convention. The abusers can be said to misuse these privileges in order to obtain the cooperation and subsequent silence of their victim. We learn about this from the victim, not usually from the perpetrator of the abuse. The therapeutic challenge then consists in helping both the abuser and, separately, the nonabusive caretaker to acknowledge to each other and to the child that this violence has occurred. It is essential that we adequately address this component of sexual abuse (which might be termed the *emotionally or psychologically abusive component* of the syndrome), because this parental misuse of power and control is not only critical to the development of sexual abuse in the first place but also represents an insidious pattern of interpersonal interaction that can lead to a recurrence of abuse after treatment. The child may need vindication of his or her experience through confronting the abuser, especially if the abuser is still consistently denying maltreatment. The child can be prepared and accompanied by the therapist to such a session in which the child tells the abuser his or her perspective of what has occurred. This may be hard—few, if any, words may be uttered by the child—but the experience of the attempt plus the support of a trusted adult can be therapeutic in itself. On occasion, the preparation the child makes will be sufficiently therapeutic to obviate the need for confrontation per se.

Acknowledging the impact of maltreatment on the child can vary from appreciation of the developmental consequences of abuse on the child's physical and emotional development to recognition of the behavioral and psychological consequences of maltreatment. Therapists may need to provide parents with a developmental perspective drawn over a long period of time in order to help them appreciate that many years of neglect and maltreatment can produce a child with many problems by the time abuse is discovered. Thus, at first sight, the parents may represent the child's problems as a justification, or at least a rationale, for their abusive behavior, but when they view these same problems over a longer timescale, a different understanding of their etiology emerges. This is not to deny the importance of temperamental characteristics as a potential trigger initiating abusive interactions in some caretakers but to emphasize the crucial importance of the developmental perspective.

It may be difficult for adult family members to appreciate and understand the impact of abuse on their children. At the same time, the process of helping children understand what has occurred is complex because they have frequently suffered many years of abuse, which has significantly distorted their view of life. For example, they may feel the need to protect their parents, in contrast to accepting protection from them. Abused children often take on a significant burden of responsibility for the health and welfare of the very adult who is supposed to be caring for them. They may also develop a conviction of their own "inner badness" through being consistently maltreated.

It may not be sufficient merely to appreciate the pattern of family interaction that currently exists. The family's biography has to be placed in its proper historical context. One approach to this is through working on the family's genealogy, either with the entire family or with specific individuals. During this process, details of the histories of parent-child attachments from conception to the present can be obtained. Emphasis on the development of different individuals enables a gradual unfolding of a full picture of deprivation, neglect, and abuse within the family, which is not solely focused on the index child. It also enables us to place a specific incident of abuse within a broader context.

So far we have considered the initial phase of treatment, that acknowledgment both of the abuse itself and of its effects upon the child. This phase is an essential prerequisite and foundation stone for the second phase of treatment.

Phase 2: Development of Increased Parental Competence and Sensitivity

The aim of this second stage of treatment is twofold: (1) to increase parents' (and caregivers') sensitivity, emotional responsiveness, and overall parental competence with respect to their children; (2) to improve the degree to which caregivers can meet their children's needs. In order to undertake this phase of therapy, parents must be well grounded in an adequate acknowledgment of their problems, as only on this basis can any real improvement in sensitivity to their child's needs and predicament be accomplished. In addition, fresh areas requiring acknowledgment may well arise during this second phase of treatment.

This acknowledgment of the impact of maltreatment can be used to help parents move to a fuller appreciation and understanding of past and current maltreatment. The essential qualities which we hope to enhance in the parents are those of empathy and emotional availability. For therapists, maintaining a child's-eye view will prove helpful in assessing and monitoring the level of progress. There is a tendency for professionals to withdraw after the acknowledgment phase, almost as though acknowledgment is all that needs to be achieved. However, much remains to be done. Old patterns of parent-child interaction tend to return: it is difficult to create true and lasting change within a family. It is not surprising that reabuse does occur; studies of the outcome of intervention have not uncommonly found some recurring maltreatment on the road to recovery (10). I will consider some themes for parents within this second phase and then consider some of the parallel issues for children.

Work with parents and caregivers often comprises several approaches in the individual case, including individual work, family therapy, marital and couple work, and therapies focused on improving parenting capacity and the broader social functioning of the family. In the individual case, emphasis may be placed on one or another approach or on all of them, depending on our assessment of the extent of dysfunction within the family. We will turn to each area of therapeutic work and select themes which illustrate common problems.

Work with Parents   Approaches with nonabusive caretakers will differ from those designed to reduce abusing behavior. However, if alcohol or substance abuse forms an important element of the case, it will be essential to address this before much progress can be achieved in the areas of family functioning and parenting ability.

Nonabusive caretakers—usually, but not exclusively, mothers—will require much support, help, and attention to their own therapeutic needs during this phase. While this theme in therapy has emerged from the study of treatment approaches within the sexual abuse field, it is just as relevant in other areas of child maltreatment. In fact, many authors consider that this area of work has been neglected in the past, yet it may prove to be the key to improving the outcome of cases. The nonabusive caretaker faces many dilemmas, quite apart from the shock of discovery of maltreatment and the public exposure which follow investigation of abuse. Her or his own needs may not be met as the investigation process searches for figures to blame and demands unequivocal allegiance from nonabusive caretakers whose world may just have been shattered.

At the same time, abusers need to be encouraged to accept direct therapeutic assistance for their problem, where this can be clearly identified. Sex offender programs are becoming more established, but equally important are programs for physically violent abusers, so that they can receive direct therapeutic help for their problem. This phase of treatment may well reveal, through careful assessment, more extensive violence among family members than the initial child abuse report implied.

The existence of mental ill health, such as significant depression, will require a direct therapeutic approach. The exploration of the parents' early experience is a natural outcome of our developmental approach to the family's current situation. Almost inevitably, the issue of the parents' own experiences of childhood and being cared for arises. The exploration of their childhood experiences can encourage appreciation of their own children's needs and increase both their sensitivity to their children and feelings of empathy for them. The therapeutic danger here is that adults may consciously or unconsciously use their own prior victimization as a means of excusing current and recent abusive behavior. Hence great care needs to be used by therapists in exploring parental childhood experiences when the aim is to improve current parenting and parental empathy for the children. Selma Fraiberg (14) in her seminal studies of these and similar processes, even went so far as to suggest that individual psychotherapy for abusive mothers should generally occur with the child in the room, to keep the focus of individual work with the adult clearly upon the needs of the infant. The implication of this is very salient for those of us working with parents who are themselves very deprived and may have been extremely badly treated in childhood. One of the easiest traps for therapists to fall into, in their understandable sympathy for a parental history of maltreatment in childhood, is to forget temporarily that the purpose of treatment is to improve the child's predicament; the adult's individual needs should come second and are addressed primarily in order to improve the lot of the child. This is an extremely difficult therapeutic stance to maintain and one which also demands integration of services as a top priority.

The issue of parents' own maltreatment and its relevance to current caretaking competence is not necessarily straightforward. In practice, many parents feel consigned to incompetence by the knowledge that their own childhood was "bad." The issue is not whether a particular adult caretaker was maltreated during his or her childhood but what subsequent meaning he or she has ascribed to these crucial experiences. The extent to which this level of self-understanding can be gained in adult life following a personal history of abuse and deprivation is an important focus of treatment—one intimately bound up with the adult's own capacity for forming attachments with others, including therapists. For many caretakers, then, the disclosure of maltreatment of their children heralds not only the need to face this painful issue about their child but also the need to explore their own maltreatment experiences. Small wonder that for many parents the prospect is too daunting, and they flee. Such recognition does underline the enormity of the task for therapists and should allow for more modest expectations of change.

Work with the Family Family work during this phase of treatment may have many foci, but a key feature will be to enable the family to operate without exploitation and violence. For this to occur, the therapist will usually move toward encouraging open communication of needs and wants between family members and toward discouraging secrecy and the unreasonable wielding of power. Not surprisingly, many abusive persons are terrified of losing control within the family and will need much help with avoiding aggressive or exploitative methods of child rearing.

Establishing boundaries between family members becomes an important focus of concern in this phase: the roles and responsibilities of each member of the family must be distinctly and clearly outlined. As a physical manifestation of such problems with blurred boundaries, there may be no doors on bedrooms or bathrooms, or family members may constantly interrupt and speak for one another, denying the value of individuality, personal feeling, or point of view. Madonna et al (15) found that families where sexual abuse had occurred were distinguishable from other troubled families along dimensions such as these.

Marital or couple work may form an important aspect of the overall family approach as disharmony, sometimes including overt violence, is not uncommon when child abuse is revealed. In reality, the discovery of child abuse frequently leads to termination of adult relationships, and much of our own family work involves a mother and her children without the participation of male partners, as fathers were either transient figures in the first place or have left or been thrown out by the mother at the time of abuse discovery. Nevertheless, we find it crucial to involve male figures in the treatment work wherever we can.

An essential theme of family work during this phase will be to avoid any sense of burdening the child with adult issues and responsibilities. Children are frequently blamed for parental feelings, overtly or covertly. Through tenuous or insecure attachment patterns, it is not uncommon for children to feel a sense of personal guilt and responsibility for having led their parent into abusing them, as they see it.

The improvement of parenting competence is a task that therapists can undertake directly. There are now many parent-training approaches in existence that aim to increase parental competence. The approaches which appear to work best are those with a clear theoretical base and with equal attention directed to both physical and emotional care of the child. Usually a broad-based method is required, one that targets several areas simultaneously and develops different techniques, with parent and child components in parallel. Interventions promoting a single behavior style have not been shown to be effective, unless they are placed in a broader context of enhancing the parenting skills. Our own use of such approaches as part of the overall treatment in cases of abuse has centered on those parent-training methods which are based in an attachment theory perspective of parent-child interrelationships. Bavolek and colleagues have based their approach to enhancing parental skills firmly upon observed deficits (16). They have grouped these deficits into findings that show a lack of empathy among abusive parents, unreasonable expectations of their children's development, and an unusually high dependence on harsh aggressive methods of obtaining control and discipline within their family. The group work which is based on this uses several different educational approaches for parents and children in parallel, with the emphasis on enhancing the qualities opposite to those which distinguish abusive families. We have also been impressed with approaches which work on the parent-child relationship per se, enhancing the quality of empathy and sensitivity between parent and child in the context of relationship play that is guided and responded to by a therapist.

My own conception of parenting qualities includes the following list of essential activities:

1. Provision of adequate food and shelter
2. Obtainment of necessary medical care
3. Protection from harm (abuse and neglect)
4. Security of affective relationships
5. Responsiveness to the child's emotional needs
6. Discipline and guidance of behavior
7. Inculcation of moral values
8. Provision of new experiences
9. Assisting the child in social problem solving

When designing a program for the individual case, therapists should tailor instruction in these parenting qualities to fit the individual assessment. Then therapists will be able to construct a list of strengths and weaknesses within the family from the perspective of these characteristics of effective parenting, to act as a fulcrum for our work (see "Treatment Planning," above).

Management of the family's social isolation can be an important part of treatment intervention. Social casework approaches focus on improving the parents' and family's social functioning and their communication with extended family, friends, and neighbors. Therapy is too often conceptualized purely in terms of individual or group meetings, ignoring the broader social dimension to treatment and outcome.

One of the great problems of describing the process of treatment in the field of child abuse and neglect is that so much else happens besides what is usually construed as treatment. For example, the influence of placement decisions and alternative care arrangements for the children, as well as the involvement of the court, can have significant effects on outcome. Whether placement considerations are handled with sensitivity and/or with an attempt to maintain a working partnership with the parents can also greatly affect outcome. It has been demonstrated that where their birth parents can maintain frequent access contact with children in placement, the probability of their eventually returning home and of ensuring their better mental health is enhanced. Sometimes, of course, this is not possible, and access contact may be overtly dangerous—but usually, if access arrangements are carefully managed, more benefit than harm will accrue.

Outside placements themselves may provide significant benefits for deprived and abused children, who can gain significantly in growth and developmental terms when they are removed from an abusive home. The therapeutic challenge then becomes to maintain any improvements that the child obtained through foster care and even to promote continuing gains when the child returns to the birth family. However, as I will suggest in the next section, family reunification may not always be possible and should not in itself be the only goal guiding the treatment process. The child's welfare and best interests come first, once again, and it is this consideration which will need to drive the direction of therapeutic endeavor toward family reunification or, alternatively, parental relinquishment.

Work with the Child   During this second phase of treatment, the work with the parents and other family members progresses in parallel to the work with the child. The accent here will often be on helping the child to express his or her feelings about the abuse itself and about any accompanying deprivation or neglect (17). Finding words and concepts for states of feeling can be especially difficult for abused children, who, it has been discovered, have significant deficits in their language for personal emotions as well as in their self-esteem and sense of personal worth. Their symptoms may require direct treatment, including the treatment of post-traumatic stress, anxiety syndromes, depression, and other emotional disorders, perhaps including specific areas of symptomatology such as sexually acting-out behavior or self-injurious behavior.

Following the public discovery of the abuse, a child may feel a profound sense of loss. The origin of this feeling may be clear—for example, he or she may miss the parental home and dislike being separated from a loved, nonabusive parent or sibling. Further, he or she may miss the emotional warmth which the perpetrator provided (even though at the cost of abuse). A more subtle sense of loss may originate from the child's realization that a parent did not meet his or her expectations. Guilt sometimes accompanies such a sense of loss, as does depression. Guilt may also derive from the child's sense of having participated in the abuse, a sense compounded by the secrecy which the victim may have been required to maintain. Exploration of issues such as this for the child can help to inform parallel approaches with the family as a whole.

Forming peer relationships and functioning in school and with siblings are often major concerns for the child. Maltreatment effects in this area are common and may require therapists to identify and educationally respond to the child's special needs. In this regard, we have found work with siblings to be very important to case outcome; although frequently forgotten and sometimes hard to work with, they can be enormously helpful in whole-family work. Their insight into aspects of family functioning and blocks in communication can bring a refreshing additional dimension to family work.

The Legal Framework and Partnership under Pressure   Severe abuse is a crime and a danger to child health and development. As such, cases of child abuse may become embroiled in both criminal and civil processes of justice. The criminal courts will be concerned about whether a crime has been committed and whether an abuser should be charged. In parallel to this, individual states and countries have a duty to protect their developing children from harm. Child protection courts within the civil jurisdiction will be concerned with identifying vulnerable children and ensuring that minimum standards of care exist and are enforced. From the criminal rehabilitation perspective, it is felt that some, but not all, of those who sexually abuse children benefit from mandated treatment. Only a few criminal jurisdictions have facilities to divert people convicted of sexual or violent offenses against children into mandated treatment programs, but there are grounds for cautious optimism that this type of approach is more beneficial than simple incarceration. From a child development perspective, the aim must be to reduce the propensity for abusers to repeat their actions. Otherwise more and more children will become victims over time, with the subsequent effects on the development of their personalities and capacities for affection. In parallel to this, we do know that making a child appear as a witness in a criminal court does have a deleterious effect on him or her (18). Whether these harmful effects are in any way open to modification through special measures designed to reduce the trauma to children has not been scientifically proved as yet, although there are encouraging signs that the use of video-link monitors and various other methods to make the process easier for the child, including changes in how children are questioned in court, does help.

We also know that the rates of refusal of treatment in the field of child abuse and neglect are high and that one important question is the extent to which civil court orders, focused on child protection concerns, can motivate a reluctant parent when abuse has been established. Studies which have examined this question, comparing the outcome for court-ordered treatment versus voluntary arrangements, have generally shown that court orders do not obstruct effective intervention and, further, are associated with better results than voluntary ones (10). So the coercive element of child protection court involvement does in fact appear to confer benefit, overall. We do not know yet whether certain subgroups of parents are relatively more responsive to court orders than others; such research would be very helpful to professionals and to the court to aid decision making. The legal approaches that appear to be effective are those which, like the elements of any effective treatment plan, link the discovery of maltreatment to a requirement for a full assessment, identification of strengths and weaknesses within the family, and specification of criteria for gauging the success of intervention, over an agreed timescale. It also seems necessary to outline the expected process of change. The challenge for all systems of intervention, including the legal, is to establish such responses to child maltreatment in partnership with parents. I (19) have emphasized that partnership with parents in this situation is not solely a question of agreement or collaborative work between parents and professionals—it is meaningful only if parents and professionals are jointly focused on the needs and welfare of the child.

Once again we return to the notion of the child's-eye view as a helpful principle through which to gauge whether partnership is truly partnership, so far as the child is concerned, or is merely a euphemism for an unfocused "working together" between parent and professional. Given this context and the available research findings, the civil court response can be usefully considered in relation to cases of child abuse and neglect. The situation is made easier in civil jurisdictions where there is a variety of possible court orders and legal responses available. Such legally mandated interventions can go a long way toward developing increased parental sensitivity to the child and competence in dealing with the child, thus moving the treatment process into its third, and final, phase.

Phase 3: Resolution

Resolution is not the end but, rather, the beginning of a more adaptive family functioning, so far as the child is concerned. The treatment intervention process may have been of long duration or relatively brief. Nevertheless, from the professional perspective two primary options emerge at this stage in treatment: (1) the child will be reunited with the family and returned to live in the family home, now deemed safe, in which the abuse originally occurred or, (2) alternative care for the child will be required. In between these two extremes are situations in which a family is reconfiguring itself, reestablishing itself with one of the original parents adopting primary responsibility for the child(ren), with or without another, new adult partner.

At this stage, the success of efforts toward family reunification or rehabilitation will depend on the assessment of risk to the safety of the child.

Reuniting the Family   In this phase, reuniting the child with his or her family will necessitate a risk assessment of the effect of the abuser's return or reintroduction into the family. This may involve a more diffuse assessment of risk, evaluating the potential danger of abuse or neglect recurring in cases in which the abuser him- or herself does not present an immediate threat but other causes for concern have been revealed. Nevertheless, the basic approach to assessing risk will in each case be to consider the various elements of the risk matrix (10):

1. Parental mental health
2. Parenting competence
3. Parent-child interaction (including type and quality of attachment)
4. Abuse factors
5. Child factors
6. Professional factors
7. Social setting
8. Family factors

There is no mathematical formula that we can apply to enable us to weight the various elements, or even the factors within each domain, to give us an unequivocal reading of the level of risk. The decision is a clinical one and based upon an analysis of these domains, considered from the point of view of both strengths and weaknesses in the family being assessed (as some factors add to or even potentiate the overall assessment of risk, while others compensate and ameliorate).

Firm rules may be required to regulate the abuser's return home. For example, in sexual abuse cases, clear guidelines may have to be established that would prohibit the abuser from bathing the child or engaging in any other intimate contact with him or her, from ever being alone with the children, and from discussing sexuality or maltreatment, at least initially. Similarly, in physical abuse cases, the abuser may have to be relieved of all responsibility for disciplining the child, at least initially. Such rules can be tailored to the individual case and will need to change over time as the case progresses.

Relinquishment of Parental Custodial Rights   Relinquishment may occur in several ways. The treatment plan for the child may not be satisfactorily completed nor the criteria for success sufficiently achieved. In other cases, the parents or caretakers may come to the decision that they do not wish to care for the child and have no desire to engage in any form of treatment or change. While relinquishment may be viewed by some professionals as evidence of therapeutic failure, we should not measure success by the attainment of family reunification but, rather, by the welfare of the child. Treatment outcomes are frequently imperfect, and the therapist has to accept this fact, together with the uncertainty involved with providing treatment for these families.

It can be difficult for therapists to decide when to stop attempting reunification and turn, instead, to a relinquishment, one with some dignity for family members. It is here that the facilitating of careful planning and the clear articulation of criteria for success or failure undertaken at the start of treatment bears fruit. The aim in such cases in which relinquishment is proposed will be to terminate treatment in a way which is understandable to the child and the natural parents. In this way, the movement into permanent placement in alternative care can be accepted by the child, and sometimes by the parents.

It is probably not reasonable to apply a rigid timescale to this process, because so much depends on the child's age and developmental status. However, if a reasonable period of time has elapsed without accomplishing either adequate cooperation or sufficient gains in treatment, then the professional system should move robustly toward obtaining relinquishment of the parents' custodial rights. It is likely that the civil court process will be needed to lend authority to the decision, which is always based upon the welfare of the child.

Conclusion

Practitioners and researchers must recognize their fallibility in predicting the outcome of treatment. In many cases, it will be most appropriate to outline the various pertinent factors in the way I have suggested above. These factors can then be set out with criteria for success or failure over a stipulated period of time, and it can then be estimated whether the outcome predictions were overly cautious or unduly optimistic. Such an approach will demand a systematic process of review of maltreatment cases for all but the most simple and straightforward ones. I would therefore strongly urge that civil child protection jurisdictions incorporate such a necessary process of review, which the uncertainty involved in working with abusive and neglectful families demands.

The stress and anxiety engendered in professionals who have to monitor and keep alert to the shifting sands of dangerousness within these cases must be acknowledged. The pressure on departments of social services to contain such anxiety, especially when resources are strained to the maximum, deserves a far greater attention and is necessary to at least mention in a chapter on treatment such as this. It is hardly surprising that turnover rates for child protection workers are so high. Much can be done to improve this situation, however, through enhancing the value of direct work by using skilled child protection practitioners and through establishing well-paid practitioner posts within social services and other agencies that provide treatment work in this area. Clinical experience indicates that treatment provision for abusive families is best organized through the medium of multidisciplinary teams of professionals, who can operate as a system of checks and balances and, at the same time, offer one another mutual support for this extremely difficult yet vital work.

References

1. Finkelhor, D., and Berliner, L. 1995. Research on the Treatment of Sexually Abused Children: A Review and Recommendations. *J. Am. Acad. Child and Adolescent Psychiatry* 34 (11): 1408–23.
2. Wolfe, D. A. 1994. The Role of Intervention and Treatment Services in the Prevention of Child Abuse and Neglect. In *Protecting Children from Abuse and Neglect,* ed. G. B. Melton and P. D. Berry, 224–303. London: Guilford.
3. Belsky, J. 1980. Child Maltreatment: An Ecological Integration. *Am. Psychologist* 35:320–35.
4. Cicchetti, D., and Rizley, R. 1981. Developmental Perspectives on the Aetiology, Intergenerational Transmission, and Sequelae of Child Maltreatment. *New Directions for Development* 11: 31–55.
5. Main, M. 1991. Metacognitive Monitoring and Singular (Coherent) v. Multiple (Incoherent) Models of Attachment: Findings and Directions for Future Research. In *Attachment across the Life Cycle,* ed. P. Harris, J. Stevenson-Hinde, and C. M. Parkes. New York: Routledge.
6. George, C. 1996. A Representational Perspective of Child Abuse and Prevention: Internal Working Models of Attachment and Caregiving. *Child Abuse and Neglect: International J.* 20: 411–24.
7. Mullen, P. E.; Martin, J. L.; Anderson, J. C.; Romans, S. E.; and Herbison, G. P. 1993. Childhood Sexual Abuse and Mental Health in Adult Life. *British J. Psychiatry* 163:721–32.
8. Clausen, A. H., and Crittenden, P. M. 1991. Physical and Psychological Maltreatment: Relations among Types of Maltreatment. *Child Abuse and Neglect: International J.* 15:5–18.
9. Jones, D. P. H., and Alexander, H. 1987. Treating the Abusive Family within the Family Care System. In *The Battered Child,* 4th ed., ed. R. E. Helfer and R. S. Kempe. Chicago: University of Chicago Press.
10. Jones, D. P. H. 1991. The Effectiveness of Intervention. In *Significant Harm,* ed. M. Adcock, R. White, and A. Hollows. London: Significant Publications.
11. Furniss, T. 1990. Dealing with Denial. In *Understanding and Managing Child Sexual Abuse,* ed. R. K. Oates. London: Bailliere Tindall.
12. Gough, D. 1993. Child Abuse Interventions: A Review of the Research Literature. London: Her Majesty's Stationery Office.

Survivors

Many children who have been abused or neglected grow up to become successful adults, capable in work, partners in happy marriages, and also excellent parents. Others grow up manifesting their earlier abuse only in failures to fulfill their potential in various parts of their lives—scars of their past experiences unnoticeable to casual observers.

The work of Rutter (19), of Mrazek and Mrazek (20), and of Zimrin (21) all identify circumstances or qualities in children who survive well, which can be helpful in considering treatment goals. A good, supportive relationship which counteracts the child's other, abusive, relationships is one of the most important of these circumstances. That good relationship may have been empathic enough to allow the child to develop a better self-image and a conviction of being valued or loved by someone and, therefore, a greater readiness to seek out helpful relationships in the future. A capacity for empathy may also be roused by someone partially dependent on the child, like a younger sibling. Caring for that sibling may take the place of a supportive relationship with an adult in providing a sense of purpose, of being needed and valued.

A quality advantageous to the child is the resourcefulness to employ his inherent cognitive abilities to learn about his environment, to recognize danger, and to work out ways to cope with it. These abilities may help with reality testing: some children are able to distance themselves enough at times to recognize the inconsistencies in the abuser and become beware that they themselves are not really to blame. Similarly, some children recognize good qualities or skills in the abuser and are able to identify with those. Even copying the aggressive qualities of the abuser may counteract the potentially self-destructive passivity of the lifelong victim and, if not adopted wholesale, may be useful in coping. Retaining some sense of identity, of control and ownership over some small part of personal life, may be very important in helping a child to protect her hope for the future. Children may also sustain hope through the ability to fantasize a better future and to remove themselves imaginatively from current fear and helplessness. Just as prisoners of war sustain themselves with meager defenses (22), some children seem able to find in their experiences or inner resources the defenses which allow them to undergo devastating experiences without losing their spirit or ability to adapt.

The Context of Treatment

Time and the Abusive Environment

One of the remarkable characteristics of very young children is their great sensitivity to environmental influences which affect their development. While this acute sensitivity is the reason children demonstrate so clearly the effects of abuse and neglect, it also makes them very responsive to treatment efforts. In contrast to this comparative adaptability of children, adults who suffered serious neglect and abuse as children may be resistant to treatment efforts that do not begin until their adult years. They may lack motivation to participate in treatment because often they have never experienced talking or authority figures as doing them any good. Even when they do participate in treatment, lifelong problems may make tolerating the anxiety of introspection and the commitment of time necessary to resolve issues a discouraging prospect. Many parents desperately want help, but they are frightened and wary of authorities taking over. These parents frequently are able to respond much more comfortably to less formal situations such as lay therapy or self-help groups where they get practical suggestions about day-to-day issues (23, 24).

The child's potential for rapid progress in a favorable therapeutic environment and the parent's relative slowness to respond can intensify the care provider's temptation to use treatment modes which bypass the parents and accept their shortcomings as inevitable. Foster care may seem to be an easy answer. While the child's development may improve rapidly in foster care, however, the relationship with the parents often becomes more and more tenuous, and the opportunity to improve attachment is lost. Sometimes therapists are left with the choice of either placing children in foster care or helping children learn to live in the difficult home environment which meets few of their needs and to gradually recognize that they must depend on themselves and others outside the family for nurturance and guidance. Whether the needs of the child and those of the family can be sufficiently met in treatment without disrupting the intact family unit is a major question, best answered during the assessment and treatment plan formulation (see chapters 8 and 12).

In this chapter, I am emphasizing treatment of the individual child. The child's treatment, whether at home or in foster care, must coincide with simultaneous treatment of the rest of the family, whether the natural family and/or the foster family, and in the context of the child's other needs at home, in day care, in school, and with peer groups. When abused or neglected children are placed in foster care to appropriately ensure their safety but no other therapeutic plan is in effect—a common occurrence—many of them continue to show their primary symptoms, and returning these children to their families, who also will not change without direct intervention, is either impossible or unsuccessful.

Parents in Treatment   One of the most urgent problems to be solved in offering therapy to abused or neglected children, no matter the age group, is how to secure the approval and participation of their parents (25) (see chapters 24 and 26). Even when treatment for both parent and child is ordered by the court, some parents tend to find many ways to avoid participation—and they will continue to resist treatment until they become convinced that it will be helpful to them. As is the case with children and therapists, so the quality of the parents' relationship with the therapist is *the* important issue. At times, enlisting the service of a lay therapist in the home, or a parent's group, may create an important intermediary step by which parents develop enough trust to become involved (23, 24).

Indications abound that when parents gain the ability to recognize and get "in touch" affectively with their own early experiences of abuse or neglect as children, they are better able not just to feel but to deal with the resultant anger and sadness so long repressed. Consequently, they also gain the ability to recognize the effect of such early experiences upon their children. The approach described by Selma Fraiberg, which uses the infant as a focus through which the parents get in touch with their own previously inaccessible experiences, requires intensive, skilled therapy (26). With such therapy, the parents' own past difficulties can become accessible, particularly those of the early, preverbal period. Such early traumas are not usually retrievable through ordinary memory and verbal description; instead, only the derivative affect related to those past experiences is apt to surface when triggered by certain situations, for instance, being rejected by a person on whom one depends. Eliciting the parents' response to the current abusive situation as a bridge to their own early experience can help them understand their child's current situation and help them develop empathy.

Other parents, whose parenting difficulties are more accessible to treatment, may respond well to family therapy, where the presence of the children serves to activate habitual behavior modes and conflicts. Encouraging communication and better understanding between parents and children in these circumstances can illuminate misunderstandings and pave the way for attaining agreement on mutually desired goals and on behavioral changes possible for both generations. Holding family sessions early in the evaluation process provides very valuable information about most children and sets the stage for treatment planning.

Behavior-oriented therapy (27), may be very useful when the child's conduct poses many problems for himself and his parents and may be one way in which the family group can function therapeutically and effectively for a time. Better behavior management allows parents and children to experience encouraging episodes of success and also allows them to continue working on relationship difficulties in a less stressful atmosphere. However behavior management by itself is usually not enough, especially when it diverts attention from the parent's or child's long-term emotional needs.

Siblings   Frequently, when a young infant is abused or neglected and the family is evaluated, the infant's older siblings may receive only passing notice, especially if they do not present obvious behavior disorders. A closer look often reveals that these children too have suffered from abuse or neglect in the past. Although they are now apparently compliant and "getting by," they also may have underlying difficulties. Many abused children recognize early in life that the rules in their home are different from the rules in the outside world and exercise great care in adapting to each environment. For them, developing a consistent and healthy self-image is an important goal. Siblings may also provide much of the support available within the family and care for one another and may also participate helpfully in family therapy.

Extrafamilial Abuse or Neglect   Children are frequently abused or neglected by persons other than their parents. Usually these perpetrators of abuse are in a position of trust, as a friend of the family, and/or responsibility, as a caregiver (for example, foster care parent, a baby-sitter, a day-care provider, or a school employee). Occasionally, the perpetrator is not the responsible usual caregiver but an employee or friend of the caregiver. In addition, more distant members of the child's or caregiver's family, including other children, may be abusers. Children in these abusive situations can be very seriously hurt physically or sexually, or they may be dangerously neglected over a long period. Intervention is needed for children abused by someone outside the immediate family, to help them deal with their feelings of vulnerability, anger, and mistrust. The family may also need the opportunity to deal therapeutically with feelings of shock and anger and to learn how to help the child.

Goals of Treatment

Intervention in the abusive or neglectful family aims first at preventing further maltreatment and providing physical and psychological safety for all members. Support for the family and treatment for the parents help achieve these goals. Specific individual treatment for the child is needed to enable her to cope with confusion and anxiety; in addition, remedial assistance is needed to assuage the developmental and behavioral effects of the maltreatment.

Some maltreated children show severe symptoms of hyperarousal, anxiety, depression, and impulsive or aggressive behavior; any of these symptoms makes change difficult, and all of them are improved with pharmacological intervention as an *adjunct* to psychotherapy (28, 29). Even young preschool children sometimes benefit from very careful and judicious use of medication for severe symptoms, as long as ongoing regular medical supervision and medical monitoring of drug levels and side effects are provided. Medication should never be used routinely, but only when warranted by the severity of the child's symptoms and the specificity and safety of the drug; medication should be discontinued as soon as no further benefit is obvious.

Although the focus of the child's therapy will be on ameliorating the child's symptoms, therapists need always to be aware of the child's total environment and to acknowledge the importance of the work of other professionals. The therapist ought not only to exchange relevant information with other assessment and treatment personnel but also to work with social services, schools, and courts in clarifying what the child's needs are and what family and community can do to meet them.

Confidentiality is always an issue in treatment and must be carefully preserved—but with thoughtful care, pertinent and helpful information can be given and received in reports or court hearings which will promote the child's and the family's progress. Such advocacy, if confined to the areas of the therapist's expertise with his or her patient, can inform and help direct the child's course toward a better permanent solution.

The Use of Foster Care in Treatment Even though a child is in foster care, treatment for the parents and child should always be part of the treatment plan. If the child has been temporarily removed from his or her home for reasons of safety, yet the prognosis for treatment of the parents seems favorable and their relationship with their child is found to be basically sound, strenuous efforts should be made to facilitate frequent visiting, to promote a healthier attachment between parents and child. While the child may well respond positively to the more skilled foster parents and the infant's developmental parameters improve, the relationship between children and their natural parents often suffers when children are placed in foster care. Parents become increasingly uncertain about their parental abilities and commitment as separation is prolonged, and children become attuned to a set of expectations of parental behavior which their birth parents may not be able to meet. In these circumstances, children's attachment to their new caretaker may supersede their ties to their original family.

Some of these results can be avoided by specially training foster parents to be an arm of therapy, understanding and helping the parents, making them welcome in the foster home, modeling child care, and encouraging attachment between parents and child. The Foster Care Enrichment Program, for example, requires foster parents who are mature, nurturing people. They should be paid more than the usual minimal foster care salaries, and they should be provided with a source of professional training, consultation, and support (30).

When older children are placed in foster care, the family services staff may unfortunately be insufficiently concerned about the children's ability to adjust to the change, not to mention their need for treatment and for long-term planning. Some relief for children may come simply from the absence of abuse and pleasure in better care, but they may also experience intense feelings of loss, intense needs to belong, guilt, anger, and fear of their future. Their own behavior may have become very difficult, perhaps to the point that they "fail" foster care repeatedly. Each new placement requires intense efforts at adjustment to a new family, and repeated placements can diminish and eventually destroy a child's capacity to adjust and to form new close relationships.

Clearly, foster care is no panacea. For many children, foster care, without vigorous treatment of the family and permanency planning, is the first step to limbo. Although some adolescents discover that foster care can be a helpful bridge to adulthood, other troubled adolescents—especially those who can no longer "invest" in a relationship with a parent figure—find the less intimate but equally safe environment of a group home more acceptable.

Common Themes in Individual Treatment at All Ages

Whatever the specific problems for which an abused or neglected child is referred to a therapist, certain common difficulties are faced by all maltreated children, no matter what their age. These difficulties, of course, are the ones which most often need to be addressed in psychotherapy. The crucial aspect of therapy with maltreated children of all ages is the development of a trusting relationship: this may be a lengthy and difficult process, but it is certainly a necessary one if therapy is to succeed. It is helped by the ability of the therapist to be empathic and scrupulously consistent in his or her supportive stance toward the child as they work through one or all of the following common themes:

1. Safety. The child's physical and psychological safety must be assured before any other concern can be resolved. Safety, for the abused child, is always an issue. He may adapt to his dangerous home life by attempting to propitiate and please his abusers or by preemptively attempting to display his own strength through aggressive behavior or through play fantasies of achieving victory through violence. Many abused children are vigilant and ever ready to assume that attack upon them is imminent; their anxiety is expressed through their play. They may manifest the acute symptoms of anxiety, hypervigilance, intrusive memories and preoccupation with the trauma, and numbing of affect usually

related to the post-traumatic stress syndrome. Dissociative symptoms mark for some children their response to traumatic stress. Many abused children, however, do not manifest these symptoms. For the child who has been abused from early childhood on, deprivation or physical attack has become a part of everyday life. She may have adapted to it by modifying her behavior, avoiding attack by accepting her parents' view of her and assuming that she is to blame and that her punishment is appropriate. Thus, the usual symptoms of post-traumatic stress may be modified if the child has become resigned to trauma and aggression and sees them as normal.

2. Unresolved fears. Maltreated children are fearful. They are usually plagued by fears of angry, inconsistent punishment or by fears of being rejected or abandoned (31, 32). Such fears derive from past or current experience, and the child may act them out directly and repetitively over many months or may disguise them through denial or displacement. Gradually the child can be helped to develop ways to handle these fears, first, through play. Eventually, with support, he may be able to recognize and cope with the underlying realities. Needless to say, the therapist tries to ensure that meanwhile, outside the therapy hours, actual improvement of the realities of the child's situation is being facilitated whenever possible.

3. Mistrust. Despite the obvious pleasure the child receives from an adult therapist's attention, the child must nonetheless struggle to overcome deep reserves of mistrust. Difficulties persist from earlier, abusive, relationships and are manifested by the child's troubles in perceiving the therapist as a consistent, caring individual. Separation from the therapist after each session often feels at first like abandonment or annihilation to the child; subsequently, the therapist is tested constantly on issues of benevolence, reliability, honesty, and interest. The therapist's vacations and cancellations of appointments are likewise important issues; even though the significance of these "lapses" may be denied by the children, their behavior will show the strength of their reaction. The significance for the abused or neglected child of forming a trustworthy relationship cannot be given too much emphasis. Being able to maintain trust even through termination of therapy may help that child reevaluate other relationships and seek help in the future when he or she needs it.

4. Need for nurturance. This is manifested in acute desires for attention, food, and possessions. These children may not readily admit the importance of the time and attention and pleasures set aside just for them, yet they react strongly if they encounter any intrusion or interruption.

5. Poor self-esteem, depression, and low capacity for pleasure. Deprivation coupled with a rigid, punitive superego derived from their parents' constant criticism diminish children's self-approval and their ability to enjoy themselves. This lack of pleasure often appears as part of a chronic depression, similar to that afflicting parents. In therapy, play and the sharing of pleasure in activities can counteract a child's depression and increase self-esteem, as can the therapist's warm acceptance of the child.

6. Tendency to regress during therapy hours. Since this tendency is more obvious in preschool children, its presence in school-age children may indicate that they are burdened by unresolved problems from earlier stages. Such children tend to seek solutions through regressing. For example, a very well behaved pseudoadult six-year-old may indulge in

occasional water play for months and eventually feel safe enough to regress to drinking from a bottle and expressing a wish to be babied. Acceptance of the wish as understandable without actually fulfilling it often helps the child be more able to meet parental demands for mature behavior.

7. Poor ability to express emotions verbally and nonverbally. Abused and neglected children often have difficulty discussing their anxiety and fears, many of which are based in the reality of their chaotic family lives. Aggression may be overtly expressed, or it may be suppressed; if suppressed, it may have considerable unrecognized influence on their behavior with peers, with adults, and also with their therapist. Children may express aggression primarily through a great deal of vivid, violent fantasy. Difficulty with feelings which children have not been able to express verbally may erupt as problems in impulse control. When therapist and child come to understand where the feelings come from and why the child feels helpless about them, the child can be lead to explore ways of dealing with them more effectively and choosing his response to them. When children at first are very fearful of the feelings they have, their expression and possible solutions for them are often dealt with only in the metaphor of play. Helping the child improve his verbal expression and find alternative ways to resolve aggressive or dependency impulses helps him acquire better impulse control and more socialized behavior. Behavior management techniques may be useful in working with the child and with the family or school; psychotherapists should incorporate into their repertoire any of these techniques that prove effective.

8. Overwhelmingly aggressive behavior. This is a special problem with some neglected or abused children who feel truly abandoned or betrayed and feel they have "nothing to lose." The therapist must find ways to contain the destructive, aggressive behavior while maintaining a steadfast stance of being completely available to help the child. These children especially need a therapist's aid in coming to terms with their own feelings, and in appropriately satisfying not only their needs (as much as possible) but also the demands of their environment (33). Sometimes this must be done in a residential setting in which the entire staff is cooperatively involved in supporting treatment.

9. Poor cognitive and problem-solving skills. Many children have difficulty applying intellectual skills on demand. They need help in acquiring confidence, in overcoming fear of failure, and in learning how to approach new tasks, as well as encouragement in catching up when they are behind in such skills as reading. The therapist's support and interest in schoolwork can occasionally help if the child is concerned about school assignments and has never experienced such noncritical interest before. In addition, therapists can assist in arranging for tutoring or special supplemental help as needed.

Treatment of the Abused or Neglected Infant

In chapter 8, the risk factors used in decision making about maintaining a very young infant at home after serious abuse or neglect are discussed. Comprehensive evaluation of the relationship between parents and child should result in a description both of the specific parenting problems which may be amenable to treatment and of the quality of attachment of the parent and child. When the abused or neglected child is an infant, treatment is aimed at providing adequately functioning parents, and a good primary attachment, in a safe environment which will meet all developmental needs.

Treatment should also attempt rehabilitation, to help the infant catch up as much as possible in physical and psychological growth. Occasionally this means that the professional is individually involved with the baby primarily for assessment purposes and that, after a treatment plan is devised, therapy is aimed at helping the parents understand the child and relate more effectively with him or her (34, 35).

Generally, however, working with the parent and infant, or toddler, together can be very effective when flexible combinations of individual therapy sessions and joint sessions elucidate the contributions of both parent and child to their relationship difficulties. Such infant-parent psychotherapy recognizes the individual characteristics of the child, his current developmental needs, and how they all intermesh with the expectations the parent derived from past relationships and experiences (36).

Keeping the abused or neglected infant in his or her own home requires that, in addition to these parent-infant interventions, a social service worker or a visiting nurse monitor the home and that regular medical assessments be scheduled to ensure that no further evidence of abuse or neglect arises and that satisfactory developmental progress occurs.

Before intervention, the therapist needs to know a good deal about the parents' own history and the reasons for their difficulty in forming a comfortable relationship with their child (see chapter 5). The parents may have never experienced a reliable, primary parenting figure in their own childhoods, or they may have had difficulty in being available to this particular child. For example, in the second situation the death of another one of their children near the time of this infant's birth may not have allowed the parents adequate time to mourn their loss and may have provoked a great deal of anxiety about emotionally investing in the new infant, leading to depression and avoidance. Clearly the capacity of parents to respond to treatment in these two situations may be quite different.

When the abused or neglected infant remains at home, simultaneous efforts to treat the parents and the child involve, in addition to medical follow-up, any or all of the following:

1. Lay supportive therapy, self-help groups, family support programs (23, 24, 37–39)
2. Parenting classes (see chapter 15)
3. Parent-infant psychotherapy (36)
4. Individual therapy for the mother and father when their personal difficulties warrant it (see chapters 24 and 26)
5. Special therapy, such as an alcoholic treatment program for either parent
6. Use of crisis nurseries or day care when the mother needs such respite (40)
7. Specialized referrals for major health problems or special training for job placement for parents

Treatment of the Preschool Child

By the time children have reached preschool age (three to five years old), they should have accomplished several important developmental tasks. Normally reared children have at this stage progressed from secure dependence on their primary attachments to their parents to some ability to relate comfortably with others. In doing so, they perceive themselves as having individual identities and feel the capacity to act independently in rudimentary ways. They have begun to feel competent in using their own bodies and in exploring toys. They have achieved an increased ability to communicate and, thereby, an improved ability to influence others. These accomplishments are constantly practiced and refined by experience, helping the child develop early control over impulses. Peer relationships and socialization skills become important as normally reared children begin to see themselves as separate entities. Major learning tasks for preschoolers are the acquisition of new cognitive and motor skills, the development of speech and language, and the expansion of social and self-help skills. Sex roles emerge as the child begins the process of identification.

Sometimes the abused and neglected preschool-age child has not yet experienced a positive attachment to one caregiving person. Basic issues of trust may not yet have been resolved, making attempts at growth and self-assertion difficult to achieve. By this time, deviant ways of coping have begun to solidify into behavior patterns that are handicapping. One significant outcome can be withdrawn or aggressive behavior, which makes it difficult for the child to get along with peers and caregivers. Abused and neglected children begin to develop serious developmental deficits by this age, which leave them poorly prepared to learn in school. Some of these behaviors have served a survival function within their abusive or neglectful family environment, but they handicap the child in a normal environment.

Treatment of the abused preschool child will more often take place outside the home in an individual or group setting, but it can occur in the home using the services of a skilled social worker, lay therapist, nurse, or developmental specialist working with child and parent together. The treatment plan might include speech and language therapy, physical therapy, specialized medical care, as well as play therapy, family therapy, behavior modification, or an individual educational plan.

Day Care

Using resources outside the home is often helpful in providing abused or neglected children with safe and nurturing care and a more stimulating environment, while also providing the parents with some relief from continuous parenting tasks. Day-care facilities vary a good deal in the sophistication of the caretakers, but considerable improvement of care may be achieved if the protective services worker consults with them and explains the special needs of the maltreated child. When an effort is being made to avoid foster care and keep children with their family, day care may be tried as the child's progress is observed and the parents are provided with help in enhancing parenting skills.

The Therapeutic Preschool

Placement in a therapeutic nursery school or day-care program is often the treatment of choice for many children aged three to five (41). Some programs are able to integrate the parents as active participants into the school's regular schedule, providing direct experience with better child care. This requires a skilled staff with sufficient time to give extra help to the parents while also giving good care to the children. Most programs do not include the parents in the school activity, but they do help parents understand their child and collaborate in setting joint treatment goals for the child. The parents should also receive simultaneous, coordinated individual therapy and/or family therapy to achieve therapeutic goals for the entire family as well as for the child.

Our experience during the 1980s in Denver at the therapeutic nursery school directed by the C. Henry Kempe National Center for the Prevention and Treatment of Child Abuse and Neglect led us to conclude that many maltreated preschool-age children exhibit serious delays and disturbances in social and emotional functioning (described in the "Developmental Effects of Abuse" section above). These children expect to be treated in school as they have been treated elsewhere and, consequently, may be frightened or easily roused to aggressive defensiveness. At the therapeutic preschool, the provision of a safe, consistent nurturing environment and a clear daily routine offers the child the opportunity to reduce anxiety and obtain aid in the integrative process. The child's physical and psychological safety is particularly emphasized. We recognize that nonverbal communication is significant and, accordingly, translate it into direct conversation. The staff uses a simple narrative style of speaking to help give the child words for his or her actions and feelings. Developing in the child an understanding of feelings and a method of impulse control is a major focus of the program. The teacher intervenes to help the child tolerate delay between stimulus and response by encouraging him to verbalize his thought process and to consider alternatives for action. The same process benefits children in their peer interactions and teaches them to communicate more effectively with one another. We liberally encourage children, to make it easier for them to deal with any initial failure and to try again.

Consistent limits of allowable behavior and clear logical consequences of exceeding those limits (including "time out" when needed) help children to cope in social situations with their peers and with adults. When the number of children in a group is held at eight to ten, the children can avoid overstimulation more easily and the staff can better provide availability and predictability. Our experience has shown that a 1:3 staff-member-to-pupil ratio works best with severely abused and neglected preschoolers, because they need much attention, nurturing, and one-to-one relationship experience. Individual play therapy helps each child cope with his or her special problems in a more explicit way; close cooperation between teachers and therapists provides continuity.

Individual Therapy

Although most abused or neglected preschool-age children benefit considerably from the group experience in a therapeutic nursery school, the therapeutic opportunities may sometimes be fragmented or diluted by the group setting. The addition of individual therapy allows the child to develop a more intense relationship with an adult in which more individual goals can be attempted. The continuity and structure of the therapy hours allow the relationship behavior (transference), play themes, and behavior patterns to be more clearly repeated, related to specific situations, and dealt with verbally or in play with the therapist (42–45).

Treatment of the School-Age Child

In school-age children (six to twelve years of age), referrals for treatment are apt to be made only when the child has serious psychiatric symptoms, is failing in school, or exhibits disruptive behavior. By this time, the child's behavior is often regarded as part of his or her personality, and its origin in a neglectful or abusive home environment may not be considered. If abuse and neglect are not evaluated adequately in the assessment phase, the child may not volunteer the information or, indeed, be aware that her home experience is unusual. The therapist may encounter similar difficulties in involving the child's parents in treatment, both in therapy with their children and in individual therapy to recognize their own needs.

Parents are sometimes more receptive to the child's entering treatment when they see the problem as the child's and when the repercussions of the child's behavior are becoming more anxiety provoking. Family therapy may be the treatment of choice for this age group, if such treatment can be flexibly combined with individual therapy sessions as required. Sometimes a behavior management approach is a useful adjunct to the family therapy early on. When parents do little to cooperate with and follow through on referrals, children who cannot function in a regular classroom have sometimes been enrolled in an experimental special school program incorporating psychotherapy (46, 47). Also, some schools provide individual and/or group therapy in the regular school setting specifically for children manifesting school-related behavior problems; many abused and neglected children may fall into this category.

Some efforts are being made to provide consulting services and special training in the dynamics and treatment of abuse and neglect for personnel in day-care centers, preschools, and grade schools (48). With such assistance, school counselors and social workers may be able to offer help to children who otherwise would not have access to treatment.

Because of cognitive and social delays, lack of readiness for cognitive learning, or behavioral problems, many abused and neglected children are relegated to the special-education classes for the learning disabled or the emotionally disturbed. On further evaluation, these children are found to be seriously handicapped by their lifelong experience with abuse and neglect and by living in an environment which is still abusive or neglectful. They may be caught in a situation in which some treatment has been attempted and they have been allowed to remain in the home, perhaps with temporary placements in foster care, but in which treatment has never become a meaningful, effective remedy for them or for their parents. If abuse continues, the child, even if placed in a therapeutic school setting, responds poorly to such inadequate measures. Only when the whole family is involved in treatment can optimum progress be made for such disabled children.

Group Therapy

Group therapy may be helpful to school-age children either by itself, supplemented by individual therapy, or in a residential setting (49). The group time can often be divided into a structured activity or a talk time, followed by free play activity, and concluded with a quiet snack time which often provides the best discussion participation. Goals for such groups vary, but they usually include development of trust in the adult therapists, improvement of peer relations, verbalization and sharing of feelings, socialization and limit setting, and especially cultivation of group respect for each child as an individual person. When they find that other group members share their problems, children may decrease conflicted loyalty to their parents and increase ability to express their feelings. Although some children may be too disturbed for this treatment mode and may require individual therapy or special placement, many children demonstrate surprisingly good improvement, especially in relief of anxiety, behavioral symptoms, and academic progress.

Individual Treatment

Psychotherapy (that is, regular individual therapy by a psychiatrist, psychologist, or social worker) or less intensive individual counseling for the school-age child should address the issues detailed above in the "Common Themes in Individual Treatment at All Ages" section; the typical slow development of trust in the therapist and the testing of the therapist's reliability might take considerable time, even in a one-to-one situation. The goals in one to-one therapy are more individual, and the pace of treatment is adjusted to the child's response (50). Neglect or abuse are, after all, experienced in the context of family relationships and ongoing events, and their meaning to the child must be understood before any change can occur. The children's interpretations of their parents' behavior toward them and the children's feelings about their families may be more readily recognized and interpreted in individual therapy: help in dealing with these stresses can be offered over time.

Participation of the parents in some kind of treatment modality is very important for the school-age child; there is more pressure on these children to reconcile their families' expectations with the different views taken by the outside world, including their therapists. This may induce conflict not just of loyalty but also of identification with parental behavior or pathology. Although mental health centers should be available as an alternative to psychiatric/psychological clinics or private psychotherapy, they do not always have the time or the trained personnel to provide individual treatment for children. It may also take special effort for the child's therapist to achieve collaboration with the therapists who undertake treatment of the parents and the family as a whole.

Treatment in Adolescence

Treatment of adolescents is more apt to be precipitated by their behavior, particularly school failure and truancy, drug use, delinquency, or running away (51). During adolescence, children's efforts at becoming independent may be jeopardized by their parents' desire to maintain a relationship in which the child meets their needs and obeys their coercive authority. The adolescent child's long years of frustration and repressed anger may find expression in delinquent behavior; the lack of loving family and healthy peer relationships may lead to gang membership or premature sexual partnerships. Truancy and school failure become increasingly serious if early learning difficulties were not resolved. Running away may be the only way some adolescents can deal with abuse at home, including sexual abuse. Recognizing this possibility may motivate the professional to arrange family evaluation and perhaps treatment. Some adolescents become increasingly depressed by their long-standing neglect or sexual abuse, or by the underlying message conveyed over the years that they are unwanted, and they attempt suicide (52, 53). Others seek surcease in alcohol or other drugs, compounding their difficulties.

Just as with younger children, the adolescent may not have adequately negotiated the most elementary developmental steps, particularly those involving close relationships. Instead of redefining relationships from an oedipal stance (the traditional psychiatric treatment of adolescence), the adolescent may still be caught in unresolved preoedipal issues, with his or her primary dependency attachment needs still unmet—a clear handicap in developing independence, trusting relationships, or any kind of mature identity.

In spite of their years, adolescents may never have learned adequately to recognize, verbally express, and cope with their own emotions or to develop social skills. They may be prey to difficulties in impulse control. Their inability to use education effectively may have left them handicapped in basic academic skills. They may not have learned how to use their cognitive skills to solve life problems nor how to trust anyone enough to ask for advice.

If they have been repeatedly criticized, belittled, abused, or ignored, they may have very poor self-esteem and very little experience (or motivation) in applying their abilities to acquire either academic or job skills. Their lack of coping skills is detrimental to both social life and work life and makes them even more vulnerable in the adult world. Often they feel comfortable only in the counterculture fringes of society, where they hope they will be accepted and valued more readily.

Many adolescents become subjected to juvenile court supervision before their need for treatment becomes obvious. Both the family and the teenager may be resistant to the idea of treatment, making the process slow and difficult, but this is an opportunity to recognize their needs. The choice of individual psychotherapy, group therapy, or residential treatment will depend on the severity of the adolescent's pathology and the presence or absence of support for a treatment program in the home. The use of foster care or a residential group home, combined with individual or group psychotherapy, may give the adolescent a second chance and an escape from continued abuse. Educational handicaps and future job training urgently require special attention, in addition to the common treatment issues and therapy goals.

Treatment of the Sexually Abused Child

Sexual abuse shares many characteristics with other forms of abuse, but there are some important differences. Societal reaction, especially in the United States, to sexual activity between adults and children often combines denial that it could happen, accompanied by a reluctance to investigate possible occurrences, with an intensely punitive response when it is recognized. Although society accepts some physical abuse with comparative equanimity (physical punishment in schools, for example) (54), criminal prosecution is considered necessary in almost all cases of sexual abuse, regardless of severity. Consequently, treatment of sexual abuse, much more than treatment of physical abuse or neglect, takes place in an atmosphere of shock and disapproval which increases the social isolation of the victim and his or her family. It also means that legal considerations, geared toward criminal punishment of the offender, often override the best ways of planning treatment for the child and for the offender.

The secrecy that is demanded by the offender serves to isolate the child from her usual sources of help. Through the authority of size, age, and experience, and by threats or seduction, the offender maneuvers the child into compliancy and often participation (55). In addition to these reasons for feeling responsible and guilty, the child often recognizes that the entire family is upset by the disclosure of sexual abuse. A child's mode of coping with sexual abuse may be very different before and after disclosure: at first, the child attempts to adapt to the secrecy and the abuse itself; later, the child must face the responses of family and community agencies, which either provide support or increase the burden through disbelief, disapproval, and disruption of family life. It must also be recognized that before disclosure the child may have enjoyed or welcomed the sexually abusive relationship if it simultaneously provided ostensible affection, companionship, or material gifts in an otherwise bleak or lonely life.

If one or both parents have been responsible for the sexual abuse, disclosure threatens the security of the entire family. Only prompt and careful evaluation can determine if the family, including the offender, can use therapeutic help to deal openly with the sexual abuse issues and to reconstitute the family relationships on a healthy basis (56). If not, either the child or the offending parent will need to be removed from the family home. The child faces loss or disruption of the family, often with the additional burden of being told it is his (or her) fault. Sometimes that child yields to family pressure, recants, and resigns himself to the sexual abuse. The more removed the perpetrator is from the parental position, the more likely the family is to be supportive of the child. Even in extrafamilial sexual abuse, however, some parents are so overwhelmed by their own response to the child's abuse that they are not able to provide the support and reassurance the child needs.

In sexual abuse, then, it is necessary to provide prompt assessment not only of the traumatic consequences to the child but also of the ability of parents and siblings to understand and help the child. Crisis intervention should include emphasis on promoting communication and understanding between parents and child and on providing supportive advocacy by the law enforcement, legal, and social agencies involved. Individual therapy sessions interspersed with family sessions allow both confidentiality and family communication (57–60).

Group therapy is often the treatment of choice for sexually abused children, in a group of children of similar developmental age and usually of the same sex (61). In a group setting, sexually abused children are reassured by the recognition that their problems are shared by others and that they are not bad or different. They find the group a safe place where they learn to talk openly about what has happened, to express their feelings and be understood, to revive trust in adults and peers, and to feel supported and valued. They learn to better understand both sexuality in general and their own future sexual identity in particular. They learn to recognize appropriate sources of attention and affection, ways of coping with problem experiences in the future, and appropriate responsibility for their own behavior.

Male and female co-therapists, when available, provide ideal opportunities for modeling relationships of mutual liking and respect between the sexes. Individual sessions with the child, and/or family sessions, should be interspersed with group meetings when there are specific behavioral difficulties or family issues which need to be resolved. Simultaneous therapy for parents, in group or sometimes individually, is obligatory in intrafamilial sexual abuse and the plan of choice in extrafamilial sexual abuse.

For sexually abused adolescents, same-sex groups provide needed peer support and promote a healthier identity, but family work may also be needed to provide better support and to remedy contributing problems in the family.

Information, advocacy, and support during the legal process which often follows sexual abuse are part of treatment for parents and child. The therapist or victim's assistance organization (many are federally funded) can aid in protective planning for the child during the court process and can contribute emotional support during court hearings. Often the frustrations of legal maneuvering, negative decisions, and delays are extremely hard for the child and family, and they need extended support during these times even after treatment has otherwise been satisfactorily terminated.

It is important for the child and her family to recognize that issues relating to sexual exploitation may have been resolved well by the child at the end of therapy but that such issues may arise again at a later time. New developmental stages or new experiences—especially when they involve sexuality, as in the onset of puberty—may require a brief reconsideration of the meaning of the sexual abuse to this individual child. This should not be considered a failure of previous treatment but, instead, a natural response to healthy development and an appropriate extension of the therapeutic process.

Treatment for Youthful Sexual Offenders

We have become increasingly aware that young boys and girls, as well as adolescents, can be sexually abusing other children (62, 63). Many but not all have been sexual abuse victims themselves; a highly sexualized environment and experiences which have led the child to feel rejected, deprived of love, and helpless may have set the stage. Even very young children may exploit other children. In a few children, the combination of sexual impulses and aggressive impulses is similar to the cognitive distortions seen in the adult rapist or sexual offender and begins to acquire an addictive quality. If a child has shown an inclination to molest others sexually (often siblings at first), treatment is necessary and usually best accomplished in a group. The longer sexually abusive behavior has continued, the more entrenched become the difficulties with understanding feelings and cognitive distortions; early treatment can make an important difference (see chapter 14).

Ryan (64) has advocated that in working with children who molest others, clear labeling and prohibition of the sexually inappropriate behaviors be accompanied by sufficient monitoring by parents to both protect the offender and keep other children from being victimized. Occasionally, this monitoring and protection can be provided only in a residential setting. In treatment, the children are helped to understand their behavior and its precursors, which may include feeling rejected, unloved, helpless, and unable to control themselves or others—and, often, growing anger. They are helped to recognize that security does not come from exerting power over others but from the ability to make choices about their own behavior. They are helped to realize why they might feel bad about themselves and to find more effective ways to develop self-esteem. Sources of anger and better ways to express and cope with that anger are discovered. Empathy for the victims of their behavior and acknowledgment of the harmfulness of their behavior are major goals of treatment.

Active family cooperation and support are vital to work with the child who molests; whenever possible, any contribution the family may have made to the development of the sexually abusive behavior needs to be understood and worked through simultaneously in family therapy.

Treatment Failure in Child Abuse and Neglect

When treatment of the family fails, the removal of the child from the family becomes the primary alternative course of action. The sooner this decision can be made, while safeguarding the interests of parents and children, the better the prognosis will be for the child.

Prediction early in the family assessment of the probability of treatment failure is often possible. Parents who are incapable of parenting because of their drug abuse or severe physical, mental, or psychiatric incapacity may not be able to change their parenting skills in time for their children to remain at home without suffering injury or developmental deterioration. In these situations, unless the clear and present danger to the child is sufficient to warrant immediate termination of parent rights, the law requires that the parents must be shown to be unable to improve their parenting skills sufficiently through therapy to care adequately for their child. It is imperative that the treatment plan be carefully developed to provide maximum assistance, that it be practical so that the parents can follow it, and that the response of the family to treatment be very well documented. Only when, after society has done its best to help the family, the parents continue to fail can termination of parental rights be effected expeditiously from the point of view of the child's future placement. If treatment efforts are half-hearted, or if the parents are allowed to delay their involvement in treatment, then no changes occur, and time is lost and never truly made up for the child who remains in an uncertain foster care situation.

The burden to respond actively to the offer of treatment is on the parents, but the burden on the protective services system is to expedite treatment for everyone, especially the child. Involvement of the court—not simply as an adversarial arena but as a participating body in approving the treatment plan and evaluating its success on the basis of the clear and detailed evidence supplied—is usually the most effective way to direct a case toward successful treatment or toward successful termination.

One of the major reasons for treatment failure is the lack of adequate follow-through on the original treatment plans. Other causes of failure of treatment are usually inadequate initial assessment and diagnosis, particularly of parental pathology, and inadequate treatment resources. These problems are dependent in part on the financial and manpower strength of a community, but they can be solved in part by creative planning and by the implementation of good standards of professional diagnostic and therapeutic work.

Treatment may be prolonged without improvement because therapists are reluctant to admit failure. Their intense wish to help the family, or their inappropriate feelings of personal inadequacy if therapy is unsuccessful, may cause them to remain unrealistically optimistic, to the detriment of the child.

Summary

If we recognize that the treatment of child and parents should begin as soon as abuse and neglect is discovered, we can help to prevent at least some of the heartbreak occasioned when an older child presents with very severe psychopathology after a long history of known but inadequately treated abuse or neglect. Successful and beneficial voluntary interventions for the child and family need to be explored as an alternative to court-ordered therapy. Earlier treatment should reduce many of the effects of abuse and neglect that cost society so much in remedial or custodial programs.

We should also recognize that many abused children and their parents receive little or no treatment because few treatment resources are available, particularly to a segment of the population which often has no ability to pay for treatment. Alternative modes of intervention, more effective and less costly, need to be explored through better evaluation of what actually works.

Always, prevention is much better than treatment. Early treatment of the child may be considered prevention of future difficulty, but it occurs only after the family is already in trouble. Many prevention programs have been identified for general use as well as for at-risk populations (see chapters 27 and 28); whatever their cost, they are cheaper than the expense of broken and distorted spirit, which is the price of child maltreatment.

References

1. American Psychiatric Association. 1994. *Diagnostic and Statistical Manual of Mental Disorders.* 4th ed. Washington, D.C.: American Psychiatric Press.
2. Van der Kolk, B. 1987. *Psychological Trauma.* Washington, D.C.: American Psychiatric Press.
3. Kluft, R. P., ed. 1985. *Childhood Antecedents of Multiple Personality.* Washington, D.C.: American Psychiatric Press.
4. Steele, B. F., and Pollock, C. B. 1974. A Psychiatric Study of Parents Who Abuse Infants and Small Children. In *The Battered Child,* 2d ed., ed. C. H. Kempe and R. E. Helfer, 103–47. Chicago: University of Chicago Press.
5. Oliver, J. E. 1993. Intergenerational Transmission of Child Abuse: Rates, Research, and Clinical Implications. *Am. J. Psychiatry* 150(9): 1315–24.
6. Haynes-Seman, C., and Hart, J. 1988. Interactional Assessment: Evaluation of Parent-Child Relationships in Child Abuse and Neglect. In *The New Child Protection Team Handbook,* ed. D. Bross, R. D. Krugman, M. R. Lenherr, D. A. Rosenberg, and B. D. Schmitt. New York: Garland.

7. Steele, B. F. 1982. Discovery of Children at Risk for Juvenile Delinquency. In *Early Childhood Intervention and Juvenile Delinquency,* ed. F. N. Dutile, C. H. Foust, and D. R. Webster. Lexington, Mass.: D. C. Heath.

8. Lewis, D. O.; May, E.; Jackson, L.; Aaronson, R.; Restifo, N.; Serra, S.; and Simos, A. 1985. Biopsychosocial Characteristics of Children Who Later Murder: A Prospective Study. *Am. J. Psychiatry* 142:1161–67.

9. Crittendon, P. M., and Ainsworth, M. D. S. 1989. Child Maltreatment and Attachment Behavior. In *Child Maltreatment: Theory and Research on the Causes and Consequences of Child Abuse and Neglect,* ed. D. Cicchetti and V. Carlson. Cambridge: Cambridge University Press.

10. Widom, C. S., and Aims, M. A. 1994. Criminal Consequences of Children's Sexual Victimization. *Child Abuse and Neglect: International J.* 18:303–18.

11. Egeland, B. 1995. Consequences of Maltreatment: Mediators and Moderators. Paper presented at the Twenty-third Annual Child Abuse and Neglect Symposium, C. H. Kempe Center, Keystone, Colo.

12. Terr, L. C. 1991. Childhood Traumas: An Outline and Overview. *Am. J. Psychiatry* 148:10–20.

13. Famularo, R.; Fenton, T.; and Kinscherff, R. 1993. Child Maltreatment and the Development of Post Traumatic Stress Disorder. *Am. J. Diseases of Children* 147:755–60.

14. Bowlby, J. 1988. Developmental Psychiatry Comes of Age. *Am. J. Psychiatry* 145:1–10.

15. Main, M., and Goldwyn R. 1984. Predicting Rejection of Her Infant from Mother's Representation of Her Own Experiences: Implications for the Abused-Abusing Intergenerational Cycle. *Child Abuse and Neglect: International J.* 8:203–19.

16. Fonagy, P.; Steele, M.; Moran, G.; Steele, H., and Higgett, A. 1993. Measuring the Ghost in the Nursery: An Empirical Study of the Relation between Parents' Representation of Childhood Experiences and their Infant's Security of Attachment. *J. Am. Psychoanalytic Association* 41:957–89.

17. Zeanah, C. H.; Benoit, D.; Barton, M.; Regan, C.; Hirshberg, L.; and Lipsitt, L. 1993. Representations of Attachment in Mothers and Their One-Year-Old Infants. *J. Am. Acad. Child and Adolescent Psychiatry* 32:278–86.

18. Pearson, J. L.; Cowan, P. A.; Cowan, C. P.; and Cohn, D. A. 1993. Adult Attachment and Child–Older Parent Relationships. *Am. J. Orthopsychiatry* 63:606–13.

19. Rutter, M. 1985. Resilience in the Face of Adversity: Protective Factors and Resistance to Psychiatric Disorder. *British J. Psychiatry* 147:598–611.

20. Mrazek, P. J., and Mrazek, D. A. 1987. Resilience in Child Maltreatment Victims: A Conceptual Exploration. *Child Abuse and Neglect: International J.* 11:357–66.

21. Zimrin, H. 1986. A Profile of Survival. *Child Abuse and Neglect: International J.* 10:339–49.

22. Segal, J. 1987. *Winning Life's Toughest Battles: Roots of Human Resilience.* New York: Ivy Books.

23. Ryan, G.; with Walters, E., and Alexander, H. 1981. *The Lay Person's Role in the Treatment of Child Abuse and Neglect.* Denver: C. Henry Kempe National Center for Prevention and Treatment of Child Abuse and Neglect.

24. Fritz, M. 1986. Parents Anonymous: Helping Clients to Accept Professional Services: A Personal Opinion. *Child Abuse and Neglect: International J.* 10:121–23.

25. Martin, H. P., and Beezley, P. 1976. Resistances and Obstacles to Therapy for the Child. In *The Abused Child: A Multidisciplinary Approach to Developmental Issues and Treatment,* ed. H. P. Martin. Cambridge, Mass.: Ballinger.

26. Fraiberg, S., ed. 1980. *Clinical Studies in Infant Mental Health: The First Year of Life.* New York: Basic Books.

27. Patterson, G. 1982. *Coercive Family Process.* Eugene, Oreg.: Castalia.

28. McAuliffe, S. M. 1994. Psychopharmacology for Preschool Children: Researchers Recommend Cautionary Approach. *Psychiatric Times,* Jan.

29. Harmon, R. J., and Riggs, P. D. 1996. Clonidine for Post Traumatic Stress Disorder in Preschool Children. *J. Am. Acad. Child and Adolescent Psychiatry* 35:1247–49.

30. McBogg, P.; McQuiston, M.; and Schrant, R. 1978. Foster Care Enrichment Program. *Child Abuse and Neglect: International J.* 3:863–68.

31. Terr, L. C. 1990. *Too Scared to Cry: Psychic Trauma in Childhood.* New York: Harper and Row.

32. Terr, L. C. 1983. Play Therapy and Psychic Trauma: A Preliminary Report. In *Handbook of Play Therapy,* ed. C. E. Schaefer and K. J. O'Connor. New York: Wiley.

33. Willock, B. 1983. Play Therapy with the Aggressive Acting-Out Child. In *Handbook of Play Therapy,* ed. C. E. Schaefer and K. J. O'Connor. New York: Wiley.

34. Helfer, R. E. 1987. The Perinatal Period, A Window of Opportunity for Enhancing Parent-Infant Communications: An Approach to Prevention. *Child Abuse and Neglect: International J.* 11:565–79.

35. McDonough, S. C. 1993. Interaction Guidance: Understanding and Treating Early Infant–Caregiver Relationship Disturbances. In *Handbook of Infant Mental Health,* ed. C. H. Zeanah, Jr. New York: Guilford.

36. Lieberman, A. F. 1992. Infant-Parent Psychotherapy with Toddlers. *Development and Psychopathology* 4:559–74.

37. Egelund, B., and Erickson, M. 1990. Rising above the Past: Strategies for Helping New Mothers Break the Cycle of Abuse and Neglect. *Zero to Three* 2(2):20–25.

38. Mollenstrom, W. W.; Patchner, M. A.; and Wilmer, J. S. 1995. Child Maltreatment: The United States Air Force's Response. *Child Abuse and Neglect: International J.* 19:325–34.

39. Weissbourd, B., and Kagan, S. 1989. Family Support Programs: Catalysts for Change. *Am. J. Orthopsychiatry* 59:20–30.

40. Beezley, P., and McQuiston, M. 1977. *Crisis Nurseries: Practical Considerations.* Denver: C. Henry Kempe National Center for Prevention and Treatment of Child Abuse and Neglect.

41. Oates, R. K.; Gray, J.; Schweitzer, L.; Kempe, R.; and Harmon, R. 1995. A Therapeutic Preschool for Abused Children: The Keepsafe Project. *Child Abuse and Neglect: International J.* 19:1379–86.

42. In, P. A., and McDermott, J. F. 1976. The Treatment of Child Abuse: Play Therapy with a Four-Year-Old Child. *J. Am. Acad. Child Psychology* 15:430–40.

43. Mann, E., and McDermott, J. F. 1983. Play Therapy for Victims of Child Abuse and Neglect. In *Handbook of Play Therapy,* ed. C. E. Schaefer and K. J. O'Connor. New York: Wiley.

44. Green, A. H. 1987. Psychiatric Treatment of Abused Children. *J. Am. Acad. Child Psychiatry* 17:356–71.

45. James, B. 1993. *Treatment of Traumatized Children.* Lexington, Mass.: Lexington Books.

46. Stein, M., and Ronald, D. 1974. Educational Psychotherapy of Preschoolers. *J. Am. Acad. Child Psychiatry* 13:618–34.

47. Graffignano, P. N., et al. 1970. Psychotherapy for Latency Age Children in an Inner City Therapeutic School. *Am. J. Psychiatry* 127:626–34.

48. Kurtz, P. D.; Gaudin, J. M.; and Howling, P. T. 1993. Maltreatment and the School-Aged Child: School Performance Consequences. *Child Abuse and Neglect: International J.* 17:581–89.

49. Corder, B. F.; Haizlip, T.; and DeBoer, P. 1990. A Pilot Study for a Structured, Time-Limited Therapy Group for Sexually Abused, Preadolescent Children. *Child Abuse and Neglect: International J.* 14:241–51.

50. McDermott, J. F., and Char, W. F. 1984. Stage-Related Models of Psychotherapy with Children. *J. Am. Acad. Child and Adolescent Psychiatry* 23:537–43.

51. Hussey, D. L., and Singer, M. 1993. Psychological Distress, Problem Behaviors, and Family Functioning of Sexually Abused Adolescent In-Patients. *J. Am. Acad. Child and Adolescent Psychiatry* 32:954–61.

52. Sabboth, J. C. 1969. The Suicidal Adolescent: The Expendable Child. *J. Am. Acad. Child and Adolescent Psychiatry* 8:272–86.

53. Letters to the Editor. 1995. *J. Am. Acad. Child and Adolescent Psychiatry* 34 (June): 700–701.
54. Bauer, G. B.; Dubanoski, R.; Yamanchi, L. A.; and Hanbo, K. A. 1990. Corporal Punishment and the Schools. *Education and Urban Society* 22: 285–99.
55. Summit, R. C. 1983. The Child Sexual Abuse Accommodation Syndrome. *Child Abuse and Neglect: International J.* 7: 171–93.
56. Furniss, T. 1991. *The Multiprofessional Handbook of Child Sexual Abuse.* London: Routledge.
57. MacFarlane, K., and Waterman, J.; with Connerly, S.; Damon, L.; Durfee, M.; and Long, S. 1986. *Sexual Abuse of Young Children.* New York: Guilford.
58. Green, A. H. 1993. Child Sexual Abuse: Immediate and Long-Term Effects and Intervention. *J. Am. Acad. Child Psychiatry* 32: 890–902.
59. Downing, J.; Jenkins, S. J.; and Fisher, G. 1988. A Comparison of Psychodynamic and Reinforcement Treatment with Sexually Abused Children. *Elementary School Guidance and Counseling* 22: 291–98.
60. Jones, D. P. H. 1986. Individualized Psychotherapy for the Sexually Abused Child. *Child Abuse and Neglect: International J.* 10: 377–85.
61. Cavanaugh-Johnson, T. 1993. Group Therapy. In *Sexualized Children,* ed. E. Gil and T. Cavanaugh-Johnson. Rockville, Md.: Walnut Creek Launch Press.
62. Cavanaugh-Johnson, T. 1993. Sexual Behaviors: A Continuum. In *Sexualized Children,* ed. E. Gil and T. Cavanaugh-Johnson. Rockville, Md.: Walnut Creek Launch Press.
63. Lane, S. 1991. Special Offender Populations. In *Juvenile Sexual Offending: Causes, Consequences, and Correction,* ed. G. D. Ryan and S. Lane. Lexington, Mass.: Lexington Books.
64. Ryan, G. 1991. Perpetration Prevention: Primary and Secondary. In *Juvenile Sexual Offending: Causes, Consequences, and Correction,* ed. G. D. Ryan and S. Lane. Lexington, Mass.: Lexington Books.

26

Further Reflections on the Therapy of Those Who Maltreat Children

BRANDT F. STEELE

In the ten years since the previous version of this chapter was published in the fourth edition of *The Battered Child,* the various kinds of child abuse and neglect, as well as the psychological and behavioral patterns of those who maltreat children, have not changed essentially. The number of abused children reported and found in need of professional care has steadily increased, as has the number of therapists, social workers, and counselors providing evaluation and treatment. The field's literature has been constantly burgeoning; many dozens of books and journal articles have appeared describing various theories and methods of treating both the victims and the perpetrators of child abuse and neglect. The very multiplicity of these publications indicates the difficulty and uncertainty of finding any pattern or mode of treatment that can be relied upon to provide effective therapy for the wide variety of perpetrators of child abuse. No one approach has proved to be uniformly applicable by the many practicing therapists, whose work is based on many different theoretical orientations, training, and experience.

Treatment can be short-term, long-term, limited, individual, group, marital, supportive, psychodynamic, psychoanalytic, cognitive, behavior modification, pharmacological, insight oriented, child oriented, client oriented, parent education oriented, specific to sexual abuse, based on hypnosis, or religious. All methods have sometimes achieved success and sometimes resulted in failure.

Treatment is usually complex and difficult, rarely easy. In addition to their problems of maladaptive parenting, the people we treat demonstrate all the same neurotic and personality disorders, even psychoses, and with the same frequency, as the general population; this accounts for part of the complexity of our cases. We may also encounter difficulties and complications arising from the concurrent involvement of the child's therapy, other social agencies, the law enforcement system, and the judicial system.

In the face of such complexity, it is useful to keep in mind a few basic principles to guide our efforts. Our primary goal is to protect children from further abuse and to enhance their future development. We can best accomplish this by improving the parenting patterns of parents or other caregivers and, simultaneously, by relieving the many forms of

BRANDT F. STEELE, M.D., is professor emeritus of psychiatry at the University of Colorado School of Medicine and serves on the staff of the C. Henry Kempe National Center for the Prevention and Treatment of Child Abuse and Neglect.

personal distress and interpersonal living problems which plague the parent-caregiver. From a biological perspective, caring for our offspring is a function we share with all other animals—but as humans we come equipped with far fewer "instinctively" determined patterns of care than even our closest primate relatives do, while our progeny, undergoing a much longer period of dependent infancy and childhood than any other species, pressures us to learn and constantly exercise intensive child-caring skills. The most basic sources of an adult's child-caring abilities are the deeply imbedded memories, conscious and unconscious, of what it was like to be a child and of how he or she was cared for then (1). It is through day-by-day experience in the first two or three years of life that we learn how people interact with each other and behave. Just as we learn verbal language (the "mother tongue") and speak to each other, we learn the "language" of interpersonal relationships and how to treat each other. These learnings persist. It is not unusual for an abusive parent to say, "I swore I would never bring up my children the way I was raised, but that's exactly what I've done."

This generational transmission of maltreatment tendencies is commonly seen in cases coming for therapy (see chapter 5) (2). Such tendencies can become manifest at any time from early childhood on. Consider, for example, the case of a four-and-a-half-year-old boy who said, when his mother asked him why he had choked and shaken his baby sister, "Mommy, that's what you used to do to me." Or take the case of an eleven-year-old youngster who was accustomed to being beaten for disobedience and was forced to baby-sit with a niece while the rest of the family went out for entertainment: he beat up the toddler when she did not obey his requests. Or a teenaged couple who declared, "We don't care what the silly pediatrician says, we'll raise our baby the way we were raised"—later, they severely injured their crying baby by harsh physical punishment. Or the child molester who repeatedly seduced latency-aged boys in much the same fashion in which he himself had been sexually abused at age nine by a "kindly" uncle. Among all the kinds of perpetrators of child abuse and across the wide spectrum of maltreatment, it is necessary to know how the perpetrator's child-caring abilities have been directed or hampered by his or her own past experiences. The behavior and caregiving patterns of perpetrators are impossible to "treat" or deeply influence unless we attempt to understand these perpetrators in relation to their own history.

Insofar as a "basic tendency" to be abusive is established in the earliest relationship between child and caregiver, it can be understood in terms of the attachment of neonates to parents and, reciprocally, the attachment, or "bonding," of parents to their new infants (see chapter 5) (3, 4). Newborn babies possess an innate biological pattern of attaching to whatever caregiving person is present and available, primarily the nourishing mother or her surrogate, and in order to survive will adapt to whatever the attachment object provides. The mother's bonding to her new infant is only marginally determined biologically, but psychologically it is based on her total life experience, beginning with the relationship she had with her own mother from birth on, and encompassing all the other people with whom she has been attached or intimately involved since childhood. Her attitudes toward her child will also be influenced by the state of her current relationships, good or poor, with her parents and with the father of the child. Deficits and distortions in the bonding process seriously hamper and interfere with the mother's subsequent ability to care empathically for her baby and thereby open the way for abuse or neglect.

Although usually not as prominent a figure as the mother is in the early attachment to the baby, a father, too, goes through a similar bonding process and can experience problems if, for instance, he is troubled by the pregnancy, labor, and delivery or by feeling the loss of the new mother's attention to him when he sees her nursing the baby. Any lack in his ability to be empathic toward both wife and child, plus any residues of unsatisfactory early experiences from his own childhood, can contribute to later abusive behaviors. In many ways child abuse can be understood as a disorder of attachment. It is through the medium of attachment and bonding that the intergenerational transmission of abusive potential occurs.

Other sources of a parent's child-caring abilities are those practices prevalent in one's culture, along with ideas and advice from relatives, friends, nurses, pediatricians, TV and radio programs, magazines, and books on child rearing, as well as direct observation of other parents. We all acquire such knowledge through cognitive learning in later childhood and adult life, and it is much more easily understood and modified through counseling and advice than are the more unconscious residues of early life experience. Inadequacies in this kind of knowledge can be addressed and corrected with rewarding results in crisis therapy or via educational methods such as parenting classes and informational material about child development.

The therapist must keep in mind that acceptable cultural and subcultural patterns of child rearing can vary widely between different countries, as well as often varying extensively and subtly between geographic, ethnic, religious, and socioeconomic subcultures within the same country. Also, in most cultures a certain pervasive ambivalence adheres to child abuse, the simultaneous beliefs that children deserve gentle loving kindness and that they cannot develop properly without strict discipline and corporal punishment. When we think of how difficult it would be to change such deeply embedded notions in a "good" parent, we realize the difficulty of changing the similarly acquired patterns of abuse.

In addition to understanding the role of early life neglect and abuse as a persistent behavioral organizer in the older abuser, the therapist needs to thoroughly explore the perpetrator's total life situation, marital relationship, sexual behaviors, recreational activities, ability to experience pleasure, and general social relationships. In particular, the therapist should cultivate an awareness of the perpetrator's specific psychological patterns and mental state, especially those concerning self-esteem and self-identity. In order to determine the type of treatment needed and its chances for success, therapists must ascertain whether or not there are signs of significant mental illness, such as serious depression, schizophrenia, paranoid personality, sociopathy, poor impulse control, sexual perversions, serious alcoholism or substance abuse, or a history of aggressivity or criminality. Devising a successful approach to an individual's problems with child care is difficult, if not altogether impossible, if his or her more pervasive total life problems are not adequately recognized and managed. It is equally important to discern if the perpetrator had, in addition to all the unhappy relationships of his or her early life, any other relationships which were good. Was there anybody—relative, neighbor, schoolteacher, or someone—whom he felt understood and cherished by, whom he felt he could love and who loved him in return? The presence of such a person in the perpetrator's life augers well for treatment; the complete lack of such persons indicates that treatment will be difficult and improvement problematical.

Episodes of maltreatment occur in a much larger life setting. The method of treatment should vary significantly to fit the particularities of each case:

> A father who is ashamed and frustrated by just having lost his job and who is now faced with the unfamiliar task of infant and child care while his wife goes out to make the family living by being a cocktail waitress.

> A teenager who is saddled with excessive amounts of housework and care of younger siblings while peers are out having a good time.

> A very depressed young mother, faced with the difficulty of having moved far away from her family and friends, alone with a crying baby, and coping with a husband who has become abusive and alcoholic.

Such are the extra strains and crises which can precipitate and perpetuate episodes of maltreatment and require immediate understanding intervention. But the discovery, recognition, and reporting of the neglect or abuse will also create a new crisis in itself. Management and treatment of the parent or other perpetrators begin at that point and must, at first, deal with the hurt feelings, denials, anger at the system, and fear of punishment aroused in the perpetrator, as well as with the disruptions, confusions, and burdens we unavoidably introduce into the family's life by carrying out the interventions necessary to protect the victimized child.

Supportive sympathetic help in the management of crisis, followed by counseling and clarification, are necessary to begin treatment of perpetrators of abuse. In some relatively benign cases, caregivers will be able to make significant changes in their child care routines, will stop neglecting or physically abusing, and will be able to maintain these changes in the future. However, for the more common, more serious situations, no significant, long-lasting change will occur unless deeper issues are addressed. The perpetrators must be helped to clearly recognize and respect their underlying needs in order to fundamentally change and improve their child-caring abilities.

The deleterious residues of early life experience which plague the perpetrator and damage his or her caregiving in adult life are essentially the very characteristics described in chapters 5 and 25 as the effects of neglect and abuse on the child. Most simply, the abusive adult needs treatment for the same things the abused child does, and, to a certain extent, the treatment of the adult is similar to that of the child. For the child, a new and better experience of being cared for is needed. The failure-to-thrive baby resumes normal physical, emotional, and social development soon after appropriate feeding and empathic care are provided, either in foster care or through coaching the mother in nurturing behavior. Depending on their developmental stage, older abused children, in addition to receiving this basic empathic care, need increasingly more complex and intellectual support; they benefit from interventions directed toward developing their cognitive awareness of what has happened to them and what they can do to improve their future. For both child and adult, the heart of successful therapy is the therapist's empathic awareness of the patient's psychological state and needs and the therapist's active, appropriate response to them. Added to this, the patient must be assured and must come to trust that he or she will be heard and understood. This therapeutic alliance is the "carrier wave" on which all other therapeutic processes must ride. Without that alliance, lasting change is unlikely.

The treatment of the child is obviously a kind of "re-parenting," and the treatment of adults has also been described as basically a "re-parenting" process. The re-parenting, in the adult case, must be carried out on a cognitive, symbolic level rather than through the literal expressions of good parenting which can be used with small children. The adult patient may very likely need to know, through our verbal response and emotional tone, that we recognize he is feeling like a lonely, frightened, three-year-old child who wants to be picked up and cuddled, even though we never actually pick him up and put him on our laps. Parental functions can be performed in this case, but without infantilizing the client.

The parental functions, over and above the provision of elementary survival needs, with which we are concerned are the reasonably consistent and reliably appropriate responses to the individual's needs and state. Such interactions validate the individual adult's or child's own growing awareness of his or her inner sensations, desires, and satisfactions. As the child grows, the parental functions also grow, from satisfying such basic needs as those for food and warmth to fulfilling the more sophisticated needs for social interactions, vocal and verbal exchanges, and motor play. Gradually, caregivers develop the parental function of interpreting reality to the child, giving the child instruction in how to deal with it safely, then both permission and encouragement to explore the world and follow, within safe limits, his or her own initiative, plus encouragement to constantly learn and to profit from inevitable mistakes.

To a varying degree, many or all of these parental functions were diminished or distorted in the adult perpetrator's early life. This invariably produces very low self-esteem, lack of self-confidence, poor sense of identity, lack of basic trust, learning difficulties, poor ability to cope with crises, and a stunted ability to find pleasure in everyday life. The therapist's function is to help this type of adult patient recognize these problems and their origin and to reopen the channels of development so that progress can be made in his or her own life. In a very simple but true sense, the parents' or other caregivers' inability to be empathically sensitive and to respond appropriately to their children is a direct result of the unempathic care they received themselves in early years. Accordingly, empathic awareness and understanding are the basis for beneficial therapy. From this basis of good communication, therapists know what interventions can be made and when to make them, they know how to help patients gain cognitive understanding of the how and why of their own feelings and behavior, and they know how to help them bring some order out of the chaotic, unhappy experiences of their early years. The most valuable assistance therapists can provide these troubled patients, beyond the intellectual insights that enable caregivers to grow and develop, is time, attention, tolerance, and the recognition of the immeasurable worth of the individual human beings sitting near to them.

Abusive caretakers are often described as immature, very needy, and dependent. These descriptive terms are essentially accurate, but too often they are used in a critical, derogatory sense rather than as valuable clues to the basic characterological difficulties which must be dealt with in treatment. The immaturity of perpetrators can best be understood as a manifestation of developmental arrest—a blockage of normal drives toward maturation and an inhibition of normal personality growth. Having been brought up under constant admonitions to be strictly obedient to external demands and to disregard their own thoughts and feelings, these individuals reached adulthood with their independent maturation inhibited. They have not been able to use their own innate abilities to develop an internal body of knowledge which would enable them to use good judgment about what to do and not to do in life. To a large extent, they have remained immature and helpless, depending upon some proper authority to tell them what to do and how to do it. Most often, the "proper authority" is what they remember of the rules of their own past childhood.

Fear of criticism or punishment for taking independent initiative can also block maturation and lead to a kind of dependency. Rather than using his or her own ideas, the person remains at the mercy of outside admonition and advice, needing to be told what to do and needing to be reassured that he is doing it well. Many persons in treatment either wait to be told or openly ask to be told what to do and how to do it, under the pretext of perfectly sensible cooperation and willingness to learn. A mother can ask, for instance, "Well, what should I do when Johnny soils his pants?" If the therapist either details specifically what should be done or follows certain rigid therapeutic rules that prohibit giving advice, the outcome will be merely a repetition of the past behavior of early life parents who either ordered the patient around or disregarded his needs entirely. The therapist can avoid this dilemma of saying too much or saying too little by replying: "I think I might do 'a' or 'b,' but other people might look at it differently and do 'x' or 'y'; I think the important thing is for you to find out which way works best for you and Johnny." Such a statement lets the mother know not only that her problems have been heard and understood but also that the therapist is not going to give her orders or make decisions for her. Instead, the therapist has involved the patient in thinking through the problem and the process of decision making and has shown respect for the patient's own ideas, all in an atmosphere where there is no threat of punishment or criticism in case of mistakes. Counseling and therapy cannot force patients to change, but it can offer a safe environment and ideas which they can use to grow and develop their own thinking process and self-esteem.

Another quite strong form of dependency, one present in every parent who shows abusive or neglectful behavior toward his or her offspring, sometimes is expressed openly and directly very early in a therapeutic relationship and sometimes is kept covered and hidden for a long time, and expressed only indirectly. This dependency is a manifestation of the patient's deep inner emptiness and a yearning for loving care and consideration. It is a persistent residue of an emotionally deprived childhood. Obviously, such intense, deep needs cannot be literally satisfied in a therapeutic situation. The therapist can, however, help patients realize the extent of their need and help them face the embarrassment of feeling so much like a small child, so empty, and so helpless and afraid. The problem of dependency is tricky. Some therapists seem to be afraid of it and avoid talking about it. Many agencies have a policy of actively discouraging patients' dependency on individual therapists, almost as if it were a kind of naughtiness that must be scolded and forbidden.

Actually, dependency is a core problem that must be openly dealt with sooner or later in order to help these parents to stop turning to their children as the sole suppliers of their enormous need for love and respect. Abusive parents need to learn to trust other adults enough to establish rewarding interactions with them. Often the intertwined problems of low self-esteem and feelings of unworthiness have made them feel undeserving of love and care and reluctant to seek it. This, in turn, merely reinforces their emotional deprivation and dependent neediness. Treatment can reverse this self-perpetuating cycle and help them broaden their social contacts in order to find acceptance, pleasure, and support in relationships with other adults.

Some perpetrators' deprivation has been so great and so prolonged that their dependency needs and feelings of emptiness appear bottomless and insatiable. They often express a sense of worthlessness, hopelessness, depression, and even suicidal ideation. Such persons should be given psychiatric care and evaluated for the possible use of psychotropic medication. Matters of child care cannot be usefully approached until the more serious psychiatric problems are resolved. Therapists without special skills should not be burdened with nor attempt the care of such difficult cases.

It must also be noted that therapists should not always take evidence of a patient's dependency on them as a sign of real trust or confidence in them. Such a dependency may have some elements of trust, but it must also be considered as an automatic submission to authority and a habitual mode of adaptation the patient assumes in order to stay out of trouble while trying to fulfill some basic emotional needs. Real trust and confidence in the therapist can develop only after the patient has experienced the *therapist's* respect, trust, and consistent attempts to understand the problem and be of help without criticism and attack. Often at the very beginning of treatment it may be helpful to say, "We don't know each other, and I expect it will take a little time before you can trust me. But I must ask you for something. Since I don't know you well, I may say something that is quite wrong or that may hurt your feelings. I have to trust you to tell me if I've made such a mistake; otherwise, I won't know." This, of course, will not really be believed, but it does set the ground rule for fielding the mistakes that will inevitably pop up sooner or later.

The residues of early neglect and disregard by insensitive caretakers leave the perpetrator particularly sensitive to desertion, abandonment, or inattention on the part of the therapist. Consequently, the therapist needs to notify the patient as early as possible about any vacations, absences, or any necessary changes in scheduled appointments. Therapists should also discuss with the patient all the appointment-related adjustments (transportation, work schedule, baby-sitters) to the patient's schedule. Although this practice is unacceptable to many agencies and therapists, giving patients one's home telephone number may be most helpful. Rarely is this privilege abused. Usually after making one or two calls in the middle of the night, patients realize they will be heard at any time if necessary and then, no longer needing to test the therapist's availability, will call during regular office hours. For lay therapists or home visitors provided by social services, receiving such at-home calls will be frequent and continued because they are performing the role of friend or substitute family—relationships which healthy adults usually have available but which the more socially isolated, abusive parents have been afraid to develop.

Not all perpetrators are cooperative and submissive at the beginning of a therapeutic relationship. Many are angry, rebellious, uncooperative, denying all problems and any need for help, and wish only that all the authorities would get out of their lives and leave them alone to raise their children they way they please. Ideally, the therapist should maintain some objective distance during such diatribes and attacks and not take them too personally but, rather, try to understand them as expressions of long-lasting feelings that originated in their childhood, were directed toward their parents, and are now transferred to all other authorities. Such angry verbal assaults may be the adult equivalent of a childhood tantrum. The therapist can best handle them by patiently waiting until the anger subsides and then saying something like, "Now what do you suppose all that was about?" and, "What can we do to straighten things out?" Therapists, like parents, are never perfect and sometimes either say or do something, quite unintentionally, that clearly belittles or disregards the patient's feelings. In such circumstances, the therapist should freely acknowledge the mistake or ineptness without being defensive or trying to blame the patient for stimulating the behavior. Such events can actually be very useful in therapy, because the therapist will be modeling behavior quite different from what the patient is used to, since most abusive parents never admit making a mistake or being wrong about anything. Such episodes can be directly helpful in exploring the long-lasting residues of childhood abuse and neglect.

To a greater or lesser degree, maltreating caretakers have had difficulty in experiencing adequate ordinary pleasure throughout their entire lives. They do not feel joy or happiness in their relationships with their spouse, their children, or even themselves. They have great difficulty in taking pleasure in social relationships. Their lives are, to a great extent, bleak and unrewarding, with only superficial, shallow attempts to enjoy themselves. It is important to encourage and assist maltreating parents in finding adequate pleasure in life, because the lack of fulfillment of this basic human need has a direct bearing on the patterns of maltreatment. The lifelong emptiness and deprivation felt by such parents leads to the well-known phenomenon of "role reversal"—instead of being a source of love and care for the child, the parent is emotionally empty and looks to the child to supply his or her own needs for the love, pleasure, approval, and respect required to bolster self-esteem. No small child, of course, can possibly meet such needs. When the child fails to meet parental expectations, he or she is considered unsatisfactory and unrewarding and is likely to be either verbally abused, emotionally neglected, or physically punished. Hence, therapy for abusive parents must be oriented toward helping them find adequate satisfactions in the world through relationships with other adults. This means that the therapists must enhance, encourage, and support, as well as cognitively understand, the abusive parent's social contacts.

Sooner or later, in one form or another, the abusive parent must be asked why he or she wanted children, what he or she expected of children, and what his or her feelings are about the specific child who has been abused or neglected. Nearly all abusive caregivers say they love children; nearly all say they love the child they have maltreated. But the further question is, What do they love them for? Is the child wanted and loved because of a normal and healthy desire to have and bring up children and to use one's ability to help a child grow? Or is the child loved and wanted just to fill up the emptiness left over from the caretaker's own early life? It is best not to approach this questioning with a moralistic, punitive, or investigative attitude that appears to be trying to establish guilt. We should not ask, "Have you beaten Charlie when he was naughty?" but, rather, "Has Charlie been a particularly difficult child for you to take care of?" This is more likely to reach the parent's feelings about the child, his relationship to him, and his expectations of him, and at the same time indicates that the therapist possesses some understanding and empathy for the parent's situation. This also opens the way for nonpunitive, noncritical discussion of what a normal child is able to do at different phases of development.

All those who work with abusive parents are familiar with two very opposing statements. The first is, "Well, I'm going to bring up my kids just the way I was brought up— that's the right way to do it." The second is, "I swore I would never bring up my children the way I was brought up, but I find I'm doing exactly what my mother and father did." Both statements stem from identification with parental care during the earliest phases of a child's attachment to primary caregivers. Both are examples of the generational repetition of maltreatment patterns, and both indicate the persistent strength of such identifications, even despite the attempt to rebel against them. Although the attachments that are made in the earliest period of infancy seem to have a basic biological, determined quality, the characteristics of the persons to whom the infant attachs can vary enormously. Too often, attachment is conceptualized as being only good attachment to a "good" object. What is thought to be a nonattachment, or a failure of attachment, may be, in reality, attachment to a "bad" object.

The behaviors related to attachment persist throughout life. Persons who were attached to kindly, good caregivers in infancy tend to seek out and relate to kindly people in adult life. Infants who had only unempathic, cruel caregivers to attach to in earliest life tend to automatically persist in this pattern both with their parents and with other adults. They are deeply attached to their abusive, neglecting parents. Even after better experiences in foster homes, such children often want to return to their parents—even knowing their parents will probably mistreat them again. The same type of behavior occurs among many battered women; they recurrently seek out or remain with an abusive partner. Much of what we call masochistic behavior is the persistence of early life attachment to sadistic caregivers. The residues of these early attachments and the identifications with these early objects of attachment are lasting. No therapy is able to eliminate conscious and unconscious memories of what actually happened in the past.

The objective of treatment in these cases is to help abusive parents become so comfortably aware of the existence of such residues that they can quickly recognize them and avoid automatically following the old patterns. In an empathic therapeutic environment, parents can learn new, more successful patterns of living, coping, and relating interpersonally that develop their own self-control and that serve the best interests of themselves as well as their children. Probably the most subtle and difficult part of treatment is helping patients relinquish their automatic submission to the authoritative figures from the earliest months and years of life. In successful treatment, patients can develop and carry away a new identification with the therapist that will enable them to cultivate empathic consideration for both themselves and others.

Often in the first weeks of treatment, especially with those patients who are less angry and negative to begin with, there is a sort of honeymoon period during which everything seems to be going very well and relationships with spouse and children are rapidly improving. Such a happy situation should neither be attacked nor accepted at face value. Instead, it should be delicately explored to determine whether it is the real improvement which *can* happen quickly in a relatively less damaged personality, or whether it is evidence of a lifelong ability to deny the self and adapt very quickly to the expectations of the environment without any real internal change taking place. Often parents who are under the supervision of social services or the court while their children are in placement say, "I'll do anything to get my kids back." Is this a statement of a real willingness and ability to change, or of a lifelong submission to any kind of rule in order to get out of trouble? Or is it even a more specifically sociopathic tendency to outwit authority and do as one pleases? Such persons are often described as manipulative, with a very derogatory implication. Manipulation, however, is a common, relatively normal method of interpersonal relationship. Most of us were manipulated a lot in our own upbringing, and we use a good deal of manipulation in rearing our own children. "You can't have any dessert until you eat your dinner first." "If you clean up your room, you can go to the movie Saturday." "You'll have to take a course in physical education before you can graduate." The task of the therapist is to make certain that the "manipulative" interaction on the part of both therapist and patient is developed as an opportunity for understanding and growth rather than exploitation.

When parents have improved in treatment during the time a child is in foster care, assessing the nature of their improvement is very important. Has the treatment produced real change in the parents' child-caring abilities, or has the improvement been related to the fact that the problem child is no longer in the family and the parents have improved because the child is absent? There may also be a honeymoon period of good interaction after a child is first returned home from foster care. The child may have developed enough emotional strength to adapt well when first sent back to his or her parents, before some of the old patterns have had a chance to resurface. Only after several weeks have passed can we validate that the therapy has produced lasting change. It is also crucial to determine, gradually, whether the parents can maintain improvement only with the support of a therapist present, or whether they have absorbed and integrated enough self-esteem and self-control into their own personalities to maintain such improvement independently, on their own, with newly developed support systems in the community.

Recurrently during treatment, reality will intrude in the form of a variety of problems: marital strife, financial problems, illness, unemployment, broken down automobiles or household appliances, school problems, conflict with relatives; the list is endless. Early in treatment, some practical help must often be given in such crises. Increasingly, more attention must be paid to the how and why of such recurring troubles. In general, maltreating families experience more crises than other families do. However, this seems more related to the poor ability of maltreating adults to cope with events and to plan for the future than to bad luck or being saddled with more than the average number of troubles. Because of their early life experiences of being taught to disregard their own inner feelings and thoughts and to remain completely submissive to outward admonitions, they have been deprived of the ability to take the initiative to think out what to do when trouble erupts.

Hence, events that are easily coped with by the average person are unmanageable to them. Because of their own distrust and consequent social isolation, they cannot seek help from others, so situations become increasingly out of control. Treatment needs to be directed toward encouraging the development of independent thought and ideas and instilling the courage to try independent action without fear of punishment or criticism. The pattern of learning to "do it yourself" which was inhibited or blocked in their childhood can be revived in adult life with very rewarding results in both crisis-coping ability and self-esteem.

It is beyond the scope of this discussion to cover all the specific problems that can arise in different modes of treatment: group therapy, family therapy, individual psychotherapy, social case work, self-help groups, crisis therapy, behavior modification, counseling of all kinds, supportive home visiting, education in child development and parenting skills, and others. Nor can it outline all the special techniques used by social workers, psychologists, psychiatrists, mental health workers, public health nurses, lay therapists, counselors, teachers, foster parents, and residential treatment centers. There is, however, a basic underlying theme in all successful treatment. Providing a facilitating environment opens up new channels of growth, development, and maturation, channels that were blocked and distorted in early life. Only by improving the abusive parents' basic life patterns can we significantly improve their child-caring potentials. This principle and the general principles of treatment discussed above are applicable, regardless of the particular treatment mode, for perpetrators of most forms of child abuse and neglect, including sexual abuse. Exceptions must be made, however, for perpetrators of pedophilia and forcible rape. Unfortunately, we have not yet found reliable models of treatment for such offenders that promise much success, nor have penal correctional systems proved very effective.

Parents must be heard and cared for themselves before they can be able, or expected, to hear and care for their children. Jolly K., the founder of Parents Anonymous, told us during the earliest years of that organization, "It is easy to help people stop physically abusing their children; we can do it in a few weeks. What is much harder to do and takes a long time is teaching them how to love." In addition to all the cognitive enlightenment that abusive parents need to put their lives in better order, they must also experience the feelings of being safe and being loved. We learn to care by being cared for. Treating perpetrators of child abuse puts new, real meaning into the well-worn adage, "You have to love yourself before you can love anyone else." Only when their parents have accomplished this will the children be in safe hands.

References

1. Benedek, T. 1959. Parenthood as a Developmental Phase. *J. Am. Psychoanalytic Assn.* 7: 389–417.
2. Steele, B. 1985. Generational Transmission of the Maltreatment of Children. In *Parental Influence in Health and Disease,* ed. E. J. Anthony and G. Pollock. Boston, Mass.: Little, Brown.
3. Bowlby, J. 1982. *Attachment.* New York: Basic Books.
4. Karen, R. 1994. *Becoming Attached.* New York: Warner.

PART

4

Prevention

Part 4: Editors' Comments

For many of us, prevention is the ultimate challenge in helping abused children, their families, and society in general cope with the personal and social toll that child abuse exacts. Part 4 in this edition of *The Battered Child* is still too short, considering the importance of prevention efforts in addressing the "national emergency" of child maltreatment. In chapter 27, by Anne Cohn Donnelly, we include a review of what is being accomplished in the area of prevention of physical abuse and neglect. Over the past decade, we have seen truly great advances in knowledge about prevention of physical harm to children. There are even budding, although still rudimentary, efforts under way to extend what we know about prevention to everyone who needs it.

Ironically, in the area of sexual abuse prevention, we have probably reached many more children, although the outcome database is much weaker for the massive efforts that have been undertaken on an national and international scale. The theoretical framework for the sexual abuse prevention effort is presented here in chapter 29, by David Finkelhor and Deborah Daro.

For theory and practice to be implemented widely and effectively, not only child protection services professionals but politicians must take action. The track record of politicians on child protection legislation worldwide is spotty. Partly this is the consequence of our having spent too much time as professionals in the lab and clinic, and too little in the halls of government. Ultimately, the prevention of child abuse and neglect will occur only when the people, through their elected officials or other leaders, decide to get involved and do something. Henry Kempe once said: "Don't be afraid of being called a do-gooder. Just go out and do some good!" It's still excellent—and timely—advice.

27

An Overview of Prevention of Physical Abuse and Neglect

ANNE COHN DONNELLY

Why should we be concerned about preventing child abuse and neglect? Every year more than a million children in the United States are seriously abused and/or neglected by their parents or guardians, and over two thousand children die from this maltreatment (1). As a nation, the United States spends hundreds of millions of dollars identifying maltreated children and providing them with medical and protective services in the hope that the immediate scars will be eradicated and the hurt will not continue or recur (1).

But in many families, regardless of the services they receive, abuse does recur or neglect continues. State agency personnel still must sometimes choose to remove children from their homes, placing them in foster care or other types of shelter. The institutional costs are great, as are the social and emotional costs of separating children from their families. Also great are the hidden costs of child abuse and neglect, seen a generation later when an abused or neglected child may himself become a perpetrator. And, of course, however intensely and effectively we do help individual families where maltreatment has already occurred, this does not result in a reduction of the prevalence of the problem in society as a whole. To save lives, to avert physical and emotional suffering—and to begin, finally, to see a reduction in the size of the problem—these are the reasons we should be concerned about preventing child abuse and neglect (2).

Defining Prevention

To ground our understanding of the concept of prevention, we will start with several definitions. Often child maltreatment prevention is described and defined by levels or layers, as follows:

- *Primary prevention:* Efforts aimed at whole population groups, addressing the underlying or societal causes of child abuse (for example, media violence, acceptance of corporal punishment as a form of discipline, poverty)
- *Secondary prevention:* Efforts aimed at individuals identified as being at risk of abuse (for instance, teen parents, parents who experienced abuse as children)—such efforts attempt to alleviate or eradicate those factors which put an individual at risk (for instance, poor parenting skills, lack of understanding of child development)

ANNE COHN DONNELLY, D.P.H., is the executive director of the National Committee to Prevent Child Abuse.

- *Tertiary prevention* (often referred to as "treatment"): Strategies directed at people who have already abused their children—such strategies attempt to get these parents (or caregivers) to stop and not repeat the abuse

While all of the above levels of prevention are important, the focus of this chapter will be on prevention efforts before any occurrence of abuse or neglect has begun, that is, on both primary and secondary prevention as defined above. Here, we will consider efforts aimed at changing behavior, attitudes, knowledge, and skills, as well as various environmental influences affecting individuals and communities, so that abuse will not occur. This includes therapeutic support for the victim of abuse as a long-term prevention strategy to help break the cycle of violence. Although prevention services offered to families on an intensive basis to help keep the family together and to avoid foster care placement after abuse has happened are very important, they are not the subject of this chapter, nor is the prevention of sexual abuse.

A Public Health Approach to Prevention

Child abuse and neglect is a major public health problem, given their incidence and prevalence in the general population. A public health approach to moving toward and designing prevention strategies is instructive. Such an approach includes a number of steps:

1. Establishing the size of the problem: developing surveillance systems to measure morbidity and mortality, define who is being maltreated, with what severity and frequency
2. Identifying those at risk: determining why children are harmed, what puts certain families at risk
3. Determining how to modify the incidence or prevalence: testing how best to reduce or eliminate the risk factors for the victim and the perpetrator, ideally through randomized trials of different interventions
4. Evaluating different interventions rigorously, in a variety of settings and for different population groups: determining the relative effectiveness of different strategies for different target groups and deciphering what makes for quality and success with different approaches
5. Implementing successful strategies on a widespread basis: using what we have learned universally

In the field of child abuse and neglect, progress has been made on many of these steps. We have been diligent in attempting to establish the size of the problem and in defining risk factors. However, our ability to do so precisely is limited for a number of reasons. First, there is a lack of consensus about the definition of child abuse and neglect. Second, our country lacks a way of gathering standard data on the problem from one state to another. And third, child abuse and neglect are such complex sets of phenomena that they involve numerous risk factors, which in turn interact variously depending upon the individual, the population group, and the community. Despite these limitations—to which many authors bear witness throughout this book—professionals have managed to find some common ground in discussing the general magnitude of the problem and key risk factors for different forms of child maltreatment.

We have been able to conduct some testing and evaluating of different prevention interventions. While our knowledge about different prevention strategies has increased dramatically during the past two decades, many questions remain only partially answered and some not addressed at all. For example, one key risk factor to be discussed at greater length later in this chapter is new parents' lack of parenting skills; various interventions—from home visitation to parent groups and family resource centers—have been devised to reduce this type of risk. Randomized trials have not been used for all approaches, however, and even when they have—as in the case of home visitation—the same intervention has not yet been used systematically across a range of population groups or assessed by varying such factors as the home visitor's degree of professional training (3). Should we be concerned about this incompleteness of our knowledge? Dr. Ray Helfer always said that if we wait for all the knowledge to come in, we will never do anything. While it is important to continue to consider these vital questions, it is also important to proceed with the implementation of prevention programs.

Our biggest challenge in the field of preventing child maltreatment has always been in accomplishing effective widespread implementation of successful strategies. In the treatment, or tertiary prevention, area, for example, the model of family preservation often called Homebuilders (that is, very intensive, comprehensive work with a family where abuse or neglect has occurred to arrive at solutions other than foster care placement) has been found in a variety of studies to be effective. Not only has it been difficult to persuade children's protective service agencies across the country to adopt this successful approach, but even when they do adopt it, they all too frequently water down the intervention process, leading to unsuccessful, unsatisfactory results (4).

Writing about public health approaches to reducing interpersonal violence, Deborah Prothrow-Stith comments, "the problem is not in proving that intervention works—it is providing intervention to the hundreds of thousands of children, millions of children, who need help" (5). To add to that thought, the problem is also in making sure when we move to the level of widespread implementation that we honor everything we have learned about what it takes to build a quality program.

Principles Underlying Prevention

When we are determining how best to approach prevention, it is essential to consider both the social and personal factors that increase the risk of abuse in parent-child relationships. In some respects, all families are vulnerable. Being a family member has its challenges for anyone, but some families have a tougher time than others. It is only by identifying and addressing those factors which increase parents' difficulties in positive functioning that we can hope to prevent child abuse. In thinking then about an effective approach to prevention, a general review of risk factors is the necessary first step.

The degree of a family's socioeconomic status is high on the list of factors that create a potential for abuse and neglect. Simply put, while child maltreatment is found at all income levels, its likelihood increases as families move down the social class ladder (6,7). Unemployment and related financial difficulties are very significant factors (8,9). Other significant factors associated with social class—for example, substance abuse, poor education, and overcrowded or inadequate housing—also bear a strong relation to child abuse (10,11). Furthermore, adolescent parenthood increases the likelihood of child maltreatment (12). This association may be partly explainable in terms of social class—most teenage parents either come from or move quickly into low socioeconomic status (13). In addition to their lifelong economic problems, many who enter parenthood as teenagers end up with large numbers of children, and large family size itself qualifies as a risk factor.

When the responsibility for caring for a child is concentrated in the hands of one person, the risk of abuse and neglect increases (14). Parents caring for young children without benefit of supplementary caregivers are especially vulnerable to becoming abusive or neglectful (15). These parents, typically mothers, are exposed to situations requiring a lot of caregiving behavior but providing little positive reinforcement for fulfilling that demanding role. The result is often depression and anger, tension and stress. All are related to child abuse.

Evidence from many sources suggests that abusive families tend to be socially isolated, having no one to turn to for support (16). The lack of financial and personal resources that place many parents at risk for child maltreatment becomes even more threatening when accompanied by lack of social supports. In addition, the behavior of parents who are socially isolated is less subject to corrective social monitoring. Research on "high-risk" neighborhoods, where maltreatment of children is especially likely to occur, indicates that in such areas parents lack social supports or social networks that set good examples of proper parenting (17). "High-risk" neighborhoods are also characterized by high rates of all forms of violence.

Along with economic, personal, and social support deficits, many abusing and neglectful parents have a lack of social skills, which frequently becomes apparent in the form of poor parenting skills (18). This most often is the result of having themselves had poor parenting models when they were children. Such parents may know little about normal child development, may be poor observers of their children's behavior, and may have unrealistic expectations of the way children ought to behave.

Stress appears as a common denominator in explaining physically abusive behavior, but the relation between stress and child abuse may not be a direct one (19). Since life crises have more of an impact on those parents with a punitive history, the life history of the parent is relevant to the link between stress and abuse. Parents who experienced rejection and a general lack of nurturance as children are more vulnerable to the disruptive effects of social stress because of their low self-esteem, poor self-understanding, and inability to distance themselves psychologically from their children. In other words, the victim of child abuse is more likely than other children to become a victimizer as an adult (20).

Some studies suggest that certain characteristics or traits of infants and children elicit abusive or neglectful behavior in adults (21,22). Such characteristics can make a child more difficult for a parent to nurture and love—a colicky infant, a mismatch in personalities between parent and child (perhaps a very active child matched with a lethargic but irritable parent), premature or low-birth-weight babies, or children with early health difficulties. Evidence also shows that physically challenged infants and children are at increased risk for abuse or neglect, as are babies with any other condition or circumstance that impedes early attachment and bonding. These risk factors must be addressed in any comprehensive approach to prevention.

Goals of Prevention

Dr. Ray Helfer (see chapter 28) guides our thinking about the goals of prevention:

> With very few exceptions, if one wishes to prevent something bad from happening, the development of something good must come first. Eliminating cholera and dysentery from our society required the development of sewers and clean water systems. Preventing polio required building polio antibody levels in the bodies of our children through vaccination. . . . Likewise, to prevent child abuse and other adverse outcomes of the breakdown in the interactional systems within our families, we must *enhance* interpersonal skills in those very folks. (23, pp. 425–26)

Because child maltreatment is such a complex set of problems with so many different causes, any approach to prevention needs to incorporate multiple ways to enhance the functioning of parents and families. Based on what we know about who is at risk, a comprehensive prevention strategy should include these goals:

- Increase parents' knowledge of child development and the demands of parenting
- Enhance parent-child bonding, emotional ties, and communication
- Increase parents' skills in coping with the stresses of infant and child care
- Increase parents' skills in coping with the stresses of caring for children with special needs
- Increase parents' knowledge about home and child management
- Increase peer support and reduce family isolation
- Increase access to social and health services, including substance abuse treatment, for all family members
- Increase parents' access to jobs, adequate housing, and safe neighborhoods
- Reduce the long-term consequences of poor parenting

Prediction as a Step toward Prevention

Given our knowledge about the risk factors associated with abuse and neglect, is it possible to predict with any accuracy who will be a child abuser and, accordingly, to direct prevention services specifically to those people? Numerous researchers and clinicians have sought to develop methods to identify high-risk parents or families (24–26). These methods generally address some combination of the risk factors listed above. Increasingly, these techniques successfully identify pools or groupings of parents at risk; however, such techniques also continue to identify some parents as being "at risk" even though they in fact never become abusers (the false positives), as well as failing to identify some parents as being "at risk" who do become abusive or neglectful.

In other words, maltreatment is a vastly complex human problem, and although it is possible to do a pretty good job of identifying groupings in which the risk is much greater than average, it is not possible to flag accurately only those individuals who will become abusers. This inability to precisely predict abusive or neglectful behavior, while not surprising, is lamentable. Researchers do find that under apparently similar circumstances, with apparently similar features and characteristics, some "at risk" parents abuse their children and some do not. But, so far, researchers remain at a loss to explain why.

The significance of this limitation, of course, depends upon what we intend to do with the information. Wisdom would suggest that even though our prevention efforts should focus on making services available to all families, or to all members of specific subgroups, which could be classified as at high risk for child abuse, our approach should be to offer all prevention services in a positive manner, without any stigmatizing population-specific labels attached.

A Comprehensive Approach to Prevention

Keeping the goals of a comprehensive prevention strategy in mind, we next should consider what the nature of our prevention interventions must be in order to achieve those goals. Again, Ray Helfer helps direct our thinking:

> Any discussions of prevention would not be complete without consideration of the question, "Does knowledge, per se, lead to prevention?" If this could be answered in the affirmative, our task would be much simpler. Teaching facts is indeed much easier and cheaper than teaching skills and influencing one's affective domain.
>
> Certainly, using the media to tell the population that child abuse exists and what to do about it has increased awareness and reporting. Telling the masses that smoking is related to cancer and speeding to fatal auto accidents seems to curtail, to some degree, these behaviors. However, most campaigns to teach parents to keep aspirin out of the reach of children did little to prevent aspirin poisoning. It was not until the tops were made hard to remove that aspirin poisoning was almost eliminated. . . .
>
> The answer to the question, "Does knowledge, per se, lead to prevention?" seems to be, "To some extent, if the behavior change required is not too complex and the attitude change is not too fundamental."
>
> For example, telling drivers to buckle their seat belts will result in a behavioral change in a certain segment of the population. Making it a law will add more to that group, but not all. In the child abuse area, one would expect that baby shaking would decrease significantly if we put as much money into the TV message "Don't Shake the Baby" as we do in teaching the public "Don't Squeeze the Charmin."
>
> Knowledge, per se, is not sufficient when the behavior change is complex and/or if the attitudes are based on a fundamental belief system. Reading a book or seeing a television demonstration on "how to parent" or "how to play golf" will not, in itself, be sufficient. One must learn these skills by modeling, coaching, one-to-one interaction, and PRACTICE. That, after all, is what childhood, in a reasonably normal environment, is all about. (23, pp. 431–32)

Because child maltreatment is exceptionally complex, with numerous causes that vary for different individuals and groups, no single preventive program can be expected to substantially reduce the incidence of abuse and neglect. A prevention approach should include a number of different strategies targeted to different populations and should reflect different phases of the family life cycle. To cope successfully with their roles in the family, both parents and children require certain supports, training, and information. Based on what we know or believe will enhance an individual's ability to function in a healthy way within a family, and keeping in mind risk factors for abuse, we should include in an overall approach to prevention the following areas:

- Support programs for all new parents, particularly those at greatest risk for abuse
- Parenting education for all parents
- Early and regular screening and health care, including prenatal care and substance abuse treatment for all children and families
- Therapeutic programs for all abused children and young adults
- Life skills training, including conflict resolution skills, for all children and young adults
- Self-help groups and other neighborhood supports—including hotlines, helplines, family resource centers, and crisis nurseries—for all parents under stress
- Direct support services, including job training, child care, and so forth

These areas begin with the child's prenatal period, furnishing prospective parents with information and skills related to child care and child development. They continue with services and support programs for parents of infants and young children and include services for the child throughout the school years.

Do we have scientific proof that all these services will prevent child abuse and neglect? No, although a great deal of clinical experience and some research point out the benefits of these kinds of services. The gaps in existing knowledge limit our ability to design the most effective prevention programs, but these gaps must not be obstacles to our getting started. Improved understanding will follow further clinical work.

Should the government offer these programs? Should they be mandatory? Certainly, there is concern that government control may become so insidious and government intervention so pervasive that the family unit as commonly accepted may become impossible to maintain. It is argued that broad, coercive intervention programs should be avoided; many professionals believe that the use of coercion diminishes the potential effectiveness of service. Because of this concern, prevention programs that provide services to all families on a voluntary basis probably have a greater chance to succeed. And governmental agencies such as health departments, which generally do not offer services to people under the force of the law, can play a significant role in making sure such services are offered universally.

There are, however, two objections to this approach. First, if services are offered only on a voluntary basis, families with the greatest need may simply choose not to accept them. Second, because of resource constraints, the more costly programs cannot be provided to all families. For these reasons, it is important (at least initially) to try to identify groups of families or communities with the greatest need for prevention programs and to make the services readily available primarily to them. Many people believe that the most important place to begin, because of the need, is with new parents.

A Place to Start: With New Parents

Drawing on twenty years of research, the U.S. Advisory Board on Child Abuse and Neglect recommended in 1991 well over one hundred different actions which they deemed necessary in order to prevent child maltreatment. The advisory board said that the logical place to begin is with new parents, helping them get off to a good start and thus head of any abuse and neglect patterns that might otherwise emerge (27).

With new parents—especially first-time parents—we have the opportunity to encourage and, if necessary, to teach good parenting practices before bad patterns have a chance to get established. New parents are often characterized as absorbing information "like sponges," anxious and ready to learn anything they can about their new babies and how to care for them. Moreover, most reported cases of physical abuse and neglect occur among the youngest children (that is, those under age five) (28). By focusing on new parents, we are reaching the target population in which the incidence of physical abuse and neglect is likely to be the greatest.

While many approaches to working with new parents have been formulated, the advisory board recommended a voluntary program of targeted home visits to new parents and their babies as the desired one. Even recognizing that intensive support to at-risk new parents is not the panacea or sole answer to the child abuse problem, the advisory board stated that no other single intervention shows the promise that home visitation does. Others—including The U.S. General Accounting Office, the Carnegie Corporation, and the American Academy of Pediatrics—concur. There are a number of reasons why.

First, home visiting has widespread appeal. It affords an opportunity to work with individuals in the family context or environment, enabling the professional or volunteer visitor to learn firsthand the parents' and child's living conditions and to respond to them directly. In other words, child protective workers are thus enabled to tailor their service (namely, the home visit) to the particular needs and characteristics of the parent and the child in their own everyday setting. In addition, home visits uniquely provide a way to reach isolated families, families that typically do not participate, families that are too distrustful or too disorganized to make their way to a center-based program or a protection worker's office—precisely those families at greatest risk to abuse. In this sense, home visiting provides a unique opportunity to engage dysfunctional families.

The public is most supportive of the home visitor concept. A public opinion poll conducted in 1992 by the National Committee to Prevent Child Abuse showed that 86% of the respondents thought it appropriate to offer home visits and other supportive services to all first-time parents (29).

Second, in addition to the widespread appeal of home visitor services, there is a solid and expanding evaluative database on the efficacy of the approach. The studies date back over two decades (30).

In the early 1970s, the C. Henry Kempe National Center for the Prevention and Treatment of Child Abuse and Neglect conducted a controlled experimental design study of home visitors with a sample of high-risk new parents. The study documented enhanced mother-infant relationships and a reduction in physical child abuse within the experimental group (31).

From the mid-1970s through the early 1980s, a number of large-scale evaluation studies of federally funded child abuse service programs, which included high-risk as well as abusive and neglectful clients, were conducted (32). The studies compared the relative effectiveness and cost-effectiveness of different service interventions. The home-visiting services of parent aides (coupled with group services such as group therapy or Parents Anonymous) and homemaker services significantly reduced child abuse potential in contrast to those clients receiving basic counseling or only out-of-home assistance.

Dr. David Olds and his colleagues (33,34) have conducted the longest and perhaps most thoroughly designed and carefully controlled studies of the home visitor model from the scientific perspective. In his initial study, four hundred first-time mothers were randomly assigned to four groups, one of which received: (*a*) intensive pre- and postnatal visits by a nurse-practitioner; (*b*) parent education on fetal and infant development; (*c*) involvement of the mothers, friends, and family in child care and support of the mother; and (*d*) linkages to health and human services. The results are powerful: this experimental group showed a 4% incidence of child abuse at the end of the study, in contrast to a rate of 19% in the control group. Members of the experimental group also demonstrated fewer accidents, less required use of the emergency room, less need to punish and discipline their children, and longer intervals between pregnancies. Dr. Olds is cautious in generalizing his findings to populations beyond the young, low-income, single mothers studied. Other research projects, however, support the value of home visitor services in various settings.

Lutzker and Rice (35) conducted a study of Project Twelve Ways, a multifaceted home-based service program in southern Illinois in which home visits to new parents were offered by graduate students. At the end of the program, abuse had been detected in 2% of those families receiving the home visits in contrast to 11% of those in the control groups. The relative effectiveness of the program continued for at least one year. In a one-year follow-up study, abuse was found in 10% of the experimental group and 21% of the control group.

Seitz and her colleagues (36) studied the impact of intensive home visits to first-time mothers for twenty months after their infants' births. Follow-ups were conducted on fifteen of seventeen matched sets of families up to ten years after the home-visiting program terminated. Seitz documented steady improvement in parenting and family life over the ten-year period.

As stated by Packard Foundation, "home visiting will never be a magic cure . . . it is however an important front end service" (3, p. 18). It does help to significantly reduce rates of reported abuse and neglect in the population serviced while also reducing the use of negative parenting practices and enhancing the capacity of parents to care adequately for their children.

The effectiveness of home visitation services for at-risk new parents appears to be linked to the degree to which such services are intensive, occur over a long period of time, are well integrated with.or into other community services, are flexible in responding to the unique needs of an individual family, and are comprehensive. The literature (3, p. 18) suggests in fact that all of the following are important or critical steps which must be implemented for effective home visitor services:

- Initiate services prenatally or at birth
- Universalize intake service for all new parents initially from a defined geographic target area (for example, educational hospital visit to all newborns in a given census tract or zip code)
- Conduct universal needs assessment using standardized protocol to identify systematically those new parents most in need of services due to the presence of various factors associated with increased risk for child maltreatment and other poor childhood outcomes
- Offer all high-risk parents home-visiting services in a positive, voluntary way
- Provide home visitation as the core service and include linkages to other community resources (for example, a medical home, a family resource center, or a substance abuse counseling program)
- Develop creative outreach (for example, persistent, positive outreach for a number of months) to build client trust in accepting services
- Schedule regular, frequent visits (for example, at least once a week), with well-defined criteria for increasing or decreasing intensity of service

Clearly, providing such services is not a simple task. For example, linkages between the home-visiting component and other community agencies, beginning with a medical home for the new baby (ensuring that each new baby is connected to a pediatrician or clinic and receives regular well-baby care such as immunizations), are critical. Collaboration of the health, mental health, social service, and education establishments does not mean merely that agency officials attend occasional meetings but, rather, that the home visitors, doctors, nurses, therapists, and social workers, working together with each family they serve, share resources and insights.

And yet, the notion of providing home-visiting services to at-risk new parents is certainly not a new one. In 1976, after testing the approach himself in Denver, Dr. C. Henry Kempe wrote:

> As a bridge between the young family and health services, the utilization of visiting nurses, or more often in most places, indigenous health visitors who are successful, supportive, mature mothers acceptable to their communities is . . . the most inexpensive, least threatening and most efficient approach for giving the child the greatest possible chance to reach his potential. (37, p. 947)

Similarly, the notion of providing intensive services is not new. Dr. Albert Solnit stated over a decade ago that policy makers always hope to find some intervention that can be given on an inexpensive one-shot basis (38). But, he points out, most services cannot and do not work like a polio vaccine; in other words, a good meal now and then doesn't create health—a consistently good diet might.

What may indeed be new, however, is the notion of offering a preventive intervention such as intensive home visitation to new parents universally, for whole population groups.

Even if those at greatest risk received the most intensive support, it would soon become a community norm rather than an intrusion or an indignity.

Recently, some communities have in fact started to establish such universal approaches. For example, the state of Hawaii is committed to using a model embracing these dimensions to reach all first-time parents. There, starting in 1985, the state's Maternal and Child Health Program pilot tested, evaluated, and has since put into place for over 50% of their new parents a program called Healthy Start. Visits by paraprofessionals to all new parents begin in the hospitals at the time of the child's birth; for high-risk parents, visits continue during the critical first months—and, if necessary, first years—of the child's life. The visits are voluntary; very few of the at-risk parents refuse the services. The home visits are complemented by an impressive array of medical, child development, and social services. The home visitors receive intensive training and ongoing supervision. Early studies suggest the program is having a very positive effect on preventing both physical abuse and neglect (39). By the early 1990s, other states across the country began looking at ways to implement a similar universal program. Just as in Hawaii, where it has taken time—eight years to reach 50% of the population—these efforts will not reach all who would benefit from them overnight. States will want to test as they go along and evaluate the relative effectiveness of the approaches their own communities adopt. But at least the experience in Hawaii, coupled with early initiatives in other states, suggests that the goal of universal coverage is not wholly unrealistic.

A Word on Preventing Different Forms of Maltreatment

Because the underlying causes of each form of child maltreatment are somewhat different, it is important to consider whether or not certain prevention strategies can effectively address all forms of maltreatment or if we need to tailor prevention efforts to fit the different ways in which parents might harm their children. The answer is, undoubtedly, a bit of both.

For example, efforts to address the prevention of child sexual abuse (see chapter 29) have not begun with new parents to help them get off to a good start. And while research suggests that teenage mothers, compared to women who become mothers at a later age, are significantly more likely to have been victims of child sexual abuse and that their children may accordingly be more vulnerable to such victimization (12), no evidence yet indicates that intensive home visits for new parents would in fact reduce the likelihood that these children will be sexually victimized. Child sexual abuse prevention efforts have instead focused on school-age children (that is, on potential victims), teaching them how to protect themselves from sexual abuse. Our theories about victimization do suggest, though, that we should not overlook the contribution new-parent programs could make to the prevention of child sexual abuse; intensive support for new parents can strengthen parent-child bonds, which can in turn protect a child from potential victimization.

At the same time, it is more clear that certain prevention strategies can and do simultaneously address both physical abuse and physical neglect even though our desired outcomes seem quite different. With physical abuse prevention, we are trying to make sure someone does not do something—namely, does not batter their child. With physical neglect prevention, on the other hand, we are working to make sure parents *do* do something—namely, clothe, feed, shelter, protect, and nurture their children. While our measures of success may differ, the means by which we get to them are quite similar if not identical. To take the new-parent program as an example one more time, intensive home visitation to new parents seeks to accomplish a number of things—support new parents, teach parenting skills, educate parents about child development, help parents enjoy their new babies—while also addressing other life stressors. The measured net result of such intensive intervention is to help a parent know what to do (nurture) and what not to do (physically assault). Our research tells us that such programs prevent not only physical abuse but physical neglect as well.

Of course, there is the broader social neglect of children in our society (and in other societies too), characterized by poverty, lack of child care, poor housing, lack of medical care, and so forth. No home-visiting program will cure this sort of widespread societal neglect: broader social reform is needed.

A Word on Tailoring Prevention Approaches to Different Population Groups

It seems readily apparent that since prevention efforts touch the very ways parents raise their children, we must consider how our prevention efforts can or should take account of the differences in parenting norms and family practices across diverse racial, cultural, and ethnic groups. In fact, we must examine many general beliefs about culture and ethnicity in order to even discuss child abuse prevention for different population groups. Differences within cultures, for example, may exceed differences between cultures. These variations, both within and across groups, result in different definitions of good parenting and good child care. Some cultural, ethnic, or class groups may appear to be similar because of similar economic stresses, but solutions to problems such as child abuse and child neglect in specific groups need to take into account more than economic issues. Also, general beliefs about groups and group behavior do not necessarily transfer directly to individual cases; in consequence, our knowing how a given population group has traditionally valued children may or may not be useful in designing prevention programs for today.

Knowledge about interpersonal and family dynamics in different cultural groups is limited. For example, although research has described mother-child relationships among various ethnic groups, less is known of father-child, husband-wife, and sibling relationships within these groups. And even less is known of how a two-person relationship may be modified in the presence of another person such as a mother-in-law.

In determining how to approach questions of prevention in the context of different cultural and ethnic groups, researchers have stressed the importance of accentuating the positive in a given community—recognizing that what is positive in one culture may be considered coercive in another. Members of a particular group should define for themselves what is functional or dysfunctional within their culture. "Positive" may simply mean building on people's best coping mechanisms. And if what is negative cannot be agreed upon, certainly the weaknesses of the community should not be overlooked when cataloging its strengths. In any case, prevention efforts must take these issues into account.

Conclusion

To turn to the thoughts of Dr. Prothrow-Stith one last time:

> If we do not provide [our children's] basic needs when they are small, they will repay us for our laxity by spending the rest of their days as predators dependent upon us all. This is not speculation. We know this to be true. A significant portion of our children are withering on the vine before they have even bloomed a little. (5, pp. 200–201)

We have no real choice but to dedicate significant resources to better understand how we can prevent abuses to children and, even as our knowledge is evolving, to proceed with efforts nationwide to put prevention interventions into place.

References

1. McCurdy, K., and Daro, D. 1994. Child Maltreatment: A National Survey of Reports and Fatalities. *J. Interpersonal Violence* 9(1):75–94.
2. Cohn, A. 1983. *An Approach to Preventing Child Abuse.* Vol. 2. Chicago: National Committee to Prevent Child Abuse.
3. Behrman, R. E. 1993. The Future of Children: Home Visiting. *The Future of Children* [the David and Lucile Packard Foundation] 3(3).
4. Schuerman, J.; Rzepnicki, T.; Littell, J.; and Clark, A. 1993. Evaluation of the Illinois Family First Placement Prevention Program: Final Report. In *Selected Family Preservation Evaluation References.* Chicago: Chapin Hall Center for Children.
5. Prothrow-Stith, D., with Weissman, M. 1991. *Deadly Consequences: How Violence is Destroying Our Teenage Population and a Plan to Begin Solving the Problem.* New York: HarperCollins.
6. Gil, D. G. 1970. *Violence against Children: Physical Child Abuse in the United States.* Cambridge, Mass.: Harvard University Press.
7. Garbarino, J. 1977. The Human Ecology of Child Maltreatment: A Conceptual Model for Research. *J. Marriage and the Family* 39:721–36.
8. Light, R. H. 1973. Abused and Neglected Children in America: A Study of Alternative Policies. *Harvard Educational Rev.* 43:556–98.
9. Gelles, R. J., and Straus, M. A. 1988. *Intimate Violence.* New York: Simon and Schuster.
10. Chasnoff, I. J. Drug Use in Pregnancy: Parameters of Risk. *Pediatric Clinics of North America.* 35:6.
11. Chasnoff, I. J. 1989. Drugs and Women: Establishing a Standard of Care. *Annals of New York Academy of Science* 562:208–10.
12. Ruch-Ross, H.; Jones, E.; and Musick, J. 1992. Comparison of One Year Outcomes for Participants in a Statewide Program for Pregnant and Parenting Adolescents with a National Sample of Adolescent Mothers. Family Planning Perspectives.
13. Chilman, C. 1981. Social and Psychological Research Concerning Adolescent Childbearing: 1970–1980. *J. Marriage and the Family* 43:109–16.
14. Bugental, D. B.; Mantyla, S. M.; and Lewis, J. 1989. Parental Attributions as Moderators of Affective Communication. In *Child Maltreatment: Theory and Research on the Causes and Con-*

sequences of Child Abuse and Neglect, ed. D. Cicchetti and V. Carlson, 254–79. Cambridge: Cambridge University Press.

15. Willis, D.; Holden, E. W.; and Rosenberg, M. 1992. Child Maltreatment Prevention: Introduction and Historical Overview. In *Prevention of Child Maltreatment: Developmental and Ecological Perspectives,* ed. D. Willis, E. W. Hoden, and M. Rosenburg. New York: Wiley.

16. Garbarino, J. 1980. An Ecological Perspective on Child Maltreatment. In *The Social Context of Child Abuse and Neglect,* ed. L. Pelton. New York: Human Sciences Press.

17. Garbarino, J., and Crouter, K. 1978. Defining the Community Context of Parent-Child Relations: The Correlations of Child Maltreatment. *J. Child Development* 49:604–16.

18. Burgess, R. L. 1979. Child Abuse: A Social Interactional Analysis. In *Advances in Child Clinical Psychology,* ed. B. B. Lahey and A. E. Kazdin. New York: Plenum.

19. Straus, M. A. 1980. Stress and Physical Child Abuse. *Child Abuse and Neglect: International J.* 4:75–88.

20. Kaufman, J., and Zigler, E. 1987. Do Abused Children Become Abusive Parents. *Amer. J. Orthopsychiatry* 57(2).

21. Egeland, B., and Stroufe, L. A. 19**. Attachment and Early Maltreatment. *Child Development* 52:44–52.

22. National Research Council, Panel on Research on Child Abuse and Neglect. 1993. *Understanding Child Abuse and Neglect: Etiology of Child Maltreatment.* Washington, D.C.: National Academy Press.

23. Helfer, R. E. 1987. An Overview of Prevention. In *The Battered Child,* 4th ed. rev., ed. R. E. Helfer and R. S. Kempe, 425–33. Chicago: University of Chicago Press.

24. Jones, E., and McCurdy, K. 1992. The Links between Types of Maltreatment and Demographic Characteristics of Children. *Child Abuse and Neglect: International J.* 16(2):201–15.

25. Altemeier, W. A.; Vietze, P. M.; Sherrod, K. A.; Sandler, H. M.; and O'Connor, S. M. 1979. Prediction of Child Maltreatment during Pregnancy. *J. Amer. Acad. Child Psychiatry* 19:205.

26. Gray, J. D.; Cutler, C. A.; Dean, J. A.; and Kempe, C. H. 1979. Prediction and Prevention of Child Abuse and Neglect. *J. Social Issues* 35:127–39.

27. U.S. Advisory Board on Child Abuse and Neglect. 1991. *Creating Caring Communities: Blueprint for an Effective Federal Policy on Child Abuse and Neglect.* Washington, D.C.: U.S. Government Printing Office.

28. American Association for Protecting Children. 1991. *Child Abuse Reporting Legislation in the 1980s.* Denver: American Humane.

29. Daro, D., and Gelles, R. 1992. Public Attitudes and Behaviors with Respect to Child Abuse Prevention. *J. Interpersonal Violence* 7(4):517–31.

30. Daro, D. 1993. Home Visitation and Preventing Child Abuse. *APSAC Advisor* 6(4).

31. Gray, J.; Cutler, C.; Dean, J.; and Kempe, C. H. 1977. Prediction and Prevention of Child Abuse and Neglect. *Child Abuse and Neglect: International J.* 1:45–58.

32. Cohn, A., and Daro, D. 1988. Child Maltreatment Evaluation Efforts: What Have We Learned. In *Coping with Family Violence Research and Policy Perspectives,* ed. G. T. Hotaling, D. Finkelhor, J. Kirkpatrick, and M. Strauss. Newbury Park, Calif.: Sage Publications.

33. Olds, D.; Chamberlin, R.; Henderson, C.; and Tatelbaum, R. 1985. The Prevention of Child Abuse and Neglect: A Randomized Trial of Nurse Home Visitation. Rochester, N. Y.: University of Rochester School of Medicine. Unpublished paper.

34. Olds, D. Improving Formal Services for Mothers and Children. In *Protecting Children from Abuse and Neglect,* ed. J. Garbarino, S. H. Stocking, et al., 173–97. San Francisco: Jossey-Bass.

35. Lutzker, J., and Rice, J. 1984. Project Twelve-Ways: Measuring Outcome of a Large In-Home Service for Treatment and Prevention of Child Abuse and Neglect. *Child Abuse and Neglect: International J.* 8:519–24.

36. Seitz, V.; Rosenbaum, L. K.; and Apfel, N. H. 1985. Effects of Family Support Intervention: A Ten-Year Follow-Up. *Child Development* 56:376–91.

37. Kempe, C. H. 1976. Approaches to Preventing Child Abuse: The Health Visitors Concept. *Am. J. Diseases of Children* 130:941–47.

38. Solnit, A. J. 1983. Foreword to *Working with Disadvantaged Parents and Their Children: Scientific and Practice Issues,* ed. S. Provence and A. Naylor, viii–ix. New Haven, Conn.: Yale University Press.

39. Daro, D., and McCurdy, K. 1996. *Intensive Home Visitation: A Randomized Trial, Follow-Up, and Risk Assessment Study of Hawaii's Healthy Start Program.* Washington, D.C.: National Center on Child Abuse and Neglect; Administration for Children, Youth, and Families; U.S. Department of Health and Human Services.

28

A Clinical and Developmental Approach to Prevention

RAY E. HELFER
RICHARD D. KRUGMAN

EDITORS' NOTE: The following chapter is an integration of two chapters written by Ray E. Helfer for the fourth edition of *The Battered Child*. In our view, the concepts Dr. Helfer presented are still highly relevant. We have rewritten and updated the "Frequency" section, for new data have been collected since the publication of the previous edition of the volume. Otherwise the core content remains unchanged. More recent studies on the prevention of child maltreatment are discussed in chapters 27, 29, and 30.

The purpose of this chapter is to build a foundation for understanding the short-term and long-term effects of child abuse and neglect on the normal developmental processes of children. The cornerstone of this foundation is based on an understanding of the "epidemiology" of this malady in our society. This approach not only enhances one's understanding of the manner in which the problems of abuse and neglect may be transmitted from generation to generation but also creates the framework for building effective and efficient treatment programs and for providing the most appropriate preventive interventions.

The Clinical Approach to Child Abuse and Neglect

When an epidemiological approach is applied to a clinical problem, one thinks of "patterns of disease occurrence in human populations and factors that influence these patterns" (1). Lilienfeld and Lilienfeld state that the general purposes of epidemiological studies are:

1. To elucidate the etiology
2. To evaluate the consistency of epidemiological data with etiologic hypothesis
3. To provide the basis for developing and evaluating preventive procedures and public health practices

As all of these principles are applied to direct clinical observations, in a large number of cases the science of clinical epidemiology can be applied (2). This approach deals with

RAY E. HELFER, M.D., who died in 1992, was co-editor of each of the four previous editions of *The Battered Child* and professor in the Department of Pediatrics and Human Development, College of Human Medicine, Michigan State University.

RICHARD D. KRUGMAN, M.D., is dean of the School of Medicine and professor in the Department of Pediatrics, University of Colorado.

analysis of group data, probability, past experiences, and the evaluation of systematic errors by sound scientific principles. The ultimate goal is to use these principles to develop treatment and preventive approaches.

Applying the concepts of clinical epidemiology to the problems of child abuse and neglect makes good sense. This does not imply, however, that this malady of our society is a "disease" in the common use of the word. Even though abuse and neglect involve more global constructs than a single disease entity does, an epidemiological approach can facilitate the understanding of this complex interactional breakdown between a child and his or her caretaker.

Several articles have been published that attempted to apply some concepts of epidemiology to child abuse and neglect (3–8). For the most part, these authors have used a very limited definition of epidemiology. Rather than presenting the total scientific approach, they reported only demographic and/or incidence data. The intent of this present review is to go further by utilizing a clinical epidemiological approach to clarify our understanding of the complex problems related to child abuse and neglect.

Definition

The working definition of this complex family problem resulting in a breakdown of the interpersonal interaction within the family unit is:

> Any interaction or lack of interaction between family members which results in nonaccidental harm to the individual's physical and/or developmental states.

Key words and phrases within this definition are:

Interaction	—in contrast to a unilateral process
Family member	—individuals who are very close to each other
Nonaccidental	—in contrast to intentional
Developmental	—to broaden beyond physical harm only (e.g., psychological/verbal abuse or neglect)

Thirty-five years ago the phrase "the battered child syndrome" was coined by Dr. C. Henry Kempe (9). This was done to draw attention to the physical aspects of "nonaccidental harm." A much broader definition is now used to describe our understanding of these problems, problems that are subsumed under the overall umbrella of "breakdown in the interaction within the family."

Etiology

Caution must be used when the term *etiology* is applied to child abuse and neglect. A similar caution is necessary when the term is used in discussing cancer and other complex maladies. Approximately twenty-five years ago the "etiology" of child abuse and neglect was proposed as a series of interacting entities, a process or sequence of events (10,11). These interactive variables are still applicable as one considers the etiologic concepts of abuse. Overt abuse and/or neglect is likely to occur when the following elements are in place:

The potential to abuse within the parent or caretaker, related to residues of child abuse or neglect in their own early life	+	A Special Child	+	A physical, psychological, or environmental stress or crisis(es) and lack of any support system due to isolation or unavailability of support services

When these interacting factors occur in sequence in the proper "amount," the outcome is often abuse and/or neglect, although the abuse may be manifested in many different forms. The etiology of child maltreatment must be seen as a complex series of circumstances beginning with early rearing experiences of the parent(s) or caregiver(s) and the way these experiences affected the parent's or caregiver's ability to develop and maintain close personal relationships.

Classification and Terminology

The definition of *interactional breakdown* can be expanded into five specific classifications or manifestations: child abuse, child neglect, sexual exploitation, psychological or verbal abuse, and spouse abuse. These parental actions or inactions can occur separately or they may occur concurrently.

Special mention should be made of three specific manifestations of interactional breakdown within the family: emotional abuse, failure to thrive, and sexual exploitation. These phrases are used and misused so frequently in the literature and daily discussions that an attempt must be made to clarify them.

The phrase "emotional abuse" should be eliminated from any classification as a *primary* entity. The abuse of one's emotions raises vague, almost indefinable constructs, often different for each individual. All five forms of parent-child interactional breakdown lead to emotional distress within a family, often causing the child or children to exhibit emotional unrest. "Verbal abuse" or "psychological abuse" more accurately describes the belittling and other attacks upon the child's self-worth and self-esteem. The phrase "emotional abuse" should be abandoned.

In like manner, the phrase "failure to thrive" is greatly misused by professionals. It means different things to different people. Failure to thrive is the failure to grow and develop, over time, as compared to predetermined standards. This term should be limited to infants under two years of age. The term "nonorganic failure to thrive" also can be found in the literature. To many, especially nonmedical professionals, this may imply something very erroneous, even mystical, that some infants do not grow for some nonorganic reason. Infants who fail to thrive do not grow adequately because they do not get enough calories (12) (see chapter 16). The reason they do not get enough calories may be due to disease, feedings methods, or lack of feedings. Using the adjective "nonorganic" is misleading and very difficult to explain to protective service workers, parents, judges, and others.

One might suggest that the phrase "sexual exploitation" be used rather than "sexual abuse" for two reasons: first, to be all-encompassing, to include the variety of interactions that adults use to take advantage of vulnerable children in a sexual manner, varying from inappropriate fondling to incest and pornography. Rape and sexual misconduct by strangers are not included in this family dysfunction classification. Second, "sexual abuse" as a term may be misleading since *physical* injury often is absent in these children. The phrase "sexual exploitation" more accurately describes the nature of this problem.

Frequency

EDITORS' NOTE: This section was written by Richard D. Krugman.

"With few exceptions, studies seeking to define the incidence (number of new cases within a specific population over a given period of time) and prevalence (total number of cases in a population in a certain period) of child abuse and neglect are fraught with innumerable complexities." A decade after Dr. Helfer began this section of the fourth edition of *The Battered Child* with that statement, we are no closer to understanding the incidence of child abuse and neglect anywhere in the world. Two decades ago, the United States Congress asked the secretary of the U.S. Department of Health, Education, and Welfare to report to Congress on the incidence of child abuse and neglect in the United States. For twenty years the data have not been forthcoming. The federal contract that gave the American Humane Association the responsibility to collect data from 1976 to 1986 was not renewed. Three "national incidence studies" have been completed (13–15). Based on the endangerment standard of *The Third National Incidence Study,* what can be said is that approximately 2.5% of American children were abused and neglected in 1993 (14a). Of these, approximately 55% are reported for neglect, 25% for physical abuse, and 20% for sexual abuse.

Prevalence data are firmer. Many studies have been conducted on the prevalence of abuse, especially sexual abuse, in a variety of populations. These data are derived by asking adults and/or adolescents about their past histories of child maltreatment. The data depend on the adult or adolescent reporting his or her *perceptions* of what occurred in the past and are subject to variation in relation to the populations surveyed and the type of abuse that occurred.

When 2,500 young women were asked to complete a standardized questionnaire at the time of hospital confinement for delivery of their baby, the overall rate of severe physical punishment used in their childhood was 20% for those in a medium-sized New England town to over 60% for those in a large city ghetto (16). Data from sixteen countries indicate that the prevalence of sexual abuse in their populations ranges from 7% to 33% of women and 3% to 16% of men (17).

The actual rates of permanent physical morbidity and mortality from physical abuse and neglect are not known. However, with the advent of child death reviews, some of the hidden deaths are being identified (see chapter 11). The permanent morbidity of sexual abuse in childhood and its companion mortality (as a result of suicide or the violence associated with rape) are similarly unknown. Retrospective studies of patients in psychiatric hospitals and among clinical populations of individuals who are substance abusers, pregnant adolescents, suicide attempters, and runaway youth indicate high prevalence rates of prior or ongoing sexual abuse (18).

Mode of Transmission

The epidemiological approach to understanding child abuse and neglect requires that serious consideration be given to how this problem passes from one generation to another (see chapter 5). The adverse effects of abuse and neglect of children are transmitted by way of developmental deficits and pathologic behaviors learned during childhood (19). A child who, over time, watches his mother being beaten by his father or her boyfriend not only experiences the fear that accompanies the witnessing of this act but also learns how two people who mean a great deal to each other resolve their interpersonal conflicts. A young girl who, over time, must assume the role of sexual partner for her older brother, father, and/or stepfather is not experiencing the developmental growth in her own sexuality which is necessary to permit her to sort out these roles during later childhood, adolescence, and adulthood. Both these children emerge from adolescence into young adulthood with very limited skills in developing and maintaining close personal relationships with significant others and ultimately with their own children.

The developmental insults affect the parents and the child(ren) in varying degrees in each of the five major pathological interactions (or lack of interactions). Through these many developmental deficits, the transmission of this form of pathological interaction is carried from one generation to another. Does every abused or neglected child run the risk of transmitting this problem to his or her family? If not, why not? These are questions yet to be answered, and key answers they will be. To date, those young adults who seem to have emerged from adverse childhood experiences less affected are those who have experienced a positive mentor relationship during their abuse and/or neglect. Someone—an aunt, uncle, teacher, or coach—said, "You're OK," during these dreadful years, or, "When you're with me, you're safe." This observation is supported only by clinical vignettes. Serious research must test the mentor hypothesis further. If this hypothesis can be supported, the concept may open new avenues for therapeutic and preventive approaches.

Epidemiological Approaches to Treatment

The primary justification for utilizing this epidemiological approach is to develop a basis for understanding the problem and to enhance our potential for developing meaningful treatment and prevention programs.

Treatment endeavors, if they are to be based upon our epidemiological understanding, must attack the basic erosion of the maltreated child's developmental process. These approaches can assist in the reconstruction of these developmental deficits. Merely understanding the deficits is not sufficient. The retraining of one's skills in interpersonal interaction, which were supposed to be learned in childhood, is crucial. The most discouraging aspect of treatment is that these approaches are rarely generalizable, that is, they are not able to be implemented on a large scale, from county to county or state to state. Unlike the building of water treatment plants and adding fluoride to the water supply or immunizing thousands against polio, transmitting a working multidisciplinary treatment program from one municipality to another, from one law enforcement agency or mental health center to another, from one county social service agency to another requires a continual reinvestment of time and energy akin to reinventing the wheel. This is extremely inefficient and not cost-effective.

The clinical and epidemiological perspective when applied to *prevention* of abuse and neglect teaches us certain basic lessons. In public health, we have known for years that the prevention of something negative occurs with the production of something positive. One prevents cholera and dysentery by cleaning our sewer and water systems. Polio is prevented by enhancing the production of antibodies by the immune system. Polio is not prevented by making more iron lungs or braces, although these are very important if one already has the malady.

While this is readily apparent to some, many child protective service agencies have not learned this approach, and most do not have an administrative methodology or adequate numbers of appropriately trained staff to implement such a program.

If the clinical approach to understanding abuse and neglect is going to be justified, it must provide information and concepts that lead to new or revised treatment and preventive approaches. It must stimulate thought, ideas, visions, and fantasies.

This review gives emphasis to the interactional construct—that is, the working hypothesis that when there is a breakdown in the interpersonal interactions of two or more people who mean a great deal to each other, the risk for maltreatment is present. The potential to abuse is flamed by stress and crisis. How the problem is manifested will vary from time to time, child to child. Even though the demographic data have significant limitations, one glaring conclusion is very evident: single, poor women of all races with young children are most vulnerable.

The frequency data, both incidence and prevalence, reveal the problem to be enormous. Since the basic mode of transmission from generation to generation is via the developmental deficits within the parent, and since these developmental scars "heal" more poorly than do physical injuries to the body, the prevalence rate is alarming. Generation after generation is affected by the limited skills of developing and maintaining long-term personal relationships.

The Developmental Process

One should perceive an individual, as he proceeds from infancy through adolescence and into adulthood, as moving through dynamic and ever-changing periods. What happens during this day-to-day process has a critical effect on one's functioning capabilities later in life. Many things are *supposed* to happen during childhood which permit a child to formulate and practice the skills necessary to function as a young adult. Those who interact with the child during these critical years have a great impact on a significant portion of this process. Some of the skills a child learns—like walking, running, and toilet training—seem to be rather "automatic," being influenced for the most part solely by time and growth. However, other developmental achievements must be carefully nurtured and modeled throughout the childhood years for the child to become a reasonably functional young adult. These include interpersonal skill, that is the ability to get along with others and to function in an acceptable and constructive manner during the interpersonal process.

Imagine that the developmental process of a child moving from infancy through adolescence is like a missile and its payload moving through a trajectory from the launching pad to its celestial goal. The launching pad is birth, and the celestial goal is adulthood. Anything that happens to modify the trajectory will have an influence on the ultimate landing site of the payload. Those who guide the path of the missile toward the celestial body must be readily available and well trained to modify any unexpected and serious deviation in the process. To complete this analogy, the actual trajectory is child development, and the parents, family members, teachers, and others who interact with the child during these critical years are those who have the responsibility for the guidance system.

Consider, for example, an infant who is separated temporarily immediately after birth because of the illness of a mother. This is a serious developmental insult in the child's life, and every means must be used to correct the potential negative effect or "scarring" if this developmental insult is to be prevented. Consider the three-year-old child who, because of serious illness, is placed in a hospital and undergoes surgery and a variety of other painful and difficult procedures, during which time she may well be separated from those who have the most impact on her "developmental guidance system." If this insult continues for a period of three or four weeks, there may be a slowing down of growth, and there certainly will be negative effects upon the developmental process occurring during this critical period. In most situations in which the child has experienced a normal childhood prior to entering the hospital and lives in an environment where modification can be made in order to overcome the insult to her "developmental trajectory," the effects of these insults probably will not be permanent. On the other hand, a child with an environment that adds little more than one insult after another to this developmental process (for example, a child reared in an environment of never-ending violence as the solution to interpersonal problems) may well have her developmental process further impaired by the hospital experience.

In the discussion that follows, emphasis will be given to those developmental traits which seem to be most deficient in young adults reared in an abusive and/or neglectful environment. Additional emphasis is given to those developmental deficiencies which affect interaction between child and parents. These, of course, are the developmental skills which demonstrate the most serious deficiencies in those reared in an abusive environment.

The Developmental Deficits: The Senses

Understanding the importance of serious developmental deficiencies of the senses experienced by those who have been reared in an abusive environment requires knowledge of the normal development of the senses (20). Dr. Wilson points out that an infant has a highly sophisticated system of touch, taste, smell, vision, and hearing, and cites the importance of the new baby's vestibular system. There are six senses, rather than five, if one considers the significance of the sense of movement. A newborn infant is not only very capable in these six sensory areas but also very dependent upon them for the establishment of a communication system with the world about him (19).

Now consider the environment which suppresses the development of this sensory system. An infant or young child is supposed to learn that use of the senses results in positive feedback, a nice feeling. Crying brings someone to hold, rock, and comfort the infant;

looking into the mother's eyes makes the child feel loved and wanted; being touched is nice, most of the time; the smells of mother's house remind the child of positive feelings, and so on. On balance, the senses should be conditioned positively; only on occasion is it necessary to have negative reactions to certain tastes, smells, and such (21, 22).

Consider what happens when touching hurts *most of the time;* smells about the house bring on very negative feelings *most of the time;* mom's eyes show the threat of a swat; when the child listens to mom and dad talk, he becomes afraid, since the messages he hears are threats, screams, and anger. Over and over, day after day, the child is bombarded with negative sensory messages, messages that truly force the senses to "shut down" (20). The child learns that it is far safer not to listen, not to look, and not to be touched, for when these senses are used, he hurts much more or receives no feedback whatsoever.

As a result, the child's senses become "muted," used only when absolutely necessary. This does not mean that if an individual reared in this manner were to have his hearing or vision tested, the results would indicate abnormalities. What is meant is that those reared to mute their senses have learned, very early in childhood, that their lives are less confused and hurt less when people do not look them in the eye, listen to what they say, touch them, or get too close.

The significance of these deficiencies in the senses is great. The ability to communicate with those about you and the environment in general is severely limited. Holding loved ones very close and looking into their eyes carries messages that few can express in words. When one enters the home where one was reared, the overall reaction to the unique smells and visual and auditory stimuli should be positive and comforting, rather than, "My God, this hurts!"

Children and adults reared in abusive environments have had their senses trained in such a way that to use them for receiving or transmitting positive messages is not part of their communication systems. While this makes it difficult for these young people to communicate with their peers, think of the results when someone with muted senses tries to establish a communication system with a newborn infant. Recall that new babies are *dependent* upon their six senses for communication (23). Little wonder young adults, reared in abuse, find interaction with their new babies so difficult. The result is a mother-baby or father-baby interaction that breaks down all too early in their relationship.

The World of Abnormal Rearing (W.A.R.)

The senses are not the only tools for learning how to interact with our environment or those about us. Many other skills must be learned in childhood, skills which enhance the young adult's ability to interact and feel that "I'm a very special person."

The concept of the "world of abnormal rearing" (W.A.R.) (23)—or in other words, the cycle of abuse, was proposed in order to better understand what occurs when one's childhood does not provide a very favorable environment in which to learn basic interpersonal skills. Those adults who are victims of the W.A.R. have truly "missed out on childhood," that is, missed learning many of the basic skills necessary to interact with others.

An awareness of the implications that this cycle has for the developing child and the adult will help prepare for the relearning phase. Understanding and then overcoming many of these basic developmental deficits require a knowledge of their origin.

Referring to children or adults who were reared in the W.A.R. cycle does *not* imply that all, or even the most, were physically beaten. For every adult who was actually beaten as a child, there are probably scores who look back at their childhood and say, "I wasn't beaten, but it really was a bad experience." Some children were beaten; some were sexually molested; others were ignored; some were constantly belittled; some find themselves so controlled that they cannot function outside of their home. Specific intervention programs are intended to help those adults who are trying to break out of the cycle. Understanding the various segments and concepts assists adults to break the cycle. Unless specific intervention programs are initiated to assist adults to escape from this cycle—and escape is possible—the future will most likely be a copy of the past.

Needs Met and Delayed Gratification

One of the most important skills that a child must learn during the brief years of childhood is how to get his or her needs met in an acceptable manner and when the most appropriate time is to seek this fulfillment. What behaviors or actions are acceptable at home, at school, or in the playground with friends? All people have needs, and we all must fall back on the foundations laid in childhood as we develop ways to have these needs met.

An infant is hungry, cold, and wet—his needs are very specific. He cries and hopes the cries bring a mother or father with food, a warm body, and dry clothes. As life progresses, crying is reserved for more extreme needs, which often are stimulated by pain or fear. A two-year-old may not cry to get the desired ice cream; rather, he may resort to a temper tantrum. Many parents find this undesirable behavior and work hard to teach the child to substitute for the hollering and kicking a "please" and "thank you."

> A young mother said to me, as she reflected on a recent disagreement she had with her boyfriend, "Isn't it interesting that my boyfriend beats me just like my husband used to?"
>
> "Yes," I admitted, "that is interesting"; I needed to hear more, so I said, "You find that interesting? Tell me, when was the last time your boyfriend beat you?"
>
> "Oh, last weekend. We went out, and he got mad at me for flirting with another guy. When we got home, he beat me."
>
> "Didn't it hurt?" I asked.
>
> "Yeah, a bit. Not too much, though. Anyway, I know he likes me," she added.
>
> Now that raised my interest; so I replied with, "How do you know he likes you?"
>
> "Why would he get jealous and beat me if he didn't like me?" she responded with great logic.
>
> That statement troubled me.
>
> A little later, this matter was discussed further with the mother. I learned more about the beatings her husband had given her and how she had interpreted them. Then I asked the key question, "*How was it for you when you were little?*"

"Oh, not bad with Mom," she commented.

"How about your Dad?"

"Well, he was pretty quiet and didn't pay much attention to me."

"Didn't that bother you?" I asked.

"Yes, and I used to bug him a lot."

"What did he do when you bugged him?" I continued.

"He'd hit me a lot," she replied.

"Why, then, did you bug him?"

She lifted her head, looked directly at me, and for the first time our eyes met as she said very slowly, "Getting hit is better than being left alone."

This young woman learned very early in life that when she had a need for a man's attention she had to "bug" him so much that he would eventually show her that he was aware of her presence by beating her. She was willing to put up with the hurt to have her needs met.

All children struggle with this critical component of development. If a child's environment is reasonably stable and secure and the parents have a good understanding of what the child's needs are and what the child must do and learn to have these needs met, then the outcome will be a child who learns acceptable skills for having these needs met and learns when the best time is to use them.

The development of the ability and willingness to delay one's gratification is a slow but steady process which progresses throughout the child's developmental trajectory. If you ask a three-year-old if he wants a stick of gum now or a whole pack on Sunday, he'll more likely than not take the stick now. Postponing the need until Sunday requires considerably more developmental skills than are present in most three-year-old children. He first must know what Sunday is, that Sunday will happen, that a pack of gum is bigger than a stick, and that he can trust you enough to be around on Sunday and to follow through with your promise. Eventually the child learns these concepts and, depending on his needs and the nature of the immediate offer, the satisfying of this need may, indeed, be postponed. Delaying gratification is a very high-level skill, one which requires considerable training and modeling during childhood to learn.

Children who are maltreated are not so fortunate. "Why wait? Tomorrow is never better than today." For them, tomorrow never comes; it is always today! These children find themselves in a world of unrealistic expectations. Their parents frequently have little understanding of childhood and make demands far in excess of a child's capabilities. Babies shouldn't cry much, should eat well, smile early, and remind mom or dad of someone the parents like; two-year-olds should shape up, not explore the cupboards and pull out the pots and pans, and not spill anything. "Look after *me*," the child is told by the parent. "To hell with your needs," he hears in a variety of ways. One of the greatest struggles for the child caught up in the abusive cycle is the constant striving to meet the parents' *unrealistic* expectations, which they have set for the child. From success at school, to caring for mom and dad, the demands are *extreme*.

A child who struggles with these issues day after day learns, as the years of childhood wear on, that his needs are not being met. Even worse, he is not learning the necessary skills to get these needs met—he is too busy looking after the needs of his parents and other adults around him. If this weren't bad enough, the behaviors that he does learn in order to meet his bare, essential needs are often extreme, inappropriate, and maladaptive.

Role Reversal and Responsibility

A child must learn during the brief years of childhood that *he* or *she* is responsible for his or her *own* actions. This is a concept that is acquired very gradually. It is tested by reality when the child reaches adolescence, as parents must accept less and less responsibility for their growing child's behavior and the adolescent begins to accept more and more. This can be an exciting and frustrating time. As the teenage years move on, one can see the maturing process. For example, "It's your responsibility to decide," was constantly heard around our home during the children's adolescent years. As a parent, I also heard, "I don't want to get up and deliver my newspapers"; "I don't want to mow the neighbor's lawn"; I don't want to take grandmother to church"; yet all were commitments which had been made previously. Responsibility and follow-through are very difficult lessons that must be learned in childhood.

Children reared in a abusive and/or neglectful environment find themselves in late adolescence ill prepared to accept responsibility for their own actions. There seem to be two extremes—either they aren't required to accept any responsibility for what they have done, or they are forced to accept responsibility for the inadequacies of their parents. This latter is so common and so confusing that it requires further explanation.

Some call this turnabout "role reversal." The child accepts the role of parent, and the parent takes on the role of the child. Role reversal is easy to understand when one sees a three-year-old soothing her crying mother and, later, the same mother ignoring her crying child. The constant need to reverse roles, which often ends in failure and frustration, may well result in "learned helplessness" for the child.

All children at varying ages of their development want to please and care for "mommy" or "daddy." This seems to be especially true in times of stress or crisis, for children really can come through and help out. However, extreme, constant, and unrealistic expectations are devastating to the developing child. Children have their own needs that have to be met.

This aspect of role reversal demonstrated by the child taking care of the parent is relatively easy to understand. More subtle and more difficult to comprehend is when this role reversal requires and trains the child to assume the responsibility for the parents' errors. This feeling is embedded into the child's mind from a very early age in a variety of ways, encouraged by remarks such as these:

> "If it weren't for you . . ."
> "If you hadn't spilled that, I wouldn't have gotten mad."
> "I hit you because you were bad."
> "You father would still be around if you . . ."
> "I could have gone back to work if you . . ."

And so it goes, on and on. This child slowly succumbs to the "guilt trip" which accompanies true role reversal. He becomes convinced that he is to blame for the parents' inability to handle crises, finances, and so forth. This guilt lasts into adulthood and manifests itself in a variety of ways. The ability to separate one's own responsibility from that of another is a learned function that develops in all children who are reared in a more normal environment. Learning that one is responsible for one's own actions and not the actions of another is *not* built into the abusive environment. In fact, it teaches the opposite.

Decision Making and Problem Solving

A child must learn the skill of making decisions during the protected years of childhood, when a "goof up" or bad decision won't be all that harmful. Options must be identified and weighed, priorities set, and a plan or solution agreed upon. Teenagers often lament, "Decisions are too tough; you decide for me." Sometimes we fall into the trap of making the decision for them. Often that is much quicker and less time-consuming than guiding them through the decision-making process—but a trap it is.

> A young seventeen-year-old mother once called me and said, "I must see you; I'm going crazy." When she arrived later, I asked, "Why do you think you're going crazy?"
>
> "I have all these things in my head, and I don't know what to do."
>
> "What things?" I asked. I thought she was going to tell me about some delusion or psychotic fantasy. Nothing of the sort occurred.
>
> "Well," she said, "I'm bleeding; my aunt is trying to get my baby; my boyfriend calls me collect, and I can't say no; my rent is due; I don't know what to do with my check; my food is almost gone . . . ," and on and on.
>
> "Betty," I said, "Stop! Tell me the last time you made a decision."
>
> She thought for a full two or three minutes and finally said, "I don't know if I ever really made any." Later she did recall she had made the decision to stop her birth control pills at sixteen so that she could become pregnant. She also decided who the father was going to be.

Children must learn, at two and four and eight and sixteen years of age, how to make decisions. *Choices, choices, choices!* This is the key. "Do you want vanilla or chocolate ice cream?" "Do you want a cookie or a piece of cake?" "Do you want your story before or after your bath?" "I don't want a bath," is the reply. "The choice is the story, not the bath," the parent responds. Choices lead to priority setting and decision making.

But one ought not to give children choices when there are none. "Do you want to shovel the driveway?" I asked my son one day after school. "No," he replied. "Shovel the driveway!" I commanded. "Why did you ask me if I didn't have a choice?" he responded. "Good point," I replied, "I'll figure out the answer while you're shoveling the driveway." It was a clear goof on my part to offer a choice that was only rhetorical.

Children reared in abusive settings rarely are given choices and rarely are allowed to make decisions. They are just told what to do or given no directions or guidance whatsoever. Even worse, they are often encouraged to decide and then are told what a stupid decision they made.

Day after day, young adults demonstrate how ill prepared they are in decision making.

What are their options and how can priorities be established? Without early experiences with trial and error in childhood, these decisions become major obstacles.

One seventeen-year-old mother related her story to me. "At nine, the sex started; by twelve, I was enjoying it; by sixteen, I hated it; and finally I hated myself." Then she added, "Do you know what one of the worst parts was? He never asked me if I wanted it." This woman not only suffered the insult of incest, she also had lost all control over her life. She had no choice.

Trusting Others

As development continues, it enters the realm of interrelating with others. Children must learn during their early childhood, and have it reinforced throughout adolescence, that there are some people who truly can be trusted and others who cannot. A two-year-old falls off his tricycle and hurts his knee; he runs, crying, to his mother or father and is picked up and consoled. "That really hurts," he hears. Two minutes later, his knee is a bit better, and he returns to his play, having learned that knees get better and people are helpful, especially moms and dads.

Trust is learned very gradually as a child moves from infancy through adolescence. Trust is built. Children not only learn whom to trust but what people can and cannot be expected to do. By the time an adolescent wants a car, a firm foundation of trust and realistic expectations should already have been laid.

Children raised in the world of abnormal rearing find themselves without such a foundation, or with a very weak one at best. Instead of learning as a young child that people can be trusted, they learn that people hurt or disappoint:

> "Don't come to me with your problems. I have enough of my own."
> "You dumb idiot, you screwed up again."
> "I drove you almost five hundred miles to play tennis in this tournament, and you
>   blew it in the first round."

Over and over the child in an abusive environment learns that when you go to others and seek help, you usually end up wishing you hadn't asked. This is especially devastating when the other person is mom or dad. If you cannot trust them when you are five or ten or fifteen years old, whom can you trust?

I asked an eight-year-old girl, reared in wealth but also abused, "What do you do when you have a problem?" Her immediate reply was, "It's best if I deal with it myself." She had learned in her brief eight years that asking others for help led to trouble.

One of the basic bail-out methods to which most adults have recourse when crises arise or a problem develops is to ask someone for assistance. When one's childhood fails to teach the basic skills of how and whom to trust, this bail-out process, so crucial to adults and children, is in serious jeopardy. The result—retreat, withdrawal, be alone! "Isn't it tough to be alone all the time?" I asked an attractive, young, divorced mother of two children. "Not really," she responded. I said nothing for a minute, and then she continued in a very soft voice directed at the floor, "No man can hurt me when I'm alone." She knew, from some very bitter experiences as a child and young adult, that being alone with a man was very risky and often led to pain. Her solution, to isolate herself from the world, was safer.

The true defense when one does not trust others is to keep people out of one's life. Keep in mind the discussion above about touching and looking. "If I don't look at you, maybe you can't hurt me as much." If all this weren't hard enough, many have the added burden of the never-ending guilt of role reversal: "If I don't take care of mom or dad, I feel awful."

One seventeen-year-old mother was having problems telling her social worker some of her personal concerns. I asked why. She said, " 'Cause if I tell the social worker about these things, then I have to tell my boyfriend."

"Tell your boyfriend?" I asked.

"Sure, that way he knows he can trust me."

Telling all was her way of gaining trust. The exact opposite is true of healthier, trusting relationships: "I trust you so much that you don't have to tell me everything." Child abuse and neglect truly distort the concept of trust.

Feelings and Actions

A child must learn on his developmental trajectory toward adulthood that how he feels and what he does are separate but related issues. This is such a crucial point for an adult to understand that it must be emphasized over and over again. Some will pick up this concept immediately; others will be very confused. The following examples may help to explain.

Two of our sons, at the ages of ten and twelve, were playing hockey on opposite teams. The younger boy skated better than the older one and regularly passed him by as the score piled up. On one of the passes, the older boy became furious, couldn't handle his anger any longer, and tripped his younger brother. The younger of the two got mad and hit his older brother with his hockey stick. They both came home angry and crying. Finally, the story came out—a golden opportunity to separate feelings from actions. After they both had settled down and I had a chance to discuss the situation with them, I said to the older brother, "I don't blame you for getting mad at your brother for skating around you all the time. I'd get mad too. *But,* that doesn't give you the right to trip him."

"I don't blame you," I said to the younger brother, "for getting mad at your brother for tripping you, *but* that doesn't give you the right to hit him with your stick." The message I wanted them to hear was, "How you felt is understandable and OK. What you did about it was inappropriate, and not acceptable."

Throughout childhood, this message must be delivered over and over:

"You *like* Susie, give her a *call.*"

"You're *mad* at Jimmy, *tell* him how you feel."

"You feel *sad, crying* may help."

"You are *excited* about the game, *tell* me about it."

As these children grow into adolescence, they gradually begin to learn that they have *control* over what they *do;* they can control their actions. Even though feelings are hard to control, some satisfaction comes from knowing that what you do about them is your decision, your responsibility, and under your control.

Adults who have been brought up in an abusive environment find this concept very difficult to understand. One mother said, "I get so mad that I scream and holler and say awful things to my kids, and then I feel awful too." Another said, "I got angry at my baby and hit her."

To both these comments, I replied, "Do you realize you are talking about two different things?" Their faces revealed confusion, and both replies were almost identical: "What do you mean, two things?" This inability to separate feelings from actions manifests itself in many ways. Children as well as adults frequently find themselves in serious difficulty because of this deficit. Anger leads to lashing out for some and to complete withdrawal and guilt for others. The extremes of actions are often used.

"How can I tell a boyfriend I like him?" one young woman asked me.

"What do you do to show a man you like him?" I replied.

"Go to bed with him," she said.

"Right away?" I asked.

"What else can I do?"

This young girl found she had no trouble finding a man to go to bed with her, but somehow it always turned out poorly. In her childhood she had missed out on learning the little innuendos of expressing her feelings. She didn't know how to touch his hand, look into his eyes, say "I like you," or smile at the right time. She replaced all of this with only one action to express her feelings of liking—sex.

The major message is that how one feels and what one does about it are separate but related issues. One can control much of one's actions. A child must learn he or she has this degree of control. When maltreated children and adults are taught that feelings and actions are the same, they mistakenly believe they have little, if any, control over their lives.

Feelings of guilt are a constant source of confusion. "Is that an OK feeling?" is a frequent question. "Certainly," I respond, "but you have to decide how to handle, how to act, on that feeling." This can be a difficult concept for many of these adults to comprehend.

And On and On It Goes

The maltreated child continues, round and round, learning fewer and fewer skills of interaction. He is "out of touch" with the world about him; control over his life is lost—actually, never gained. What better way to train a child to become a nonentity, functioning in the extremes, than to:

Mute his senses.

Fail to teach him how to get his needs met.

Teach him he is responsible for the actions of others.

Give him little practice in problem solving.

Convince him he cannot trust others.

Show him day after day that feelings and actions are one and the same.

The results? The results are contained in this book. The W.A.R.—the world of abnormal rearing—has convinced its victims that they are "no damn good"; unable to help others; have minimal skills for finding and keeping real, close friends, much less a soul mate; and are easily discouraged and depressed.

At some point in their young adult lives, they may enter into the "I think I'll have a family" route as a solution to their loneliness. Some bypass this option and go on to work or school, trying to cope as best they can, using what few skills they learned in their childhood. Some make it; many do not.

Considerable work can be done to facilitate breaking this cycle of abuse and teaching them the skills they have not learned during their childhood. Even more can be achieved if the cycle is interrupted before its damage is too severe.

Prevention

The goal of any individual or group working in as difficult a field as child abuse and neglect is prevention. While this goal is truly admirable, the very thought is overwhelming. Preventing a phenomenon that occurs more than a million times each year, that adversely affects children's physical growth and emotional development, and that eats away at the very foundation of our society—the family—is a goal that must always be before us.

What Is Being Prevented?

In a narrow sense, the answer to this question is very clear: physical abuse and neglect. Limiting the goal to these two manifestations may simplify research studies in the field. Expansion of the answer to include the prevention of adverse forms of parent-child interactions complicates the research picture considerably, yet prevention strategies to prevent child abuse are neglect as well as interventions to enhance parent-child interactions have been studied.

O'Connor et al. demonstrated that rooming-in after delivery of a newborn decreases the risk of physical abuse, abandonment, and failure to thrive (24). Burgess pointed out that mother-child interactions are more negative in abusive families than in nonabusive families (25). Both extremes of the interactional continuum can be measured and the prevention intervention assessed. To prevent child abuse and other adverse outcomes of the breakdown of the interactional system within our families, we must *enhance* interpersonal skills in those very folks who like each other the most, those who will make up our future families, the mothers and fathers to be. This raises two critical questions: (1) What programs must be implemented to enhance interpersonal interactions? (2) How, in order to implement these programs, does one gain access to individuals before they become parents?

Before we consider these two issues, an important though obvious consequence of this approach must be acknowledged. Child abuse prevention programs should *not* be expected to result in an immediate decrease in the incidence of child abuse. While a decrease is desirable, the ramifications of family dysfunction and the manifestations of abuse are too massive, and our ability to identify and measure the incidence is too inaccurate, for such a decrease to be identified within a short period of time. What can be expected of prevention programs is the *improvement* of interactional skills between those individuals to which the programs are being aimed. Their interactional skills can improve, as demonstrated by Bristor et al. (26) and Lutzker et al. (27).

What Programs Enhance Interactional Skills

In a review of the literature on the prevention of abuse (28), the following components of primary prevention programs were identified as necessary:

1. A community consortium committed to the dictum that family violence in their community is unacceptable
2. A never-ending mass media campaign to educate the public
3. A major change in our health services to include some form of training for *all* new parents in the art of communicating with their baby
4. A home health visitor program for *all* new parents for the one to two years after the birth of their firstborn child
5. An early child development program for all preschool children, run by churches, schools, community colleges, or whomever
6. An interpersonal skills program (how-to-get-along curriculum) in the public schools (K–12) built upon interpersonal skills in grade school, advancing, in middle and high school, to courses on the topics of sexuality and parenting
7. An adult education program for two levels of young adults—those who had a positive childhood experience themselves and want a refresher course on childhood before they become parents, and those whose childhood experiences were negative, who need a "crash course in childhood" before parenting is undertaken

Various intervention programs have already been initiated, and the list of these programs below, accompanied by a brief description and appropriate references, will assist readers as they review the literature.

A. *Perinatal coaching.* New parents are provided training in the interactional skills necessary to communicate with their newborn (19, 29–31).
B. *Home visiting program.* New parents are provided a home visitor to assist them in resolving day-to-day issues and health problems, and in increasing interpersonal communication skills with their infants (32, 33).
C. *Expanded well-baby care.* The proposal here is that physicians and nurses must better meet the needs of young parents when they bring their new babies in for traditional well-child care. No longer is it appropriate to limit the services provided to those which simply demonstrate that the child is physically well (34).
D. *Interpersonal skills training for middle and high school.* This program, a fantasy at this time, is an achievable one. Schools should be teaching how-to-get-along skills—how to get along with peers, teachers, parents, girls, boys, dates, mates, and one's own children. No good study of this concept has been found by the author.

E. *Interpersonal cognitive problem-solving skills.* Techniques have been developed by Spivack and Shure (35, 36) to teach young children (ages four to ten years) how to solve everyday problems. These can be taught by preschool and primary school teachers.

F. *Crash course in childhood for adults.* Some young people have arrived at adulthood by way of a childhood which, to say the least, was less than optimal. These young adults need a second chance to learn the skills of interacting, skills which they did not learn during their childhood. This relearning and retraining is best done before one arrives at the pre-parent stage of life (19).

G. *Pre-parent refresher.* Many of the young adults, both men and women, who had positive childhood experiences and those graduates of the "crash course in childhood" will decide to enter the pre-parent stage (getting ready for pregnancy and parenthood). Some will have placed many years of cognitive learning (college and graduate school) between their childhood and parenthood. These soon-to-be parents will benefit from a refresher course in the concepts of interacting with children and mates (19).

The most encouraging programs to date, of those listed are the new parent–newborn communication training, the home visitor programs, and the school age training by Spivack and Shure.

Classification

The question of the appropriate goal for prevention programs is usually resolved by inserting the word *primary* in front of *prevention,* thereby indicating prevention before the fact. While this should help, our knowledge that child abuse is a cyclical event, frequently passed from one generation to another, adds complexity to this terminology. Treatment of parents after the child has been abused (see chapters 24 and 26) would be considered secondary prevention as far as the child is concerned (preventing recurrence). Treatment of the child, on the other hand (see chapters 24 and 26) would be primary prevention as far as the child's future children are concerned. Providing a new mother, formerly abused, with special training in how to interact with her baby is primary prevention for the baby and secondary prevention for the mother.

All this can be summarized as follows:

Primary prevention: providing training and services to enhance those skills necessary to keep abuse and its many ramifications from ever occurring (for example, perinatal coaching programs)

Secondary prevention: providing training and services to enhance those skills necessary to keep abuse and its many ramifications from occurring in the next generation and services (for example, programs for the child or adolescent who is treated after being the victim of abuse)

Tertiary prevention: providing training and services to enhance those skills necessary to keep abuse and its many ramifications from recurring once it has been identified (for example, after-the-fact interventions)

At Whom Are Prevention Programs Directed?

The ability to initiate any program that enhances parent-child interactions and has the potential to prevent outcomes of serious breakdown in these interactions—such as failure to thrive, abuse, and neglect—inevitably raises the question of preselection or screening. Who should receive such a program? How should they be chosen?

The simplest, and most effective, answer is that all mothers and fathers should have the benefit of perinatal coaching. If not all, then certainly all new mothers and their infants. While this may be an idealistic goal, realistically many new programs cannot service such a large number at the outset. How then would those who are to receive perinatal coaching be selected? The distinct advantage of universal access for all new mothers is that it would not adversely label the recipients. This would also protect the program itself from receiving a label that may be inappropriate—for example, "only mixed-up or high-risk parents and babies are helped." Labels must be avoided.

What are the methods available to screen or identify those who may benefit the most from or really need extra services? Five such techniques have been tested and reported. These five fall into three distinct categories: the self-administered questionnaire (37, 38), the standardized interview (39), and the observational checklist (40, 41). All of these techniques have been studied and show encouraging results.

Each of these tools is useful in research studies, especially when one wishes to determine the presence or absence of high-risk parenting dysfunction in both the study group and the control group. The utilization of instruments with so-called predictive capability on a "routine" basis carries a considerable burden. At best, these have an 80% to 85% sensitivity and specificity. One must use great care not to adversely label or make invasive intervention decisions solely on the basis of the results of these tests. Their use in clinical decision making mandates that services be available for referral and follow-up for those in need of them. At the current level of validity, these instruments should be reserved for well-designed studies approved by human research committees.

Access to the Population

Marketing programs which focus on enhancing interpersonal skills is much easier and more acceptable than promoting a program focused on those who have been identified as abusive or neglectful. Such programs are nonthreatening, nonlabeling, and eliminate any concerns about cultural or religious bias. They even override the concern of those who feel "parenting should be taught in the home," since interpersonal skill training programs teach *how* to interact, not the form the interaction should take or on what belief system it should be based.

An additional advantage to giving emphasis to the enhancement of interactional skills rather than the prevention of abuse is that gaining access is much easier. The key places in our society where it is feasible to obtain access to a large number of people *before* abuse has occurred are hospital newborn centers and schools at every level. Initiation of programs to improve interpersonal interaction is more acceptable to the boards and committees who "guard the entrance gates" to these institutions, and the populations involved are attracted to these "self-help" programs. Very few new parents have turned down the perinatal coaching program when asked if they wished to learn how to interact better with their baby.

Emphasis on enhancement rather than prevention decreases the need to screen for the "high-risk" population. All new parents can benefit from improved skills in interacting with their baby; some, of course, need them much more than others. Involvement in the program does not, in itself, adversely label the parent or the child.

Any discussion of prevention would be incomplete without consideration of the question, "Does knowledge, per se, lead to prevention?" If this could be answered in the affirmative, our task would be much simpler. Teaching facts is indeed much easier and cheaper than teaching skills and influencing parents' affective domain. The answer to the question seems to be, "knowledge does lead to prevention, to some extent, if the behavior change required is not too complex and the attitude change is not too fundamental." Reading a book or seeing a television demonstration on "how to parent" or "how to play golf" will not, in itself, be sufficient to learn these developmental skills. One must learn these skills by modeling, coaching, and PRACTICE. That, after all, is what childhood is all about.

References

1. Lilienfeld, A. M., and Lilienfeld, D. H. 1980. *The Foundations of Epidemiology.* 2d ed. New York: Oxford University Press.
2. Fletcher, R. N.; Fletcher, S. W.; and Wagner, E. H. 1982. *Clinical Epidemiology— The Essentials,* 2–4. Baltimore: Williams and Wilkins.
3. Baldwin, J. A., and Oliver, J. E. 1975. Epidemiology and Family Characteristics of Severely Abused Children. *British J. Preventive Social Medicine* 29:205–21.
4. Christoffel, K. K.; Liu, K.; and Stamler, J. 1981. Epidemiology of Fatal Child Abuse: International Mortality Data. *J. Chronic Diseases* 34:57–64.
5. DeJong, A. R.; Hemada, A. R.; and Gary, A. 1983. Epidemiologic Variations in Childhood Sexual Abuse. *Child Abuse and Neglect: International J.* 7:155–62.
6. Gonzalez, P., and Thomas, M. 1977. Child Abuse and Neglect: Epidemiology in Kansas. *J. Kansas Med. Soc.* 78:65–69.
7. Greenberg, N. H. 1979. The Epidemiology of Childhood Sexual Abuse. *Pediatric Annals* 8:289–99.
8. Newberger, E. H., and Daniel J. H. 1976. Knowledge and Epidemiology of Child Abuse: A Critical Review of Concepts. *Pediatric Annals* 5:15–25.
9. Kempe, C. H.; Silverman, F. N.; Steele, B. F.; Droegemueller, W.; and Silver, H. K. 1962. The Battered Child Syndrome, *JAMA* 181:17–24.
10. Kempe, C. H., and Helfer, R. E., eds. 1972. *Helping the Battered Child and His Family,* xiv–xv. Philadelphia: Lippincott.
11. Helfer, R. 1973. The Etiology of Child Abuse. *Pediatrics* 51:777–79.
12. Goldbloom, R. B. 1982. Failure to Thrive. *Pediatric Clinics of North America* 29:151–66.
13. National Center on Child Abuse and Neglect. 1981. *Study Findings: National Study of Incidence and Severity of Child Abuse and Neglect.* Washington, D.C.: U.S. Department of Health and Human Services.
14. National Center on Child Abuse and Neglect. 1988. *Study Findings: Study of National Incidence and Prevalence of Child Abuse.* Washington, D.C.: U.S. Department of Health and Human Services.
15. Sedlak, A. J., and Broadhurst, D. D. 1996. *The Third National Incidence Study of Child Abuse and Neglect.* Washington, D.C.: U.S. Department of Health and Human Services and National Center on Child Abuse and Neglect.
16. Schneider, C.; Helfer R. E.; and Hoffmeister, J. K. 1980. Screening for the Potential to Abuse: A Review. In *The Battered Child,* 3d ed., ed. C. H. Kempe and R. E. Helfer, 420–30. Chicago: University of Chicago Press.

17. Finkelhor, D. 1994. The International Epidemiology of Child Sexual Abuse. *Child Abuse and Neglect: International J.* 18:1–5.
18. Finkelhor, D. 1990. Early and Long-Term Effects of Child Sexual Abuse: An Update. *Professional Psychology: Research and Practice* 21:325–30.
19. Helfer, R. E. 1991. *Childhood Comes First: A Crash Course in Childhood for Adults,* 3d ed. East Lansing, Mich.: Helfer Publications.
20. Wilson, A. L. 1987. Promoting a Positive Parent-Infant Relationship. In *The Battered Child,* 4th ed., ed. R. E. Helfer and R. S. Kempe, 434–43.
21. Stern, Daniel. 1971. Mother and Infant at Play: The Dyadic Interaction Involving Facial, Vocal, and Gaze Behaviors. In *The Effect of the Infant on Its Caregiver,* ed. M. Lewis and L. Rosenblum. New York: Wiley.
22. Montague, Ashley. 1971. *Touching.* New York: Columbia University Press.
23. Helfer, R. E. 1974. Presidential Address, Ambulatory Pediatrics Association. *Pediatrics Basics* 10 (Feb.): 4–8.
24. O'Connor, S.; Vietze, P. M.; Sherrod, K. B.; and Altemeier, W. A. 1980. Reduced Incidence of Parenting Inadequacy Following Rooming-In. *Pediatrics* 66:176–82.
25. Burgess, Robert. 1979. Private communication.
26. Bristor, M. W.; Helfer, R. E.; and Coy, K. B. 1984. Effects of Perinatal Coaching on Mother-Infant Interaction. *Am. J. Diseases of Children* 138:154–57.
27. Lutzker, J. R.; Megson, D. A.; Webb, M. E.; and Darkman, R. S. 1985. Validating and Training Adult-Child Interaction Skills to Professionals and Parents: Indications for Child Abuse and Neglect. *J. Child and Adolescent Psychotherapy* 2:91–104.
28. Helfer, R. E. 1982. Preventing the Abuse and Neglect of Children: The Physician's Role. *Pediatrics Basics* 23:4–7.
29. Helfer, R. E. 1980. Perinatal Coaching Guide. *Pediatrics Basics* 26:10–14.
30. Helfer, R. E., and Wilson, A. L. 1982. The Parent-Infant Relationship. *Pediatric Clinics of N. America* 29:249–60.
31. Bristor, W. B.; Wilson, A. L.; and Helfer, R. E. 1985. Perinatal Coaching: Program Development. *Clinics in Perinatology* 12:367–79.
32. Gray, J., and Kaplan, B. 1980. The Lay Health Visitor Program: An Eighteen-Month Experience. In *The Battered Child,* 3d ed., ed. C. H. Kempe and R. E. Helfer, 373–78. Chicago: University of Chicago Press.
33. Kempe, C. H. 1976. Approaches to Preventing Child Abuse: The Health Visitor Concept. *Am. J. Diseases of Children* 130:940–47.
34. American Academy of Pediatrics. 1986. *The Well Child.* City: Elk Grove Village, Ill.: AAP.
35. Spivack, G., and Shure, M. 1974. *Social Adjustment of Young Children.* San Francisco: Jossey-Bass.
36. Spivack, G.; Pratt, J.; and Shure, M. 1976. *The Problem Solving Approach to Adjustment.* San Francisco: Jossey-Bass.
37. Bavolek, S. J. [n.d.] *Adult-Adolescent Parenting Inventory.* Schaumburg, Ill.: Family Development Association, Inc.
38. Hoffmeister, J. [n.d.] *Michigan Screening Profile of Parenting.* Boulder, Colo.: Test Analysis and Development.
39. Altemeier, W. 1982. Antecedents of Child Abuse. *J. Pediatrics* 100:823.
40. Murphy, L. S., and Orkow, B. 1985. Prenatal Prediction of Child Abuse and Neglect: A Predictive Study. *Child Abuse and Neglect: International J.* 9:3.
41. Rosenberg, N. M.; Meyers, S.; and Shackleton, N. 1982. Prediction of Child Abuse in an Ambulatory Setting. *Pediatrics* 70:879.

29

Prevention of Child Sexual Abuse

DAVID FINKELHOR AND DEBORAH DARO

Sexual Abuse Prevention Adopts a Different Approach

Initiatives to prevent child sexual abuse have followed a very different course from those aimed at preventing other forms of child abuse. A typical sexual abuse prevention program, for example, is a class for elementary school children on how to identify abusers, say no to them, and disclose any abusive episode to an adult. A typical program for preventing physical abuse, on the other hand, identifies a group of high-risk parents—for example, in a hospital maternity ward—and offers them education about child rearing, or the support of a home visitor, or a respite center where they can leave their children in times of stress.

The differences can be characterized more schematically. While a variety of strategies, including public education, have been adopted in efforts to prevent child abuse generally, the most common approaches are distinguished by several qualities:

1. The primary strategy has been to identify situations with a high risk for child abuse, such as the families of young, poor, or stressed parents.
2. The intervention has focused on the potential perpetrators themselves, changing their attitudes and their coping styles or providing them with additional resources that facilitate good parenting.
3. The services provided, although referred to as prevention, have been relatively similar in form to the "treatment" that would be provided to individuals who had already been abused.

In contrast, efforts at preventing sexual abuse, which developed independently and much later in the 1980s, have taken a different direction.

1. The main focus of sexual abuse prevention has been the dissemination of school-based curricula for elementary-school-aged children.
2. The strategy has been targeted toward the potential victims, not perpetrators; accordingly, the intervention has been aimed at all children, not just those at high risk.

DAVID FINKELHOR, Ph.D., is co-director of the Family Research Laboratory and research professor of sociology, University of New Hampshire.

DEBORAH DARO, D.S.W., is director of the Center for Child Abuse Prevention Research at the National Committee to Prevent Child Abuse.

3. With its educational focus, this intervention bears very little similarity to the treatment offered to victims or families who have actually suffered sexual abuse.

The Roots of the Sexual Abuse Prevention Strategy

The very different strategy utilized to prevent sexual abuse has grown out of a number of
realities surrounding the problem and the people organizing the response to it.

First, child sexual abuse was first identified as a social problem and mounted as a
public concern by the women's movement in the late 1970s and early 1980s (although it
had been recognized as a medical problem earlier in the 1970s) (1). This contrasted with
the movement involved with the issue of physical child abuse and neglect, which up until
that point had primarily included professionals—physicians, nurses, and social workers.
The sexual abuse activists had broader goals and a community organization focus. Consequently, the strategies they devised were not therapeutic but educational and were addressed to the widest possible audience, with the goal of changing the basic socialization
of children. It was these activists who conceived the first sexual abuse prevention programs
and developed many of the curricula that have since been disseminated.

Another reality about child sexual abuse that strongly conditioned the prevention
strategy it elicited was the enormous stigma involved. The commission of sexual abuse or
even the suspicion of such behavior is more roundly condemned, subject to more punitive
social sanctions, and considered less remediable than other forms of child abuse. This has
made it harder to craft prevention programs that would attract or retain potential perpetrators voluntarily, because no one wants to be treated as though they harbor even the slightest
tendency toward sexual abuse. Moreover, few adults, however predisposed to sexual abuse,
identify themselves as being in need of assistance. The fact that the majority of sex abusers
are men, and that men are more difficult to recruit into seeking help, also contributes to the
problem significantly. As a result, the strategy of building programs specifically for potential sex abusers has seemed impossibly challenging.

Third, more problems emerge in identifying and targeting the populations at high risk
for sexual abuse than those for physical abuse. Fewer high-risk perpetrator groups have
been clearly profiled through research—and to the extent that they have been identified,
they have been more difficult to reach. For example, stepfathers may be a risk category, but
they are certainly harder for professionals to reach than are young mothers without partners
in maternity wards.

At the same time, a fourth reality about sexual abuse that favored a broad school-based
approach to prevention was the fact that parents were generally more worried about the
vulnerability of their children to sexual abuse than to other forms of abuse. This was particularly the case because many parents believed a substantial threat existed outside their
own family. Parents readily accepted a school-based approach to alerting children about
sexual abuse that might have seemed insulting to parents had the topic been physical abuse.

Prevention Education: Strengths and Weaknesses

These fundamental realities have conditioned much of the first generation of prevention programs in the area of child sexual abuse. The programs have targeted potential victims, not perpetrators: have not attempted to identify a high-risk population; and have relied primarily on an educational approach. As a strategy, this approach has a number of advantages that recommend it:

1. The programs are inexpensive, easily implemented and disseminated, and can be administered by a wide variety of providers, including nonspecialists. In many places, regular classroom teachers or other school personnel have become the providers.
2. The programs reach a broad segment of the population. A recent national survey suggested that 67% of American school children have been exposed to a program, 32% in the most recent year for which figures are available (2).
3. The programs affect the primary socialization process and, therefore, influence children when they are most susceptible. General prevention theory suggests that intervention early in life, as in Head Start, is more likely to be effective.
4. The programs are nonstigmatizing: they do not label or suggest anything pejorative about participants. In fact, evidence suggests that children have very positive reactions to the programs (2).

The approach also has a number of identifiable drawbacks:

1. As many have pointed out, this approach puts the responsibility of prevention on potential victims—that is, on children. This seems morally unfair as a sole or primary strategy, and it certainly should not distract society from building lines of defense that give children more than just their own resources for protecting themselves against sexual abuse.
2. It is hard to make such interventions very intensive. The moment they become intensive, they also become prohibitively expensive because such large numbers of clients are involved. Thus most children receive only a few hours of prevention education over the course of their childhood.
3. Inexpensive though the widespread educational approach may be, it may also represent a diversion of resources away from truly high-risk situations that require concentrated preventive interventions.
4. Simply because this approach is being applied so widely, any negative effects it generates, even small ones, can have an enormous social cost.

Emerging Critiques of Prevention Education

Sexual abuse prevention education for children has been accepted very rapidly, in part because the problem triggered a high level of public concern but also because such programs were low in cost and easy to implement. After witnessing a period of rapid and enthusiastic dissemination, however, we saw in the late 1980s the beginning of a more critical view of these programs. The criticisms tended to focus around three issues.

The most fundamental challenge to sexual abuse prevention programs has been the argument that children have little power over abusers. Research on offenders has been interpreted by some (see 3, for example) to suggest that many are highly motivated and very canny—or, in the case of family members, very powerful. In this line of argument, little of what children do in the way of saying no, trying to run away, or threatening to tell will have an impact, at least not when confronting such perpetrators (4).

A second line of criticism accepts the possibility of abuse prevention but believes that many of the existing initiatives are ineffective (5). Such critics have argued that many of the concepts are developmentally inappropriate or too abstract—like "body ownership," for instance—or cannot be adequately taught or retained in many of the current brief, didactic, instructional formats.

A third concern is that prevention education programs actually cause harm, however unintentionally. Speculation has focused on whether programs may, in the course of warning children about sexual abuse, make them afraid of adults in general, afraid of the benign forms of touch and affection, or instill generally negative long-term feelings about sex and sexual touching (6).

Research Evidence

As a response to these concerns, researchers have amassed a rapidly expanding fund of empirical evidence about the child sexual abuse prevention programs. Although it yields generally reassuring conclusions, many of the more serious and troublesome issues have not yet been fully evaluated.

Knowledge Acquisition

Most of the research has focused on the question of whether children learn the concepts that the programs try to convey. A review of twenty-five such studies (7) found overwhelmingly that children who have received formal training have, as a group, more accurate knowledge than untrained children. However, the knowledge differences are sometimes small, they are not uniformly distributed among all children, and there is evidence that some of the more problematic concepts—for example, the idea that abusers can be people the child knows—are not always retained several months later (8).

The big debate in this literature centers on whether or not the prevention concepts can be learned by preschool children. It is apparent from a number of studies that younger children learn less than older children (9). But a widely publicized study concluding that such instruction was futile (3) has been contradicted by a number of other studies (10, 11) that suggest that even young children appear to learn some things from the programs.

Practical Efficacy

More important than whether children learn prevention concepts is the question of whether they are able to put them into practice. In the view of some, children cannot be expected to thwart a motivated offender, especially an adult offender, no matter what they do. In the National Youth Victimization Prevention Study, designed to address this issue, Finkelhor et al. (12, 13) found in a retrospective survey that children with quality prevention instruction from parents experienced fewer victimization attempts that turned into completed victimizations, an indication that the trained children had indeed short-circuited some perpetrators' attempts to abuse them. However, enrollment in school-based prevention programs alone was not associated with equivalent success in thwarting completed victimizations, although it was associated with usage of such preferred self-protection strategies as threatening to tell. Another study also found that training could be translated into actual behavior: children, before and after training, were approached by an adult confederate who tried to lure them away, and more of the trained children refused to be lured (14).

Another indication of whether prevention education influences behavior itself can be seen in the number of children's disclosures. Although these education efforts are labeled "prevention" programs, promoting disclosures of sexual abuse that has already occurred is one of their primary objectives. Even people who are skeptical about the capacity of these programs to thwart abuse admit that prevention programs may help children to disclose previous incidents of sexual maltreatment. Research generally confirms that this is in fact what happens: studies that have compared schools or classes with and without training programs have indeed found increased reports of sexual abuse follow in the wake of prevention programs (15, 16). Similarly, the National Youth Victimization Prevention study (12) ascertained that children who received exposure to higher-quality school prevention programs were more likely to have told someone about victimization and victimization attempts.

Other Outcomes

A variety of other potentially positive outcomes of prevention training remain to be researched well. For example, prevention education units may give children a greater sense of empowerment and security and may possibly protect children from negative effects even if they are sexually victimized. The National Youth Victimization Prevention Study (12), did find that children who participated in higher-quality school-based prevention programs perceived themselves as having been successful in coping with actual victimizations that had occurred to them. Such perceptions of efficacy have been associated with better recovery from trauma in other research (17).

Prevention programs may have other more diffuse positive effects that have not been studied at all. For example, they may raise the general level of awareness—not just of children but also of parents and adults in the community—about sexual abuse and thus improve general prevention efforts. The implementation of prevention programs may stimulate schools and communities to improve their procedures for detecting, reporting, and treating victimized children. All these positive effects have been noted anecdotally but not analyzed in formal evaluation studies.

The programs may also exert direct deterrent effects on perpetrators, effects that do not depend on the actual behavior of specific individual children. For example, a potential abuser (a father or an uncle, say) may avoid approaching a child who he knows has received prevention training for fear the child may disclose the incident, whether or not the child actually learned anything from the program or would be able to put it into practice. These programs may also instill enough knowledge and sensitivity about abuse to deter some of its child recipients from ever becoming abusers themselves. Such effects, although difficult to evaluate, are important to consider and weigh in the balance.

Negative Consequences

To attain a balanced view, we need to weigh the evidence of positive effects against the possibly negative consequences of these prevention programs. Some have questioned whether the programs produce unnecessary fear, anxiety, negative feelings about sex, the potential for malicious reports, and a sense of failure among those children who, despite prevention training, actually become victimized sexually.

Some concern was precipitated by an early study (18) in which over a third of the children reading a Spiderman comic book about sexual abuse reported being worried about abuse afterward. This study has been criticized for using a very crude questionnaire to evaluate a very untypical type of training situation, one using a medium and a character that may inspire more worry than others (particularly in girls unfamiliar with comic book action figures. More important, evidence suggests that the worry that children express, when they do express worry, in the wake of prevention training is not a negative outcome but a functional one—and is even viewed by children, not to mention their parents, as a sign that they are taking the program information to heart. In the National Youth Victimization Prevention Study (12, 13) the children who told researchers that prevention programs had made them worry more about abuse were the very children who reported, and whose parents reported, the most enthusiastic reactions to the programs. The parents had noted their children's worry and were not alarmed. In general, the better-designed studies, and those investigating parent observations of children's behavior, have found very few overtly negative reactions (19, 20).

In addition, some have wondered whether these programs might instill in children not only fears but negative attitudes about sexuality or intimacy, especially in the absence of positive sex education or information. Gilbert et al. (3) noted that preschool children in their study had more negative attitudes not just toward negative touches like hitting but also toward rather benign or natural touches such as tickling or bathing. Whether this finding represents a change in these children's perceptions of touching or an artifact of the particular research methodology utilized, the issue of how children generalize the concepts of sexual abuse prevention needs to be further studied.

In summary, the debate over the effectiveness of prevention programs has raised many important issues that invite detailed empirical examination. To date, however, the research that has been conducted, limited though it may be, has yielded reassuring conclusions that children in abuse prevention programs learn concepts, put them into practice, and experience some psychological benefits while at the same time not appearing to suffer much harm.

Program Improvement

Beyond covering the issue of program effectiveness, the research has also provided some conclusions about what are the more effective modes and methods of prevention training.

One of the important conclusions from several studies is that programs that offer children the opportunity to practice and to role-play do a better job of teaching concepts than programs that rely primarily on more passive modes such as lectures and films (21). Another conclusion is that with school-based programs, it does not appear to matter whether the instruction comes from the regular school personnel or specially trained outside staff.

Prevention education may be more effective when presented by or at least reinforced by parents than when children's only exposure to it occurs entirely in school. In the National Youth Victimization Prevention Study (12, 13), good parent instruction was associated with more positive outcomes—that is, more use of preferred strategies, more thwarting of attempted victimizations, and more disclosure—than was instruction limited only to good quality school-based instruction. Moreover, the school programs appeared to achieve their effectiveness at least in part because they stimulated parental instruction. These findings suggest that communities should institute more parent-focused prevention programs and that even school-based programs might want to strengthen their parent-outreach components.

Other Approaches to Sexual Abuse Prevention

School-based educational programs have thus far been the focus of sexual abuse prevention efforts, but a focus increasingly considered too exclusive. Whether supportive or critical of such prevention programs, all observers agree about the need to widen the scope of our work. Various goals and strategies are possible for such efforts; we will briefly sketch some of these possibilities suggested by theory and research.

Parent Education

Several lines of research suggest that parents should be the target of much more of the sexual abuse prevention effort. One research finding (cited in the section above) is that parent-initiated prevention instruction is simply more effective. But there are several other reasons to focus on parents.

First, poor parenting seems to be a major risk factor for sexual abuse. Numerous studies indicate that when children have poor relationships with their parents or when parental supervision is compromised by absence, illness, or alienation, children are more vulnerable to abuse in general (22). Other research shows that father-daughter bonding may actually serve as a deterrent to the commission of abuse (23).

Second, in addition to protecting children against victimization, good parenting seems to help children recover from victimization. Studies have found maternal or parental support to be the most consistent and crucial factor in predicting how much long-term negative impact an experience of abuse will have on a child (24).

Sexual abuse prevention targeted at parents should become a priority and should develop a number of general and specific goals. At the most general level, parent-child bonding and good parenting practices need to be fostered during all the phases of children's development. Certain specific parenting skills may need some particular emphasis, especially

1. How to monitor children and their contacts with adults and other children
2. How to talk to children about sexual abuse, sex in general, and the avoidance of sexual victimization
3. How to detect signs of sexual abuse in children

Parents need to know how to make themselves trustworthy to children so that children will be comfortable disclosing to them. Parents also need guidelines to help them to deal with children's disclosures and their aftermath. The importance of listening to children without expressing judgment and without hysteria needs to be stressed. Some of the more frightening stereotypes about the inevitability of irremediable long-term consequences need to be revised to help keep parents from overreacting. Parents need to be informed about the importance of supportive responses and where they can go to get help and support for themselves.

With these general goals in mind, we may find it beneficial to target for prevention education certain parents and certain families—in particular, those whose children may be at higher risk for abuse. The evidence is quite strong, for example, that children in families undergoing divorce or children living in stepfamilies are at increased risk (22). Children in families where parental supervision is compromised by substance abuse or mental illness may also be at risk. In programs dedicated to helping parents and children adapt successfully to these conditions, specific sexual abuse prevention education ought to be included.

Perpetration Prevention

Another target of expanded prevention efforts should be the prevention of abusive behavior and abusive proclivities (25) (see chapter 14). What we know about the development of sexually abusive behavior suggests a number of preventive goals and strategies.

Sexual abuse seems to develop among individuals who have themselves experienced various kinds of sexual trauma and humiliation, particularly trauma compounded by a climate of shame and an environment of social isolation and poor role models. This certainly suggests that the provision of positive sexuality education and the allaying of fears and guilt feelings could make a difference. Parents, in particular, need instruction in how to create more positive climates for sexual development early in life. More children, especially adolescents, should have the opportunities in school, among their peers, and with adult professionals to communicate about sex, to discuss their hidden concerns and questions about sex, and to be listened to in a nonjudgmental context.

In addition to the promotion of positive sexual development, specific education needs to be included to deter sexually abusive behavior (26). Gail Ryan and her colleagues, for example, have developed a program to help adults to recognize abusive behavior and its precursors in children and adolescents, giving concerned adults ways to discuss, confront, and extinguish the abusive behavior without reinforcing children's shame and humiliation. Programs have also been introduced to help children (particularly adolescents) gain skills to short-circuit their own tendencies to abuse. These programs have emphasized the development of empathy, knowledge about what others may find offensive, and the ability to get their needs met through negotiation rather than coercion.

Public education campaigns aimed at potential abusers have also been initiated. These have included advertisements warning potential abusers about the negative consequences of sexual abuse on young victims and urging potential abusers to seek help for their problem. Other education campaigns have tried to publicly confront and debunk some of the rationalizations and stereotypes that abusers use to justify their behavior.

Researchers have recommended various means of identifying and targeting children who may be at particular risk for developing abusive patterns (25). Children who were themselves abused in any way, not just sexually, and their siblings are an obvious risk group. It is important, however, not to exaggerate the efficacy of this kind of approach to prevention. Research suggests that less than one-third of those victimized as children go on to abuse others, and victims suffer under enough stigma without the additional burden of being treated as potential powder kegs.

Other high-risk groups may exist. Research suggests that very isolated children and adolescents and those who prefer to associate with children much younger than themselves may be more vulnerable to abusing.

We know something about high-risk adults as well. Adults whose judgment is compromised by substance abuse problems may be one such group. Adults who have committed any prior sexual offense not involving children may be more likely to offend against children. And, obviously, adults and adolescents who have offended against children before are among those at highest risk to offend again.

Changing Social Structure

A problem as pervasive as sexual abuse needs to be countered by a broad program of social change, not simply an assemblage of educational and therapeutic programs. It is crucial for us to recognize the variety of underlying social structures that are in part responsible for the problem, help perpetuate it, and need to change for the problem to be fully eradicated. This social structural analysis is speculative, but it has potentially important implications.

Social change is needed in several domains if we are to undermine those social structures that support sexual abuse. The first concerns creation of a healthier culture around human sexuality. Sexual abuse clearly is a problem that thrives in a context in which sexuality is burdened with shame, secrecy, and exploitation. It is at one extreme end of a continuum that includes many minor experiences of sexual trauma and sexual exploitation that are part of the lives of almost everyone in our society. Social changes are needed that make sexual information more readily available to children and others, that work toward acceptance rather than stigmatization of sexual diversity, that reduce feelings of shame and inadequacy, that enhance communication between people and the ability to empathize with another's sexual reality, and that model sexual activities in the context of mutual respect and affection. All these changes would help curtail the culture that feeds sexual abuse and increases the trauma that it inflicts.

A second domain concerns the nature of gender roles. That men preponderantly commit sexual abuse and women preponderantly suffer the abuse is almost certainly related to deeper social stereotypes that need to be changed. For example, notions of dominant masculinity support attitudes of sexual entitlement and exploitation in our culture. They also pose obstacles to men's forming healthy relationships with children. As men come to empathize better with children and become better, more involved fathers, we might see a reduction in the amount of sexual abuse.

Stunted gender roles for women contribute to sexual abuse as well. In a culture that still socializes girls to value themselves primarily for their sexual attractiveness and to seek approval and affirmation from men, girls will be more vulnerable to being manipulated by abusers. As women come to value assertiveness, independence, and their own physical strength, their vulnerability to abuse may decrease.

A third domain concerns the role of children in society. In spite of the recent abundance of pro-child rhetoric, there is considerable evidence that the rights of children in our society are not well protected. Children are vulnerable to sexual abuse when they are neglected, poorly supervised, and when potential perpetrators sense that children do not have credibility. As we transform institutions like the courts to make them more accessible to children and as we work to guarantee children the right to schools, families, and day care where they will be well cared for and protected, we will almost certainly reduce children's risk for sexual abuse.

Conclusion

The enormity of the problem of child sexual abuse has been one of the most discouraging discoveries of our era. It is all the more discouraging in that it reveals our past failure as a community of researchers and child welfare professionals to detect and recognize a major source of suffering in the lives of our children. Yet in the brief history of our organized response to the problem, we can discover great reasons for optimism as well. The rapid professional mobilization around the problem suggests that we live in a social climate much more willing to confront and much less willing to tolerate the maltreatment of children. The higher level of general social knowledge and the transformed public attitudes about sexual abuse, along with a host of new programs, have set in motion a process of social change whose manifold effects we cannot fully anticipate but whose ultimate impact may be profound.

In the face of what seem like ever multiplying social problems, it is easy to be discouraged. But there is no doubt that we have made enormous strides in this century toward the improvement of the condition of life for many groups of children. We have seen vast increases in scientific and professional knowledge about childhood. There is good reason to believe that we will eradicate the problem of child sexual abuse just as we have routed other scourges of childhood: child labor, infectious diseases, and whippings. In preventing the trauma of child sexual abuse, we will also build a society more humane and livable for everyone, victims and nonvictims, children and adults.

References

1. Finkelhor, D. 1984. *Child Sexual Abuse: New Theories and Research.* New York: Free Press.
2. Finkelhor, D., and Dzuiba-Leatherman, J. 1995. Victimization Prevention Programs: A National

Survey of Children's Exposure and Reactions. *Child Abuse and Neglect: International J.* 19(2): 125–35.

3. Gilbert, N.; Duerr Berrick, J.; LeProhn, N.; and Nyman, N. 1990. *Protecting Young Children from Sexual Abuse: Does Preschool Training Work?* Lexington, Mass.: Lexington Books.

4. Melton, G. B. 1992. The Improbability of Prevention of Sexual Abuse. In *Child Abuse Prevention,* ed. D. Willis, E. Holder, and M. Rosenberg. New York: Wiley.

5. Krivacska, J. J. 1990. *Designing Child Sexual Abuse Programs,* Springfield, Ill.: C. C. Thomas.

6. Reppucci, N. D., and Haugaard, J. J. 1989. Prevention of Child Sexual Abuse: Myth or Reality? *Am. Psychologist* 44 (10): 1266–75.

7. Finkelhor, D., and Strapko, N. 1992. Sexual Abuse Prevention Education: A Review of Evaluation Studies. In *Child Abuse Prevention,* ed. D. Willis, E. Holder, and M. Rosenberg, 150–67. New York: Wiley.

8. Plummer, C. 1984. *Preventing Sexual Abuse: What In-School Programs Teach Children.* Durham, N.H.: University of New Hampshire.

9. Conte, J.; Rosen, C.; Saperstein, L.; and Shermack, R. 1985. An Evaluation of a Program to Prevent the Sexual Victimization of Young Children. *Child Abuse and Neglect: International J.* 9:329–34.

10. Daro, D. When Should Prevention Education Begin? *J. Interpersonal Violence* 4(2):257–60.

11. Harvey, P.; Forehand, R.; Brown, C.; and Holmes, T. 1988. The Prevention of Sexual Abuse: Examination of the Effectiveness of a Program with Kindergarten-Age Children. *Behavior Therapy* 19:429–35.

12. Finkelhor, D.; Asdigian, N.; and Dziuba-Leatherman, J. 1995. The Effectiveness of Victimization Prevention Instruction: An Evaluation of Children's Responses to Actual Threats and Assaults. *Child Abuse and Neglect: International J.* 19(2):137–49.

13. Finkelhor, D.; Asdigian, N.; and Dziuba-Leatherman, J. 1995. Victimization Prevention Programs for Children: A Follow-Up. *Am. J. Public Health* 85(12):1684–89.

14. Fryer, G.; Kraizer, S.; and Miyoski, T. 1987. Measuring Actual Reduction of Risk to Child Abuse: A New Approach. *Child Abuse and Neglect: International J.* 11:173–79.

15. Beland, K. 1986. *Preventing Child Sexual Victimization: A School-Based Statewide Prevention Model.* Seattle: Committee for Children.

16. Kolko, D.; Moser, J.; and Hughes, J. 1989. Classroom Training in Sexual Victimization Awareness and Prevention Skills: An Extension of the Red Flag/Green Flag People Program. *J. Family Violence* 4 (1):25–45.

17. Janoff-Bulman, R., and Lang-Gunn, L. 1988. Coping with Disease, Crime, and Accidents: The Role of Self-Blame Attributions. In *Social Cognition and Clinical Psychology,* ed. L. Y. Abramson, 116–47. New York: Guilford.

18. Garbarino, J. 1987. Children's Response to a Sexual Abuse Prevention Program: A Study of the Spiderman Comic. *Child Abuse and Neglect: International J.* 11:143–48.

19. Hazzard, A.; Webb, C.; and Kleemeier, C. 1988. *Child Sexual Assault Prevention Programs: Helpful or Harmful.* Atlanta: Emory University School of Medicine.

20. Wurtele, S. K.; Marrs, S. R.; and Miller-Perrin, C. L. 1987. Practice Makes Perfect? The Role of Participant Modeling in Sexual Abuse Prevention Programs. *J. Consulting and Clinical Psychology* 55:599–602.

21. Wurtele, S.; Saslawsky, D.; Miller, C.; Marrs, S.; and Britcher, J. 1986. Teaching Personal Safety Skills for Potential Prevention of Sexual Abuse: A Comparison of Treatments. *J. Consulting and Clinical Psychology* 54:688–92.

22. Finkelhor, D., and Baron, L. 1986. High-Risk Children. In *A Sourcebook on Child Sexual Abuse,* ed. D. Finkelhor, 60–88. Beverly Hills, Calif.: Sage.

23. Williams, L. M., and Finkelhor, D. 1995. *Paternal Caregiving and Incest: A Test of a Biosocial Model. Am. J. Orthopsychiatry* 65(1):101–13.

24. Kendall-Tackett, K. A.; Williams, L. M.; and Finkelhor, D. 1993. Impact of Sexual Abuse on

Children: A Review and Synthesis of Recent Empirical Studies. *Psychological Bulletin* 113:
164–80.

25. Ryan, G. D. 1991. Perpetration Prevention: Primary and Secondary. In *Juvenile Sexual Offending: Causes, Consequences, and Correction,* ed. G. D. Ryan and S. L. Lane, 393–408. Lexington, Mass.: Lexington Books.

26. Ryan, G.; Blum, J.; Sandau-Christopher, D.; Law, S.; Weher, F.; Sundine, C.; Astler, L.; Teske, J.; and Dale, J. 1989. *Understanding and Responding to the Sexual Behavior of Children: Trainer's Manual.* Denver: University of Colorado Health Sciences Center.

30

Child Protection Policy

RICHARD D. KRUGMAN

The role that government plays in the protection of children from abuse and neglect has received increased attention over the last several years in the United States. In the early 1990s, the U.S. Advisory Board on Child Abuse and Neglect issued a series of reports (1–4) detailing the status of the child protection system in the United States. The findings and recommendations of these reports are of great interest, since several countries around the world have patterned their child protection systems on the American one, thus demonstrating that the issues faced in the United States have wide applicability. In this chapter, I will chronicle the events that led to the formation of the advisory board, review its findings and recommendations, comment on the response, and suggest the need for a universal approach to policy development and implementation. The deliberations and process of the board provide a good case study on policy development which can be instructive for those working in the area of child abuse and neglect.[1]

The Setting

In the 1960s, every single state in the United States passed legislation mandating that all cases of *suspected* as well as known child abuse and neglect be reported to a designated agency (usually departments of social services). At that time, it was estimated that there might be several thousand children who were "battered" each year. Some states developed statewide approaches to child protection; others gave jurisdiction to counties. Thus across the country there are several thousand different agencies charged with this responsibility and, as a result, literally hundreds of different "official" approaches to protecting children, depending on the number and experience of the professionals living and working in each jurisdiction.

By 1974, when the federal Child Abuse Prevention and Treatment Act (CAPTA) passed, testimony suggested that each year as many as 60,000 children were being abused

---

1. Melton and Flood have recently published a helpful review of research policy in the United States (5), which I recommend to those interested in that related field.

RICHARD D. KRUGMAN, M.D., is dean of the School of Medicine and professor in the Department of Pediatrics, University of Colorado.

The author appreciates Anne Cohn Donnelly's critical review of and suggestions for this chapter.

and neglected. Gil estimated that there were 2 million such cases annually, based on extrapolation from his prevalence survey (6), but this figure was not taken seriously by many. CAPTA required states to enact child abuse reporting statutes if they were to receive federal money under the act. It established a national research and demonstration grant program and required the Secretary of the Department of Health, Education, and Welfare to publish annual data on the incidence of child abuse and neglect.

CAPTA has been reauthorized several times, with more requirements added each time. In 1978, the development of a program to prevent sexual abuse was stipulated. The 1978 amendments also required that family reunification receive particular emphasis, in response to the plight of children left languishing for many years in foster care after they had been removed from abusive homes. Another noteworthy amendment was the 1984 "Baby Doe"[2] language, which broadened the definition of *abuse* to include the withholding of medically indicated treatment from infants born with severely disabling conditions. Each reauthorization added more work or requirements but rarely appropriated more money.

CAPTA created the National Center on Child Abuse and Neglect (NCCAN) in 1974 to carry out the purposes of the legislation. NCCAN was placed within the Children's Bureau of the Administration of Children, Youth, and Families (ACYF) in the welfare area of what was then the Department of Health, Education, and Welfare (HEW). Later, after education was split out into a separate cabinet position in 1979, ACYF was relocated to the Office of Human Development Services of the renamed Department of Health and Human Services (HHS). The naming and renaming and the various permutations of the reorganized department were less important than the fact that NCCAN, which was to be the federal government's lead agency on child abuse and neglect, was buried within the welfare side of the massive HEW and HHS bureaucracy.

During NCCAN's first seven years, it was successful in channeling a fair amount of money out into the field. It funded many research and demonstration projects (including dozens of home visitation projects), conducted several evaluation studies, and published a series of "user manuals" that provided practice guidelines for social workers, law enforcement officers, and other professionals. It also set up ten regional resource centers that provided support and consultation to child protection workers in the field, and sponsored national conferences to bring research findings and training opportunities to the field.

However, in 1982, the first year of the Reagan administration, NCCAN—and nearly all HHS agencies—suffered a 30% cut in personnel and budget. The impact of this was devastating to the agency and substantially slowed the advancement of knowledge in what had been a steadily developing field.

During the decade of the 1980s, a variety of events conspired to create serious problems for the United States' child protection system:

1. The combination of an economic recession with rising unemployment and in-

---

2. "Baby Doe" was an infant born with esophageal atresia, who was not expected to live. In consequence, life-giving fluids were withheld, leaving the infant to starve and dehydrate. The amendment required that all states set up Infant Review Boards to assess such cases and required that, at a minimum, all infants should be provided fluids and other minimal support.

creased poverty put a significant strain on the ability of states and the federal government to maintain welfare programs for needy clients.

2. The print, radio, and television media were filled with reports of physical and sexual abuse cases and the inability of the child protection system to stop them. Public awareness of the problem skyrocketed, and reports of abuse cases escalated from 60,000 in 1974, to 669,000 in 1979, to 3 million in 1994.

3. The increased recognition of sexual abuse as a significant problem facing children complicated the task of child protective services agencies in the 1980s. Unlike physical abuse and neglect, which were handled almost exclusively by child welfare agencies and the civil court, child sexual abuse is a criminal offense. As such, it requires a law enforcement investigation in addition to the social work assessment. A criminal investigation is harder, more time-consuming, and certainly raises the stakes for the family that is being investigated.

4. Over the course of the 1980s, as a result of the budget cuts that plagued federal and state government, the child protection system, broadly defined,[3] was decimated. Public health nursing, for example, moved away from offering supporting care in maternal and child health to staffing fee-for-service home health care agencies. These public health nurses ended up spending most of their time caring for ill adults, and even they needed a diseased organ or a doctor's prescription before a visit from a public health nurse could be authorized. The mental health system also became unavailable for most of the child protection system as a result of the successful implementation of the government's policy to "de-institutionalize" the chronically mentally ill. Although this policy might have been good for some of those long-term patients, the resulting overcrowding of community mental health clinics made it almost impossible for thousands of maltreated children and their families to obtain needed therapy.

5. As reports of child abuse rose, the pressure to investigate the reports grew. Soon, the efforts of most child protection services agencies were directed almost entirely into investigating; few resources were left for treatment, much less prevention.

6. In addition, as the economy faltered, more mothers joined the work force, the links to extended families disappeared, and neighborhoods, especially in the larger cities, began to disintegrate.

7. Substance abuse significantly increased and was associated with both a similarly significant rise in crime and violence and a concomitant deterioration of family and neighborhood life.

8. Finally, recognizing the growing crisis, Congress passed an amendment to CAPTA in 1988 that created the U.S. Advisory Board on Child Abuse and Neglect by reconstituting the former National Advisory Committee on Child Abuse and Neglect.

It was for all these reasons, plus the grim reality that the United States was spending

3. The U.S. Advisory Board on Child Abuse and Neglect defines the *child protection system* as the multidisciplinary network of medical, public health, mental health, child welfare, law enforcement, court, and education professionals. Child protective services are a part of this system, and the services' staff members are the professionals who work in the agencies that investigate reports of child abuse and neglect.

billions of dollars on a system that wasn't working, and billions more on the downstream consequences of the failure to treat and prevent child abuse and neglect, that the advisory board labeled the situation in 1990 "a national emergency" (1).

Recommendations

The thirty-one recommendations of the advisory board's first report—which was entitled *Child Abuse and Neglect: Critical First Steps in Response to a National Emergency* (1)—were presented in eight general steps, or areas (see table 30.1). Each step laid out several specific recommendations. The first two areas called on the public, professional groups, and elected officials at all levels to *recognize* and *acknowledge* that the emergency existed. It is striking too note how silent nearly all public officials are about this problem. It is rare that the words "child abuse and neglect" are even uttered in public unless an especially terrible case has made the news, and rarely do reporters ask those seeking public office about their record of policy on child abuse and neglect.

The third step called for *coordination of efforts* by agencies at all levels of government. For several decades, professionals working in the field have recognized that the best, most effective approach to recognizing, treating, and preventing child abuse and neglect is multidisciplinary, drawing from the perspectives and methods of many areas (psychology, social work, medicine, the law, and so on). Nonetheless, few efforts at the federal or state level have routinely been practiced this way.

The fourth and fifth general areas called for the *generation of knowledge* and *diffusion of knowledge*. The research base for practice in the field was (and remains) very thin. The availability of evaluation or outcome data on the thousands of daily interventions administered by the child protection system in the United States is quite undeveloped. The quality of individual practice and the system's impact on children have rarely been assessed. The media have an important role to play here in assuring that the public is informed not just about sensational cases or tragic failures of the child protection system but also about the complexity of the problem—the broad-based approaches to solving it need to be much more widely known. This simply is not a field that lends itself to quick fixes.

The sixth step called for *increasing human resources,* not just for more money. The board felt that a new profession—child protective services caseworker—needed to be

TABLE 30.1
Steps Required to Address the National Emergency

1. Recognize that the emergency exists.
2. Acknowledge the emergency in public statements.
3. Coordinate existing efforts.
4. Generate knowledge (research and evaluation).
5. Diffuse knowledge through all professions and the public.
6. Increase human resources (human and fiscal).
7. Improve programs that are already in existence.
8. Plan for the future.

developed, with commensurate training, support, and salary; that the curricula of schools of social work, medicine, law, and other professions needed to be revised to include the child abuse and neglect issue; and that aggressive efforts needed to be made to recruit members of ethnic minorities to this profession.

The seventh area called for *improving programs* in social work, law, and education. This would require additional resources, including the infusion of more money into abuse prevention—money that was not to be reallocated from existing identification and treatment programs.

Finally, the board's first report called for government and professionals to *plan for the future*. Two things were requested: (1) a study of the direct and indirect costs of the child protection system in the United States, including the cost of *not* preventing or treating the problem, and (2) a planning process, to involve all levels of government, that would ultimately restructure the entire system into one that was comprehensive, child-centered, family-focused, and neighborhood-based.

The relevant members of Congress, the national media, and most of the professionals in the field were excited about the report. It was clear that the board had been comprehensive and had also been careful to follow a "no-fault" approach. The board's view was that neither major political party, nor any profession, was to blame for the emergency and that little was to be gained for children by engaging in a partisan political battle. In truth, no one had done much that could be pointed to with pride in regard to child protection. The secretary of the Department of Health and Human Services, in whose lap most of the recommendations fell, promised to study the report. Regrettably, several key lower-level officials felt the report was too critical of *their* administration, and they successfully managed to blunt and slow the response of the agency. Three months after the report was released, the secretary said he "accepted" much of what it said and had "launched an initiative" to address the problems.

This initiative consisted of the secretary "using his bully pulpit" to raise awareness of child abuse and neglect; he included a paragraph or two on the subject in his speeches; he convened one national and ten regional conferences to increase awareness throughout the country; and he prepared a memorandum of understanding, signed by most cabinet secretaries, pledging to coordinate interagency child abuse treatment and prevention activities. Although this was more than had ever been done before by a secretary, it seemed to the board that it was not a very vigorous response to an "emergency."

Before the national conference to launch the secretary's initiative was convened (in December 1991), the board had released a second report. This one was as specific as the first was general. It focused on the role that the federal government would need to play to enable the country to move away from the current child protection system to the envisioned new one. This report considered six general areas and made thirty recommendations, each accompanied by several "options for action."

The first area was, in many ways, the most important. In its efforts to assess the child protection system in the United States, the board noted that nowhere in federal or state statute was there a written child protection policy. This failure of policy development suggested (as was indeed the case) that the child protection system had grown in an unplanned, heterogeneous way that had left the responsibility for protecting children up to a whole range of professionals but without giving them any guidance as to whether the approach they should take should rely on rescue of children or rehabilitation of parents, civil intervention actions or criminal prosecution of abusers, educative efforts to prevent abuse in the first place or therapeutic treatment to help children and families after the fact. Thus the second report's first recommendation called for the United States to *state its child protection policy*. To assist the government in this effort, the board provided a model policy, based on the United Nations Convention on the Rights of the Child, and suggested that this policy be incorporated into CAPTA and become the driving force behind all child protection policy in the United States (see the appendix to this chapter).

The second area called on the federal government to act to reduce the level of child maltreatment in this country by *strengthening neighborhoods and families*. These efforts, the board recommended, should be implemented by relevant cabinet agencies (for example, the Department of Housing and Urban Development, the Department of Agriculture) and should summon the involvement of volunteers as well as professionals, especially those in the religious community. The board contended that the erosion of neighborhood and family support systems was a critical factor in the increasing incidence of child maltreatment and that repair of this frayed network would require broad-based action.

The third area called again for all federal agencies and programs that have an impact on the problem of child abuse and neglect to develop a focus on the strengthening of families. This was a call for a *federal multidisciplinary effort*, analogous to the multidisciplinary approach that was in place clinically at the local level.

The fourth area also repeated a still ignored call, one for *better data*. Data on incidence and outcomes were sorely lacking, and funding for better research was badly needed. Accordingly, the board proposed (1) instituting a peer-review process for awarding grants; (2) establishing qualifications for and standards of practice so individual professionals could participate in a quality-control process; and (3) funding of resource centers throughout the United States to provide technical assistance and training to local and regional professionals.[4]

The fifth area called for the *development of an agency at the federal level* that was multidisciplinary and would be responsible for planning and coordinating all federal efforts. This recommendation really enraged officials at the Department of Health and Human Services—they not only reacted extremely defensively but accused the board of "tinkering" inappropriately with their turf! It was the board's view that unless *someone* at a high enough level of the federal bureaucracy took responsibility for coordinating all that needed to happen, nothing *would* happen.

The final recommendation of the board's second report called for the federal government to initiate a "dramatic new initiative" to prevent child maltreatment—*piloting universal, voluntary, neonatal home visitation*.[5] Through it, the board was responding to some

4. At the present time, NCCAN funds two "national" resource centers—one for physical abuse and neglect, one for sexual abuse. Neither can possibly meet all the needs.

5. I have surveyed and analyzed the developments and debate surrounding this recommendation elsewhere (7).

criticism from Congress and the media that the first report had been too "global." Several congressional staffers had asked for "*something concrete*" that could be written into legislation. The board was wary of a history of legislation passage that had fiddled around the margins of federal and state law and meant little or nothing to either the child protection system or children and families. Although home visitation was not considered a panacea, the board felt that it was the best-studied maltreatment prevention measure and that, as such, it held great promise. The government was urged to initiate a series of pilot programs that would not merely study the efficacy of the home visitors but would also assist in projecting the measures needed to take an intervention that had proved successful for several hundreds of families at a time and universalize it to the county, state, and national levels. *That* step has still never been accomplished to this day in the United States.

There was little response by the administration to the board's second report. Congress never passed any home visitation legislation, and few if any of the recommendations were ever acted upon. During the following two years, the board developed the "blueprint" discussed in the first report, which had outlined a strategy for rebuilding the child protection system in the United States. This plan called for the replacement of the then current child protection system with a new, neighborhood-based, comprehensive, child-centered, family-focused child protection strategy.

The primary need for this strategy was to change the primary orientation of the child protection system in the United States from investigating alleged incidences of child abuse to assisting families in need. The purpose of the new strategy was to make it as easy for troubled parents to pick up the telephone and get help to prevent them from abusing their children as it currently was to pick up the telephone and report the parent after the abuse had occurred.

The Response

As I discussed briefly above, the response by the national media to the board's first report was very positive. The "child abuse emergency" was widely reported throughout the print and broadcast media. Part of the reason for this was that the U.S. Supreme Court had decided two pertinent cases on the same day the board released its report in Washington, D.C. The combination was big news. In contrast, the second report was released in Denver, and the national media were absent. Furthermore, rather than foregrounding the state of emergency, the second report was focused on detailing what the national government had failed to do and on suggesting many changes. Such useful information is rarely deemed newsworthy by a media looking for crises.

The efforts of the board to induce congressional action on several of the recommendations were actively opposed by the Bush administration. Meanwhile the secretary of HHS had begun his "initiative"—fifteen months after the release of the first report and several weeks after the second. The initiative may have increased general awareness of the national emergency, but it was a response to the first report, not the second. Neither the second nor third reports received much attention at all from the federal government.

The private sector, on the other hand, did respond. Several national agencies used the report to advance their own efforts in implementing home visitation. The National Committee for the Prevention of Child Abuse (NCPCA) and the National Parent Aide Association supported the board's recommendation and mobilized the private sector. NCPCA obtained $1 million from the Ronald McDonald Foundation and began "Healthy Families America," which is an initiative, patterned on Hawaii's Healthy Start system, that operates neonatal home visitation programs throughout the United States. These efforts were supported by several national professional organizations such as the American Hospital Association and American Nurses Association (see chapter 27).

In January 1993, the presidential administration changed. Many child advocates in the United States believed that the lot of children would be improved since the new president and first lady had a long record of child advocacy in Arkansas. In the subsequent years, however, there was little or no federal response to the board reports and no direct action on any of the recommendations. Finally, in 1994, Congress passed, and the president signed, "Family Preservation" legislation, which authorized the appropriation of $1 billion over a five-year period. Some of these funds can be used for home visitation services that are preventive in nature, but the main thrust is for treatment of identified abusive families. It is a start, at least.

The Lesson

In examining the half decade spent in child protection policy development in the United States, certain lessons appear to emerge. As professionals throughout the world look to make the world safer for children and address the problem of child abuse and neglect, the child protection system in the United States continues to struggle. Reported incidents of child abuse have surpassed 3 million a year, and deaths from maltreatment now exceed two thousand annually. Treatment and prevention programs are scarce. A new administration swears in a new board, another report is issued—this one on child maltreatment fatalities (8)—and children continue to wait for action.

How should societies respond to child maltreatment? The experience gained from efforts to comprehend and remedy the problem in the United States since 1989 seems to offer some lessons. It is clear that even though the media, politicians, and the public would like to believe that quick fixes can be found, the nature of child maltreatment, the depth to which it is ingrained in our society, and the complexity of the problem all defy simple solutions. If progress is to be made, however, we must resolve to take the following courses of action.

First and foremost, we must formulate and clearly state a universal, generally accepted child protection policy and do so for each of the forms of child maltreatment. The United States has, without public discussion of the ramifications, followed a therapeutic approach to dealing with the physical abuse and neglect of children, and a punitive approach to child sexual abuse, focused on prosecution of offenders. The problems inherent in our failure to adopt a coherent written policy are several: (1) the individual members of multidisciplinary professional teams, community agencies, and government may act differently if their aim is prosecution rather than protection; (2) without a policy, assessment of whether the intervention effort is successful or not is impossible; and (3) those looking to "solve" the problem will respond to the crisis of the week with "knee-jerk" legislation. A classic example of this third problem occurred in 1993, when Congress passed the "Oprah" bill. Oprah Winfrey, a television talk show host and herself a survivor of child sexual abuse, asked the Congress of the United States to institute a program requiring background checks of child care providers after she read about a child who had died in child care in Chicago at the hands of a previously convicted abuser. This bill was the only legislation of note to pass the Congress during the years in which the board was advocating that a comprehensive overhaul of the entire child protection system was urgently needed. Oprah herself stated that her bill was just a tiny step. At that time, it must be noted, several states had already passed laws requiring such background checks, and the state programs that had been implemented were costly and not shown to be effective. Furthermore, even though the members of Congress congratulated themselves and Oprah for "doing something" about child abuse and neglect, they never appropriated the funds to actually implement a nationwide program. If the policy of the United States is to try to identify and target all child abusers, then this bill makes sense. On the other hand, if our policy is mainly to protect children, then this costly, ineffective legislation probably should not have been considered, let alone "enacted."

A second lesson from our experience in the field since 1989 is that those of us who seek change should recognize how important it is to have leadership at the national level and how difficult it is to develop it. The centuries of denial and the general disinclination to recognize the problem except in the most lurid of cases cannot be overcome unless our elected leaders and other public figures acknowledge the problem. In this regard, C. Henry Kempe's public statement about battered children in 1961 and Marilyn Van Derbur Atler's[6] public statement about incest empowered professionals and the general public to begin to address the problem more openly.

In 1987, Ray Helfer, to whom this volume is dedicated, spoke of the child protection system of the next century (9). He fantasized that at halftime of the Super Bowl game in 2007, a star player and his wife asked all those in the stands who had been abused and neglected in childhood to rise. Twenty thousand stood up, and the blimp above the field captured the moment for the nation and the world—and, finally, the magnitude of the problem and the need to address it became clear to all. Short of this, having the president or first lady of the United States lead the way would also mobilize policy. In the United States, that is the *ultimate* in leadership. Sadly, it has been missing.

The longer any country goes without open, public discussion of child abuse—with the actual words being spoken—the longer it will take to develop an effective child protection system. If we are to have a child protection policy, we will need to discuss it in public. Reporters and voters will need to ask their elected officials what their child protection

6. This former Miss America of 1958 publically announced in 1989 that she had been sexually violated by her millionaire, socialite father from the time she was five years old until she was eighteen. This extraordinary public statement led to literally thousands of adult incest survivors coming forward. If it was OK for Miss America to speak about incest, many women and men felt that they could speak out too.

policy is. Since most officials probably have not thought about such a policy, asking the question may get them to realize we should have one. Ultimately, public awareness must be turned into public policy.

The final lesson of the recent experience in the United States is that the absence of a continuing, effective program of research and evaluation at the national, state, and local levels will retard the development of effective policy. Few human services have done so much to help children and families on the basis of so little data than the child protection system. And this is true for child protection systems all over the world. In Catherine Marneffe's chapter in this volume (see chapter 23), an alternative way of dealing with abuse and neglect is presented. This "confidential doctor" approach is close to what the U.S. advisory board recommends in its fourth report (4), but it should be noted that there are no evaluative studies of that system either.

Clearly, a concerted effort to build a research program that will inform policy and practice is needed not just in the United States but in every country. Otherwise, the abused and neglected children of the world will have no choice but to wait until the public, their elected officials, and caregiving professionals can offer them more than just a report—in every sense of that word.

Appendix: Proposed National Child Protection Policy

NOTE: This document is an extract from *Creating Caring Communities: Blueprint for an Effective Federal Policy on Child Abuse and Neglect* (2). Underlined language which appears here is drawn from the United Nations Convention on the Rights of the Child, sometimes with minor revision for grammatical form.

Definitions:

Child protection system refers to the entire system that serves children and their families in cases where:

- risk of child maltreatment exists,
- maltreatment has been reported, or
- maltreatment has been found to exist.

The child protection system includes but is not limited to **child protective service,** the State or County child welfare agencies mandated by law to protect abused and neglected children. Other components of the child protection system include law enforcement, education, health and public health, mental health, developmental disabilities, and court agencies. The system includes public, private, and voluntary agencies and organizations.

A **comprehensive** child protection system is one that incorporates the provisions identified [elsewhere in this proposal].

A **child-centered** child protection system is one that:

- takes children seriously as individuals,

- gives primary attention to their best interest, as reflected in their needs and experiences,
- provides opportunities and such representation as may be necessary for children to be heard in matters pertaining to them (when children are capable of such expression), and
- responds flexibly to the diversity of their cultural backgrounds and the circumstances in which they find themselves.

Adoption of the perspective of the child will lead in most instances to a concern with strengthening families.

A **family-focused** child protection system is one that . . . recognizes the paramount importance of the family for the development of children.

A **neighborhood-based** child protection system is one in which:

- primary strategies are focused at the level of urban and suburban neighborhoods and rural communities.
- social and economic supports for troubled families and children are developed at the neighborhood level, where neighborhood is defined by geographic boundaries, and
- both formal and informal services (e.g., volunteer, professionally facilitated self-help programs) that are based on the principle of voluntary help by one citizen for another are widely available, regardless of whether access to such services is determined by place of residence.

Declarations:

Respect for the inherent dignity and inalienable rights of children as members of the human community requires protection of their integrity as persons.

Children have a right to protection from all forms of physical or mental violence, injury or abuse, neglect or negligent treatment, maltreatment or exploitation including sexual abuse, while in the care of parent(s), legal guardian(s), or any other person who has the care of the child, including children residing in group homes and institutions.

Children have a right to grow up in a family environment, in an atmosphere of happiness, love, and understanding.

The several Governments of the United States share a profound responsibility to ensure that children enjoy, at a minimum, such protection of their physical, sexual, and psychological security.

The several Governments of the United States bear a special duty to refrain from subjecting children in their care and custody to harm.

Children have a right to be treated with respect as individuals, with due regard to cultural diversity and the need for culturally competent delivery of services in the child protection system.

Children have a right to be provided the opportunity to be heard in any judicial and administrative proceedings affecting them, with ample opportunity for representation and for provision of procedures that comport with the child's sense of dignity.

The duty to protect the integrity of children as persons implies a duty to prevent assaults on that integrity whenever possible.

Findings:

Each year, hundreds of thousands of American children are subjected to abuse, neglect, or both.

Often the child protection system fails to protect such children from further maltreatment or to alleviate the consequences of maltreatment.

The child protection system has developed largely in unplanned fashion, with resulting failure (a) to reach many of the children in need of protection and (b) to provide effective services to them and their families.

Substantial gaps exist in knowledge about child abuse and neglect, the diffusion of that knowledge, and the development of a pool of trained professionals who are specialized in child protection.

Tolerance of child abuse and neglect threatens the integrity of the nation because of its inconsistency with core American values: regard for individuals as worthy of respect, reverence for family life, concern for one's neighbors (especially those who are dependent or vulnerable), and competence in economic competition.

Failure to provide an effective system of child protection also imperils the nation by increasing the risk of crime and physical and mental disability, diminishing the level of educational achievement, and threatening the integrity of the family.

Such consequences of child abuse and neglect cost the nation billions of dollars each year in direct expenditures for health, social, and special educational services and in long-term loss of worker productivity.

Deterioration in the quality of urban neighborhoods and rural communities increases the isolation of the families from their neighborhoods and, therefore, the rate of child abuse and neglect; child maltreatment itself tears the social fabric of the community and thus escalates the decline of neighborhoods and communities in crisis.

Although the family remains the most fundamental unit in American society, the family has undergone substantial change in recent decades, and the nature of child maltreatment has become more complex. The complexity of the task of child protection has increased commensurately.

An effective response to the problem of child abuse and neglect requires a **comprehensive** approach that:

- integrates the contributions of social service, legal, health, mental health, and education professionals,
- provides for coordinated roles of (a) private child welfare, mental health, and advocacy agencies, (b) civic, religious, self-help, and professional organizations, and (c) individual volunteers,

- assures the protection of children while in each of the relevant service systems,
- provides for coordinated roles of all levels of government, in cooperation with the private sector, and
- ensures that adequate provision is made in the child protection system for prevention, investigation, adjudication, and treatment.

The prevention and treatment of child abuse and neglect are most effective when they are organized and delivered at a neighborhood level.

Failure to provide a comprehensive child protection system integrated across and within levels of government (in cooperation with relevant private-sector organizations) results in waste of many of those resources now allocated for child protection.

Substantial reduction of the prevalence of child abuse and neglect and alleviation of its effects when it occurs are matters of the highest national priority.

The Following Tenets Are Hereby Declared to Be the Child Protection Policy of the United States:

The child protection system should be comprehensive, child-centered, family-focused, and neighborhood-based.

The principal goal of governmental involvement in child protection should be to facilitate comprehensive community efforts to ensure the safe and healthy development of children.

Federal authorities should exercise due care to ensure that standards and procedures for public financing of child protection efforts promote and do not inhibit flexible, integrated approaches to child protection in all of the systems of service (e.g., education, mental health) for children and families.

Because of (a) the link between poverty and some forms of child maltreatment and (b) the limited resources available in impoverished communities, Federal aid for child protection should be distributed with due regard to relative financial need of States, their political subdivisions, Tribes, and community health and mental health catchment areas.

Recognizing the complex nature of child maltreatment, Federal authorities should stimulate, integrate, and coordinate leading child protection programs, at least in those public, private, and voluntary agencies that have responsibility for carrying out Federal efforts in social services, health, mental health, advocacy, education, law enforcement, corrections, housing, cooperative extension, volunteer action, and the administration of justice.

Federal authorities should ensure that direct child protection services to children and families within Federal jurisdiction (e.g., military families, Native Americans) are exemplary in quality and that relevant Federal agencies provide models of culturally competent child protective strategies that may be adopted in other communities.

The child protection system should incorporate all appropriate measures to prevent the occurrence or recurrence of child abuse and neglect.

The child protection system should incorporate all appropriate measures to promote physical and psychological recovery and social re-integration of a child victim of any form of neglect, exploitation or abuse; such recovery and reintegration should take place in an environment which fosters the health, self-respect and dignity of the child.

As the fundamental group of society and the natural environment for the growth and well-being of all its members, and particularly children, the family should be afforded protection and assistance necessary for it to assume its responsibility fully within the community. The several Governments of the United States, in cooperation with private organizations, should act:

- to strengthen families in general to minimize the circumstances that may cause or precipitate child abuse and neglect,
- to provide intensive services to avoid the removal of children from family environments at times of crisis, and
- to make all reasonable efforts to reunify families when abuse or neglect has resulted in removal of a child.

Comprehensive child protection plans should be developed regularly at all levels of government and should show due sensitivity to the cultural diversity and individual needs of children and families.

Child protection efforts should be integrated with broader child and family policy, pursuant, e.g., to the recently-enacted Claude Pepper Young Americans Act.

Federal Agencies Are Hereby Directed to Use All Means Practicable, Including Financial and Technical Assistance—in Cooperation with State, Tribal, and Local Governments and Other Concerned Public and Private Organizations—to Fulfill This Policy and to Act with Due Urgency in Doing So:

To that end, the several agencies of the Federal Government with responsibility for child protection should take all steps necessary to ensure that every community in the United States has the resources—fiscal, human, and technical—required to develop and implement a child protection strategy that will:

- ensure the safety of children,
- prevent child maltreatment, whenever possible,
- result in timely, sensitive, and accurate investigation and assessment, whenever child maltreatment is suspected or known to have occurred,
- result in treatment to ameliorate the effects of abuse and neglect on children and family members,
- aim, whenever possible, to rebuild the families whose ties have been frayed by maltreatment, and
- assure safe, stable, and nurturing substitute family environments when children are temporarily or permanently unsafe in their biological families.

Among the steps that should be taken by the Federal Government to assist communities in their child protection and family strengthening efforts are the following:

- facilitation of community planning;
- generation and diffusion of knowledge relevant to child protection, including models for prevention and service delivery;
- strengthening of States' capacities to assist communities, particularly with respect to moving toward more voluntary preventive services as opposed to emphasizing investigation and foster care;
- stimulation of the growth of human resources (professional, paraprofessional, and volunteer) that communities may use in fulfillment of their plans for child protection;
- sharing of financial resources necessary to implement community plans;
- leadership in uniting caring communities unwilling to tolerate the abuse and neglect of their youngest members.

References

1. U.S. Advisory Board on Child Abuse and Neglect. 1990. *Child Abuse and Neglect: Critical First Steps in Response to a National Emergency.* Washington, D.C.: U.S. Government Printing Office.
2. U.S. Advisory Board on Child Abuse and Neglect. 1991. *Creating Caring Communities: Blueprint for an Effective Federal Policy on Child Abuse and Neglect.* Washington, D.C.: U.S. Government Printing Office.
3. U.S. Advisory Board on Child Abuse and Neglect. 1992. *The Continuing Child Abuse Emergency: A Challenge to the Nation.* Washington, D.C.: U.S. Government Printing Office.
4. U.S. Advisory Board on Child Abuse and Neglect. 1993. *Neighbors Helping Neighbors: A New National Strategy for the Protection of Children.* Washington, D.C.: U.S. Government Printing Office.
5. Melton, G. B., and Flood, M. F. 1994. Research Policy and Child Maltreatment: Developing the Scientific Foundation for the Effective Protection of Children. *Child Abuse and Neglect: International J.* 18 (supp. 1):1–28.
6. Gil, D. G. 1973. *Violence against Children: Physical Child Abuse in the United States.* Cambridge, Mass.: Harvard University Press.
7. Krugman, R. D. 1993. Universal Home Visiting: A Recommendation from the U.S. Advisory Board on Child Abuse and Neglect in "Home Visiting." *The Future of Children* 3:184–91.
8. U.S. Advisory Board on Child Abuse and Neglect. 1995. *A Nation's Shame: Fatal Child Abuse in the United States.* Washington, D.C.: U.S. Government Printing Office.
9. Helfer, R. E. 1991. Child Abuse and Neglect: Assessment, Treatment, and Prevention—October 21, 2007. *Child Abuse and Neglect: International J.* 15 (supp. 1):5–15.

Contributors

Marla R. Brassard, Ph.D.
Associate Professor
Department of
  Developmental and
  Educational Psychology
Teachers College
Columbia University
New York City, New York
  10027

Donald C. Bross, Ph.D., J.D.
Professor, Department of
  Pediatrics
Director of Education, The
  C. Henry Kempe National
  Center for the Prevention
  and Treatment of Child
  Abuse and Neglect
University of Colorado
  Health Sciences Center
1205 Oneida Street
Denver, Colorado 80220

Hendrika B. Cantwell, M.D.
Clinical Professor Emerita
Department of Pediatrics
School of Medicine
University of Colorado
  Health Sciences Center
4200 East Ninth Avenue
Denver, Colorado 80262

Deborah Daro, D.S.W.
Director, Center for Child
  Abuse Prevention Research
National Committee to
  Prevent Child Abuse
332 South Michigan Avenue

Suite 1600
Chicago, Illinois 60604

Howard A. Davidson, J.D.
Director, Center on Children
  and the Law
American Bar Association
740 Fifteenth Street, N.W.
Washington, D.C. 20005

Anne Cohn Donnelly, D.P.H.
Executive Director
National Committee to
  Prevent Child Abuse
332 South Michigan Avenue
Suite 1600
Chicago, Illinois 60604

Donald N. Duquette, J.D.
Clinical Professor of Law
Director, Child Advocacy
  Law Clinic
University of Michigan Law
  School
801 Monroe Street
Ann Arbor, Michigan 48109

Kenneth Wayne Feldman, M.D.
Clinical Professor
Department of Pediatrics
University of Washington
  School of Medicine
2101 East Yesler Way
Seattle, Washington 98122

David Finkelhor, Ph.D.
Co-Director, Family Research
  Laboratory

Horton Social Science Center
University of New Hampshire
Durham, New Hampshire
  03824

James Garbarino, Ph.D.
Professor, Human
  Development and Family
  Studies
Director, Family Life
  Development Center
College of Human Ecology
G-20 MVR Hall
Cornell University
Ithaca, New York 14850

David B. Hardy
Statistical Consultant
P.O. Box 60051
Florence, Massachusetts
  01060

Mary Edna Helfer, R.N.,
  M.Ed.
Director, Continuing Medical
  Education Outreach
University of Colorado
  Health Sciences Center
4200 East Ninth Avenue
Denver, Colorado 80262

David P. H. Jones, Mb.Ch.B.,
  F.R.C. Psych., D.C.H.
Park Hospital for Children
Old Road
Oxford OX3 7LQ England

Ruth S. Kempe, M.D.
Associate Professor Emerita
Department of Pediatrics and
   Psychiatry
School of Medicine
University of Colorado
   Health Sciences Center
4200 Ninth Avenue
Denver, Colorado 80262

Robert H. Kirschner, M.D.
Clinical Associate
Departments of Pathology
   and Pediatrics
University of Chicago School
   of Medicine
6822 South Euclid Avenue
Chicago, Illinois 60649

Jill E. Korbin, Ph.D.
Professor
Department of Anthropology
Case Western Reserve
   University
Cleveland, Ohio 44106

Richard D. Krugman, M.D.
Professor of Pediatrics and
   Dean, School of Medicine
University of Colorado
   Health Sciences Center
4200 East Ninth Avenue
Denver, Colorado 80262

Catherine Marneffe, M.D.,
   Ph.D.
Barakkenbergstraat, 9
1540 Herne, Belgium

R. Kim Oates, M.D.
Douglas Burrows Professor
   of Paediatrics and Child
   Health
Department of Paediatrics
University of Sydney
Sydney, Australia

Susan K. Reichert, M.D.
Medical Director
Kids Intervention and
   Diagnostic Service Center
1375 Kingston Avenue, N.W.
Bend, Oregon 97701

Marguerite M. Rheinberger,
   J.D., M.P.H.
Allina Foundation, Allina
   Healthsystem
9800 Bren Road West
Minneapolis, Minnesota
   55343

Donna Andrea Rosenberg,
   M.D.
Donna.Rosenberg@UCHSC.
   edu

Gail Ryan, M.A.
Director, Perpetration
   Prevention Project
The C. H. Kempe National
   Center for the Prevention
   and Treatment of Child
   Abuse and Neglect
University of Colorado
   Health Sciences Center
1205 Oneida Street
Denver, Colorado 80220

Elizabeth A. W. Seagull,
   Ph.D.
Professor, Department of
   Pediatrics and Human
   Development
College of Human Medicine
B-240 Life Sciences Building
Michigan State University
East Lansing, Michigan
   48824

Inspector Jack R. Shepherd
Executive Assistant,
   Investigative Services
   Bureau

Michigan Department of
   State Police
714 South Harrison Road
East Lansing, Michigan
   48823

Wilbur L. Smith, M.D.
Professor
Departments of Radiology
   and Pediatrics
University of Iowa College of
   Medicine
Iowa City, Iowa 52242

Brandt F. Steele, M.D.
The C. Henry Kempe
   National Center for the
   Prevention and Treatment
   of Child Abuse and
   Neglect
University of Colorado
   Health Sciences Center
1205 Oneida Street
Denver, Colorado 80220

Robert W. ten Bensel, M.D.,
   M.P.H.
Professor
Department of Pediatrics
University of Minnesota
   School of Public Health
420 Delaware Street, S.E.
Minneapolis, Minnesota
   55455

Michael W. Weber
Associate Director
National Committee to
   Prevent Child Abuse
332 South Michigan Avenue
Suite 1600
Chicago, Illinois 60604

Index

schooling (education) (*continued*)
    fore eighteenth century, 8; home schooling, 349;
    for neglected children, 367–68; neglectful par-
    ents' attitude toward, 364; in sixteenth and sev-
    enteenth centuries, 9; unwarranted denial of
    medical care and, 393, *395*
schools: after-hours supervision at, 355; in family
    assessment, 155; sexual abuse prevention pro-
    grams in, 616, 619, 621; therapy programs in,
    556
Schreier, H. A., 418
scintigraphy, skeletal, 207, *208,* 211, 231
Scotland, dispute resolution mechanism in, 495
Scott, Sir Walter, 16–17
Scott County (Minnesota) cases, 120–21, 123
screening of child abuse reports, 128, 142
scurvy, 244
SDH. *See* subdural hemorrhage
Seattle (Washington) CASA program, 463
secondary (reactive) depression, 114
secondary prevention, 579, 611
second-degree burn injury, 189
Seitz, V., 587
self and identity: and communication, 107; employ-
    ment and male identity, 51; sense of, in child
    abusers, 88–91; sexual abusers protecting sense
    of, 333
self-discipline, neglect of teaching, 353
self-esteem, low. *See* low self-esteem
self psychology, 79
semen, tests for presence of, 262, 315–16
sentencing of child abuse offenders, 494
setting limits, neglect of, 353
severe emotional disturbance, 402–3
sex education, 157, 163, 167
sex roles: emergence in preschool children, 554. *See
    also* gender
sexual abuse: in abusive parents' childhood, 163;
    acknowledgment of, 530–31, 532; age-of-con-
    sent laws, 15; anatomically correct dolls, 130,
    159, 299, 306, 318; assessment of, 296–312; in
    autopsy, 262–63; behavioral indicators of, *315;*
    blurred family boundaries and, 535; bowel per-
    foration caused by, 243; case history of, 95–
    100; in child maltreatment complex, 73; child
    sexual abuse accommodation syndrome, 297;
    constant factors in, 336; in context of other
    abuses, 443–44; as criminal act, 492, 558, 629;
    cycle of, 330, 336, *337,* 340; defined, 83, 296;
    early warning of, 297–98; emotional or behav-
    ioral difficulties following disclosure, 308, 559;

evidence of, 122; flagellation as, 16; genital ma-
    nipulation, 7, 85; group therapy for victims,
    559–60; historical indicators of, *314;* in history,
    11–18; incidence of, 313, 597; interviewing the
    child, 156–60; investigation of, 130, 299–307,
    302; medical evaluation of the child, 313–28;
    medical interview of the child, 317–20; mind-
    altering techniques in, 443; as multi-agency
    problem, 303; Native American concern about
    European agencies, 41; and neglectful parenting,
    370; nurturant function distorted by, 165; out-
    comes of, associated with family environment,
    399, 524; physical examination of the child,
    320–26; physical symptoms of victims of, *315;*
    practitioners avoiding involvement in, 313;
    presentation of, 297–98, 314; prevalence of,
    35–36, 597; prevention education programs,
    617–18; prevention of, 342–43, 589, 615–26;
    professionals having little control over outcome
    of, 326; protective laws against, 22; psychody-
    namic and biological factors in, 83–88; recogni-
    tion of, 122, 313–17; research findings on pre-
    vention programs, 618–21; risk factors for, 616,
    622; and satanic rituals, 169, 443; Scott County,
    Minnesota, cases, 120–21, 123; sequelae of,
    87–88; sexual exploitation as preferable term
    for, 596–97; sexual sadism, 16, 444–45; social
    change required for preventing, 623–24; and so-
    cial development of adolescents, 155; socializa-
    tion function distorted by, 167; stages of investi-
    gative process, 301–7; stigma of, 616; talking
    with children about, 300–301; teen pregnancy
    associated with, 370; treatment for the child,
    558–60; varieties of, 85. *See also* fellatio; in-
    cest; pedophilia; sexual abusers
sexual abusers, 329–46; abstinence violation effect,
    336–37; assessment interview of alleged, 309;
    attachment disorders in, 338–39; characteristics
    of, 84; childhood living conditions of, 84; clini-
    cal assessment of, 334; current research on,
    338–41; deterring, 331–32, 619–20; effective-
    ness of treatment for, 340–41; empathy in, 339;
    etiology of abusive behavior, 86, 342; four-fac-
    tor model of, 330; group treatment for, 337; in-
    terventions with, 332–38, 342–43; monitoring
    of, 335–36; motivation of, 330–31; multidisci-
    plinary approach to, 334–36; neurological func-
    tioning of, 339–40; perpetration prevention,
    341–42; pharmacological interventions for, 338,
    340; prevention programs as deterring, 619–20;
    prevention programs targeted at, 616, 622–23;